THE SOVIET

POLITICAL SYSTEM

A Book of Readings

THE SOVIET
POLITICAL SYSTEM

A Book of Readings

edited by
RICHARD CORNELL
York University

PRENTICE-HALL, INC., *Englewood Cliffs, New Jersey*

PRENTICE-HALL INTERNATIONAL, INC., *London*
PRENTICE-HALL OF AUSTRALIA, PTY. LTD., *Sydney*
PRENTICE-HALL OF CANADA, LTD., *Toronto*
PRENTICE-HALL OF INDIA PRIVATE LTD., *New Delhi*
PRENTICE-HALL OF JAPAN, INC., *Tokyo*

© 1970 by Prentice-Hall, Inc., *Englewood Cliffs, N.J.*

Current printing (last digit):

10 9 8 7 6 5 4 3 2 1

C 13-823831-6
P 13-823823-5

Library of Congress Catalog Card Number: 71-105446

Printed in the United States of America

PREFACE

It is the intention in this volume to provide something of a more contemporary, more analytical approach to the study of the Soviet political system. It is an attempt to go beyond description and the institutional setting, and to integrate within a more meaningful frame of reference our knowledge of Soviet politics. This is not to say that a competent presentation of the "facts" is unnecessary or superfluous. On the contrary, an awareness of the historical developments, the institutional structures and the writings of Marx, Lenin, Stalin, Khrushchev, and others is an absolutely essential preface to any sort of meaningful analysis. Thus, this volume would ideally be utilized in conjunction with a good text and a selection of the Marxist-Leninist "classics" by someone who has had a thorough grounding in the history of the Soviet Union.

I would not wish to pretend that the selections and commentary here included are, taken together, anything resembling a definitive statement about the nature of the Soviet political system. They do, however, present a reasonably accurate summary of the state of our knowledge at this time—what we think we know and do not know, and the questions which scholars are now asking. Certainly, few of the judgments of the individual authors would go without challenge. Indeed, the articles included are most provocative in areas where our knowledge is least sure.

A number of very useful selections had to be left out because of space limitations. Some of these include discussions of: the use of rewards by the political elite to assure compliance and to maximize legitimacy; a more elaborate discussion of the role of law in Soviet society emphasizing the persistence of regularity of procedure in the more apolitical

v

areas of life, even during the height of the purges; the impact of foreign policy questions on domestic policy; and further examples of how various "groups" or "interests" have played a role in the decision-making process. Numerous current issues or problems—such as agriculture—have not received the attention they deserve.

I should like to thank my former colleagues and students at the State University of New York at Buffalo, two of my colleagues at York, Grey Hodnett and B. Michael Frolic, the editorial and production staff of Prentice-Hall, Inc., and most of all, my wife Bodil, for their constructive comments, assistance, and patience.

RICHARD CORNELL

Toronto
January, 1970

CONTRIBUTORS

ARTHUR E. ADAMS:

Professor of History and Director of the Russian and East European Studies Center at Michigan State University. Author and editor of numerous works on Russian history.

VERNON V. ASPATURIAN:

Research Professor and Director of the Slavic Studies Center at Pennsylvania State University. His most recent book is *The Soviet Union in the World Communist System* (1966).

JEREMY AZRAEL:

Associate Professor of Political Science at the University of Chicago and author of *Managerial Power and Soviet Politics* (1966).

FREDERICK C. BARGHOORN:

Professor of Political Science at Yale University. His most recent book is *Politics in the USSR* (1966).

DANIEL BELL:

Professor of Sociology at Columbia University and co-editor of *The Public Interest*. Author of numerous books and articles, including *Marxian Socialism in the U.S.A.* (1967).

ZBIGNIEW BRZEZINSKI:

Professor of Government and Director of the Research Institute on Communist Affairs at Columbia University, Mr. Brzezinski has written many books and articles on Soviet, East European, and world politics.

L.G. CHURCHWARD:

Reader in Political Science at the University of Melbourne and author of several articles on Soviet local government.

ROBERT CONQUEST:

A British scholar noted for his poetry and literary criticism and his studies on Soviet affairs. Mr. Conquest has written, among other works, *Power and Politics in the U.S.S.R.* (1961) and *The Great Terror* (1968).

ALF EDEEN:

A member of the Directing Staff of the Royal Swedish National Defense College, Mr. Edeen has published several works on the Soviet administrative bureaucracy.

JEROME M. GILISON:

Mr. Gilison is an Assistant Professor of Political Science at The Johns Hopkins University.

PAUL HOLLANDER:

Associate Professor of Sociology at the University of Massachusetts. Editor of *American and Soviet Society: a reader in comparative sociology and perception* (1968) and author of several articles.

JERRY F. HOUGH:

Professor of Political Economy at the University of Toronto and author of *The Soviet Prefects* (1969).

SAMUEL P. HUNTINGTON:

Frank G. Thomson Professor of Government and Chairman of the Department of Government at Harvard University. Author of *Political Order in Changing Societies* (1968) and other books and articles.

ALEX INKELES:

Professor of Sociology and Director of Studies in Social Relations at the Russian Research Center of Harvard University. Author of, among other works, *What is Sociology?* (1964).

EUGENE KAMENKA:

Mr. Kamenka is Senior Fellow in the History of Ideas at the Australian National University and author of *The Ethical Foundations of Marxism* (1962).

ALLEN KASSOF:

Associate Professor of Sociology at Princeton University and Executive Director of the International Research and Exchanges Board. Author of *The Soviet Youth Program: regimentation and rebellion* (1965).

JOHN H. KAUTSKY:

Professor of Political Science at Washington University (St. Louis) and author of several articles and books on communism and political development.

ROY D. LAIRD:

Professor of Political Science at the University of Kansas and author of several works on Soviet agriculture.

CARL A. LINDEN:

Is on the faculty of St. John's College, Annapolis, Maryland. He is the author of several articles on Soviet politics, as well as the longer study, *Khrushchev and the Soviet Leadership, 1957–1964*.

LEON LIPSON:

Professor of Law at Yale University and former chairman of the American Bar Association's committee on Soviet law. Author of several articles on Soviet law and the Soviet legal system.

RICHARD LOWENTHAL:

A professor at the Free University of Berlin, Mr. Lowenthal is the author of many articles on contemporary Soviet and communist affairs.

TIMOTHY MCCLURE:

The author is a British observer of Soviet affairs who has preferred to write under the pseudonym of "Timothy McClure."

ALFRED G. MEYER:

Professor of Political Science at the University of Michigan, Mr. Meyer is the author of several books on marxism, communism, and Soviet politics, including *The Soviet Political System: An Interpretation* (1966).

BARRY M. RICHMAN:

Professor at the School of Business, University of California at Los Angeles, Mr. Richman is the author most recently of *Industrial Society in Communist China* (1969).

HENRY L. ROBERTS:

Former Director of the Russian Institute at Columbia University, Mr. Roberts is now Professor of History at Dartmouth College. His works include *Rumania: Political Problems of an Agrarian State* (1951) and *Russia and America* (1956).

W.W. ROSTOW:

Professor of Economics and History at the University of Texas and former special assistant to the President of the United States. Author of many books and articles, perhaps most notably *The Stages of Economic Growth* (1960).

H. GORDON SKILLING:

Professor of Political Economy and Director of the Russian and East European Centre at the University of Toronto, Mr. Skilling has written extensively on Soviet and East European affairs. He has edited a volume on interest groups in the Soviet political system which is forthcoming.

MICHEL TATU:

East European correspondent for the Parisian daily *Le Monde* and author of *Power in the Kremlin* (1969).

CONTENTS

INTRODUCTION

The readings included in this volume have been selected and organized to serve two purposes: first, to provide the reader with a perspective on the Soviet political system that emphasizes its dynamic character—its state of continuing change, second, to enable one to compare more meaningfully the Soviet political system with other political systems.

Until recently, communism was perceived of essentially as a highly unified and directed phenomenon. Changes were thought of not as the result of any inherent pressures for differentiation, but rather as a consequence of personal idiosyncracies or gradual adaption of the less essential features to changing reality. The surprise with which observers have reacted to the unfolding disintegration in the international communist movement in the years after 1953—the failure, with a few notable exceptions, to foresee with any clarity the course of developments—is a commentary on the inadequacy of the image of communism that had been presented by most analysts, communist and non-communist alike.

One can make this same criticism of our perception of the Soviet political system as a specific example of the more general political phenomenon, communism. Failing to take account of what would seem to be the simple fact that all political institutions, organizations, and systems change over time, the old concepts and models developed to explain Soviet politics tended to produce a static, and thus unrealistic, picture. By stopping, analytically, the process of historical development at one point in time, through the choice of political and societal influences emphasized as decisive for determining the nature of the political system, the old approaches provided only a chronological cross-section of the changing political system. The effort to uncover the sources and processes of change was de-emphasized, as were steps to re-evaluate on a more or less continuous basis what were considered to be the persistent, fundamental elements of the system.

Perhaps we forgot, as well, the imprecision of our knowledge about the Soviet Union. A lack of humility seems now apparent in those who offered theories in explanation of Soviet developments. Too much, in too assured a fashion, was made from too limited evidence. Even today, it is enormously difficult to acquire reliable information upon which to build interpretations and evaluations of Soviet society. Conversely, opportunities remain limited indeed for the testing of theories through observation of the Soviet system. Secrecy and an environment not overly conducive to Western notions of academic inquiry—at least in the social sciences and concerning the political processes—remain characteristic of the Soviet Union.

The uncertainties created in scholars of Soviet politics in recent times as to the "truth," as to how best to describe and evaluate the Soviet system and to relate it to other political systems, have led increasingly to diversification of approach. One thing that is clear, however, is that all approaches share the desire to understand not only the state of affairs at any given moment, but more importantly, to uncover the forces both producing and resisting change. New analytical tools are being sought. There are efforts to bring to Soviet studies some of the conceptual and methodological insights uncovered within the traditional academic disciplines. An effort is being made to revise and rephrase the older explanations. The readings in Part I are representative of the diverse approaches to the study of the Soviet political system, and of the debate over what may fruitfully be discarded and what should be retained from the earlier approaches.

It is of great benefit to view political actions and activities within the Soviet Union as a "system"[1] By so doing, one emphasizes properly the high degree of interdependence among all areas of Soviet society. Action or change in one area will most often have consequences in other areas. For example, changes in economic organization and administration in the name of efficiency not only have affected the demands placed upon the decision-making agencies, but could well produce changes in the structure and membership of these institutions. Or further, a lessening of the efforts to direct and guide consciously the process of political socialization—control over writers and artists, for example—can affect the legitimacy of the existing decision-making structure in the Soviet Union.

This need not imply any necessary harmony, or that political life in the Soviet Union unfolds according to some mechanistic, deterministic process. Rather, the concept of "system" serves as a useful way of ordering reality so as to emphasize the notion of change which characterizes any society. The concept of "system" is a vague one, difficult to define precisely and to everyone's satisfaction. It can, however, be a useful device by which one can describe the inter-relationship between conscious action and the environ-

---

[1] See Marian D. Irish and James W. Prothro, *The Politics of American Democracy*, 4th ed. (Englewood Cliffs, N.J., 1968), pp. 6–17, for a brief but illuminating discussion of political activities as a political system.

ment. The political "system" is not "the more or less fatalistic outcome of environmental or 'ecological' factors"[2] as some scholars perceive it, rather the political system encompasses and describes the interaction between environmental influences and the directing, guiding, or shaping forces of political institutions and political leaders. Political systems differ from society to society (as well as show varying degrees of similarity) because of differences in the environmental influences which exist in each society, and which are of consequence for politics in that society, and in the character of the political institutions and leaders and their responses to the environment.

The Soviet political system can best be described as a process of interaction between certain environmental influences and the consciously directed actions of a small elite group of individuals working through a highly centralized institutional structure. The latter seek to modify or limit the effect of the former, or put them to their own use. Concurrently, the former appear increasingly to be providing a challenge to the latter: to be setting limits within which behavior can be consciously directed, and to be producing social forces that in turn create demands on the political process dominated by the elite group. As will be noted in the readings, an important question at the moment concerns the pace and scope of this development and the ability of the elite to cope with it. Is the ability of the elite to impose its will on society in fact being circumscribed or changed so severely that it is in danger of losing its position of leadership and direction?

Many observers appear agreed that the elite[3] has essentially given up its

----

[2] Joseph LaPalombara, "Macrotheories and Microapplications in Comparative Politics: A Widening Chasm," *Comparative Politics*, I, No. 1 (October 1968), 59.

[3] The term "elite" has acquired many conceptual meanings, often depending upon the interests, values, and perspectives of the user. It is the more specific form of an elite, a "political elite," in which we are interested here. For the purposes of the discussions in this volume the concept of "elite" will at times refer broadly to the entire membership of the CPSU, to the party as such, if only because any more specific elite which may exist professes, at least, to be acting for, and in the name of, the party. In addition, the requirements for admission to the party, the demands placed upon party members, and the rights and duties of party members create an important separation between the party and the rest of society. There is, however, a need for a more specific definition of the "political elite," given the hierarchical structure of power in the Soviet Union. The definition offered by Seweryn Bialer seems most appropriate, and will be followed here. He has suggested that the Soviet political elite is "a relatively small group of the most influential participants in the Soviet political process" [Seweryn Bialer, "Soviet Political Elite: Concept, Sample, Case Study" (unpublished Ph.D dissertation, Faculty of Political Science, Columbia University, 1966), p. 61], or those "officials who occupy strategic positions in the exercise of authority" [p. 39]. As an *indicator* of membership in the political elite, Bialer suggests "occupancy of a high office in the hierarchy of authority, . . . combined with participation in such symbolic institutions as the Supreme Soviet (or the Party Congress)" [p. 42]. The highest *nomenklatura* list—those positions and individuals whose appointment is within the exclusive jurisdiction of the Politburo or the Secretariat of the CPSU—would describe the outer limits of the political elite [p. 42].

efforts to impose its will on society. They argue that the party is no longer engaged in a revolutionary transformation of Soviet society so as to achieve a certain ideologically defined utopian social order. In place of the "revolution from above" that the party has waged, beginning in the late 1920s, the party is content now to "shape and manage economic and socio-political conflict within [the existing] social structure."[4] The utopian goal—communism—will be achieved through successful efforts to raise economic productivity and provide material abundance. One might reply that even if this view is merited, the elite as yet retains (and continues to seek to justify) the authority to determine the appropriate means for achieving economic growth and development. It also retains the authority to set the limits within which individual social and political behavior is acceptable or permitted. The readings included in this volume all bear on this issue of the changing role of the party, the elite, and its efforts to transform or lead society.

The environmental influences in the Soviet Union against which conscious action plays are fivefold: (1) history, custom, and tradition; (2) the multinational character of Soviet society; (3) a political culture composed of a persistent pattern of traditional values, expectations, and aspirations regarding the social order, as well as a set of values, often in conflict with the traditional values, imposed on society by the small, elite group; (4) the spontaneous processes of social change within the society, arising from the social structure; and (5) the external environment—the impact of and response to developments outside the society. The readings in Part II explore the importance for politics within the Soviet Union of some of these environmental factors.

Parts III, IV, and V concern themselves with the efforts of the ruling party elite consciously to guide, lead, and direct Soviet society. Each of these parts is concerned with one of the roles performed by the Communist Party of the Soviet Union: political leadership (including the making of decisions), control over the application or administration of decisions, and efforts to assure compliance with and enforcement of these decisions.

In the Soviet Union a self-perpetuating political elite within a single-party system exercises a monopoly over political leadership in that it defines the goals of the society (sets out a utopian vision towards which the society shall struggle); defines the organizational forms and the roles and duties of individuals, and allocates the tasks thought necessary to achieve the

---

Bialer argues that at least for analytical purposes the membership of the Central Committee of the Communist Party provides the best sample of the Soviet political elite [Ch. 3].

[4] Henry W. Morton, "The Structure of Decision-Making in the U.S.S.R.: A Comparative Introduction" in Peter H. Juviler and Henry W. Morton, *Soviet Policy-Making* (New York: Frederick A. Praeger, Inc., 1967), p. 13.

vision; and seeks to motivate and induce the individual to participate in the effort. By arrogating to itself the right to set goals and establish priorities, as well as by controlling participation in decision-making activities, it determines many of the demands placed upon the decision makers. By restricting opposition and monopolizing the process of political socialization, it seeks to assure support for its role by controlling the attitudes and behavior of the individual. It decides which interests in society are to be satisfied and which not. It co-opts individuals into the leadership by a selection process designed to perpetuate not only one-party rule, but elite predominance.

Because the way in which decisions are implemented can itself be a form of decision making, the political elite is concerned with controlling the institutions through which decisions are applied or put into practice. This has always involved separation of party and state, and a search by the political elite for the appropriate relationship between the two. Of particular importance now is the question of adaptability: can the administrative bureaucracy display the creativeness and innovativeness necessary for further, efficient development of the Soviet economy? Can the existing form of administrative organization—by which those skilled in managing and developing the modern industrial Soviet society are unable to exert influence in the decision making process in proportion to the importance of their role —cope with the pressures from the economic and social environment?

In a political system where all activities are justified and tolerated only to the extent that they further established societal goals, the individual must comply with decisions made in pursuit of these goals. Compliance means more than just passive acquiescence; it means, ideally, a positive, active commitment to struggle for the goals set for society by the ruling elite and to follow the policies established for fulfillment of these goals. Thus, a wide variety of measures designed to coerce, compel, persuade, and induce the individual to comply with and to actively support decisions is characteristic of the Soviet political system. The efforts to secure compliance are designed, more basically, to achieve that measure of legitimacy which even so centralized a political system as that in the Soviet Union requires.

As suggested earlier, pressures from the environment and challenges from within the institutional structure have called these traditional roles of the party into question. It is to be hoped that the readings offered here in this volume will not only emphasize the provisional nature of our knowledge concerning the Soviet political system, but increase the reader's awareness of the fact that the system, as all political systems, is changing. The way in which institutions and processes are changing, and the pressure for change, as well as the forces resisting change, are the focal point of most of the selections. This is not to say that any particular form of change, or basic, structural changes in any specific institution, is a foregone conclusion.

Change is occurring, but the direction, pace, motivation for, and significance of this change is a matter of conjecture. The discussion in Part VI gives some evidence of the range of this conjecture.

As a system, the Soviet political system exhibits many similarities, if not identities, in structure and function with other political systems. There appear to be enough significant differences, however, in the role of various institutions and in the manner in which certain functions are performed to set it apart as a special type. In addition, an almost total mobilization of society, led by a few, for the purpose of complete transformation of the environment has been a twentieth-century innovation. The Soviet example of conscious action shaping the environment has been significantly different in degree, if not indeed in kind, from the experience of other societies in the past. It may well be serving at present as an example in other, newer societies. When deciding upon each selection to be included in this volume, an essential criterion was that it demonstrate either an aspect of the Soviet political system held in common by all political systems, or the unique way in which a common structure or function is manifested within the Soviet system, or both.

With the readings in such a framework, the reader should be in a better position to make some comparisons between politics in the Soviet Union and political activities in other countries. Of course, the selections will in addition give evidence of recent and current policy issues and problems, as well as speculation on future development. It will soon become apparent to the reader that most of the problems and issues found in the Soviet political system are reflections of the pressures for change, stability, or both. The selections are oriented predominantly to the recent past, the present, and the future. Missing is the broader historical perspective found in such studies of Soviet politics as Merle Fainsod, *How Russia is Ruled*, (Cambridge, Mass.: Harvard University Press, 1963). This volume should thus be considered as complementary to, and certainly not a substitute for, study of the historical development of the Soviet political system.

It is to be hoped that by focusing a presentation of the current state of knowledge about the Soviet political system on the areas where both the forces of change and stability are observable, the reader will have a better perspective from which to understand the evolution of Soviet society.

I UNDERSTANDING THE SOVIET POLITICAL SYSTEM

Interest in learning about the Soviet Union has grown dramatically since World War II. Until this historical turning point, awareness of the nature and character of the Soviet political system, apart from that of a handful of scholars, diplomats, and journalists, was limited and polarized. Most others viewed the Soviet regime with either sympathy or antipathy, vaguely held but often passionately expressed. The fact and fiction surrounding events in the Soviet Union, in particular the form of rule under Stalin, either severely abused one's sense of political morality or served to reinforce preconceptions about how to achieve social justice and economic development. With the emergence after the war of the Soviet Union as a large and powerful country playing a major role in international politics, it became evident that moral righteousness, whether condemnation or approbation, could not substitute for a more dispassionate understanding of the Soviet political system. For whatever reason, more and more interested individuals have come to want to know not only what the Soviet political system is like, and how the political processes function, but also *why* things happen as they do. Most important, they wish to know, on the basis of the *why*, what might happen in the future.

Unfortunately, there is neither an easy explanation for the way in which Soviet politics unfold, nor a ready-made key with which we can unlock the secrets of future Soviet behavior, internal or external. Ever since the Bolsheviks assumed power in Russia in 1917, observers have been offering theories in explanation of events and as the basis for predictions about the future. Over the years, a wide variety of such theories, or approaches to the study of the Soviet Union, has been developed. Many, if not all, of these approaches are still with us today in greater or lesser degrees of respectability. No one approach has received a sufficient degree of acceptance and confidence to enable us to give up the search for some better way, or ways, of explaining and predicting events.

It has been only in the last ten to fifteen years that scholars have begun to criticize systematically the existing approaches to the study of the Soviet Union—to evaluate their adequacy, utility, and continued relevance—and to set forth the problems involved in undertaking analyses of Soviet society. Two early studies that remain important are John Reshatar, *Problems of Analyzing and Predicting Soviet Behavior,* and Daniel Bell, "Ten Theories in Search of Reality," *World Politics,* April 1958. A more recent volume is that edited by Walter Z. Laqueur and Leopold Labedz, *The State of Soviet Studies.* This process of criticism by now has become endemic within the field of Soviet studies, with older approaches being challenged and defended and new approaches being offered.

What the readings in this section provide is some evidence of the course of this debate, and an illustration of some of the approaches in use, or coming into use, today. Broadly speaking, the debate is characterized by a challenge to the approach that has dominated the field of Soviet studies for the last twenty-five years and more, the concept of totalitarianism or the totalitarian model.[1]

Starting from the premise that a conceptual scheme or model is a prerequisite for fruitful further study of any social or political phenomenon, Alex Inkeles in his article on the use of models discusses the strengths and weaknesses not only of the totalitarian model, but also of the two models coming increasingly into use: the developmental model, and the model of the mature industrial society. While recognizing the continued utility of the totalitarian model, Professor Inkeles argues that "for analysis of the recent past and the contemporary scene in the USSR we need a model different from that developed to deal with totalitarianism." In this regard, he is giving voice to the increasing concern found among many scholars of the Soviet Union as to the role, if any, that the concept of totalitarianism should play in our studies of changing Soviet society.

Not all scholars, however, are of the opinion that the totalitarian model must either be abandoned or share its role as orderer and explainer of Soviet reality with other, newer models. Carl Friedrich, an early and prominent advocate of the totalitarian model, has recently restated his belief in its relevance as "a *relative* rather than an absolute category."[2] Professor

---

[1] For an explication of this concept see, among others, Hannah Arendt, *The Origins of Totalitarianism* (2nd ed.), (Cleveland: Meridian, 1958); Carl J. Friedrich, ed., *Totalitarianism* (Cambridge, Mass.: Harvard University Press, 1954); Carl J. Friedrich and Zbigniew Brzezinski, *Totalitarian Dictatorship and Autocracy* (Cambridge, Mass.: Harvard University Press, 1956). For a critique of the concept see A. J. Groth, "The 'Isms' in Totalitarianism," *American Political Science Review,* LVIII, No. 4 (December 1964); Robert C. Tucker, "The Dictator and Totalitarianism," *World Politics,* XVII, No. 4 (July 1965); and Robert Burrowes, "Totalitarianism: The Revised Standard Version," *World Politics,* XXI, No. 2 (January 1969).

[2] Carl J. Friedrich, "Totalitarianism: Recent Trends," *Problems of Communism* (May–June 1968).

Friedrich argues that the concept of totalitarianism must be understood in dynamic rather than static terms. A cyclical pattern of "alternation of intensification and relaxation of autocratic power" is inherent in totalitarianism. He suggests that "perhaps the most important change in the theory and practice of totalitarianism, in the conception we have of it as an ongoing process of government, is the realization that totalitarianism, like other political phenomena, is a *relative* rather than an absolute category. Instead of worrrying about an 'ideal type,' the comparison of a number of different regimes, all corresponding to the model as defined earlier, reveals that it is quite meaningful also to speak of totalitarian trends."[3]

Paul Hollander, also writing in defense of the continued relevance of the totalitarian model, sets forth what he sees to be its virtues. Reiterating a point made by Professor Inkeles, he also notes that "the emerging consensus, at any rate, among students of Soviet society, lies in combining several models, several approaches depending upon the interests at hand." He quite appropriately remarks that the question of which model one uses depends upon one's interests and values.

Allen Kassof introduces "a variant of modern totalitarianism" in his article on "the administered society." Professor Kassof has made an effort to bring the concept of totalitarianism into line with the observable changes in Soviet society—to take account of the fact that in recent years the Soviet leaders have sought to make the political system more efficient. This attempt has resulted in a decline in the use of terror and the secret police, and a search for economic rationality. Professor Kassof argues that the concept of the "administered society" best accounts for the overwhelming concern of the Soviet political elite for the total coordination of society (totalism). It "recognizes that the changes in the Soviet Union have been real and vast (after all, totalism without terror is something new); but it insists that far from developing alternatives to totalism, Soviet society is being subjected to new and more subtle forms of it, and that the Stalinist past is being streamlined rather than rejected." The concept of "the administered society," so Professor Kassof suggests, provides a general framework for depicting the Soviet system today, "sensitizing us to interpretations that otherwise might go unnoticed and enabling us to see patterns in apparently unconnected trends."

As much a method or mode of analysis as a model, "sovietology" is an approach to the study of the Soviet Union owing much to the totalitarian model. While not denying the existence of large-scale social forces, totalitarianism emphasizes the primacy of politics. One noted sovietologist has suggested that in Soviet society large-scale movements "are not given any direct political expression: they figure simply as influences, competing with

---

[3] *Ibid.*, 43.

other and often more powerful influences, on the moves made in the only area where political change is possible—the central group of politicians."[4] The continuing struggle for power and the issues associated with it is the arena in which the sovietologist seeks answers to the questions of who the Soviet decision makers are, why they behave as they do, and how they are likely to behave in the future.

Arthur E. Adams defines sovietology as "the study of all matters that help us to understand the meaning of current, politically significant Soviet-communist behavior and to forecast its future course." Emphasis should be placed on the words *current* and *politically* in this definition, for sovietology is oriented to the present. It is the conscious behavior of individuals now occupying politically significant positions that is the subject of attention for the sovietologist.[5]

The sovietologist assumes that an oligarchical policy-making process exists. He assumes that decisions are made by a few leaders at the apex of the political system, who are relatively unfettered by society or the population as a whole. Within this oligarchical structure, conflict persists among individuals and among groups. To understand how decisions are made and which issues are important, and thus ultimately the direction of Soviet society, one must study the power struggles and the decision-making process within the elite. The sovietologist points to evidence indicating the existence of an "esoteric code of communications" through which leaders at the top of the power pyramid communicate to the broader levels of the party and state. By acquiring the necessary skills, an outsider can learn to read these communications, and thus learn a great deal about political behavior within the elite of the Soviet Union. In at least part of their work, most contemporary observers of Soviet society engage in some form of sovietology.

T. H. Rigby has noted the absence of a separation of "politics" and "administration," and the existence of "government without public, institutionalized politics," in the Soviet Union. He suggests that in the Soviet Union "conflicts of interest and aspiration ... denied a special political sphere of operation [characteristic of liberal-democratic societies], tend to give a political coloration to processes ostensibly executive and administrative in character, that is, to generate a distinctive *crypto-politics*."[6] It is the

---

[4] Robert Conquest, *Power and Policy in the U.S.S.R.* (New York: Harper Torchbooks, 1967). Another illustrative example of sovietology is Donald Zagoria, *The Sino-Soviet Dispute, 1956–1961* (Princeton, N.J.: Princeton University Press, 1962).

[5] Professor Adams makes the distinction between the sovietologist and the expert on Soviet politics. He is vague on this point, but seems to be implying that there are aspects of political life in the Soviet Union at a distance from the immediate elite, conflicts he associates with the decision-making process. Why these are important and why they merit study by political scientists, if they do not help in predicting the future, is not made clear.

[6] T. H. Rigby, "Crypto-Politics," *Survey*, No. 50 (January 1964), pp. 144–55.

task of the sovietologist, suggests Rigby, to follow the political conflict within the Soviet leadership. In order to do so adequately, a general picture of the conditions of *crypto-political* activity in the USSR must be sketched out. In so doing, one can profitably learn "from experience acquired in studying bureaucratic politics in other systems."

A challenge to traditional Soviet studies, especially the totalitarian model and sovietology, comes from within the discipline of political science. Alfred Meyer and John Kautsky, for example, prefer to view the Soviet political system from within a broader, more comparative perspective—to understand communism in the Soviet Union by uncovering the social forces affecting the nature of the system, and by relating it to other political systems.[7] Their views presented here, along with those of Paul Hollander, were part of the Symposium on the Comparative Study of Communism, and the discussions that ensued therefrom, which ran in several issues of the *Slavic Review* in 1967.

Meyer and Kautsky argue generally that Soviet studies should be integrated with contemporary political science. Specifically, Professor Meyer argues that the accumulation of concepts developed for the comparative study of political systems should be applied to the Soviet Union, and to the communist world more broadly. Both articulate the view held by many scholars today that knowledge and understanding of the particular (the Soviet political system) can most fruitfully be attained or approached through relating it to the general (communist systems as a whole, or non-communist systems). Both have attempted to do so, in similar ways. Implicitly or explicitly, both assume a process of development through which every political system passes, although not necessarily at the same pace, or through exactly the same stages.

Professor Kautsky suggests that the communist movements, beginning with Russia, are best understood as modernizing movements that share numerous characteristics with non-communist modernizing movements (the social composition of the leadership and the following: acceptance of Western ideologies and models; the goal of rapid industrialization). He argues further that to understand the dynamics of politics within the Soviet Union, one would be served best by understanding the dynamics of "modernization" and "development." There are political phenomena that are a result of, or associated with, modernization or development. Any

---

[7] See also the discussion between Zbigniew Brzezinski, Alfred Meyer, and Robert C. Tucker on the nature of the Soviet system in the *Slavic Review*, XX, No. 3 (October 1961). Professor Meyer has applied his bureaucratic model at length in *The Soviet Political System: An Interpretation* (New York: Random House, Inc., 1965). Professor Kautsky has collected his writings on communism and the process of development in *Communism and Political Development* (New York: John Wiley & Sons, Inc., 1968).

society that is modernizing or developing (such as Soviet society) will manifest these phenomena, with differences, but also with considerable similarity. "Political systems, movements, and ideologies can usefully be compared when they are at roughly equivalent stages of economic development, regardless of whether they are communist or not." A continuum of societal forms is implied, ranging from premodernization, through modernizing, to modern. Knowledge of the dynamics of movement along this continuum, and location of a given political system therein, will best enable one to understand why things happen as they do, why certain institutions and processes exist in a given society. Most important, one will have a better idea of what to expect in the future.

In describing why he prefers the "bureaucratic" model, Professor Meyer speaks of communist societies as developing societies; of the development of communist systems and periods of "growing pains"; and of "system-building," as well as a "presumably much longer period of settled existence within a well-established system." Having passed through a period of development, through "a succession of political systems differing from each other in purpose, structure, and functioning," the Soviet Union is presumably at or approaching the ultimate level of modernization, a mature industrial society. Although Professor Meyer does not reject the totalitarian model—in fact he states that it and his "are complementary rather than mutually exclusive"—he believes that one can best understand the Soviet Union by comparing it with complex modern bureaucratic organizations anywhere. "Like modern bureaucracy, communist rule is essentially an attempt to impose rational management over social life by means of complex organization. This attempt leads to the emergence of structural forms, political processes, psychological adjustments, as well as malfunctionings which make communist systems look remarkably similar to bureaucratic organizations in other parts of the world."

There is an even sharper challenge coming from within the discipline of political science. It comes from those who would emphasize the methodology, techniques, and empirical theory of the social sciences in general as they have developed over the past twenty or thirty years. Their concern is not primarily with the application to the Soviet Union of concepts already formulated for the comparative study of political systems. Indeed, Robert Sharlet, in his contribution to the Symposium on the Comparative Study of Communism, though arguing for joining communist area studies with "the main lines of the discipline of political science," cautions against an uncritical and unsystematic application of basic concepts taken from political science and applied to communist area studies.[8] Rather, they seek to restructure inquiry about Soviet society.

---

[8] Robert Sharlet, "Systematic Political Science and Communist Systems," *Slavic Review*, XXVI, No. 1 (March 1967). See also Robert Sharlet, "Concept Formation

A noteworthy statement of this view, and a critique of traditional Soviet studies from this perspective, is Frederic J. Fleron, "Soviet Area Studies and the Social Sciences: Some Methodological Problems in Communist Studies," *Soviet Studies*, XIX, No. 3 (January 1968). In Fleron's words, "the methodology spoken of here is sometimes called the methodology of science. There are compelling reasons for believing that this methodology of science offers the best means for gaining systematic knowledge." What this entails is "scientific concept formation, empiricism, verification, and theory-construction"[9] and "the systematic collection of data and the construction of empirical theory."[10] Professor Fleron does not offer his own explanation or description of the Soviet political system. Rather, he argues that the inadequacies of past and present explanations can be remedied, and new, more reliable explanations constructed, only if scholars reorient their thinking and accept certain assumptions about how intellectual inquiry can best be undertaken.

Professor Fleron perceives several methodological problems relating to Soviet and communist studies. Seeking "to promote a more vigorous and systematic study of communism," he discusses problems of concept formation, the logical status and methodological utility of empirical theories and theoretical models, and the use of certain patterns of explanation. He calls for precision in the definition and use of concepts, and provides specific definitions and uses of the terms *theory, model,* and *ideal-type.* He specifically criticizes what he believes to be the vagueness in the use of such terms by many of the authors included in Part I of this volume.

As Professor Fleron notes, the philosophical basis for the methodology of science approach is essentially that of neo-logical positivism. It is an approach that searches for the "universal laws of human behavior." From these, using the appropriate techniques for classifying and measuring data, one might develop a level of explanation and prediction considerably more precise and reliable than is the case at present. This raises important epistemological issues, for there is by no means complete agreement as to "the rules according to which systematic inquiry is conducted"; or whether all questions humans ask, or unknowns about which they inquire, can be subsumed under *a* set of rules; or what it means to be "systematic." Are there general or universal laws expressing uniformities or regularities of human behavior? Must one refer to, or apply, general laws as the most appropriate means of explaining events? These are related questions over

---

in Political Communist Studies," *Canadian Slavic Studies*, I, No. 4 (Winter 1967), and his forthcoming study, *Building a Communist System: The Soviet Union as a Developing Country.*

[9] *Ibid.*, 22.

[10] Fleron, 315. See also Frederic J. Fleron, ed., *Communist Studies and the Social Sciences* (Skokie, Ill.: Rand McNally & Co., 1969) and Roger E. Kanet, *The Behavioral Revolution and Communist Studies* (New York: The Free Press, 1970).

which there is great debate among philosophers and social scientists. Professor Fleron clearly comes down on one side.

Despite possible objections to Professor Fleron's argument, his call for precision and for concern with first principles is long overdue. His comments are part of the growing self-criticism within the field, which can only have a salutary effect on the state of Soviet studies.

MODELS AND ISSUES IN
THE ANALYSIS OF SOVIET SOCIETY

ALEX INKELES

I recently completed a small book, essentially a long essay, called *What is Sociology?*, the writing of which made me acutely sensitive to the fact that most social scientists approach the subject they are studying with some kind of conceptual scheme which we may call a model. These models play an enormously important role in deciding what is taken into consideration and what is left out, what weight is assigned to one factor as against another, which sets of interrelationships are assumed to exist and which will go largely unnoticed. There is a great deal of debate about models, most of which deals with the question of whether or not a particular model is right or wrong. In my opinion there is no such thing as a right or wrong sociological model. There are richer and poorer ones. There are the more sensitive and less sensitive. There are those which are more appropriate to one time or place than another. All have a piece of the truth, but it is rare that any *one* model is really adequate to the analysis of a richly complex concrete historical case. The object of my talk is to present three important models with a word

about the strengths and weaknesses of each, viewed for the most part historically, as we have approached them in Soviet studies.

The first, the model which dominated Soviet studies in the past, may have different labels applied to it but it will be readily recognised as the model of the totalitarian society. We may also speak of it as the model of the Stalinist terror, of the implementation of the concept of the Leninist society, of the distinctive communist polity, or the model of the betrayal of socialism. All these variant perspectives have in common the essential idea that there was created in the Soviet Union under Stalin a fairly distinctive type of social structure with more or less unique characteristics. I am, at this point, reminded of an idea of Henry Murray and Clyde Kluckhohn, who said we should always keep in mind that each man is in some respects like all other men, in some respects like some other men, and in some respects like no other man. The totalitarian model, although it accepted the notion that the Soviet Union was a society like all other societies, and acknowledged it

Survey, No. 60 (July 1966), 3–14, reprinted by permission. Footnotes omitted.

also as one *type* of society, mainly stressed the *uniqueness* of the USSR. Belief in the distinctiveness of the Soviet system, concentration on the special combination of events that made it what it was, was quite reasonable. The Soviet Union was, after all, the first society on the world scene to represent the attainment of power by a group of men who were dedicated to and organised around the principles of communist thought.

The central elements in the totalitarianism model are well known. These are the themes we regularly write about in our books and refer to in our lectures. If I give you only the key terms, that will suffice. One of the key concepts is the central importance of a concern with power. As we see it, according to the model, the Soviet regime imposed by force, on a nation and a people, an alien system, but one which was self-contained and complete. The themes that we have dealt with in elaborating the model of totalitarianism include the mobilisation of the entire population for the purposes of building a new type of social structure. This mobilisation was characterised, to a very important degree, by the fact that the population did not choose to build this society, but rather was organised for this purpose by the political leadership. Many of the tensions of Soviet society stemmed from this fact. In promulgating the totalitarian model we give great attention, of course, to the central role of the communist party, not only its monopoly of power, but its special internal structure, its peculiar semantics, its history of personal rule in the form of Stalin, its unique reliance on propaganda, its very special use of force as in political terror.

This totalitarian model had great strength. It answered to many of the really basic and distinctive characteristic facts of the situation. The essence of being a Soviet expert, the thing that set them apart from everybody else, was their feeling that here in this model they had the key to Soviet reality. Many a Soviet citizen said that if *Pravda* carried reports of food shortages in Africa, he knew that the next day there would be difficulty in buying grain and meat in Moscow. Just so Soviet experts felt that unless one came to understand the semantics, the complex double-thought, unless one knew how to read *Pravda* and *Izvestiya* between the lines, and possessed the key provided by the model of totalitarianism, one could not be considered qualified to discuss Soviet affairs.

This model also had certain weaknesses. One of the difficulties was that it was relatively insensitive to the sources of social support for the Soviet regime. It represented a screen which did not permit the intrusion of this kind of information, because, naturally, such information was a challenge to the adequacy of the model. Every scientific model is, to a certain extent, an ideology, which screens out information too challenging to the premises of the model. A second great difficulty with the totalitarian model, it seems to me, was that it seriously neglected the degree of Soviet development, or what in Soviet language is called 'socialist construction'. The model was not sufficiently attuned to the fact that, within the Stalinist framework, a very large-scale, complex, and in some ways enormously creative process of building new social forms and new institutions was going on.

There is a term which we could not use for a long time because of its popularity with certain naïve English political commentators who did not understand the totalitarianism model, but who rather referrred to the Soviet Union as an 'experiment'. I am delighted to hear that word come back. It should be in our vocabulary, because to an extraordinary degree the Soviet Union, even though perhaps an *evil* experiment (as perhaps Stalin was an *evil* genius), *was* an extraordinary experiment. It is true that the experiment rested on the exercise of absolute power, and was perhaps motivated by very unattractive objectives. Nevertheless, the Soviet Union was and continues to be a place in which, to an extraordinary degree, a continuous process of social experimentation, or, in different words, planned change, is going on. Sometimes the experimentation was of the most disastrous sort for the people involved, as for example in the collectivisation of agriculture, or in the purge-trials, each a gruesome kind of social invention. (I always think of the trials in terms of the statement made about Stalin being a pragmatic man. It was said that he proceeded by trial and error. It seemed to me that he did indeed proceed by his error and someone else's trial.)

A fourth defect I would like to mention is that this model, as all models, is historically limited. After the death of Stalin there were profound changes in the Soviet social structure. What was formerly a system limited to one country and therefore inextricably identified as parochial, is now becoming to a great degree world-wide; not merely a 'movement', which it had been for a long time, but a standard form of institutional organisation which has been established in many places. Therefore anyone who wants to understand contemporary politics or contemporary social structure in many of its aspects,

must confront the new forms which this system has taken.

In going to conferences on Soviet affairs I sometimes have the feeling that all the Soviet experts were once put in a kind of sealed chamber, something like a bathysphere, and then put on the bottom of the sea where they remained permanently locked up in their small world, breathing their special form of rarefied atmosphere. Occasionally new men were put in and others taken out, but otherwise the basic circle and its standard dialogue has gone on for decades. I suggest we get some new themes, new ideas, new models into the discussion, not just for the sake of novelty, but because I think we are really dealing with a system which is in an important degree changing. But even in our interpretation of the past, new models of analysis may enrich and correct interpretations we have already made. I am reminded here of a statement I heard recently about a corpulent British writer and critic. He said, 'Inside every fat man, there is a thin man crying to get out'. Perhaps we should think of the Soviet system in the same way. Inside its bloated totalitarianism there may all along have been a quite different system struggling to be born.

I suggest that for analysis of the recent past and the contemporary scene in the USSR we need a model different from that developed to deal with totalitarianism. This is not to say we must entirely abandon the model we have been using. In many respects it answers extremely well. But we need to put an *additional* model into our work. I think we can best refer to it as the 'development-model'. This model either deals with certain problems common to all developing societies, or tries to treat the distinctive problems of a particular society, but always from the perspective of development. It is quite a different perspective from one which sees society mainly in terms of power and politics. I personally feel that we have seriously neglected looking at the Soviet Union in these terms.

Martin Lipset recently wrote a book about the United States called *The First New Nation*. Perhaps he put the origin of newly-developed nations too far back. If you insist on locating such developments in the more recent past, the Soviet Union probably represents, with the possible exception of Japan, the prime example of the new kind of social and economic development which preoccupies the leaders and the people of many countries and has become one of the central problems of the post-Second World War period. The Soviet Union was the first nation which confronted us with the kind of preoccupation with *growth* which characterises the developing nations, and its history foreshadowed the kinds of solutions which have been typically adopted to meet the distinctive problems facing developing countries (granted that often the problems which are distinctive are so because the leaders have made them so).

The long-standing central concerns of the Soviet regime are in many respects similar to the central concerns of the governments of many of the developing nations of the world. For one thing, the Soviet leaders were enormously preoccupied with developing a highly flexible system of administration responsive to central authority rather than to the general population. In that they are not so different from the leaders of many other developing countries. One of the fundamental con-

cerns, one of the central preoccupations, of the Bolshevik leaders was to organise things so that they really ran. We have been insensitive to the challenge that this would have presented to any Russian government. Another concern they had was to organise political loyalties around a central national image. I shall always remember Professor Karpovich telling me that when the First World War began, he was in a small Russian village to which he often went for vacations. A peasant who knew Karpovich to be a man of learning came up to him and said he hoped he would not mind if he asked a question. The peasant had heard that the Kaiser and the Tsar were at war, and he wondered did that mean that his village and he himself also had to consider themselves at war with the Kaiser. Such an incident had become unthinkable by the time Hitler went to war with Stalin. The analogue to this situation is found all over the world now in the developing countries. For example, in East Pakistan, in a survey I am now conducting, we asked people how they would respond if they were travelling in a foreign country and were asked: 'To what *country* do you belong?' About 24 per cent of the people we interviewed named their village or subdivision of origin as the country to which they belonged. Some 66 per cent named their county district. Only 7 per cent named Pakistan!

To take another theme; consider the integration of diverse religious and ethnic groups around a cohesive new sense of national identification. We have usually approached the Soviet nationality problem almost exclusively as an example of the forced imposition on various peoples of membership in an alien national society, of which they very often do not feel a significant part and in which they often do not wish to participate. In part this image is true. But it developed not merely out of Soviet totalitarianism. The process of more or less forced integration of diverse ethnic and religious groups into new amalgams is going on all over the world. It arises inevitably in the course of nationbuilding.

We may also profitably look at the realm of education. The Soviets were obviously enormously concerned with raising the level of literacy, and then of widely introducing advanced and higher education. I do not think this can be explained exclusively in terms of power, although power surely played a part. No doubt the Soviet leaders wanted to get more people to read and write so that they could be reached by the message of the communist party. But the leaders also encouraged literacy because it was obvious that Soviet Russia could not develop into a modern society unless everyone had equipment so fundamental for participation in the modern world. The Soviet campaign for literacy was an instrument for *modernisation* as well as a tool of political purpose. Similarly, in the case of Soviet preoccupation with establishing a broad base for science and technology, this can be explained by reference to Marxist ideology, which certainly expressed a positive interest in science and technology. But we should also recognise that central to the Soviet leadership's concern for science was its desire to establish a technological basis for the development of a modern society.

Turning, finally, to the realm of economy, we see again that many of the central preoccupations of the leadership can be better understood if we think in terms of a group of men who, quite apart from the fact that they also happened to be Marxists and communists interested in certain semantics and in the possession of power, were also concerned with developing their country as a great industrial nation. This surely had something to do with the broadening of the central industrial base and the intimately related problem of the neglect of agriculture. Sovietologists have made all kinds of efforts to explain the depressed condition of Soviet agriculture in purely political and economic terms. It is also possible, however, that the Soviet leaders were victims of the same misconception about the 'natural' path of economic development as we find among the leaders in almost every underdeveloped country in the world today. This is something that goes beyond Marxism. Among the leaders of developing nations there is a widespread mystique about the central role of large-scale industry in nation-building. Ultimately some kind of psychological symbol is involved, and it has led Soviet leaders—as it has led others since—to grossly neglect agriculture in favour of building industry. Their preoccupation with the establishment of new distribution systems, however ineffective they may have been, represents another typical concern. The Soviet leaders' interest in planning is something which is obviously shared in almost all the developing countries. Surely I need not provide more illustrations.

The strengths of the development model are several. This approach is responsive to certain important facts, and it must be given its due. Lenin and Stalin were deeply preoccupied with the problem of development.

They were dedicated not merely to seizing and holding power, but also to social development and the construction of a new society, however unattractive many of its features may be to us. The Soviet self-image was above all else the image of the developing society. Furthermore, leaders of most of the developing countries of the world see the Soviet Union mainly as a model of development rather than as a model of politics. They often regard those political issues which are the objects of the Sovietologists' past and present attention as quite incidental. They are, unfortunately, not always impressed by our treatises on liberty and freedom and our strictures on the dangers of totalitarianism. They are more interested in how rapidly they can have good, effective administration, how they can learn to build a school system, to get bridges across rivers, even to get trains to run on time. They want to know what are the devices whereby you build an elite, develop an intelligentsia, or establish a stable bureaucracy. In this connection they see the Soviet Union as a relevant model whereas, interestingly enough, the United States, Germany, England, and even Japan are often not so regarded even though they, too, once went through a comparable phase of development. Unless we engage ourselves with this issue, we are putting ourselves more and more in the position of talking to ourselves. We are back in the bathysphere! If we wish to find grounds for understanding and communicating with the people in the developing countries we must view the Soviet Union as a problem in development, acknowledge it as one strategy for development, and argue about it on those terms. I do not think that as

a rule we do this, nor indeed, are we now well equipped to do it.

The development approach also has some weaknesses. It might be that the model is in fact inappropriate, that the situation is a little bit like the Red Riding Hood tale. The wolf (for whom you may substitute the Soviet Union) has come along and eaten grandma (who to us represents, perhaps, the displaced colonial powers). Now the wolf is in bed with grandma's hat on when little Red Riding Hood (the developing countries) comes along. The wolf looks like grandma, but is in fact about to devour Red Riding Hood. There may well be some justice in the analogy. It may also be true that it is inappropriate to speak of Russia as having been a truly underdeveloped country at the time of the Revolution. Russia in 1917 was certainly very far ahead of the point at which most developing countries now start out, and in addition it had a long European tradition. Nevertheless, in many ways Russia was the most backward country in Europe, despite the fact that its industry at the time of the first world war was perhaps the newest and included many of the largest plants in Europe. I do not think it inappropriate, therefore, to think of it as having been a 'developing' country. Certainly Lenin thought of development as perhaps the main problem facing his regime.

Second, it may be argued against the development model that the alleged status of the Soviet Union as a developing country, even if a fact, is a quite incidental one. The most important consideration is the conditions in which this development took place, namely under communist party domination. My answer to this is yes, of course, but development always takes place in *some* conditions. Whether the conditions in which it takes place, or the development itself is the predominant factor, or whether the interaction between the two is more important, constitutes an historical problem which can be solved in each concrete case only by detailed analysis. The most important challenge to the development model, consequently, remains the one I used about the model of the totalitalian system, namely, that this is also an historically limited model.

If we study the Soviet Union and what is happening in it, we must recognise that a third model is becoming relevant. It is unfortunately the least developed and least used model. Yet if the development model is the model of the present, this one will be the model of the future. This third is the model of the Soviet Union as a mature industrial society. The industrial model has been used a little at Harvard, where I have emphasised it in my teaching and research. In this, Professor Sorokin anticipated me a long time ago. In his book on *Russia and the United States* (1944), his chief argument was that the correct approach to the Soviet Union was to see it mainly as a large-scale industrial society like the United States. He said there, as a matter of fact, that only foolish people would be preoccupied with what he considers the minor differences between the two nations.

I can more readily accept being a fool than I can accept the differences between the United States and the USSR as minor. Nevertheless, I consider the industrial society model one which can greatly contribute to our understanding of Soviet society. In this perspective politics is no longer the sole, nor indeed the universally determining

force operating; nor is the fact of political *development* the central problem. Instead this approach stresses such things as size, complexity, forms and levels of such social realms as education, stratification, urbanisation, community organisation, social mobility, mass communication, and the like. In the industrial society perspective, we see all these as having a pattern of effects on the social order not mainly because of but often regardless of the political system which prevails.

I know many of you will think it rash—if not a form of madness—for me to assert such 'independence of the political system' when talking about the Soviet Union. I would rest my main case on the data and reasoning presented in *The Soviet Citizen*. There we showed that in most areas of life the best way to predict the attitudes, values, and orientations of men in the Soviet system is to draw on the general knowledge that we have about men holding comparable positions in western industrial societies. This is not to say there are not some areas of life where the fact of communist party domination is not the prime predictor. Nor would I say that there are not other areas where knowing that we speak of a Russian rather than a Ukrainian is crucial in judging a Soviet man's life-situation and his resultant attitudes. But on most questions, knowing his relative position in a modern large-scale industrial social structure seemed more useful in understanding the attitudes of a Soviet worker or manager than was knowing his party history or his ethnic membership.

The significant advantage of the industrial-society model is that it highlights certain neglected problems. For example, none of the other models provides the possibility of anticipating, or the means of dealing with, the sudden appearance in the Soviet Union of a kind of *jeunesse dorée*. The other models are helpless to explain phenomena such as the middle-class delinquency exemplified by the children of ministers who steal money from their parents, even snatch pocket-books to raise funds for joy-rides to certain fabulous hotels and bars in Minsk, Kiev, Leningrad, and Moscow. There are many aspects of the stratification situation in the Soviet Union which can be understood only if we see them in terms of the problems facing most large-scale industrial social systems.

If we examine the work on Soviet industrial managers, we can see a large number of elements in the life-situation of these men and in their response to it which are indistinguishable from the situation and response of industrial managers in many other parts of the world. Of course this is not to say that this makes them identical. Among the themes spontaneously mentioned in an interview with an industrial manager in the West, labour relations is always one of the most frequent. In the Soviet Union it is a theme seldom mentioned, and that fact is connected, obviously, with important differences in the socio-economic structures of the systems being compared. But there are many other ways in which a manager from the USSR *is* like one from any western industrial nation. This is so because there are factors in the managers' life-situation as members of an industrial society which over-ride distinctive political and cultural differences. Soviet managers now exert pressure for the adoption of a more rational system of allocation, and increasingly recognise the necessity for using computer techniques out of kinship of experience

with managers elsewhere which arises independently of political context and stage of economic development.

The reports that we hear about young people further confirm the appropriateness of the industrial model. We have heard that young artists in the Soviet Union are now ready to say: 'Leave me alone, I am doing serious work'. This cannot be explained in terms of the other models; rather this must be understood by reference to the fact that the Soviet Union is reaching levels and entering realms and beginning to face problems which arise mainly from its maturation as an industrial society. Or consider the role of science and the intellectuals. It is significant that there has been a final end of Lysenkoism. The effort to work out new relationships between science and government in the Soviet Union involves many parallels with the problems scientists report in places which are presumably as different from the Soviet Union as is the United States.

The industrial-society model is especially relevant for the future. As the Soviet Union continues to mature, it is acquiring more and more of the characteristics of the western type of social system. This is accompanied by the erosion of some of its own previously distinctive characteristics like the political terror. New problems will emerge, which again do not eliminate the old but must be dealt with. For example, the problem of the youth culture and the weak integration of the young in all the large-scale societies in the western world, is a problem which requires serious attention. As we have discovered in Berkeley, California, and in Jakarta, it can sometimes have very explosive consequences.

Other shared problems include the results of technological change and consequent unemployment. The Soviet Union is beginning openly to acknowledge what we have known for a long time, namely, that there is enormous underemployment in the Soviet economy. They are entering a new phase in which they openly admit that they do not know what to do with the surplus people who are thrown on the labour market as a result of improved technology of production. The problem of leisure-time and the threat that it poses; the changed nature of old age and the social issues which it presents —more and more of these issues will come to the fore in the Soviet Union as they have in other industrial societies.

If we want to continue to deal with the Soviet Union as a society, we must deal with these questions and issues. We can of course, if we wish to, remain pure sovietologists, and say: 'No, I'll not deal with that sort of thing. It has nothing to do with communism or the purely Soviet'. I can understand that choice. I am trying here to delineate it, to clarify it, to ask us to face consciously the choice we are making. My feeling is that we will miss a great deal of what is important if we do not accept responsibility for studying these contemporary and newer issues in Soviet development. But to the extent that we do we will be obliged to draw on analytic models other than the totalitarian or even the developmental.

This is a highly-compressed account, and therefore, before leaving the subject of models, I should like briefly to make a few points which may forestall misunderstanding. I should like to stress, first of all, that the models I have presented are certainly not the only relevant ones for the analysis of Soviet society. Some of you may know the article by Daniel Bell, in which he differentiated ten different approaches to the study of the Soviet Union, and that is by no means exhaustive. I did not put the historical model in the centre here, but I think one certainly might. I personally am a great believer in the relevance of what is sometimes called the 'characterological' or the 'national character' model. This is perhaps another way of stating the historical. I cannot believe that the study of Soviet society can be complete if it does not consider some long-term and deeply-rooted aspects of the Russian orientation to authority-figures. Nor, indeed, can we leave out so general a theory as that which Professor Erlich proposes, since he presumably has in mind some model of human nature which he conceives of as inherently opposed to the nature of the Soviet system. There are, of course, other models of human nature which would argue just the contrary, namely that the Soviet system is the one which most *corresponds* to human nature. The point I am making, of course, is that there are many models, and the three that I selected were by no means meant to exhaust the number of those available, in fact not even to exhaust those that I have myself used at different times.

Second, I should also make it clear that I have no special preference for one model over any of the others. I think they are all interesting and useful, each in its place and time. I am not prepared to commit myself exclusively to one; my purpose has been rather different. I wanted to highlight the existence of the models, and to help us realise that these are the ways in which some of us, indeed all of us in varying degrees, have been thinking about the Soviet Union. My purpose was to make us aware of our thought patterns, sensitive to the strengths and weaknesses of all three of the models.

Third, I want to stress that these models are abstractions and not reality. In other words, we take these as sets of ideas or concepts which have a certain unity, and then ask how far does reality fit them. They are, therefore, heuristic devices to aid communication and analysis. If I know the model you are using, and you know the same model that I know, and we know the terms in which it is couched, it facilitates our ability to communicate. We are thus brought closer to the style of communication which is characteristic of mathematics, where one works with very precise terms and everyone knows the symbols which represent them and the laws governing their combination. Our great problem in the social sciences is that so much of the time we are so imprecise in our language and so casual in our use of it, not because we are incapable of doing better, but because we have not developed the technique or habit of exact and precise expression.

My fourth point concerns the time factor and the outmoding of models. This is related to the issue of preference. I am not saying that any of these models, in particular the first, is at present *irrelevant* to the analysis of Soviet society. This would be nonsense. The totalitarian model is still highly relevant. Yet if we keep it in mind as a model, we can see how far the Soviets have been moving from it. This also requires that we be more honest, or if you like more precise, in specifying what exactly each model represents. We must somewhere write down exactly what we consider the elements of the model to be, and then later on accept the test of whether something has departed from it or not. Professor

Brzezinski at one time defined Soviet totalitarianism to include the terror as we knew it in the thirties as an *essential and defining* feature of the Soviet system. I think he would acknowledge today that the terror, although obviously not eliminated entirely, no longer plays anything remotely like its former role in Soviet society. Now, since we agree on the facts, the problem that he and I would face in a dialogue would be, should we still call the Soviet Union 'totalitarian'? If we would still call it totalitarian, would we not have to go back and revise the earlier model? And if we did not want to revise the model, would not the path then be to elaborate some conception of totalitarianism of the type A, B, or C or a combination of these? This would get very complicated. I think we learn something from this kind of review. Yet to point to the inadequacy of a model as an exclusive or exact guide is not to say that it has completely lost its relevance. My aim was to get a hearing for models which I felt had been relatively neglected, and not mainly to impugn the great relevance in the past of the other models.

A fifth point concerns the combination of models, which Professor Fainsod in particular stressed as being desirable. I am reminded here of a theme that much preoccupied us in the early days of the Russian Research Centre when we talked about the integration of disciplines as a way of studying the Soviet Union. Cylde Kluckhohn used to say that the objective is not to have several skulls under one discipline, but rather to have several disciplines under one skull. Now we face something of the same problem when we consider the combination of models. We all generally agree that a combination of models is desirable. But I am not sure we should automatically argue for the combination of models because, as I have tried to point out, every model has its distinctive perspective. By combining the models we inevitably lose the possibility of highlighting some element that we consider critical. I do not, therefore, necessarily make an unreserved plea for the combination of models. I am in favour of both their combination and their maintenance in their distinctive conditions, depending upon the kind of problems we are dealing with and the historic time in which we are operating.

I wish to reiterate that I do not think it necessary to give up the particular insights and contributions of one model in order to bring another one to bear. In order to acknowledge the increased importance and autonomy of the scientific community, it is not necessary to deny the fact that the Soviet Union is still overwhelmingly dominated by the communist party. To be aware that freedom of expression is extraordinarily limited in the USSR, it is not necessary to blind yourself to the

fact that in the realm of the family there are currents which are highly spontaneous, quite uncontrolled by the regime, and reflecting something of Russian character and tradition. Indeed, this family may for its members increasingly represent a structure of life which they do not particularly interpret in Russian or communist or totalitarian terms, but rather treat as another situation of life with all its human opportunities and uncertainties. If we take responsibility for Soviet studies rather than for the study of communism more narrowly defined, we must accept an obligation to deal with all the areas and dimensions of Soviet life.

Finally, the time dimension is very much in my mind. If you look at the problem historically, you can see that new models had to be introduced because the old ones no longer served when used exclusively. As Soviet society developed and changed, so we have been obliged either to develop and change our models or continue to analyse Soviet affairs with conceptual tools which did not answer to reality.

THE ADMINISTERED SOCIETY: TOTALITARIANISM WITHOUT TERROR

ALLEN KASSOF

"As an orchestra conductor sees to it that all the instruments sound harmonious and in proportion, so in social and political life does the Party direct the efforts of all people toward achievement of a single goal.

"Each person must, like a bee in the hive, make his own contribution to increasing the material and spiritual wealth of society. People may be found who say that they do not agree with this, that it is coercion of the individual, a return to the past. To this my answer is: We are living in an organized socialist society where the interests of the individual conform to the

World Politics, XVI, No. 4 (July 1964), 558–75, reprinted by permission. Footnotes omitted.

interests of society and are not at variance with them."—Nikita Khrushchev, March 8, 1963.

More than a decade after Stalin's death, the time is ripe for a fresh view of Soviet society. Many of the conventional patterns of analysis, developed largely during the period of Stalinist absolutism, seem to be no longer adequate for this purpose. This article proposes that a new concept, the "administered society," may be useful in summarizing and evaluating recent changes in the Soviet system and in identifying current trends.

Like other ideal-typical concepts, that of the administered society by no means pretends to account for all of the concrete detail of a social order. Instead, it draws attention (through emphasis, and hence a certain exaggeration) to very general features which constitute a society's ethos or prevailing themes—in the Soviet case, centering around the drive of the regime to establish a highly organized and totally coordinated society, and the consequences of that drive.

The administered society can be defined as one in which an entrenched and extraordinarily powerful ruling group lays claim to ultimate and exclusive scientific knowledge of social and historical laws and is impelled by a belief not only in the practical desirability, but the moral necessity, of planning, direction, and coordination from above in the name of human welfare and progress.

Convinced that there should be complete order and predictability in human affairs, the elite is concerned not merely with the "commanding heights," but also to an overwhelming degree with the detailed regulation of the entire range of social life, including those institutions which, in the West, typical-

ly have been regarded as lying beyond the legitimate scope of public authority and political intervention. The rulers of the administered society refuse to grant the possibility of unguided coordination; they believe, on the contrary, that not only the masses but responsible subgroups (for example, the professions) are incapable of maintaining a viable social order on their own, without the precise and detailed supervision of an omniscient political directorate. The elite believes, and through a far-reaching program of education and propaganda tries to teach its subjects, that the only possible good society is one that is *administered*.

The administered society is thus a variant of modern totalitarianism, with the important difference that it operates by and large without resort to those elements of gross irrationality (in particular, the large-scale and often self-defeating use of psychological terror and physical coercion as basic means of social control) that we have come to associate with totalitarian systems in recent decades.

The administered society, however, should be distinguished from the conventional welfare state in that it is not involved simply or principally in creating minimal conditions of social welfare within an otherwise pluralistic political framework, but instead treats welfare as an incidental—and instrumental— element in the larger scheme of social planning and reform. While an administered society may display more or fewer welfare features of a material or service nature, they are neither final goals nor the most important determinants of overall policy. To put it another way, the elite regards the promotion of total coordination as itself the ultimate form of welfare under modern conditions.

Plainly enough, the administered society is not the authentic good society of faithful Marxists, for it is characterized by the growing size and importance of an elite party and state bureaucracy, in contrast to the withering-away of governmental apparatus which Marxism predicts and upon which it insists.

Nor, finally, should the administered society be confused with a rational technocracy, even though here there are some superficial parallels. The leadership of the administered society, to be sure, is forced to rely on scientific and technical cadres as sources of essential information and in the execution of highly complex economic and social planning. But the political elite is not bound solely or principally by considerations of technical rationality; the technicians and experts operate only under license of the political elite and in terms of the latter's self-proclaimed ultimate knowledge about the proper uses of science and technology in the larger socio-historical setting. The experts, in short, are servants rather than masters or even independent practitioners. They lack the power of veto on grounds of technical rationality over political decisions (though in the end the limits of technology itself, if not the will of the technocrats, of course impose certain restraints). And their potential for independent influence in the society is decisively cut short by the elite's consistent practice of defining *all* decision-making as political and therefore beyond the competence of any group other than itself. Similar considerations are applied—if anything, with more vigor—to the producers of the more "esoteric" goods and services—the artists and writers, professors and critics

and journalists. Like technicians in the more literal sense, they are construed by the elite as turning out "commodities" whose creation, distribution, and consumption demand coordination from above in the pursuit of order and planned progress.

Let us see how this preliminary definition of the administered society can be applied to an understanding of Soviet developments, and with what advantages.

I. Totalitarianism Without Terror

By now it must be clear even to the most reluctant analyst that the cumulative change in Soviet society since Stalin's death is too great to dismiss as merely superficial. The transformation of Soviet society during this period, though by no means a wholesale departure from earlier patterns, nevertheless has been extensive. The conventional label for this change has been "liberalization." The reference point is to the state of Soviet totalitarianism under Stalin and to the degree of departure from that condition.

To be sure, the totalitarian model could only approximate the underlying reality. Even at the zenith of Stalinism, we know, there were major and numerous exceptions to the effective realization of absolute despotism. Piecemeal information such as the testimony of refugee informants showed that many individuals were able to preserve for themselves or to create tiny islands of privacy and to maintain attitudes of doubt and skepticism about the system in the face of the relentless propaganda that penetrated every corner of the society. We know, too, that in the midst of what was surely the most thorough-going system of political and social controls ever devised, there were widespread and patterned evasions of official demands in places high and low. The factory manager engaged in self-defensive falsification of production statistics; the peasant stealing time from the collectivized sector to work on his private plot; clandestine listeners to forbidden foreign radio broadcasts—these and other types are amply familiar to students of Stalinist Russia. For those who were caught (as well as for many of the totally innocent) the costs were horrendous, often final. But even at its most extreme the system of surveillance and punishments did not stamp out pockets of resentment, awareness, inner resistance.

Nevertheless, if Soviet totalitarianism under Stalin was not exactly an Orwellian 1984 and if, in important respects, it departed from the analysts' model of the totalitarian society, it came very close indeed (perhaps as close as is possible in a modern complex society) to approximating that model. Extraordinary was the near-completeness, if not actual totality, of the invasion of society by Party and State. The efforts to regulate in minute detail cultural activity, patterns of material consumption and taste, attitudes towards love and friendship, professional routine and aspiration, scholarly research, moral virtue, recreation and leisure, informal social relationships, sex and childbearing and childrearing—these efforts, though far from always successful, had the most profound effects in creating a condition of unfreedom. If one also recalls the elaborate development of control mechanisms designed to promote the institutionalization of anxiety (that state of affairs in which even the most

innocent act is likely to be arbitrarily greeted with harsh and capricious punishment), then it is clear that the Soviet system under Stalin, by any practical definition, was totalitarian.

It is also clear that substantial liberalization has taken place since the dictator's death. But this measure, useful in many ways, creates very serious problems in analysis and evaluation. For although liberalization tells something about where the Soviet system has come from, it does not say very much about where it is *going*. To say that the system is being liberalized is like walking away backwards from a receding reference point, a procedure that gives too little information about what lies on the road ahead. After all, if the society has become less totalitarian, then what is it? To conclude, in effect, that it is still more of the same but somehow less so than it used to be may be essentially correct, but it is not a very satisfactory answer. And the understandable fascination with the political drama of on-and-off again de-Stalinization has led to a partial neglect of its *social* consequences—in some quarters, too, to an imprecise assumption that political liberalization (the moderation of one-man despotism and the probably genuine efforts to avoid extreme abuses of absolute power) also spells some kind of broad social liberalization (even leading, perhaps, to a form of society more familiar—and less antagonistic?—to the Western experience).

Indeed, it may be that the use of liberalization as the key criterion for measuring changes in Soviet society is responsible for some of the confusion and disagreement among analysts of various persuasions. Thus, those of a conservative or pessimistic disposition have been inclined to deny that the changes are so significant (or that some of them have really taken place) because of the implication that liberalization also means *liberation*, a prospect they reject as too unlikely; while their more optimistic colleagues (especially those who see in Khrushchevism the harbinger of a welfare state) have attached far more significance to the same developments.

The core of the difficulty lies in the fact that, under Stalin, there was an amalgamation of totalism with terror and coercion, and that we may have overlearned a lesson about the necessary association between the two on the basis of that highly convincing record. The concept of the administered society is proposed as a way of saying that there can be totalism *without* terror; it recognizes that the changes in the Soviet Union have been real and vast (after all, totalism without terror is something new); but it insists that, far from developing alternatives to totalism, Soviet society is being subjected to new and more subtle forms of it, and that the Stalinist past is being streamlined rather than rejected..

The implications of this assumption will have to be explored, but first a few illustrations are in order to give a necessarily rather abstract discussion some concrete grounding.

II. Some Examples

The case for the administered society is not subject to proof of an absolute kind, for not only is such a concept more or less useful rather than right or wrong, but its application to the affairs of a live society cannot possibly cover all contingencies. It does, however, provide a general framework for depicting the Soviet system under Khrushchev (and probably his successors as well), sensitizing us to interpretations that otherwise might go unnoticed and enabling us to see patterns in apparently unconnected trends. The following examples (at this early stage it would be too much to call them evidence) are chosen from a number of important areas of the Soviet system: social stratification, educational policy, administrative shifts in industry and agriculture, the youth program, Khrushchev's position on art and literature, and the recent activity of Soviet sociologists.

Social stratification

Under Stalin, the differences in income, life-style, and perquisites of the various occupational strata came to be very wide indeed, certainly so in contrast with the Marxist vision of the classless order, also in absolute terms. By and large this development could be accounted for by the functional importance of differential rewards in maximizing output and performance, particularly among the technical and managerial cadres, among symbol-makers and bureaucrats, and in assuring the loyalties of these strategic groups during the critical periods of economic expansion and political consolidation.

Under Khrushchev, however, this trend towards increasingly sharp social stratification has come into question and concrete measures have been adopted to slow its progress, if not to reverse it. And so in recent years we have seen reductions in income and privileges of some of the highest groups, along with serious efforts to improve the lot of the most deprived peasants and workers. Certainly these steps have not been sufficient to over-turn the established order of priorities, a revolutionary change that would in-volve long-range costs and penalties too great for a system still bent on rapid expansion and dependent on a proven, if quite un-Marxist, system of motiva-tions. But the official talk has revealed an apparently deep concern over the excesses of the stratification system given impetus under Stalin.

The Soviet explanation for these changes is that they represent a re-newal of Marxist intention now that the requisite material base for estab-lishing full communism, and with it full equality, has been achieved. A somewhat more likely explanation is that the regime under Khrushchev is making strenuous efforts to enhance its popularity by easing and improving living conditions, and probably this is true as far as it goes. But neither ex-planation accounts for the simultane-ous attack against the privileged groups: in purely practical terms, the redistribution of part of their share of the national income could hardly have much of an impact on millions of new recipients and would also threaten to undermine the good-will of the strategic strata towards the post-Stalin regime.

Then what does lie behind this new policy? The most convincing answer has been given by Robert Feldmesser, an American student of Soviet affairs who has for some years carried on pain-staking studies of social-class policies. Feldmesser's examination of the evi-dence leads him to the conclusion that class policy under Khrushchev repre-sents an effort to prevent the forma-tion of vested interest groups, in the form of durable social strata, that might interfere with the Party's free-dom to plan and manage the affairs of society in its own way. According to

Feldmesser, the growing privileges of the upper strata "... threatened to contravene the cardinal dogma of the Soviet system, which has come to be known as Stalinism though it could as well be called Leninism or Khrush-chevism: that ultimate power belongs exclusively to the party—or more ac-curately, to the head of the party. Whenever any group jeopardizes that principle, it must be struck down, and that is what Khrushchev is doing. Stalin, in other words, forgot his Stalinism; and Khrushchev is not re-pudiating Stalinism, he is, if anything, reinstating it."

The significance of this development, then, is very great. The growth of pluralism, or at least of the capacity of a population to erode the mono-lithism of a social system, seems to depend to a considerable degree upon the opportunities available to various social groupings (especially, perhaps, in the upper ranges of the stratifica-tion system) to develop over the gen-erations, without undue manipulation and interference from the outside and with reasonable probabilities of con-tinuity, their own traditions, expecta-tions, and behavior patterns—in short, upon opportunities to develop into subcommunities of interest. This is why sociologists and others have sometimes looked to the possibilities of an inci-pient "bourgeoisification" of Soviet society as an important clue to the easing of totalitarianism, on the grounds that an increasing concern among a growing professional and middle class with preserving advantages once gained might lead to restraints on the freedom of the Soviet regime to pursue harsh programs at home or to engage in risky overseas adventures. But the Soviet record shows us how important it is not to confuse a bourgeoisification of taste and style (which undoubtedly is taking place) with a realignment of power and influence stemming from the interests of this stratum. Public displays of affluence and refinement, which in other times and places have been associated with the political ascendancy of a middle class, do not have this meaning in the contemporary Soviet Union.

It is precisely the prospect of such an ascendancy that is so intolerable to the leadership; it would make it more difficult to administer the society from above. The regime depends upon the privileged groups—else they would not be privileged—but refuses to allow them the kind of long-run security of position that might dilute power. And so the Khrushchev policy can be seen as part of the drive to administer from above.

Educational policy

A parallel development has taken place in educational policy. Although the reforms of recent years, beginning in the late 1950's, reflect in part the influence of practical problems of manpower allocation (one intended consequence of the reforms is to reduce the pressure on university admission by shunting more aspirants into the labor force instead), they are also designed to enhance administration from above. That the educational system continues to be construed as a preparatory instrument for quite specific and narrow adult occupational roles rather than as an agency of general enlightenment is highly revealing. Moreover, the new provisions requiring most applicants for admission to higher education to have spent some years either at work or in the military forces are quite consistent with the ethos of a system in

which the official emphasis is on treating people as aggregate resources and elements of planning rather than as individuals whose voluntaristic impulses will be sufficient to keep the system running.

In the same connection, the efforts currently under way to establish the new boarding schools on a more extensive basis are, by Soviet assertion, designed to prepare children from the earliest possible age for the institutional atmosphere of the highly organized society. And it is no accident that the main theme of recent Soviet pedagogical and youth literature centers now about the task of raising the new generation in a spirit of "group and collective life" that will surpass in scope and intensity the experiences of the earlier generations. Such bold intentions, of course, may not be effectively realized (and this is a question that will have to be taken up later) but the intentions are unmistakable.

Controls in industry and agriculture

An especially convincing example is to be found in the record of industrial and agricultural organization. Early reaction to the widely publicized administrative reorganizations that gained momentum in the latter half of the 1950's saw in them a kind of decentralization that might lead to the development of an incipient grass-roots autonomy on the local level. The announced desire to improve productive efficiency by granting more discretionary powers to plant and farm managers, it was speculated, also held forth the possibility of autonomies that would go beyond the intended area of purely economic or managerial decision-making; that is, might lead by tiny but cumulative steps to local patriotisms whose long-run effect would be to encourage a modicum of genuine political independence.

The proposition is reasonable enough, for there is a connection between one kind of autonomy and another, even though the actual political consequences of such a situation are necessarily difficult to forecast. However that may be, we now know that the new independence of industrial and agricultural managers has turned out to be largely illusory. As early as 1960, Arcadius Kahan could conclude in a study of agricultural reorganization that the practical consequence of administrative shifts had been to *tighten* Party control by reducing the overweight bureaucratic machine between Moscow and the farm, thereby enhancing the Party's effective presence in local operations. He writes: "The new collective amalgamations, the influx of agricultural specialists and former MTS personnel (often party members) into the farm organizations, along with a drive for new party recruits in rural areas, have made it possible to organize party cells on most collective and state farms. The consequent opportunity to exercise control from within, and to represent the party to the mass of peasants as a local rather than an alien force, has undoubtedly increased the party's influence over the behavior of the farm population."

On the industrial side, Herbert Ritvo has made a similar point even more emphatically: "... the economic bureaucracy has undergone a series of sweeping reorganizations designed to improve its efficiency and to strengthen direct controls. There can be little doubt that not only the power of leading representatives of this group, but also many of their personal privileges, have diminished as a result of

Khrushchev's administrative changes and reforms. As one reads the familiar complaints of industrial managers, it becomes only too apparent how little the 'rights of managers' have been expanded since the decree of August 9, 1955. In addition, this sector, more than any other, has felt the greater severity of the new penal laws of 1961–1962; thus, the reorganization of management has revealed that the opinions of this part of the bureaucracy could be silenced and ignored in a matter affecting its vital interests; the harshness of the revised penalties for economic crimes has demonstrated that, despite the importance of the technical elite in an industrial society, their prerogatives are limited—not least by an educational system which can now provide a sufficiency of replacements."

These are not only the conclusions of Western analysts; the fight against the dangers of local autonomy is a matter of high-level policy in the USSR: "... from the very beginning Comrade N. S. Khrushchev, to whom belongs the initiative for the reorganization, directed the attention of our economic cadres to the impermissibility of localism in any form and cautioned them against understanding an integrated economy as self-contained and autarchical. Was such a warning necessary? Undoubtedly it was. The relatively small size of many of the economic administrative regions was an objective basis for attempts to develop a self-sufficient economy within the framework of the economic councils."

Both in industry and agriculture, then, the Khrushchev reforms have been liberalizing insofar as they attempt seriously to amend the rigid and inefficient Stalinist pattern of multiple, overlapping, and crosschecking hierarchies between the center and the localities. But at the same time they have given the Party a freer (because more direct and efficient) hand in administering its own interests within the production units.

The youth organizations

An additional illustration comes from the Soviet youth organizations. Far from loosening their grip on the new generation in comparison with their practice in Stalin's time, the Komsomol and Pioneers have been involved in intensive efforts to extend their network of influence, both in membership coverage and in the range of youth activities that they originate or supervise. It is true that some steps have been taken to reduce some of the most extreme consequences of excessive bureaucratization and neglect of local interests and, at the most recent Komsomol Congress in 1962, there was some guarded talk about democratizing the internal structure. But a close examination of the recent Komsomol record suggests that the impulse for such changes comes not so much from a serious intention to democratize the the youth program as to alter its widespread reputation as boring, repressive, and offensive in order to make it more appealing to youth. At the same time there has been no sign at all of a withdrawal from interference in personal life; if anything, the reforms are meant to make that interference more effective by replacing swivel-chair organizers with energetic enthusiasts who will not be afraid to grapple directly with problems of youthful nonconformity.

Certainly it is true, as in other areas of Soviet life, that the resort to coercion and threat has become less important than under Stalin. But their replacement with more reasoned tactics of persuasion should not be taken as a surrender of the principle of total involvement and control. On the contrary, the youth program is now regarded as more essential than under Stalin, for it has become increasingly important to remind the new generation—which does not share the caution born of experience in the old days—not to confuse the relatively more benign outward character of Khrushchevism with a grant of autonomy. A genuine test of change in the youth sector would be a surrender (more realistically, a partial surrender) of the organizations' claim to a monopoly over formal and informal youth activities. Concretely, such a step might take the form of allowing youngsters (especially in higher educational institutions) not to join if they have no desire to do so. But there has been no change in the Komsomol's policy of covering an ever-larger proportion of those of eligible age, including 100 per cent of the university students and large majorities of key categories of young professionals. And the Pioneer organization, as before, continues to maintain total coverage in its group. Finally, the content of the youth program (as revealed in recent policy literature) centers around renewed efforts to exercise total control over the young on the grounds that the reforms now make the organizations such benign and authoritative agencies of society that no one could possibly object to their paternalistic concern.

Literature and art

In art, literature, and intellectual affairs generally, recent events in the Soviet Union have attracted such intensive scholarly and journalistic coverage in the West that it is hardly necessary to review them here. Most analyses have stressed the alternating thaws and freezes in the intellectual world since Stalin's death, seeking to discern in them an overall trend or to attribute cyclical changes to shifting alignments in the Party leadership or to general characteristics of the political climate.

Granting that the end of this complex story is yet to be told, Khrushchev's now famous speech of March 1963, in which he upbraided errant artists and writers, must stand as a landmark in the publicly proclaimed policy of the administered society. The essence of his message is that the Party's willingness to allow at least some frank discussion of the Stalin period and the decision to loosen somewhat the straitjacket of rigid conformity must not be understood as permission to stray from Party control; that what the more optimistic members of the artistic and intellectual communities have taken for liberalization, or liberation, is only a readjustment in the form and content of Party supervision. In effect, said Khrushchev, either the writers, artists, and others must work out a satisfactory system of self-censorship conforming to the needs of the Party, or the Party will do the censoring itself.

Khrushchev made it clear, then, that artistic and intellectual output is a commodity to be mobilized as the regime sees fit in furthering its domestic and international programs, and that the leeway granted in the process of de-Stalinization has been a measure to improve the quality of the product for these purposes—not a signal that the instrumental approach has been modified or abandoned. The thaws and freezes, that is, have been generated by uncertainty as to how the product could be improved without violating unchanged political requirements. So long as this uncertainty remains, the ups and downs of the artistic and intellectual communities may be expected to continue as the limits of experimentation are redefined in practice. But the basic principle has been reiterated, and unmistakably so.

Khrushchev's statements on that occasion are in fact more interesting for what they reveal about his idea of social order than merely as strictures against disobedient poets. He could not have expressed more precisely the ethos of the administered society when he said that the denunciation of the Stalin cult does not signify that "... a time of drift has set in, that the reins of control have been slackened, that the ship of society is drifting at the will of the waves, and that each person can follow his own whim and behave in whatever way he sees fit. No. The Party has pursued and will consistently pursue the Leninist course it has mapped out, irreconcilably opposing any ideological waverings and attempts to violate the norms of life in our society." And he said in the same speech, "... among certain people one can hear talk about some kind of absolute freedom of the individual. I do not know what they have in mind, but I believe that there will never be absolute freedom of the individual, even under full communism.... And under communism the will of one man must be subordinated to the will of the entire collective. Unless this is so, anarchic self-will will sow dissension and disorganize the life of the society. Without the organizing, directing principle, neither socialist society nor any other society, even the smallest collective of people, can exist."

To give him proper credit, Khrushchev is probably quite right in an elementary sociological or philosophical sense when he denies the possibility of absolute individual freedom. But there is an enormous difference between saying this as an abstract assertion about the limits of human experience and the active promotion of an all-encompassing social policy dedicated to the proposition of individual subordination to a superorganized society. And Khrushchev is not speaking as a sociologist or philosopher, but as a man of action.

Sociology

A final illustration concerns the current work of Soviet sociologists. Sociological writing and research were taboo in the Soviet Union until recent years, and even the word "sociology" was regarded as a synonym for "bourgeois apologetics." But beginning in the late 1950's, a number of academics began to identify themselves as sociologists and to write under the heading of sociology. Much of what they have produced up to now consists of little more than political slogans of old dignified with a new professional vocabulary; this aspect of their work need not concern us here. More revealing are their research and their conception of the proper uses of sociology.

It is only a slight oversimplification to conclude that, so far, the principal assignments of the sociologists have been to prove the "superiority" of the Soviet Union over "bourgeois" societies and to provide policy-makers with how-to-do-it information of a rather limited scope. Conspicuously absent are even the most timid efforts at criticism, evaluation, or basic questioning about social structure. That is, there is no sign of an uninhibited, nonpolitical search for answers that are not already predetermined by general dogma.

There is also an intriguing (and probably not altogether accidental) parallel with the kind of industrial and personnel research that is popular in some American corporations, where the micro-techniques of the social sciences are applied to the purposes of administration and manipulation. (So far, it must be said, the Soviet sociologists have barely begun to develop the kind of technical sophistication displayed by their Western counterparts, but they have declared their intention to do so.) In particular, there is a strong resemblance between the organizational ethos that is becoming increasingly evident in Khrushchev's Russia and the internal behavior of some American corporations depicted by observers such as William Whyte. The concrete, human consequences of "being administered" may be more or less benign for the individuals involved—but that it takes place at all is the critical fact. On the one hand in a large corporation, on the other in an entire society, the insistence on the superiority of superorganization emphasizes the relevance of the whole life for the task-oriented area and results in efforts to bring together into a coherent pattern —under influence and guidance from above—such a wide variety of roles that social character and individual aspiration become increasingly a public affair. Probably it is no accident that, at a recent international sociological conference, a Soviet participant is reported to have said that David Riesman's "other-directed man" (that modern type whose behavior is motivated by what others think of him more than by a stable core of inner values) comes very close to the ideal of responsible social behavior so ardently fostered by the Soviet educational and propaganda systems.

III. Some Implications

These illustrations go only a small way towards showing the potential applications of the concept of the administered society to an understanding of contemporary currents in Soviet life. Others, no doubt, would be equally appropriate—for example, the growing emphasis on "public" participation in social control through voluntary assistance to the militia, the Komsomol street patrols' enforcing of dress, decorum, and taste, the quasi-judicial comrades' courts, and so forth.

There are also *a priori* reasons to expect the Soviet leadership to stress this approach. The organizational problems of the Soviet economy, for example, become more rather than less complex with technological advance; if economic successes under Stalin solved a number of relatively primitive problems of accumulation and investment, they in turn have created new problems of organization and coordination that are less easily solved. When Khrushchev rejects the notion that the ship of society can sail wherever the waves carry it, he refers not only to the narrow problem of political unity and ideological correctness but to the large, underlying issue of how to manage a modern industrial order. In one sense the Soviet case is a qualitatively extreme example of the problem of coordination faced in all modern industrial societies, aggravated by the peculiar ferocity with which the issue of backwardness was handled under Stalin.

The passion for organization, for perfect coordination and integration of social life—a kind of compulsive's dream of beehive order projected upon an entire society—has partly replaced the original impetus of Bolshevik ideology. The denial that there can be any real conflict in the good society, the belief that all legitimate human needs can be satisfied simultaneously, that interest groups are subversive, that only uninformed selfishness or disregard of organizational principles stands between the present and the utopia of the future—these are some of the ingredients of the new ideology. If it lacks some of the romantic appeal of barricade-storming, it is perhaps no less revolutionary in its consequences, for its purveyors insist that they will not rest until all societies have undergone the transformation to superorganization. Its potential impact on an audience, say, of hard-pressed political leaders and court philosophers of developing nations may be considerable, for the idea of total coordination must tempt many of them as the answer to problems and frustrations of economic backwardness and the awkward necessities of coping with competing political interests. And for mentalities especially sensitive to the real and apparent disarray of human affairs or philosophically intolerant of ambiguity in social structure, there is, after all, a great utopian charm in such an image: much like the classical Marxist formula of salvation, it seems to promise a final answer to the centuries-old dislocations generated by modernism and science and a return to a latter-day version of a medieval world where everything—and everyone—apparently had a proper place in the universe.

Assuming this assessment of the basic aspirations of the Soviet regime to be correct, there is the quite different question of how far they are likely to be realized in practice. Naturally it would be unrealistic to expect complete and literal fufillment of the dream, any more than one could have expected totalitarianism to exist under Stalin. The issue, then, is how closely it will or can be approximated. Without going into the kind of detailed discussion that is far beyond the scope of these early notes, the best that can be done is to suggest some of the factors in a balance sheet of probabilities.

In the background is the ancient dilemma of how to combine personal with public interest in such ways as to put an end to politics. If the record of other complex societies (not to mention the history of the Soviet Union itself) is a guide, we may be excused for having serious doubts about such a grandiose conception. To deny that there is social conflict, as the Soviet leadership essentially does, is not to be rid of it. Even the most superficial reading of the Soviet press daily provides an endless catalogue of the stresses and strains arising from the pursuit of private or group interests against the demands for conformity emanating from the center. Some of the examples are petty, more of them are serious, all of them reflect the underlying tensions of an imperfectly coordinated society; they usually fall short of posing immediate threats to the political directorate but often have cumulative consequences of an unplanned and unintended nature. Moreover, broad areas of deviant behavior and subversive attitudes which once were suppressed by the application of prophylactic terror now have to be handled by more patient and indirect means. It is too early to say whether the new machinery of social control will be as adequate to the task as was pure Stalinism.

Then there is the paradoxical discovery, finally dawning on the regime, that the gradual alleviation of extreme material want that has been behind so many traditional problems may produce new and more subtle issues of control over a long-deprived population experiencing relative affluence for the first time. Failures to satisfy these wants are the obvious danger; success breeds more subtle risks, however, for a rising standard of living (as we have seen in the case of other industrial nations) often results in new forms of emotional investment that are to a great extent antithetical to the high level of public commitment obviously essential in realizing the administered society. We already have some evidence of this in the form of a troublesome youth problem in the Soviet Union: one of the greatest headaches of the post-Stalin regime has been how to prevent the drive for individual advancement and the intoxication with consumption from becoming the basis for a privatism that could easily wreck long-term intentions. So far the problem has been most visible among youth, but there is reason to believe that is widespread.

To these and equally powerful impediments in the road to the administered society—for example, the articulate and sometimes effective objections of at least parts of the scientific, artistic, and intellectual communities to being as totally mobilized as they were under Stalin—must be added the even more vexing "technical" problem of *how* to administer and coordinate an entire enormous society effectively even in the absence of any special opposition. Yet when all this is said, what stands out is the remarkable success of the Soviet regime, during and since Stalin's day, in making a very impressive start.

Most important is the fact that, during almost half a century of Communist rule, the possibilities for alternative institutional forms have been largely wiped out. Even were the will to democratic or pluralistic institutions substantially present—and it is not—it is highly doubtful that the resources currently available by way of formal structures, source philosophies, or practical experience would go very far. The Bolshevization of a society, if it goes on long enough, is an irreversible process, because it is so intense and so total that it indelibly alters not only earlier institutional forms but the entire pattern of a population's expectations of reasonable and workable alternative possibilities for social order. This is not to say that the Soviet leaders have mastered history, for even a process that is irreversible can move forward in unintended and undesired directions. But the prospects of developing viable substitutes for a social system that has so long been based upon extreme and centralized organization are very poor. Ironically, the regime is probably correct—at least in the case of Soviet society—when it insists that any form of pluralism is impossible. The best that can be expected is a more or less benign totalism within the limits of the administered society, with a very slow erosion of the Bolshevik heritage; the worst, a surrender of good intentions to manage the society without terror and a return in some form to the excesses and cruelties of classical Stalinism.

How one evaluates this situation depends on his general political outlook and his preferences about the good society. Surely no one will deny that the Soviet citizen is, in the elementary sense, better off today than he was under Stalin. And certainly no one will claim that the Soviet citizen prefers to be brutalized as he was then. Still, the thoroughgoing bureaucratization, the superorganization, of social life contains a special nightmare quality of its own even when shorn (as probably it must be if it is to operate efficiently) of raw psychic brutality and terror. And the easing of the terror, while an obviously welcome development, also has the consequence of diminishing the awareness of living in an essentially closed society and of reducing the capacity to act from moral indignation towards a freer life.

Perhaps the concept of the administered society, in this preliminary form, errs on the side of pessimism by making too much of the dream and not enough of the sheer confusion of reality. Daily life in the Soviet Union is far richer, far more problematical to its rulers, far less certain than an abstraction can depict; no doubt the framework of this modest idea will have to be considerably filled in before it can be of much use in practical analysis. But it does call attention to the inadequacy of the liberalization formula in understanding contemporary Soviet developments and the new ideology driving the regime. And if this is the dream of the post-Stalin leadership, then the Soviet system under Khrushchev may be moving not towards its Western counterparts but even farther away from them. If Khrushchev and his heirs succeed, the developments of the last decade in the Soviet Union will have been only a tactical regrouping on the march from a relatively primitive to a far more advanced variety of twentieth-century totalitarianism.

THE HYBRID ART OF SOVIETOLOGY

ARTHUR E. ADAMS

Before embarking upon some new campaign in Gaul or Britannia, Roman generals used to consult their augurs. Salaried Etruscan *haruspices* pored over the steaming entrails of slain animals, studied code books on the meaning of signs, and foretold disaster or success. Other eras have employed a great profusion of oracles, soothsayers, prophets, and fortune tellers. The present is little different. Today we have the electronic computer, which does all and more than haruspication could do, and without bloodshed; generals fight global nuclear wars on computer paper, calculating the number and character of the new weapons that will be needed to win a real war. But robot brains are not yet omniscient; because there are subtle political, moral, and psychological factors that defy exact formulation, we continue to base decisions concerning such matters as our national security on evidence so elusive that it cannot be fed into machines. Man must still depend upon man for much of his most vitally needed divination. To say this is to explain a great deal about the nature and practice of sovietology.

Sovietology is the study of all matters that help us to understand the meaning of current, politically significant Soviet-communist behaviour and to forecast its future course. There is great need for such study. Since the end of the second world war a para-mount problem for the Western world has been represented by the dynamic growth of the Soviet Union and by the continuing spread of world communism from what was, until recently, its Soviet centre. In response, Western governments and their peoples demand reliable estimates of communist intentions and capacities.

Seeking to answer such demands, sovietology works against a number of odds not common to the research of social scientists in most other areas. While we know a great deal about communist ideas and various aspects of Soviet life, cardinal political facts are hidden. Too often Soviet documents are designed to mislead and the student of Soviet affairs must use an elaborate set of lie-detectors to extract their significant elements. Almost all inter-communist affairs are clothed in secrecy, so that the relations of the Soviet Union with its allies and with the communist parties of Western Europe, Latin America, and Asia, are largely matters for conjecture. Nevertheless, the sovietologist persists, and the past twenty years have witnessed a great deal of (sometimes rather wild) experimentation, with all the social sciences lending a hand.

The British cultural anthropologist, Geoffrey Gorer, argued that tight swaddling of Russian babies tends to make Great Russians unduly submissive to autocratic authority, yet ever ready

---

Reprinted from *The State of Soviet Studies* by Walter Z. Laqueur and Leopold Labedz (eds.) by permission of the M.I.T. Press, Cambridge, Massachusetts. Copyright © 1965 by the Massachusetts Institute of Technology. All rights reserved. Footnotes omitted.

to erupt in violent explosions. Irreverent observers have since dubbed this theory *diaperology*, and some Soviet refugees questioned on the subject for the refugee study of Harvard University contemptuously refused to answer the question when they understood its implications. Psychology, too, has had its day, for example in the work of Nathan Leites, who suggested that the key to Bolshevik character (and therefore to communist behaviour) is the Bolsheviks' fear of their own latent homosexual proclivities and an exaggerated emphasis upon the father-image, Lenin. Bypassing sound efforts to explain the determining factors of Soviet conduct on the basis of ideology and power, some sovietologists have devised and published theories quite at odds with known facts: the regime's imminent collapse is regularly prophesied by men who exaggerate the degree of influence exercised by popular dissatisfactions; and at least one renowned kremlinologist believes that what he writes about the Soviet Union influences the decisions of Soviet policy-makers. Such theories have created a bad image for sovietology by making it seem to be a field of study where irresponsible guesswork and the wildest theorising are standard practice. It so happens that sovietology does welcome guesses and theorising (though only when based upon much sound knowledge and careful analysis), for it looks into what is essentially unknowable—the future.

It is not possible to talk about *the* method of sovietology because there are many methods available to the individual practitioner, and naturally each man's training, whether in economics or politics, in literature, anthropology, journalism, or statistics,

has much to do with the particular combination of skills he may develop for his work. Yet it is both necessary and possible to sketch at least in outline the methodological framework within which every sovietologist carries on his research.

Since the ultimate purpose of sovietology is to chart the course of political decision-making and to predict the future, the sovietologist is interested above all in the policy-making processes at the apex of the party-state pyramid in the Soviet Union and in the inter-relations of party leaders around the world. Within the Soviet Union events inside the Presidium and Secretariat are of the greatest significance, for these bodies alone make the decisions that determine Soviet conduct; here also are the men who make the policy and whose struggles for position, prestige, and power directly influence every decision. But while it is a truism that sovietology is concerned primarily with decision-making and the power struggle in the highest circles of the party, it is just as true that such decisions and struggles do not take place in a vacuum. Policy decisions are made on substantive issues—economic problems, administrative difficulties, military affairs, and foreign relations. Leaders support one or another side of each issue for a variety of reasons. A man may defend the point of view that seems to have the most merit; he may use the issue to attack an opponent or to mend his fences by supporting a factional group that may help him in the future.

Clearly, to one who hopes to comprehend the all-important events in the Kremlin, virtually anything concerned with communist party and Soviet affairs may be of use. The sovietologist must be thoroughly familiar with all that is known about the structure, organisation, and operation of both party and state. He must know the history of their development, keep abreast of structural changes, and estimate their intent and consequences. He must know the men in office, their professional abilities and factional relationships; and, since these change, such knowledge must be kept constantly under review: a rapprochement of two former enemies at the Presidium level may change the course of history.

While secrecy in high party affairs is extreme, the same cannot be said of other areas. The volume of economic information published by the Soviet Union and made available to the West is immense: the sovietologist must master economic facts, the latest budget figures, the current plan, the causes and consequences of agricultural failure. He must understand, as exactly and concretely as any military strategist or professional economist, the stresses created by the conflict between limited resources and ambitious economic and military plans. So, too, he must be familiar with opposing theories (sources of conflict) within the party on such matters as the proper emphasis to be given to heavy industry, nuclear testing, or collective farm reorganisation. He must be an advanced student of Marxism-Leninism, familiar with fresh developments in theory as well as their probable significance in the minds of party leaders. He must have a profound knowledge of the social system, of the past and its traditions—the Orthodox faith, the writings of Pushkin, Tolstoy, and Dostoevsky, the revolutionary tradition, and the early history of the party.

There are some who argue that to

be thoroughly grounded for his work the sovietologist must have been at one time or another an active communist, preferably in one of the communist-ruled countries. This is not the case. While lengthy party experience can be immensely helpful, early enthusiasm for the Marxian deterministic outlook and communist utopianism has in some cases proved a permanent hindrance to rational analysis. The crux of the matter lies with the knowledge, objectivity, and analytical capacity of the man.

It is self-evident that the sovietologist must be deeply informed on matters of Soviet foreign policy and that here, as in other fields, his information must be up to the minute. This latter requirement is one of the essential characteristics distinguishing the sovietologist from the expert in Soviet politics or economics, or the scholarly historian of party affairs—the sovietologist's information is up to date and he has some idea of what is coming next. His job is to inform and advise foreign ministries, prime ministers and presidents, the scholarly community, and a vast world of newspaper readers. Most of these clients are peremptory in their demand for immediate interpretations of current events. Therefore, the sovietologist reads and analyses Khrushchev's latest speech the moment it becomes available; he keeps up with *Pravda, Izvestia,* and *Kommunist,* with the Chinese *Red Flag* and *People's Daily,* and with a mass of other materials.

All this study is possible and finite; it deals with information that can be acquired by intelligent industry. But there is a second and far more difficult part of the sovietologist's work, which is to learn what ranges from the less knowable to the almost totally unknowable, to reach conclusions about important matters for which only little direct evidence is available or for which there are no sources of direct evidence.

Although both phases go on concurrently, the sovietologist's work with what is knowable is preparation for the more demanding work in the less knowable areas. By learning everything he can about the known areas, he narrows the limits of the unknown, eliminating some of the empty squares on his chart, identifying within others precisely what it is he doesn't know and what he needs to learn before he can answer certain questions.

Given his operational model of the Soviet Union, which provides most of the information needed for run-of-the-mill analysis and prediction, how does the sovietologist make his approach to the less knowable areas? For this he has developed special techniques, whose usefulness and reliability are often questioned because they have been mishandled. The nature of the problems these techniques are fitted to solve and the question of their proper application deserve careful attention.

Foremost among the problems is the subject of policy-making and the concomitant power struggle that we assume is taking place among the top policy-makers. We know almost nothing about how Soviet decisions are reached; nor do we know what roles are played by the various members of the Presidium and Secretariat. We seldom learn what issues are debated while some new policy is being made, for, with rare exceptions, extreme care is taken to suppress every hint of dissension. When policies are announced as decrees or resolutions of the Central Committee and/or the Council of Ministers, we are given to understand that the decision was unanimous, the implication being that the truths of communism are not only superior but

also manifest, to which there is always only one way of doing practical justice. But are these decisions really unanimous? Is it true, for example, that all members of the Presidium equally approved Khrushchev's decision to place intermediate range missiles on Cuba and then agreed with equal unanimity to pull them out in late October 1962, after President Kennedy's warlike demonstrations? Is it true that all members of the Presidium unanimously approve the first secretary's present policy vis-à-vis China?

Given our fairly extensive knowledge of the past history of power struggles among communist leaders, involving dissension over a variety of issues, it is necessary to assume that in fact unanimity rarely exists, that on the contrary rivalry for place and power among communist leaders is constant and intense. For Western policy-makers the precise degree of friction and the exact strength of the party leader's authority are of tremendous interest. It is the task of the sovietologist to identify the issues, to anticipate the probable outcome, and to interpret the significance of the conflict in terms of its probable effect upon the strength or weakness of central authority.

Consider another example of a less knowable area. What is the real degree of unity between the Soviet party and its sister parties in the bloc? How does the Soviet leader exercise his predominance and to what degree? Does he possess greater personal authority in Sofia than in Warsaw? And, to reverse this line of questioning, to what extent, if at all, do the strongest leaders of the bloc countries influence the policies of the Communist Party of the Soviet Union?

Add another series of crucial questions: What is tomorrow's Sino-Soviet relationship to be? And how will this relationship affect the Soviet party's policies vis-à-vis other community parties? Will the Soviet party slow down the revisionist pace, and move towards more rigid controls or will the opposite course be followed? What of the idea, widely discussed in the Western press, that the Soviet Union must ultimately turn to the West for an alliance against China?

Given the Soviet Union's limited resources and international political ambitions, will she continue to go all-out for greater nuclear armaments? Or is there a possibility that she will turn to disarmament in earnest? And what of Russia's desire for influence in Africa, Asia, and Latin America? Will the strain of economic assistance, both upon her own and upon the Eastern European economies, prove too great to be supported? Who will be the next supreme leader of the Soviet Union? Will his policies follow those of the present incumbent, or are there good reasons for believing that major changes of direction may be expected?

The first special method the sovietologist employs in trying to answer these questions is that of analysing what he somewhat pretentiously calls 'esoteric communications.' It is a known and demonstrable fact that Russia's communist elite (as well as those of other communist countries) talk to each other in the press by means of a highly formalised and changing set of symbols which only members of the group fully understand. While some of this veiled language can be deciphered only by the most sophisticated members of the ruling group, the hidden messages in others may be brought to light by the outsider who has carefully learned as much as he can about the codes used.

The little signs the sovietologist must know how to interpret are innumera-ble. Of first importance are the party's many ideological formulas; whilst at any one moment they represent sacrosanct dogma, over a period of time many of them undergo evolution and reinterpretation. Assuming that the smallest alteration is never inadvertent, the sovietologist attempts to unearth its hidden significance, which in ideological affairs can be extremely exacting.

When Ilya Ehrenburg writes boldly in *Pravda* about the effect of Stalin's terror upon writers, the sovietologist surmises that Khrushchev has given the go-ahead signal for the literary exploitation of Stalin's purges and labour camps. When an economic theory, hitherto blacklisted, is discussed at length in *Pravda* by a little known professor of economics, it is safe to assume that the party is either reviewing its theory or has already done so. Typically, this assumption would entail a search through learned and technical economic journals for corroboration and a scanning of industrial news to learn if the theory in its revised form is already in practice.

The sovietologist may need to know a whole detailed history of events simply to catch the full import of a single word or phrase used by a party leader. For example, during his visit to Bulgaria in May 1962, Khrushchev made a speech at Varna in which, speaking warmly of Soviet-Yugoslav relations, he clearly implied that he considered Yugoslavia to be 'building socialism.' Now from 1948, when the Soviet-dominated Cominform read Yugoslavia out of the world communist movement, until the Varna speech, good communists had said of Tito many a curious thing, but building socialism was not one of them, because that phrase had been reserved exclusively for nations with Soviet-approved communist regimes. Although Khrushchev had made efforts at rapprochement in 1955 and 1961, Yugoslavia was still condemned for deviations from orthodoxy in a number of official edicts. Khrushchev's statement that co-operation with the USSR would help the Yugoslav peoples to 'consolidate their socialist positions' and would 're-dound to the benefit of all countries that are building socialism and communism,' was a bold announcement of a new policy, an order to the bloc to fall into line, a slap in China's face, and a clear indication to Western governments that Yugoslavia might be leaning rather more heavily eastwards than they had suspected. The indirect acknowledgment that Tito's regime was building socialism formally reversed fifteen years of history.

These are but the briefest illustrations of what the analyst may find under the surface in the Soviet press, in documents and speeches, in the rare statements made by Soviet leaders to distinguished Westerners, or in the planted 'leaks' to Polish, Yugoslav, and Italian communists, who dutifully whisper them into the ears of Western diplomats and journalists. For the man sensitive to the political significance of slogans, catchwords, theoretical formulas, and the nuances of communist phrasing, the Soviet press, while not quite an open book, is full of information the layman cannot see. Carried out systematically, used always in conjunction with other sources of information, and guided by a sovietologist prepared to admit the role of accident even in Soviet political life, the interpretation of enciphered language is an invaluable aid to exegetics.

Certain of its practitioners tend to emphasise the difficulty of unscrambling esoteric signals and to resent the fact that their efforts are not sufficiently appreciated. It is true, of course, that the scrap of evidence presented by a change of formula is often difficult to recognise and interpret; yet the process of ferreting out the hidden meaning of an official document, a literary work, or a rumour is certainly not new to scholarship. Every good British constitutional historian, piecing together a picture of England from the Anglo-Saxon laws and the *Doomsday Book*, has carefully extrapolated his way to what he believes to be the true meaning of his texts. So, too, every competent interpreter of the Bible, whether his approach be literal, or mystic or allegorical, has practised with varying success the technique of deciphering the hidden implications of his text. So, too, the young lover, who reads the answer to his hopes in the flushed cheek of his maiden, is deciphering an esoteric communication, while the man who waits for an explicitly worded answer may live unrequited all his life.

The common man has long had to guess what it is his king is trying to tell him with those formal, awkward-sounding phrases kings use, and the king or his soothsayers must painstakingly examine the official communiqué of another ruler to judge whether its threats are inspired by bombast, fear, genuinely murderous intent, or the malice of some bilious clerk in the enemy's foreign office. The sovietologist, an outsider, seeks to fathom hidden significance of what one communist leader or faction is saying to another, to various sub-sections of the party, to other communist parties, or to the West. The acumen and intuition needed for deciphering these coded messages, while undoubtedly considerable, is certainly not so great as to defy intelligent minds trained in the academic disciplines.

Kremlinology is another special technique used for plumbing the less knowable areas of Soviet life. It relies heavily upon the art of breaking the code of Soviet jargon, but its attention centres primarily upon the power struggle at the top levels of the party and government and upon the rise and fall of the party and state leaders. *Murder will out*; this is the working hypothesis of kremlinologists, who assume that prolonged struggles between members of the ruling circles must sooner or later surface in the Soviet press and in the actions of Soviet leaders. At its most macabre this activity verges on the ancient art of anthropomancy—divination by the entrails of a human sacrifice.

For the West the value of knowing who is rising and who falling in the central decision-making bodies is great. Internal dissensions may mean hesitant foreign policies; or in certain circumstances, over-aggressive policies; a ruling party torn by violent conflicts may become too weak to react intelligently or forcefully to domestic and external pressures; and since we are seldom able to perceive conflict and change in the Kremlin by other means until it is too late to matter, the sovietologist's ability to detect the struggle and foresee its outcome by using the technique of kremlinology is too valuable a trick to ignore.

While the Kremlin seldom publishes information on these struggles, scattered information is nonetheless provided, most often in what is called 'protocol evidence.' Who among the members of the party Presidium were present at Vnukovo Airport to welcome the head of the Polish party, and

who was absent? Who stands atop the Mausoleum for the May Day parade, and where are others placed in relation to the First Secretary? While such evidence may seem at first glance too primitive to be of real value, it should be remembered that the sovietologist making use of kremlinological techniques brings with him the benefit of other knowledge. There is more to kremlinology than *Pravda* photographs of men all wearing the same kind of hat and standing on Lenin's Mausoleum.

Day after day the names of party leaders are listed in *Pravda* and *Izvestia* for one reason or another. The order often varies, but it is seldom accidental, and the kremlinologist ignores it at his peril. Major revisions mean major changes in the leadership and probably in policy. Even minor changes may represent an alteration in the balance of forces within the ruling group. It is of course perfectly true that men age, become ill, retire, or simply do not measure up to a job; therefore, while assuming that the changes he records have political significance, the sovietologist reminds himself constantly that accident plays a role in all human affairs, and much that happens, even in the Kremlin, has little political import.

To be more specific, everyone seems to understand that in certain conditions, official reference to a communist leader without the word 'comrade' preceding his name, may mean that he has been disgraced. In his secret speech at the 20th congress in 1956, Khrushchev gave another excellent example of protocol evidence which even the lowest party member could decipher:

I can remember how the Ukraine learned about Kosior's arrest. The Kiev radio used to start its programme thus: 'This is Radio Kosior.' When one day the programme began without naming Kosior, everyone was quite certain that something had happened to Kosior, that he had probably been arrested.

Should a young careerist like Alexander Shelepin (appointed head of the important party-state Control Committee in November 1962) turn an obscure phrase that appears to attack a policy identified with a respected elder statesman, the sovietologist would look for other evidence that Shelepin had taken a new step upward. And if such evidence were discovered, there would be need to reconsider a whole spectrum of relationships in the Presidium, the Secretariat, and the higher echelons of the apparat—the permanent, paid workers of the party.

As with the deciphering of esoteric language, much has been made of the blackness of the art of kremlinology. Some hold this to be the least respectable of the techniques employed by the sovietologist, yet this method of research is neither new nor bizarre. The Kremlin is not the first court to decide its affairs in secret. Nor is it the first court where the middle and lower nobles have had to study incessantly the careers of their patrons, anxiously scrutinising protocol signs in order to know when to desert a loser and attach themselves to a new and rising figure. In this age-old struggle the ambitious noble has always known how to indicate to his supporters that his favour at court is growing. Nor is Moscow's the first court in history where men fall out of grace over-night where the leader maintains his strength by surrounding himself with favourites and by playing one powerful baron against another. Finally, Moscow is hardly the first capital city to witness

constant intrigue and strife between the cliques that hold power. That the kremlinologist's study has been considered unique in the history of scholarship reflects badly upon our memory of the past.

A third technique of prediction upon which the sovietologist relies very heavily is common to all men. This is simply the technique of defining current trends of development, in order to estimate their probable effect upon related institutions, ideas, and men, and to envisage something of their future. Simple enough when it concerns the harvest, or an estimate of railroad freight with detailed statistics of past traffic loads at hand, such trend study and projection become infinitely complex in other fields.

Khrushchev's destalinisation, for example, has been accompanied by a limited liberalisation of the party's control over certain intellectual and artistic affairs. What will be the effect next year and the year after? By permitting men in the sciences, in literature and art a limited freedom to think and discuss, the party appears to be encouraging a process that must inevitably undermine its authority. Conceivably, at some time in the foreseeable future, the advance of intellectual freedom may so weaken the party's power to arbitrate in intellectual affairs that it might find itself unable to lay the ghost it has raised without more cost to itself than it would wish to pay. A reversion to earlier practices would probably find little favour with the leaders, for it could revive the dysfunctional tensions of Stalin's era. But can we believe that the party will voluntarily limit its right to step in and decide any intellectual or artistic issue it considers politically important? What, in short, will be the political and social consequences of intellectual liberalisation five or ten years from now?

Manifestly, such questions must be the subject of serious study. Men must do their utmost to foresee the future, but there are no particularly fine techniques for making such work easy or accurate. What is needed is intelligence and knowledge, patient industry, sound judgment, and recognition of the openness of history.

THE COMPARATIVE STUDY OF COMMUNIST POLITICAL SYSTEMS

ALFRED G. MEYER

The intent of this article is to join in the slowly rising chorus of voices expressing dissatisfaction with the methods used so far in the analysis of Communist political systems. I shall argue, perhaps in rather circuitous fashion, that political scientists in the West have failed, by and large, to apply to the Communist world the rich store of concepts developed for the comparative study of political systems and that the concepts that have been used have been applied in ways that are objectionable. If, as is at times maintained, our discipline tends to be provincial or ethnocentric in its methods, this tendency has been most pronounced, perhaps, in the study of Communist systems. As a result, very little work done has been genuinely comparative. The discipline has failed to place the Communist world into any of the several systematic conceptual frameworks it has developed.

I shall begin by offering a definition of Communist systems but shall then suggest differences between them. My point will be that the similarities between various Communist systems are less salient than the dissimilarities; hence, merely because two systems are called Communist (by Communists or others) need not mean that they are similar. Let me rephrase this by saying that perhaps there is no such thing as *the* Communist political system. Having thrown out that challenge, I shall, finally, make some suggestions concerning methods for exploring these differences further and, at the same time, for discovering similarities between Communist and non-Communist systems.

Communist polities are born in revolution. Since every political system arises out of violence, this is a banal statement. It must be made, however, because it leads at once to questions about the nature of the revolutions that bring Communist parties to power; the nature of the systems that preceded Communist rule; the reasons for their disintegration and fall; the strategies employed by all parties concerned in the struggle for power and the civil war (if there was any); the size, composition, leadership, and program of the Communist party at the time; and many other quite obvious questions. I mention them only in order to show that there are significant differences between Communist revolutions and

Slavic Review, XXVI, No. 1 (March 1967), 3–12. Reprinted by permission. Footnotes omitted.

between the societies in which they occur. Indeed, the differences are more easily stated than the similarities.

If we are interested in similarities, several come to mind at once. One is the doctrine of Marxism-Leninism, an ideology which all Communist leaders profess to share, even though it does not in fact imply an identical program of action for all of them. More generally, the precise relationship between the professed ideology and the policies actually pursued is complex and uncertain, nor have matters been simplified by the recent trend toward the disintegration of whatever ideological unity prevailed in the Communist world. The fact remains that Communist systems are ruled by parties avowing allegiance to a doctrine and program that even in its diverse interpretations retains some unity. Moreover, Communist parties are organized very much according to a common model. Decision-making and administrative processes within the parties are, on the whole, quite similar, and so are the patterns of organization, manipulation, and mobilization which ruling Communist parties have elaborated for the purpose of managing entire societies. From the principles of democratic centralism to constitutions and mass organizations, Communist systems bear remarkable structural similarities.

They are similar to each other also in regard to less formal matters of substance and style. A conventional way of stating this would be that Communist systems have predominantly shown totalitarian features. We are all familiar with the syndrome or model of totalitarianism: it includes one-man dictatorship and a political system designed specifically for the purpose of protecting the dictator from his as-sociates; these associates are drawn from the leadership of a single ruling party, which again structures the polity so as to perpetuate its sovereign position in society. On the whole, totalitarian systems cannot be reformed except from outside. The chief instrument of totalitarian rule is terror, that is, lawless violence and the threat of violence, applied to supporters as well as dissenters of the regime; one of the fringe benefits of the use of mass terror is that it makes for social mobility in an otherwise rigid and self-perpetuating society.

Totalitarian systems, according to the theoretical model from which this summary is drawn, furthermore are characterized by having an ideology, meaning a doctrine sharply critical of present social relations and institutions and demanding radical changes in them. This ideology serves as a guideline for decision-making, a blueprint of the future, a source of legitimacy in the present. Totalitarian rulers act under a strange compulsion to indoctrinate all citizens with this ideology; hence totalitarian systems devote much energy to a frantic effort at total re-education. Totalitarian systems, in addition, seek to control and mobilize all citizens by means of a complex and all-embracing network of party-sponsored or party-dominated organizations and associations. They tolerate no autonomous group life within the community. In the realm of economic activities, they have a similar distaste for free enterprise; hence totalitarian economies are nationalized and managed from the center on the basis of a national plan.

I have repeatedly expressed doubt concerning the usefulness of the term totalitarianism. The model I have presented in its briefest outlines above may read like a caricature. Yet it was not intended to be one. Obviously, totalitarianism is an ideal type, an abstract construct, to which no system has ever conformed totally. Moreover, the growing degree of changeability and differentiation in the Communist world forces us to look increasingly to the many incongruities between the model and reality.

In my search for an alternate model I have argued in recent works that at least one Communist system can be understood adequately by comparing it with complex modern bureaucratic organizations anywhere. Like modern bureaucracy, Communist rule is essentially an attempt to impose rational management over social life by means of complex organization. This attempt leads to the emergence of structural forms, political processes, psychological adjustments, as well as malfunctionings which make Communist systems look remarkably similar to bureaucratic organizations in other parts of the world. An important difference which remains is that Communist systems are sovereign bureaucracies, whereas other bureaucracies exist and operate within larger societal frameworks, so that a Communist state becomes one single bureaucratic system extended over the entire society, or bureaucracy writ large.

The totalitarian and the bureaucratic models of communism are complementary rather than mutually exclusive. They highlight different elements of the Communist world and may well be applied jointly. In using the former, we stress the novelty and uniqueness of Communist rule as well as the terroristic, coercive, and manipulative methods of rule; in preferring the latter, we point to striking similarities the bureaucratic model has with organizations familiar to all of us, and we imply that in criticizing the Communist way of life we should not be blind to analogous failings in our own. The main reason, however, why I prefer the bureaucratic as against the totalitarian model of communism is that the latter, if at all adequate, probably applies to Communist systems only for a limited period of their development, a period of growing pains, of system-building, a period devoted to the "primitive accumulation" of both the means of production and the authority to rule. In contrast, the bureaucratic model more likely applies to the presumably much longer period of settled existence within a well established system.

Whatever model we may use, several features more readily associated with the democratic way of life than with the totalitarian or bureaucratic have to be added. Among these I should mention the effort made by Communist ruling parties either to educate the citizens for a certain measure of self-government or at least to draw them into active participation in public life. A second feature is the egalitarian ethos which expresses itself foremost in the virtually universal opportunities for upward social mobility given to all citizens, and guaranteed by a system of free public education. Finally, Communist states, within the restrictive limits of their economic potential, are, or try to be, welfare states. Although the Communist world is primarily interested in rapid industrialization and a strong national defense—pursuits which require heavy investment yielding no (or no immediate) return to the consumer—and although the level of economic development from which most Communist states were forced to start is relatively low, the ruling parties at least try to put a floor under the general living standard through social security schemes, free medical care, and various other public services.

Despite the strong egalitarian ethos, however, Communist societies have shown tendencies toward the development of new patterns of social stratification. In the attempt to mobilize all citizens for a maximal effort on behalf of the goals established by the party, the leaders of the Communist world have learned that they cannot rely solely on revolutionary enthusiasm, nor on mere terror, but must give their citizens tangible incentives to work. Methods of coercion and persuasion must be supplemented by rewards. Nor can these rewards be given indiscriminately, equally to all, but instead must be differentiated on the basis of the individual's performance, or his worth to the regime. In short, Communist rulers, however reluctantly, have felt the need to establish systems of managed inequality in which material welfare, power, status, and honor are distributed unequally.

If the task of providing a summary description of the structure of Communist systems has become controversial, a summary of their aims has always been a subject for dispute. While some regard Communist states as political machines devised for the fulfillment of a millennial ideology, other interpretations see them primarily as political machines devised by amoral operators and power-seekers. Once they have attained power, the system turns into a control mechanism geared to the task of keeping rival leaders and the masses at bay. My own contribution to this controversy is to offer entrepreneurship as the overriding motive force of Communist rule; that means that the chief aim (or, perhaps, the chief effect) of communism is perhaps the promotion of industrialization.

Interest must focus not only on the aim but also on the manner in which it is pursued, as well as on the subsidiary aims which this pursuance places on the agenda. The manner, or style, of industrialization favored by Communists is the crash program. The subsidiary pursuits and effects include strict consumer austerity, dictatorial rule, and an ambitious attempt to re-educate peasants and other preindustrial cultures for the twentieth century and the industrial way of life. The unwanted and unplanned consequences of the attempt to industrialize backward countries as rapidly as possible are remarkably similar to the growing pains of capitalist industrialization in the West.

One other preoccupation of Communist ruling parties must be added; it is very obvious, hence easily overlooked. Let me call it system-building. This effort is required in all societies which are the products of revolutions. All revolutions, in turn, can be divided into at least three distinct phases. The first phase is that of system-destruction. The second usually is an interregnum marked by various kinds of disorder, false starts, failures, and retreats. The third is that of system-building. In this phase a new social order is in fact created and establishes itself.

This act of creation, again, entails a number of processes which the revolutionary (or, better, postrevolutionary) leadership must promote. They include (a) society-building, that is, the creation of a new social structure, a new system of political institutions, and new organizational forms which become standard for the society's entire organized and associational life. (b) This effort can succeed only if it is accompanied or preceded by the primitive accumulation of authority and legitimacy, meaning a process by which the Communist party and the entire new authority pattern it seeks to create come to be accepted as legitimate by the citizens. Since Communist parties have either come to power as unpopular minorities or have managed to make themselves unpopular by some of the policies they pursued after coming to power, their need for legitimacy was desperate; and their reliance on terror as well as their commitment to total and unceasing indocrination are indications of this desperation. (c) Finally, system-building entails the creation and institutionalization of social traditions and social myths, which take the form of systematic and articulate "official" doctrine and must also be seen in doctrinal taboos, that is, unmentionable topics glossed over or left out of the official ideology.

Even a cursory examination of any one Communist system will reveal that the brief summary description given so far is a gross oversimplification. At the same time, any elaboration might be unsatisfactory because it would add details that do not fit all Communist systems. The fact is that Communist states differ from each other. Another fact is that Communist states have changed, and at times dramatically and drastically. They have changed their aims and their structures. I would, indeed, assert that they have undergone systemic changes. As far as the Soviet Union is concerned, I would be prepared to argue that it is in fact a succession of political systems differing from each other in purpose, structure, and functioning. The same may be true of China, Yugoslavia, Poland, and the Czechoslovak Socialist Republic, and other Communist nations.

The statement just made could be rephrased as follows: The summary description of Communist systems offered above may be acceptable. All the features enumerated may be present in most or all Communist-led societies. But—and this is a very important reservation—the relative strength of these features has varied greatly from one Communist state to another and, within the same state, from one period to another. The precise mix of the various ingredients has in fact shown so much variety that a mere enumeration of the ingredients is unsatisfactory. Instead, our attention should concentrate on the variety of Communist experience and on the variability of Communist political systems.

I find it a bit strange, really, that the changeability of Communist polities has not been given greater emphasis and that it has not been incorporated into theoretical models of communism. After all, they are revolutionary systems, and major revolutions do not, as a rule, establish their results at once. Instead, it may take decades of false starts and long periods of system-building before a relatively stable new political order has emerged. Further, the process of system-building or even the false starts may be preceded by a prolonged destructive phase of doing away with the residues of past systems. In short, Communist societies are developing societies. To be sure, some features, such as the doctrinal framework and the political monopoly of the Communist party, remain relatively constant. But despite the continuities, some of which are merely formal, systemic change takes place.

One can, of course, conceive of political systems which restructure themselves in response to changing inputs, in the manner of self-regulating automatic machines. Some Western scholars have been inclined so to view the Communist systems, which then become institutionalizations of revolution-making; and the ideological spokesmen of Communist regimes likewise describe their orders as self-adjusting democracies. My reason for rejecting this model is that it gives a false image of spontaneous, smooth, and effective self-adjustment; it presents a picture of a political machinery so finely devised that it does in fact regulate itself. In reality, however, Communist systems have shown little talent for smooth self-regulation. On the contrary, they have manifested recurrent tendencies toward institutional, procedural, and ideological rigidity and conservatism, in short, toward self-entrenchment. Major adjustments therefore had to be made in near-revolutionary (or near-counterrevolutionary) fashion. They have usually been violent, and they could be accomplished only because at the top of the system a powerful dictatorship or oligarchy was operating with few restraints. Every readjustment was a major crisis, usually provoked by the top leadership. For some scholars this unrestrained dictatorship, with its ability to rework the entire system, is the essence of Communist politics. But this, too, is unconvincing, not only because it is too one-dimensional a view of a political system but also because this very sovereign ability of the Communist parties is in the process of being challenged. The checks on arbitrariness, hence on permanent revolution, seem to be getting stronger in most of the existing Communist states, which thus may be entering a phase in which self-regulating adjustments or grand restructuring by dictatorial fiat becomes more difficult.

Under the impact of de-Stalinization, intensified polycentrism, and the growing awareness of the need for innovation, the countries of East Europe are at the moment going through an evolution that is similar to post-Stalinist trends in the USSR; and each of the East European systems is going through these changes at its own pace. I should like to summarize the nature of this evolution by arguing that throughout the European Communist world the societal base is tending to reassert its sovereignty over the political superstructure; the native political cultures are regaining some influence; the political systems are forced to adjust themselves to their several political cultures and social structures. The Communist world therefore is rapidly becoming more and more heterogeneous. We must distinguish not only between Western and Asian Communist systems (with Latin American communism as a possible third variant). We must also separate industrial from preindustrial Communist systems. Furthermore, we ought to pay attention to many other variables distinguishing one Communist system from another. Let me name a few at random: different degrees of social stratification and bureaucratization; different patterns of participation, representation, and indeed democracy; different institutional structures; different attitudes toward authority; different interest groups and subcultures.

I am arguing that polycentrism was a reality even before the leaders of the Communist world acknowledged its possibility. And polycentrism means heterogeneity. I see this as a growing trend. We already have Communist regimes in countries as highly developed as Czechoslovakia and as underdeveloped as Albania and North

Korea, not to mention the Mongolian People's Republic. If the experience of the past two decades is at all indicative of a trend, then we must expect the differences between levels of industrialization and modernization to become even greater. The affluent among the Communist nations seem to be growing more affluent, leaving the poorer neighbors further and further behind. This will doubtless lead also to greater and greater differences in policies and outlook. What polycentrism therefore implies is the increasing vagueness and meaninglessness of the term "communism." Today, when a person calls himself a Communist, it is impossible to conclude merely from this confession of faith precisely what his political views are. Similarly, merely to state that a given political system is Communist no longer gives us sufficient information for classifying and understanding it. At the same time, the differences between Communist and other systems lose whatever sharpness they may have had in the past.

I have defined communism as the application of the corporate pattern of entrepreneurship and management to modernizing countries. This makes it appear as a system which serves as a bridge between the traditional and the modern world, hence as one which is likely to share salient features of the most divergent systems. In turn, this may enable us to state differences. One difference from the Western corporation is easily stated: in the Communist society, corporate patterns of organization and rule have been extended to the total social life, so that one might define communism as the corporation writ large.

The difference between communism and the systems of other developing nations is less easily stated, though one might venture a few general observa-

tions. One would be that, on the whole, the countries of the Communist world have started from a somewhat higher level of development. At the time of their revolutions, they had a somewhat more industrial economy than, let us say, Ghana or Indonesia at the time of their emancipation from colonial rule. They had a more numerous and influential intelligentsia, and one might add that contacts with the West had been more ancient and intimate, and Western influence more significant. A second difference lies in the fact that Communist parties have come to power in countries which already had national consciousness, whereas the newly emancipated former colonies, as a rule, have to engage in nation-building simultaneously with other aspects of system-building and economic construction. There is, in addition, the obvious ideological difference: the Communist world confesses its adherence to Marxism-Leninism; other developing nations do not, even though in fact their leaders may think along similar lines and may indeed often use the vocabulary of Marx and Lenin, whether they are aware of it or not. The question whether the ideological differences are essential or whether they are, perhaps, merely ideological is exceedingly intriguing but cannot be answered here. Some scholars might add to this that communism has shown itself, on balance, more efficient in attaining its objectives than other developing nations. I am not sure whether there is sufficient evidence to prove or disprove this assertion; and even if it is correct, one might visualize that in the future some other developing societies might outstrip the Communist world in this regard.

Some years ago Gordon Skilling called for the development of a new subdiscipline—comparative Communist systems. What I have been suggesting, by implication, is that such a subdiscipline has finally emerged. Or, if you wish, I am simply echoing his suggestion, though perhaps in stronger terms. What must be done by political scientists is implicit in my definition of Communist systems. First, we must intensify our efforts at comparing Communist systems with each other. In this connection, many approaches hitherto neglected should be used. In doing so, the time dimension should be added to that of space; we must not only compare, say, the USSR with China, but also the USSR in 1966 with that of 1926 or 1946. In making comparisons, many approaches hitherto neglected should be used. For instance, we need comparative studies of Communist elites; and these should be systemic studies, based on the realization that different types of elites function within different structures and in different styles. In other words, to the extent that the comparative study of political elites has come up with hypotheses or models about the different kinds of elites and other salient variables within political systems, we ought to apply them to the study of Communist systems. Again, if I am correct in stressing the bureaucratic nature of Communist governments, we should seek to place Communist systems within the comparative study of bureaucracies. John Armstrong, in his recent article "Sources of Administrative Behavior: Some Soviet and Western European Comparisons,"[1] has shown how useful this can be. Similarly, it is time to fit the social structures of Communist systems into comparative studies. The relation between the social structure and the political system has been so

changeable that the field of comparative Communist systems, with this particular focus, will turn into a study of contrast. The same may be said about the relation of Communist systems to their interest groups as well as to their national political culture and subcultures. In all these areas we are only at the beginning of comparative studies, and the list could be extended.

Second, the same techniques, hypotheses, models, and other intellectual devices should be applied far more systematically than heretofore to the comparison of Communist with non-Communist systems. Some beginnings have been made with attempts to account for Communist experiences by fitting them into models of modernization. We are beginning to be aware also of the need for studying the structuring effect which the industrial economy and the social psychology of industrial life have on political systems. The rather unfortunate concept of convergence is a token of this awareness. We are still sorely deficient in applying the functional approach to this field; by that I mean the notion that all political systems must serve certain definable functions but may develop different structures for the purpose.

What I am suggesting is, very tritely, that the students of Communist systems become more thoroughly acquainted with the state of the discipline, that they re-think their knowledge in terms of current methods and models, and that they endeavor to do truly comparative work. And that means fitting Communist systems into models of the political system which are sufficiently abstract to have general validity.

Most work done in the past, I would submit, has not been comparative in this sense but has been ethnocentric. In dealing with the Communist world, our notions of what a political system is and

---

[1] *American Political Science Review,* LIX, No. 3 (Sept. 1965), 643–55.

does have been suspended. For describing that world we have used concepts and models reserved for it alone or for it and a few other systems considered inimical. Thus one might almost say that the Communist world was analyzed outside the framework of comparative political science. Or else we used one set of concepts for Communist countries and another for the rest of the world. Most American political scientists would reject the elitist models of Pareto, Mosca, and Michels and would criticize a sociologist like Mills for seeking to apply them to the United States. Yet have not most studies of the Communist world described Communist states in the crudest Paretan terms as the rule of self-appointed elites striving to perpetuate themselves and structuring the entire system to this purpose? And I stress the crudeness of these interpretations, which neglect most of the subtleties and sophistication of both Mosca and Pareto.

Much criticism is now beginning to be leveled against the concept of totalitarianism, and I have occasionally joined in on this criticism. There are few remarks I wish to make about it here. One reason why it is of limited usefulness is that it is a residual category, lumping together a variety of mass mobilization systems simply because they are neither constitutional nor traditional. Residual categories purvey false notions of sameness where in fact there is a heterogeneity. Moreover, the concept of totalitarianism implies that the systems to which we apply the term are unique. But this notion of uniqueness, I think, is an ethnocentric myth which conceals innumerable precursor systems in the Western world.

It is hardly necessary, I am sure, to point out the ideological implications of my strictures, and therefore the bias on which my arguments are based: the concepts and interpretations I find inadequate were used for reasons— good reasons perhaps. One might enumerate the reality of Stalinist rule, the inaccessibility of Communist systems to Western researchers, and perhaps even the public statements made by Communist spokesmen. But one of the reasons for our failure to view Communist societies through the gridwork of commonly used concepts and theories has surely been the ideological climate of the cold war. In urging that we integrate the study of these societies with the discipline to which we profess to belong, I am perhaps suggesting nothing else than that we sweep the cold war out of this undertaking.

COMMUNISM AND THE COMPARATIVE STUDY OF DEVELOPMENT

JOHN H. KAUTSKY

First of all, I should like to support as strongly as I can Professor Meyer's plea that the study of the Soviet Union and of communism be integrated with the study of comparative politics. For a number of reasons Soviet and Communist studies have developed apart from the rest of political science in this

Slavic Review, XXVI, No. 1 (March 1967), 13–17. Reprinted by permission. Footnotes omitted.

country. Among these reasons is probably the general growth of area studies with their noncomparative stress during and especially after World War II. More particularly, the government's need for information about Communist countries and the mobility of personnel in this field between government agencies and universities have bent some of the scholarly work in it in the direction of intelligence work. Also, in the study of these countries, refugees from them have played a significant role. Quite naturally, they have been more inclined to deal with the countries of their origin alone and to see them as unique than to compare them with non-Communist systems. Finally, there is a long tradition in Soviet and Communist studies of stressing Marxist-Leninist ideology, perhaps because Communists themselves stress it and because so many engaged in such studies are ex-Communists, Marxists, or ex-Marxists. But their ideology is precisely the element that sets Communist systems apart from others (though not as clearly as is often suggested), and emphasis on it therefore inhibits comparison with non-Communist systems.

However, the *rapprochement* and eventual integration of Soviet studies and comparative political science will have to come from both sides, for most of the very people who have made the greatest contribution to the advancement of comparative politics have avoided analysis of Communist systems. They have been as guilty as Soviet and Communist specialists of implying by this omission that Communist systems are unique and not comparable with other systems. Thus, Almond and Coleman's authoritative volume on *The Politics of the Developing Areas* contains no section on the Soviet Union or even China, as if the

mere fact that Communist parties rule these countries removed them from the scope of generalizations about developing areas. Panel meetings on comparative politics at the 1966 meeting of the American Political Science Association, which should to some extent reflect the state of the discipline, were divided into three categories: "Developed Systems," "Developing Systems," and "Communist Systems." Evidently Communist systems, being Communist, are neither "developed" nor "developing"!

To Professor Meyer's plea that students of Communist systems join the disclipline of political science, not just in name but by using the concepts developed by political scientists, I would, then, like to add my plea that political scientists who are developing and using concepts valuable for comparative analysis begin to apply these to Communist systems. Indeed, there may be more hope for an improvement in the analysis of Communist systems in this approach, for it may be intellectually easier to apply concepts with which one is familiar to new substantive material than to analyze material with which one is familiar with the aid of new concepts, to think in new ways about what one has thought about for many years.

Secondly, and more particularly, I should like to express my agreement with what I think is implied throughout Professor Meyer's paper, that is, that Communist and general comparative studies should be integrated in a developmental framework. Let me briefly make some points on one way this might be done, most of which I have already spelled out elsewhere at greater length.

The revolutions that brought Communist parties to power took place in traditional societies disrupted by the impact of early industrialization. They were led by intellectuals, that is, people with a Western education, whose chief aim was, as Professor Meyer says, the promotion of industrialization. Obviously, this makes Communist revolutions far from unique. They share these characteristics and many others that accompany them with the general upheaval throughout the underdeveloped world in our time.

I would suggest, then, that Communist revolutions, including the Russian, be placed, for analytical purposes, in the context of revolutions in underdeveloped countries. This type of comparison has so far been obstructed in large part by the use, both by participants and by observers, of certain labels and symbols that have stressed differences between Communist and non-Communist revolutions. Thus, most non-Communist revolutions in underdeveloped countries have been referred to as "nationalist," a term that, as used with reference to underdeveloped countries, seems to mean little more than anti-Western.

Communist revolutions, on the other hand, are, of course, made in the name of communism and of the more immediate goals of "socialism," of proletarianism, and even of internationalism (which sounds very different from nationalism). Again, the meaning of these symbols with reference to underdeveloped countries, including those where Communist parties have come to power, is very vague.

For purpose of comparative analysis, we can put revolutions in underdeveloped countries in a common framework by calling them "modernizing" instead of nationalist or Communist. They are all led by intellectuals who both are anti-Western and wish to Westernize, that is, above all, to in-

dustrialize their countries. Being anti-Western, they are, in a vague sense, nationalists; and since industrialization in underdeveloped countries can only take place, if at all, with the government playing a large role in the process, they are, in a vague sense, socialists. Indeed, in recent years Communist revolutions have increasingly made use of nationalist symbolism, as in the terms "national liberation movement" and "national democracy," while non-Communist nationalist regimes have widely referred to themselves as socialist. If they can minimize the distinction for political reasons, so can we for political science reasons.

What I have just said applies also to non-ruling Communist parties in underdeveloped countries in comparison with non-Communist so-called nationalist movements. Here, too, it has been generally—and, I feel, wrongly—implied that a sharp line of distinction can be drawn, as is clear from recurrent debates as to whether Castro and Lumumba, Sukarno and Sékou Touré, revolutionary movements in Zanzibar and the Dominican Republic and in Viet Nam are or are not Communist, as if every leader and movement had to be clearly one or the other. Here, again, the practicing politicians have in a sense been ahead of the political scientist. The old myths and symbols that stood in the way of recognition of the common character of Communist and non-Communist movements have slowly begun to yield. The two types of movements have been converging and, in a few cases, have in effect merged, most notably in Cuba, but also to some extent in Algeria and Egypt. Communist parties and the Soviet government generally support non-Communist modernizing movements, and the Soviet Union has virtually adopted some of them, such as those of Ghana, Guinea, and Mali, as surrogate Communist parties. It may be time that political scientists caught up with reality and began using the concept of modernizing movement, along with that of modernizing revolution, as a tool for the analysis of both Communist and non-Communist movements.

Turning from Communist revolutions and movements to Communist regimes and systems, I would like to join Professor Meyer in his doubts concerning the usefulness of the concept totalitarianism. It was understandable that in the 1930s the two most striking deviations from what was then regarded as the democratic norm—German and Italian fascism and Stalinist Russia—should be lumped together under the concept of totalitarianism. Today we know—or we ought to know if we focus on the interests represented by the various so-called totalitarian regimes—that there are also vast differences between them. In our context here I refer only to the commitment of Communist regimes, led by modernizing intellectuals, to rapid industrialization, as contrasted to the rise of fascist regimes out of groups reacting to and afraid of industrialization.

This contrast between Communist and fascist systems in turn points to the similarity between Communist regimes and other regimes of intellectuals committed to industrialization in underdeveloped countries, which the concept of totalitarianism tends to obscure. To be sure, there are also great differences among such regimes, but these are not necessarily differences between the Communist and the non-Communist ones. Professor Meyer stresses quite rightly that there is no

such thing as *the* Communist political system, that there have been and are several different types, and that they cannot be clearly distinguished from other political systems, particularly from those in other developing countries.

I would say that even Professor Meyer's very cautious observations on differences between Communist and other developing countries assume too much uniformity within each group of countries and overemphasize the differences between the two. Thus, that Communist systems had their revolution at a more advanced industrial stage than non-Communist countries is, no doubt, true of Russia as compared to Ghana or Indonesia. But is it equally true of China as compared to Mexico? Similarly, the Russian intelligentsia was no doubt more numerous and influential than the Ghanaian or Indonesian intelligentsia. But was the Chinese or Vietnamese more numerous and influential than the Indian intelligentsia? Contacts with the West were ancient and intimate for Russia and Cuba. But were they more so for China and Viet Nam than for Turkey and Mexico? As to national consciousness, which is said to have been present when Communist parties came to power but not at the time of anticolonial revolutions in other underdeveloped countries, the concept would seem to have little meaning with respect to the peasantry, that is, the vast majority of the populations, of tsarist Russia and pre-Communist China. With reference to the intelligentsia, however, we need not necessarily assume that national consciousness was greater in China or even Russia than, for example, in India or Egypt at the time of their emancipation from colonialism.

Finally, Professor Meyer points to the ideological difference: Communist systems adhere to Marxism-Leninism; other developing systems do not. On the one hand, this is, as he himself adds, not quite true, because the intellectual elites of many non-Communist countries also think and talk along Marxist-Leninist lines, and, of course, leaders of different Communist countries can think and act quite differently from each other though they all profess adherence to Marxism-Leninism. On the other hand, the statement is no more than a truism: Of course, Communist systems adhere to Marxism-Leninism, because that is what defines a Communist system. Thus, Cuba became a Communist country when and because Castro announced—evidently to the surprise and perhaps the dismay of Soviet leaders—that he was a Marxist-Leninist and that his movement would be Communist. But did this announcement, this change of symbols, make his regime more different from those of, say, Ben Bella, Nasser, or Nkrumah than it would have otherwise been? In some respects, yes, for symbols and myths play a great role in politics, but not in others. Particularly with regard to its economic development and the consequent development of the major social groups in the population, Communist Cuba looks much more like non-Communist Egypt than like Communist Russia.

Again, we may note that in the political practice of the elites of Communist and non-Communist developing countries the sharp distinction between them is being obscured—Soviet theoreticians recognize some non-Communist countries as "national democracies"; Ben Bella and Nasser were made Heroes of the Soviet Union; Yugoslavia and Cuba have partici-

pated in conferences of non-aligned countries; Afro-Asian conferences have united Communist and non-Communist countries with even the European Soviet Union trying to participate. Political scientists should have seen similarities of developing political systems across the so-called ideological dividing line long before those caught up in their respective ideologies did. At least we should now not lag too far behind them.

I have suggested, then, that political systems, movements, and ideologies can usefully be compared when they are at roughly equivalent stages of economic development, regardless of whether they are Communist or not. Thus, one can, for instance, come closer to establishing the function of Communist ideology in a comparison in which the factor of economic development is held constant. I am not suggesting, however, that all countries are passing through stages of developing at the same rate or that they must even necessarily pass from one stage to the next one at all. I am not suggesting that, since Mao and Castro, Nasser and Ben Bella, Sukarno and Nkrumah are in some ways functional equivalents of Lenin, all their countries must and will have their Stalins and eventually their Khrushchevs and Brezhnevs. It is precisely one of the functions of comparative analysis to help discover why Russia did and others may not.

But if and when a so-called developing system does develop, that is, does become an advanced industrial society wtih the inevitable social and political concomitants this process implies, as has been most notably true of the Soviet Union and could become true of at least a few other developing countries (for example, Mexico), then comparison with other advanced industrial systems will be in order. Just as communism must not be a barrier to the comparative analysis of underdeveloped or developing countries, so it must not prevent the development of models that can be usefully applied to the study of both Communist and non-Communist advanced countries. Professor Meyer's bureaucratic model is certainly an extremely suggestive one, which should be most useful in the study not only of Communist but also of other systems dominated by intellectuals who are bent on rapid industrialization if and when and especially after their dreams have been realized.

OBSERVATIONS ON BUREAUCRACY, TOTALITARIANISM, AND THE COMPARATIVE STUDY OF COMMUNISM

PAUL HOLLANDER

Though I am a sociologist rather than a political scientist, I share with Professor Meyer an interest in Soviet society, convergence, totalitarianism, and the comparative study of communism and have followed the development of his views on these matters. I therefore welcome an opportunity to comment on his recent paper (in the Symposium of the March 1967 issue of the *Slavic Review*), having felt both critical of and sympathetic toward the views put forward in it. His thoughtful analysis of the study of Communist societies is all the more worthy of discussion since it reflects not only the current misgivings about the subject but also some broader contemporary issues in American social sciences and in our general thinking about communism.

First, I want to make clear that I am in sympathy with his call for comparative studies of Communist societies as well as with his championing a more discriminating use of the concept of totalitarianism. We are at a stage in the study of Communist societies, the Soviet society in particular, when the old model has lost some of its validity, whereas a new model of similar explanatory power has not yet arisen. The emerging consensus, at any rate among students of Soviet society, lies in a preference for combining several models, several approaches depending on the purposes and interests at hand. The question of the day is not so much which models to use but what emphasis to give any one of them. In agreement with those who call for a more restricted use of the totalitarian model, I would stress its growing inapplicability to areas of life which lie outside the realm of politics proper. It is in itself an indication of change that today we can speak with more certainty of such areas. In particular I have found that totalitarianism cannot adequately explain what sociologists call social problems, for example, juvenile delinquency, crime, family instability, problems of leisure, alcoholism, and rural migration. When deal-

Slavic Review, XXVI, No. 2 (June 1967), 302–7. Reprinted by permission. Footnotes omitted.

ing with these features of Soviet society (and some other Communist societies) we are compelled to fall back on concepts or processes which have no direct political relevance or derivation: secularization, urbanization, social mobility, the decline of informal social controls, and so forth—concepts which are unrelated to totalitarianism. At the same time I would like to argue that we have not yet reached the stage at which the totalitarian model can be abandoned or even demoted to a very subordinate role in the analysis of Communist societies. I would also like to argue that its declining popularity is associated with circumstances other than the changes in Communist societies usually cited as the main justification for its abandonment.

First, I would like to suggest that, American social sciences being as dynamic as American society itself, we tend to be impatient with concepts, models, or theories which have been around for a long time; they make us restless and even anxious. We social scientists (sociologists probably even more than political scientists) want to be in the mainstream of the latest developments. We are fearful of being left behind with an old, obsolete "model"; we long for the latest. The analogy is deliberate—the fear of becoming obsolete is as pervasive in the social sciences as in the realm of consumption. The quest for new models and theories is not its only expression. We are also addicted to verbal innovation and to the spurious sense of novelty that comes with each new publication. None of this has any direct relevance to the issue at hand, least of all to Professor Meyer's work and opinions, for which I have much respect. I have made the above observation merely to indicate the broad

background against which the current debate might be considered and to increase the appreciation of our receptivity to innovation.

To trace further the general context in which we confront the call for comparative studies of Communism and new models with which to carry it out, I would like to comment on the influence of the cold war which Professor Meyer mentioned. It seems to have become almost axiomatic, for Professor Meyer and others, that the concept of totalitarianism is inextricably linked to the cold war and that this relationship has been detrimental to the development of scholarship on the Soviet Union and Communist countries in general. We hardly need to be reminded that the emergence of the concept of totalitarianism preceded the cold war, having evolved originally from the experiences of Nazism and fascism. It is true, however, that subsequently it has been wholeheartedly applied to the Soviet system and that the early applications coincided with the beginning of the cold war. What remains to be demonstrated is that use of this model did any lasting or temporary damage to the study of Communist societies. It so happens that to date the best studies, of Soviet society at any rate (of which I know most), made use of the concept of totalitarianism and were employed by authors of such divergent views as Merle Fainsod, Alex Inkeles, Barrington Moore, and Adam Ulam, and by many others. I am sure Professor Meyer would agree with me that their use of the model did not impair their scholarship, their objectivity, or the value of their work. And I would agree with his probable rejoinder that, if in the past there was justification for the model, this may not hold for the present. In any case I merely wanted to draw attention to the fact that the concept of totalitarianism in itself need not carry the stigma of the cold war and an attendant unscholarly ideological fervor.

In relation to the effects of the cold war on Soviet studies I would like to take up another point Professor Meyer implies in his paper and has made more explicit elsewhere. I feel that his diminishing liking for the totalitarian model is closely linked to a belief that its use inclines us to self-righteousness and blindness to the defects of our own society. His remark in support of the bureaucratic model supports this proposition: "In preferring the latter [that is, the bureaucratic model], we point to striking similarities the bureaucratic model has with organizations familiar to all of us, and we imply that in criticizing the Communist way of life we should not be blind to analogous failings in our own." I am in complete agreement with Professor Meyer's feeling on this subject. The study of foreign societies, Communist or otherwise, should not become a vehicle for an indulgent evaluation of our own. Yet I do not think that the overgenerous use of the bureaucratic model necessarily saves us from this temptation. I submit that neither in the American nor in the Communist case is bureaucratization the major evil which should provoke the sharpest social criticism. This does not mean that we should ignore the ill effects of bureaucratization, American or Soviet. I simply suggest that each society has far more serious shortcomings than those which can be derived from the bureaucratic model and that adopting it for the analysis of Communist societies may not be of much utility in redressing the balance between self-in-dulgence and the stern criticism of others.

I would now like to offer more direct criticisms of the model and the approach Professor Meyer prefers—sometimes, it would seem, in contradiction to his own insight into both the differences between Communist and non-Communist societies and the similarities between the Communist societies. It seems to me, in brief, that the totalitarian model is not quite as obsolete, and irrelevant to the political landscape, as he and others believe. The model suffered most because of its emphasis on coercion, or, more precisely, permanent mass terror. The question remains: does this invalidate the model entirely or can it be "patched up"? While the decline of coercion has had far-reaching social consequences and while the purge turned out to be impermanent, massive and highly differentiated coercive institutions have not been eliminated, nor have new institutional arrangements been made to place obstacles in the path of arbitrary force. I would nonetheless agree with Professor Meyer that, despite this, a return to Stalinist forms of government is for many reasons unlikely. In any case, however, the potentiality of coercion remains a major incentive to conform in Communist societies. These features cannot be reduced to the characteristics of complex bureaucracies. This brings me to my central contention, namely, that replacing the totalitarian model with the bureaucratic is not an improvement. To be sure, Professor Meyer did say at one point that the two are complementary rather than mutually exclusive and may well be applied jointly. If this is the case I have little to disagree with. I might even be inclined to suggest a verbal innovation such as a model of pluralistic versus totalitarian bureaucracy. Still, on the whole Professor Meyer explicitly prefers the bureaucratic model.

Should we decide to abandon the middle-aged and decreasingly useful concept of totalitarianism in favor of one that focuses on the bureaucratic model, we would do little to sharpen our understanding of Communist societies viewed either in isolation from each other or jointly. It would achieve, however, what I think Professor Meyer favors, a lowered estimation of the differences between Communist and non-Communist societies. Even if one aspired to construct a scheme to accommodate both Western and Communist societies, I wonder whether the bureaucratic model is a more promising starting point than the concept of convergence. I have argued, together with Ezra Vogel, that Communist bureaucracies—at any rate the Soviet and Chinese—are radically different both from the classical sociological models of bureaucracy and from contemporary Western bureaucracies. While many counter-arguments are possible and many similarities between all bureaucracies can be noted, we concluded that the differences outweigh the similarities. This is not the place to repeat my arguments (or to draw on those of Vogel) but merely to recall that we both found the decisively distinctive feature of Communist bureaucracies to be their thorough politicization, from which follow many other features setting them apart from Western bureaucracies. What I am suggesting here is that we cannot provide a unifying conceptual scheme for the analysis of Communist and non-Communist societies which is based on the alleged similarities of all complex, large-scale bureaucratic organizations once such similarities, or their importance, are open to serious question. We might end up with a situation worse than that which faces us currently with the totalitarian model: we would have to qualify the generalizability of the bureaucratic model out of existence.

I would now like to say something positive to recommend the retention of the totalitarian model, at least until we have something better or until further changes in the Communist world reduce its usefulness more significantly. I see the remaining virtues of the totalitarian model in that it draws together the following features of Communist systems: (1) strong ideological commitment of the leadership combined with apparent belief in a quasi-utopian social order (some participants in the Symposium referred to this as a drive to create a new man); (2) intensity of controls, which, even if not outright terroristic, cannot be adequately described as bureaucratic; (3) concerted drive for industrialization (Nazi Germany obviously is a special case); (4) absence of legitimate and significant pluralism; and, most important, (5) deliberately created interdependence of all social, economic, political, administrative, and cultural institutions and activities. I am aware that some of these features of totalitarianism might be found in non-Communist, developing societies and that we might end up with the unsatisfactory finding that totalitarianism is more than ever a matter of degree and not a pure type. However, the same objection can be made to the use of any other ideal-type concept: democracy, capitalism, bureaucracy, feudalism, underdeveloped, modernizing, and so on. The present time is characterized by such a high degree of interchange and mutual borrowing between different societies that pure types are increasingly difficult to find. In the final analysis, the question of which model we find the most useful boils down to often intangible factors of personal interests, disposition, and values. The preference for the totalitarian or bureaucratic model clearly depends on whether we are more interested in discovering similarities or differences between Communist societies, whether we consider their internal similarities more important than their resemblances to non-Communist societies. Unavoidably, the issue of the distinctiveness of Communist versus non-Communist societies does have ideological implications, but the differences discerned need not be viewed in terms of superiority and inferiority, even when we compare our own society with Communist societies.

What I am suggesting is that we can and should recognize and study the differences between Communist societies without falling back on the bland, homogenizing approach toward all modern societies, Communist and non-Communist alike, implied by the bureaucratic model. Little is gained if we exchange one set of oversimplifications for another.

I would also like to comment on Professor Meyer's perception of the ethnocentrism which, in his opinion, has characterized Western, and presumably primarily American, studies of communism. He says:

Most work done in the past, I would submit, has not been comparative in this sense but has been ethnocentric. In dealing with the Communist world, our notions of what a political system is and does have been suspended. For describing that world we have used concepts and models reserved for it alone or for it and a few other systems considered inimical.

I would like to propose exactly the opposite. To apply without reservation the concepts and models developed in the context of Western political institutions and traditions to Communist and other non-Western societies might be a good deal more ethnocentric than the practice criticized by Professor Meyer. By following his advice we would project terms and perspectives which derive from a particular and limited historical experience and scholarship and which may have little relevance to the new phenomena they try to describe. It seems to me more ethnocentric to build and apply concepts on the assumption that "basically" all societies are like our own (of course it depends on what is "basic"). Consequently, one could argue that the concept of totalitarianism arose not out of the desire to arm ourselves with a new pejorative term with which to describe our enemies but from the recognition that a somewhat new sociopolitical phenomenon had appeared which could not be described adequately by the traditional vocabulary Western social scientists had developed and applied to their own societies. In addition, I sense a contradiction between the plea for sharper distinctions between Communist societies, on the one hand, and, on the other, the proposal to analyze them with concepts which would make them less distinctive in comparison with non-Communist societies.

In the end, the major and the most sensitive issue that emerges is not so much the variability of Communist societies but the degree and the ways in which they differ from non-Communist societies. (I am in full agreement with Professor Meyer concerning the growing differentiation of European Communist movements and societies as their respective social-cultural bases reassert themselves.) I submit that we can retain and even increase our appreciation of the differences between Communist systems without overestimating their similarities to Western societies (which may occur through undue reliance on the bureaucratic model) and also without succumbing to the even stronger temptation of lumping them together with all "developing" countries. The lure of the latter is particularly strong because it promises to maximize the yield of theoretical generalizations in the framework of a subtle revival of evolutionary theory.

To sum up, I believe that as of now the comparative study of Communist systems in itself does not necessitate a rejection of the totalitarian model, which, while timeworn, continues to direct our attention to many important features these systems have in common. Moreover, although the model can be improved upon (or supplemented by others), little will be gained by treating Communist systems as modern, complex bureaucracies. Finally, if we wish to promote greater sensitivity in distinguishing between Communist systems, the developmental model might not be the most useful, unless we are content with a more sophisticated version of economic determinism.

Perhaps it might be justifiable to conclude that—as is often said in scholarly disputes—our manifest disagreements are more matters of emphasis than of substance.

II THE ENVIRONMENTAL INFLUENCES

The philosophical and ethical self-justification of the Bolshevik assumption of power in 1917 was that they were carrying out an historically inevitable class mission. Defining society in terms of antagonistic classes, the Bolsheviks behaved as self-appointed representatives of those class interests that they defined as nonexploitative. They avowed an intention of transforming society so as to root out, and forever prevent a return to, an exploitative social order. They expected to put into practice certain ideas and beliefs, to order reality to fit certain values, to change social, economic, and political institutions so as to create a more just, materially abundant society. Through conscious action, through the force of human will, the environment would be shaped to coincide with the beliefs and values.[1]

Over the years since 1917 this emphasis on social transformation or regeneration has remained as an important, if perhaps no longer directing, influence within the Communist Party of the Soviet Union (CPSU). In addition to providing the fundamental purpose underlying the assumption of power, this goal served to stimulate the move toward rapid industrialization and the enforced collectivization of agriculture initiated by Stalin in the late 1920s. Many observers interpret the Twenty-Second Congress of the CPSU (October, 1961), and the new party program that was adopted at the congress, as signifying a more conservative turn, away from (but not abandoning) the goal of social transformation and toward managing the existing social system;[2] nevertheless, an important legacy remains. The rationale offered by the party for its role in Soviet society—a total monopoly over the institutions of authority—remains anchored in the notion of social change through elite (i.e., party) control of the environment. Only through party leadership can the positive steps already taken towards a socially just

---

[1] See Alfred G. Meyer, *Leninism* (Cambridge, Mass.: Harvard University Press, 1957).

[2] See Robert Tucker, "The C.P.S.U. Program: A Credo of Conservatism," *Problems of Communism* (September–October 1961), pp. 1–4.

and economically abundant society be preserved in the face of reactionary pressures and retrogressive instincts, and further gains made. That it has been possible within the Soviet Union for political leaders to shape the environment is clear from even a casual observation of history. The issues raised in the readings in this volume give evidence of the changes brought by conscious action. However, it is almost a truism to say that individual will is not the sole determinant of political behavior and political decision making. The goals that man, in society, sets for himself—such as harmony, tranquillity, security, material abundance, social justice—are not reached through a simple progression from desire to power to achievement, from will to means to ends. To an important, but unfortunately elusive, degree, the environment imposes limitations upon conscious action, upon politics as the expression of man's effort to control his own destiny. Each generation finds something left over from the preceding with which it must cope, and which circumscribes its opportunities to shape its own future. As a prominent scholar has noted,

Even the most revolutionary political systems have their roots in history. A country's institutions and behavior patterns can be seen as the products of the social and economic development in which every phase and every conflict, every issue and every resolution of an issue have left, like geological deposits, some laws, some institutions, traditions, or methods of administration. Every historic event leaves sediments, and the political system is composed of such sediments and crystallizations.[3]

At the least, a tension develops between man's efforts to guide his own fortunes and the social, economic, political, cultural, and spiritual forces that are the result of his past actions or his physical surroundings. The selections here in Part II emphasize some of the more important environmental aspects of the Soviet political system. It is hoped that they will illustrate and provoke:—illustrate the types of environmental influences that appear to shape the nature of politics in the Soviet Union, as well as the considerable gaps in our knowledge, and provoke the reader to further thought and study about how these influences do affect the system.

Two rather obvious environmental limitations, which are of importance for all political systems and need little discussion, are physical conditions, broadly speaking, and external developments. Within the territorial boundaries of the nation-state called The Union of Soviet Socialist Republics live a certain number of human beings (about 240 million), with varied skills and, with variations, a certain level of cultural and technological sophistication. Included in this territory are certain natural resources—a relative lack of arable land, a near self-sufficiency in minerals, still untapped power sources. Because of its particular location, this territory is subjected to a certain pattern of climatic conditions. All of these factors serve as

---

[3] Alfred G. Meyer, *The Soviet Political System*, p. 21.

the raw materials upon which the political system is built. They affect the conditions in which people live, and are a frequent natural source of demands to which the political system must respond.

One particular human factor within the Soviet Union that has had a continuous effect upon political life is the existence of many different nationalities. The Soviet Union is by no means an ethnically homogeneous society. Although the three main Slavic peoples—the Russians, the Ukrainians, and the Byelorussians, the first two with a distinct national pride of their own—constitute over three-fourths of the Soviet population, the country contains around two hundred nationalities, tribes, and linguistic groups. These vary from the Baltic peoples, the Estonians, Latvians, and Lithuanians, through the peoples of the Caucasus and Central Asia, to the Chukchis in the frozen tundra of northeast Siberia. There are many differences in cultural development among these peoples.

This multinational environment has made it extremely difficult, if not impossible, for the party to unify society from above by imposing a new culture. Latent traditions of an independent existence and pride in cultural differences or singularities are a major source of problems for the elite, and they affect political institutions and political processes throughout the Soviet system.

The continuation of the forms and facade of a multinational federalism as the constitutional basis for the Soviet state give overt testimony to the impact of nationalism on the Soviet political system. The multinational chracter of the Soviet state and its imperial Russian predecessor has been formed and historically maintained less by consensus, than by coercion. This has led to continuing political and social tension and conflict. As Vernon V. Aspaturian notes in his discussion of the nationalities problem, the disaffection of the major non-Russian nationalities was a principal factor in the revolutionary events of 1917. By structuring the Soviet state on a multinational basis, while retaining power in the hands of the highly centralized party, and not eschewing coercion entirely, Lenin and his successors have attempted to develop a sense of legitimacy sufficient for the building of what Professor Aspaturian refers to as a "multinational sociopolitical system."

Multinationalism affects the Soviet political system in other important ways. The *national* demands on the decision makers force choices that can be either irrational, in terms of established goals, or threatening to the political position of the decision makers. More broadly, the often centrifugal forces of nationalism pose a threat to both the centralization of the party and the dominance of the Russians as the by far most numerous nationality. Professor Aspaturian points in this regard to the effect of modernization and industrialization of Soviet society on the various nationalities, and thus on the political structure.

The political system of any society does not function in a vacuum created by its national boundaries. There appears to be an extremely important mutual relationship between the domestic determinants of a nation's foreign policy and the external environment. The Soviet decision makers formulate foreign policy not only to reach some predetermined universalist goals, or in response to certain domestic pressures, but also in response to developments in the world at large outside their control; actions of other states, the United States, for example; or fundamental developments such as the anticolonial independence movement, or the scientific-technological revolution. The external environment thus affects the Soviet political system by creating issues for decision outside the control of the decision makers.

It is the contention of W. W. Rostow that "the precise forms which Soviet society has taken ... have been partially determined by an inescapable historical continuity imposed upon the regime." As he notes, his discussion focuses "on the manner whereby those physical and cultural factors which have determined the nature of Russian civilization in general have also had their influence on the policies, techniques, and mannerisms of the Soviet state." Professor Rostow suggests that certain aspects of life even in Soviet society are governed by traditional values, and that "on balance ... the regime has tended to recognize its incapacity to alter radically the anthropological foundations of human life." He also notes that on the one hand the environment, in the form of a prevailing tradition of autocratic rule and weakly developed democratic traditions, can *aid* those who exercise autocratic power. On the other hand, he suggests that a deeper trend, extending back considerably before 1917, has been at work *against* autocratic rule. This trend can perhaps be viewed as a pressure against which those who exercise power must continually be creating defenses. At the least, autocratic rule must appear in public in democratic clothing.

Many would not wish to go so far as Professor Rostow in emphasizing the effect of the past, or of the human and physical factors, on contemporary Soviet politics. One does run the risk of sliding into historical or cultural determinism, by which present political behavior is explained away more or less simply as the inevitable product of environmental conditions very little, if at all, controlled or controllable by man. Certainly the leadership in the Soviet Union would not accept this view, although it finds itself in a somewhat ambivalent position in this regard because of its propagation of Marx's dogma of historical materialism on the one hand, and its insistence on the other that under party leadership the environment can be shaped and directed.[4] One need not accept all of Professor Rostow's arguments,

---

[4] See Meyer, *Leninism*, for Lenin's reconciliation in theory of this contradiction. See also Richard Pipes, "Communism and Russian History," in Donald W. Treadgold, ed., *Soviet and Chinese Communism: Similarities and Differences* (Seattle: University of Washington Press, 1966) and Cyril E. Black, "The Modernization of Russian

however, to be persuaded that an awareness of the past is important to an understanding of the Soviet present. How important, and in what ways traditional values influence the present, is difficult to say with precision. Much remains to be done in this area.

Political culture—the sum of those fundamental beliefs, customs, habits, values, aspirations, and expectations of a society that refer to authority, political goals, political processes, political leaders, and political institutions —appears to be as important an influence in the Soviet Union as in any other society. As with other of the perceived environmental influences, however, it is extremely difficult to say with any precision just what are the critical beliefs and what their social functions are.[5] How do they affect behavior; how do they serve to stimulate or to limit conscious action as expressed in the programs and policies of the party? Even more difficult is an evaluation of whether or not the effects of political culture on the political system, or the political culture itself, are changing.

What makes a study of the Soviet Union so interesting is that it was one of the first societies in which a conscious effort was made to change radically the political culture. From the moment the Bolsheviks acquired power in 1917, they and their successors have sought to impose a new belief system on society, eradicating that which had developed partly spontaneously, partly under the weakly organized efforts of the church and the autocracy over the preceding centuries.

As Daniel Bell points out so clearly in his article on ideology, every society needs and has a belief system to provide the rules of the game, to give legitimacy to the political system and the decisions made. In the Soviet Union, there has been a conscious effort by those who have exercised power to impose a particular set of values on all of society—a belief system, derived in part from the Russian past[6] and in part from the ideas of Marx and Lenin, according to which the party claims to know the "truth" and the direction of history. This belief system, the dominant political culture,[7]

Society," in Black, ed., *The Transformation of Russian Society* (Cambridge, Mass.: Harvard University Press, 1960) for other discussions of historical developments and the Soviet political system.

[5] See David Joravsky, "Soviet Ideology," *Soviet Studies*, XVIII, No. 1 (July 1966), for a stimulating discussion of ideological thought and its social functions, as well as Robert G. Wesson, "Soviet Ideology: The Necessity of Marxism," *Soviet Studies*, XXI, No. 1 (July 1969).

[6] See W. W. Rostow, *The Dynamics of Soviet Society* (New York: W. W. Norton & Company, Inc., 1967), pp. 24–27.

[7] See Frederick C. Barghoorn, *Politics in the USSR* (Boston: Little, Brown and Company, 1966), Chap. 1, and "Soviet Russia: Orthodoxy and Adaptiveness," in Lucien W. Pye and Sidney Verba, eds., *Political Culture and Political Development* (Princeton, N.J.: Princeton University Press, 1965); Meyer, *The Soviet Political System*, Chap. 3; and Zbigniew Brzezinski and Samuel P. Huntington, *Political Power: USA/USSR* (New York: The Viking Press, Inc., 1964), Chap. 1, for discussions on political culture and the role of ideas in the Soviet political system.

sets forth the goals of society and seeks to mobilize the members for social change. Ideally, each member of Soviet society would subscribe to this belief system and would internalize the goals and values that derive from it. Each would spontaneously accept the decisions of the party and the role of the party in society, and display an eagerness to become a highly productive member of society.

In such an ideal situation the effect of conscious action, of party leadership and mass following and support, would be to shape the environment —to transform society and human nature. The reality, however, has been something less than the ideal. Although the party has had successes in its effort to replace old values with new, it has failed to impose completely its belief system on Soviet society. Observers of Soviet society would like to know the extent to which the imposed or dominant culture has succeeded in eradicating the older, prerevolutionary, traditional values. One would also like to know to what extent remnants of the traditional inhibit the extension of the dominant, imposed culture.

One evident fact is that the belief system that formally dominates Soviet society can serve as a constraining influence on the political process. The commitment to doctrine can lead to behavior that is irrational in terms of the needs and demands imposed by reality. The effective and efficient resolution or satisfaction of the latter is necessary if the goals laid down in the imposed belief system are to be achieved. Thus, important sources of tension and political problems in the Soviet Union are the contradictions that have developed (1) within individuals in the party elite between commitment to the accepted values and the persistence of traditional values, (2) between the accepted values and reality, and (3) between the elite and the masses as a result of the effort to enforce a belief system over not only the traditional values, but also the individual's "own motivational needs as a personality."

Daniel Bell and Roy Laird are concerned with how much the dominant culture is changing and why, and what effect this change has, or can have, on the political system. Bell argues that doctrine has changed, that "while dogmas such as dialectical materialism, historical materialism, the superiority of collective property, and the nature of scientific communism remain on a formal level, the doctrinal core, the central fact is not any specific theoretical formulation *but the basic demand for belief in the Party itself.*"[8] For Bell, it is belief in the party, in its historic mission and fitness to lead,

---

[8] Joravsky (fn. 5) argues that both "grand" ideology (vague and sweeping unverifiable beliefs appealing to the emotions) and "petty" ideology (verifiable but unverified beliefs) have been giving way to political "realism" in the thinking of the Soviet elite. He does not equate political realism with pragmatic or empirical behavior, however. On the contrary, he argues that the political "realist" is as ideological as the ideologue, but in a different way.

inculcated in the individual, upon which the party itself leans to provide legitimacy for specific programs and policies. Questioning how the party can maintain this notion in a mature industrial society such as the Soviet Union has become, Bell argues that the role of the party may diminish, understandably with significant consequences for the political system of the Soviet Union. In this regard, Professor Bell is representative of a growing number of scholars who question the extent to which the ideas of Marx and Lenin serve as a significant influence on political behavior in the Soviet Union.

Written in response to articles by Alfred G. Meyer and Alec Nove in *Soviet Studies* on the role and the functions of ideology in contemporary Soviet society,[9] Roy Laird's article challenges the view that the efforts of the party to maintain a belief system essentially in accord with the dogmas of Marx and Lenin, and their reinterpretations over time, have foundered almost completely. Although changes have taken place, admits Laird, "not all the new Soviet values [introduced after 1917] are being discarded.... For any foreseeable future Marxism-Leninism cannot be ignored as a vital (perhaps the most important) source of the public myth."

The difference in opinion among observers as to the contents of the dominant belief system is not just a scholastic argument. Assuming some connection between the belief system and the institutions and processes that society will support as being legitimate, it becomes important for the party to assure the maintenance of a belief system that accepts the role and functions the party has defined for itself.

The rationale for Bolshevik insistence upon a small, elite party was their desire to maintain unity of will and purpose. The elite, which was privy to the "truth," would force a transformation of society over the innocence, vacillation, or opposition of other groups. This role presumed an extremely high degree of homogeneity. Whether as a small band of revolutionaries, an expanded party extending its control over all of the territory of the former Russian empire, or a bureaucratic party dominated by a professionalized corps of full-time party workers, it was assumed that the elite was somehow united against the environment, struggling to shape the environment to its own image of the ideal society.

This elite-environment dichotomy had considerable relevance in earlier times. It is argued by some, however, that today a situation is developing whereby the environment may be transforming the elite. Although the environment is not *preventing* the efforts of the Communist Party of the Soviet Union to influence the course of developments in Soviet society, it

---

[9] Alfred G. Meyer, "The Functions of Ideology in the Soviet System: A Speculative Essay Designed to Provoke Discussion," *Soviet Studies*, XVII, No. 3 (January 1966), 273–85, and Alec Nove, "Ideology and Agriculture," *Soviet Studies*, XVII, No. 4 (April 1966), 397–406.

may be seriously *inhibiting* or *constraining* them. Vernon Aspaturian has directed attention to the fact that the character of the elite itself appears to be changing in response to certain environmental influences, which themselves have been created by past policies. The elite, the party as a whole, is displaying a heterogeneity based upon diverse social forces arising from the new social structure created by the party itself. "During the party's nearly five decades' existence as a ruling structure, it has not only transformed the social order but has fundamentally transformed itself by the very social forces which it brought into being."

Thus, a question of greatest importance is how the various social forces in Soviet society, especially the diverse manifestations of the new Soviet intelligentsia, relate to one another and to the instruments of authority in the Soviet political system. The elite, the party seeking to impose its will on society, is broadening, in social composition if not in numbers, so that the "will of the elite" is difficult to find. Aspaturian suggests that the groups associated with the various social forces are struggling not against the party, but rather "for its control or a share of its control," for dominance over the more specific political elite. The party as an arena in which these group struggles are reconciled, with the assumption of some degree of mutual limitation, is already a far cry from a homogeneous elite dominating and sweeping aside the environment on the way to creation of a totally new society. This question of the role of groups in the Soviet system is discussed further in Part III.

NATIONALISM AND THE POLITICAL SYSTEM

VERNON V. ASPATURIAN

The most striking characteristic of the Soviet population is its ethnic diversity: the Soviet Union is a country of more than 100 different nationalities, tribes, and linguistic groups, according to the 1959 census. To be sure, there is a propensity for the Soviet authorities to exaggerate the ethnic heterogeneity of the U.S.S.R. for propaganda purposes by even including "nationalities" numbering fewer than 1,000 souls. Nevertheless, the ethnic diversity of the country remains impressive. Twenty-

two of the nationalities enumerated in the 1959 census number more than 900,000 each, and account for 95 per cent of the total population. The other 80 or more "nationalities" total fewer than 10 million, and only 20 of these number more than 100,000 people each.

The Soviet multinational population was a legacy of the Tsars, whose expanding empire absorbed but never fully digested this variegated and mutually antagonistic collection of races and nationalities. In Imperial

From "The Non-Russian Nationalities" in Allen Kassof, ed., *Prospects for Soviet Society* (New York: Frederick A. Praeger, Inc., 1968), pp. 143–60, 190–98. Reprinted by permission. Footnotes omitted.

Russia the Russians were not only numerically preponderant but the ruling nationality as well. Russia was a "prison of nations," not a multinational commonwealth in fact or fiction. It is generally acknowledged that one of the principal factors contributing to the Revolution of 1917 was the disaffection of the major non-Russian nationalities, and especially of their educated classes. All the revolutionary parties of Russia counted among their leaders outstanding individuals of many nationalities. The failure of Imperial Russia to grapple intelligently with the nationality question was instrumental in accelerating its demise in the midst of national agony and crisis.

When Lenin assumed power in 1917, the Bolsheviks fell heir to the "prison of nations" and its unresolved problems. Of all the revolutionary parties, the Bolsheviks were perhaps best prepared to deal systematically with the nationality question, since they alone had devoted serious attention to it. Both Lenin and Stalin were specialists on the national question, and Lenin must be accounted one of the chief and original expositors in the twentieth century of the principle of national self-determination, a concept which found its way into President Wilson's famous Fourteen Points some years after the Bolsheviks had incorporated it into their own political program.

Lenin shrewdly recognized the qualitative distinction between the defensive character of the nationalism of oppressed nationalities and the chauvinistic and aggressive nationalism of a ruling nation. He refused to condemn all nationalism as equally retrogressive and perceived in the aspirations of the smaller nationalities of Russia a progressive character and a revolutionary potential. To this day, Communist doctrine continues to draw a basic qualitative distinction between the nationalism of the oppressed, which is praised and supported, and that of ruling nationalities, which is condemned as retrograde. It is a distinction often overlooked by Western observers and statesmen. Although Soviet behavior sometimes resembles oppressive chauvinistic nationalism, and Soviet leaders are notoriously unable or unwilling to acknowledge it, this should not obscure either the objective significance or the moral implications of the perceptive Marxist-Leninist distinction between the nationalism of oppressed and oppressing nations.

Lenin also recognized that under conditions of Tsarist oppression the Bolsheviks could attract the support of the discontented nationalities only by promising them the right to secede and form their own national states, although he was, in principle, against the dismemberment of the Russian Empire once it passed under Bolshevik control. As early as 1903, when national self-determination was incorporated into the Bolshevik program, Lenin acknowledged that it "cannot be interpreted otherwise than in the sense of *political* self-determination, i.e., the right of secession and the formation of an independent state." Since then, the right of secession has remained a cardinal principle of Soviet nationality policy and has continued to find juridical expression as a fundamental tenet of every Soviet constitution.

The Bolshevik espousal of national self-determination was designed to achieve four interrelated purposes: (1) to prove to the non-Russians that the Bolsheviks were not simply another Great Russian party; (2) to diminish the attractiveness of the local nationalist movements and recruit their intellectuals into the Bolshevik organization; (3) to encourage secessionist movements which would weaken the Empire and hasten the revolution; and (4) to prepare the foundations for a future reconciliation between the Great Russians and their former subjects on the basis of equality, once the revolution was accomplished. It is noteworthy that except for point (3), which is recognized abstractly in the Constitution but is ruthlessly suppressed in practice, current Soviet nationality policy continues to pursue essentially the same aims, but in order to stabilize and preserve the *status quo*, not to disrupt it.

Although Lenin was more perceptive than most in recognizing the moral distinction between the nationalism of the oppressed and the oppressing nations, he completely miscalculated its unreasoning, visceral, emotional side. He hoped that Bolshevik policy would be sufficient to persuade the leaders of the national minorities of Bolshevik sincerity and that, once given the right to secede, the nationalities would suddenly recognize the wisdom of not exercising it. After the Bolsheviks assumed power, Lenin and Stalin issued *The Declaration of the Nations of Russia*, which virtually invited the border nationalities to secede by gratuitously recognizing "the right of the peoples of Russia to dispose of their own fate even to the separation and establishment of an independent state." The impotent Soviet regime was cruelly disappointed when the border nations, taking the invitation at its word, responded with declarations of secession and independence. Countries like Georgia, which before the Revolution rarely thought of independence, and

people like the Byelorussians and Cossacks, who were hardly aware of their separate national identity, suddenly discovered that they were invested with the right to secede. So-called National Councils sprang up all over Russia, even in purely Great Russian areas, and under the guise of "regional national self-determination," asserted this new-found right.

If the policy of national self-determination accelerated the disintegration of the Tsarist system, it was now an even greater threat to the existence of the Soviet state. Secession quickly spread to all parts of the country. Lenin failed to foresee not only the irrational character of nationalism, but also the inherently disruptive and centrifugal nature of the doctrine of national self-determination for a multinational state. Valuable as an instrument of revolution, it was equally a menace to stability and, once set into motion, assumed an undirected and uncontrollable momentum of its own. In order to preserve Bolshevik power, it was necessary to arrest the disintegration of the Soviet state by introducing a countervailing principle, which would halt though not repudiate the disruptive course.

The magic formula was federalism, an idea generally spurned by Marxists as incompatible with their imperative of a centrally organized and planned society, but now seized upon by Lenin as a device which could arrest secession and promote re-amalgamation in the name of national self-determination. To implement the first aim, the R.S.F.S.R. came into being, while the second purpose was served by forming the U.S.S.R. after the Red Army had successfully installed Soviet regimes in some of the disaffected border regions, notably in the Ukraine, Byelorussia, the Caucasus, and Central Asia. The reassembling of the fragmented parts of the Russian Empire into a multinational federal state was substantially accomplished by 1925, after the reincorporation of the Far East Republic and the full integration of Bukhara and Khorezm into the Soviet state.

The Ethnic Composition and Distribution of Soviet Society

Most of the Russian Empire was preserved intact as the U.S.S.R., although Poland, Finland, and the three Baltic states managed to secure their independence, and Bessarabia was annexed by Rumania. The federal solution to the nationality problem, however, was eventually subverted by the political policies and ideological goals of the Soviet regime and could only be considered a limited success before World War II. The nationality problem is in many ways a matter of life and death for the Soviet state because of the strategic location of the border nationalities. The geographical balance and distribution of the nationalities of the Soviet Union give rise, in fact, to a "Russian" problem as well as a "Soviet" problem (see Table 1).

The Great Russians, occupying the continental interior of Eurasia, are fringed on all sides by a virtually uninterrupted belt of non-Russian nationalities which form a buffer on the international borders of the Soviet Union. Along virtually the entire Baltic coast of the U.S.S.R. are the Estonians, Latvians, and Lithuanians, while the Byelorussians, Ukrainians, and Moldavians inhabit the territories bordering Poland, Czechoslovakia, and Rumania.

In the Caucasus, the Georgians, Armenians, and Azerbaidzhani Turks inhabit the regions bordering on Turkey and Iran, while in Central Asia, the Turkmen, Uzbeks, Kazakhs, and Kirgiz occupy the border areas adjacent to Iran, Afghanistan, and the Sinkiang Province of China, and a multitude of Turkic, Mongol, and Tungusic tribes occupy the border regions with Outer Mongolia. Only in the Soviet Far East do Russians inhabit territories adjacent to international frontiers, and this is a region remote from the heartland of the Russian nation.

Because of the strategic location of the border nationalities, their loyalty to Moscow and their relationship to the Russian people has always been a vital factor in Russian and Soviet security considerations. The federal solution whereby each major nationality was organized into a separate republic with its own language, culture, constitution, and other symbols of nationhood, was only a partial success in winning the loyalty and reliability of these nationalities. During World War II, the Germans were welcomed in some of the border regions, and hundreds of thousands of Soviet prisoners of war of many nationalities agreed to enlist in Nazi-organized National Legions to fight against the Soviet Union. The nature and intensity of this defection still remains the subject of considerable speculation and controversy, since it is not exactly clear whether the motivations were basically anti-Soviet, anti-Russian, anti-Stalin, or just simple self-preservation, but undoubtedly all of these elements were involved.

Of the 21 non-Russian nationalities which had 900,000 or more people each in 1959, fourteen are organized into union republics with constituent federal rights and are recognized as quasi-sovereign nation-states. Two of the 22 major nationalities, the Poles and Germans, are considered national minorities of other nations, while a third, the Jewish, is territorially scattered and does not occupy a defined national territory. Four other nations, the Tatar, Chuvash, Bashkir, and Mordvin, being located in the interior of the Union and surrounded by Russians, are organized as Autonomous Republics, since one of the criteria for status as a Union Republic is that it must be located on the border so that the abstract right to secede does not become a technical absurdity.

The Russian presence

The Russian nation accounted for slightly more than one-half (115 million) the total population in 1959. The ethnically, linguistically, and culturally related Ukrainians and Byelorussians followed with 37 million and 8 million, respectively. Thus, the Soviet Union is still an overwhelmingly Slavic country with nearly 160 million, or 80 per cent, of its people made up of the three closely related Slavic groups. The Russians, or more properly Great Russians, are concentrated in the huge central plain around Moscow, the North Caucasus, and the Volga regions, and are settled across Siberia to the Pacific. According to the 1959 census, more than 85 per cent of the Russians were found in the R.S.F.S.R. Elsewhere they constituted from more than 43 per cent of the Kazakh Republic to 10 per cent of the Moldavian. Only in the Byelorussian, Lithuanian, and Armenian republics did they account for less than 10 per cent of the population (see Table 2).

TABLE 1. Major nationalities of the U.S.S.R. 1939–59

Nationality	1939	1959
Russian	99,019,000	114,500,000
Ukrainian	28,070,000	36,981,000
Byelorussian	5,267,431	7,829,000
Uzbek	4,844,021	6,004,000
Tatar	4,300,000	4,969,000
Kazakh	3,098,000	3,581,000
Azerbaidzhani	2,274,805	2,929,000
Armenian	2,151,884	2,787,000
Georgian	2,248,566	2,650,000
Lithuanian	—	2,326,000
Jewish	3,020,141	2,268,000
Moldavian	—	2,214,000
German	1,423,534	1,619,000
Chuvash	1,367,930	1,470,000
Latvian	—	1,400,000
Tadzhik	1,928,964	1,397,000
Palish	626,905	1,380,000
Mordvin	1,451,429	1,285,000
Turkmen	811,769	1,004,000
Bashkir	842,925	983,000
Kirgiz	884,306	974,000
Estonian	—	969,000

The presence of substantial numbers of Russians in most of the republics guarantees a minimum political and ethnic ballast in the non-Russian regions to counter separatist sentiment. Their diffusion throughout the Union serves, moreover, to accelerate and intensify the process of Russianization. The large influx of Russians has been due not only to the industrialization and modernization program, but also to the collectivization of agriculture, when millions of recalcitrant peasants were uprooted in the European parts and deported beyond the Urals. The major cities of Soviet Asia are heavily populated with Russians, while Ukrainians are sprinkled across the rural areas.

Ukrainians and Byelorussians

The Ukrainians constitute a compact unit in the southwestern region of

TABLE 2. Distribution of major nationalities in the non-Russian republic—1959 census

Republic	Total	Per Cent
Ukrainian	41,869,000	100.0
Ukrainians	31,852,000	76.1
Russians	7,400,000	17.1
Jews	840,000	2.0
Byelorussian	8,055,000	100.0
Byelorussians	4,444,000	80.0
Russians	729,000	9.1
Poles	539,000	6.7
Uzbek	8,106,000	100.0
Uzbeks	5,026,000	62.0
Russians	1,101,000	13.6
Tatars	445,000	5.5
Kazakhs	335,000	4.1
Tadzhiks	312,000	3.8
Kazakh	9,310,000	100.0
Kazakhs	2,755,000	29.6
Russians	4,014,000	43.1
Ukrainians	762,000	8.2
Georgian	4,044,000	100.0
Georgians	2,558,000	63.3
Russians	438,000	10.8
Armenians	443,000	11.0
Armenian	1,763,000	100.0
Armenians	1,552,000	88.0
Russians	56,000	3.2
Azerbaidzhani	3,698,000	100.0
Azerbaidzhanis	2,481,000	67.1
Russians	515,000	13.9
Armenians	442,000	12.0

TABLE 2. (*Continued*)

Republic	Total	Per Cent
Lithuanian	2,711,000	100.0
Lithuanians	2,151,000	79.3
Russians	231,000	8.5
Poles	230,000	8.5
Moldavian	2,885,000	100.0
Moldavians	1,887,000	65.4
Russians	293,000	10.2
Ukrainians	421,000	14.6
Latvian	2,093,000	100.0
Latvians	1,298,000	62.0
Russians	556,000	26.6
Kirgiz	2,066,000	100.0
Kirgiz	837,000	40.5
Russians	624,000	30.2
Uzbeks	219,000	10.6
Tadzhik	1,980,000	100.0
Tadzhiks	1,051,000	53.1
Russians	263,000	13.3
Uzbeks	454,000	23.0
Turkmen	1,516,000	100.0
Turkmen	924,000	60.9
Russians	263,000	17.3
Uzbeks	125,000	8.3
Estonian	1,197,000	100.0
Estonians	873,000	72.9
Russians	260,000	21.7

the Soviet Union. Except for a very brief existence as an independent state immediately after the Revolution, the bulk of the Ukraine has been united with Russia for many decades. The Ukrainian population of Eastern Galicia, however, has had little political or cultural contact with Russia, having been ruled by Austria since the partitions of Poland in the eighteenth century, and before that by the Poles. The people of this area are predominantly Uniate Catholics who accept the spiritual authority of the Vatican. After the war, the Soviet government forced a renunciation of their ties to Rome and their return to the Eastern Orthodox Church from which they had been separated by the Poles in the sixteenth century. The Western Ukrainians have been exposed to varying degrees of Polonization. The strongest sentiment for an independent Ukrainian state is found in this region.

The Byelorussians occupy the marshy areas of the Pripet River and their republic also borders on Poland. The idea of Byelorussian nationality hardly existed before the Revolution, since the region was one of the most backward in all Europe, and national consciousness was largely absent. The Byelorussians in the west also have been subjected to varying degrees of Polonization, while these in the east are virtually indistinguishable from the Great Russians. Byelorussian nationhood came virtually as a gift of the Soviet regime and in many ways remains artificial.

The Turks and Tatars

The second largest bloc of ethnically related people are the Turko-Tatar nationalities, which total more than 20 million and are divided among nearly a score of tribal and linguistic groups. Nine of these nationalities number more than 900,000 people each. They are predominantly Moslem in faith and Islamic in culture, although some groups have been exposed to Russian cultural influences for longer periods of time than others. Many of the Russians in the Volga and Ural regions appear to be assimilated Tatars or possess varying degrees of Tatar infusion. Most of the Turko-Tatar languages are mutually intelligible.

Culturally associated with the Central Asian Turks are the Iranian-speaking Tadzhiks, found in the Pamir mountains on the borders of Iran and Afghanistan. Dominated by the Uzbeks for many centuries, large numbers have been Turkicized, but under Soviet rule their basic Iranian traditions and culture have experienced a resurgence, and they share cultural and historical traditions with the Persians, Afghans, and Pakistanis.

The Turko-Tatar nationalities are not a single compact group, but are separated in three distinct geographical regions. The largest concentration of Turks is in Central Asia, and they represent the groups which have experienced the shortest period of Russian rule (dating from the mid-nineteenth century). The major Central Asian Turks are the Uzbeks, the Kazakhs, the Kirgiz, and the Turkmen. The second heaviest concentration is in the Middle-Volga and Urals region, whose most important representatives are the Volga Tatars, the Bashkirs, and the Chuvash. The third concentration is located in the Caucasus, with the Transcaucasian Azerbaidzhanis being the most numerous and significant, while smaller tribes are located in the North Caucasus. Other Turko-Tatar groups are found sprinkled across the vast expanse of Central Russia (European and Asian) and represent the backwash of the retreating Tatar tribes after their period of domination was broken by the Grand Dukes of Moscow and they in turn were subjected to Russian expansion eastward.

The most ethnically diluted of the national republics is the Kazakh, where the native population accounts for less than 30 per cent of the total, whereas the Russians and Ukrainians account for more than half. The reduction of the Kazakhs to minority status in their own republic is due not only to the tremendous influx of Russians into the republic in recent years, but also to the fact that, more than any other nationality, the Kazakhs have suffered great population losses under Tsarist and Soviet rule. The 1926 census reported 3,968,289 Kazakhs, but by 1939, the Kazakhs suffered a net loss of nearly a million people, when their number was reported at 3,098,000. The 1959 census shows that the Kazakhs still number 400,000 fewer than they did in 1926.

The Kirgiz are also a minority in their own republic, where they constitute only 40 per cent of the population, whereas the Russians and Ukrainians account for about 37 per cent. Another significant factor in the ethnic distribution of Central Asia is the presence of a substantial number of Uzbeks in all the Central Asian republics, ranging from slightly more than 8 per cent in the Turkmen to 23 per cent in the Tadzhik. The ruling nationality of Central Asia before the

Revolution, the Uzbeks are once again emerging as a stabilizing influence in association with the Russians.

The Caucasus: Georgians and Armenians

The Caucasus represents one of the most complex ethnic areas in the world. Although the total population is relatively small, there is an extraordinary number of nationalities and mountain tribes who have tenaciously clung to their separate identities despite their small numbers. The two most important non-Turkic Caucasian nationalities are the ancient Christian nations of Georgia and Armenia, whose people are culturally and racially, but not linguistically, related. Each numbers approximately 3 million, but whereas the Georgians are for the most part concentrated in the Georgian Republic, nearly half the Armenians reside outside the Armenian Republic, which is, however, the most nationally compact of the republics, with 88 per cent of the inhabitants being indigenous. Both nations have strong ties with Russia, which has traditionally posed as their protector from the Moslem Turks, although each maintains its own distinctive alphabet, national tradition, and its autonomous church. The role of individual Georgians and Armenians in Soviet cultural and political life is far greater in proportion to their numbers than that of any nationality including, ironically, the Russians. This was particularly true during the long period of Stalin's rule. Stalin and his secret police chief, Beria, who were Georgians, naturally relied upon kinsmen in the Caucasus as instruments of their rule. Despite the death of Stalin and the execution of Beria, Georgians and Armenians are still in many im-

portant secondary positions in the government, the Communist Party, the armed forces, and cultural and educational institutions, although their proportion is decreasing.

The Baltic Nationalities

The three Baltic nations of Estonia, Latvia, and Lithuania form another small, but important, cluster of nationalities. The Latvians and Lithuanians are linguistically related members of the Balto-Slavic group, while the Estonians belong with the Finns. The three nations are the most Westernized of the Soviet national groups; all use the Latin alphabet, but whereas the Latvians and the Estonians are largely Lutheran, the Lithuanians are Roman Catholic. All three share a common background of long Russian political rule and German social and cultural domination. Under the Tsars, the Baltic Germans, descendants of the Teutonic Knights, constituted a local ruling aristocracy, while the indigenous population was largely peasant in character. The cultural life of the three countries thus represents a curious blend of German, Russian, and indigenous elements.

The three countries enjoyed a brief twenty years of political independence between the wars. There was a genuine resurgence of national culture and tradition, and while the political systems were far from democratic, they were indigenous and far more preferable to the local population than foreign rule.

Since the three states cut Russia off from the Baltic Sea, it was axiomatic that once the Soviet Union had recovered its strength it would again seek to open a window on the Baltic —one of the most persistent aims in foreign policy from Ivan the Terrible to Joseph Stalin. The three states were annexed in 1940, after the German elements of the population were returned to the Reich in conformity with the Nazi-Soviet Pact of 1939.

Russian rule, whether Tsarist or Soviet, is deeply resented. With Soviet occupation, the native elites were arrested and either executed or deported to Siberia as were thousands of others who betrayed overt signs of opposition to Soviet control or ideas. Of all the nationalities of the Soviet Union, sentiment for separation is most pronounced in the Baltic countries because the bonds of mutual benefit, protection, language, culture, gratitude, and religion are largely absent. The Ukrainians and Byelorussians are related to the Russians; the Georgians and Armenians accept the Russians as their protectors; and while the resurgent non-Russian nations of Siberia and Central Asia owe their modernization and elevation from social and economic backwardness to the Soviet regime, the Baltic nations do not owe their high cultural and material standard of life to the Russians or to the Soviet regime. In this association, all of the benefits flow in a single direction, to Moscow.

The Alien Nationalities

Four of the 22 major nationalities (the Germans, Poles, Moldavians, and Jews) are in a separate category in that states of the same nationality are located outside the frontiers of the U.S.S.R.; hence, they constitute true national minorities. Before World War II, the largest concentration of Germans was in the Volga-German Autonomous Republic, and other German communities were scattered in the Ukraine and the North Caucasus. After the German attack, they were all gathered and deported to Central Asia and Siberia, because of both real and imagined pro-German sympathies. According to the 1959 census, half of the 1.6 million Germans are reported as living in the R.S.F.S.R., most likely the Siberian regions; the location of the other half is unreported, but evidence from other sources indicates that they have been relocated in the Kazakh and other Central Asian republics. Since the Soviet census has meticulously enumerated the breakdown of various national groups in the individual republics if they numbered 10,000 or more, the failure to account for the location of 800,000 Germans can only be a deliberate attempt to conceal their present whereabouts.

The Moldavians are linguistically indistinguishable from the people of neighboring Rumania, although under Soviet rule their language is written in the Cyrillic rather than in the Latin alphabet. They inhabit portions of the historical province of Bessarabia, parts of which have been assigned to the Ukrainian Republic, while the remainder has been organized into a separate Moldavian Republic. Actually, the Moldavians are a minority, politically and territorially separated from their national state of Rumania, which is now showing a renewed interest in them.

The Jews

The 1959 census reported a population of nearly 2.3 million Jews, a catastrophic drop in the total number of Jews who lived within the prewar frontiers of the Soviet Union and in the areas annexed from Poland. The decimation of the Jews resulted from

Nazi policies, and since the war, their existence as a separate national group in the Soviet Union has been precarious. Their position in Russia has never been an enviable one, and the Tsarist pogroms were largely responsible for the migration of Russian Jews to the United States and the organization of the Zionist movement. After the Revolution, the Soviet government took energetic measures to stamp out anti-Semitism, accorded the Jews recognition as a separate nationality with rights of cultural autonomy, legalized the use of Yiddish as the language of instruction in schools located in centers of Jewish population, and encouraged and supported a Yiddish press and theater. Since the Jews were scattered in various urban centers of the country, a genuine Jewish republic could not be established, while the contrived Jewish Autonomous Region organized in a remote area of the Soviet Far East failed to flourish. Despite the cultivation of a Jewish nationality centered around the Yiddish language, most Soviet Jews were on the road to voluntary assimilation before the war.

Two events brought about a fundamental transformation in the status of Soviet Jews. The first was the Nazi occupation, which succeeded in rekindling the ancient and latent anti-Semitism of the Ukrainians and Russians, which had been submerged by Soviet policies. The second was the establishment of the state of Israel, which apparently had an electrifying impact upon many Soviet Jews, indicating to a suspicious Stalin the possibility of a psychological attachment incompatible with Soviet ideological and foreign-policy objectives. The immediate result was the disestablishment of Jewish cultural autonomy. All Jewish organizations, the Yiddish press, theater, publishing houses, and schools were dissolved. Prominent cultural leaders, as well as some political personalities of Jewish origin, were imprisoned and some were executed, while the Soviet press marshaled a thinly veiled assault against Jews in general, calling them "passportless wanderers" and "homeless cosmopolitans," implying that they were malingerers, speculators, black-marketeers, and social parasites.

Jews were purged from sensitive political positions, and informal quotas for admission to institutions of higher learning were set, although the eminently practical Stalin tolerated their continued participation in literary, professional, and scientific activity. One of his objectives was to terrorize the Soviet Jews into recognizing unambiguously that the Kremlin would not tolerate the faintest shadow of sympathy for Israel. Although the ferocity of the campaign has relented since Stalin's death, his successors have continued the policy of extinguishing Jewish cultural autonomy. This official attitude has once again made anti-Semitism acceptable in Russia; and vandalism and excesses against Jewish religious institutions often go unpunished. Judaism and Jewish believers are vilified periodically in the local press and Jewish religious life rendered virtually impossible.

If Israel were a Soviet republic within the U.S.S.R., Jewish religious and national loyalties might not be incompatible with Soviet interests. But Moscow takes special measures against any religion whose spiritual center is located in a foreign country. Since the Soviet government has itself manipulated to political advantage the Russian and Armenian churches, whose spiritual centers are located on

Soviet territory, it expects other powers to do the same. Dual loyalties, whether they be sentimental, psychological, cultural, political, or spiritual, are not tolerated by the regime if it cannot manipulate both loyalties. Cultural and national pluralism are compatible with the Soviet system only as long as they are unambiguously subordinated to Soviet ideological and political objectives.

The Quality of the Soviet Multinational State

One of the ironies of the Stalinist legacy is that while the stated purpose of Soviet nationality policy has been to further the development of national and cultural autonomy, in fact it has been used to suppress particularistic political self-expression and identity. But the fact that the Soviet nationalities must subordinate their political and national activity to higher social and political goals is far from unique. All states made up of distinct ethnic, regional, or historical constituents characteristically follow such a course. This important fact should not be obscured simply because the norms imposed upon the Soviet nationalities are Communist norms.

The Soviet Union, no less than Canada, India, Switzerland, Belgium, or any other multinational state, frowns upon all manifestations of national separatism; while this may merely testify to the effectiveness of totalitarian controls, it remains the only binational or multinational state in the world which recognizes even the abstract right of its constituent nations to secede and to establish separate national states. History has amply demonstrated that the voluntary charac-

ter of federations and multinational states is largely a fiction which no state is ready to put to the test. This has been stated most candidly by the Soviet leaders themselves. In the words of Stalin, which have been quoted *ad nauseam* by critics of Soviet nationality policy as eloquent evidence of Soviet hypocrisy, the Soviet position was articulated as follows: "We are in favor of the separation of India, Arabia, Egypt, Morocco, and the other colonies from the Entente. . . . We are *against* the separation of the border regions from Russia."

Although Western countries have not expressed their double standard of national self-determination as systematically or as frankly as have Soviet leaders, it would not be inaccurate to say that they were precisely in *favor* of what Stalin was against and *against* what he favored at the time these words were written. Soon thereafter, the border regions of Russia (Poland, Finland, Estonia, Latvia, Lithuania, Bessarabia) did manage to separate, with the assistance of the Western powers, while at the same time the colonial dependencies of the European powers were increased. The fact that at present all of the countries named by Stalin, and many more, have become independent states, while Russia's border regions, with the exception of Poland and Finland, have been recovered, is a token of the growth of Soviet power and the diminution of West European influence.

In recent years Western spokesmen have attempted, without signal success, to pin the label of colonialism on the Soviet Union and have been mystified and frustrated by the conspicuous lack of favorable response on the part of the new states of Africa and Asia. Perhaps this is because the decline of

Western colonialism and the parallel rise of Soviet imperialism are more the consequences of fundamental shifts in the world balance of power since 1945 than reflections of the ideological and political contrasts between East and West with respect to the ethical imperatives of the age. The dismantling of the British Empire is frequently held up as an example of the Western adherence to the principle of national self-determination in contrast to the forcible preservation of the Soviet empire. But the more painful and violent decolonialization processes which overtook the French, Dutch, and Belgian colonial empires and the continuance of Portuguese colonies are often conveniently overlooked.

There is another universal characteristic of multinational states which is sometimes ascribed to the Soviet Union alone. Specifically, it is alleged that Russia enjoys far more rights and advantages than the other nations making up the U.S.S.R. Actually, such charges have been made in connection with virtually every existing multinational state: the French Canadians allege that the English dominate Canada; the Flemish similarly accuse the Walloons in Belgium; the Slovaks (both before and after Communist rule) complain of Czech domination; the Croats and Slovenes traditionally protest Serb control of the Yugoslav state; and the Hindus are charged with seeking to impose their norms upon the rest of India.

There is a kernel of truth, of course, in all these charges to the extent that in any multinational state the benefits and advantages of the union do not flow evenly or register equally. When the balance of benefits becomes disproportionate to the point where the aggrieved partners perceive the possi-

bilities of greater satisfaction in independence than in partnership, then the consensus upon which the state is based begins to erode.

There is little question that under Stalin the Soviet Union was increasingly reverting to a Russian imperial state, though with some significant reservations, and that residues of the Stalinist era continue to color the Soviet multinational system today. The Soviet multinational experience is especially complex because, although in absolute quantitative terms the Russians enjoy more benefits than any other nationality in the union, it is probably also true that in relative or qualitative terms the Georgians and Armenians derive the greatest benefits and advantages. The Soviet contention that the leading role of the Russians burdens them with responsibilities and duties to the other nationalities is undoubtedly true in a sense. In assessing the value of the union to the non-Russian nationalities one must also consider whether as a nation collectively and as individual citizens their aspirations and interests would be better served by an option other than being part of a Soviet state. No doubt, attitudes would vary widely from one Soviet nationality to another.

Molding the Soviet Multinational State: Sovietization, Russianization, and Russification

The Bolsheviks inherited a *Russian* state, not an abstract state devoid of ethnic, cultural, or historical identities. They fell heir to Russia's geography, its multinational population, its culture and traditions, its memories of misery and glory, its friends and enemies, and, above all, its complex of collective behavioral responses summed up as "national character." The nations of the former empire, with their diverse religions, cultures, skills, knowledge, ignorance, prejudices, fears, animosities, superstitions, anxieties, and legacies, now became peoples of the Soviet Union. This was the human raw material upon which the ideological norms of Marxism were to be imposed and from which the elite wished to fashion an embryonic universal Communist state. Most of the new leaders were Russians, and the non-Russians among them were drawn, for the most part, from the nationalities which played influential roles in the cultural and political life of the empire: Ukrainians, Jews, Georgians, Armenians, Germans, and Balts. It was multinational, but far from international, even though the new Soviet state intended to play a role on the historical stage which transcended Russia itself. Thus, the universalism of the Bolshevik state was putative from the outset because it was ruled not by the Communist International but by the Russian Communist Party (later All-Union Communist Party). Although the Soviet state was originally envisioned as the spearhead of the international proletariat, no Soviet leader seriously suggested placing the former Russian Empire under rule of the Comintern.

A state gripped by messianic and universalist pretensions but ruled by Russians was inherently imperialistic, the rhetoric of its leaders and apologists notwithstanding. In the process of reshaping the Russian Empire into an embryonic universal state, they in fact created an authentic multinational commonwealth. This was not, however, the ultimate purpose of the leaders, simply a means to an end. Nonetheless, some of the peculiar characteristics of

the Soviet multinational system today are legacies of its original universalist aspirations.

Since the new leaders were predominantly Russian, as was the population, the universal state was bound to be heavily and disproportionately influenced by the Russian element. The Bolsheviks had inherited an existing imbalance between the Russian and non-Russian nationalities, and ultimately succumbed to its objective dictates.

In the shaping of the multinational state, three distinct though closely interrelated (but often mistakenly equated) processes were set into motion: Sovietization, Russianization, and Russification. Sovietization is here defined as the process of modernization and industrialization within the Marxist-Leninist norms of social, economic, and political behavior. Russianization is defined as the process of internationalizing Russian language and culture within the Soviet Union. While Sovietization was the ultimate objective of the regime, Russianization was regarded initially as a means rather than an end. Sovietization and Russianization, however, became inextricably intertwined and the two processes mutually reinforced and contaminated one another.

Finally, Russification, which is often confused with Russianization, is a more limited process; it was not initially conceived as either an end or a means, but occurred as a sociological by-product or consequence of Sovietization and Russianization. It is defined as the process whereby non-Russians are transformed objectively and psychologically into Russians, and is more an individual process than a collective one. Thus while Sovietization is universal in its effects and Russianization almost so, Russification is more restricted.

There is, of course, an obvious evolutionary relationship between Russianization and Russification. Russianization is a prerequisite to Russification, but it can be a terminal process as well, just as were the Hellenization of the Near East in ancient times and the Hispanicization of Latin America. Near Easterners were not transformed into Greeks, nor were the Indians of the New World into Spaniards or Portuguese. Rather, they became Greek-like or Hispanic-like, and their culture became a stabilized blend of indigenous and nonindigenous elements. Whereas Russification is restricted mainly to the educated elites of the non-Russian nationalities, Russianization affects all social classes and groups in Soviet society. Russification is more than a mere intensification of Russianization, since it involves qualitative psychological transformations and can be legally institutionalized by an explicit change in national identity.

All three processes have proceeded at different paces and with different levels of intensity among the non-Russian nationalities, depending on their prior stage of development and the degree of national resistance and immunity to alien doctrines and cultures. The intensity of Russianization which the non-Russian nationalities have been able to endure without succumbing to Russification also varies from nationality to nationality....

The Soviet Union as a Multinational Sociopolitical System

The Soviet multinational state, as a sociopolitical system, has been subjected to characterizations ranging from condemnation as a colonial empire to glorification as a model of multinational, multiracial harmony. This disparity is due, at least in part, to the fact that the Soviet system has been in flux since its inception five decades ago, and not always moving in a single direction. Like other aspects of Soviet life, the multinational system has moved through a number of phases, each marked by its own peculiar characteristics. The system and the policy must be examined as dynamically evolving phenomena.

The Soviet Union has undergone three distinct phases in its evolution as a multinational state, and is now well along in the fourth. While each phase has been accompanied by an evolutionary change in the juridical and constitutional structure of the state, the phases are not defined in terms of these formal alternations, but rather by the content of Soviet nationality policy.

The first period, 1917–28, was characterized by the organization of the Soviet state into a formal federal system designed to liberate the non-Russian nationalities psychologically and physically from Russian domination. It was marked primarily by a deliberate policy of restraining and curtailing the natural tendency of the Russians to assume dominance in the new state and simultaneously encouraging the non-Russian nationalities to assume greater responsibility and power. Great Russian chauvinism was considered the main danger to the Soviet order and, while local nationalism was frowned upon, it was nevertheless indirectly encouraged by the regime. During this period, however, the Soviet Union was still largely an illiterate, economically and culturally retarded, agrarian, polyglot state. Vast social, cultural, and political voids separated the various nationalities, who were equal only in the most formal sense. The Russians were the most numerous, the most advanced culturally and economically, and the most habituated to political rule. But, under circumstances in which their natural superiority was artificially suppressed and other nationalities were encouraged to come forward, a curious, limited, authentic multinational sociopolitical system soon materialized.

It soon became evident that an authentic multinational sociopolitical system would be impossible unless there was an approximate economic and cultural equality among the various nationalities. The second period, 1929–36, was characterized by vigorous efforts to modernize the underdeveloped nationalities. The Soviet regime chose more advanced nationalities to act as tutors. As the most numerous, the Russians inevitably contributed the largest number of tutors, but the presence of large numbers of non-Russians somewhat mitigated the appearance of a revived Great Russian colonialism. Russians, Jews, Georgians, Armenians, Ukrainians, and Balts assumed key positions in many of the underdeveloped republics, usually in secondary administrative positions, where the real power was vested, rather than in the formal posts occupied by indigenous leaders. The ruling Communist Party was a genuine multinational ruling elite, but again highly selective and not always indigenous to the particular republic. It was thus not a precise microcosmic reflection of the multinational spectrum of the Soviet population. Indeed, the well-known failure of Stalinist policy to reshape dedicated indigenous Communists out of former "bourgeois nationalists" led, by 1936,

to an apparent revival of the Russian Empire in Soviet form.

The decapitation of the indigenous leadership of the non-Russian republics signaled the inauguration of the third, or "Russianization," phase, which continued from 1936 until Stalin's death in 1953. The least understood period in the development of Soviet nationality policy, it is primarily responsible for the characterization of the Soviet Union as a Russian colonial empire. An essentially transitory phase in the evolution of the Soviet state was mistakenly assumed to be a terminal phase, and the sharp departure in political policy from the pre-1936 period effectively obscured the uninterrupted continuity in social and economic policies which were to have long-range implications for the evolution of the Soviet multinational state into a multinational commonwealth.

Three sub-phases of the period (prewar, war, and postwar) constituted a distinct escalation in the Russification of the Soviet *political* order, but not necessarily the *social* system. As a result of the pre-1936 experience, Stalin was thoroughly disenchanted with the prospect of a quick materialization of reliable national cadres. The Soviet generation would still take some time to mature. Hence, this consummate specialist on the nationalities question shrewdly reasoned that Sovietization in the non-Russian areas would have to be executed principally by Russians and nonindigenous cadres. Stalin decided to shift the *national* base of his support to the Russian nation, since it was to become the national instrument of Sovietization. Inevitably, this meant Russianization, and even some Russification. (The Cyrillization of the non-Russian languages was carried out during the prewar sub-phase.)

Stalin's secondary *national* base was the Caucasus, since Georgia and Armenia were the only two countries which Stalin felt could be reliably governed by their own indigenous elites. They, like the Russian nation, were particularly favored during this period, and some of the favoritism rubbed off on neighboring Moslem Azerbaidzhan. Georgia and Armenia supplied large contingents of loyal Stalinists to serve in his various apparatuses throughout the country. The secret police, for example, was virtually "Caucasianized" by Stalin's compatriot L. P. Beria, as Georgians, Armenians, and some Azerbaidzhanis assumed key positions in the Soviet secret police empire.

It should be emphasized, however, that the basic Soviet social and economic policy of modernizing the underdeveloped nationalities continued without serious interruption or deviation. The various republics were industrialized and urbanized; more and more indigenous children were enrolled in schools; and a new Soviet-educated native intelligentsia was slowly and painfully squeezed through Russianization and Russification screens. But Stalin was implacable in denying the indigenous nationalities any kind of real *political* autonomy, and the formula "national in form, socialist in content" was ruthlessly executed. Local nationalism of any kind was ruthlessly stamped out, as were anti-Russian sentiments and condemnations of Great Russian chauvinism.

This was one aspect of the Great Purge trials of the 1930s when non-Russian party and administrative leaders in all of the non-Russian republics were purged, incarcerated, or executed on sundry charges of "bourgeois nationalism," secessionist aspirations, and collusion with the enemies of the Soviet Union. The purges reached their climax in 1938 when the two Uzbek leaders, Faizulla Khodzhayev (Chairman of the Uzbek Council of People's Commissars) and Akmal Ikramov (First Secretary of the Uzbek Communist Party), K. C. Rakovsky and G. F. Grinko of the Ukraine, and V. F. Sharangovich of the Byelorussian Republic were tried along with Bukharin and the "Rightists" and executed for alleged treason and separatist activities. The indictment implicated local leaders in virtually all ten of the non-Russian republics which had been established by the new Soviet Constitution only two years earlier. Since Sovietization in Central Asia and other underdeveloped republics was carried out principally by Russians and Russianized non-Russians from other regions, and the Moslem religion was suppressed by nominal Christians, Islamic culture was subjugated to Russian, and local nationalism was stifled by alien bureaucrats assigned by Moscow; Sovietization, so far as the natives and the outside world were concerned, was indistinguishable from colonialism, a fact which Stalin himself periodically noted with distress and chagrin.

The German attack on the Soviet Union served to accelerate and intensify the trends which were set into motion before 1936. It was more essential than ever to secure the absolute loyalty of the Russian population, the most numerous of the nationalities and the backbone of the Soviet armed forces. The war period witnessed a positive glorification of Russia and a powerful resurgence of Great Russian nationalism in all aspects of Soviet life. After the war, the glorification of Russia was not much toned down, but the Marxist-Leninist norms of Soviet life, which had been relatively de-emphasized, were revived with renewed force. Marxism-Leninism-Stalinism was emphatically transformed into Russified Marxism. At the same time, it must again be emphasized that, even under Stalin in the postwar period, the social and economic modernization of the underdeveloped republics was stepped up. During the war, when the western territories of the Soviet Union were devastated, the Caucasian and Central Asian republics experienced accelerated development. While this intensified indigenous political development in the Caucasus, it resulted in accelerated Russian political control in Central Asia because of the large influx of refugees from the west. The industrialization of the Central Asian republics brought in hordes of Russians to the metropolitan centers, just as collectivization earlier had resulted in decimating the nomadic Kazakhs and repopulating their lands with Ukrainian peasants deported from the west. But by the time of Stalin's death, a new generation of Central Asians had matured under Soviet rule, a comparatively young and reliable group of native leaders had been recruited. They were Russianized and bilingual; and while probably not completely immune from infectious local nationalism, they seemed to have a greater stake in the Soviet system than in separatism.

The death of Stalin inaugurated the fourth and current phase: transformation of a Soviet Russian empire-state into an authentic multinational, multilingual, federal commonwealth, preparatory to its conversion into a Russianized unilingual, multinational, *unitary* commonwealth.

Beria was the first of the post-Stalin leaders to perceive that the nationalities

had come of age: their dissatisfactions and latent national resentments provided a possible power base from which to move against his rivals. Molotov, Kaganovich, Malenkov, and the "anti-party group," if Khrushchev can be believed, still viewed the non-Russian cadres as unreliable and opposed giving them more political responsibility and power, locally as well as in all-union affairs. Among the charges leveled against Beria after his arrest was that he sought to mobilize the non-Russians against the Russians:

Beria and his accomplices undertook criminal measures in order to stir up the remains of bourgeois-nationalist elements in the union republics, to sow enmity and discord among the peoples of the U.S.S.R. and, in the first place, to undermine the friendship of the peoples of the U.S.S.R. with the Great Russian people.

On the other hand, it was charged four years later that the anti-party group sought to preserve the national *status quo* and opposed a greater role and participation of the nationalities in the Soviet system:

They were against the extension of the rights of the union republics in the sphere of economic and cultural development and in the sphere of legislation and against enhancing the role of the local Soviets in the fulfillment of these tasks. Thereby, the anti-party group resisted the party's firm course toward the more rapid development of economy and culture in the national republics, a course ensuring the further promotion of Leninist friendship between all peoples of our country.

And at the Twenty-First Party Congress, the Uzbek leader N. A. Mukhitdinov charged: "The anti-party group ... showed elements of [Great Russian] chauvinism and did not believe in the ability of the cadres of the national republics to solve tasks of the state."

Khrushchev and his successors appear to have adopted a policy midway between the extremes of complete national autonomy and nonindigenous control: to steer a prudent course between the vices of "local nationalism" and the excess of Great Russian chauvinism. The key elements in this policy are: (1) to strike a more equitable numerical balance among the nationalities in the distribution of posts in the structure of Soviet power; and (2) to enhance and expand the authority and responsibilities of the national republics. The national elites will increasingly assume greater direction of their national republics and at the same time become co-opted and more fully integrated into a multinational all-union ruling elite. Simultaneously, however, the Russianization of the multinational commonwealth and the multinationalization of the union republics have also been accelerated.

Reconciling Ideology, Russian Nationalism, and Local Nationalism

The modernization and industrialization of Soviet society has not only introduced a new system of social stratification and created a new urban-rural equilibrium, but also altered the social equilibrium among the various nationalities. The Soviet political structure is only now beginning to reflect these changes in the basic social and national distribution of power and influence. The changing nationality equilibrium is reflected first in the shifting relationship between Russians and non-Russians, and among the non-Russian nationalities. During the current phase in the evolution of the Soviet multinational state, when national distinctions are still conspicuous (even while eroding and withering in the face of Russianization and Russification), two basic trends reveal themselves: (1) the steady and disproportionate increase of Russian participation and influence in all sectors of Soviet life; and (2) a move toward proportionate participation and influence for the other nationalities (except possibly for the Byelorussians and Ukrainians, who will be encouraged to Russify themselves). The first trend establishes Russia as *primus inter pares* in the union during the transition, while emphasizing the direction in which the Soviet multinational state is ultimately moving; the second stresses the principle of national equality, or proportionate balance, as long as national distinctions continue.

Since the Soviet Union no longer conceives of itself as an embryonic universal state, its ultimate transformation into a terminal, multinational, unilingual commonwealth deprives it of its former open-ended imperialistic character. With the transformation of the Soviet state into such a multinational unilingual commonwealth, the importance of separate national republics will diminish significantly. The implications of such a development are already being examined by Soviet jurists from a variety of perspectives.

The nationalities now enjoy some latitude in registering their national demands upon the system and upon one another. They can legitimately demand greater representation in local and national organs and institutions of the state and party, greater local control over their own national territories, greater investment and resource allocations for services and enterprises in their national locality, and territorial adjustments and claims against other national republics or foreign states. So long as these demands threaten neither the social imperatives of the system nor the external security and territorial integrity of the Soviet Union, they are considered legitimate expressions of national interest. Their realization, however, will continue to depend upon the leverage which each nationality can command, and the degree to which national demands impinge upon the interests of pure social constituencies, particularly the elites.

In recent years, the Soviet government has tried deliberately to eliminate points of friction where the interests of social constituencies intersect with those of national constituencies. The major evidence of this sensitivity to national interests has been the national quota system, which the Soviet regime has been adopting, formally and informally, in recruiting and staffing state and party institutions from top to bottom; in the enrollment of students in institutions of higher learning; and in the periodic adjustments of territorial claims between various national units. The tendency, then, has been to establish proportional national representation in all political and social institutions. The tempo with which this is accomplished varies among individual nationalities in accordance with their significance, size, and development, as well as the degree to which their interests serve the higher social, foreign policy, and security interests of the state.

The interests of the basic social constituencies—namely, the various functional elite groups—continue, however, to enjoy the highest priority in the decisions and policies of the Soviet Union. Consequently, it is the social

elite groups within the various nationalities who are likely to benefit most immediately from the new nationality policy. By according the social elites greater influence and participation on the local and national level, the Soviet regime hopes to raise their "loyalty calculus" by creating a bond of common interest among the elites of various nationalities stronger than the bonds among different social classes of the same nationality. Given its ultimate social and ideological goals, the regime hopes that, as social classes are progressively eliminated and all Soviet citizens are raised to the status now enjoyed only by the social elites, national borders and distinctions will gradually decline in importance, and nationalism will automatically lose its force. It is in this spirit that one must interpret the 1961 Program of the CPSU:

The boundaries between the union republics of the U.S.S.R. are increasingly losing their significance.... Full-scale Communist construction constitutes a new stage in the development of national relations in the U.S.S.R., in which the nationals will draw still closer together until complete union is achieved.... Communism will call for still greater interconnection and mutual assistance between the Soviet republics. The closer the intercourse between the nations and the greater the awareness of country-wide tasks, the more successfully can manifestations of parochialism and national egoism be overcome. ...There is a growing ideological unity among the nations and nationalities and a greater *rapprochement* of their cultures. ...An international culture common to all Soviet nations is developing.

Switzerland has demonstrated rather effectively that a multinational state based upon a common economic interest can inspire a loyalty which prevails over centrifugal loyalties, but this was accomplished without the extinction of national identity or the imposition of a common language. The United States, on the other hand, has demonstrated that it is possible to forge a new nation by transforming the national identity of millions of citizens of a score of different nationalities, by imposing a common language and culture and thus inspiring a loyalty to the new nation stronger than the old loyalties. The American nationalities, however, were uprooted and transplanted from their national patrimony, and this may have been the decisive factor. It is noteworthy that the Americanization process has been least successful where it affects indigenous and territorially rooted American nationalities such as the Indians, Mexicans, and Puerto Ricans.

The Soviet Union aims to forge a new nation out of more than a score of indigenous nationalities; that is, to effect a transformation similar to that of the United States by imposing a common language and culture upon nationalities rooted, however, in their own national territories, like those of Switzerland. Unlike the latter, which considers itself a permanent multinational state, or the United States, which has never considered itself a multinational state, the Soviet Union considers itself to be a transitional multinational, multilingual state which will ultimately fuse into a unilingual state. Whether the Soviet objective succeeds or not depends upon whether the nationalities can be persuaded that it is more in their interest to give up than to preserve their national identities, and this is by no means a certainty. The evolution of the Soviet multinational state is sure to provide some surprises as the nationalities respond to evolving policies with a curious and ambivalent mixture of acceptance and resistance. If the amalgamation process is pressed too fast, it may intensify rather than attenuate local nationalism among some nationalities. In any event, the nationalities are bound to respond and react unevenly, with the balance between acceptance and resistance varying considerably from one nationality to another.

THE ROLE OF RUSSIA IN THE EVOLUTION OF THE SOVIET STATE

W. W. ROSTOW

1. The Russian Heritage

It is the burden of this essay that the current state of Soviet society is to be understood in terms of the complex interaction over time among the sectors of that society, consequent upon the creation of a bureaucratized dictatorship dedicated to the maintenance and enlargement of its power within Russia and vis-à-vis the external world. The nature of this interaction and, there-

Reprinted from *The Dynamics of Soviet Society* by W. W. Rostow. By permission of W. W. Norton & Company, Inc. Copyright 1952, 1953 by Massachusetts Institute of Technology. Copyright © 1967 by W. W. Norton & Company, Inc. Footnotes omitted.

fore, the precise forms which Soviet society has taken, have been partially determined by an inescapable historical continuity imposed on the regime. This continuity arises, simply, from the fact that the whole process occurred in a specific country, Russia, at a particular stage of its long history, under specific conditions and in relation to certain cultural forces not susceptible to rapid change. This chapter seeks to summarize briefly the nature and mode of operation of such distinctively national elements. It aims to account for certain Russian aspects of Soviet society and Soviet policy. In particular the discussion seeks to focus on the manner whereby those physical and cultural factors which have determined the nature of Russian civilization in general have also had their influence on the policies, techniques, and mannerisms of the Soviet state.

Even the extremely powerful instruments which a twentieth-century dictatorship has at its command leave largely outside the control of the state certain important aspects of the life of the people. In fact, one of the weapons which dictatorships exploit is the fact that the priority of motivations among ordinary citizens places politics and the exercise of political power relatively low on their scales of interest.

In most societies human beings appear to be concerned, in the first instance, with the adequacy of food and shelter for themselves and their families, with their personal lives, and with their security. A modern dictatorship can, indeed, interfere with these intimate human pursuits; and such interferences contribute to the tensions which exist within Soviet society and which can be noted in other modern dictatorships. Nevertheless, any general evaluation of Soviet society must

recognize that it is made up for the most part of people who continue to talk; to live; to govern their marriage, family, and home lives, and tastes, along lines which remain largely continuous with a past much longer than the Soviet regime.

This fact has contributed significantly to the social, cultural, and intellectual policies which the Soviet regime has come to regard as efficient instruments for dealing with its peoples. The criterion of efficient short-run operation, in a given society, imposes on its dictatorial rulers a discipline which is similar to, but distinguishable from, the discipline involved in societies where the identification of the ruler and the people's interest is more direct.

There has been in recent years some speculation as to the relationship between certain elements in Russian culture and the present dictatorship. Hypotheses have been advanced which would imply that extreme Russian individualism may be, somehow, linked to a requirement for absolute authority. Russian habits with respect to the swaddling of infants have also been advanced as basic to a predilection for dictatorial rule from above. These hypotheses—modestly advanced as clues rather than conclusions and by no means accepted generally by anthropologists—have not been developed in such a way as yet to make a persuasive link between the cultural characteristics asserted and the Russian political process. In particular, it is evident that many societies, in the past and at present, have found themselves under political dictatorship. In each case, looking backward from the existence of dictatorship, it is possible to isolate a good many factors in the history of the society which made it likely and possible, if not inevitable, that some form of political dictatorship would emerge. It is also evident that the political outcome might have been different if forces less profound than those rooted in the society's culture had not been what they were. In short, there is as yet no firm basis for moving directly from observations about real or alleged aspects of the Russian culture, in its anthropological sense, to its recent political experience.

It is clear, however, that certain aspects of the Russian position as of 1917, less significant than its cultural foundations, but, perhaps, ultimately related to them, contributed to the possibility of violent revolution and to successful Bolshevik exploitation of it. There were, in the first instance, the setbacks in the field of the tsarist armies and the incapacity of the tsarist regime to adjust to the forces set in motion by these defeats. Secondly, the antitsarist, non-Communist groups were split among themselves and were incapable of unifying or of mobilizing enough power to defeat the Bolsheviks in the cities where power was seized. Thirdly, those who led the civil war were incapable of offering any alternative except anti-Bolshevism at a time when the Russian people apparently felt the need for fundamental changes in the objectives and organization of their society. As a contemporary observer of the civil war has recently written: "... there was no reason to suppose that any substantial part of the population desired a return to the pre-revolutionary order. That is the primary reason for the failure of the 'White Guardist' movement which offered the people no better prospects than return of the discredited Tsarist regime."

It may be concluded, then, that the weakness and narrowness of the democratic tradition in Russia as of 1917 significantly contributed to the possibility of the Bolshevik *coup d'état* and to ultimate Bolshevik victory in the civil war. No realistic alternative was effectively crystallized out of the diverse non-Communist majority interests and offered to the Russian people.

2. The Imperatives of the Pursuit of Power in Twentieth-Century Russia

Having seized power, the Soviet regime soon confronted a range of forces which strongly influenced the real possibilities open to it. These fundamental facts of Russian life helped determine the forms which an effort to consolidate and enlarge the regime's power would assume. The Bolsheviks were operating, in the first instance, within the physical boundaries of the Russian Empire. The natural resources available were given, as were the existing agricultural and industrial potential. The level of education and the skills of the people under their control were at a stage determined by prior Russian history. Put another way, the exercise of power from the geographical, social, and economic base of Russia as of 1917 (and the several decades thereafter) determined largely the forms which the pursuit of power would take both at home and abroad.

At home the enlargement of power meant an acceleration of the industrialization process which had been going on rapidly in Russia for some decades before World War I, notably since the mid-1890's. It meant seeking increased productivity in Russian agriculture and coping with the aspirations of the peasantry for their own land, problems long familiar in prerevolutionary Russian history. It meant coming to terms with the nationalities question which, as in the case of the peasantry, Lenin did by making important concessions in 1921 with the installation of the NEP. And it required making some sort of policy toward the heritage of Russian culture, including religion. As described earlier, this was ultimately accomplished by abandoning, to a degree, the substantive radicalism of the Bolshevik Revolution and making important compromises with the persistent facts of Russian cultural life. Repeating an old tsarist pattern, the general formula adopted has been to permit a degree of cultural and religious latitude while insuring not only that the political power of the state has not been obstructed, but also that if possible, it has been strengthened by the presence of traditionalist strands.

To some extent, however, the regime has sought to change the patterns of Russian culture at its roots. Populations in the nationalities areas—notably the Ukraine and the Caucasus—have been moved, and they have been diluted by the Great Russian immigration; antireligious propaganda has been sustained; extraordinary efforts have been made to project and imprint the image of the New Soviet Man, energetic, disciplined, unquestioningly loyal to the state. But the New Soviet Man is, after all, a version of the ideal tsarist subject, placing loyalty to the state above any other standard for action, although transplanted into a changing industrial society where energy and an ability to adapt have been added to the continuing and overriding criteria of discipline and loyalty to the state. In a throwback to deterministic Marxism the regime has flirted in recent years with the notion that

the moving of the peasant to larger more urbanized concentrations might diminish his attachment to the concept of private ownership of land and other traditional aspirations which have resisted two decades of preponderantly collectivized life. On balance, however, the regime has tended to recognize increasingly its incapacity to alter radically the anthropological foundations of Russian life; it has sought, rather, to neutralize them or to put them positively to its use.

Geographically, any regime seeking to maintain and, if possible, enlarge its power from the Russian base would be confronted with similar, if not identical, concrete issues. Russian history and, in a wider sense, Russian civilization, have been profoundly influenced by the problems of organizing internally a coherent state over a vast area and defending that state from external assault along its extensive and vulnerable frontiers. From the Muscovite Grand Duchy forward the physical problems of governing, in the primitive sense noted above, have obsessed the Russian state.

Externally, toward the West there was the problem of the European balance of power and especially of relations to Germany. Any Russian regime attempting to increase its power vis-à-vis the outside world in the years after 1918 might well have explored the possibilities of agreement with Germany with a view toward sharing of power in Eastern Europe. Any Russian regime might well have confronted also the danger that Germany, in its pursuit of power, might encroach on Russian spheres of influence and might even be tempted to conquer and annex important parts of the Russian Empire. Similarly, increased power over the Dardanelles and in the Baltic might well have emerged as part of the substance of the pursuit of power for any Russian regime; and so also in the Far East, with Manchuria, Korea, Sakhalin, etc. Whatever the motivations or techniques employed, the maintenance and pursuit of power from geographical bases leads to similar forms of enterprise. As indicated at the end of this section, however, it is, in our judgment, incorrect to draw from these observations the conclusion that the Soviet regime is simply another example of Russian autocracy.

3. The Pattern of Russian Autocracy and Soviet Rule

The national characteristics of a society, created by a very long process, are bound to leave their mark on its political techniques—even when political rule is arbitrarily imposed. The extent of historical continuity in Russia is indicated by comparing the operative character of the Soviet regime with the main characteristics of tsarism over the years 1500–1900, as summarized by B. H. Sumner:

(a) The semi-sacrosanct personification of authority in a supreme ruler whose power, though closely circumscribed by the weight of custom and dependence on the landed and military classes, never became explicitly limited by clearly formulated or regularly operative checks of a legal or institutional kind, and frequently was of decisive consequence.
(b) The conception of service to the state to be enforced in some form or other, first from all land, later from all groups of subjects, a conception that was never fully realized in practice, though it was more and more effectively applied until the middle of the eighteenth century.
(c) The application of this conception of service to the landed class in such a way

that not only must no land go out of service, but all land must be in service, with the result that all land came to be regarded in the last resort as under some control of the Tsar.
(d) The linking up of the idea of service with that of the omnipotence of the state, of its unlimited range of action (except, prior to Peter the Great, in regard to the church), of the state as the creator and not merely the regulator of all associations within it, other than the church.
(e) The lack of differentiation between legislative, administrative, and judicial functions and the development of a centralized bureaucracy on an exceptionally large scale, corresponding to the exceptionally wide range of state control and extent of the empire.
(f) The paramountcy of the military needs of the state, which made the army, directly and indirectly, the first concern of tsarism and intensified the use of force and arbitrary police action in government.

These six characteristics inevitably took on various hues in the course of four hundred years, and in the nineteenth century a seventh appeared—the attempt to impose uniformity in the greater part of the vast and polyglot Romanov empire.

There is no doubt that the prevailing formal tradition of Russian government over the past five and a half centuries has been autocratic. The Soviet regime is, in an important sense, in the direct line of succession to Muscovite rule. Mobilization, in the context of an unstable world balance of power, of wide-spread resources and a heterogeneous population (including self-conscious nationality groups) has helped make chronic in Russian history highly centralized regimes which have demanded the subordination to their needs of the interests of all elements of society.

Despite persistent efforts by various powerful elements of Russian society to decentralize authority, grand dukes and tsars were proved able to effect their claim to ultimate authority. No competing institution could gain sufficient sustained support. Through councils and assemblies, the bureaucracy, the military, and various strata of the nobility shared considerable authority from the sixteenth century on. They legislated and even designated who the autocrat would be; but they were never able to control him for long or to overthrow the principle of autocracy.

At times—usually in periods of weakness or crisis—the ruling family and various elements of the nobility in the Royal Council, the Assembly of the Land (Zemsky Sobor), the Privy Council, and Senate shared the authority of the state. The Assembly, which legislated infrequently and appointed tsars, was without juridical foundation and had lost all real authority before Peter arbitrarily abolished it. The Ruling Senate, like the bureaucracy, was never more than a consultative administrative and judicial body. In the eighteenth and early nineteenth centuries the nobility, through its strategic control of the palace guard, was able to designate the autocrat; but it was unable to maintain its control. It failed signally, in the revolt of December 1825, to achieve fundamental change in the structure of the state.

In the half-century before 1914, however, pressures increased for a system of government with greater distribution of power. It is misleading to identify governments autocratic in conception and form with the substance of autocracy, i.e., the effective centralization of key decisions and the predominance of the state's own interest in the content of those decisions. In these terms there is little doubt that, while the forms of autocracy re-

mained virtually to 1917, deeper Russian trends ran strongly in the other direction. The substance of autocracy has varied over Russian history; and, even at its peak, as Sumner notes, it was tempered by "the weight of custom and dependence on landed and military classes."

In general, the nineteenth-century Council of State enjoyed only a consultative influence, but in 1905 that body was transformed into a controlled upper house along the lines of Prussia's parliamentary system. The increasing influence of liberal Western ideology in court circles, the nobility, and intelligentsia was reflected in the designation of local authority to the Zemstvo organizations. The acts of these organizations were always subject to the veto of the provincial governor, and their authority was progressively restricted by the bureaucracy. Nevertheless, in them an element of grass-roots democracy had taken limited hold on the Russian scene. The spread of the concepts and values of Western liberalism and socialism, as well as the appearance of a small but growing industrial and commercial middle class, had evident consequences. The new groups demanded a greater influence on national policy; but they evoked, at first, only a firmer insistence by autocracy on its divinely ordained absolutism. The growing antagonism between these Western-oriented elements, backed by growing peasant discontent, and the central authority, with its swollen bureaucracy (staffed largely with the declining nobility), contributed to and provided leadership for the 1905 upheaval and its achievement of a Western parliamentary structure in the Duma. This body, too, however, was subject to increasing restriction and the imperial veto, and could not influence cabinet appointments or other decisive acts of government. Thus the actual operation of the autocratic machinery persisted much as before 1905 until its patent incapacity to deal with the war crisis swept it from the scene in 1917.

The parliamentary tradition dating, somewhat arbitrarily, from the French Revolution, had evidently grown rapidly in Russia in the pre-1914 decades. But it had struck insufficiently deep roots in the popular consciousness to dominate the chaos of 1917. Its liberal and socialist leadership was split and indecisive in the face of peasant and worker demands released by the March Revolution and the urgent requirements of either fighting the war effectively or making peace. In these circumstances the Bolshevik minority of about 25 per cent, with a positive program, a unified command, and a keen sense of power tactics, won support among key urban groups, as well as elements among soldiers and peasants, and took over power with comparative ease. The balance of forces represented in the Constituent Assembly certainly reflected the aspirations of Russia more nearly than did the Bolsheviks. The majority simply proved incapable of making itself effective in the anarchy of 1917.

There is an important sense, then, in which the Soviet state is a reversion, in Russian history, away from a historic trend. The half-century before 1914 had seen the rise of ideas and reluctantly-granted institutions which moved Russia away from the deeply imbedded autocratic tradition. The Zemstvos, Zemgor (a popular institution which more or less took upon itself certain important aspects of military provisioning during World War I), and the Duma were in being and

were demonstrating their ability, in a limited way, to meet and especially to articulate popular needs. Widening elements of the population were becoming aware of the meaning of democratic ideas.

Evidently, the strength of this evolving democratic pattern of thought and behavior was inadequate to master the situation in 1917. Russia reverted to an extreme version of autocracy. The verbal concessions of the Soviet Constitution reflect, nevertheless, the underlying popular vitality of elements in the democratic tradition. It is by no means unthinkable that, in the long run, the trend of the pre-1914 decades will resume and triumph over the older tradition of absolute centralized state power in Russia, although the timing, the process, and the vicissitudes of such an evolution can not be predicted. The analogies between Stalin, Peter the Great, and Ivan the Terrible are real enough. It is partly because Soviet rule is a throwback that such analogies are so persuasive. But Russia's history has not been static. The evolution of Russia from 1861 to 1917 resulted from forces which the Soviet regime has contained or distorted but not eliminated from the operative determinants of Russia's future.

4. Russian Nationalism and the Soviet Regime

The written record of Russian history reveals a long tradition of awareness of nation, or at least of common culture. This strand of national attachment was associated with and developed by the long struggle for national security, internal and external, and by a reaction against, as well as an acceptance of, Western cultural infiltration. Russian nationalism has persistently incorporated a profound, primitive attachment to the Russian land. The expansion of education and the growing influence of Western ideology in the nineteenth century gave modern Russian nationalism a fairly broad popular base by the outbreak of World War I.

The practical significance of Russian national feeling was made evident to the Soviet regime during the period of foreign intervention after the Revolution; and by the mid-thirties the Party leadership revealed a determination to transform it into an asset of the regime. The force of this feeling was made apparent by the reaction of Russian troops and peoples both before and after German policy in Russia had defined itself in 1941–42. The large-scale defections in the first phase of the war and the initial reaction of certain nationality groups were matched by the profundity of the nationalism (and notably Great Russian nationalism) which asserted itself as Hitler identified himself as perhaps the most ruthless in the long succession of foreign invaders. The regime apparently made an appraisal along the following lines:

1. The Russian peoples are quite unprepared to fight for a Communist regime as such, and they might even be prepared to defect in large numbers to a foreign enemy in the hope that the Soviet regime might be overthrown and an alternative Russian government installed.
2. On the other hand, the Russian people appear prepared to rally around a strictly nationalist effort to overcome a foreign invasion when the foreign power fails to offer a dignified national alternative to the Soviet system.
3. Of all the peoples of the Soviet Union those of Great Russia are, in the national sense, the most reliable.

Major and dramatic concessions were thus made to Great Russian nationalism in the course of the war. The conclusions drawn concerning popular motivations, which were continuous with the line of thought underlying Stalin's policy since 1934, appear to have been carried over into the postwar period, despite the re-assertion of ideological conformity which has also marked the past several years. Efforts to identify the regime with Russian nationalism in the face of a hostile world have been accentuated, even as compared with the mid-1930's. This has involved in particular a systematic effort to portray American purposes with respect to Russia in the image of Hitler's actions. Finally, a decision has been made to rely heavily on the nationalism of Great Russia. A purposeful appeal to this majority element has been made, and such costs as may be involved in exacerbated feelings among the nationality groups have been accepted.

5. The Russian Heritage and the Priority of Power

The human and physical materials of Russia have thus strongly affected the content of Soviet policy. They have helped alter almost beyond recognition the character of the regime's ideology. They have helped determine the concrete objectives, internal and external, which the regime has sought in its efforts to consolidate and enlarge its power.

There is, moreover, a significant interweaving of Russian elements with the patterns of Marxist thought. Three major points of convergence between Marxism and the Russian heritage can, in particular, be noted.

First, the concept of conflict between the socialist state and its capitalist environment links well to the history of Russia's awkward relations to the Western world, with its differing religious and cultural foundations, periodic conflicts and invasions. It is notable that, while both Marxist and national elements are invoked in Soviet propaganda (for example, by Beria in his speech of November 7, 1951), the weight of emphasis falls increasingly on the danger of a recurrence of a historical menace to Russia rather than on the capitalist encirclement of a socialist state.

Second, the pattern of Russian history as well as the concepts of Marxism would suggest restraint by the Soviet state in launching an external military campaign with Russian troops. Russia has been only cautiously aggressive outside its borders in the past. Its major military excursions have been as riposte to invasion.

Third, this traditional caution may link with another fact of Russian history; namely, that Russia now stands at an intermediate state of transition to industrialization, with its period of maximum relative economic strength still some decades off. To the extent that an element of Marxist faith prevails within the regime, these national characteristics might support a Marxist historical perspective on a future in which ultimate Communist victory is, if not guaranteed, regarded with sufficient confidence to make it advisable to avoid the risks of defeat in major war at the present intermediate historical stage.

Despite the complex infiltration of the present regime with elements of substance and behavior derived from a long Russian past, it is the burden of the present argument, taken as a whole, that the motivation of the leadership, and the institutional arrangements into which they have now crystallized, are not to be understood in terms of the interests of the Russian peoples or the Russian nation, but in terms of the continuity and enlargement of the regime's own power, narrowly defined. Only to the extent that the enlargement of Russia's strength and power was required for this prior goal has the regime pursued Russian ends—although it has increasingly sought to identify its policy, in the minds of the people, with the Russian national interest and with the national heritage. The distinction appears important for an understanding of the Soviet past—and it may be decisive to the Russian future.

The nature of the distinction stems from the whole dynamic process by which the Bolsheviks gained and then consolidated and enlarged their power. It stems, in fact, from Lenin's adaptation of the Marxist ideology. That adaptation served as a rationale for the seizure of power in the face of a hostile national majority, and for the maintenance of the Party leadership in power against probable majority opposition within the Party. The decision, taken definitely by 1921, to perpetuate the regime in power in the face of both Party and popular opposition placed the regime in a position of virtually permanent hostility and suspicion with respect to its own people. Step by step the regime institutionalized the forms of administration of power which would, as it were, make good its initial choice to seize power and maintain it under such circumstances.

As noted earlier, this *ad hoc* process has yielded a systematic result. Forms of political, social, and cultural policy, as well as modifications of ideology, have emerged in which the state has sought to create those conditions which would guarantee the efficiency of its own operations and, especially, its perpetuation in power. The institutional process, in turn, has bred habits of mind which deny a sense of identity between the leaders of the regime and the Russian peoples. The citizens of the Soviet Empire, including its European satellites, are regarded as units to be molded if possible, but certainly to be controlled, so as to contribute to goals determined independently of their inclinations. The system is designed to operate indefinitely in the face of the wishes of its citizens while doing what it can to identify the wishes of the citizens with the goals of the regime.

The imposition of state policy from above is no new thing in Russia or in other countries. A modern instance was Turkey under Ataturk. What is distinctive about the Soviet regime is the extreme priority it accords to the pursuit of the goal of its own power, as opposed to a national program reflecting the aspirations of its citizens. In particular, the regime is marked by an almost total lack of inhibition in the means it is prepared to use to effect this priority. Stalin's totalitarian state lacked the common-law restraints and compromises which softened earlier Russian autocracies, and had at its command more modern and efficient instruments of surveillance, communication, and control. A program of popular education, industrialization, and mechanization of agriculture in Russia after 1917 might have had its rationale in a strictly national definition of the Russian interest; and some such policies would, almost certainly, have been pursued by any Russian regime after 1917.

Soviet action in these and other directions was taken, however, mainly as a reflex to its own power goals. It never had the advantage of the historical, emotional, and religious connection with Russian peoples and their culture which even the least popular of the tsars enjoyed. It came to power and held power in defiance of the bulk of the Russian peoples. Although time has passed, the mark of this deep insecurity remains with the regime in relation to Soviet citizens. The divorce of the regime from the nation it governs is firmly crystallized in attitudes and institutions whose change now would constitute virtually another revolution.

A similar foundation exists for the maintenance of a relation of extreme and persistent hostility to the outside world. In the first instance, important elements in the Bolshevik regime regarded its victory as merely a tactical phase in a world revolutionary uprising. This view of the matter was appreciated abroad and led to a certain amount of ill-feeling toward the Bolsheviks as well as to counter-revolutionary intervention in Russia. The reaction of the Soviet state, in turn, was a compound of ideological and national feeling. The success of Soviet resistance at this early stage dramatized the value of an external enemy as a rationale for the internal policy of the regime. And thus the external enemy came to be virtually institutionalized as a permanent feature of Soviet policy.

The Russian mannerisms of the Soviet regime are, then, to be regarded as the consequence of the tactics of pursuing power from a Russian base; they represent more nearly the long-run infiltration of an occupation regime by the area and society it rules than a direct national phenomenon determined by the aspirations of the

Russian peoples or by an emotional identification of the rules of the state with those peoples.

To put this conclusion another way, Russian geography, culture, and its historical position as of 1917 certainly set limits within which any regime would have had to operate over the succeeding three and a half decades. Forces were at work that any regime would have had to cope with and, in one form or another, reflect if it were to remain effectively in power. The Soviet regime is deeply marked by certain stable or slow-changing elements in the cultural life of Russia. But it appears analytically important to remember that Russian life had and has the capability of producing, from the same limiting foundations, other forms of government and societal organization. And it appears important in the making of policy toward the Soviet Union not to confuse the operative motivations of the regime toward its own peoples or the outside world with the national mannerisms it has acquired.

IDEOLOGY AND SOVIET POLITICS

Daniel Bell

The word *ideology*—it has so many ambiguous meanings and emotional colorations. What is not an ideology today—ideas, ideals, beliefs, passions, values, *Weltanschauungen*, religions, political philosophies, moral justifications, and so on, and so forth? One hears about "communism and capitalism as competing ideologies," about the "ideology of the small businessman," about the "failure of the United States to develop an ideology," and *pace*, "the end of ideology." In an essay in *Partisan Review* on pornography, ideology is defined as "fantasy cast in the form of opinion or assertion," a loose and associative form of thought "sharing qualities in common with pornography itself." A front-page essay in the *Times Literary Supplement* on pre-Christian religious tracts discusses the effects of trafficking in "hostile ideologies" (early Epicureanism) on Christian apologists. A sociology colleague sends me an essay entitled "Change, Ferment, and Ideology in the Social Services."

Surely by now some specific meaning should have developed out of common usage. And yet it has not. The word remains both descriptive and pejorative, both analytical and normative. The word does not remain neutral. Neither do people who are influenced by ideology. (In talking about the "end of ideology," one is accused of calling for an end to ideals!) Ideologies, because they somehow catch up one's passions, move people to action. This is the source of their initial power, for in a world committed to change, often quite violent change, ideologies become prime agencies of movements. But this is also the seed of their decay, for when pas-

Slavic Review, XXIV, No. 4 (December 1965), 591–603. Reprinted by permission. Footnotes omitted.

sions are spent or betrayed, or when harsher realities confound initial promises, ideologies also can wane or, if used coercively, induce cynicism.

And yet, although the meaning of the word has shifted so much over time, there is need for some working definition which will allow us to pin down this elusive term. Let me begin by distinguishing, historically, four usages of the term "ideology" in order to see how the concept has functioned in different ways and to see if by this sorting some further clarity can be achieved.

A first meaning of ideology, as, for example, Marx used it in *The German Ideology,* is to deride the proposition that ideas are autonomous or the belief in the power of ideas to shape or determine reality. In this sense ideology is a "false consciousness," and the "end of ideology," as Engels used the phrase in his essay of *Ludwig Feuerbach and the End of Classical German Philosophy,* meant the time when men would achieve "true consciousness," or the awareness of the direction of history and the material basis of society. But that would also be the "end of history," for then men would no longer be subject to causal laws (that is, necessity) and consciousness would be free to change social circumstance. But "during history" ideology can only be a masquerade, and the critique of ideology, *an evaluative critique,* is therefore to denounce the claims of autonomous ideas.

A second use of the concept is the argument that all ideas are conditioned —class-conditioned, *zeitgebunden,* language-bound; thus, all ideas are socially determined. Though Marxism, in one important sense, is a source of this idea, as it was developed scholastically, the

chief stimulus was the idealist school of historical relativism, in particular, Wilhelm Dilthey. From this point of view all knowledge is a function of the concepts selected to organize the meaning of events; but if in human actions these a priori concepts are not absolute (as space and time were thought to be) but change over time, if all ideas, thus, are time-bound or conditioned in some other fashion, how does one know about a previous period of history, or objectively know the truth about the present? Such questions led, in the work of Scheler, Durkheim, Sorokin, Mannheim, and others to the sociology of knowledge. When Mannheim, for example, speaks of thought as *ideological* or *utopian,* he is distinguishing two modes or styles of thinking in relation to time perspectives. Lukacs, when he distinguishes types of consciousness, does so from a class perspective. But the effort in all these instances, whether by invoking science, or contrast perspectives, or history, is to *transcend* the partialities of conditioned ideas.

A third, by now quite common usage is to see ideologies as justifications which represent some specific set of interests. Thus, ideas are looked at not to see whether they are true or false but in terms of their function. The analytical intention is not to uncover the origin of ideas or to test their validity but to assess their consequences. In this respect, elements of the positivist, pragmatic, Freudian, and Marxist traditions all converge in regarding the concept of ideology in these terms. The intention here is not to debase ideas; yet the effect, in many instances, is to assert that ideas really have no influence in social action and to challenge the notion that ideology carries much weight in the affairs of politics. In the crudest version politics is seen largely as *qui gagne*, or *kto-kogo*, or who gets what when and how. Ideas are not regarded as instrumental but as epiphenomenal.

Finally, there is the viewpoint which sees ideologies as social formulas, as belief systems which can be used to mobilize people for action. Here the instrumental and functional aspects are fused. Now all social movements to some extent use ideas in an instrumental sense: to reorganize old habit patterns and to provide new means of comprehending experience. But in revolutionary politics ideology becomes completely instrumental, becomes, in fact, a way of life. And the prize example of this is Leninism. In Lenin's terms, ideologies are belief systems fashioned by intellectuals or professors for use in organizing the masses. In *What Is to Be Done?* it is clear that Lenin uses the term "ideology" to mean the combat of ideas. (Ideology, in fact, becomes simply another term for "consciousness.")

"All those who talk about 'overrating the importance of ideology,'" he wrote, "about exaggerating the role of the conscious element, etc., imagine that the pure working-class movement can work out, and will work out, an independent ideology for itself, if only the workers 'wrest their fate from the hands of their leaders.' But this is a profound mistake."

And, continued Lenin:

Since there can be no talk of an independent ideology being developed by the masses of the workers themselves in the process of their movement, the *only* choice is: either the bourgeois or the socialist ideology. There is no middle course (for humanity has not created a "third"

ideology, and, moreover, in a society torn by class antagonisms there can never be a non-class or above-class ideology). Hence, to belittle socialist ideology *in any way*, to *turn away from it in the slightest degree* means to strengthen bourgeois ideology.

While it is doubtful whether Marx ever would have accepted the designation of his set of ideas as an ideology (after all, he believed it was science), Lenin, by concentrating on the mobilization of ideas, talked a language of conflicting belief systems in the same temper as the previous wars of religion. He spoke of the Zubatovs who were dragging the working class "along the line of clerical and gendarme 'ideology.'" He described the German working class as "broken up among a number of ideologies." The bourgeois ideology had prevailed, he wrote, because "it possesses *immeasurably* more opportunities for being spread."

By casting ideology in these "either-or" terms Lenin, more than any other thinker or leader, gave politics its *totalistic* framework and made ideology synonomous with total belief.

But one does not have to accept the concept in these terms. If ideology is an aspect of behavior, a sociologist has to fit it into some social framework which shows how it is linked to other aspects as well, and which allows one to understand the limits of ideology as well as its functions. And an analytical framework has to specify the level of generality as well as the range of application of a conceptual term. The sociological analysis of ideology gains coherence only in relation to the value system of a society, and it is by understanding the complicated interplay of the operation of the value system with ideology that one can identify some specific social processes and see how they shape social action.

Ideology and the Value System

Every modern society has to justify itself in one way or another to its members. Even the most coercive of societies has to establish some justification of the coercion; it has to transform *Macht* into legitimacy in order to govern without turning an entire society into a concentration camp. As Rousseau wrote in the third chapter of *The Social Contract,* "The strongest is never strong enough always to be the master unless he transforms strength into right and obedience into duty." In that sense, perhaps, one understands the meaning of Emile Durkheim's statement that "every society is a moral order." In more formal terms, as Talcott Parsons has put it: "All human societies embody references to a normative cultural order which places teleological 'demands' upon men," an allegiance to something beyond themselves. And this normative order is expressed in the central value system of a society.

The value system of the society is the implicit creed subscribed to, or unquestioningly accepted by, the members of the society which defines for them the good society and which shapes the evaluative judgments on actions taken by members of the society. The values are formulated in "sacred" pronouncements (for example, the French Declaration of the Rights of Man, the United States Constitution, the Communist Party Program), become exemplified in history, are presented as tradition, and act to facilitate or inhibit change to the

extent that the innovation can be reconciled with established doctrine. The values define what it means to be a member of the society (what it means, for example, to say, "I am a Bolshevik" or "I am an American"), just as a religious creed defines what it means to be, say, a Catholic or a Moslem, and a professional credo defines what it means to be a physician or a scientist. The value system legitimates the distribution of authority and the performance of roles in a society.

Now it is true that a creed, broadly defined, can be compatible with a large number of different political policies, that one cannot deduce one, and only one, course of action from necessarily abstract formulations. Societies guided by a belief in natural law or divine justice have as much difficulty defining the moral correlate of an act as secular societies encounter in rationalizing political actions. So one cannot take ideational formulations as concrete guides to political policy.

But neither can one ignore them. For each society needs some creed, intellectually coherent and rationally defensible, both to justify itself and to meet the challenges of—or to challenge —other creeds. The value system, like the rule of law, provides a set of standards to evaluate actions, but, being the most abstract level of the normative order, these standards are directions of actions, not directives. In societies (or social movements) that seek to mobilize people for the attainment of goals, some sharper specification of doctrine is necessary. The function of an ideology, in its broadest context, is to concretize the values, the normative judgments of the society. And in some instances, as in the Soviet

Union, ideology indicates the direction of the future, and the realization of some further values in that future.

In sum, within every operative society there must be some creed—a set of beliefs and values, traditions and purposes—which links both the institutional networks and the emotional affinities of the members into some transcendental whole. And there have to be some mechanisms whereby those values can be not only "internalized" by individuals (through norms) but also made explicit for the society—especially one which seeks consciously to shape social change; and this explicating task is the function of ideology.

An *official* ideology is both a principle of inclusion and a principle of exclusion. It defines the official creed, and it identifies the enemy or heretic against whom sentiments must be mobilized. By its very formulation of a public creed it requires an overt statement of allegiance from those who occupy responsible positions in the society.

Thus, ideologies also are forms of legitimation, a link between the generalized values of the society and the institutionalized action of the collectivities (for example, government) in order to set the limits of action. And, if authority is defined as the regulative pattern which is relevant, too, to the normative control of political functions, then ideology can be seen as an aspect of authority, and part of the control system of the society.

Ideology and Reality

We have accepted the proposition, advanced by Talcott Parsons, that "a system of value-orientations held in common by members of the social system can serve as the main point of reference for anlayzing structure and processes" of that system. To this we have added the function of ideology as the mobilization of these values through a codified system of beliefs and, thus, the explication of the goals of the society.

With this in mind, the value system of the Soviet Union might be characterized as one of "ideological activism," that is, a self-conscious set of directives to change the society in accordance with a generalized theoretical doctrine. This involves a constant scrutiny of canonical texts, a testing of achievements by the double standard of practical results and concordance with doctrine, and a constant specification of goals in order to spur the people to the ends set by the regime. Such a society has a high, built-in drive toward social change and a great flexibility in the choice of means. But the stress on ideological conformity also creates a rigid submission to authority and evasions of responsibility, both of which serve to inhibit change and create great tensions in the society.

For the individual, values are grounded in the existential beliefs about the world, his own motivational needs as a personality, and his relation to others in a society. Ideology serves to organize the cognitive validity of the ideas and to demand a practical commitment—putting one's interests at the service of the beliefs. But an ideology, to be effective, must be "congruent" with reality. Official actions must conform to the ideological tenets or be rationalized in some acceptable way. When elements of the doctrine are "utopian"—that is, promise performance in the future rather than the present—the present actions must be justified as moving in the expected direction. When the doctrine conflicts with performance, some "textual answer" must be found to justify a change. Thus ideology is in constant revision in the society. The discrepancy between ideology and reality becomes a continuing source of strain.

For the elites, the very possession of authority forces them to maintain a conscious relationship to the official creed. No society, however, is so completely homogeneous, nor a creed so monolithic, that the different segments of the elite must maintain an allegiance to the creed with the same degree of intensity. Clearly the different social strata within the elite display variable sensitivities to the vicissitudes of ideology. For the hierophants, the interpreters of ideology, the strains are masked, for one of the chief tasks of these pulpiteers is to provide a seemingly unbroken line of continuity in the validity of the doctrine. For the scientific and intellectual members of the elite, however, who, as members of the wider international scientific and intellectual community, are subject to counterdoctrines or independent interpretations, the vicissitudes of ideology become an important source of support for their efforts to make the ideology more consonant with the common standards of professional belief. The differential degrees of attachment, or alienation, on the part of the scientific and intellectual elites to the creed thus become significant indicators of the cohesion of the society and its ability to mobilize support for its stated goals.

The major ideological problem for a regime, then, is to maintain the central core of the creed, or to be able to redefine it successfully when it is challenged, so as to achieve a continuity with the past and a realistic orientation to the present. In the Soviet Union the core doctrines have come under increasing attack from within the system, and the crucial questions are whether it will be able to maintain the given doctrine, modify significant sections successfully (that is, control the consequences for the existing elite's power as well as rationalize it with other elements of the creed), or face an erosion of doctrine that would result in the alienation of a substantial segment of the scientific and intellectual elites from the system as a whole.

To put the questions in more substantive form: Do the current debates in science, philosophy, economics, sociology, and literature portend a revision of Marxist-Leninist dogma to bring it in line with the mainstream of Western rationalist thought (as so much of Marxism actually was, in its pre-Stalinist phase)? Will there be a more open forum of intellectual discussion and literary and philosophical "experimentation" so that some new doctrinal commitments will emerge? Or is the current ferment simply an "accommodation" on the part of the regime to momentary pressures, an accommodation that might be revoked by the ruling elite when it feels that the changes have gone too far? In short, is the process of ideological change irreversible, or can it be halted? If the evolution continues, will it be toward the creation of a doctrine sharing a common intellectual foundation with Western thought and values, or will it be toward some new doctrinal formulations of Marxism-Leninism? No complete answer can be given on the ideological plane alone; a "surrender" of the Russians to the Chinese line might result in new controls and the effort to reassert particular dogmas, or intensified conflict between Russia and China might result in more rapid changes moving toward newer ideological formulations. One can deal here only with "immanent" tendencies, rather than with the total political context in which the major changes will be played out.

Accommodation or Change?

The fact that a doctrine or an ideology is changing does not necessarily mean the disintegration of faith, a loss of the power to hold or move believers, or inability to sustain an intellectual argument against outside challenges. The history of the great faith-systems of the past—Catholicism, Islam, Buddhism, and others—illustrates their remarkable ability to re-order their doctrines, assimilate diverse intellectual currents (Platonism and Aristotelianism, for example, in the case of Catholicism), and maintain a following among the faithful—though it is a moot question whether the survival of a faith can be attributed to the intellectual flexibility of its doctrines or to the fact that these religions were embedded within powerful economic and social systems that allowed them to wield temporal as well as spiritual influence.

A number of people, Professor Joseph Bochenski, for one, argue that the present changes in Soviet doctrine do not portend the disintegration of a powerful faith or the loss of allegiance among the elite but represent simply a complex process of accommodation that is the feature of every doctrine-centered system. In the paper he presented to the 1964 Hoover Institution conference, Bochenski sought to demonstrate the process of change. The Communist countries, he admitted, face a dilemma in that every Marxist-Leninist "must hold that everything in science, art, morals, and so on" has to conform to the "absolutistic standards of the totalitarian state doctrine," while at the same time "he must face the developing realms of thought, and more generally of spiritual life."

The regime, he argues, seeks to overcome the dilemma by a tactic, so to speak, of "three truths." First, there is the basic dogma that is stated in simplified terms for public consumption. Second, there is a "speculative superstructure," consisting of statements in a technical, Marxist terminology that must be acknowledged by everybody but which can be interpreted freely. And, finally, there is a third kind of statement ("on the borderline between ideology and pure science"), "declassified doctrines" (such as the legitimacy of mathematical logic), about which there can be "practically unlimited freedom of discussion."

By this balancing act the regime seeks to accommodate the different elements in Russian society. But Dr. Bochenski is dubious about the prospects of the revision of "basic faiths." "A generation of truly Marxist-Leninist thinkers has been formed," he argues, "and its control is strong enough to assure that no radical breach with the past will occur. . . . Changes may be slow, all the slower in that this doctrine has now become a unifying ideology of a great and proud nation."

Dr. Bochenski, as a philosopher and a scholastic, assumes that a system of faith containing an intellectually coherent creed has to be articulated in all its parts so as to embrace every aspect of intellectual activity. Like Father Wetter, a good Thomist, he assumes that dialectical materialism, despite its intellectual primitiveness, is a sufficiently articulated, comprehensive system (and for that reason more dangerous, intellectually, than Western thought, with its eclectic hodgepodge of idealism, Kantianism, empiric-criticism, positivism, naturalism, and the like) which, in scholastic fashion, can and does serve as a unifying feature of Soviet thought.

My principal objection to Dr. Bochenski's argument is that the picture he draws is too static. Even the image of "three truths" (one more than Plato's) is cast in the mold of a settled system that has discovered how to make harmless accommodations and now exercises this device as a subtle means of social control. My own feeling is that Marxism-Leninism as a unified doctrine is becoming disjointed and losing its *élan*; where significant philosophical changes are in the offing, they point in the direction of rejoining the diverse traditions (naturalism, positivism, philosophy of science) of Western thought.

There are four broad factors, intellectual and sociological, that put Marxism-Leninism increasingly on the defensive these days: (1) the inherent contradictions that appear in the logic of the doctrine (particularly the "dialectic" and its conflict with science); (2) the incompatibility of the doctrinal structure with the complex differentiation of Communist society—expressed, on the one hand, in the inadequacy of Marxian economic theory and, on the other, in the idea of the "laws of socialist development" as they apply to different countries; (3) the influence of Western thought, partly through the emergence of a world community

of science, partly through the interchange of literature and ideas; and (4) the crumbling of the "walls of faith," as a result of Khrushchev's 1956 speech and the bewildering reversal of his own fortunes. The sense of betrayal about the past and the uncertainty about how far present leaders can be trusted undermine the certitudes of the faith. Marxist-Leninism is no longer an all-embracing, aggressive ideological doctrine. As in the breakup of Islam, perhaps, different elements of the doctrine may now become of differential importance for different groups in various Communist countries.

Within the Soviet Union there are three currents of change that work to modify, reshape, or erode Soviet doctrine: first, the role of science as a new legitimating agency in challenging older orthodoxies; second, the disillusionment of the young intellectuals, particularly the literary, with the old doctrines, and the adoption of a negative attitude toward all ideology; third, the need of the new intellectual elites, no longer believing in "historical reason," to confront the existential questions—the meaning of death, suffering, anguish, and the "ultimate" questions about life.

The "End of Ideology"?

In the face of all these changes in doctrine, what is the central core of Soviet ideology? It should be clear here (as in my more extensive review) that no single element of doctrine is a keystone whose removal would cause the collapse of Soviet ideology. In his book *Soviet Politics* (subtitled "The Role of Ideas in Social Change") Barrington Moore sought to compare the prerevolutionary expectation and ideology of the Communist Party with the Soviet reality and concluded that, among all the aspects of Bolshevik doctrine, the transfer of the means of production to the state represented one of the few instances of congruity between anticipation and fact. In the expectations concerning the organization of industry, social and economic equality, the school, the family, the power of the state—basic themes of the socialist vision—reality has turned out to be far different. Equality of wages and workers' management of industry have turned into sharp differentials and managerial authority. The 1919 Party Program demand for the organization of the army as a people's militia faded long ago before the stratified organization, ranks, and epaulets, no different from those in any other army. The schools, once organized along the lines of progressive education, have become authoritarian institutions (in the jargon of sociological pedagogy, "teacher-centered" rather than "child-centered"). The themes of equality and sacrifice, nobly sounded during the Revolution, turned into class distinctions so severe that when drastic food rationing was introduced in 1941, in the month after the Germans invaded Russia, the population was "split up into favored, semi-favored and unfavored categories, the rations of the latter being already extremely meager." Could the abandonment of revolutionary ideology be more dramatic? By 1941 such conditions were accepted as "normal."

But does this mean, as Robert Daniels has maintained, that ideology, or any description of the Soviet system in terms of direction or purpose, is meaningless? In reviewing the trends of Soviet thought, Daniels argued in

1956: "The pattern of changes within the core of official ideology, the official-purpose system, cannot convincingly be written off as a series of mere tactical ruses or strategic zigzags. The Soviet regime has no higher conception of society or social purpose or of the objectives of its own existence than the ideology which has been under discussion here—which ideology has been reduced to an instrument for rationalization after the fact. It has apparently lost all long-run directing power, no matter what the direction. There is no fixed star for the Soviets to steer by; they have no ultimate pattern which has not thus been subject to reshaping over the years."

Thus the question is polarized: Is Soviet doctrine a "unifying ideology," or it is only a "rationalization after the fact"? Neither answer is suitable, not because each represents an extreme and the truth is always the happy middle but because each misunderstands the nature and function of ideology.

Every society, as I have argued earlier, has some value system, implicit or explicit, reflecting the underlying moral core that is the "irreducible" source of legitimacy and emotional affinity. To the extent that the society has to mobilize its people (for war, for economic development, and the like), it has to create an official ideology—some creed, intellectually coherent and rationally defensible, to justify that set of actions and to meet the challenges of other creeds. To the extent that a society does not mobilize its people and becomes pluralistic and diverse, the ideology becomes more diffuse. The question of legitimacy remains then on the more general and abstract level of the value system (for example, in the American system, the belief in equality, achievement, and so forth), which is compatible with a wide range of practices and even attenuated loyalties. But some ideological base always remains. The meaningful question, therefore, in view of all the changes that have taken place in the content of Soviet doctrines, is this: What is the persistent or underlying thread of Soviet ideology, and under what conditions might one expect that element to change, if at all?

I think the underlying thread is fairly simple: the claim to a "historic mission" (to realize "communism") and the legitimacy of "the chosen instrument" (the "leading role" of the Party). To this extent the vicissitudes of ideology in the short forty-eighty-year history of the Soviet regime have not been different, in sociological principle, from the vicissitudes of dogma in the history of the Catholic Church. (In comparing the two, of course, the change of time scale must be kept in mind. Because of the nature of communication and feedback the Soviet time period has been vastly compressed.)

While dogmas such as dialectical materialism, historical materialism, the superiority of collective property, and the nature of scientific communism remain on a formal level, the doctrinal core, the central fact is not any specific theoretical formulation *but the basic demand for belief in the Party itself.* Any movement based on a creed, but hierarchically organized encounters this blunt necessity when it is forced, through the pressure of experience or doctrinal challenge, to surrender one or another contradictory element in the creed: it is not the creed but the insistence on the infallibility of the interpreters that becomes the necessary mechanism of social control. Thus, the

crucial feature of Soviet ideology is not any formal doctrine but the idea of *partiinost'* itself—that Party direction is essential in all fields of work. Only in this way can the Party rationalize the abandonment of once-hallowed doctrines and adopt new doctrines that may have little justification in the old dogma.

In the Soviet Union the legitimacy of Communist rule derives in great measure from the claim of the Party to know the truth and direction of history. But, as Zbigniew Brzezinski has asked, what is the role of the Party in a technical-managerial society; more specifically, what is the role of the pure Party functionary—the *apparatchik?* He has no functional role in such a society, whether technically competent in industry or as an administrator in government.

In the formative years of Soviet society the role of the Party was solidary (through "Bolshevik man" to provide a coherent social identity), ideological (to formulate goals for the future and to rationalize changes in doctrine), instructional (to train elites and supply the cadres to replace the bourgeois elements), and regulative (to set up a "control apparatus" to push and prod functionaries in other sectors). In the army, for example, Party men long served as "political commissars." But the system of "dual power" was inherently unworkable, and the purely political officer has been withdrawn; the Party "trusts" the higher army officer, as a Party member, but his primary role is that of the army man. In factories today few successful managers listen to the *obkom* Party secretary as a guide or controller. At the top of the Party, in fact, more and more of the Party leaders are drawn from among the engineers and technicians rather than, like Khrushchev, from the *apparatchik* cadres. But the question is not just one of social composition, but of structural relations. What role remains for the Party when technical functions begin to predominate, and these are located in technical and governmental institutions?

None of this is meant to suggest that the Party will disappear. Since the society lacks any other mechanism, the Party remains, crucially, as the arena where factions can coalesce to put forward one policy rather than another as decisive for the society. But a role as a decision-*making* center is already different from one as a decision-*administering* center; and in all this the role of the Party—and with

it perhaps, the role of mobilizing ideology—may diminish.

All of these are tendencies; in a complex society their consequences take many years to unfold. But the direction is clear—the breakup, on all levels, of a monolithic society and the consequent fact that different groups will have, as in any diverse society, a differential degree of attachment to and alienation from the society. This does not mean that ideology, in the sense of a formulated creed or an articulated belief system, will disappear. But in the abatement of the *dynamism* of a creed, and the reduction of the role of ideology as a "weapon" against external enemies, it may signify the "end of ideology" in the sense that this polemical idea has been postulated.

THE NEW SOVIET MYTH:
MARX IS DEAD, LONG LIVE COMMUNISM!

ROY D. LAIRD

Eminent theologians in the Christian West for some time now have been taking seriously the argument that 'God is dead'. Indeed, some even imply that He never was. Similarly, the observations made concerning the current status of communist ideology in the Soviet Union by such leading scholars as Professors Alfred G. Meyer and Alec Nove are important contributions to a growing assertion among Western scholars that if Marxism-Leninism ever was seriously regarded by USSR leaders as providing the corpus of a secular religion—their

'science of society'—this is no longer the case.

'Are They Really Communist?'

Professor Meyer implies a view that the deterioration of Marxist-Leninist ideology has reached the point of having produced a schizophrenic (he does not use this term) leadership whose 'ideological output' is largely a matter of 'talking to themselves', an act of 'self-deception' that may well have no more impact on Soviet society

Soviet Studies, XVIII, No. 4 (April 1967), 511–18. Reprinted by permission. Footnotes omitted.

than 'American advertising' has on United States citizens. The comparison with American advertising is of value, but does American advertising (and Soviet ideological propaganda) really have so little impact upon society? On the contrary, American advertisers spend millions of dollars each year employing Pavlovian techniques so successfully that manufacturers who do not employ such methods find they cannot compete in the national market. Of course, the American consumer does exercise some selectivity among the products advertised; so undoubtedly does the Soviet citizen exercise a selectivity among the items of Soviet ideological propaganda, but in the USSR, too, the ideological advertisers have created a virtual monopoly over the market. Moreover, the latter is a market that cannot be dispensed with since common beliefs are the essential strands for binding a society together in peaceful relationships. No society ever has become stable without evolving a common public myth.

There is little quarrel over the particular observations set forth by either Professor Meyer or Professor Nove. Moreover, one can agree with the implication by both gentlemen that if Communist dogma ever was a rigid ideological guideline for Soviet leaders' actions, this no longer is the case. Marx is dead! Indeed, the probable date of the fatality was the end of the 'honeymoon of the revolution' in early 1918, and Lenin was the executioner. Lenin's highly pragmatic political sense, coupled with the early discovery that utopia could not be realized just because a society had experienced a revolution in the name of Marxism, surely inspired a growing awakening that Communist doctrine is an insufficient guideline for organizing and

managing society. Yet such arguments can be carried too far.

Rejecting repeated Soviet assertions of doctrinal fealty, one should resist the tendency of swinging to the opposite extreme and attempting to impose a standard of rigid adherence to doctrine upon the Communist that has not been observable in other belief systems. God may never have been, but, at least since the Reformation, devout Christians have openly quarrelled over the content of their dogma. Indeed, the very churchmen who today join the argument that God is dead do so while simultaneously expressing a conviction that facing up to new reality will help to strengthen the church. While a modern theologian may believe that Christ was mortal, he also believes that Christ's ministry was inspired teaching that still provides the best possible direction for human relationships. Left out by too many atheist and un-Marxian critics alike is an adequate accounting for the reality that in all times men, by necessity, have been believing animals, forced by their emotions to create personal and social myth systems which may or may not be scientifically verifiable, but which do provide the tentative answers and guidelines necessary for coping with the problems of life. As the psychiatrist Jung observed, these myths (his term, 'the great religions') have always been essential for the preservation of individual sanity. Moreover, when key elements of such myths are collectively shared by the members of a society, the warp and woof of meaningful communication is supplied from which the fabric of a community or nation can be woven. When serious disagreements over beliefs arise among segments of a society, the seeds of revolution are sown.

In his previous writings, Professor Nove correctly pointed out that there were important economic reasons for Stalinist terror, yet the most important (though unspoken) reason of all behind Stalin's method of rule may have been that fear was the key ingredient that allowed the Bolshevik leadership to hold the potentially revolutionary elements of Soviet society at bay, until a new society-binding myth of Soviet nationalism could be created. By 1953, enough of the strands of a new belief system had been created for Soviet society not to fly apart when Stalin's successors abandoned terror as a key element of Soviet rule.

Western social scientists need to spend more time identifying the strands of the new Soviet nationalism. Nevertheless, there is enough evidence at this point to conclude that the key sources of the new myth are traditional Russian nationalism (largely let back in by Stalin during World War II), Marxist-Leninist doctrines, and axioms derived from the pragmatic lessons of Soviet success.

Undoubtedly, the party leadership is disturbed by such findings as that of a recent survey of a representative agricultural area where 57% of the ordinary collective farm members were found to have icon corners in their homes. (However, in the homes of the skilled agricultural workers, only 7% had such icons.) Evidently, something like half of the rural society (perhaps the most dissident segment of Soviet life) gives evidence of having evolved a new belief system. Moreover, even among those who retain their icons, there is reason to assume that important elements of the Communist propaganda have been absorbed. After all, Western anthropologists have repeatedly discovered that among once-pagan peoples converted to Christianity there almost always exists an amalgam of beliefs in which the old gods still play an important part. More to the present point, the extensive Harvard interviews of early post-World War II Soviet émigrés revealed that even among this most disenchanted element from Soviet society a remarkable number of Communist values were carried over into their new lives.

Again today, as in Tsarist times, there is evidence of widespread dissent among the intellectuals, as expressed in private conversations and the underground circulation of manuscripts. Here again, however, the careful observer will discover that not all the new Soviet values are being discarded. Indeed, a favourite theme seems to be an agonizing over the failure of the leadership to live up to the ideology's promises. Any society's patterns of belief must be altered if the challenge of changing circumstances is to be met, but where is the example of a society, that, without a prolonged and bloody revolution, engaged in a wholesale abandonment of the beliefs championed by its political élite for as long as half a century?

Certainly, in 1917 only a small number of revolutionaries subscribed to Bolshevism. However, the area of common Marxist belief, not only between the Bolsheviks and Mensheviks, but among most of the revolutionary groups was impressive. Surely the Soviet ideology has been transformed, but hardly to the point of becoming relatively meaningless as implied by Professor Meyer. He concludes that the 'Soviet leaders do believe in communism as they understand it', yet, he asks, 'are they really Communist?' Can Soviet society be expected to take Marxism-Leninism lightly when, in but a half-century, the leadership has guided the transformation of backward Tsarist Russia into the world's second major power, all in the name of the ideology? Moreover, with all the serious failings in the system, and the inhuman sacrifices imposed by Stalin, the lot of the individual citizen has improved. Can the beliefs that sponsored the sacrifices for improvement be repudiated or easily forgotten? Undoubtedly, both the doctrinal rigidity and certain specific elements of the earlier doctrine are now privately doubted by many if not most of the citizens and leaders alike. Yet, short of another revolution, Khrushchev surely was right in asserting that the Soviet Union will abandon communism 'when shrimps learn to whistle'.

Perhaps the academic's relative isolation from his own society, plus the scholar's laudable tendency to struggle against falsely rooted social myths in his own society, may tend to insensitize the Western intellectuals to what may be happening both at home and in Soviet society. Specifically, Professor Meyer writes, 'but as a mere ritual, [Communist] ideology will tend to be almost as removed from actual life and its activities as Sunday sermons'. Sunday sermons, in American churches, have been increasingly dealing with such things as business ethics, civil rights and personal relationships, and less with biblical dogma. As piously removed from intellectual reality as many (perhaps most) such dissertations may seem to be for many academics, this observer is persuaded that the Sunday sermon serves as a vital reinforcement for the average communicant's personal and social myth. This writer is a practising atheist-agnostic (a Unitarian), but an interest in beliefs led to pursuit of religious discussions

with intelligent acquaintances who regularly attend traditional churches. Perhaps the most common answer is that much of the strength of such people's ties with their church is due to the ability of their particular minister to express in his sermons a meaningful discussion of problems that they face in their lives. For the churchgoer, Sunday morning may well comprise the major confrontation he has with his own and society's emotional problems. Perhaps the people's courts, and even some factory party lectures, provide a similar social catharsis in Soviet society.

A colleague recently suggested that Khrushchev's secret speech not only destroyed the deity of Stalin, but since so much of Soviet history had been Stalin's brand of Marxist-Leninism, the ideology may well have been destroyed as well. Perhaps, but if Stalin's wrathful, Old Testament Marxism is dead, what is the new social myth that has taken its place? Soviet ideology may be undergoing radical change, yet now that the flames of the conflagration created by Khrushchev's speech are dying down, the new corpus of Soviet beliefs that is emerging may prove to be striking similar to the old phoenix.

'Ideology Cannot Determine What They Do'

Professor Nove's negation of any positive impact of ideology upon agricultural policy is convincing. He documents his argument that economic or political reasons were more compelling than ideological considerations in the examples of agricultural decision-making that are cited, thus maintaining that, at best, ideology has had only a 'negative' influence, merely limiting the range of possible decisions.

Perhaps, however, decision-making may be more complex than Professor Nove seems to indicate. In discussing the most crucial of all Soviet agricultural decisions, Professor Nove is quite correct in noting that Stalin used a 'lie' in attempting to prove Leninist support for forced collectivization. However, as this writer has documented elsewhere, while a review of Lenin's writings will show that he repeatedly argued that collectivization could be satisfactorily achieved only by persuasion, i.e., *sans* coercion, he also emphasized that the need to adopt large-scale, collective and mechanized agriculture constituted an 'indisputable theoretical truth'. True, collectivization offered Stalin an attractive economic promise for extracting from the peasantry the necessary capital for industrialization, but noting that Stalin was stupid enough to lie about Lenin's views on the use of force does not prove the lack of doctrinal imperative that sooner or later agriculture must be in some way collectivized. Had Lenin lived another score of years without bringing the peasant majority of society into some form of a collective system, such a failure surely would have destroyed any meaningful argument that the new system was building communism.

As implied earlier, a closer look at the evolving Soviet agricultural myth will reveal roots in the growing amalgam of pragmatic experience, traditional nationalism and Marxist-Leninist doctrine. For example, the tradition of the *mir*, the commune, and the very village way of life was so strong that important distinctions existed between Russian peasant culture and that of the more individualistic Western farmers. Marx was not all wrong in seeing parallels between Communist prognostications and Russian rural experience.

Professor Nove is probably right in asserting that for every major agricultural decision economic or political explanations can be found. However, does the demonstrable presence of such rationale prove that material or power considerations always have provided the prime motivation in decision-making? Is it not possible that for even the non-Marxist the more tangible nature of economic and power factors may make them seem to be important out of proportion to reality? The following incomplete list contains examples wherein such relatively tangible explanations seem so weak, or where the actions taken seem to be so contrary to the alternatives which a relatively objective outsider might have selected as best serving the needs of the system, that Soviet myths must be credited with having provided the primary motivating factor:

1. Professor Nove rightly argues that if ideology were the prime determinant of policy the more ideologically pure state farms should have been created in the beginning rather than a system predominantly made up of collective farms. Yet, in the early years Stalin did set up huge 'state grain factories' which failed. Furthermore, although the asserted ideological superiority of the *sovkhozy* over the *kolkhozy* has been played down somewhat in the post-Stalin years, there is still indication of a widespread belief among the party leaders that the *sovkhozy* are at least somewhat closer to the ultimate agricultural form. However, when state subsidies and other preferences given to the *sovkhozy* are allowed for, there remains no indication that the *sovkhozy* have been more efficient than the *kolkhozy* as production units. Furthermore, not since

the heavy infusion of the party into the collectives in the 1950s has there been any indication that state farms are more politically responsive than collectives. Yet, precisely in the post-1950 period the *sovkhozy* have been greatly expanded, much (but not all) of which has been at the expense of the *kolkhozy*. What more satisfactory explanation of this phenomenon is there than that belief largely has guided the decision makers?

2. Both the size of the farms and the size of the brigades as work units can be explained up to a point by the need for controls over the peasants and their product. However, particularly in face of evidence indicating a much higher level of efficiency of the small *zveno* work units, there is hardly any compelling economic argument that the other extreme, the present huge brigades (probably averaging over 100 individuals), is the most desirable form of organizing the work. A review of the evolution of both the farms and the brigades into ever larger units supports the conclusion that agricultural gigantomania—rooted both in Marxian and traditional Russian beliefs—has been the primary motivating factor.

3. A combination of the authoritarian leadership's insatiable seeking of ever tighter controls, along with Stalin's decision to concentrate virtually all effort on industrial growth, was probably behind many of the post-World War II rural administrative reforms. Will such factors, however, account for either the frequency of the reforms or the fact that each time such reforms were announced the leadership indulged in grandiose predictions of success, thereby exposing themselves to later criticism because of failure? Of course, the Western observer would be partially right in answering, 'But this was a form of irrationality. Have not Khrushchev's successors finally admitted that agriculture has long needed a substantial increase in investment?' Irrationality, however, is the point. Since science cannot provide men with all the needed answers, other less supportable elements of the web

of belief must fill in. Surely, many attitudes towards rural reforms can be explained only by the leadership's conviction that the *kolkhoz-sovkhoz* system really is superior; therefore if only the magic formula of ordering local (and local-central) relationships can be found, the system will achieve the Communist promise.

4. Finally, in our opinion, the most important of all the myths that must be regarded as having a positive influence over Soviet agricultural decisions is a belief or attitude, fashioned from a wedding of scientism and the asserted science of Marxism-Leninism, which reached a peak in Lysenkoism. Surely there is a basis for worry over the growth of scientism in the West—i.e., the widespread hope that just as the natural scientists have used their mathematical disciplines to build super weapons and produce wonder drugs, so such precise techniques can be employed to solve the major problems of human relations. Yet, in addition to the optimism in the West there is a long tradition of religious and philosophical scepticism involving a belief that there are limits both to the knowable and to human achievement because man is not perfect.

In contrast, communism is dominated by faith in material and human perfectibility. Perhaps most of the present Soviet leaders no longer believe in the utopian dream of communism, but the over-optimistic belief in the promise of progress seems to remain. Lysenkoism may at last be laid to rest, but all the extravagant promises of science for agriculture are not. For example, the asserted decisive advantages to be gained from a wholesale adoption in agriculture of manufacturing production processes and industrial administrative forms comprised one of Lenin's major claims as a scientist of administration. From his time to the present not only has there persisted a belief that the industrial experiences are wholly adaptable to agriculture, but also that when such a marriage has been successfully consummated, the union will unleash an exploitation of scientific discoveries that will result in a growth in agricultural production rivalling the rates of growth achieved by industry. Perhaps the Soviet adherents of scientism are right, but such views are not in line with those of Western agricultural authorities who point to the relative limitations on rates of food production growth. For example, although undoubtedly there are outer limits on the number of pins a factory can produce, when the plant area is confined to only one hectare of land, modern machinery, when compared with human hands, can multiply the rate of output by the million. In comparison, a hectare that had been producing only some ten centners of grain, even if put under glass and tilled with the use of all known scientific aids, could not be induced to increase its output by as much as ten times.

Undoubtedly, if confronted with such a statement of the relative promise of dimensions of growth, the individual Soviet agricultural scientist (even the individual party leader) would admit its validity. Yet, the past and present record leads one to expect a stress upon the promise science holds for food production that is out of proportion to similar expectations in the West.

What do we conclude? This writer recalls Professor Nove's apt description of the Soviet Union as the 'most highly industrialized of the underdeveloped nations'. The descriptive term used here is Soviet nationalism. The emotional fires of nationalism seem to be more intense than ever before in the present world, especially in the new developing states which are struggling to achieve a social identity that will peacefully cement the dissident elements of their societies together. When compared with most of the new nations, the Soviet Union is ahead both in industry and in evolving a meaningful web of beliefs. Furthermore, these beliefs are probably more important, more passionately held, and yet more passionately doubted in the USSR, than in the more stable Western societies. After a half century of Communist rule, the official party ideology cannot claim a monopoly over Soviet beliefs. Nevertheless, for any foreseeable future Marxism—Leninism cannot be ignored as a vital (perhaps the most important) source of the Soviet public myth.

SOCIAL STRUCTURE AND POLITICAL POWER
IN THE SOVIET SYSTEM

VERNON V. ASPATURIAN

In all social systems a profound relationship exists between the social structure of society and the political dynamics of the system, irrespective of formal institutions and processes. The Soviet Union is no exception to this rule, although the relationship between the social structure in Soviet society and its political processes are in many ways *sui generis*. In the systematic analysis of the power structure of a given society and its relationship to the hierarchy of social groups, one is almost always confronted with a social order which has been in existence for some time and the precise relationship between power and society has been obscured by the passage of time and complicated by the reciprocal feedback between the political system and the social order it serves. The Soviet social order offers a unique opportunity to examine a developing social system whose beginnings are within the memory of living generations and has yet to run its course and stabilize itself along more or less permanent lines. Historically we know how the Soviet system came about; how the social order was transformed in response to preconceived ideological norms and objectives; how the state and party have calculatedly engineered the social system into what it is today. During the first four decades of its existence, the Soviet social order was at the mercy of essentially voluntaristic political and ideological forces, although increasingly the emerging social system spasmodically fed back influences and pressures which were deterministic or at least quasi-deterministic in their impact. As the Soviet social order achieves its definite configuration, we can expect the political system to increasingly serve as a structure for articulating the interests of crystallizing social groups and to provide a more predictable process for the orderly resolution of interest conflicts into concrete decisions reflecting a consensus among them rather than being simply the instrument of a dominant ideological elite imposing its social norms upon society in response to an alleged historical imperative.

Thus, although the Soviet political system is a creature of the Communist Party which seized power in 1917 and the Soviet social order was shaped by the party from above, the relationship of the party to the social system it created has undergone and is continuing to undergo a fundamental transformation. One of the most intriguing problems involved in relating political power in Soviet society to social and class formations is that whereas politi-

From a paper prepared for delivery at the 1963 Annual Meeting of the American Political Science Association, New York City, Commodore Hotel, September 4–7, 1963.

The paper has been reprinted in its entirety in U.S. House of Representatives, Committee on Foreign Affairs, Subcommittee on Europe, Hearings—*Recent Developments in the Soviet Bloc*—Part II, (88th Congress, 2nd Session). Reprinted by permission of the author. Footnotes omitted.

cal power is in fact highly centralized and identifiable in certain personalities operating through defined political institutions, the social foundations of political power and their impact on the political process remain elusive, fluid, and nebulous. To say that power is lodged in the Communist Party and specifically in its central organs, while transparently true, contributes little to an understanding of the social configurations of power. To proceed further and assert that the party reflects the articulated interests of the intelligentsia and legitimizes the distribution of power among the elites within the intelligentsia is equally true, but no less deficient in establishing the social sources of power in the Soviet system.

Much of the difficulty stems from the historical fact that the social groups which dominate and benefit from the existing Soviet social order are not those which shaped Soviet society to conform to their interests, but rather were themselves the products of the system. The Soviet system did not evolve spontaneously and erratically in response to fortuitous events and forces in a mechanistic way as was the case in previous social orders, but rather was calculatedly molded and shaped—a process which is still continuing, in contrast to other existing social systems, whose basic character has been shrouded by the mists of time and obscured by successive overlays of myth, legend, and rationalization.

Thus, while it is indisputable that the Soviet intelligentsia, which is the principal beneficiary of the existing Soviet order and is the social formation from which Soviet decision makers and power holders are recruited, came into being as a social class after the Communist Party and the Soviet state were

established, it is also equally clear that the Soviet intelligentsia bears an ineluctable sociohistorical relationship to the Bolsheviks who seized power in 1917.

Historically, power was seized by an organized group, the Bolsheviks, in a limited armed insurrection through intuitive reliance upon a part of the working class as its main social base, with the larger peasantry as a secondary source of social support. The social power provided by these two social classes was acquired in return for definite promises made by the Bolsheviks which accorded with the fundamental interests and aspirations of these two deprived social groups in Russian society. This social power was direct, raw, crude, primitive and amorphous, yet sufficiently effective when manipulated by individuals skilled in organization and agitation and having an intuitive flair for grasping the essentials of power in a disorganized society. The crude and direct power of the masses prevailed because the refined, intricately complex and fragile instruments of rule upon which a small ruling class must rely in order to keep large and amorphous masses of humanity under control had been shattered by a power external to society itself in a violent war. The middle class, who first surged to fill the resultant power vacuum, constituted the main social prop of the provisional government, but its social interests were not sufficiently broad to accommodate those of the workers and peasants. Since it was numerically small as well, it also required for the preservation of its power access to refined instruments of rule which could not be readily fashioned because of the military and economic conditions which prevailed. It could rely on the direct and crude power of the masses only by striking compromises which it was either unwilling or incapable of making and thus could not muster sufficient social support to preserve its authority.

The Bolshevik Party can be viewed in retrospect as the embryonic manifestation of what was to become the future Soviet intelligentsia, emerging after power, first as the party apparatus, which then expanded and proliferated into various social elites as a consequence of its interaction with other social groups in Soviet society. Although it was the self-appointed advanced detachment of the working class and the self-proclaimed paternalistic custodian of the interests of the Soviet peasantry, it was in actuality a distinct and separate social formation, with its own interests and aspirations, separate from those of the social classes over which it exercised a unilaterally assumed leadership disguised as a "dictatorship of the proletariat." It did not constitute a "ruling class" in the sociohistorical sense but resembled more a potential "ruling class" as described by Gaetano Mosca:

The ruling class may also be vanquished and destroyed in whole or in part by foreign invasions, or, when the circumstances just mentioned arise, it may be driven from power by the advent of new social elements who are strong in fresh political forces. Then, naturally, there comes a period of renovation, or, if one prefers, of revolution, during which individual energies have free play and certain individuals, more passionate, more energetic, more intrepid or merely shrewder than others, force their way from the bottom of the social ladder to the top-most rungs. . . . When social life begins in such environments, there is no readymade ruling class, and while such a class is in the process of formation, admittance to it is gained very easily.

II

According to Marxist doctrine, however, a ruling class is defined in terms of its ownership of the means of production and that once private ownership in the means of production is disestablished, the economic basis for a division of society into ruling and exploited social classes vanishes and with it the class struggle as well. By vesting ownership of the means of production in society, initially in the form of public or state ownership, new social relations of production would arise in which a ruling class would be functionally superfluous and empirically impossible since private ownership of the means of production would be rendered legally inaccessible and ethically impermissible.

The most conspicuous characteristic of the Soviet social order is that it is the first social system in history in which private ownership of property is not a major foundation or source of either social or political power. In all preceding civilized social systems, whether slave-holding, feudal, or capitalist in character, private property has been a major, and in some cases the paramount, source of social and political power and a basis for the stratification of society into social classes and groups. "Property," Clinton Rossiter observes, "is power," and in the words of Sidney Hook, "That property which gives power over land, instruments of production, and the things that human beings need to live, is power over the human beings who must live by use of them. The more absolute the power over such things, the more absolute the power over people."

The interests of the Bolsheviks, however, were historically unique in that they were conceived as neither material nor personal in character, but ideological. Thus Lenin and his party did not seize power in order to establish themselves as a new ruling class, and legalize a new redistribution of private property in order to enrich themselves personally and thus preserve a dominant position for their offspring in a new social order. Rather they seized power in order to transform Russia and ultimately the entire world so that it might conform to the apocalyptic norms of Marxist prophecy. They sought to establish what might be described as an ideocratic system, whose closest parallels were the theocracies of the Middle Ages and classical antiquity. The party was to rule, not as a distinct social class, but as a priestly elite with exclusive custody over the keys to the future.

Alongside private ownership of the means of livelihood as a social source of political power other social foundations for political leverage have always existed in society. These include specialized knowledge, intelligence, certain skills and talents, physical strength, association with symbols of legitimacy, and even good looks and beauty. In social systems which permit unequal private accumulation of property and wealth and its transmission from one generation to the next, private ownership of property tends to dwarf all other social sources of power since it is more directly connected with the means of livelihood and can be exchanged for the services of those who have access to other sources of power. These various social resources of power are not mutually exclusive and are most effectively used in combination with one

another. Over the long run, however, particularly in stabilized societies, private property becomes the dominant, most reliable and decisive source of power and individuals whose sources of power are other than ownership of property increasingly endeavor to transmute this type of power into ownership of property. Throughout history, individuals and groups have used their knowledge, intelligence, skills, and talents to accumulate private property, since not only is it most readily transformed into other forms of power, but is cumulative in its effects as well.

In Soviet society where private ownership of the means of livelihood is legally proscribed and where definite limitations are imposed upon the accumulation of any kind of property or tangible material wealth, private property has been eliminated as a social source of power. This is also becoming increasingly true of some underdeveloped countries where private ownership of the means of production is severely circumscribed. Under these conditions, other traditional social sources of power assume decisive significance in the struggle for control over the means of livelihood, and in particular is this true of functional sources of power such as specialized skills, knowledge and talents.

In the Soviet Union, private ownership of the land and what the Marxists call the means of production, as well as ownership of the media of distribution, communication, transportation and even recreation has been legally abolished and forbidden in favor of a system of total, absolute and permanent public ownership, whether through the state or state-sponsored societies and organizations. All citizens in Soviet society bear an identical relationship to the instruments of production and the means of livelihood in the sense that they cannot be distinguished as owners and nonowners. This universal relationship to the means of livelihood provides the legal basis for the ideological assertion that the exploitation of man by man has been eradicated in the Soviet system.

While the Soviet system, for the first time in history, has ruptured the venerable and durable connection between private ownership of property and the possession and accumulation of power, there still remains a highly unequal distribution of power based upon the relationship of various social groups to the control of the means of livelihood. Historically, private ownership emerges as one method of control over the means of livelihood and not as the generic source of social and political power as was assumed by Marx and some other writers. In the Soviet Union, ownership of the principal means of production is permanently vested in an institution, the state, or an abstraction, "society," for while the state is a temporary agent, it is, in fact, the executive and administrative arm of the Communist Party. Control of the party assures control of the state and through it control of the land, the economic establishment, the coercive instruments of society (the armed forces, police, courts, and legal system), the means of transportation, distribution, and communications.

Control of the party, however, is not governed by law, for it flourishes outside and above the framework of legality, which is its creation, but rather is governed by its own inner rules and the primordial canons of power politics. When control of the party changes hands, there is a corresponding turnover and rotation of personalities in the state apparatus as well, which is invariably followed by changing patterns of control over rewards and priorities in the distribution of the fruits of production.

All Soviet legality is thus bound up with the processes and institutions of the state and remains a somewhat intact and self-contained unit, with no rupture of legal continuity or relations, even though control of the party itself may at any given moment remain an object of strife and struggle. The struggle for power is thus conducted outside the structure of the law, institutions, and processes of the state, although of course the latter may become involved as instruments of the struggle itself. Irrespective of the course and outcome of the struggle, ownership of the means of production is never an object of the struggle for power, for ownership remains permanently vested in the state and there is never a redistribution of ownership but only of control. While power vacuums are inevitable in the Soviet system, the possibilities of legal vacuums or lapses of authority are reduced to a minimum, and in any event ownership of property cannot become a source of political power in the Soviet order. The state, for example, is not employed for the purpose of transferring ownership of property from one hand to another or from the state to private possession, or for the purpose of facilitating the accumulation of private property by various individuals or social groups through manipulation of the legal system, or for preserving the existing pattern of property distribution among private individuals and groups of society.

The animating interests of the Bolsheviks were ideological, in the sense that they sought power in order to transform the social order in accordance with predetermined social norms, masquerading as the interests of the working class. An ideological interest, however, no matter how tenaciously held or powerful a motivating force in order to preserve itself as a viable political force must coincide with the material interest of some social formation in society. As long as the immediate interests of the workers and peasants fortuitously coincided with the ideological interests of the party, these two groups constituted its social foundations of power. Once the ideological interests of the party deviated from the more mundane and earthly interests of the masses as social groups—not as abstract historical conceptions—a hiatus soon developed betwen the interests of the party and the immediate interests of the workers and peasants.

The survival of the party and the integrity of ideological goals were now threatened by the very disorder and chaos which it had taken advantage of to seize power, and the social basis of party rule was gradually shifted to new social forces being created as a consequence of the transformation of society itself—social forces, whose tangible interests were more in tune with the ideological goals of the party. The power potential of the working class was nullified by destroying the trade unions as an autonomous social force and subordinating them to the control of the party apparatus, which effectively deprived the working class of its historical instrument of power, the strike. The traditional power lever of the peasantry was control over the food supply; this was effectively nullified by the liquidation of the kulaks as a social force and the collectivization of the farms. To this day, the only form of association permitted the working class is the trade union, while the only form of organization permitted

the peasantry is the collective farm, both of which are dominated from alien social elements recruited from the intelligentsia. Shifting the social foundations of party rule required in effect a "second revolution," or "revolution from above." The new social force upon which the party relied was the intelligentsia, which was spawned by the party and proliferated in response to the industrialization and modernization of Russia. As the intelligentsia expanded and diversified, given increasingly greater privileges and rewards in return for its support and loyalty to the system, it was increasingly assimilated into the party structure. The social foundations of the Soviet system were correspondingly strengthened and broadened, but in the process, these new privileged elites within the intelligentsia crystallized into amorphous yet distinct functional interest constellations with outlooks which were discretely at variance with one another yet compatible with the Soviet system as a whole and generally united in their interests as opposed to those of the working class and collective farm peasantry. The numerical growth and functional diversification of the intelligentsia and its accelerated enrollment into the party resulted in correspondingly reducing the numerical proportion of the party apparatus within the party, and enabled them to articulate their social interests more forcefully within the political structure. These new elites threatened to become separate sources of social and political leverage which might challenge the supremacy of the apparatus for control of the party. Stalin dealt with this threat by further co-opting members of these elites into the apparatus itself and periodically purging the intelligentsia, producing an artificially induced rapid upward social mobility for younger members of the intelligentsia and the more vigorous and ambitious elements in the peasantry and working class. This artificially induced circulation of sub-elites strengthened the hold of Stalin and the apparatus but at the expense of unsettling the Soviet system as a whole and thus could serve only as a temporary device at best. The elites continued to grow numerically, while their role and function became increasingly critical in the operation of a complex industrial society. Their challenge to the party apparatus for a share of power commensurate with the importance of the social functions which they performed in Soviet society continued as they sought to transform social privileges granted to them by the apparatus into absolute social rights independent of the whims of the apparatus.

Although the intelligentsia is the most important social formation in Soviet society, its existence is still considered to be purely transitory, for it is destined for automatic self-liquidation once the distinctions between physical and mental labor wither away in an advanced stage of communism. Accordingly, Stalin in 1935, rejected a proposal that the intelligentsia be mentioned in the constitution along with the working class and peasantry on grounds that "the intelligentsia has never been a class, and never can be a class—it was and remains a stratum." This remains the current official view and constitutes a source of anxiety and uneasiness for the intelligentsia. As a social group, neither its status and privileges nor its very existence is safeguarded in law. It can be assumed that renewed pressure will be exerted to provide it with juridical recognition in the new constitution so that the legal organization of Soviety society will reflect more realistically the role of the intelligentsia in the social order and in the power structure of the Communist Party.

III

Thus, during the party's nearly five-decade existence as a ruling structure, it has not only transformed the social order but has been fundamentally transformed itself by the very social forces which it brought into being. Broadly speaking, there have been four distinct phases in the evolution and transformations of the party since its inception as a separate entity in 1903.

During the first phase of its development, the party was a semi-illegal revolutionary organization seeking to seize power on a more or less monopolistic basis, independently from other revolutionary parties and organizations with which it was engaged in ideological conflict. The basic psychological and operational configurations of the party were shaped during this period and the prime personality characteristic demanded of party members was idealistic, fanatical, and monolithic devotion to the purposes and objectives of Marxism as interpreted by Lenin. The prototype of the Bolshevik during this period was the brilliant intellectual revolutionary with a consuming passion for action in the interests of social justice.

The party entered into its second phase after the seizure of power in 1917, when it was transformed from a semi-illegal conspiratorial organization seeking to seize power into the only legal political instrument in society, whose primary function was to maintain power against all internal and external challenges to its authority.

During this period, the party was inevitably divided into factions and cliques over questions of ideology, policy, and personalities. Only the massive prestige of Lenin kept the party together during the early stages of the second phase, but with his death the party was further transformed as an arena of struggle between various factions and cliques for supremacy. During this stage of the second phase, factions were entirely intraparty in character and were relatively isolated from social groups and the population at large. The political process at this stage had very little relationship to the social order, which was in a state of transition and imminent convulsion.

During the second phase of its development, the first discrete intraparty group emerged as a power instrument distinct from the party itself, yet a part of it—the party apparatus. With the victory of Stalin and the emergence of the party apparatus as the chief instrument whereby to control the party and manipulate its symbols of legitimacy and authority, the party entered into is third phase. During its third phase, covering roughly the years of the Stalinist primacy, 1928–53, the party itself was reduced to an instrument of the party apparatus, which in turn was subservient to Stalin. During this era, it was converted into a vehicle of social transformation, economic modernization, and cultural progress. The industrialization and modernization of Russia created a new social order, out of which new social groupings and elites emerged, armed with special skills, knowledge and techniques, which were assimilated into the structure of the party but not necessarily into the party apparatus. Under the impact of social change, the party apparatus itself split into various factions and cliques and monolithic control was assured only after Stalin purged all potential opponents in and out of the apparatus within the party.

While the purges delayed the political transformations which were inexorably dictated by the social changes wrought in Soviet society, these new elites and emergent interest constellations created distinct, but not independent, potential power structures which might rival that of the party apparatus for control of the party and hence of political power in the Soviet system. The party apparatus under Stalin became an instrument for maintaining the subservience of these new potential loci of power, although he skillfully employed one apparatus against the other by devious juggling of personalities and policies.

The structure of power and the party's role in it under Stalin was roughly as follows: Stalin controlled the party apparatus and through it the party, into whose leading organs the leaders of the emerging elites were coopted, kept under surveillance, and thus reduced to subservience. These parallel power structures, the state bureaucracy, the economic-managerial bureaucracy, the armed forces, the police, and the cultural elites, each had its own division of labor in regulating and controlling the social system as a whole. The apparatus had its representatives in all of these groups, through its network of party cells, secretaries, and political administrations, while the apparatus itself was in turn checked by agents of the secret police, as were the other structures.

Stalin stood at the apex of this structure of power as secretary-general of the party, chairman of the council of ministers and generalissimo of the armed forces, thus combining in his person direct control over the party, state, and military establishments.

During his later, but by no means declining, years, these potential centers of power, whose development had been stultified by Stalin's repressive measures were clearly crystallizing into semiautonomous entities, with their own intra-organizational cliques, which would make informal alliances and associations with rival cliques emerging in other organizations, to create a bewildering pattern of artificially frustrated political behavior, since this activity was outside the bounds of legality. But the old dictator had not yet lost his touch. The institution of the purge, his reputation for ruthlessness and instantaneous decisiveness, his irrational suspicions, and his astute manipulation of personalities, cliques, and organizations had performed efficiently in the past. A purge now and then at lower levels and high, in the center and the periphery; an execution here a "suicide" there, coupled with a few conspicuous "disappearances"; the periodic rotation of personnel, and the exploitation of the greed, vanity and ambitions of his subordinates resulted in a system of terror from which no one was immune. The Soviet system, by the time of Stalin's death in March 1953, had become a frozen social monolith, a monstrous leviathan on the threshold of devouring its second generation in the form of a new blood purge being conspicuously hatched in clear public view, the infamous "doctor's plot" of January 1953, which, according to Khrushchev, was part of a plan designed to set the stage for "the future annihilation of the old Political Bureau members."

The death of Stalin lifted the incubus of terror under which Soviet so-ciety was smoldering and these new social formations shaped in the crucibles of the Soviet system emerged to engage in rivalry with the party apparatus for control of the party, its symbols of legitimacy and authority, and to make known their will and demands upon other groups. Thus, in the fourth and current phase of its development, beginning in 1953, the party is being transformed into a crucible of conflict and resolution, out of which emerges policies and decisions reflecting whatever equilibrium exists among various factions, cliques and groups within the party's higher organs, which continue to pursue their political aims within the party and not outside. The struggle is not against the party but for its control or a share in its control.

Contrary to current Soviet views, the post-Stalin factions in the party do not simply represent differences over ideology or policy of a personal nature, which was more characteristic of factional conflicts during the early years of the Soviet regime, but rather they reflect the profound social differentiation which has developed in the Soviet system and the different ways in which various social groups perceive their interests, role, and function in Soviet society in relation to other social constellations. While this explanation of factional conflict in the party is vehemently denied by Soviet authorities, there is much implied in Soviet behavior which more than suggests that Soviet leaders are aware that factional differences in the party find their source in the social structure of Soviet society. The most important indication of this realistic assessment is the decision to retain the ban on factional activity in the new party rules. This is justified on the grounds that ideological penetration from the outside and psychological survivals of the past are remaining residual sources of factionalism in the party. Thus F. R. Kozlov's justification for the retention of the ban against factions is much more significant for what it denies than it affirms:

Under present circumstances, need the statutes contain any formal guarantees against factionalism and clique activity? Yes ... such guarantees are needed. To be sure, there is no social base left in Soviet society that could free opportunistic currents in the party. But the sources of ideological waverings on the part of particular individuals or groups have not yet been entirely eliminated. Some persons may fall under the influence of bourgeois propaganda from the outside. Others having failed to comprehend the dialectics of society's development and having turned ... into dying embers, will have nothing to do with anything new and go on clinging to old dogmas that have been toppled by life.

IV

Differences and conflicts within the party arise as a result of both personal ambitions for power and conflict over doctrine and policy, which increasingly reflect the experiences, functional orientation and interests of various elites in the Soviet system. Personal rivalries and conflicts over doctrine and policy are so intricately interwoven that attempts to isolate distinctions between the two are bound to be a sterile exercise. The rival cliques within the party hierarchy which had taken shape during Stalin's later years, and may have indeed been encouraged by him so as to play off subordinates against one another, evolved into factions, each with its own aspirations, policies, and social foundations of power outside the party structures.

Contrary to the official Soviet view that factions within the party do not arise from social conflicts within Soviet society but are rather the deviationary expressions of personalities seeking power, it is at once obvious that factions could neither arise nor flourish unless they received sustenance and nourishment from powerful social forces in Soviet society. Just as party factions do not organize themselves into separate political organizations challenging the supremacy of the party for political power, so social groups with their own interests and functional orientation do not constitute themselves into separate social bodies demanding formal representation in the party, but rather seek to make their demands upon other groups as formless clusters of vested interests.

Within the context of Marxist-Leninist ideology a social group with its own distinctive interests can only be a social class with economic interests that conflict with the interests of other classes. After the revolution, the interests of the working class alone, as determined by the party, were considered to be legitimate and the interests of other classes were suppressed pending their ultimate annihilation as social formations. Factional groupings within the party were ascribed by Stalin to the attempts of classes slated for oblivion to worm themselves into the party, while deviations were described as ideological expressions of these class interests articulated through the party. In 1936, Stalin proclaimed that class conflicts in Soviet society had been eradicated, but he continued to recognize the existence of separate social classes, whose interests had merged into a single identity. The Communist Party was verbally transformed from a party representing only the interests of the working class into one representing the transcendental interests of all Soviet social classes. Consequently, Soviet ideology and party doctrine continue to deny the legitimacy of competing interest groups and refuse to tolerate their autonomous existence. In Soviet jargon, a social group which develops interests which deviate from that of the party is an incipient hostile class; the faction that represents it in the party is an embryonic party within a party; its articulated views on policy and doctrine constitute an ideological deviation. Yet, even this is no longer sufficient, since current party mythology insists that even the social foundations for factions within the party no longer exist in the Soviet system, but since they do in fact exist, they must represent, in the words of Khrushchev, "dying embers . . . which go on clinging to old dogmas that have been toppled by life."

Separate social groups with their own distinctive interests, however, continue to flourish in Soviet society, but in conformity with neither the doctrinaire and contrived contours of 19th century Marxism, nor entirely with the synthetic social groups which have received official sanction. The collective farm peasantry and the working classes constitute the numerically preponderant groups in Soviet society, but they are effectively decapitated politically and cannot directly articulate their views or interests in the Soviet political process. The social groups in Soviet society who are actively involved in the political process and whose views are articulated through the party do not

follow the artificial social configurations of Soviet ideology. Rather, in accordance with the unique dynamics of the Soviet social system, these groups find their social differentiation within a single recognized social group, the intelligentsia, which is denied the status of a class in Soviet ideology and is euphemistically called a stratum.

Although the Soviet intelligentsia is a variegated congeries of differentiated elites, they all have a common desire to perpetuate the Soviet system from which they have sprung and in which they benefit as privileged groups. Within this broad common framework of interests, however, these elites are concerned preeminently with the social status of their own group within the Soviet social system and they seek to shape doctrine and policy to assume the contours of their own special interests reflecting their own perspective concerning their role and function in Soviet society. They are officially recognized as occupational categories, but they are not officially endowed with either political or social characteristics which can distinguish them from one another. Since they do not enjoy official sanction as interest constellations, they cannot formally organize themselves into political organizations outside the party or as explicit factional groupings within the party, but must exert their influence and make their demands through the Communist Party as amorphous entities. Since they cannot legitimately articulate a separate interest inside or outside the party, they are inevitably forced into competing for control of the party's decision-making organs and its symbols of legitimacy to articulate their interests as those of society as a whole. Because Soviet ideology demands conformity with the official myth that there exists a single monolithic social interest in Soviet society, conflicts among social elites and their factional representatives in the party's leading organs cannot be resolved within an institutionalized framework of political accommodation and compromise, but by a process whereby one interest group or faction asserts its supremacy over the others and imposes its interests as those of society as a whole. In the event one group cannot subdue the others, an uneasy and temporary coexistence ensues, and the party, under the pressures of diverse groups seeking political articulation, becomes a cover for a conglomeration of interests whose incompatibilities are only partially and temporarily obscured by a transparent veneer of "monolithic unity."

What in effect masquerades as the "monolithic" interests of society as a whole is in reality what is characterized as an ideological consensus in other societies. This consensus in the Soviet system, as elsewhere, represents not the common denominator of acceptance embracing all strata in society, but includes only those groups who demonstrate sufficient power and consciousness to enter into the political process and make their influence felt. Just as in a feudal social order, the clear dominance of one social class in society does not preclude conflicts of interests and personal rivalries within the ruling group, so in Soviet society, the fact that the Soviet elites are united in accepting the Soviet social system does not mean that they are united at all times on how status and rewards in the system shall be distributed among both the elite groups and those outside the framework of political activity.

In dissecting the political process in the Soviet system, the basic political actors can be isolated as the elites within the intelligentsia. Their informal organizational expressions within the organs of the party are factions, while divisions and rival groupings within factions can be called cliques. In Soviet parlance, however, factions are characterized as formalized groupings within the party which engage in cabalistic intrigue, conspire to take concerted action within the party, and offer a program and slate of candidates in opposition to those of the official party line. A faction constitutes, in effect, a "disloyal opposition," since a loyal opposition grouping is not yet recognized as legitimate. True enough, some factions may have very little social support, as is officially maintained, and may represent only the views of individual party leaders.

Social classes and interest groups within them in Soviet society have highly uneven opportunities for articulating their interests inside and outside of the party, although all social classes and many subclasses within the intelligentsia are formally recognized as having special interests which are reflected in officially approved institutions, associations, and organizations. Political power in the Soviet system remains largely a monopoly of the intelligentsia, but its distribution among various elites within the intelligentsia is also sharply uneven, and favors those elites which largely coincide with political institutions and are organized into hierarchical structures of power. Unlike the various subclasses within the intelligentsia, none of the subdivisions within the working class or peasantry are permitted separate associational existence. Trade unions are not organized along craft, functional, or horizontal lines, but vertically by enterprises and include managers as well as unskilled workers in the same organization. The only association permitted the peasantry is the collective farm, which is a rural institution designed to control the peasants rather than to articulate their interests.

The working class and peasantry are thus effectively decapitated politically, but they do participate or rather are involved in the political process through ritualized periodic elections to the Soviets, in which they are given the privilege of electing to government positions candidates selected for them by the elites who dominate the party. The proliferation and expansion of interest conflict within the intelligentsia, however, could draw the masses more directly into the political process if the latent power of the workers and peasants could be mobilized to good advantage by one faction or another within the party structure. Once the elites openly compete for the "goodwill" of the peasantry and the workers, it will signify their formal entry into the Soviet political system as active rather than passive actors. Under these conditions, Lenin's perceptive definition of a "revolutionary situation" might be a valid approximation of how the workers and peasants might be drawn more actively into the Soviet political structure:

What are, generally speaking, the characteristics of a revolutionary situation? We can hardly be mistaken when we indicate the following as one of three outstanding signs: (1) it is impossible for the ruling classes to maintain their power unchanged; there is a crisis of the 'upper classes' taking one form or another; there is a crisis in the policy of the ruling class; as a result, there appears a crack through which the dissatisfaction and the indignation of the oppressed masses burst forth ... (I)n consequence of the above ... there is consider-

able increase in the activity of the masses ...who are drawn both by the conditions of the crisis and by '*the upper classes*' *themselves* into independent historic action.

It should be recalled that the power and position of the Communist Party in the Soviet system is unilaterally asserted. It is impossible legally to vote the Communist Party out of power and to disestablish its monopoly or political action. This is entirely outside the framework of formal elections. While government officials may be formally elected by the entire adult population, members of the party are not elected by the electorate, they are co-opted and selected by the party hierarchy. Thus, a wide chasm exists between the power vested in the organs of the party and the electorate which cannot be legally or socially bridged as long as the party is an exclusive and selective organization from which the overwhelming mass of the citizenry is calculatedly excluded. While theoretically, the central decision-making organs of the party represent the will of the party through the system of indirect election of higher bodies by lower institutions, the 9,700,000 party members themselves are not elected by any electorate but are selected and screened by the party organization itself.

The Communist Party is thus not an "open" party nor does it conduct anything like a "primary" election in which the electorate chooses among various nominees for office from within the party. The more than 140 million Soviet voters are excluded from participation in the party and have no votes in the selection of party officials; they can only cast their votes for candidates selected for them by a party from which they are systematically excluded.

The net effect of this practice is to impart to the party a distinctive social configuration which is totally out of focus with the social structure of Soviet society and this distortion becomes increasingly exaggerated as one moves up the party pyramid. The proportion of workers and peasants in the party represents a small fraction of their members in Soviet society and their presence in most instances is more formal than real.

The party, in effect, remains the property and instrumentality of the elites within the intelligentsia, a fact which was given formal affirmation when the party was transformed from a party of the working class into a party of all classes in Soviet society.

V

Interest groups in the Soviet system do not readily lend themselves to ready-made classifications, and in any case must be related to larger social groupings such as social class. Within the three broad social groupings in Soviet society are to be found three types of interest groups—some of which are purely intra-class while others are interclass in character. The party as a whole can no longer be accurately described as an interest group because of its artificial numerical dilution by working class and peasant members, who have little tangible common interests with the intelligentsia aside from vague common ideological bonds. The members of the intelligentsia within the party clearly have more in common with those of the same class outside the party than with the workers and peasants within.

The principal political actors in the Soviet system are four political institutional groups, all found within the intelligentsia, and identifiable with diminishing institutional precision, as: (1) the party apparatus; (2) the professional military; (3) the state bureaucracy; and (4) the managerial-technical bureaucracy, or economic bureaucracy. Theoretically speaking, both the managers and the military are part of the state apparatus, but they seem to operate as relatively separate structures nevertheless. The police also constitute a distinctive institutional structure within the state apparatus, but it no longer plays a significant role as a major political actor in the system. The totalitarian character of the Soviet system with its continuous interaction and interpenetration of the social order with the political order renders it difficult to always establish precise and clear-cut distinctions between some groups as to whether they are operating as social formations or as political institutions, since they may largely coincide. The institutional interest groups in Soviet society are essentially social groups operating as political structures and their interests may reflect at different times that of the social group, of the institution, or of subgroups, cliques, and individuals of various social groups in control of various institutions. The institution itself may also serve as the arena where inner clique conflicts among various personalities and factions take place within the organization for paramountcy, just as the Communist Party serves the same function for all social groups in Soviet society. No attempt will be made here to provide detailed descriptions of the various institutional groups nor their internal divisions and political processes. It should be noted at this point, however, that these four institutional groups vary considerably in size of membership, functional diffusion, and institutional coherence. The party apparatus and the professional military are more clearly defined institutional structures, in terms of function and organization, than either the state bureaucracy or the managerial technical bureaucracy. The latter is perhaps only marginally an institutional group, but because of its pivotal role in the economic establishment and because the generally uniform training its members have received and the almost deterministic impact which their function in society performs in shaping their social outlook, it is more institutional than noninstitutional in its behavior. Some institutions, like the party apparatus, because of its small numbers, key location in the party, and its more defined group spirit, have been more successfully employed as instruments of subgroups and individual leaders, while the military has articulated its interests largely as an institution rather than as a vehicle for the specific interests of this clique or individual personality. The professional military seem to arrive at a distinctively uniform outlook irrespective of individuals and cliques which may be most visible at the summit of the military establishment—a phenomenon which is not restricted to the Soviet military by any means. As the sole remaining organized structure of physical destruction and violence in the Soviet system, the temptation of individual military men to employ it as a vehicle for personal or clique power may increase, particularly in the event of another succession crisis.

The most imposing institutional rival of the party apparatus is the state bureaucracy, which legally encompasses both the military and the economic bureaucracy. Its principal distinguishing feature, which separates it from the military and the economic bureaucracy as a group, is that it is the only institutional group which has custody of important symbols and credentials of legitimacy. The state is the source of all law in the Soviet system; it is in fact the corporate embodiment of the Soviet legal order. Only the state can authorize legal rewards and punishments. To the extent that law and legality are associated with legitimacy, the state bureaucracy possesses a powerful political lever of great potential and long-range significance. Whereas in other existing political systems, legitimacy is embodied in the state, in the Soviet system, legality only is embodied in the state, whereas legitimacy is an ideological concept vested in the party. Since the Soviet state represents physically and psychologically an extension of the historic Russian state, with its powerful emotional appeal, it possesses a latent force to be ultimately reckoned with. Stripped of all refinements, the party apparatus represents a structure of legitimacy, the state bureaucracy, a structure of legality, the professional military, a structure of coercion, and the managerial-technical bureaucracy, a structure of production and distribution. While individuals have freely moved from one structure to another and considerable overlapping and rotation of personnel continues to take place, these four structures represent distinctive and separate avenues of power in the Soviet system.

III THE PARTY AND POLITICAL LEADERSHIP

The fundamental justification for the leadership role that the Communist Party plays in Soviet society, indeed the rationale for the party's very existence, has been the assertion that in it, and only it, resides the "true," the "correct," the "scientific" world outlook. On the basis of this wisdom, the party is to provide the leadership necessary for movement toward the ultimate, utopian state—a communist society. Thus, it is the task of the party to guide the development of society. As stated in the party Rules,

> ...the Party...is the highest form of socio-political organization, the leading and guiding force of Soviet society. The Party directs the great creative activity of the Soviet people and imparts an organized, planned, and scientific character to their struggle to achieve the ultimate goal, the victory of communism.

This definition of the role of the party as the "leading and directing force of Soviet society" is a direct consequence of Lenin's perception of the party as an elite of professional revolutionaries, serving as the "general staff" of the revolution. It was given explicit form after the revolution, even before the party had overcome its opponents for succession to the old system, when the tasks of governing society became an increasingly important concern of the party. In the unstable conditions of civil war, the growing system of soviets was becoming the institutional source of political legitimacy, and thus a serious challenge to the party and its leaders. The Party Program adopted by the Eighth Congress in March 1919 institutionalized the measures necessary to establish and preserve the dominant role of the party. Party bodies were divorced from the soviets and given resources with which to direct and control the administrative apparatus. Under Stalin, this function of leadership of society became even more concentrated, essentially in his own hands, at a minimum in the form of an ultimate veto power. Within certain constraints imposed by the environment, the general form of Soviet society from the late 1920's until 1953 reflected either what Stalin personally thought best, or what he permitted. It was in these years, apart from World War II, that conscious action in the form of political leadership produced the greatest impact upon Soviet society. A great transformation indeed took place in the social and economic conditions in the Soviet Union.

Although Stalin's successors have limited the opportunity for another individual to concentrate as much power as did Stalin, they have not repudiated in theory or in practice the doctrinal justification upon which not only Lenin, and then Stalin, but they themselves have based the right to exercise power. The party's assumed leadership role has been reiterated and justified frequently in contemporary terms in various party publications. It is asserted that, led by the party, the Soviet people have achieved "the complete and final victory of socialism" as the "greatest result of . . . [their] revolutionary transforming activity." The people follow and "tie their destiny to the Party." The party guides "the country's economic, sociopolitical and spiritual life," and defines "specific tasks for the new stage of communist construction."[1]

A major function of the Communist Party of the Soviet Union, a fundamental expression of the nature of the leadership role that the party perceives for itself and seeks to perform, is goal definition and the setting of directions for society. This is clearly a task of leadership. The party, monopolizing the process by which the broader goals of society are established, claims that these goals represent the best interests of all society. The party Rules take it for granted that Soviet society is struggling for "the victory of communism" as the "ultimate goal," and that it *should* do so. The new party Program adopted in 1961 asserts that "the building of a communist society has become an immediate practical task for the Soviet people."

More importantly, the party defines the more specific goals to be achieved on the way to the ultimate goal of communism. In fact, it is only by so doing that the party is able to give some substance to the extremely vague notion of a "communist society." The party has set economic goals, first by deciding on industrialization and how it was to be achieved, and then continuously by formulating the Five-Year and Seven-Year Plans. The latter, by setting production targets and allocating resources, define the shorter-range goals to which all of Soviet society is directed. The Directives on the Five-Year Plan, 1966–1970, issued by the Twenty-Third Congress of the CPSU in April, 1966 provide a good illustration of the extent to which the party sets the goals and directions in society affecting the everyday life of the average Soviet citizen.[2] Included in these directives is a statement of the "chief tasks" of economic development and instructions for

---

[1] From the editorial "The Party Carries Lenin's Banner," *Pravda*, October 10, 1967, translated in *The Current Digest of the Soviet Press*, XIX, No. 41, 28–29.

[2] *Pravda*, April 10, 1966, 2–7; *Izveitia*, April 10, 1966, 2–6, translated in *The Current Digest of the Soviet Press*, XVIII, No. 16, 3–20.

implementation. The bulk of the directives were concerned with more specific goals for industry, agriculture, transportation and communications, capital construction, improvement of the people's living standard, the distribution of productive forces, and the development of the economies of the union-republics and the foreign economic relations of the Soviet Union. Goals ranged from the number of tons of "cheese and sheeps-milk cheese" to be produced to improvement in pension insurance for workers, employees, and collective farmers.

The party also defines broad goals in other areas of life. Intrusion into family matters and the arts, for example, is a form of goal definition in that it limits the freedom of the family or the individual to aspire to a future set by themselves. Ideally, the future character of the family or state of the arts are matters for party planning rather than spontaneous evolution. Control over admissions policy to institutions of higher learning, and the assignment of jobs to graduates, can often have a serious effect on individual career goals. The individual's opportunities to reach personal career goals determined by his own interests, though by no means totally absent, and though admittedly limited or influenced by many outside factors in all societies, are clearly subordinate in the Soviet Union to the broader societal needs and goals as determined by the party.

The setting of goals for society by the party, and the prohibition of other channels through which the direction of society can be set, should not be taken to imply automatic commitment to these goals on the part of each individual in the Soviet Union. Nor does it mean that there are no differences over what these goals and directions should be. As will be evident as a thread winding through many of the readings in this volume, frictions and tensions, if not potential sources of conflict, have arisen at least *within* the party, if not between the party and the broader masses, over these fundamental questions.

The preceding comments have refered to "the party," perhaps implying a monolithic or undifferentiated entity with a readily identifiable will of its own. This clearly is not the case. The party is made up of individuals with different personalities, attitudes, opinions, backgrounds, interests, ambitions, and styles. Some of them rise to higher position of authority, power, or influence than others. Few Soviet citizens become members of the party. Individual party members relate to each other, and to non-party members, in various ways. To understand more correctly the leadership role of the party one must ask who the leaders in Soviet society are, how one becomes a leader, how the higher leaders succeed one another, what the nature of the relationship between the leaders is, and, ultimately, how decisions are made. Change, or the absence of change, in each of these areas can provide clues to the development of the Soviet political system.

In an increasingly complex society like the Soviet Union, how much is the environment transforming the political system? How much is conscious leadership being circumscribed by the new social forces associated with changes in society? Different observers put these questions in different ways, but in the end they come to the same thing. Does the transformation of the Soviet Union into a complex industrialized society require changes in the way in which the Communist Party exercises its leadership role? Can one have a "modern" society that is *not* pluralist, in the sense of Western liberal democracy? One thus studies the character of the political leadership in the Soviet Union for signs of how it might be changing, and why.

The question of who is a leader in the Soviet political system can be answered very broadly by referring to the membership of the CPSU. Given the party's role as "the leading and directing force of Soviet society," the individual party member performs a leadership role by giving "guiding directives" to or within various institutions, by supervising or coordinating the implementation of the directives, or by helping to mobilize the masses for their fulfillment. T. H. Rigby, in the first comprehensive and systematic analysis of recruitment into the party and party social composition, has found a direct relationship between party membership patterns and policies and the party's leadership role in society.[3]

The performance of the party's leadership role depends upon the type of individual recruited into the party, and the dispersal pattern of party members through the various institutions of Soviet society. In the first instance, the party needs to recruit individuals who will be "loyal." To be "loyal" means all acceptance of the traditional centralized structure of the party, and the party's self-defined place in society. On the other hand, the party also needs to recruit individuals who are competent and capable of performing leadership functions. Increasingly, this has become a problem for the CPSU as the Soviet economy and social structure have become more sophisticated and complex. To issue directives and oversee their implementation requires a technical competence far greater than was necessary in the 1920s before rapid industrialization began.

If the party is to perpetuate its established role in society as an elite that leads, and maintain the "mystique of the party as an order of men set apart from and above the masses,"[4] as Rigby notes, it is important that the party be selective in its recruitment. Equally important is a dispersal of party members such as to assure dominance of all "elite" segments of society.[5] In contrast with this need, however, is a need generated by the political socialization and mobilization functions of the party. These functions re-

---

[3] T. H. Rigby, *Communist Party Membership in the U.S.S.R., 1917–1967* (Princeton, N.J.: Princeton University Press, 1968).

[4] Rigby, *Communist Party Membership*, p. 524.

[5] Rigby, *Communist Party Membership*, pp. 510–11. Elite defined as the internal order-maintenance and rule and policy-making functions.

quire, ideally, a larger, relatively less selective membership and "a party membership broadly representative of the social categories (occupational, ethnic, educational, sex, age, etc.) of which the population is composed."[6] They also require a pattern of dispersal that places a heavy concentration of party members in those auxiliary organizations (educational institutions, Komsomols, trade unions, soviets, and so forth) serving to socialize and mobilize the population. For fifty years the CPSU has sought unsuccessfully a way out of the dilemma created by conflicting demands from its leadership functions on its recruitment and dispersal policies. The specific problem has been the extrafunctional and dysfunctional features associated with alternation between periods of low recruitment and increased expulsion (elitism), and rapid growth in membership (representiveness).

Given the centralized and hierarchical character of the CPSU, the search for "leaders" in the Soviet political system cannot end with the individual party member. Some party members exercise more power than others, and participate more directly or significantly in the crucial policy and rule-making functions. The precise pattern according to which power is distributed in the Soviet Union is by no means clear, probably not even to the most informed individuals in the Soviet Union itself. The search for clarification of this issue occupies a great many observers and analysts of the Soviet political system. As discussed in the Introduction, however, one can distinguish a political elite, a "top leadership", in which authority has been concentrated.

If one were to note the way in which the Soviet political system has developed over the course of fifty years, one might well be justified in assuming that the goal definition and rule-making functions are at the heart of political leadership in the Soviet Union. Thus, to get a clearer answer to the question of who is a political leader, one would like to know who participates in these processes. Do all members of the political elite participate in these processes? If so, do they do so equally?

An answer has been offered by Zbigniew Brzezinski and Samuel P. Huntington in their pioneering comparative study. It is one segment of the political elite, the professional politician, or *apparatchik*, who superseded the professional revolutionary during the 1920s, who they say is the political leader. Brzezinski and Huntington discuss the character and role of the professional politician in both the United States and the USSR. An important consequence of the expansion and bureaucratization of the party under Stalin was the creation of a corps of professional politicians, "individuals who attempt to make a career of political leadership." Thus for Brzezinski and Huntington, it is the *apparat* that is the locus of effective political leadership.

---

[6] Rigby, *Communist Party Membership*, p. 512.

The important question in many observers' minds is the degree to which the predominant role of the *apparat* in providing political leadership may be changing, either in terms of challenges from groups or institutions outside the *apparat*, or in terms of the changing attitudes and perspectives of the *apparat* itself. Indeed, there are some who question the utility of continuing to speak of the *apparat* as such, as if it exhibited a cohesiveness that it may not in fact possess. Are the Politburo and Central Committee, for example, institutions of the *apparat* when they contain, in addition to the highest full-time party officials, the highest full-time governmental executives as well?

There are those who argue that the *apparat* must change if it is to be able to perform its leadership functions in a "modernizing" or "modernized" society. The political leaders in the *apparat* must acquire by one means or another the increasingly complicated technical skills that would enable them to make rational decisions. Otherwise, either the task of political leadership will inevitably fall in a modern society to those who possess the skill to make the decisions required, or the system will degenerate to the point of crisis. Others are more optimistic about the prospects of acheving a separation of "political" from "technical" decisions. Such a separation would leave the political leaders to make broad policy decisions, presumably on the basis of information provided by the technicians, leaving implementation to the latter. This view assumes such a separation can be made in a modern society.

Still others see the challenge to the *apparat* in group or institutional terms. Social forces in modern society, they argue, are leading to the formation of groups competing with the *apparat* for predominance. In all cases, the key issues are: the social composition, attitudes, and cohesion of the existing *apparat*; the manner in which recruitment into the *apparat* may be changing, and how these changes may be affecting its character; and the role of the *apparat* and how it may be changing.

The *apparatchik*, as Brzezinski and Huntington implicitly define him, has personal characteristics and a career pattern such that he can successfully manipulate and control people. He has acquired the broad administrative and integrative experience, and "knowledge of the distinctive pattern and characteristics of behavior" in Soviet society, necessary for his "generalist" role as a professional politician. It is thus not so important that the career pattern of the professional politician be *solely* within the party organization. What is of crucial importance is that he be an integrator and "reconcilor," with broad horizons, rather than primarily an advocate or polemicist for more parochial professional or institutional interests. Though the evidence is as yet limited, it seems unlikely that the latter becomes co-opted into the *apparat* and thus exercises political leadership.

An integrator or reconcilor in the Soviet context is not a leader who is necessarily "opinion-free." Rather, at lower levels in particular he is one who ideally can bring together different specialized views on the same issue, producing a specific policy that is in accord with established goals and broad policy directives. The difficulty comes at the top of the system; who ultimately is to make the basic decisions and reconcile different appeals to serve as the basis for policy?

The formal process of acquiring a particular position in the *apparat* is through selection or co-optation by a party secretary or secretariat to fill a post included in the *nomenklatura* for that party body. All posts of importance in the Soviet Union are included in some party secretariat's *nomenklatura*, or "list of appointments." This is true for both the state administrative apparatus and the party *apparat*. Higher party secretaries control appointment to the lower party and state posts. The informal process, however, is of greater importance. How does one come to the notice of a party official seeking to fill an office? One has become a leader and moved up in the *apparat* by becoming a member of the party; by serving an apprenticeship in the party (or one of its auxiliary organizations—Komsomol, trade union, secret police), or in the party and in administrative work in industry, agriculture, or an executive body of a local soviet; by performing well in the extensive and intensive program of in-service training and education sponsored by the party, by demonstrating *partiinost'*, a fundamental commitment to, and belief in, the party, its hierarchical structure, and its right to lead or govern; by showing certain skills; and by being "in the right place, at the right time."

The conditions of skill and "timing" would include: intelligence and knowledge; the qualities of talent and personality that enable the individual to persuade others to do what he wants them to do; a sensitivity to the informal "rules of the game" and to shifting demands from the top; skill in private intrigue; being associated with another individual or a higher leader who is rising in the hierarchy; and being on the "right" side in policy disputes. To reach the pinnacle of power today, one must have built up a sufficiently prestigious personal following, most immediately within the Central Committee, or be closely associated with a strong personality, to enable one to claim a power base sufficient to be accorded the respect of membership in the Politburo.[7]

---

[7] There is some speculation that a situation is developing in which the occupants of certain key party and state offices may *ex officio* become full or candidate members of the Politburo (for example, general secretary of the party, chairman of the USSR Council of Ministers, key republic party first secretaries, and chairmen of certain republican councils of ministers). If so, this would be a highly significant institutionalization of power in the Soviet Union. The question would still remain, however, as to how a particular individual comes to occupy each of these posts. For discussions of the process of recruitment and advancement in the party *apparat* see Alfred G. Meyer, *The Soviet Political System* (New York: Random House, 1965), pp. 143–50, and Frederick C. Barghoorn, *Politics in the USSR* (Boston: Little, Brown and Company, Inc., 1966), pp. 205–12.

Are these criteria changing? Are individuals with skills different from those necessary in the past coming into the *apparat?* Must one rise through the *apparat* in order to acquire a place in the higher institutions of authority in the Soviet political system (the party Central Committee, Politburo, and Secretariat)? Here, too, there is a difference of opinion among Western scholars of the Soviet system. Some argue that the traditional political/personal/bureaucratic skills remain the essential ones. Others argue that rational/technical criteria are becoming most important (who has the skills necessary to perform the technical leadership functions?), with a consequent decrease in the role of the professional politician, and an increase in pluralism and bargaining in the decision-making process.

Brzezinski and Huntington note that " ... it would be an important clue to change in the Soviet Union if at the political apex one saw the appearance in significant numbers of individuals whose careers had been primarily associated with a non-political bureaucratic profession." The question, of course, is how many constitute a "significant number." Presumably the party could tolerate in important positions of decision making a certain number of individuals whose careers in a professional elite had not prepared them for the generalist role of professional politician, but if too many rose to the apex of power, where would the professional politicians come from? The function of the politician must be performed, and the doubt that remains for some as to the prospects for fundamental change in the role of the *apparat* is that there is no evidence that either, other groups, institutional or professional, are prepared to do this, or that the individuals from professional elites brought into the party *apparat*, or into the higher party bodies, display a perspective significantly different from the body into which they are co-opted.

A recent study by George Fischer indicates that the above criteria may not be incompatible.[8] He suggests that there is a trend among top party executives toward men whose skills combine the characteristics of both the professional politician and the technician.[9] Professor Fischer refers to such an individual as a "dual executive," one in whom "leadership" and "administration" tend to merge. The obvious consequence of such a development would be to provide the professional politician who monopolizes power in the Soviet Union the necessary technical skills for directing a complex society, thus maintaining a special kind of "monist," as opposed to the development of a "pluralist," political system.

Jerry Hough seeks to "find revealing clues to the direction in which con-

---

[8] George Fisher, *The Soviet System and Modern Society* (New York: Atherton Press, 1968).

[9] As Professor Fischer notes, " ... a deep gulf exists between a leader who might bring to a high party post some economic experience, and a factory manager, businessman, or higher economic executive." *Ibid.*, p. 16.

temporary Russian society is moving by studying the changing composition of the Soviet elite." (Professor Hough defines elite here to include all elected party committees at the All-Union and the Republic levels.) He sees in the 1966 party elections the continued primacy of the party apparatus, and argues that in the short run there is little evidence of an erosion in the "directing" role of the *apparat* as compared with governmental institutions. In effect, the party apparatus has taken note of the growing importance of the specialized institutions and subinstitutions, found increasingly in Soviet society, by including specialized administrators in the elected party bodies. This represents an increase in status for these individuals and the institutions they represent. The question, of course, is whether this increase in status as a result of growing representation in the essentially honorific bodies will lead to a greater role in the exercise of political leadership.

One might also ask if this development was the product of genuine elections, reflecting a growing bargaining between the old professional politicians in the *apparat* and the specialized administrators, or whether the professional politicians in the *apparat* were merely co-opting skills for their own purposes. The long-term effect of this inclusion of technical skills will depend upon any broader criteria for inclusion imposed by the *apparat*. Why, for instance, in choosing between various available specialized administrators, did the *apparat* select who it did, to the exclusion of others possessing the desired skills? One might suggest that those included had shown the characteristics of the professional politician mentioned earlier. Perhaps they are the prototype of Professor Fischer's "dual executive."

One key group of *apparatchiki* in which one might look for changes as a sign of change in the role and position of the *apparat* in society, and its adaptation to the demands of contemporary Soviet society, is the corps of first secretaries of the *oblast* party committees (*obkom* first secretaries). Grey Hodnett has analyzed the backgrounds and career patterns of this group of functionaries from just before the party reorganization (October, 1962) to just after its termination (December, 1964).[10] He concludes that the Soviet leadership may well have succeeded in producing "an entrenched, agriculturally oriented (but not pro-peasant) middle-rank elite whose capacities and scope of interests are not in full alignment with the thrust of urban-industrial life." There remains, says Professor Hodnett, a need to recruit younger, better-trained personnel for the party apparatus, especially in light of the perceived need for party initiative in stimulating innovation in both industry and agriculture, but particularly in industry.[11] Despite the

---

[10] Grey Hodnett, "The *Obkom* First Secretaries," *Slavic Review*, XXIV, No. 4 (December 1965).

[11] As will be noted in Part V, in the apparent absence of effective party control over industry at the *oblast* level, the party leadership has emphasized control at the grassroots level of the party, the primary party organization.

organizational changes and reversals of Khrushchev's later years, no transformation has occurred in the basic characteristics of one body of important full-time party executives.

As has been suggested earlier, the multinational character of Soviet society provides an environmental constraint on the party, and at least a potential source of tension within the political system. One might argue that the greater the degree of participation by the national minorities in the political system, the less likely any potential tensions will be to explode into conflict. Most particularly, the greater the representation of a national minority in the political leadership, the greater should be the sense of identification of that minority with party policies and programs. This assumes, however, a "nationalist" perspective on the part of those from each national minority group found in positions of leadership, as well as some degree of "representativeness" in fact between such individuals and the national group from which they come.

As Professor Aspaturian has noted, Khrushchev and his successors have sought to find a nationality policy that occupies a middle ground between the pressures for national autonomy and the tendency toward Great Russian domination.[12] He suggests that in the distribution of offices "in the structure of Soviet power" there has been an effort to achieve a more equitable balance among the various nationalities. He also predicts that "the national elites will increasingly assume greater direction of their national republics and at the same time become coopted and more fully integrated into a multinational all-union ruling elite." If this indeed should be the course of developments, the centrifugal pressures within the Soviet system generated by nationalism may well be contained within manageable bounds. It may be the case, however, that the source of nationalism in the Soviet Union lies not within the party or the administrative bureaucracy, but rather within the intellectuals and broader circles of the population. In that case, changes in the composition of the leadership would not affect nationalist pressures.

Yaroslav Bilinsky has analyzed the degree of political participation by the diverse nationalities "as measured by their representation in the major organs of political rule in the USSR."[13] He emphasizes the desire of the national minorities to run their own national affairs, at least in the sense of *administering* state affairs. The "more equitable balance" referred to by Professor Aspaturian would perhaps take the form, in Professor Bilinsky's

---

[12] See Grey Hodnett, "What's In a Nation?" *Problems of Communism* (September–October 1967), and "The Debate Over Soviet Federalism," *Soviet Studies,* XVIII, No. 4 (April 1967), for discussions of the current debate on nationality policy.

[13] Yaroslav Bilinsky, "The Rulers and the Ruled," *Problems of Communism* (September–October 1967). See also Seweryn Bialer, "How Russians Rule Russia," *Problems of Communism* (September–October 1964).

eyes, of the *limited* quota system for filling offices which he sees existing. This system works increasingly less satisfactorily for the national minorities the closer one gets to the center of political leadership—the central organs of the party and the state. "The really crucial positions in the party Secretariat ... are now held exclusively by Russians." Together with the Ukrainians and the Byelorussians, the Russians dominate the central party organs.

In contrast to changes of leadership in the established, constitutional systems in Western Europe and North America, such changes in the Soviet Union have not in the past taken place according to any institutionalized procedures. The result has been considerable disruption to the political system, and the existence of instability and insecurity within the political leadership itself. The absence of any formal structure for transferring power automatically led to severe crises within the CPSU after the deaths of both Lenin and Stalin. In each case the individual himself had been the source of effective political leadership, although the leadership arose on the one hand from personal prestige and authority, and on the other from coercion and sycophancy.

Neither the party Rules nor the Soviet Constitution recognize the problem of the transfer of leadership when an individual leader passes from the scene. Both maintain the myth of a homogeneous party governed by collective leadership. Under these conditions, individuals come and go, but the collective remains. No office bears any particular authority, because the occupant is supposedly only an agent of the collective—party Congress or Central Committee, or in the state apparatus, the Supreme Soviet or Council of Ministers. In reality, power in the party until the recent past has gravitated in varying degrees into the hands of one man (Lenin, Stalin, Khrushchev) and into one or two offices, first and foremost, the party general secretary or first secretary. When the primary leader passed on, a more or less raw struggle for power developed in the absence of any institutionalized procedures for filling top offices. To what extent is this a systemic feature of Soviet politics? Is this something that is bound to recur, given the structure of the party, or is there evidence surrounding the fall of Khrushchev to lead one to conclude that more regularized procedures are developing as a result of changes in Soviet society? Is it inherent in the Soviet political system to have one more or less supreme leader emerge? Is a factional struggle for power underway behind the scenes in the Soviet Union today, through which one leader will rise to preeminence? Or is the system stabilizing, becoming more oligarchic as the condition of stability, with the question of who occupies the positions of top leadership—Politburo, Secretariat, Central Committee—being answered by negotiation, bargaining, and compromise between readily identifiable institutions, more vaguely identifiable "interest groups," or still more vague coalitions put together on an *ad hoc* basis solely for acquiring power. Will a generational change, away from an emphasis on revolutionary social change and toward economic efficiency, lead to changes in succession procedures? Henry Roberts raises these questions in his provocative piece.

With political leadership, and the accompanying power and authority, concentrated in the Soviet Union within the Communist Party and within the party in individuals occupying positions in the top party organs, relations between individuals and groups within the leadership acquire particular significance. The official Soviet view of homogeneity and continuous agreement within the party never has been a realistic description of leadership politics. This is not to say that there are no ties binding party members together, or that there are no similarities in perspective and interests among party leaders. The official view, however, would have one believe that conflict was not present, or present only at exceptional times as an expression of "antiparty" activity.

If the official view is unrealistic, what can one say more meaningfully about the nature of the political process within the leadership? During the first half of 1965, shortly after the removal of Khrushchev from his until then apparently preeminent position of leadership within the party, there was a continuing discussion in the pages of *Problems of Communism* between observers of Soviet politics on the reasons for, and implications of, the fall of Khrushchev. This exchange is of interest not so much for its specific explanation of Khrushchev's downfall, for there is much as yet unknown about that event. Rather, its utility lies in its representation of the variety of opinions as to the nature of leadership politics in the Soviet Union. The selections by Richard Lowenthal, Carl Linden and Robert Conquest represent perhaps the most often expressed points of view.

The outward division of opinion into adherents of a "conflict-model" and a "non-conflict model" reflects differences of view expressed before Khrushchev fell. Some viewed Khrushchev's position as inherently unstable, challenged by competing groups and individuals, with conflict the basic condition of leadership politics. Others, not necessarily denying opposition to Khrushchev or the existence of conflict, were more sanguine as to the prospects of Khrushchev's maintaining himself in power.

The division of opinion into conflict and non-conflict models is not really a useful description of the differences that do in fact exist. All observers agree that conflict exists. The issue in dispute concerns the nature of this conflict. Is conflict within the top party organs fundamental, endemic, a constant? Is it, as Robert Conquest suggests, "the dynamic force activating Soviet political life at its highest reaches"? Or is conflict spasmodic, emerging from time to time in association with factional rivalries within the leadership? Who are the participants in the conflict—individuals or factions struggling for power, for the top positions; or "interests" or policy groups seeking representation or to substitute their views for those that predominate? Is conflict the by-product of struggles for power, or it is the inevitable result of broad social changes within the society as a whole? Did Khrushchev's policy goals elicit a contrary response, did they lead to a coalition opposed to him on policy grounds, did his policy goals step over "a generally more conservative consensus"? Or was the conflict evidenced by his removal essentially an internal leadership conflict in which secondary leaders succeeded in limiting (in fact, confiscating) the powers of the principal leader? Was his removal a *coup de parti*, and if so, was it the result of power and institutional considerations or of policy differences? Was his removal rather the culmination of a process of social and economic change in Soviet society? Thus, different analysts draw different conclusions as to the implications of conflict within the political leadership.

For purposes of illustration only, one can distinguish three general positions in the controversy among analysts of Soviet affairs over the nature of leadership politics. Few, if any, individuals could be associated completely with any one position. The "power" explanation does not admit of the likelihood of a fundamental change in the nature of the Soviet political system as a result of adaptation to, or accommodation with, broad underlying social forces making for change. The existence of the latter are not denied but are not accepted as "uncontrollable" influences, forcing a change in the political system such that the role of the party, and the party *apparat*, is threatened seriously. Policy issues, to the extent that they are the product of the social and economic dynamics of the society, are instrumental rather than causal. They are important not because they lead to factions and the existence of conflict, but rather because they are useful to individuals or amorphous or temporary groupings in power struggles.

The "policy" explanation describes the political process in terms of conflict between well-defined policy orientations or groups, some representing the old, established forces, some the emerging social forces—a "conservative"/"reformist" dichotomy. The struggle for power is more a by-product than a cause of the formation of groups. This explanation puts a heavy emphasis on the influence and effect of the environment, and the social and economic forces. The observable conflict within the political leadership exists over the representation of "interests." New "interests" have been created as a result of the changes in the social and economic environment over the last forty years, and these strive to be influential or dominant against the "interests" vested in maintaining the *status quo*.

A variation of the "power" explanation, which in some ways bridges the gap with the "policy" explanation, holds that under contemporary Soviet conditions (neither a supreme arbiter, nor institutionalized procedures for filling offices and reconciling differences) instability of political leadership is a fundamental characteristic. Disagreements over policies do exist, leading to struggles for control of the top positions. However, these disagreements do not lead to the formation of permanent and enduring political group-ings ("reform" "conservative"; "pro-Khrushchev," "anti-Khrushchev"). Rather, shifting coalitions are formed as a result of different opinions, de-pending upon the particular issue under debate. Conflicts exist over policy differences between temporary groupings for power—a limited relationship to the broad social forces. Struggles for power are more the product of policy conflicts than an inherent need for one man to rise to the top, but policy differences are not so clearly associated with deeper social forces, with readily identifiable interests.

The conflict/non-conflict dichotomy has taken on a new dimension since the fall of Khrushchev. The question now is: can, or will, a more stable situation of oligarchic cohesion develop within the Soviet leadership? If so, on what basis: tacit understandings, institutional restrictions? Will oligarchic cohesion lead to stability, or to further instability because of the need to make room for new "interests"? Or will another preeminent leader or "supreme arbiter" emerge out of what may now be a highly unstable situa-tion?

The exercise of leadership by the Communist Party of the Soviet Union manifests itself ultimately in the making of decisions. The rationale for monopoly by the party of political leadership includes control over the individuals, groups, and institutions that participate in the decision-making process. The setting of goals and directions for Soviet society by the party clearly involves the making of decisions. The questions of interest to ob-servers of the process of decision making in the Soviet Union include: How are decisions made? Who participates in decision making? What influences exert themselves on the decision-making process, and where do they come from? Are changes occurring, and if so, what might be their consequences for the political system?

The questions of interest concerning *how* the political leadership in the Soviet Union is formed, and the relationships *between* the leaders, are inter-woven with these questions concerning decision making. Are decisions the result of bargaining and negotiations leading to compromise? If so, between and among whom? Clearly not between the party and the mass of the population. If political leadership is concentrated within the party, then any bargaining must take place within the party. But within what institu-tional framework? Most important, which individuals and groups are participants? Is there a more or less well-defined process by which decisions are made within the party for all of society?

The variety of opinion with respect to decision making in the Soviet Union can be resolved essentially into two points of view. Each shares certain points of agreement with the other, but basically they provide distinctly different explanations. One view, represented by Jeremy Azrael, is that the party *apparat* "continues to exercise an extensive power-political hegemony." Even under Brezhnev and Kosygin and the appearance, at least, of collegial rule, "effective access to the ultimate decision-making arena remains very strictly circumscribed." Although the party elite may at a maximum have to share its power informally with state bureaucrats, economic managers, and other specialized and professional experts as a result of the elite's dependence upon the latter for information and for implementation of decisions, the authority structure remains distinctly hierarchical. It is the few leaders at the top who decide when and with whom they will consult, rather than a process of bargaining between autonomous groups. Tendencies for the observable "groups" or "interests" to demonstrate cohesiveness or unity of outlook, to act autonomously as a group, and to seek to exert enough power or influence so as to be able to bargain, are still very limited. The important decisions and discussions are still initiated at the top by the party leaders rather than from below by the organized pressure of interest groups and experts.[14]

A second view, represented by Gordon Skilling, argues that issues requiring decisions are increasingly raised by society or social groups, rather than by the party or its top leaders. It is these more or less readily identifiable groups, ranging from broad, amorphous social groupings to the "policy groups" and the "sectors of the intelligentsia," which have become the effective participants in the decision-making process. The party *apparat* represents only one of several groups participating in a bargaining situation. Thus, Skilling suggests that there *are* interest groups in the U.S.S.R., which on the basis of one or more shared attitudes make certain claims upon other groups in society through or upon the institutions of government (in the Soviet case, the higher party bodies).

In contrast with the first view, which holds that the party *apparat* need only consult with experts and policy groups in the name of efficiency, with initiative remaining in its own hands, this view argues that the increasingly evident diverse social forces have created a situation in which the party leaders must more and more be concerned with forming a consensus among the groups. Initiation increasingly rests not with the top leaders, but spontaneously from more or less organized pressures from below.

The importance of the difference in perspective is that each viewpoint carries implications for future development of Soviet society and the Soviet political system. The first implies no necessity for, and probably more skepticism about the prospects for, the emergence of a significant degree of

---

[14] For a further elaboration of this point of view, see Henry W. Morton, "The Structure of Decision-Making in the U.S.S.R." in Juviler and Morton, *Soviet Policy-Making*. For a very illuminating exchange of views on the decision-making processes in the Soviet political system see T. H. Rigby and L. G. Churchward, *Policy-Making in the U.S.S.R., 1953–1961* (Melbourne: Lansdowne Press, 1962).

pluralism in the Soviet Union—of democracy as defined in the context of Western liberal democratic constitutional systems, for example. The second implies that social forces are at work that will inevitably lead to the existence of autonomous groupings, to pluralism, and perhaps to a convergence of Soviet and Western democratic societies. Thus, whereas both viewpoints recognize the existence of groups or "interests," they differ as to the ability of the top party leaders to cope with them and to maintain their position at the top of the power pyramid.

A third, intermediate view argues that the "interests" of various social groups, most particularly the professional and technical specialists necessary for the functioning of a modern industrial society, will become represented in the arenas of decision making through increased recruitment of such individuals into the party *apparat*.[15] This increased representation would affect the political system not by substituting some other group, or groups, for the *apparat*, or forcing the latter to share its decision-making authority with other groups, but rather by broadening the character of the apparat *itself*. If this is not pluralism as understood in a liberal democratic sense, it would at least be different from a condition whereby the small elite of professional politicians monopolizes the decision-making authority. As discussed earlier, this view assumes that the perspective on politics of the individual specialist recruited into the *apparat* would retain significantly more in common with other specialists than with the full-time party politician with whom he is now working. It also assumes that the recruited specialist and the career party executive would be on equal terms in the context of appointments to positions and offices of higher authority within the *apparat*.

Which are the significant institutional and professional-occupational groups in contemporary Soviet society? What evidence is there that they have played some role in the decision-making process? A considerable number of studies of individual groups—the economic planners, administrators, and managers; the military; the national minorities; and the writers and artists—have been made. Others that could be included are the lawyers, the scientists, the "experts" (technical and specialist intelligentsia), and

---

15 Another suggested way by which those groups offering "expert" judgments can influence decisions is through communication of their judgments to individuals at the top of the hierarchy who *are* in a position to influence outcomes. See Joel J. Schwartz and William R. Keech, "Group Influence and the Policy Process in the Soviet Union," *American Political Science Review*, LXII, No. 3 (September 1968), 840–51. Such group influence, the authors suggest, will be greatest in conditions of policy conflict within the leadership. The essential questions remaining here, however, are whether or not "expert" judgments can be rejected by those who solicit them, and most important, whether or not "expert" judgments initiate policy, or merely refine or "operationalize" a decision already taken by higher political authorities. Furthermore, evaluation of the influence of "expert" groups must always consider the fact that the evidence shows the "experts" to be divided among one another far more often than they are united, whether against the professional politicians or not.

agronomists and farm managers. What is evident in each of these studies is the existence of a policy "debate" in which members from various groups, including the party bureaucracy, participate. What may also be seen is a division in counsel in many cases; the military divided into traditionalists and modernists; the economic administrators into those who favor centralized management and those who are for increased autonomy at the level of the enterprises; some "conservative" writers accepting the role laid out for them by the party, others not. This tempts one to conclude that the politically significant groups in the Soviet political system are the informal, shifting coalitions found within the higher party organs and the political elite in general, and made up of individuals from various institutional and professional-occupational groups, and based on either shared views on policy issues, or personal followings, or both.

CINCINNATUS AND THE APPARATCHIK

Zbigniew Brzezinski/Samuel P. Huntington

I. Political Leadership in Modern Society

"Kto kovo?" asked Lenin. "Who governs?" echoes a contemporary American political scientist. The question is of perennial interest. The "who's" have the capacity to influence the behavior of others. They include *political leaders*, who customarily exercise power through public or governmental bodies, and *non-political leaders*, who may exercise power through the command of other values, such as wealth, income, expertise. Political leaders and non-political leaders together constitute the *elite*; they lead the masses, who, needless to say, greatly outnumber the elite.

Political leadership in modern industrialized societies differs significantly from that in pre-modern agrarian societies. In the latter, typically, the functions of political leadership and non-political leadership are exercised by the same people. The primary distinction is between the elite or ruling class or aristocracy, on the one hand, and the mass of the people, on the other. The political leaders of society are also it military, economic, cultural, and religious leaders. Certain individuals, of course, may spend more of their lives in politics, or in the church, but they are all recruited from the same relatively limited social class and in many cases the same individuals are leaders in more than one field of endeavor. The gap between elite and mass is vast. Few members of the lower class climb into the elite; the division between the two is usually fixed by heredity. The numerous lower class possesses neither wealth, education, culture, authority, power, status, nor, in many cases, liberty. The elite pos-

World Politics, XVI, No. 1 (October 1963), 52–78. Reprinted by permission of the authors. Footnotes omitted.

sesses all of these. The system is, in Professor Dahl's term, one of "cumulative inequalities."

In varying forms this pattern of organization appears in agrarian societies where landownership is concentrated in a few hands. It was the prevailing pattern in Western Europe until the nineteenth century. It was the prevailing pattern in Russia until 1917. It is the prevailing pattern in many parts of Latin America and the Middle East today. It was also, in less rigid form, the pattern in the United States until about 1820. The principal political impact of industrialization is to diversify the pre-modern agrarian ruling class. It replaces the system of "cumulative inequalities" with one of "dispersed inequalities." It gives rise to new forms of wealth and power, and it eventually produces a complex society characterized by a multiplicity of functions and a highly developed division of labor. The functions and institutions of military leadership, educational leadership, economic leadership, religious leadership, and political leadership become more specialized. Mass armies develop, commanded by professional officer corps. Specialized economic institutions—corporations or trusts—are created by government or private entrepreneurs and, in due course, themselves give birth to a new class of industrial managers. Scientific and technical knowledge multiplies, giving rise to a variety of experts. The ability of any one individual to be a Renaissance (or Enlightenment) man diminishes, and the ability of any one social class to monopolize the positions of leadership within society also is weakened.

A simple society does not need elaborate or highly differentiated leadership institutions. A complex organization, however, contains within itself many specialists, subgroups, and functional types. Hence, it requires yet another type to coordinate and integrate their activities. This is the role of the political leader; to perform this role he requires some degree of power over others in society. Hence, unlike other individuals who may exercise power, the political leader is formally invested by society with authority to exercise power. He is the general manager of the modern state. His function is comparable to that of the line officer in an army, the broad-gauged executive in a corporation, or the dean in a university. Because he is a specialist in the general direction of society, the political leader faces problems in ordering his relations with the specialists in other areas of activity. In pre-modern agrarian society, political leaders and non-political leaders were identical. In the complex modern society, the relations between political leaders and non-political leaders equal in importance those between the leaders and the masses.

In modern societies, political leadership is the product of achievement. The problem is: What type of achievement? Who are the political leaders and where do they come from? To a large extent they are recruited from the class of professional politicians—i.e., individuals who attempt to make a career of political leadership. The expansion and differentiation of society give rise to specialized political institutions and specialized political practitioners. The state bureaucracy expands and is rationalized; cabinets and legislatures develop and acquire more distinctive roles; and, most important, the political party emerges as the key institution for the representation and integration of competing interests and the recruitment and selection of political leaders. Political parties in the sense of divisions or factions are as old as history; political parties in the sense of organized institutions, however, date from the late eighteenth century. Only in the nineteenth century did Western societies evolve a distinct class of professional politicians. Only in the nineteenth century did politics, in Weber's phrase, become a vocation. The professional politician operates the party system and operates through the party system to achieve positions of political leadership in the state.

The history, ideology, and culture of a society shape the character of its political leadership and, particularly, the extent to which that leadership is composed of professional politicians or individuals drawn from other sources, usually the non-political leaders of society. In the modern state all professional politicians are not necessarily political leaders, and all political leaders are not necessarily professional politicians. The pattern in each society is different. In addition, while each modern society has an identifiable class of professional politicians, the characteristics and skills of that class vary from one society to another. They too are a function of the overall character of the society. The professional politician is thus a less universal figure than most of the other specialists in the modern world. Technical skills are universal; social skills are peculiar to particular societies. The skills of a nuclear physicist are the same in the Soviet Union and in the United States; presumably a physicist from Moscow or Leningrad University could easily make himself at home in the laboratories at Harvard or Columbia. A surgeon transferring from a Moscow hospital to a New York hospital also would have little trouble in adjusting to his new institutional environment and job. The manager of a machine tool factory, on the other hand, might have a more difficult time of it: the technical skills would be similar but the social context would be very different. He would have to learn how to negotiate with autonomous labor unions and labor leaders. The professional politician, however, would probably have the most difficult time of all. The specialized knowledge of the politician is almost entirely social in character; it is, in part, knowledge of the universal characteristics of human behavior, but it is, even more, knowledge of the distinctive patterns and characteristics of behavior in a particular society. The professional politician is concerned with the manipulation and control of people. The means and skills for accomplishing these ends may differ greatly from one society to another, and, indeed, in any one society they change over time as the underlying social and political character of the society changes. The leader of a small group in one context and with respect to one set of problems may well be a follower in another context and when the group is confronted with a different set of problems.

II. Leaders, Politicians, and Bureaucrats

Professional politicians

In the United States, the old colonial-Federalist ruling class declined during the nineteenth century and was replaced by a more diversified social-economic elite including new frontier wealth, new merchants, and new industrialists. The decline was also marked by the development of the party system, the extension of the suffrage, the multiplication of elective offices, and the emergence of the American-style professional politician. Confronted with an almost infinite variety of elective offices in local, state, and national governments, the American politician's career consisted of campaigns for elected offices with successively bigger constituencies and broader responsibilities. The key decisions in such a career were frequently ones of selection and timing: which office to run for in which year. The American electoral politician thus differed significantly from his British counterpart, whose election interests were simply to get into the Commons and to stay there. The American professional is an electoral politician, the British professional a parliamentary politician. In America, the term "professional politician" still conjures up the image of a person who is running for elective office, a person who is in elective office, or a person (party chairman or campaign manager) whose job is to get other people into elective office.

In Russia, the ruling class first declined and then was overthrown by an organization of professional revolutionaries. The resulting vacuum in political leadership was filled by the rapid expansion of the party apparatus and the transformation of Lenin's organization of professional revolutionaries into Stalin's organization of professional rulers. In the United States, the professional politician is the product of the democratization of the government. In the Soviet Union, he is the product of the bureaucratization of the party. As professional politicians the Soviet apparatchik and the American electoral politician have some similarities. To some degree each may develop expertise in a particular set of policy problems important to his oblast or constituency. But the distinctive character of each is that he is a generalist, an expert in dealing simultaneously with a variety of issues and pressures, balancing one off against another, attempting to resolve problems at the least cost to the greatest number of interests involved. In addition, the politician in both systems must be flexible in viewpoint, adaptable in outlook, and contingent in loyalties. He must reward his friends and punish his enemies, but he must also be aware that today's friends may be tomorow's enemies and vice versa. He must be able to adapt to a variety of different circumstances and responsibilities. He must be a mobile individual, committed wholeheartedly to the position or institution he is in at the moment but also able to move quickly on to a different position in a different institutional context. The higher party authorities shift the promising apparatchik every few years from one oblast to another and one type of responsibility to another. The vagaries of the voters and the variety of the opportunities of the American political system require a comparable degree of mobility on the part of the American electoral politician.

Apart from these generic characteristics, the apparatchik and the electoral politician are rather different political animals with different habits and habitats. They differ especially in their degree of political professionalization and their commitment to politics as a career. The typical American politician is really only a semi-pro: he usually combines his public career with the simultaneous pursuit of a private career in law, business, education, or journalism. If circumstances or the voters retire him from his public career, he can still pursue his private one with little loss and perhaps with considerable benefit. His commitment to politics is thus nowhere near as profound as that of his Soviet counterpart. Even for the professional, politics in America is still in many respects an avocation rather than a vocation. Only five of 513 top political leaders in the United States from 1789 to 1953 had no career other than politics. Indeed, the professional politician may well make a public career out of politics with the thought that the primary benefits of this career will be in other fields, that the political ladder may be used to scale non-political heights in business and society. For his Soviet counterpart, on the other hand, a political career is normally a more-than-fulltime commitment for life. The Russian enters upon it as an American might enter the priesthood or the army. He becomes engulfed in the life of the apparatus. Lacking a private career upon which to fall back, he would find escape difficult even if it were conceivable. His life is more focused, his loyalties more exclusive, his commitment more intense than those of the American politician.

Not only is the apparatchik's career commitment exclusive but the career itself is highly professionalized. The apparatus is a sort of cross between the Hague machine and the United States Army. The apparatchik's career in many ways resembles that of the military officer. Although practice has varied, certain minimum educational attainments are usually required. As for the officer, entry is normally at the bottom of the ladder. Like the successful officer, the successful apparatchik moves up the hierarchy to posts of broader and broader responsibility: raion to oblast or krai to Union Republic or to major party organizations such as those of Moscow and Leningrad and eventually to the Central Committee Secretariat. The apparatchik can also move upward in the type of responsibility at each level: from a position as second secretary in one oblast to a post as first secretary in another. At various points in his career he will be "seconded" to positions in the state or industrial bureaucracy. He will be expected to improve his education regularly through correspondence courses. Like the army officer who goes to a staff school or war college, he may also be sent for a four-year course at the Party School in his Union Republic or to the Higher Party School of the Central Committee in Moscow. The schools were founded in 1946 and during the first decade of their activity some fifty-five thousand individuals were trained in the local Party Schools and nine thousand by the Higher Party School. Party officials under the age of thirty-five and with a good record in party work are nominated for the four-year course at the Inter-Oblast Schools; more senior officials under the age of forty may be assigned for two years to the Higher Party School, which also offers courses by correspondence. (In 1956, two hundred officials were in attendance at the Higher Party School and three thousand more were studying by correspondence.) Several of the younger top party leaders, such as Polyansky, Mazurov, Furtseva, have already received their training there.

The party official assigned to such advanced party studies will receive intensive training designed to improve his political and ideological knowledge, as well as his adeptness at handling economic and technical-managerial issues. Of the 3,200 hours prescribed in 1957 in a typical curriculum of a four-year Inter-Oblast Communist Party School, 41.5 per cent were assigned to strictly political subjects, such as "diamat" and history of the CPSU; 15 per cent to economics, economic organization, and planning; and 43.5 per cent to such varied specialties as industrial technology, agriculture, regional planning, and statistics. The training is obviously designed to develop *professional political leaders of society,* capable of providing expert social-economic direction within the framework of the ideological goals and political vested interests of the ruling party. After "graduation" the rising party official keeps in touch with the latest organizational guidelines and techniques by receiving the regular party journals and through various "handbooks," issued by the Central Committee, containing detailed instructions on how to act in various contingencies.

"Alternation of intensive training with practical experience," one scholar has observed, "is a basic principle of the process of moulding the apparatus official." While he may hold some jobs longer, his normal tour of duty, like that in the United States Army, is three or four years. If he develops a reputation as a trouble shooter in industrial production, agricultural problems, or construction projects, he may well be shifted from one trouble spot to a similar but worse one. Even so, if he demonstrates his ability he will eventually take on jobs with more varied responsibilities. He may also serve on the political staff supervising the military. His success depends upon his political and administrative abilities and his affiliations with more powerful patrons who can speed his way up the apparatus hierarchy. If he does not succeed at the oblast level, he will be shunted off to a low-level secondary post.

The career histories of two Soviet officials, both of whom represent the new apparatchiki, are good illustrations in point. They illustrate graphically the generalizations made above:

PANTELEIMON K. PONOMARENKO
b. 1902;
joined CPSU in 1925;
1918–31, various posts in the Red Army and in industry;
in 1932 finished the Moscow Institute of Transport Engineers;
1932–35, in the political apparat of the Red Army; then again in industry;
1938 joined C.C. apparat and in 1939 elected to the Central Committee, CPSU;
1938–47, 1st Secretary of the Byelorussian Republic C.C.

LEONID I. BREZHNEV
b. 1906;
joined CPSU in 1931;
in 1935 graduated from the Dneprodzerzhinsk Metallurgical Institute;

1936–41, Party work

during the war served as a political commissar on the Southern Front, and in 1946–50 served as a regional [oblast] Party Secretary in the Ukraine [during 1947–49 Khrushchev was in charge of Ukrainian affairs];
1950–52, 1st Secretary of the Moldavian Republic C.C.;

1948–53, Secretary of the C.C. of the

CPSU, and during 1950–53 combined this with a ministerial post;

February 1954, appointed 1st Secretary of Kazakhstan Republic C.C., an agriculturally critical area, which proved to be his undoing;
also identified with Malenkov; after latter's resignation as Premier in 1955, appointed to increasingly less significant ambassadorial posts;

1961, dropped from membership in the Central Committee, CPSU.

1952, elected to the Central Committee, CPSU;
1953–54, head of Political Administration of the Navy;
1954, appointed a Secretary of Kazakhstan Republic C.C., under Ponomarenko;

1956, Secretary of the C.C., CPSU, and candidate member of the Presidium;

1957, elected full member in reward for supporting Khrushchev during the June 1957 crisis;
1957–58, trouble shooter in charge of industrial reorganization;
1960, elected Chairman of the USSR Presidium [nominal Head of State]—the man to watch.

Contrast this highly professionalized career pattern with that of the "professional" American politician. The American may or may not start in at the bottom rung in politics: the higher his social-economic status before entering politics, the higher will be the first office for which he runs. If he starts in with some local office—city council, district attorney—he may then move on to the state legislature, from there to state-wide office or Congress, and from one of these positions to governor or senator. If he is elected governor in a small state, he will probably eventually run for senator; if he is elected senator in a large state, he may run for governor. He may also be content to rest on a lower rung of the complex ladder of American politics and to make his career within his city government, the state legislature, or Congress. If, after creditable service in a lower elective office, he runs for a higher one and loses, he can be reasonably assured of appointment to an executive or judicial position in the government. No higher power consciously shapes his

career pattern. It is up to him to make the most of what the American political system offers.

The Soviet professional politician functions exclusively in a bureaucratic environment. Since the party apparatus is the most important bureaucracy in Soviet society, the power of the apparatchik depends upon his position in the party bureaucratic structure. Organizational positions are to him what votes are to the American politician. The immediate environment of the latter is, indeed, one of the least bureaucratized segments of American society. The United States has industrial, administrative, military, educational bureaucracies, but it does not have a political one. Hence, the skills which are required of the Soviet politician differ considerably from those of the American politician. The apparatchik requires executive traits: the hard-driving, promoting, bulldozing abilities of the old-style American entrepreneur, plus the flexibility in trimming his sails and blending with his environment of the organization man. He must also be adept at bureaucratic in-fighting, anti-cipating changes in the party line and party priorities, identifying the rising apparatus stars and the falling ones, and choosing the right side of the critical issue while maneuvering his opponents onto the wrong side. Crucial to his success is not so much the sup-port of large numbers of people as the backing of the right man at the right time.

The American politician, on the other hand, needs to sense the trend of public opinion rather than Presidium opinion, to articulate common symbols which have wide appeal, to avoid com-mitment on issues where his constitu-ency is divided, and to negotiate satisfying compromises among the in-terests making demands upon him. He must be expert in the strategy of the forum, the apparatchik expert in the strategy of the closet. In campaigns and in legislatures the American politician functions in an egalitarian environment in which the ability to help and harm operates in both directions. The Soviet apparatchik, however, works in a more asymmetrical bureaucratic environ-ment. While power never flows ex-clusively in one direction, he is none-theless largely at the mercy of his superiors while at the same time he exercises extensive controls over his subordinates. The American politician must persuade equals; the apparatchik must please superiors and prod sub-ordinates. When confronted with an-other politician, the American asks himself, "What's he got to offer?" while the Soviet thinks, "Who is to be master?"

Politicians and leaders

The differences in the character of the professional politician in the So-viet Union and the United States are matched by the differences in their roles in the system of political leader-ship. Most of the political leaders in the Soviet Union are apparatchiki. Only a relatively small number of the political leaders in the United States are professional politicians. In the So-viet Union the apparatchiki furnish the Leader for the system, form a majority in the Presidium and the Central Com-mittee, often fill the top posts in the state bureaucracies, and monopolize the Central Committee Secretariat and the party apparatus. In the United States, the electoral politician shares the positions of political leadership with many other types. The profes-sional occupies many posts in state and local government and he usually domi-nates legislatures at all levels of gov-ernment. He may also fill the Presi-dency. With that exception, however, he is rarely found elsewhere in the Administration or in the governmental bureaucracies or in the private bu-reaucracies of the Establishment. The governmental and private bureau-cracies are usually headed by their own products, and Administration leaders are in large part recruited from these products. In addition, of course, even the professional electoral politician usually combines a public and a pri-vate career. The model political leader in the Soviet Union, in short, is the apparatchik who has devoted his life to the party. The model political leader in the United States is the Cincinnatus-like distinguished citizen who lays aside other responsibilities to devote himself temporarily to the public service.

On the national level, professional politicians always occupy the top po-litical position in the Soviet Union and they usually occupy it in the United States. Lenin was a professional revolutionary; Stalin and Khrushchev, both apparatchiki. Of their four principal rivals for power, Trotsky, Kirov, Malenkov, and Molotov, the first was a professional revolutionary and the other three apparatchiki. Of the eight American Presidents since 1917, five had almost exclusively political careers; one moved from education into electoral politics; one moved from business into Administration position; and one spent most of his life in the army.

At the next level the difference in the roles of the professional politicians becomes more apparent. Forty-four men and one woman have been on the Politburo or Presidium between 1919 and 1961. At the time of their appointments, five had served most of their careers as underground professional revolutionaries; seven combined revolutionary experience with work in the party apparatus; five combined revolutionary experience with work in the state bureaucracy; one combined revolutionary experience with work in the military establishment; 19 had worked primarily within the party apparatus; six had worked primarily as officials in the state bureaucracy; one was primarily an economist; and one was a military officer. Similarly, of the 175 members of the Central Committee elected in 1961, 66 had spent their careers almost exclusively in party positions, 42 combined experience in party and government, 33 were in industry or commerce, and 34 were specialists in other branches of governmental or technical work.

Unfortunately for the social scientist, the United States has no Central Committee. One social scientist, however, attempted to identify one by asking knowledgeable people to name the "top leaders in the development of policies affecting the nation." The soundness of this method is not beyond dispute; the result is an arbitrary sam-

TABLE 1. Primary occupations of top political leaders (in per cent)

	Soviet Union 1961 (N–175)	United States 1958 (N–100)
Total politics and government:	61.7	37.0
Politics (party bureaucracy: SU; electoral politics: US)	(37.7)	(19.0)
Private career and politics	—	(8.0)
Politics and government bureaucracy	(24.0)	(1.0)
Private career and government bureaucracy	—	(9.0)
Total commerce and industry	18.8	40.0
Total other occupations:	19.5	23.0
Military (including one military and business: US)	(8.2)	(7.0)
Journalism, mass media, writing	(3.4)	(4.0)
Education and sciences	(1.7)	(4.0)
Labor organizations	(1.7)	(3.0)
Law	(.6)	(3.0)
Diplomacy	(1.7)	—
Religion	—	(1.0)
Farming	(1.1)	(1.0)
Factory worker	(1.1)	—
Total	100.0	100.0

ple of national leaders; but it is probably as reliable a sample as any other means would produce. In 1958 these 100 leaders were strewn across the commanding peaks of politics, government, business, and the professions. Forty-three were in the national government and two others were ex-Presidents. The only state governor (Harriman) had previously occupied important positions in the national government. Thirty-nine were in business, the majority (26) of them in industry. The remainder included five editors and publishers, two lawyers, four educators, three labor leaders, and one cardinal. Table 1 compares the primary occupations of 175 Central Committee members in 1961 with those of these 100 top American leaders of 1958.

These two leadership samples dramatically suggest the expertise required to run a modern society. With a few minor variations, the same skills and experiences are present in each elite. Approximately one-fifth of each elite consists of individuals with primary careers outside politics, civil government, commerce, and industry. The representation of some of these careers is remarkably similar. Professional military officers, for instance, constitute about 7 to 8 per cent of each elite; each group also includes three trade unionists, and one (SU) or a few (US) persons who have followed exclusively legal careers.

The great difference in the composition of the two samples concerns the balance between politics and government, on the hand, and commerce and industry, on the other. Thirty-eight per cent of the Soviet leaders were professional party politicians, compared with 19 per cent for American leaders whose careers had been primarily in

electoral politics. An additional 8 per cent of the American sample combined careers in electoral politics with private careers in business (4%), education (2%), and law (2%). Twenty-four per cent of the Soviet leaders combined careers in the party and governmental bureaucracies, while only 10 per cent of the American leaders had filled extensive government appointments as well as engaging in business (7%), law (2%), and electoral politics (1%). Thus, the careers of almost two-thirds of the Soviet leaders were primarily political and governmental, compared with somewhat more than one-third (37%) for American leaders whose careers included extensive governmental and political service. Only one-fifth (20%) of the American leaders had careers devoted primarily to politics or civil government. Of these 20 individuals in 1958, 15 were in Congress, three in the executive branch, one on the Supreme Court, and one (Harry Truman) was an elder statesman. Forty per cent of the American leaders, on the other hand, had primary careers in commerce and business and 11 per cent more combined a career in business with one in either politics or government. In contrast, only 19 per cent of the Soviet leaders had careers primarily in industry.

Two possible qualifications should be mentioned in connection with these figures. First, many Soviet party and governmental bureaucrats spent much of their careers dealing with industrial problems. When the party bureaucrats dealt with industry, however, it was usually as one aspect of the city, region, or Union Republic for which they as secretary had overall responsibility. Industrial problems might demand much of their time, but their responsibility was an overall political one. Those who combined government and party work may have had more extensive exposure to industry, but their careers also included a variety of other unrelated responsibilities. Only 19 per cent of the Soviet sample had careers devoted exclusively to industrial management. Secondly, on the American side, it could be argued that many of the individuals whose primary occupations were in business and industry also at times held important posts in government. In all cases, however, these governmental responsibilities were either brief (e.g., three or four years at the subcabinet level and thirty-five or forty in business) or additional to their principal business activities (e.g., service on a presidential commission). These marginal governmental responsibilities are more than compensated for by the fact that 17 per cent of the 37 per cent among the American leaders whom we have classified as primarily in government and politics actually spent about half of their careers in private pursuits. Thus, the broad tendencies suggested by the figures are valid. One-fifth of each leadership sample is composed of representatives from the more specialized elite groups present in the modern state. In the Soviet Union, the other top political leaders consist overwhelmingly of professional party politicians and governmental bureaucrats. In the United States, half the remainder is composed of business executives, and the rest is split between electoral politicians and individuals with mixed private-and-government careers.

The more important the office in the Soviet system, the more likely it is to be occupied by an apparatchik. At the 22nd Party Congress, for instance, 26 per cent of the delegates occupied positions in the party apparatus. Forty-nine per cent of the Central Committee elected by that Congress, however, consisted of party officeholders. At the very top, 81 per cent of the members of the Presidium and Secretariat were apparatchiki. In the American system, apart from the Presidency the situation is almost exactly the reverse. The more important the post, the less likely it is to be filled by an electoral politician. Only 19 of Hunter's 100 top leaders were electoral politicians and 14 of these were in Congress. Only three held office in the Administration. At the state and local levels, the proportion of electoral politicians in key jobs—elected and appointed—is much higher. Less than 10 per cent of the governors elected between 1870 and 1950, for instance, had held no previous public office, and over 50 per cent of them had served in the state legislature. Over 30 per cent had served in elected or appointed law enforcement offices, 20 per cent in local elective office, 19 per cent in state-wide elective office, and 14 per cent in federal elective office. In many communities the withdrawal of the "economic dominants" from politics has left the key positions in local government to professional politicians, representing new ethnic groups and often coming from lower middle-class and low-class background. The owner of a family business, on the other hand, who, unlike his grandfather, steers clear of politics in his local community may well turn up in Washington as an Assistant Secretary. The low status of state and local government compared with that of national government is both a cause and a consequence of the prominent role which the electoral politician plays in the former.

During the forty-five years after 1917

the role of the apparatchiki in the Soviet political system tended to increase in importance. In terms of sheer size, the growth of the apparatus kept pace with the growth of party membership. In 1922 there were 15,325 responsible officials in the party, approximately 4 per cent of the party membership. In 1962 the professional paid party workers numbered about 150–200,000—or less than 4 per cent of the total membership. The total number of apparatchiki was much larger, however, since many held temporary assignments in the government and specialized bureaucracies. Much more significant than simple numerical growth was the movement of the apparatchiki into most of the key positions of leadership in the Soviet political system. During Stalin's struggle for power in the 1920's, the idealistic revolutionaries and intellectuals were gradually eliminated from the leading party bodies and replaced by Stalin's adherents from the apparatus. Of the 14 new members of the Politburo between 1925 and 1940, 12 were full-fledged apparatchiki, while two (Voroshilov, Kalinin) combined careers in both the party and other bureaucracies. Since then the apparatchiki only declined in importance when the apparatus itself was subordinated during the last years of Stalin's dictatorship and the first years of the succession struggle. Between 1947 and 1953, five new members were appointed to the Politburo or Presidium, no one of whom was primarily a party worker: Voznesensky was an economist; Bulganin was an industrial and then military administrator; Kosygin, Saburov, and Pervukhin were industrial administrators. The victory of Khrushchev, like that of Stalin, brought a new flood of apparatchiki into the Presidium.

While the role of the apparatchiki in the Soviet political system has increased in importance, the role of the electoral politician in the American system has tended to decline. In 1888 Bryce could argue that a distinctive aspect of American politics was the large class of professional politicians who constituted the real governing class of the country. His observations, however, applied primarily to the state and local level. The emergence of the professional politicians was accompanied by a decline in the political experience of leaders at the national level. Prior to the Civil War, the top leaders of the national government (President, Vice-President, cabinet member, Speaker of the House, Supreme Court Justice) spent more of their careers in politics than in other pursuits, the peak being the generation of 1801–1825, which devoted 65 per cent of its working life to politics. Since the Civil War the top members of the national government have usually spent more of their working life in non-political occupations. Between 1901 and 1921 only 28 per cent of the careers of these national political leaders was devoted to politics. A similar decline has taken place in the proportion of top national leaders who have risen primarily or in part through elective office, the percentage who have held state or local office, and the percentage who have served in state legislatures. As the apparatchik rises to dominate the Soviet political system, the electoral politician slowly fades from the American scene.

The same factors responsible for the rise of the apparatchik were also responsible for the decline of the traditional American electoral politician. The fundamental cause was the bureaucratization of modern society. The electoral politician is at home in the state legislature or Congress but he is sadly out of place in an administrative, industrial, or military bureaucracy. The skills of the bureaucrat are not those of the electoral politician. Few men in recent American politics have been able to perform successfully in both worlds. Averell Harriman, for instance, demonstrated a sustained ability in a variety of national government posts: NRA administrator, presidential adviser, ambassador, cabinet member, foreign aid director, Assistant Secretary of State. But he conspicuously failed to achieve the same level of success as governor of New York. Those who follow electoral careers must identify themselves with a single constituency or state. Those identified with national institutions find it difficult to sink the local roots necessary for an electoral career. In many cases they see little reason to do so. "Although they were policy makers," Hunter remarks of the businessmen among his 100 top national leaders, "with rare exceptions they did not wish to run for public office, and they held themselves superior to the men who seek office." The decline of the electoral politician is thus both directly and indirectly the result of the growth of large national institutional bureaucracies. The leaders of these bureaucracies are necessarily political leaders of the nation. The electoral politician, however, is excluded from these new centers of power. In addition, the leaders of the new bureaucracies have moved in on the executive branch of the national government and dislodged the electoral politician from positions which he once normally occupied. Relegated to Congress and to state and local government, the electoral politician operates primarily at the middle reaches of

power. Given the American system of government this development was a natural one. It is not, however, an inevitable feature of twentieth-century democratic government. In Great Britain, for instance, the parliamentary politician maintains his pre-eminence in the cabinet and ministry. The road to the top positions in the British government is still the traditional career of the professional politician.

In most political systems an individual achieves the top office by winning the support of the key political figures with whom he will work when he is in office. To win out in a succession struggle, a Stalin or Khrushchev gains majorities in the Presidium and Central Committee made up of the people who will be his principal colleagues and subordinates in governing the country. Similarly, in Great Britain, an M.P. normally becomes Prime Minister by first being chosen Party Leader by the members of his party in Parliament. The top party figures both in and out of the Commons whose support he requires to become Party Leader will fill his cabinet when he becomes Prime Minister. In the United States, however, the gap between electoral politics and Administration politics produces a gap between the individuals whom a presidential candidate depends upon to win office and those whom the President depends upon to discharge his office. The first group includes the political leaders and bosses in key states and cities: governors, mayors, state and county chairmen, and perhaps U.S. Senators. They are professional electoral politicians whose national functions are limited to, first, the nomination of the presidential candidate (they appear in full glory at the nominating conventions), and, second, electing him to office.

They are the Daley, the Lawrence, the Crotty: local satraps who emerge for a few months every four years to shape the course of the nation. Once the candidate is elected, however, they can be of little help or hindrance to him. To capture the Presidency, the only resources needed are those which can be directly translated into votes. To govern the country, much else is required. The success of the President depends, in part, on the leaders of Congress, who (with some exceptions, like Harry Byrd), because they are leaders in Congress, are usually not the dominant political figures in their parties at home. The President's success also depends, however, on the cooperation of the leaders of the Establishment and his ability to mobilize political and technical expertise in a wide variety of policy fields. This need leads him to segments of American life which he may never have penetrated in his electoral career. Even someone as well-connected as John F. Kennedy, it was reliably reported, "suddenly discovered he didn't know 'the right people.' During his campaigning he had, of course, met practically every politician in the country. But as far as picking a cabinet was concerned, his large circle of acquaintances seemed inadequate. The truth of these remarks, made matter-of-factly and with no suggestion of regret, was subsequently borne out when Mr. Kennedy appointed men not previously known to him to several key posts in his administration." "Nine strangers and a brother" did not quite accurately describe Kennedy's cabinet, but it did acutely suggest the problem which faces an incoming President.

Whatever inner feuds may rack it, the Soviet Presidium, in terms of shared experience, is in a real sense a team. Although its average membership has vacillated from 10 to 15 members, only 45 individuals have served on it between 1919 and 1961, for an average tenure of approximately a decade. The situation of the British cabinet is somewhat similar. When a party comes to power, the choices which its leaders can make in forming the cabinet are relatively limited. With a few exceptions, its members are in the Commons; rarely have they been there for less than a decade; and most of them have functioned together for several years as a "shadow cabinet." The Prime Minister can shuffle the chairs among them and decide who will have the more important and who the less important offices, but the nature of his government is in general clear to the electors before he is returned to power. In contrast to the Soviet Presidium and the British Ministry, the American Administration is a completely *ad hoc* body. As a group, its members share no common previous experience. A President must honor his political debts and achieve some balance of interests in his Administration. But within these limits he can appoint almost any individual whom he can persuade to accept office. Soviet political leaders come up through the common channel of the party apparatus. As the figures in Table 3 will suggest, however, the President's principal subordinates can come from the most diverse backgrounds. American executive leaders are drawn from the four corners of the nation, and at the close of the Administration they disperse to the four corners of the nation. No other major country draws its political executives from such diverse sources. And in no other major country do individuals move back and forth so often between positions of leader-

TABLE 2. Primary institutional connection of top Soviet leaders; party presidium and secretariat combined

	Stalin 1949 (N–15)	Malenkov 1953 (N–18)	Bulganin-Khrushchev 1956 (N–21)	Khrushchev 1962 (N–21)
Professional apparatchik	54%	61%	67%	81%
(Ideologue)	(7%)	(11%)	(14%)	(20%)
State bureaucracy	33%	28%	23%	19%
(Industrial)	(20%)	(17%)	(14%)	(5%)
Police and military	13%	11%	9%	—
Total	100%	100%	100%	100%
Educational Background				
Higher	40%	56%	71%	76%
(Technical; scientific institute)	(33%)	(45%)	(53%)	(52%)
(Economics, Marxism-Leninism, and humanities)	(6%)	(11%)	(18%)	(24%)
Incomplete higher and secondary	34%	21%	14%	19%
(Seminary)	(13%)	(5%)	(5%)	(5%)
(Technical)	(13%)	(11%)	(5%)	(10%)
Primary	13%	11%	5%	5%
Less	13%	11%	9%	—
Total	100%	100%	100%	100%

ship in the executive branch of the government and positions of leadership in the great institutions of society. In eighteenth-century societies, the social-economic leader, the aristocratic land-owner, might also because of his status command a regiment in the army and a seat in the government. In the late nineteenth century, Americans re-luctantly abandoned this reliance on amateurs in their army. In the late twentieth century, they still continue it in politics.

In contrast to the heterogeneity of the American leadership, the political homogeneity of the Soviet leaders is illustrated by their institutional origins, as shown in Table 2.

The data warrant some qualifica-tions and a few further observations. First of all, it must be stressed once

again that the division of the top leadership echelons into party or state bureaucracy is quite arbitrary. Most of those who are listed as owing their primary institutional connection to the state bureaucracy were or still are high party officials—e.g., Beria or Mikoyan. However, they were assigned to the category whenever it could be assumed that their responsibilities were such that they concentrated primarily on some specific operation of the state machinery and were not directly in-volved in internal party affairs.

The table graphically illustrates the steady growth in the preponderance of the apparatchiki. It is noteworthy, however, that this increase was achieved entirely by the enlargement of the Presidium and Secretariat, and by the disappearance from the scene of military and secret police "representation." (In 1949 and 1953 there was one of each; in 1956 there were two persons with military association, although it may be assumed that Voroshilov's links with the military were tenuous in all three cases; in 1962 there were none, although Shelepin, an apparatchik who for a while headed the secret police, may be in charge of supervising security affairs.) The absolute number of individuals associated with the state bureaucracy remained constant, suggesting that this number was considered functionally desirable.

Noteworthy also is the steady increase in the number of professional ideologues in the top leadership, an indirect reflection of the new emphasis on social indoctrination and perhaps even of concern over recent challenges to ideology. Furthermore, in some respects the later phases of Stalinism were marked by the absence of socio-economic innovation, and static orthodoxy requires fewer ideological interpreters than a period marked by considerable experimentation. The definition of goals and the choice of new means are also ideological issues. In 1949 there was only one such professional ideologue in the top ranks; in 1953 there were two; in 1956, three, including one now in the Presidium; in 1962, four, with two in the Presidium. Their institutional origin and educational background can serve to offset any excessive tendency toward a purely "pragmatic" or technical orientation. Their growth can be contrasted with the gradual fading of the industrial bureaucrats, although the importance of this decline should not be overrated. Many of the top apparatchiki have had industrial experience while more than half have had technical-scientific training, and some have

had occasional industry-related assignments (e.g., Brezhnev supervised the industrial bureaucracy's reorganization in 1957–1958). More important still, some of the others may promote industrial interests, either for ideological reasons or because they see in industrial development the basis for the party's continued primacy.

Table 2 supports the view that the trend in the Soviet leadership is toward greater predominance by the professional apparatchiki, assisted on the one hand by the professional ideologues, and on the other by the experts. To think of an American analogy, one would have to imagine an Administration dominated by a combination of the old-time city-machine bosses and high civil servants, with Senator McCarthy or General Walker setting the ideological tone on one side, and a group of industrial executives providing the technical counsel on the other. The educational data (in several cases quite arbitrary classifications were made because of the imprecision of available information) also support the view that the composition of the leadership is becoming increasingly undifferentiated. Stalin's Politburo of 1949 involved a variety of institutional backgrounds and educational levels, with one-fourth of the Politburo lacking any formal education (the self-made man). Khrushchev's Presidium of early 1962 was four-fifths apparatchiki and almost four-fifths had a higher education. In that, too, its composition was in keeping with the trends inherent in modern professional bureaucracy.

While the Presidium and the Secretariat do not strive to "represent" the various institutional segments of the Soviet system or the varied geographical and national interests of the

Soviet society, and some (for instance, the military) are currently altogether unrepresented, the members perforce do specialize in particular functions and in that sense may be said to reflect indirectly certain specific considerations. Furthermore, an effort is usually made to have two or three non-Russians in the top party organs. However, it is always important to bear in mind that the organizational tradition and discipline of the party inhibits the formation of a narrow, specialized outlook among the Presidium and Secretariat members. Like the cardinals on the Vatican Curia, they are predominantly professional politicians, sharing a common organizational outlook, common interests, and increasingly common background.

In the United States, on the other hand, the sources from which Presidents recruit their Administrations vary considerably. The interests represented in Congress are arbitrarily determined by geography. The great, vital interests of the country are directly represented in the Administration, and it is precisely this characteristic that is responsible for the growth in the power of the executive at the expense of the legislature. Unfortunately, no studies have been made of the representative functions of Administrations, but even the limited data in Table 3 indicate that each Administration embodies a slightly different combination of interests. Almost half the top personnel in the Truman Administration in 1949 had pursued careers in the civil or military administrative branches of the national government, a proportion twice that of the personnel in either the Eisenhower or the Kennedy Administration. As successor to a President who had held office for twelve years, Truman recruited his top subordinates from among the middle-aged bureaucrats who as bright young men fresh out of college or law school had

TABLE 3. Primary occupations of administration leaders*

	Truman 1949 (N–65)	Eisenhower 1953 (N–68)	Kennedy 1961 (N–75)
Electoral politics	5%	6%	14%
Government bureaucracy	48%	23%	21%
Civil	(35%)	(10%)	(12%)
Military	(13%)	(13%)	(9%)
Private	39%	53%	41%
Business	(15%)	(28%)	(11%)
Law	(14%)	(13%)	(11%)
Education	(3%)	(6%)	(16%)
Other	(6%)	(6%)	(4%)
Mixed	8%	17%	23%
Private—electoral	(5%)	(7%)	(10%)
Private—gov't. bureaucracy	(3%)	(10%)	(13%)
Total	100%	100%	100%

* For 1949, 1953, and 1961, respectively, Administration leaders were distributed as follows: Executive Office of the President (including President and Vice-President): 14, 14, 14; heads of executive departments: 9, 10, 10; State Department officials: 4, 6, 9; Defense Department officials (including JCS): 11, 11, 12; subcabinet officials in other departments: 8, 9, 10; heads of non-cabinet agencies: 19, 18, 20.

flocked into Washington in 1933. "The most noticeable difference between the present Administration and the New Deal," John Fischer observed, "is about eighty pounds, comfortably larded around the bureaucratic paunch." The Truman Administration was also able to call upon the large numbers of senior military officers who had demonstrated their abilities during World War II and were available to staff the rapidly expanding Cold War foreign policy agencies at a time when the wartime volunteers in government service were heading back into private life. The Truman Administration thus reflected extensive government experience, if not electoral experience. In European terms, it was a "government of technicians." Yet this was also an indication of its political weakness. It was unable to recruit substantial numbers of individuals who had made careers in business, law, education, and other private pursuits. Only 47 per cent of the top leaders in the Truman Administration had pursued private careers, in whole or in part, as compared with 70 per cent in the Eisenhower Administration and 64 per cent in the Kennedy Administration. The Administration, in effect, was divorced from the principal non-governmental sources of power and influence. It could enlist the support of neither the Counting-House, the Forge, nor the Academy. The political stature of an Administration thus varies inversely with the proportion of career governmental employees in its top ranks.

The Eisenhower Administration, in contrast, placed little reliance on professional government administrators. Over 50 per cent of its top leaders in 1953 had private careers and well over a quarter had spent most of their lives in business. The proportion of professional businessmen in the Eisenhower Administration in 1953 was almost twice that in the Truman Administration in 1949 and two-and-a-half times that in the Kennedy Administration in 1961. "We're here in the saddle," Ike's Secretary of the Interior said, "as an Administration representing business and industry." He was right.

The Kennedy Administration in its first year assumed a still different pattern. Unlike the earlier Administrations, no single source of leaders predominated. Three types of leaders, however, were present in much higher proportions than they had been under either Truman or Eisenhower. Many members of the Kennedy Administration combined private and governmental careers. In large part this reflected the extent to which Kennedy was able to draw upon the experience of the Democratic Administration eight years before: 29 of his top 75 leaders had served under Truman. Secondly, the Kennedy Administration was, in one sense, a more political Administration than its predecessors. Fourteen per cent of its leaders had careers in electoral politics, more than twice the proportion in the Administration of either Truman or Eisenhower. Only 13 of its 75 top leaders, however, had actually held previous elective office at the national, state, or local level, as compared with 10 of the 65 top leaders in the Truman Administration and 13 of 68 top leaders in the Eisenhower Administration. The higher proportion of specialists in electoral politics in the Kennedy Administration reflected not so much a return of the old-style electoral politician as the presence within the Administration of the new-style campaign assistant and political manager, of whom the President's brother was the arch-type. A third distinguishing characteristic of the Kennedy Administration was the high proportion of professors and educators. While businessmen were two-and-a-half times as prevalent under Eisenhower as under Kennedy, the proportion of educators in the Kennedy Administration was two-and-a-half times that in the Eisenhower Administration and five times the proportion of the handful in the Truman Administration. The "Irish mafia" and "Harvard" were statistics as well as stereotypes.

III. A New Professionalism?

The absence of a corps of professional bureaucratic politicians is the most important feature distinguishing political leadership in the United States from that in the Soviet Union. The top political leader in the Soviet Union is a politician and a bureaucrat. The top political leader in the United States is either a politician or a bureaucrat. John Kennedy had fourteen years in politics but none in bureaucracy. Dwight D. Eisenhower had thirty-five years in bureaucracy but none in domestic politics. Khrushchev, in a sense, combines the experience of both. Here is the crucial problem of political leadership in the United States. The modern society is a bureaucratized society: it needs bureaucratic politicians to run it. In the United States the traditional type of professional politician is retiring into the legislatures. To what extent is the United States likely to develop a type of professional bureaucratic politician to replace the declining electoral politician? Can the non-political leader from the Establishment become a successful bu-

reaucratic politician and political leader in government? He is probably more likely to succeed in Administration posts, apart from the Presidency, than is the electoral politician. But if his career has been primarily or exclusively in industry, banking, education, law, or the military, is he likely to bring into government the principal skills and experience required there? To some extent, of course, all bureaucratic organizations are similar, and the skills required to lead them are the same. The successful military commander can transform himself— not entirely painlessly—into a successful corporation executive officer. But adjusting to shifts from one specialized bureaucracy to another may well be easier than shifting from any one specialized bureaucracy to leadership in the Administration. Within a specialized bureaucracy, advancement is normally a product of pull, influence, and contacts, on the one hand, and ability judged by fairly objective standards of technical knowledge and achievement, on the other.

In a political bureaucracy such as the Communist Party of the Soviet Union or any single American Administration, these two grounds become both more general and less distinguishable. Access and contacts are, in a sense, technical criteria for judging politicians. Achievement on the job is measured in terms of social, political, and ideological values which, unlike the standards in the specialized bureaucracy, are diverse, subjective, and controversial. The cabinet officer who is a success to a conservative may be a dismal failure to a liberal. Thus the factors which may bring a man to the top of a specialized bureaucracy do not necessarily prepare him for the wide-open competition in a political bureaucracy. Not having made a career of the struggle for governmental office and power, he may well have his problems in adjusting successfully to that struggle. In general, the more technical and specialized his experience in private life, the more difficulty he will have in government: hence the common observation that Wall Street bankers seem to do better in Washington than Midwestern industrialists. Inherent in the American amateur tradition has been the assumption that individuals who are leaders in one area can also be leaders in another area, that leadership consists of certain traits which some may develop while others do not. Leadership abilities, however, are not universal but specific to particular situations: the leader in one environment may be most inadequate in another.

Successful political leaders thus are likely to be those with experience in political bureaucracy. To some extent, the United States may be slowly developing such a group of bureaucratic politicians. The immense expansion of the federal bureaucracy has multiplied the number of "political offices" at the top of it. It is not inconceivable that a new type of American professional bureaucratic politician is emerging—a man who may have gotten his start in one of the private institutions of the Establishment, but moved into a junior position in government at a still relatively early age, and then worked himself up to a top position in the Administration. Apart from the normal risks of politics, the key problem in such a career is that no Administration lasts longer than eight years. Hence, a career as an Administration political executive is not likely to be a lifetime one. Three alternative patterns are possible. First, if one Admin-

istration is succeeded by another of the same party, undoubtedly many of the bureaucratic politicians in the first will also find places in the second. Second, even if the other party comes to power, a few individuals may still continue their governmental careers. (They would, under Galbraith's definition, be the true "Establishment men": Republicans serving a Democratic Administration or Democrats serving a Republican one.) Or, third, if the other party does come to power, many of the political bureaucrats from the previous Administration may temporarily return to private institutions and come back to government when the parties change once again. That the United States may be developing such a corps of "ministrables" is suggested by the fact that 13 per cent of the leaders of the Kennedy Administration had mixed governmental-private careers, as compared with 10 per cent of the leaders of the Eisenhower Administration and 3 per cent of those in the Truman Administration. The fact that almost 40 per cent of the leaders of the Kennedy Administration had held some post in the Truman Administration also suggests that in the future the elite of one Administration may frequently be recruited from the subelite of the last previous Administration of that party. Extensive governmental service interlaced with some private experience may be the pattern for the new American apparatchik.

It is unlikely, however, that the new professionalism of the American political leadership will result in the emergence of a type of leadership similar to the Soviet. The more ideologically oriented Soviet system requires much more selectivity in recruitment and far greater emphasis on personal commitment to a particular and overt orientation than can be justified by the purely functional requirements of a political system of an advanced industrialized society. But since that selectivity and commitment are vital to the elite's hold on power, it is likely that the ruling elite will continue to stress it, using the device of party membership to siphon off the politically oriented and ambitious elements of society into its own professional bureaucratic network. Lateral entry into political leadership from non-political posts of high responsibility will continue to be viewed as dangerous to the homogeneity of the leadership and hence to its power. In fact, it would be an important clue to change in the Soviet Union if at the political apex one saw the appearance in significant numbers of individuals whose careers had been primarily associated with a non-political bureaucratic profession. But until that happens, the exercise of power and the making of policy in the Soviet Union, unlike the United States, will remain a matter of bureaucratic professionalism and ideological homogeneity. The Soviet leadership still heeds closely Machiavelli's injunction (in which we substitute the word "politics" for "war") : "A prince should ... have no other aim or thought, nor take up any other thing for his study, but politics and its organization and discipline, for that is the only art that is necessary to one who commands.... The chief cause of the loss of states, is the contempt of this art...."

GROUPS AND INDIVIDUALS

JERRY F. HOUGH

Although we may never have the answer to Chichikov's century-old question: "Russia, where are you speeding?", we can find revealing clues to the direction in which contemporary Russian society is moving by studying the changing composition of the Soviet elite. An examination of the "elected" committees and bureaus of the all-union and republican party organizations, for example, reveals interesting information on the relative status of different individuals, officials, and such institutional groups as the police, the industrial managers, the local soviets, and the party apparatus itself. Although the committees, if not the bureaus, are largely honorific bodies composed of prominent workers, peasants and key administrators, they do include the most important officials of the area. Membership on them is considered a prized status symbol and constitutes, with its various gradations of membership, a more sensitive indicator of status change than election to the soviets.

The most obvious index of the relative importance of top officials and the institutions they represent is membership in the All-Union Central Committee and the Auditing Commission of the CPSU. However, it is often difficult to ascertain whether an individual's selection to these bodies reflects his institutional position or his own

Problems of Communism (January–February 1967), pp. 28–35. Reprinted by permission. Footnotes omitted.

personal stature. For example, the increase in the proportion of military
officers on the Central Committee from
five percent to eight percent between
1952 and 1966 may mean an increase
in the influence of the armed forces in
Soviet political life, but it could also
reflect a desire to honor particular individuals who were heroes of the victory over Germany and, in a decreasing number of instances, of the civil
war of the 1920's.

To a considerable extent, a study of
the membership of the republican
party central committees helps to overcome the problem of distinguishing
between personal and institutional
status. To be sure, the election of an
individual to a particular republican
central committee may reflect his
services to the party rather than his
institutional connections, but these
peculiarities tend to cancel out in a
composite summary of the status of a
particular job in the fourteen republics
examined by this author. A change in
the overall pattern may be quite revealing even when there are exceptions
to that pattern.

This article will review the results of
recent party elections—the first comprehensive elections since the fall of
Khrushchev—and attempt to ascertain, by investigating the relative standing of institutional groups such as the
party apparatus, plant managers, the
police, light versus heavy industry, and
of those individuals directly engaged
in the much discussed economic reform, whether they do indeed provide
some clue about the course Soviet
society is taking.

The Role of the Police

To many observers, the most striking
development of the post-Stalin period

was the reduction of police terror, a
development clearly reflected in the
dramatic decline in influence of the
police in the party bodies. Despite
the recent speculation about a possible
return to Stalinist practices, there is no
evidence in the 1966 party elections
that the police have benefited from
Khrushchev's removal. On the contrary, the status of the police has fallen
even farther since the 1961 party elections.

To a large extent, the number of
police officials on the all-union party
bodies had been reduced to a minimum
by 1961, and the fall of Khrushchev
brought no reduction in police representation at this level. In 1961, no
deputy chairman or deputy minister of
the police was named to the all-union
party bodies, and only the Chairman
of the KGB (the Committee for State
Security) remained a voting member
of the Central Committee. That same
year, the highest official of the republican Ministries of Public Order (which
replaced the all-union Ministry of
Internal Affairs), the RSFSR Minister
of Public Order, was demoted to the
level of candidate member of the
Central Committee.

This year the 1961 pattern was repeated, the KGB chairman being made
a full member of the Central Committee, and the RSFSR Minister of
Public Order, a candidate member.
The first deputy chairman of the KGB,
N. S. Zakharov, was not elected a
candidate member of the Central Committee nor a member of the Auditing
Commission, and the author has not
identified any other police officials
among the members of these bodies.

While the decline in the status of the
police in the post-Stalin period was not
as rapid in the republics as it was in
the center, it is most significant that
this decline is still continuing. The

Composition of the republican party bureaus

Professional Functions	1954 Memb.	1954 Cand. Memb.	1956 Memb.	1956 Cand. Memb.	1961 Memb.	1961 Cand. Memb.	1952–64 Memb.	1952–64 Cand. Memb.	1966 Memb.	1966 Cand. Memb.
FULL-TIME PARTY APPARATUS	56	10	79	6	83	12	86	13	75	20
Republican secretaries	44	0	67	0	68	2	70	1	70	1
Republican Department Heads (usually Party Organs Dept.)	7	4	3	3	3	7	0	3	0	5
City Regional Secretaries	5	5	9	3	12	3	3	8	5	14
Chairmen, Party-State Control	—	—	—	—	—	—	13	1	—	—
Chairmen, Party Control Committee	0	1	0	0	0	0	0	0	0	0
REPUBLICAN STATE APPARATUS	62	4	55	6	56	8	33	11	48	15
Chairmen, Council of Ministers	14	0	14	0	14	0	14	0	14	0
Chairmen, Presidium Supreme Soviet	14	0	14	0	13	1	14	0	14	0
Deputy Chairmen, Council of Ministers (Agriculture)	5	1	8	2	4	1	1	4	5	2
Ministers (Agriculture)	4	1	1	0	1	0	0	0	0	0
Deputy Chairmen, Council of Ministers (Industry)	9	0	6	2	9	0	1	2	6	2
Chairmen, Sovnarkhozy	—	—	—	—	9	2	1	0	—	—
Ministers (Industry)	1	1	0	0	0	1	0	0	0	0
Deputy Chairmen, Council of Ministers (Culture)	1	0	2	0	0	1	0	1	0	0
Ministers (Culture)	1	0	0	0	1	0	0	0	0	0
Heads of Police	11	1	9	1	5	2	2	4	3	3
Chairmen, State (People's) Control	1	0	0	0	0	0	—	—	8	6
Miscellaneous	1	0	1	1	0	0	0	0	0	1
OTHER	13	15	10	17	11	24	7	17	8	14
Military	5	2	6	1	5	3	5	2	6	1
Republican Komsomol Secretaries	0	9	2	7	1	8	1	6	1	5
Republican Trade Union Chairmen	4	1	2	3	3	8	1	9	1	8
Newspaper Editors	2	2	0	6	1	5	0	0	0	0
Miscellaneous	1	0	0	0	1	0	0	0	0	0
Unknown	1	1	0	0	0	0	0	0	0	0
Total	131	29	144	29	150	44	126	41	131	49

republican party bureaus still contain a number of police officials, but their representation has dropped consistently.

A similar picture emerges from an examination of the central committees of six republics which were studied in detail. The leaders of the two police organizations, the Committee for State Security and the Ministry of Public Order, are still full members of the central committees, but the lesser police officials have not fared as well. Although lower police officials were mentioned very infrequently in the Soviet press in the mid-1950's, it was possible to identify three of these men among the full members of the six republican central committees chosen in 1956. In 1961 and 1966, when the names of these officials appeared more often in the press, there were no police deputy ministers among the full members and never more than one of them among the candidate members of the republican central committees and the members of the auditing commissions.

The inability to identify all of the members of the republican party committees makes it impossible to draw accurate conclusions about the status of lower police officials. A few examples, however, are illuminating. In Uzbekistan the deputy chairman of the KGB was a full member of the republican central committee in 1956. In 1961, however, while still deputy chairman of the KGB, he was demoted to the status of central committee candidate member, which the elections of 1966 have not changed. In Byelorussia A.D. Rudak was elected a full member of the republican central committee in 1956 when he was head of a central committee department, and in 1960 when he was Head of Affairs (*upravliaiushchii delami*) of the republican Council of Ministers. When

he later became deputy chairman of the republican KGB, however, he was demoted to the auditing commission at the 1961 party congress. The elections of 1966 have not changed his status either, although he was first deputy chairman of the republican KGB at the time.

Economic Reform

If the major domestic problem in the years immediately following Stalin's death was the relationship of the police to the party and later to the population, the central question of the present period surely is that of economic reform. While the reforms undertaken thus far can best be described as cautious, a number of interesting experiments have begun. At the present time there are a number of indications —some rather vague, some quite direct —that we shall see many more radical changes in the future.

To this observer, the most startling fact about the 1966 party elections was that they failed to give recognition to the men directly associated with the economic reforms or those who might be expected to gain new importance as a consequence of those reforms. None of the major advocates of the reform were included in the all-union party bodies, and only one of the lesser advocates was named to a republican party committee. (This man was V. M. Glushkov, a mathematician, whose inclusion in the Ukrainian Central Committee no doubt is based on the fact that he is Director of the Institute of Cybernetics and Vice-President of the Ukrainian Academy of Sciences.)

Indeed, the party elections gave little recognition to any of the economists who, as a result of the reforms, would seem likely to play a larger role in economic decision making. None of the economists among the deputy chairmen of Gosplan, none of the directors of the economic institutes, and not even the chairman of the crucial Committee on Prices, was included among the 439 men named to the all-union party bodies. I have been able to identify 16 directors of republican economics institutes, and of these only one was selected a member of a republican party committee—the auditing commission, at that. Both at the center and in the republics, the top posts in the councils of ministers, the planning organs, and the ministries (and the corresponding memberships in the central committees) have been given rather to men with engineering, plant-manager backgrounds, in other words, the same group that has dominated Soviet industrial administration for years.

Except for men such as Suslov, the only economists we can identify among the members of the new All-Union Central Committee are F. A. Tabeev, a young obkom first secretary, and A. M. Rumiantsev, at the time of his election acting head of the economics division of the Academy of Sciences. Rumiantsev, in particular, is a most interesting and instructive case. Now more widely known as the liberal chief editor of *Pravda* for a year after Khrushchev's ouster, and recently named Chairman of the Scientific Council on Problems of Concrete Social Investigation, Rumiantsev left the Ukrainian Commissariat of Justice to become a research economist in 1930, the year in which the creative economic work of the 1920's was suppressed. In the 1940's he was transferred to party work, ultimately becoming the ideological secretary of the Kharkov

obkom. In the last years of the Stalin period he was named director of the Ukrainian Institute of Economics and then academic secretary of the social sciences division of the Ukrainian Academy of Sciences.

Although Rumiantsev is now said to be a vigorous supporter of empirical sociological research, Soviet economists must find it ironic, at least, to find a man with his background as the leading economist on the Central Committee in these days of the rebirth of economic science. It is, of course, possible that his selection reflects a desire to find an advocate of economic reform who most nearly speaks the language of the "orthodox" economists and who can reconcile the differing factions. However, one cannot avoid the suspicion that Rumiantsev's election denotes some ambivalence on the part of the leadership.

Some ambivalence is also suggested by the treatment given plant managers in the party elections. The central and republican party bodies do contain a great many administrators and regional party secretaries who formerly were plant managers, but surprisingly few of their members are plant managers at the present time. Indeed, despite intimations that managers of enterprises are to be given greater decision-making authority, the number of directors of civilian plants on the all-union Central Committee and Auditing Commission fell from five in 1961 to four in 1966, and the number among the full members of the six republican central committees from 18 to 16. The leading plant directors involved in the recent economic experiments received no recognition at all.

It would, of course, be premature to conclude that the proposed economic reforms will be abortive. However, one can point to a problem which surely must be resolved in the next few years. In quasi-Marxist terms, we might almost say that there is a "contradiction" between some of the professed goals of the reforms and the personnel chosen for the top posts in the councils of ministers, gosplans, and ministries—or to be more exact, between these goals and the relative positions accorded to key groups. It is a "contradiction" which is not likely to last long, however, for unless there are changes in personnel policy, the men called upon to implement the reforms will not have the prestige or authority to do so.

Heavy vs. Light Industry

While the results of the party elections raise questions about the intensity of the commitment of the leadership to radical reforms in the planning system, the announced decision to bring light industry somewhat closer to equality with heavy industry does find greater reflection in the election results.

To be sure, the elections (as well as the directive on the new Five-Year Plan itself) leave no doubt about the continued primacy of heavy industry. Fourteen Ministers of Industry were elected full members of the All-Union Central Committee, none of whom head light industry ministries. With the exception of the Ministry of Electronics (essentially a defense industry), even the ministries on the periphery of light industry (those concerned with the production of chemicals and machinery for light industry) won representation only at the level of candidate members of the Central Committee.

A similar situation prevails within the central party secretariat. The head of the heavy industry department (A. P. Rudakov, who died July 10, 1966) was given the rank of secretary and full membership in the Central Committee, while the secretary for industry with the highest status (D. F. Ustinov, a candidate member of the Politburo) is a former Minister of Defense Industry. On the other hand, the head of the light industry department is only a candidate member of the Central Committee, and the heads of the chemical industry department and the trade organs department are only members of the Auditing Commission. (The heads of the departments for machine building and for defense industry are also only candidate rather than full members, but Ustinov's and Rudakov's prime responsibility in these realms must be taken into account in evaluating this fact.)

In the republics, the differentiation of status between officials of heavy industry and those of light industry is not as marked, but it is still quite visible. While republican ministers in charge of branches of heavy industry which have always had low priority (notably the timber industry and the building-materials industry) continue to be accorded rather low status, those in charge of oil, coal, and metallurgy are, as always, full members of the central committees. By contrast, less than half of the ministers of the various branches of light industry have been granted full membership. Similarly, only four out of 11 heads of light industry and food industry departments of the republican party central committees were given full membership on the central committees, while all but one of the heads of heavy industry departments (or industrial-transportation departments in cases where there is no department for heavy industry alone) received this honor.

Nevertheless, in spite of the higher status still accorded to officials connected with heavy industry, the recent elections do reveal that for the first time in the postwar period the ministers in charge of light, consumer-goods industries have been given a significant place among the party elite. In 1952 three of the four ministers in charge of consumer industries were not even elected to the Auditing Commission; in 1956 only two of these four were included on the Central Committee and the Auditing Commission; and in 1961 the number of light industry administrators in these bodies remained at two. In 1966, by contrast, three of the four consumer industry ministers and the deputy chairman of the RSFSR Council of Ministers in charge of light industry were elected candidate members of the Central Committee, and the fourth consumer industry minister was made a member of the Auditing Commission. In the republics also, ministers in charge of consumer industry received substantially increased recognition in the party's governing bodies. In the six republics sampled, 18 such ministers were elected full members of republican party central committees in 1966, as against 13 in 1956, and 10 in 1961.

Even more dramatic has been the elevation in the status of the ministries concerned with consumer services. In both 1956 and 1961 only seven heads of such ministries were given places on the All-Union Central Committee and Auditing Commission, whereas 11 of them received this honor in 1966. In the six sample republics, the total number of ministers concerned with consumer services who were elected to the key republican party bodies rose from 21 in 1956 to 24 in 1961, and to 35 in 1966.

The substantial rise in the status of the consumer-oriented ministries from 1961 to 1966 is indeed striking in comparison with the relative lack of change between 1956 and 1961. In retrospect, the 1961 party elections appear to be a truer index of Khrushchev's actual investment priorities (that is, the priorities he adopted when faced with a hard choice) than were his many statements about "goulash Communism." The 1966 party elections could, therefore, presage a more determined and effective effort to achieve the new targets for consumer-goods production than was made to meet these targets as set in the preceding seven-year plan. If the Soviet citizen now hears little about a transition to communism by 1980, perhaps he has greater reason to hope that the country is at least moving closer to a consumer-oriented economy.

The Role of the Party

Anyone who speculates about the development of Soviet society must investigate the changes, if any, that are taking place within the Communist Party itself. Is there any evidence of an erosion in the "directing" role of the party apparatus as compared with the role of the governmental institutions? Is the process by which party decisions are made becoming more pluralistic? Are men with new and different backgrounds and perspectives coming to the fore in the directing party bodies?

The Soviet press in the post-Khrushchev period has carried a multitude of warnings that party organs should not attempt to "replace" (*podmeniat'*) the soviets or state organs of economic administration and should not interfere in detailed administrative questions. Some observers have concluded from these statements that while Khrushchev "tried to expand [the party apparatus] from an ideological organization into an operational organization involved in day-to-day management of all aspects of the economy," his successors "have withdrawn the party organization from the detailed operation of government and society."

In an earlier article published elsewhere* the author pointed out that the significance of such warnings against party encroachments on the administrative functions of the soviets and state organs has often been exaggerated. After all, such warnings had been uttered periodically in the last two years of the Khrushchev period as well as earlier. Rather than implying a restriction of the authority of party organs, these warnings are intended to remind republican and lower-level party secretaries of the broad scope of their responsibilities and of the consequent necessity to leave relatively routine problems to the state administrators. The party first secretary at the republican or provincial level has been depicted in party theory as a prefect-like official—that is, an official who is an integral part of the administrative system with the responsibility of representing the center in his area, of coordinating the work of the local agencies of the specialized ministries, of seeing that the decisions of these agencies reflect a broader perspective than might flow from narrow departmental

---

* See Part IV [Ed.].

interests, and of promoting a balanced development program in the region.

Nothing in recent Soviet official statements indicates that there has been any curtailment of the basic authority or responsibility of the party organs, and the 1966 elections provide corroborating evidence of the continued primacy of the party apparatus. Republican and regional party secretaries continue to constitute the largest single group in the all-union Central Committee, as do lower-level party secretaries in the republican party central committees, and they continue to dominate the all-important bureaus. Nevertheless, there has been a slight decline in the percentage of acting party officials elevated to membership of key party committees and bureaus, a decline which might possibly foreshadow a gradual change in the role of the party organs but more probably reflects the necessity of representing the larger number of central ministries required by the major reorganization of the central government apparatus last fall.

It should be noted that the Khrushchev period saw a drastic increase in the representation of the professional party apparatus in the republican party bureaus. Following a 1952 decision to reduce the republican and regional party secretariats to three men, party officials held a majority of the voting seats in only two (or possibly three) out of 14 republican party bureaus. In 1956, however, party officials constituted a majority of the voting members of party bureaus in nine republics; in 1961, in 11 republics; and in 1962–64, in all the republics.

The 1966 party elections did not reverse this trend. At the present time, party officials have a majority on all but one of the republican party bureaus, and in this one exception (Latvia) five of the ten bureau members are party secretaries. Moreover, in over half of the republics, one of the "state" members of the party bureaus is the chairman of the People's Control Commission, a position invariably filled from the career party apparatus.

The significance of the high percentage of party officials on the republican party bureaus does not lie in the existence of a common apparatchik viewpoint. It is doubtful that any such thing exists any longer in view of the increasing scope and diversification of functions within the party apparatus. In many bureaus, specialized party officials who work in intimate contact with one another and with the first secretary constitute a majority. It is virtually inevitable under these circumstances that on many problems a compromise will have been informally, perhaps even unconsciously, reached before the question is even considered by the bureau as a whole. In this sense there is a danger of the party secretariats supplanting the bureaus, and the danger is not merely a hypothetical one.

At the center, few of the specialized secretaries sit on the Politburo, but Khrushchev's practice of giving a majority of Politburo voting memberships to party officials has been continued. Six out of the full Politburo members are all-time party officials, and four of the "state" administrative officials now on this body spent most of their careers in party or Komsomol work. No doubt reflecting the nature of the Politburo's work, nine of its voting members have had the coordinative administrative experience of a republican or obkom party first secretary.

While party officials are still the largest single group in the party committees and bureaus, there has been, as already noted, some reduction in the strength of their representation on these bodies, although at certain levels it is difficult to make a distinction between purely government and purely party leaders. At any rate, the enlargement of the all-union and republican central committees has meant a decrease in the percentage of seats held by individuals identifiable as purely party leaders.

The decline in the proportion of party officials on the committees and bureaus appears to have little practical significance for the short run. The change in the central Politburo primarily reflects the decision to divide the two major positions held by Khrushchev between two men, while the shift in the republican bureau can be explained by the transformation of the former Party-State Control Committees (regarded as primarily party organs) into People's Control Commissions (now classed as state agencies). If this is taken into account, the actual change from 1964–66 is very slight, nor does the reduced proportion of seats occupied by party apparatchiks on the All-Union Central Committee seem likely to have much impact on the decision-making process. With party officials continuing to constitute 42 percent of the Central Committee membership and with many former party secretaries now in the state administration, there is little reason to believe that the Central Committee could be used as a vehicle to reduce the role of the party apparatus, or that important differences of opinion on other issues will involve representatives of the party apparatus on one side and those of the state apparatus on the other. In fact, any divisions are likely to cut across both groups rather than to follow party-vs.-state lines.

If the decline in the proportional representation of the party apparatus is unlikely to have any immediate practical impact, does it have any broader, longer-range significance? To answer this difficult question, it becomes necessary to examine what particular groups have benefited most from the expansion of the central committees. When we take a long look at the all-union Central Committee over a period of years, for example, we find that there was a sharp rise in the representation of the military in the period 1956–1961, of industrial administrators in 1961–1966, and of foreign affairs officers throughout the last decade. At the republican level, there have been considerable variations from the pattern of change in the all-union Central Committee, but increases in the representation of state administrators in consumer-oriented fields and of rank-and-file peasants and workers have been generally conspicuous.

Rather than seeking to explain each of these changes individually, it is perhaps more useful to treat them as a whole and to relate them to what is doubtless the fundamental long-term trend in the evolution of Soviet society —the increasing specialization in the decision-making process. Because of the growing number of specialized institutions and sub-institutions and the increasing complexity of the decisions

to be taken, it becomes inevitable that an ever greater number of these decisions should in fact be left to those individuals with specialized knowledge, regardless of changes in the top political leadership. From this perspective, the gradual rise in the number of specialized administrators seated on the party central committees no doubt reflects recognition of the growing importance of the decision-making role of the institutions which these administrators represent.

In any event, it seems clear that the resolution of conflicts between the major interests in Soviet society continues to be carried out primarily by party officials. Certainly, despite statements about an increase in the role of the soviets, there is no indication of any increase in the status of their chairmen since 1961. Furthermore, it is worth noting that every republican party first secretary was named a full member of the Central Committee, while only five of the chairmen of republican councils of ministers received this honor.

In a subsequent article* I will examine more closely the categories of party officials who are becoming increasingly important and attempt to see whether new men with different backgrounds and perspectives are coming to the fore in the directing party bodies.

---

* *Problem of Communism*, March/April 1967 [ed.].

THE PASSING OF POWER:
REFLECTIONS ON THE FALL OF KHRUSHCHEV

HENRY L. ROBERTS

Khrushchev's abrupt removal from office and power last October was, for me, but another in a sequence of unanticipated events in Soviet affairs, a sequence that has made the study of modern Russia both fascinating and perplexing. It is not the failure to foretell the occurrence that causes me chagrin—the contingencies surrounding any particular event are so great that I am content to await the fact—but rather such an event has a way of badly muddying one's general picture of what is going on in the Soviet Union. The victory of one American Presidential candidate over another, or even such a shocking interruption of our political process as the assassination of President Kennedy, does not, it seems to me, produce this disconcerting sense of derailment, this rueful "back to the drawing board" mood, in which one's general notion of the Soviet political process seems badly awry.

Now this may merely reflect the professional warping of the specialist—too much squinting at and brooding about the Soviet Union. The answer may be, as Yeats advised regarding another "bitter mystery":

Young man, lift up your russet brow . . .
And brood on hopes and fear no more.

Surely it is true that we are inclined to ask more of the craft of Sovietology than can be reasonably expected. Precisely because the subject is important and the stakes are great, we have a strong compulsion to demand greater perception in our appraisals of the Soviet scene than we might expect to gain in connection with our own society—given our still limited knowledge of political processes. I am afraid, however, that there are also problems in the subject itself, not merely in our level of expectation as observers. In broadest terms these perplexities concern the gaining, maintenance, concentration, and transfer of political power and authority. In examining such difficult abstractions here, my intention is less to produce a coherent pattern than to reflect upon the Russian past, to emphasize, perhaps even to caricature, certain features of perversity in Russian affairs that I find so troublesome.

For a number of years now, with the evident actuarial likelihood that Nikita Sergeevich would not be on the premises indefinitely, the question of Khrushchev's successor has been much discussed: Brezhnev was considered the favorite though a general turmoil was expected to follow. But of course the singular feature is that Khrushchev *was* ousted. However we may rate the extent of his control after 1957, however "first" he may have been among his "equals," this is still the first time in Soviet history that the man apparently firmly in the saddle was unseated by means other than death or disablement. I am not at all sure that

Reprinted from the *Columbia Forum*, Summer 1965, Vol. VIII, No. 2, Copyright 1965 by the Trustees of Colombia University in the City of New York.

there will not be, nevertheless, a struggle for power among Khrushchev's successors, but the simple fact that his career was terminated in a fashion different from Lenin's or Stalin's suggests prudence in basing expectations on the earlier models. And it is just here that the would-be student of Soviet affairs begins running into what strike me as rather serious analytical difficulties.

It is, of course, from the post-Lenin and post-Stalin experiences that we derive the notion that a succession crisis is a hardy perennial in the Soviet way of politics. In these two "classic" cases, the death or disability of an unchallenged leader led to bitter struggle among his chief lieutenants until a new leader emerged from the contenders: Stalin with his victory over the Right opposition in 1928, Khrushchev with his victory over the anti-party group and Marshal Zhukov in 1957.

Now this pattern of struggle has presented a problem for political analysis. Myron Rush, who has devoted much thought to it, recently summarized his views with respect to the likelihood of future crises, as follows:

A succession crisis *is* to be expected. This conclusion is not simply grounded in history; the nature of the Soviet political system appears to make such crises inevitable. There are two reasons why this is so. First, in the Soviet system, there is no established decision-making center whose authority is recognized at all times. Second, for this reason, and for others to be cited, no orderly method of succession has been or is likely to be devised. . . .
There is a paradox here. The Soviet system has been most stable until now when it has had a dictator, yet dictatorial authority inheres in no office or title. It is unprovided for in the fundamental laws of Party and state, which establish collective organs of leadership without exception. As a result there is no rule for establishing the legitimacy of the dictator. . . .
In the USSR, then, the new ruler evidently comes to his office not by an orderly transfer of authority but by arrogating power to himself. As a result, for a time, at least, the functions normally performed by the ruler go undone. Moreover, the process by which this state of affairs can be rectified, namely, the concentration of great power in the person of the successor, is disruptive. It is these two consequences of the failure to provide for succession that produce political crisis in the Soviet system. . . .

I have no objection to this analysis, for it is evident that the Soviet regime maintains an intimate connection with its revolutionary origins, which were the antithesis of a "legitimate" assumption of power. There is a connection, too, with the determination of the Bolsheviks not to be trapped by constitutionalism or by established ways.

It can be argued further that an ideology with pretensions to absolute correctness must ultimately rest upon a single source and symbol lest pluralism and relativism arise. From this it is concluded that, so long as the ideology is active and operative, any shift in authority will be impelled away from collegial efforts toward one-man control. Such a system does not necessarily imply a succession crisis, as is clear from the election of Popes. But it does suggest that in the absence of an orderly sequence of power transfer—whether by inheritance and the divine right of kings, or election by a College of Cardinals, or through a more secular form of election in Presidential politics—a succession crisis will take the form of this compulsion toward the reestablishment of one-man supremacy.

While one may feel that for these and other reasons the post-Khrushchev leadership in the Soviet Union may not prove particularly stable, there are two considerations that do not seem to me to fit simply into any neat picture. One is analytical, the other historical.

As I said, unlike Lenin and Stalin, Khrushchev was thrown out while apparently holding power. Mr. Rush observes: "Khrushchev, to my surprise, failed to preserve the power he had concentrated, perhaps because his overconfidence enabled his intended successors to acquire too much power. Fundamentally, however, his overthrow illustrates the double dilemma ... of a ruler in the Soviet Union who attempts to govern without terror and to arrange for his own succession...."

The analytical problem, as I see it, is that the introduction of terms such as "overconfidence" or "govern without terror" at once raises some exceedingly problematic, human questions. And while they are quite proper—surely Khrushchev's human foibles and the human decision whether to employ terror must be granted as relevant—the more significant one sees their role to be, the more one undercuts an analysis based on abstract considerations of power, authority, and sovereignty. If after his successful scramble to the top in a succession struggle, a man who enjoys such a great concentration of power can be toppled, not through an act of God but just through blunders, does not our entire theory of power become a bit insubstantial?

Insofar as we formulate the succession problem in the Soviet Union as a systemic oscillation between stability under an established dictator and instability during periods of contending aspirants—the stability of the former deriving from the lack of effective challengers—then Khrushchev should not have been ousted. On the other hand, once we grant that a dictator at the height of his sole power is sufficiently subject to human error to lead to his downfall, perhaps in preparation for his own succession but presumably at any time, then our formulation becomes correspondingly uncertain.

Nor do we gain much insight by reference to the undoubted fact that Khrushchev lacked Lenin's "moral authority" or charisma, or Stalin's ability to use terror effectively. Indeed, I am increasingly troubled by our tendency to believe that such terms as "charismatic leadership" or "rule by terror" advance us very far analytically. These are clearly descriptive terms for uncustomary but observable phenomena; but when we inquire just *how* a leader succeeds in exerting his charismatic or terroristic influence, or *why* his people respond appropriately (rather than shrugging their shoulders to the charisma or putting a knife in the back of the would-be terrorist), we must seek the answer in a very particular set of circumstances. "Charisma" or "moral authority," to be effective, must evoke a response; otherwise a leader is simply crying in the wilderness. The application of terror requires both a populace that can be cowed by it and henchmen to exercise it who will not turn and fall upon the leader. These are not, I think, simple or easy circumstances to create, nor are they accounted for by general models of political power.

Indeed I have long nourished a suspicion that any rigorously systematic model of the political process—most obviously those employing mechanical or physical analogies such as power, balance of forces, and the like—ultimately becomes involved in self-contradiction. This strikes me as a fatal flaw in all such efforts from Machiavelli and Hobbes on down.

In the present example I rather suspect that precisely because the Soviet regime and ideology are themselves so power-conscious and power-motivated, we are more than usually inclined to seek a systematic explanation in terms of power. But I am not at all sure that we can make a self-sufficient argument, on the basis of the Lenin and Stalin successions, that there is a formal or internal necessity for further succession crises in the Soviet Union. Khrushchev's ouster, *by its prematurity*, can be used as an argument against, as well as for, such a necessity.

Yet, this being said, I will grant that power and its transfer do somehow constitute a rather special problem in Soviet Russia. Could it be that the reason is *historical* rather than *systematic*? To examine this possibility, I should like to make a few random excursions into Russian history. I must say at once that my examples are from earlier rather than immediately pre-Soviet history; and this raises the question whether we are in fact dealing with the same problem. Still, let us look at some examples and see what they suggest.

Regarding the dim Kievan past, we are told that among the rulers of the Rurik dynasty, the pattern of inheritance and succession was a rather unusual one: not from father to son, but through a series of lateral transfers in the various holdings by seniority among the members of the dynasty. In time the system broke down, not surprisingly it seems to me: between the years 1054 and 1224 no less than 64 principalities had a more or less ephemeral existence in which 293 princes came forward with succession claims, and their disputes led to 83 civil wars.

With the emergence of Muscovy, however, we get a reversal of the pattern, a move—whatever the causes and occasion—toward autocracy, combined with the "ingathering" of domains previously lost or distributed through civil conflict and foreign invasion. Autocrats not only emerged, but managed to pass along the succession of autocracy, sometimes under extremely difficult circumstances. For example, Ivan IV, known as the Terrible, came to the throne at the age of three. How in the world did this infant, despite nobles and boyars, manage to re-establish the autocracy, indeed to strengthen it? Not a medievalist, I remain perplexed by this phenomenon, which seems inexplicable by mechanical means.

Following the death of Ivan's weak heir, Muscovy was convulsed—by the Time of Troubles—but again an autocracy emerged, under the Romanov dynasty. Why not an oligarchy of chieftains? The Polish habit of whittling away the Crown's power whenever there were breaks in the regular succession might seem more natural. Admittedly, there were places in Western Europe where after weak or infant kings, or civil wars, autocracy was able to re-form: Louis XIV after the Fronde, the House of Tudor after the War of the Roses. But the examples seem somewhat less extreme, less persistent. Peter the Great seemingly repeats the pattern of Ivan the Terrible —a youngster without power somehow contrives to retrieve and extend absolute authority.

In the 18th century, the absence of a clear line of inheritance fearfully confused the succession question. It is worth noting that at the accession of Anne, in 1730, the lady was obliged to sign a document limiting autocratic power and providing for control by a grand council. This proved to be very unpopular and she, too, was able to restore at least the principle of unlimited autocracy. According to a contemporary source, one of the nobles who helped her said:

That he was deputed by the whole nobility of the empire to represent to her, that she had been, by the deputies of the Council of State, surprised into the concessions she had made; that Russia having for so many ages been governed by sovereign monarchs, and not by council, all the nobility entreated her to take into her own hands the reins of government; that all the nation was of the same opinion, and wished that the family of her Majesty might reign over them to the end of time.

Then, from the beginning of the 19th century, the succession question seems less a prominent feature of the Russian political landscape, partly because of regulated inheritance. The confusion at the time of the death of Alexander I, connected with the Decembrist uprising, appears rather a problem of communication than a real question of succession. Mr. Rush has suggested that the "succession" crisis "played a role, though not a great one, in the fall of the tsarist regime in 1917, which was somewhat hastened by the refusal of Archduke Michael to assume the throne left vacant by the forced abdication of Nicholas II." I personally doubt whether that belated episode played any significant part in the onset of the revolution or the course of Russian history. By the time of Nicholas II, a weak man with a hemophilic son and a brother whose chief recommendation for the throne apparently was his stupidity, the pattern of monarchial succession in the Romanovs was pretty well played out.

What conclusions, if any, may be legitimately drawn from these scattered episodes from Muscovite and early imperial history? They do bear certain resemblances to succession issues in the Soviet period: a political system with an enormous concentration of authority; a less than satisfactory method of transmitting it in an orderly fashion; and finally, a tendency to reconcentrate power. In considering possible parallels I do not wish to suggest that Russians "by nature" love despots; nor that Bolshevism has been an atavistic throwback to Muscovy—such leaps are persuasive only if some plausible means of transmittal from one age to another can be advanced.

I should, however, like to suggest one explanation that may have some bearing on contemporary concerns. As we have noted, the periodic crisis of succession and re-establishment of autocracy tended to fade out in the 19th century. Simultaneously, although the Tsar remained an autocrat at least up to 1905, during that century Russian society became far more articulated: between the sovereign power and the populace there grew a complex of intermediate elements—middle class, intelligentsia, new formation of bureaucracy. While this development was not adequately reflected in corresponding constitutional or political change, I have the impression that even so vigorous a reactionary as Alexander III was not, in reality, the autocrat that his 17th- and 18th-century predecessors had been. Some revolutionaries hoped that getting rid of the individual monarch might topple the system, but there was a growing belief that this alone would be insufficient—that the system was held together by many other forces.

In other words, I am suggesting that, whatever the reasons for the peculiar concentration of authority and its transmittal in earlier Russian history, the 19th and early 20th centuries were witnessing a significant growth of elements making for political pluralism, whether recognized or not. Then came the 1914 war, the Revolution, and the Civil War—vast upheavals demographically and socially as well as politically—which had, I believe, the effect of scraping away, through deposition, death, confiscation, and emigration, a very considerable part of these new intermediary elements, not to speak of the autocracy itself.

Thus I would venture to say that the beginning of the Soviet period was in certain respects a historical retrogression. It was not only that, through revolution, elements in the lower strata of society had been flung to the top, but also that a great many of the cushioning or modulating social elements had been removed. The objects of governmental policy—the Soviet citizenry—were in large measure once again the premodern peasantry.

Under these circumstances the ideological impulses of Marxism-Leninism could easily lead, in their concrete application to society, to that curiously atavistic despotism we know as Stalinism. For all of Stalin's ferocious talents, the fact that he was *able* to impose his will tells us as much about Russian society of his time as it does about his aims and abilities.

If this suggestion has merit, we might look to its recent application. Whatever our judgment of the human cost, Russia has gone far since the 1920s in modernization and industrialization. Against the wreckage of those early years a highly articulated society has again been erected, even though there has not as yet been adequate political or constitutional reflection of this change. Within Soviet society im-

portant new groups have emerged: managers, intellectuals, bureaucrats— an increasingly large percentage of whom, as time passes, have been spared the scarifying effect of the Stalin era. In this "re-articulation" of Russian society, are we witnessing a healing, after half a century, of the great social rift or amputation resulting from the Revolution? If so, it may then follow that the dictator/succession crisis/dictator sequence could fade away, not because of ideological erosion (though that, too, should not be excluded), but because of changes in Soviet society. The lord may pull the bell-rope, but the servants may not come.

Do these suggestions find either support or refutation in the post-Khrushchev period, a matter of eight months? I am afraid not. I am uncertain whether Khrushchev's replacement by Brezhnev and Kosygin is a step in a progressive direction or merely another turn in the cycle of Communist infighting atop an inert society. I am impressed by the persistence of the Stalinist heritage, especially among the *apparatchiki* now at the top, whose school of advance was the late 1930s.

Still, my impression is that the Khrushchev ouster, for all its obscurity and dubious legality (if the term has meaning here), may be considered as more positive than negative. Admittedly, this can be challenged. Leonard Schapiro, for example, has argued that Brezhnev and Kosygin "seem to lack even the kind of legitimacy that Lenin, Stalin, and Khrushchev all had." And of course within the framework of the revolutionary tradition this is quite true: Lenin made the Revolution, Stalin played a part in the Revolution and laid claim to being the legitimate heir of Lenin; even Khrushchev, in his anti-Stalinism, had some claim to maintaining the Leninist tradition. The element of continuity is far less apparent in the case of Brezhnev and Kosygin, men of a younger generation who rose under Khrushchev, and the lack of it could well lead to instability.

On the other hand, the very fact that such men were willing and able to take power from Khrushchev—a not unimpressive First Secretary of the Party—suggests that, even now, the political ground rules may be changing, to something hectic, perhaps, but perhaps also something more familiar.

THE REVOLUTION WITHERS AWAY

RICHARD LOWENTHAL

The overthrow of N. S. Khrushchev, who for eleven years was First Secretary and for seven years the undisputed leader and spokesman of the Soviet Communist Party, by the Presidium and Central Committee of that party is an event without precedent in the annals of modern party dictatorship. The deposition of Benito Mussolini by the Fascist Grand Council in July 1943 —the nearest formal analogy that comes to mind—took place under the impact of military defeat, with enemy troops on Italian soil; and even then, it was only made possible by the collusion of the dictator's inner-party opponents with the King and the leaders of an army that had never been brought under effective party control —that is, by the fact that Fascist rule over Italy had never become fully totalitarian. Khrushchev's "resignation," on the other hand, came about in the absence of any acute external crisis of the Soviet state; and whatever role the armed forces and the security services may have played in his removal —a subject on which the amount of Western press speculation is in striking disproportion to the paucity of reliable

evidence—must have been performed by them in the framework of their formal subordination to the party as the only bearer of legitimate political power. It was, after all, as the successful champion of the party's claim to indivisible supremacy that Khrushchev had established his own position of undivided leadership of the Soviet Union between 1953 and 1957; the institution whose victory he had then helped to assure was now the one to oust him.

Who Was Right?

That it could in fact do so was nonetheless a surprise—not only for Khrushchev himself, but also for Western students of the Soviet political system. We knew, of course, that one of the differences between Khrushchev's rule and Stalin's personal despotism was that Khrushchev had to operate within the institutional mechanism of the party; we also knew that he was far from enjoying Lenin's unique authority over his colleagues. Evidence that some of his policies could be opposed with impunity and

Problems of Communism (January–February 1965), pp. 10–17. Reprinted by permission. Footnotes omitted.

occasionally defeated within the leading organs of the party had accumulated over the years and was not seriously in dispute. Yet, against this, one had to set the fact that he had defeated all apparent rivals of substance and reputation—men like Malenkov, Beria, Molotov, Zhukov and Bulganin—within a few years; had cumulated the office of First Secretary of the party, the chairmanship of its newly-created Bureau for the RSFSR, and the premiership; and had taken care to work with different deputies in each of these roles, and even to change his "heirs apparent" in the Secretariat from time to time.

From this, many Western observers (including the present writer) had concluded that while Khrushchev might have to yield to adverse majorities within the party Presidium on specific issues, his position was strong enough to prevent the formation of any faction that was systematically opposed to his leadership or general policy, and to remove the instigators of any attempt in that direction. Another school of thought had interpreted the evidence of inconsistencies and zigzags in Soviet policy as proof of a persistent and systematic challenge to Khrushchev's leadership within the Presidium, but had identified the challengers as a faction of "conservative" opponents of his "reforming" policies.

Clearly, the outcome has not been consistent with either hypothesis. For though there is much to indicate that Khrushchev's policies were indeed seriously challenged by a "conservative" opposition headed by F. R. Kozlov during the winter and spring of 1962–63, it is obvious that he successfully survived that crisis and subsequently reinforced his position through the entry of L. I. Brezhnev

and N. V. Podgorny, two loyal supporters of his policies, into the Secretariat. What is more, he has now been replaced, not by his "conservative" critics, but by his own designated successors—men who have hastened to renew their commitment to the decisions of the three Khrushchevian party congresses and to the "revisionist" program of 1961, in the teeth of all "dogmatist" attacks from Peking. This suggests that the basic cause of Khrushchev's overthrow was not any major difference over foreign or domestic policy, but rather the institutional question of the relative powers of the leader and the highest constituted organs of the ruling party. In fact, the party bureaucracy seems to have developed a degree of oligarchic solidarity and asserted a measure of collective control not hitherto observed in any totalitarian state.

The Man and the Apparat

In retrospect, it is possible to view much of the internal history of the Khrushchev era as having revolved around this institutional question. In denouncing Stalin's arbitrary rule not only for its lawlessness and cruelty, but also for its failure to respect the party statutes and to submit all policy decisions to regular meetings of the party congress, Central Committee and Politbureau, Khrushchev had in fact given the party bureaucracy a double pledge: that he would not use the secret police against them, and that he would consult them according to the statutory rules. In establishing the party's supremacy over the other power machines which Stalin used to balance its influence, Khrushchev had in fact become increasingly dependent on the support of the party machine. That dependency and those pledges were the price he had to pay for rising to unrivaled power as the exponent of the ruling party; and many of his subsequent actions, beginning with his assumption of the premiership in March 1958, can best be understood as part of an effort to free himself from these self-imposed shackles.

One of the characteristic features of Khrushchev's style of rule was his fondness for appealing to "the people" against "the bureaucrats"—and it would be quite wrong to assume that "the bureaucrats" were not intended to include the *apparatchiki* of the party, at least during the later years. This anti-oligarchic element was particularly strong in Khrushchev's educational reform—one of his most sternly-resisted policies.

The early struggles over the treatment of the defeated "anti-party group" should be seen in the same light. There is considerable evidence that an attempt to force the expulsion of Malenkov, Molotov and Kaganovich from the party, with a possible view to their subsequent trial for complicity in Stalin's crimes, was made and defeated at the 21st Congress in early 1959. The view that Khrushchev favored such an attempt appears highly plausible in the light of his published remarks at the preceeding Central Committee plenum of December 1958. Yet it does not follow that the victorious opponents of that attempt—who seem to have included the bulk of the party Presidium—were politically opposed to destalinization: prominent among these were Anastas I. Mikoyan, who had been the very first publicly to criticize Stalin at the 20th CPSU Congress, and M. A. Suslov, who—despite frequent allegations to the contrary—has been an equally consistent critic of the Stalinist past but seems to owe much of his prestige within the party oligarchy to his vigilant defense of the party's institutions against the tendency to develop a "personality cult" of Khrushchev. Not factional resistance to destalinization, but collective Presidium opposition to measures that might place the dangerous weapon of the purge into Khrushchev's hands seems to be the explanation of his failure to achieve the expulsion of his rivals in 1959.

Further, beginning in December 1958, Khrushchev sought to reduce his dependence on the Central Committee by turning the meetings of this body into semi-public shows, attended by hundreds or even thousands of outside experts on whatever happened to be the main subject—kolkhoz chairmen and agronomists, industrial managers and technicians, economists, scientists, or literary men. Some parts of the CC meetings were still reserved for members and candidates only, and their debates remained secret; but minutes of the enlarged sessions were published, including Khrushchev's frequent interruptions of speeches by other party hierarchs. This dilution of the Central Committee meetings amounted to a serious depreciation of their deliberative character: the pledge to submit all major issues to regular meetings was formally honored, but their policy-making authority was skilfully undermined.

Pressure and Resistance

It was thus inevitable that the small Presidium, shielded as it was from the glare of demagogic publicity, should become the main focus of oligarchic resistance to the First Secretary's efforts at achieving personal rule. In contrast to the Central Committee, its members were all responsible for specific sectors of party or state affairs and had a working knowledge of other issues as well. In contrast to the Secretariat, the Presidium was not an executive organ for the disciplined implementation of decisions, but a policy-making organ whose members voted as equals. Even so, it was often challenged by the outside political speeches of the First Secretary, who sought to anticipate its decisions by publicly defending his own and attacking opposing points of view. In the last two years, Khrushchev had even begun to publish some of the policy memoranda he had circulated to the Presidium members before critical sessions—thus allowing readers to admire his initiatives and, by comparing the First Secretary's memoranda with the subsequent decisions, to deduce the extent of resistance to them.

But the major blow intended by Khrushchev both against the oligarchic cohesion of the party bureaucracy in general and against the authority of the Presidium in particular was undoubtedly his dramatic reorganization of the party in November 1962, its division into separate industrial and agricultural sectors up to the level of the national republics, and the simultaneous creation of a new organ for party and state control, which was vested with very considerable powers. There were, of course, other reasons for this move as well: as will be discussed below, the reorganization also constituted an attempt to maintain the party's rule in a period of concentration on the non-revolutionary tasks of economic construction—to adapt it to those tasks, and to shift its legitimation

to the economic field. Yet, implicit in the scheme of reorganization was an all-round reduction in the role of the formally elected, policy-making party committees in favor of new, quasi-managerial bureaus for industry and agriculture appointed from the top and controlled by the central party Secretariat.

Further, the resulting upheaval was bound to give rise to a massive turnover of the party's bureaucracy on all levels, again with the selection in the hands of the Secretariat. Finally, the new Party-State Control Committee, whose purpose was to collect the complaints of the public against state and party bureaucrats and to purge them if it thought fit, was to be headed by A. N. Shelepin—a member of the Secretariat, who was also appointed a deputy premier in connection with his new task, yet did not—at that time—become a member of the party Presidium. It was without precedent for any man to hold simultaneously, posts in both the Secretariat and the government without sitting in the party Presidium, and it clearly indicated Khrushchev's wish to keep the head of the new control organ as his personal subordinate, outside the discussions of the highest policy-making body. The intention to bypass this body was indeed so tangible that during the decisive Central Committee meeting, only two other Presidium members—Podgorny and Voronov—spoke up in favor of Khrushchev's scheme.

Danger Signals

But Khrushchev's intended *coup de parti* was never fully consummated. In the months that followed the Central Committee plenum of November 1962, the division of the party organization into industrial and agricultural sectors was indeed carried out, but the Presidium succeeded in considerably limiting the changes of personnel as well as the power of the Party-State Control Committee. During the same period, a campaign to bring Soviet literature and art under more effective party control, which Khrushchev himself had helped to set in motion, was effectively used for the most serious counterattack yet on the First Secretary, whose halo had already been seriously dimmed by his repeated failures in agriculture, foreign policy, and the world Communist movement. This time, the attack was political as well as institutional: it was accompanied by calls for a halt to destalinization, and Khrushchev was driven to the point where he had publicly to defend his own record during the Stalin era. But his opponents seem to have overplayed their hand, and by the spring of that year Khrushchev was able to defeat a faction whose platform was out of tune with the real interests of the Soviet Union, and to get approval for his policy on the nuclear test-ban and emancipation from Chinese pressure.

Even so, the danger sign had been clear: it was still possible for Khrushchev to retain his leadership despite the various setbacks suffered by his policies, but not to increase his personal power and to free himself from institutional controls in the face of these setbacks. Yet with the more favorable atmosphere created by the 1964 harvest, Khrushchev again seemed to embark on a policy of enhancing his personal power. Towards the end of September, while preparations for a Central Committee session in November were in progress, he convened a combined meeting of the party Presidium, the Council of Ministers, the heads of the various planning bodies, the provincial party secretaries, and the chairmen of the regional economic councils—but without the full membership of the Central Committee—and used this highly irregular gathering as a sounding board for his proposed directives for a long-term economic plan along highly popular pro-consumer lines.

The report on Khrushchev's speech which finally appeared in *Pravda*—after a delay of several days—is a good indication of the struggle that must have been going on at that time. Khrushchev succeeded in placing the constituted organs of the party under popular pressure before they had come to a decision, but even that victory was rather abortive, since the full text of his remarks was never allowed to appear in print. It may well have been this specific action, combined with Khrushchev's reported plan to put his son-in-law in charge of a new agricultural reorganization, that finally precipitated his overthrow—not just by the opponents of the policies advocated, but by a common front of the oligarchy in defense of institutional procedures.

With Khrushchev out of the way, the victors hastened to undo what was left of his November 1962 reorganization: they decided to merge once again the industrial and agricultural party units on a territorial basis; they reserved the necessary changes in personnel for the collective authority of the Presidium; and they promoted Khrushchev's protégé, Shelepin, who had presumably joined them at the critical moment, to membership of the Presidium—thus bringing the controller under control.

But if in the light of the outcome,

this interpretation of the politics of the Khrushchev era as a persistent but vain struggle by the leader to break out of the institutional limitations of his power may well seem plausible, it remains unsatisfactory by itself. Why, we must ask, could a totalitarian system that from its inception had been geared to one-man leadership, and that was clearly still in need of a visible, personal embodiment of its authority, develop an oligarchic cohesion that proved, again and again, strong enough to defeat the ambitions of a leader of Khrushchev's vital energy and demagogic gifts? For an answer, we must look beyond the mechanics of institutional power to the underlying changes in the social and political dynamics of the system as a whole—changes that may well be regarded by future historians as the chief result of the Khrushchevian era of transition.

Revolution Without Terror

The starting point of these changes was the abandonment of mass terrorism as a method of government. Stalin had understood that totalitarian rule could only be maintained in the long run by ̄ver new revolutions from above—by the ruthless use of state power to transform society in the direction of the ideological goal and to prevent its structure from setting into any firm and stable mold. In 1937, he had expressed this *arcanum regni* in his notorious doctrine of the necessary sharpening of the class struggle as socialist construction progressed; in 1952, he had insisted in his last pamphlet, *Economic Problems of Socialism,* that the transition to the higher stage of communism could not be achieved by a mere improvement of productiv-

ity and organizational efficiency, but required another structural transformation to turn the kolkhoz farmers into state laborers. If the next turn of the wheel of permanent revolution had required another massive dose of violence, Stalin would not have shrunk from it.

Yet, the economic cost of repeated violent upheavals, which had been bearable during the period of Russia's forced industrialization, was bound to appear prohibitive once an industrially mature Soviet Union had to strive for further advances in productivity in competition with other mature industrial powers. In dissolving the forced labor camps and taking steps to raise the incomes of the mass of kolkhoz peasants and unskilled workers, Stalin's heirs deliberately shifted the balance of their levers of control from coercion to incentives. In repudiating Stalin's doctrine of the progressive sharpening of internal class struggle as well as practice of blood purges, Khrushchev proclaimed the end of the role of mass terrorism as a basic element of the Soviet political system.

This repudiation of government by massive violence did not then mean, in Khrushchev's mind, the renunciation of further revolutionary changes in the social structure of the Soviet Union. An ideological believer as well as a modernizer, he was convinced that the ideological imperative of state-directed social transformation could be reconciled with the economic imperative of a continuous growth of production stimulated by material incentives: was not this the only possible justification for restoring the supremacy of an ideological party, yet pressing for the modernization of its method of rule? When, in late 1958, Khrushchev responded to the challenge of the Chinese "people's communes" by elaborating his own program for the "building of communism," he emphasized that the goal could only be reached on the basis of the most advanced technology, but he stuck to Stalin's view that the disappearance of the structural difference between collective farms and state farms was a precondition for reaching the "higher stage."

True, the concrete road forward was to be quite different. For while Stalin had envisaged centrally organized barter between the collective farms and state industry as a way of overcoming the remnants of kolkhoz independence, Khrushchev believed in the need to raise kolkhoz productivity by making all costs and returns comparable in monetary terms; hence, he actually strengthened their independence by allowing them to acquire the equipment of the Machine Tractor Stations and converting their various types of delivery obligations into sales to the state at a unified price. Nevertheless, in his speech to the 21st Party Congress in early 1959 and as late as the December Central Committee plenum of the same year, he insisted that the transition to communism required structural changes in the collective farms, and that concrete measures must be taken not only to replace the "labor day" system of remuneration by fixed monthly cash advances, but also to reduce the role of the peasants' private plots and herds and to prepare for their resettlement in "agrotowns" in which the private plots would be eliminated altogether.

Totalitarianism Without Revolution?

In practice, however, the structural changes propagated by Khrushchev proved incompatible with a steady growth of productivity. Wherever the peasants were "persuaded" to sell their private cattle to the kolkhoz, the results were so discouraging that propaganda for such sales was soon followed by warnings to local party officials to avoid undue pressure. The requirements of economic rationality and of ideological transformation were thus manifestly in conflict, and a choice had to be made. The answer was given in the new Party Program of 1961: here, the reduction and eventual abolition of private plots and herds and the creation of agrotowns no longer appeared as concrete tasks for party action, but were merely forecast as future byproducts of an eventual rise in kolkhoz productivity which would eliminate the peasant families' need for their own private produce. For the first time, the task of "building communism" was no longer defined in terms of structural change, but merely in terms of the struggle for steady quantitative improvements in both productivity and the standard of living.

The 1961 Party Program thus marked the end of the Soviet Communists' commitment to imposing a "permanent revolution from above" on Soviet society; indeed, a commitment to stop this permanent revolution was implied in the Program's political thesis that, owing to the disappearance of hostile and exploiting classes, the Soviet state had ceased to be a "dictatorship of the proletariat" and become a "state of all the people"—in other words, that the internal class struggle in the Soviet Union had ended. Contrary to Khrushchev's original belief, it had proved impossible to continue transforming the social structure in accordance with preconceived ideological blueprints without mass terrorism; for the first time since the consolidation of totalitarian party rule in Russia, the economic dynamism of Soviet society had proved stronger than the ideological dynamism of the totalitarian system. The program amounted to an assurance to all Soviet citizens that henceforth they could go about their business without fear of further social upheavals imposed by the ruling party; in however obscure terms, it announced the "withering away" of the revolution. The Chinese were thus right in denouncing it as a "revisionist" document.

Yet the program was *not* intended to announce the withering away of one-party rule; on the contrary, it claimed that this rule, now exercised by a "party of all the people," was no longer dictatorial, and that the party's "leading role" would even outlive the attainment of full communism and the disappearance of the state. In fact, the party's monopoly of power was to be maintained indefinitely—if under another name—even though the original justification of this power by the revolutionary transformation of society had expired. This raised the problem of finding a new legitimation for maintaining Communist party rule in the Soviet Union. Nor could this need be evaded by putting more stress on the international aspect of the party's revolutionary task, for in this field, too, Khrushchev's attempt at a Leninist revival had ended in disillusionment. By 1962, hopes of a Soviet-led revolutionary breakthrough in world politics were finally sunk in the Caribbean, while the course of the Sino-Soviet conflict proved beyond doubt that not every advance of Communist revolution would necessarily redound to the greater glory of the Soviet Union. The CPSU, having lost its former international authority, had compelling reasons also to renounce its claim to world revolutionary leadership just when it recognized that its revolutionary role had ended at home.

Khrushchev's solution to the problem of a new legitimation for the party's power was his 1962 doctrine of the primacy of constructive economic tasks, bolstered by the timely discovery of an unpublished Lenin text and dramatized by the radical reorganization of the party on a production basis. If the party could no longer aspire to transform society at will, it had to make itself useful to society; if its officials were not to be looked upon increasingly as phrase-mongering parasites, they had to prove themselves effective animators of economic progress—and the party organization had to be revamped in order to enable and even force them to do so. The wheel had indeed come full circle: instead of changing the structure of society in accordance with the ideas of the party, the structure of the party was now to be changed in accordance with the supposed needs of society! But the solution was more apparent than real; for the *apparatchiki* of the party were often unqualified for the performance of strictly economic tasks and reluctant to make the necessary adjustment, while the real need of the Soviet economy was not for more production-minded bureaucrats, but for greater managerial freedom from bureaucratic interference—as, indeed, Khrushchev's successors have recognized.

Dynamism Manqué

If we look back on Khrushchev's persistent but ultimately unsuccessful struggle against the oligarchic tendencies of the party apparatus in the light of these changes in the evolutionary trend of the Soviet system, the basic reason for his failure becomes plain: Khrushchev tried to furnish dynamic leadership at a time when the totalitarian dynamism of the Communist regime was running down. He offered new experiments and a revival of faith to a bureaucracy exhausted by the historic horrors of Stalinism and longing ever more strongly for stability and routine. He imagined he could be a milder, more benevolent Robespierre when the time had come for the *Directoire.*

Though Khrushchev helped to start the new trend by turning his back on Stalin's methods, he was not its conscious architect and master, and he ultimately became its victim. Indeed, the resistance he encountered, far from always being motivated by a nostalgia for Stalinism, was often more in tune with the new times than were his own proposals. It was a merit of the party oligarchy that it welcomed—and perhaps exacted—his pledge to end terroristic rule, yet refused to let him use his criticism of the past as a purge weapon against his rivals. Again, his colleagues seem from the beginning to have been doubtful about his plans for reducing the peasants' private plots and resettling them in agrotowns—the resolution of the 21st Congress was far less outspoken on these points than his own report, and the plots have indeed now been restored to their pre-Khrushchevian size. Generally, the routine-loving bureaucrats may have been more willing to listen to scientific advice on plant biology and agricultural management than was a would-be charismatic leader seeking miraculous results by perennial campaigns, be it for the extension of corn cultivation, the ploughing-up of virgin soils, or the reduction of fallow periods.

Yet Khrushchev was both sincere and consistent in his conviction that a modern party dictatorship can only survive if it remains an agent of dynamic change; and once he had reconciled himself to the fact that change could no longer be imposed according to ideological prescriptions, he sought to counter the regime's tendency towards bureaucratic inertia by making himself increasingly the spokesman of genuine social needs—of the demands for more food, more and better consumers' goods, better housing, and so on. But the more he identified his own struggle for personal authority and for a permanent circulation of the elites with those popular demands, the more his activities must have come to appear to the entire party bureaucracy as a threat to their rule.

When Khrushchev came to power, he had been determined both to restore the institutions and to revive the dynamic faith of the regime; in the end, it was the growing rigidity of the restored institutions that defeated his own dynamic faith. The contradiction, basic to the present phase of the Communist regime in the Soviet Union, may well be implicit in the nature of long-term totalitarian rule. Totalitarianism may be defined either by the institutions of single-party government, combined with a monopoly of organization and information, or by the dynamics of permanent revolution from above—of ever new social transformations enforced by political power in accordance with an (unattainable) ideological goal. In theory, it can be shown that the dynamics of permanent revolution require these institutions, and that the institutions can only be justified by this kind of dynamic purpose. Yet in practice, the maintenance of the dynamism requires an all-powerful leader who, while using the institutions, remains above them and often even disorganizes them to assure his personal power, as Stalin (and Hitler) did, while the institutions become stable only as the supposed *perpetuum mobile* is grinding to a halt and oligarchic rigidity sets in.

The fall of Khrushchev means that this stage has been reached in the USSR. The formal continuity of the party regime remains unbroken, but the erosion of its ideological dynamism is far advanced. The new men are both objectively and subjectively unable to continue the revolution; they will have to be content with administering its results. When all necessary reservations about historical analogies are made, the comparison wrongly applied by Trotsky to Stalin's rule seems to fit

the *Directoire* of Khrushchev's successors much more closely—a regime of "Thermidorian" bureaucrats. As the revolution withers away, its heirs are reduced to the conservative role of stabilizing its institutions and defending their oligarchic privileges. No outside challenger to their domination is in sight. But perhaps it is not too sanguine to hope that their regime may prove more calculable and even more nearly legal, as well as less inspired and inspiring, than that of their predecessors, and that it may thus at last give a chance for the quiet maturing of new minds and forces that will one day break out of the shell of a dead tradition.

AFTER THE FALL: SOME LESSONS

ROBERT CONQUEST

For the past few months political observers have studied the events surrounding the fall of Khrushchev for clues to future trends in Soviet domestic and foreign policy. The purpose of this brief inquiry, however, is different: it is to examine Khrushchev's fall for the lessons it may teach us regarding the general nature of Soviet leadership politics.

If the principals in the latest upheaval had been specifically asked to provide us with a dramatic illustration of how Soviet politics works, they could not have chosen a more auspicious time. For during the past few

years a certain air of accord had seemed to emanate from the Soviet political scene, and it had again become possible for those so inclined to dismiss as fantasy, interpretations of Soviet events that pointed to discord at a high level.

This view, which does not recognize conflict as the dynamic force activating Soviet political life at its highest reaches—and which may be conveniently called the "non-conflict model" of Soviet politics—had made its appearance in the pages of this journal itself. To be sure, other observers were quick to combat it.

Problems of Communism (January–February 1965), pp. 17–22. Reprinted by permission. Footnotes omitted.

In 1961, this writer stated in his *Power and Policy in the USSR:*

To assume that harmony now prevails among the Soviet leadership would be to assume that a very extraordinary change had taken place in the system. This is not, perhaps, impossible, but at least one can say the assumption is the most speculative that could be made. It would be uncharitable to name the sources, but I have seen the assumption that stability has been achieved at last and that a collective leadership based on mutual restraint has finally emerged, put forward after the death of Stalin; after the fall of Beria; at the time of the 20th Congress; and at almost every other critical point in recent Soviet history. . . .

Perhaps a momentary lapse from charity will be conceded, just to provide one recent, if extreme, illustration of a basically erroneous attitude toward Soviet politics. In *Problems of Communism* of May-June 1964, a correspondent (A. Allison) expressed notions which in a general way still affect some students. He held that those who find Soviet political life permeated with conflict rely on "inferential and selective evidence while heavily discounting what appear to be simple and obvious realities." Such "realities" included the public appearance of harmony, or at any rate of political stability, in the highest party councils.

But it is ancient history that public figures are capable of public behavior —indeed of private behavior—which conceals their political aims. An example among thousands that come to mind is to be found in Lytton Strachey's *Elizabeth and Essex:*

Raleigh himself was utterly unsuspecting; there seemed to be a warm friendship between him and the Secretary. . . . His earlier hopes had been shattered by Essex; and now that Essex had been destroyed he was faced by a yet more dangerous antagonist. In reality, the Earl's ruin, which he had so virulently demanded, was to be the prologue to his own.

That is, a skilled operator was capable of deceiving not merely the public but even fellow-members of the Council! In any case, we *know* that similar practice has been common in the USSR. Malenkov and Beria were in public—and perhaps in private—notable cronies until the moment of truth; and similarly with Khrushchev and Bulganin. No, to take such superficial observance of the conventional amenities as meaning anything at all in any political society is to mislead oneself.

All this is far indeed from the cold-bloodedness of the Soviet oligarchy and the harshness of the struggle for power which recent events have just revealed in all their true crudity. We recognize the complexity, and the idiosyncrasies, of the polity to which we are accustomed, but we are all too apt to oversimplify our ideas of societies of which our knowledge is more indirect. We are inclined to construct models of strange political systems on too simple a basis, especially when the true facts are not readily available. Our notions about the Soviet polity are distorted by the fact that these events are taking place in the 20th century, among people who wear flannel suits and are called "Minister." If they wore turbans and were known as "Wazir," we would be less inclined to make mistakes about them. And similarly, their "Marxism" is a dialect, however debased, of the political language of the West.

What is more, a faint notion of people discussing scientific propositions still attaches to the political polemics of the Kremlin; this, too, is to some extent delusive. In any society, even the most primitive, policy matters are debated in a more or less rational way, but this in itself does not necessarily mean that the political style resembles that of the advanced democracies. It is quite inappropriate to think of Soviet politics in anything like Western terms, if only because there is no mechanism in the USSR for the social forces to express themselves. In advanced countries, society and polity virtually coincide; in the Soviet Union, the political world is limited to a few thousand members of a self-perpetuating elite. Moreover, this elite was originally formed, and has been trained for decades, to force its will upon society as a whole.

In the overthrow of Khrushchev, one of the most striking things of all was the absolute passivity of the Russian masses. Another was the absolute inattention of the leaders to the views of the people; the citizens' right to information, let alone participation, seems to have occurred to no one in the Kremlin. The gulf between this sort of attitude and anything resembling democracy is going to be a major crux as the Soviet Union faces problems which can scarcely be settled without the genuine involvement of the public. In fact, far from democracy being anywhere visible, it became clear from the pronouncements of the new regime that not even rational and consistent oligarchy could be found at the basis of the system. For Khrushchev had, it was now alleged, put through a whole series of hastily prepared and ill-considered schemes, disrupting industry, agriculture, and the party organization itself over the past few years, without the other leaders being able to do anything effective to stop him.

In his *L'Esprit des lois* (Book XI, Chapter 4), Montesquieu wrote: "C'est une expérience éternelle que tout homme qui a du pouvoir est porté à en abuser: il va jusqu'à ce qu'il trouve des limites." In democracies these limits are fairly well defined. In the Soviet Union there is no such specificity, no properly established institutional bar. The ruler goes as far as he can until *ad hoc* opposition is mustered in sufficient strength to stop him.

The *mode* of Khrushchev's dismissal is in itself a great demonstration of the nature of Soviet politics. It was carried through with all the correct Moscovite trappings—almost to the point of caricature: the complete secrecy; the sudden coup; the issuing of a short and almost perfunctorily misleading statement about age and health; the simple cessation of reference to the name of the man who had just been the most powerful in the country; the oblique, but obvious, attacks on his methods; the removal from office of his closest adherent (Adzhubei) without comment or announcement until his replacement was mentioned casually a week or so later.... In particular, the evident absence of any idea on the part of the new rulers that such procedures might be found odd by anyone (including foreign Communist parties) shows flatly a complete, unself-conscious attachment to the traditionalisms of Soviet politics.

But to return again to Western analysis. The non-conflict model of the Soviet political system is defective on three counts. First, there is no such thing as non-conflict politics. "To govern is to choose," and so there will always be "conservative" and "progressive," "left" and "right" divisions in any political grouping, however narrow its spectrum of ideas. The only exception must be a one-man dictatorship so pure that no subordinate dare venture an opinion at all. Even Stalin's Russia did not reach that position.

Second (and still arguing *a priori*), the Soviet system is especially susceptible to conflict because it is constructed to force ideological solutions upon the recalcitrant crises it must continuously deal with; because it is based on an ideology that is liable to various interpretations and subject to fissiparous trends; and because its leaders have over the years been selected for their ruthlessness, ambition and intrigue. Third (and at last *a posteriori*), evidence showing or suggesting conflict within the system is continually available.

Against all this, there is only one serious consideration. Since Soviet convention demands that all party decisions be the product of monolithic agreement, evidence of dispute at the highest level is not allowed to appear in open form—or at least not at the time of the agreement. Thus, those who take the view that conflict does not occur are free to regard the obliqueness of the evidence as a sign of its nullity.

But there are many circustances, in many fields, where evidence must be indirect. The logic of the other way of thinking is as follows: "The visible part of the iceberg must constitute the whole of it. It is true that some observers claim to see something below the waterline, but even they admit that the submerged part is only obscurely and temporarily visible, and that it may well be something else really, such as a reflection, or a delusion, or a whale. Then again, they deduce from the movements of the visible portion and the laws of dynamics that there

must be something below; but after all, this is mere deduction. In fact, the whole evidence is circumstantial, and I prefer to believe what I can see with my eyes." Such a view is not simply mistaken at a superficial level; it reflects a wholly and basically erroneous notion of the nature of Soviet politics.

"In the West ... there is a lack of knowledge about the different situations in different Socialist countries. ... Some situations seem difficult to understand. In many cases one has the impression that there are differences of opinion among the leading groups, but one does not know if this is really so, and what the differences are." So wrote Togliatti (if only for public consumption) in the memoir composed shortly before his death—and not long before the overthrow of Khrushchev. His basic conclusion was right; and so were his feelings about the difficulty of following the course of the political struggle in the Soviet Union. Nevertheless, throughout the period he was concerned with, much evidence of disunity at the top was available.

Item: There have been issues in Soviet political life on which it has been impossible to make any decision at all. For example, no official account, true or false, of the 1936–38 trials has been available for eight or nine years.

Item: There have been sudden shifts from one policy to another, associated with the rise or decline in prominence of a particular spokesman. Note, for example, the tough approach to literature in early 1963, associated with Kozlov, and the change of the May 1st, 1963, slogan on Yugoslavia, coincident with his fading-out.

Item: There have been sudden unexplained promotions and demotions, such as the relegation of the then heir apparent, Kirichenko, from all his posts in 1960, or the demotion of Kirilenko from the Presidium and the promotion of Spiridonov to the Secretariat at the 22nd Congress (October 1961)—followed, in early 1962, by a reversal of both moves.

Item: There have been violent agitations in favor of policies which nevertheless were either never carried out or effected only much later. Take, for example, the calls at the 21st Congress (1959) for the expulsion from party membership of Molotov and Malenkov, which was only to be announced in 1964.

Item: Discussions have taken place in which different party organizations have taken different lines. For example, at the 22nd Congress, delegates from only half the republics called for the expulsion of the "anti-party" group.

Item: Plans to which the head of the party and government has publicly committed himself, while admitting that "some comrades" opposed him, have been abandoned: *e.g.*, the issue of the fertilizer target for 1970.

Item: Individual party leaders have made remarks which, though couched in terms within the protocol of collective leadership, can best be interpreted as political criticism of another faction. For example, after the reorganization of the party into industrial and agricultural sections, Kozlov commented that this could "not in any circumstances be allowed" to split the urban and rural party organizations—just what it obviously was doing—and we now know that Kozlov was expressing the reservations of many members of the Presidium. Again, at the 22nd Congress, Kosygin declared that the "antiparty" group was not a present danger, and was only being attacked

to show the party and the people once again what the personality cult leads to. ... We must and will do everything in our power to insure that our party and our society have no room for a personality cult in the future either....

This writer commented at the time— and surely it was reasonable to do so —that "this was an obvious criticism of the Khrushchev cult."

It is true that this sort of evidence requires delicate handling and considerable confirmation from the context. But it is not to be dismissed out of hand and will be disregarded only by those who have inadequately studied the tone of Soviet pronouncements. To be sure, alternative explanations *can* be found for all types of evidence we have listed, but though it may be fragmentary, inadequate, and sometimes even misleading, it is the only evidence we have, and properly interpreted, it has always led to sounder conclusions than have assumptions of its meaninglessness.

So much, then, for the non-conflict model. But this is not the only relevant issue which has been debated over the last years in these pages as well as in others. For, it may be urged, even a good old-fashioned, non-Platonic, down-to-earth conflict model admits of various interpretations. There is, for instance, nothing in it that would necessarily have prevented one from concluding that Khrushchev is bound to win any conflict. And some such position was widely maintained.

As one of the contributors to this journal who did not hold that view, and as one who is on record as putting forward the possibility that Khrushchev might fall, I should say that the key word is "possibility." There were many good arguments about the strength of

Khrushchev's position, and it was perfectly reasonable to give him the odds. It was simply a methodological error to construct a model of Soviet politics in which a possibility was excluded. It turned out that Khrushchev's ouster was precisely the possibility that happened to become a fact, and so the thesis proved self-refuting. But if Khrushchev had won, that would not have proved the inevitability of his victory. The lesson of the recent events is that in dealing with Soviet politics we must never think that a restricted view of the possibilities is prudent, or commonsensical, or respectable, or admirable in any other way. From the vantage point of 1953, the major events of the first post-Stalin decade would have been contrary to "reasonable" anticipation. We should realize once and for all that communism is in a state of continuous crisis, and that it is basically unhistorical to predict for it a smooth and logical evolution. If we do not allow for even quite extravagant possibilities, we are bound to be taken by surprise. Serious consideration of Soviet prospects must deal with every variation that is formally possible.

Meanwhile, we can at least predict further struggle. For it is clear that the frictions of the past few years were not polarized between Khrushchev on the one hand and all the other members of the Presidium on the other. There must have been some support, besides Khrushchev's, for the political acts now most condemned, and there must certainly be some who were less opposed to him than others. In any case, the conspiracy against him would scarcely have waited until it had attained absolute unanimity in the Presidium. Rather, the conspirators struck as soon as their forces were adequate; the

alternative would have been appallingly poor security. So there must now be vulnerable men at the top.

But even the allies who mounted the coup, and are now benefiting from it, are united only in their opposition to Khrushchev. In the Soviet past, every group that has risen against a rival has, after victory, quarreled over the disposal of the spoils, as well as on policy grounds. It is hard to see how the present rulers, even if they see the advantages of an agreed share-out, could possibly find a formula adequate to end this old tendency, this law of Soviet politics.

There are all sorts of elements in the current situation—the provocative and anomalous power of the Ukrainian contingent in the leadership, for example—which augur continued struggle. But rather than start, at this stage, on a detailed Kremlinological analysis, it may be worth registering a general point which seems to distinguish this period from earlier ones.

When Shamil, the great leader of Caucasian resistance to the Russians, asked his council who would succeed him, the answer was: "Venerated Imam, your successor will be the man with the sharpest sword." Conditions in the Kremlin are different from those in the *auls* of Daghestan and Chechenia, and it might be suggested that the knife in the back, rather than the scimitar at the breast, is the symbolic weapon more appropriate to Kremlin conditions. In any case, there are certain qualities specially required of a man if he is to become, in any true sense, Khrushchev's successor as the leader of the Soviet Communist Party and the Soviet state.

In the first place, political prestige seems essential. We saw in 1957 that a great concentration of such prestige is not adequate in itself; there must be credibility about a man's assumption to the leading position. And he must also, in the ordinary course of events, have the necessary skill and experience in the required infighting and manipulation of the *apparat*.

Strictly speaking, Khrushchev was the only member of the Presidium who had all these qualities. The immediate future must then involve either a series of attempts to maintain collective leadership—a situation which is automatically unstable in Soviet conditions; *or* the calling-in of fallen leaders with greater prestige; *or* the rather quick development of the necessary leadership qualities by one or another of the present contenders. Meanwhile, we are entitled to regard the period as inherently unstable.

In the post-Stalin succession crisis, a handful of leaders in the Presidium had so much more experience, confidence and prestige than the rank-and-file members of the Central Committee that none of the latter could have reasonably entertained the possibility of an early rise to the top. But when the leading contenders are a Brezhnev or a Podgorny, there are a score or so, at the very least, of officials who only a few years ago ranked with the men currently at the front, or even above them, and they are unlikely to think of the Brezhnevs as in any way their superiors. The thought must be natural that the way to the top is now open,

or might be open, to any ambitious provincial secretary. As Finlay writes of a Byzantine ruler,

he had risen to the highest rank without rendering himself remarkable either for his valor or his ability; the successful career of Romanus therefore excited . . . the ambition of every enterprising officer.

In dealing with the membership of the present Presidium and Secretariat, we should never fail to keep in mind the fact that, over the past six or seven years, membership of these bodies has been precarious, and that they contain a number of men whose advancement over their contemporaries is recent and unlikely to be thought of as part of the established nature of things by either their seniors or their juniors.

Although Khrushchev, with his erratic and changeable policies, has to some degree shaken the old solidarities and certitudes of the party, he has, nevertheless, provided the main element of political stability and continuity in the recent period. For the regime has at least been centered in one man of long experience and political credibility. With his removal, we now see the disintegration, which has long marked the economic and intellectual spheres, reach into the political realm as well. Although it would be going too far to say that this development is irreversible, it yet seems quite probable that the Soviet system has thereby entered a general crisis from which it can only emerge transformed out of all recognition.

POLICY CONFLICTS AND LEADERSHIP POLITICS

CARL LINDEN

With the dust barely settled after the shock of Khrushchev's fall, Professor Lowenthal has leapt into the breach with a thought-provoking interpretation of that event. In his article ... he sees the issue of Khrushchev's "institutional" powers *vis-à-vis* those of his associates as the "basic cause" of the Soviet leader's downfall. Conceding that he overrated Khrushchev's power position in the past, he now develops a picture of a Khrushchev struggling and ultimately failing to break through the institutional barriers limiting his power, barriers successfully defended by the party oligarchy. This viewpoint seems unexceptionable as far as it goes, and it generally accords with arguments offered here by the present writer in 1963.* Nevertheless, Professor Lowenthal's analysis adds up to something less than an explanation of "the basic cause" of Khrushchev's fall. Rather, it would be more accurate to say that the question of the former First Secretary's powers arose as a consequence of his relentless pursuit of certain basic *policy* goals.

This writer argued in [1963] ... that, in addition to a conflict over Khrushchev's power, there was a conflict in the leading group over his policy—a conflict describable in terms of a conservative-reformist cleavage—and that,

---

* See also Carl A. Linden, *Khrushchev and the Soviet Leadership, 1957–1964* (Baltimore: The Johns Hopkins Press, 1966).

moreover, this cleavage was a crucial aspect of the leadership battle during Khrushchev's incumbency. It is here that Professor Lowenthal and I diverge. While Professor Lowenthal concurs in the view that Khrushchev faced a "conservative" challenge led by Kozlov (I would also add Suslov) in late 1962 and early 1963, he says that Khrushchev's overthrow in October 1964 had little to do with his policy, or with a "conservative" opposition to his "reforming" policies. He bases this conclusion on the view that Khrushchev's "designated" successors remain at the helm and that they remain loyal to his policies.

Yet, if one examines what the new regime has said and done so far and what had been the sources of conflict in the leadership during the former First Secretary's last two years in office, one is driven to the opposite conclusion —namely, that the explanation of last October's upheaval must include a consideration of the policy issues that agitated the later stages of Khrushchev's incumbency. That his successors are neither pristine Stalinists nor "internal" Chinese does not negate—as Professor Lowenthal suggests—the proposition that the repeated and energetic attempts of Khrushchev to reorient the party's political direction provoked a basically conservative resistance. Recognition of this is essential to an understanding of Khrushchev's fall.

First, let us go beyond the new regime's public assertions of loyalty to

Problems of Communism (May–June 1965), pp. 37–40. Reprinted by permission. Footnotes omitted.

past policy. A sharp reaction against Khrushchev's reform projects has colored the statements of the new leaders from the outset. They not only have criticized the fallen First Secretary's style of leadership but have condemned him for going too far too fast. Attacks on his "subjectivism," "harebrained schemes," "immature conclusions" and "reformism," while a criticism of his methods, also add up to the charge that he pursued an overly radical policy. The recent refrain has been that policy must not go beyond what "objective" conditions permit—a favorite saw of the defender of the *status quo*.

The consensus of the present leadership found striking expression in the immediate dismantling of Khrushchev's 1962 party reform—an action vindicating the traditionalist, and incidentally Kozlovian, view that the party's primary role must be political and ideological. The criticism audible in the party at the time the reform was introduced—namely, that it tended to depoliticize and deideologize the party by reducing it to a mere instrument of economic management—re-emerged almost instantly upon Khrushchev's removal. *Pravda* struck then at the Khrushchevian view of the party's role by asserting that the practical problems of Communist construction "cannot be divorced" from the party's political-ideological work and that Lenin's stricture against "dismissing theoretical questions" in party practice now had "special force." The repeal of the reform cannot thus be counted among the symptoms of ideological erosion in the USSR which Professor Lowenthal discerns; rather, it represents a striking measure of the resistance to change in the party apparatus.

In order to put Khrushchev's party reform in perspective, it is necessary to

recognize that it was intimately connected with his long-term battle to shift the focus of party policy to agriculture and the consumer, and away from steel and defense. He had met repeated frustration in this effort; the 22nd CPSU Congress, for example, had registered a conservative consensus on economic policy that was clearly not to his liking. It is against this background that Khrushchev attempted to reshape the party apparatus into a more responsive instrument of his purposes and at the same time to undercut and replace those who had raised obstacles to his aims. His effort to base the party structure on the "production" principle, however, was not a "harebrained scheme," but flowed logically from his view of the party's role which he had tirelessly propounded since the 20th CPSU Congress. He had then stated that "problems of practical economics" must hold the center of party work both in theory and in practice. The new Lenin document which was subsequently unearthed to buttress the 1962 reform similarly asserted that the "economic organizer," not the "political agitator," must take the lead in the party.

Thus the 1962 reform was not the product of a belated decision on Khrushchev's part that in modern Russia the role of the party must be revised—a decision based, as Professor Lowenthal suggests, on the final collapse in the Carribean of all hopes for a Soviet-led revolutionary breakthrough in world politics. Rather, the reform was intended to *coincide* with the hoped-for breakthrough. Khrushchev, after all, had unveiled the reform plan in the CPSU Presidium a month and a half *before* his Cuban gamble foundered. When the defeat came in Cuba, not only did it deny him the massive political momentum which a victory would have given his domestic policy, but he was forced into retreat, facing within the party a dangerous challenge from which he never fully recovered. His leadership suffered a blow at the very time the proposed reform was producing a profound reaction among the party's ideologues and *apparatchiki*.

That all was not well even after Khrushchev regained his footing in the wake of Kozlov's incapacitation was apparent in signs of continuing resistance to his policy initiatives right up to the time of his fall. His sweeping scheme for priority development of the chemical and fertilizer industries provoked opposition that led to a scaling-down of his fertilizer goal. His "wheat deal" provoked objections from associates who favored belt-tightening rather than importing "capitalist" grain to cushion the effects of the 1963 harvest disaster. His effort to get funds for his chemicals program at the expense of defense aroused military protests. Indeed, the complaints reached such a pitch that in early 1964 Khrushchev felt compelled to defend the very premises of his course and insist that the "comrades" understand that his chemicals drive was not a "craze" or "fad" but fundamental policy. His proposal at the end of September 1964 to revolutionize planning to favor the consumer turned out to be the straw that helped break the camel's back.

To the last a gambler who subscribed to the precept that a good offense is the best defense, Khrushchev in his last year rapidly unfolded a refurbished strategy of détente abroad and reform at home. The test-ban agreement, the chemicals program, and his new consumer project were part and parcel of a new assault on the *status quo* in policy. Concurrently, he sought to force a decisive break with his Chinese enemies and revived the issue of his defeated "anti-party" opponents at home. Thus, in April 1964, Soviet plans for a world Communist meeting were announced, and it was disclosed that "Molotov and others" had been expelled from the party. Both actions must be counted among Khrushchev's Pyrrhic victories: the first foundered in the face of foreign party opposition, and the second only strengthened the resolve of various members of the leading group to prevent Khrushchev from acquiring purge powers over them.

One thing should be obvious. Khrushchev's zeal for reform and the risks he undertook in this connection offended too many vested interests within the regime too often. The new group, characteristically, has displayed a wariness of reform schemes that might upset the existing political and institutional balance within the regime. For policy execution, new reliance is being placed on the managerial and administrative bureaucracy of the state, which under Khrushchev's long-term policy was to play an ever-diminishing role. Consistent with this trend is the regime's emphasis on "scientific" management, efficiency, improved quality of production, and the use of economic "levers" to induce better economic performance.

Also not to be ignored is the effort of Khrushchev's successors to get off the collision course with the Chinese. This seemingly vain endeavor follows up past criticism of the former First Secretary for pressing a personal vendetta against the Chinese—criticism to which Khrushchev himself appeared to refer in April 1964 when he quipped that one day he might be censured for "subjectivism" on account of his sharp personal attacks on Mao. Peking, nevertheless, continues to scorn all offers of accommodation short of Moscow's full surrender to the Chinese political line, and Khrushchev may yet have the last laugh on this issue.

Furthermore, the new regime has shown a strong inclination toward the view that world revolution, rather than Khrushchev's "communism-in-one-country" policy, must hold first place in Communist strategy. The themes of anti-imperialism and national liberation have been upgraded, and the Khrushchevian emphasis on coexistence, economic competition, and détente has dropped several notches. It is worth recalling in this connection that a similar shift in emphasis emerged temporarily when Khrushchev was in retreat after Cuba. A CPSU letter of February 1963 to the Chinese party, proposing an agenda for Sino-Soviet talks, favored the CCP position by listing the subjects of anti-imperialism and national liberation ahead of coexistence; a later letter, however, reversed the agenda items, putting coexistence and economic competition first.

To sum up, Khrushchev insisted on imposing upon the party policies that flew in the face of traditional practice. Moreover, to attain his goals, he persistently sought to use and to expand his power, and in the fall of 1964 this brought to a head the "institutional" question of his power relationship to his associates in the Presidium. By attempting to overstep the bounds of a generally more conservative consensus in the leading group, he finally alienated even his former supporters.

None of the foregoing conflicts with the obvious fact that the present caretakers of power in the USSR represent an unstable and diverse coalition of leaders. The reformist forces which Khrushchev sought to lead did not disappear with his fall any more than did the more conservative forces Kozlov

once sought to marshal against him. Any new contender for power will have to operate in this context, seeking to forge a program that could win support from both ends of the political spectrum. The conflicting pressures for continuity and change are already clearly visible in the new regime and mark the renewed and far from resolved battle over the regime's policy direction. Just as post-Stalin party politics revolved around Stalin's political and doctrinal legacy, so after Khrushchev the controversy revolves around the latter's revisions of that legacy.

The new regime's task of assuring party hegemony in the Soviet system is now complicated by the fact that it is precisely during periods of divided leadership, such as the present one, that the party's ability to contain the social forces striving to free themselves from political tutelage is least effective. As various party figures search for sources of political support, the professional, managerial and intellectual elites gain opportunities to press for reform and extended freedom of action —not, however, within the party framework as Khrushchev envisaged, but outside it.

Khrushchev carried the CPSU through its perilous post-Stalin transition, but his concept of the party's long-range role has clearly foundered. He tried to purge the party of Stalinist practices, yet himself remained their prisoner in some respects. While he helped make a return to full-blown Stalinism improbable, he failed to overthrow the forces of orthodoxy and conservatism embedded in the regime. The underlying instability of Soviet leadership politics which infected the atmosphere during his own incumbency persists, and it beclouds the future of his successors. He leaves an ambiguous legacy.

DECISION-MAKING IN THE U.S.S.R.

JEREMY R. AZRAEL

Essays on the legislative process ordinarily seek to describe and analyze the role of legislative institutions within the broader political system. Frequently they are addressed to the so-called "crisis of parliamentarism"—the multidimensional threat to parliamentary supremacy that is posed by such developments as the growth of mass society, the emergence of a self-aggrandizing military-industrial complex, the rapid progress of science and technology, and the rise of an administrative state. In the Soviet context, however, these conventional themes are of dubious analytical utility. To put the case summarily, the "legislative branch" of government plays only a marginal role in Soviet political life, and the idea of a "crisis of parliamentarism" is meaningless in a political system where parliamentary supremacy has never existed—or, more accurately, where it has existed only in name.

*I. Parliamentary Supremacy:
Doctrine and Reality*

Such a qualification is necessary because the *doctrine* of parliamentary supremacy *is* an integral part of Soviet constitutional theory. Thus, Article 30 of the Soviet Constitution explicitly designates the Soviet "parliament", the so-called Supreme Soviet, as "the highest organ of state power in the U.S.S.R." Similarly, Article 32 provides that "the legislative power of the U.S.S.R. is exercised exclusively by the Supreme Soviet". And Articles 48 and 64 stipulate that the federal executive power, including both the so-called Presidium of the Supreme Soviet (a kind of collective president) and the Council of Ministers or cabinet, is directly responsible to the legislature. In point of fact, however, neither these provisions nor the equivalent provisions pertaining to the organization and distribution of power at the republican and local levels of the system have ever had real operational significance. That they should exist at all is somewhat ironic in view of Marx's and Lenin's insistence that socialists should discard the "bourgeois" concept of "separation of powers", but their interest as examples of ideological "deviationism" is diminished by their practical irrelevance.

*The Political and Parapolitical
Functions of the Soviets*

Far from exercising sovereign power, the Supreme Soviet has never played an appreciable role in the Soviet decision-making process. With a few minor exceptions of recent vintage, its "lawmaking" activity has been confined to the endorsement—usually *ex post facto*—of decrees in whose preparation it has had no meaningful voice. Moreover, this endorsement has never been preceded by serious deliberation or debate and has invariably taken the form of unqualified ap-

Jeremy R. Azrael, "The Legislative Process in the U.S.S.R.," in Elke Frank, ed., *Lawmakers in a Changing World,* © 1966. Reprinted by permission of Prentice-Hall, Inc. Footnotes omitted.

proval. It suffices merely to report that the Supreme Soviet is only in session for a few days a year, that these few days are almost entirely occupied by official speeches, and, finally and most indicatively, that the Supreme Soviet has never witnessed a negative vote or even so much as an abstention. According to official sources, of course, this remarkable unanimity testifies to the monolithic solidarity of Soviet society and the universal support that the Communist regime enjoys among the Soviet people. In fact, there is no doubt that what it actually signifies is the purely nominal and ritualistic character of the Supreme Soviet's legislative functions. And, what is true of the legislative functions of the Supreme Soviet at the center is true also of the legislative functions exercised within their particular areas of jurisdiction by the various lower level soviets (i.e., the republic-level, provincial, city, and district soviets).

Where there is an appreciable difference between the Supreme Soviet and its local counterparts is in the role of the standing organs that represent these bodies when they are not in session—to wit, the so-called *executive committees* and *permanent commissions*. Thus, whereas the "executive committee" of the Supreme Soviet, or as it is now called, the Supreme Soviet Presidium, plays virtually no independent role in the policy process, the executive committees of the local soviets play a significant part in the administration and direction of certain local enterprises and communal services. Similarly, whereas the permanent commissions of the Supreme Soviet are only nominally analogous to the legislative committees with which we are familiar in the West, the permanent commissions of the lower level soviets

do appear to play a significant "watch-dog" role and may even initiate a certain amount of local legislation. Even at the local level, however, the permanent commissions are only marginally involved in the policy process and the executive committees operate quite independently of the local soviets to which they are ostensibly responsible. In essence, they are merely low level adjuncts of the centralized ministerial system, and it is provable that the only thing that has prevented their formal incorporation into the latter is a lingering reluctance to discard all pretense of commitment to the Marxist-Leninist idea of a complete fusion of legislative and executive authority. Accordingly, despite certain salient differences between the pattern at the center and at the "peripheries", it can be said both of the Soviet political system as a whole and of each of its constituent territorial units that the "legislative branch" of government is almost completely devoid of effective political power.

To stress the powerlessness of Soviet parliaments is not to deny that these bodies serve some important political or parapolitical functions, the very stress on parliamentary supremacy in official constitutional theory suffices to invalidate any suggestion, and the elaborate institutionalization of parliamentary forms makes it clear that the soviets are useful to the regime in a variety of ways. For one thing, the soviets provide the leadership with a ceremonial sounding board for important statements of policy and purpose, as well as with a highly visible forum for prosecuting the unending campaign of "criticism and self-criticism" which is so integral a part of Soviet life. In addition, the soviets provide an arena for giving status rewards to particularly diligent "activists" on the various "fronts" which comprise Soviet society, while simultaneously recruiting new "activists" and opening up new "fronts". Again, by lending the appearance of reality to the fiction that the regime is at once popularly based and genuinely representative, the soviets help disarm both foreign and domestic criticism. In this connection, the fact that the soviets are composed so as almost perfectly to replicate the ethnic, sex, and other demographic differences in society stands the regime in particular good stead. It is not every parliament, after all, that can boast so high a proportion of women, or members of minority groups; and it is not every observer who can discern that parliamentary recognition is not necessarily correlated with political representation. Moreover, just as the soviets create an illusory sense of meaningful political representation, they also create an illusory sense of meaningful political participation. Thus, there is little question that the operations of the soviets and the elaborately organized plebiscitary elections whereby their members are selected provide some of the population with an illusion of effective access to the policy process—an illusion which, in turn, strengthens political consensus and support.

It is doubly important that these functions be acknowledged at the present time because it is only when they are understood that one can properly evaluate the effort to "revitalize" the soviets that has been so prominent a part of recent Soviet politics. This effort has taken many different forms and has found expression in the recall of certain soviet delegates by their constituents, the rejection of certain candidates at the polls, the criticism of certain executive committees which

fail to convene sessions of local soviets on schedule, the introduction of minor revisions in legislative proposals after "hearings" before the permanent commissions of the Supreme Soviet, the organization of more and more public auxiliary bodies attached to local soviets, and—most strikingly—the bruiting about of suggestions that electors be offered a choice of candidates instead of having no option than to vote for or against a single nominee. In all of these instances what is involved is an effort to enable the soviets to perform their various legitimation, communication, and mobilization functions more effectively. What is really at issue is a desire on the part of the ruling elite to make the soviets more effective "transmission belts" or better "schools of communism", as official parlance has it, and attempts to depict these measures as steps toward "liberalization" or "democratization" cannot bear close scrutiny. As before, so now, the soviets and the population they ostensibly represent are deprived of almost all effective voice in the formulation and implementation of state policy, and this situation is unlikely to change in the near future.

II. Dynamics and Sources of Soviet Law

Who then does participate in the legislative process in the U.S.S.R.? What structures and what groups in the Soviet political system do play a meaningful role in the making of law —that is, in the formulation of "principles, regulations, and policies prescribed under the authority of the state or nation?" Instead of going on to a more detailed examination of the soviets as such—instead, for example, of expatiating on the relationship between the two chambers of the Supreme Soviet, the reasons for the existence of a unicameral system at the subnational level, the rules and procedures governing parliamentary debate, and other similar topics—the remainder of this essay will be addressed to these two questions. Because the primary focus of political analysis is the organization and distribution of power and because the soviets are largely powerless, it seems appropriate to move from matters of form to matters of substance and to inquire into the actual dynamics of Soviet politics and the real sources of Soviet law, broadly defined. To repeat, who actually does participate in the legislative process in the U.S.S.R., given that the nominal legislators and the vast majority of their constituents do not?

Exercise of Political Power in the Stalinist Period

The "classical" answer to this question is, of course, that virtually no one except the dictator and the members of his immediate entourage exercises appreciable political power. Moreover, there is no doubt of the fundamental validity of this answer where the Stalinist period is concerned. To be sure, some devolution of power occurred even under full-fledged Stalinism. Indeed, it could not have been otherwise, for no single individual or small group can possibly exercise a complete monopoly of power in a complex modern society covering one sixth of the earth's surface. In any such society, some decisions have to be delegated to middle and lower echelon officials, and even those decisions that are reserved to the central leadership must rest in large part on the advice

and judgment of technical experts and administrative specialists. Because they alone possess the "relevant facts," such experts and specialists inevitably control many of the critical "premises" on which adequate decisions must be based, and from time to time such control is bound to be utilized to effect official policy choices and aggrandize political influence. However, if one can exaggerate the concentration of power that obtained under Stalin, it is nonetheless true that the Stalinist system was an unprecedentedly close approximation of the totalitarian "ideal-type"—that is, of a type of political system in which there are no institutional or societal restraints on the exercise of central power.

Under Stalin, the politicization of society reached unprecedented lengths, and virtually all secondary associations and groups were converted into political "transmission belts," harnessed to the goals and purposes of the dictatorial regime. Hypercentralization was the norm in all spheres, and the dictator made every effort to guarantee that no one who enjoyed a measure of delegated authority was in a position to translate that authority into political independence. Authority was organized in "parallel, competing bureaucracies" which merged only at the top and were purposely assigned vaguely defined and overlapping spheres of jurisdiction. While the *principle* of "collegial administration" had long since been replaced by the *principle* of "one-man management," in practice virtually every "one-man manager," whether plant director, army commander, or university rector, had to share his authority with a party secretary and a secret police official who were responsible to different superiors through independent chains of command and who felt free—indeed, obliged—to intervene in virtually all of the given institution's affairs. This entire system, in turn, was subjected to constant arbitrary terror and a relentless "permanent purge" with results that fully justify calling it a system of "institutionalized cross-espionage, fear, and mutual-suspicion." As such, moreover, it was by no means confined to the lower and middle levels of authority. On the contrary, the members of the ruling elite were at least as vulnerable to sudden arrest as their subordinates, and Stalin went out of his way to cultivate rivalries and conflicts among his top lieutenants, thereby maximizing his own power and insuring that politics was confined to competition for his grace and favor.

The insecurity and subservience (not to say servility) that Stalin inspired among even his closest associates is now well known, thanks *inter alia* to his successor Khrushchev's "revelations." In this connection Khrushchev's reports of the constant humiliation that Voroshilov endured at Stalin's hands and of the pleasure that "the Leader" took in examining his lieutenants to see if they had "shifty eyes" are particularly revealing. They leave no doubt that the atmosphere in the Kremlin was that of a despotic oriental court. For present purposes, however, one of Khrushchev's less lurid and less familiar stories is even more relevant because it relates directly to the policy process as such. We refer to Khrushchev's report of a Council of Ministers' meeting at which Stalin suddenly proposed a production plan that ran directly counter to the advice of his industrial ministers, and then, having watched the ministers vote unanimously in favor of his proposal, openly gloated over his success in keeping his subordinates in their "proper" places. No doubt such scenes were not regular occurrences in that Stalin was ordinarily probably somewhat less imperious in his approach. However, what is of concern here is not Stalin's leadership style, but the fact of his unchallenged leadership; not the tact with which he treated his top aides, but his readiness to ignore or dismiss their advice and his ability to do so with complete impunity. Given this kind of dictatorial power, it is clear that even the upper stratum of the Soviet ruling elite enjoyed only intermittent and highly contingent access to the policy process, and there is no question that the law which emerged from this process came very close indeed to expressing the arbitrary will of a single, omnipotent sovereign.

The Reemergence of Politics After Stalin

It was, of course, inevitable that Stalin's death would leave a huge vacuum of power at the very core of the Soviet system. The demise of the absolute dictator was bound to touch off a major realignment of forces within the ruling elite and to unleash intense pressure for the redress of accumulated grievances. In short, the situation was ripe for change, and it is not surprising that the period following Stalin's death witnessed a marked growth in the political assertiveness of major social groups and a sharp increase in official responsiveness to popular claims and demands. Nevertheless, though this reemergence of conventional politics represented a fundamental and dramatic change, and one whose momentum has yet to be exhausted, its scope must not be exaggerated. The bulk of the

population remained politically inartic-
ulate and unorganized while effective
access to the system's power processes
remained very highly circumscribed. In
the final analysis, almost all major decisions continued to be made by a small
circle of Stalin's ex-lieutenants, and the
ability to exert a significant influence
on critical policy choices remained confined to the leading members of four
strategic elites: the secret police, the
managerial elite, the officer corps, and
the full-time party functionaries or
apparatchiki. Moreover, by 1955 it was
evident that a countertrend had set in,
and the next several years saw a substantial reconcentration of power and a
gradual curtailment in the access of all
groups except the *apparatchiki* to the
power-political arena.

The party *apparat* had, of course,
traditionally occupied a position of
political primacy within the Soviet system. It had acquired this status while
Lenin was still alive, and it was above
all thanks to his control of the party
apparat that Stalin had been able to
succeed to Lenin's mantle and to aggrandize autocratic power. However,
as he moved closer to his goal, Stalin
had sought simultaneously to reduce
his dependence on the *apparat* and to
enhance his direct control over the
other major power structures in the
system. Only in this way could he hope
to attain total domination, and the war
and postwar years consequently witnessed an almost uninterrupted rise in
the relative authority of the state bureaucracy and the secret police. This
process had apparently not yet gone
far enough to satisfy Stalin, who seems
to have been planning a further downgrading of the *apparat* at the time of
his death, but it had nonetheless gone
quite far—far enough that by 1953 the
apparat appeared to be merely one of

a number of coordinate and nearly
coequal instruments of rule. Moreover,
while Stalin's death gave the *apparatchiki* more room to maneuver, it
was by no means certain that they
would be able to recoup their position
and reestablish their traditional primacy under the new regime. On the
contrary, it was apparent that most of
the major elite groups in Soviet society
favored a further curtailment in the
authority of the *apparat*, and the manner in which power was divided at the
apex of the system, among Stalin's
immediate heirs, was clearly calculated
to reinforce the pressure that these
groups exerted.

As is well known, Stalin's heirs
affected a division of power along essentially bureaucratic lines, with Khrushchev emerging as First Secretary
of the party, Malenkov as premier and
head of the state machine, Beria as
head of a newly re-consolidated secret
police apparatus, and so on. This alignment of forces, in turn, made it almost
inevitable that conflict within the
ruling elite would exacerbate the already considerable tension among the
regime's principal instruments of rule
and cast a number of top leaders in
the role of spokesmen for bureaucratic
groupings that were inimical to the
aspirations of the *apparatchiki*. Indeed
with the conspicuous exception of
Khrushchev, who clearly had an overriding interest in the maintenance and
enhancement of *apparat* primacy, virtually all of the top leaders now
found themselves in institutional positions that forced them either to surrender all hope of playing an independent power-political role or else to
assume a more or less vigorously anti-
apparat posture, for only such a posture
would enable them effectively to mobilize the support of their principal

"constituents." Accordingly, when the "collective leadership" which had been established after Stalin's death disintegrated, Khrushchev was in a somewhat isolated position, and it was uncertain that the *apparat* would be able to hold its own, let alone reclaim its former authority. In the event, however, Khrushchev was able to play his rivals off against each other until his own dominance was assured, and his success in this regard was, *ipso facto*, a success for his supporters.

Apparat *Primacy and Collective Leadership*

Although the period 1953–1958 witnessed major challenges to *apparat* primacy from the side of the secret police (Beria), the state bureaucracy (first Malenkov and then Bulganin), and the armed forces (Bulganin to some extent and, above all, Zhukov), all of these challenges failed. Aided by their still unrivaled organizational resources and their control over the symbols of legitimacy (a critical variable in any succession struggle), the *apparatchiki* were able not only to contain their opponents but to move more and more onto the offensive. Slowly but surely, they reasserted their sovereignty within the power-political arena, and the end result of their self-aggrandizement was a massive extension of the political and administrative hegemony of the party machine. Suffice it to say in this regard that the successive stages of the post-Stalin succession struggle culminated in a drastic political emasculation of the secret police, a complete dismantling of the system of centralized economic ministries (the system from which the managerial elite had derived its power),

and a substantial purge of the officer corps in a context characterized by much increased emphasis on the importance of political and ideological—as distinct from professional—criteria in the determination of military organization and policy. In short, by 1958, the record revealed that in a contest with the party *apparatchiki* the other key elite groups in Soviet society were apt to fail not only as counterelite or power-political "constituency groups," but even as "veto groups" where their own most vital interests were at stake. In doing so, it clearly ran counter to the expectations of those who had confidently predicted in 1953 that the Soviet system would undergo a rapid evolution toward a system of "countervailing power" or even toward genuine political pluralism—that is, toward a polity in which the decision-making process is characterized by extensive bargaining among truly autonomous groups representing discrete institutional and professional interests. However, if the outcome of the succession struggle did not confirm the more optimistic projections of the "pluralists," it left room for doubt regarding the validity of claims that the "natural" configuration of Soviet political life is one-man dictatorship or monocratic (autocratic) rule.

Developments subsequent to Stalin's death clearly indicate that the Soviet political system embodies a strong *tendency* toward monocratic rule. The rapid breakdown of the initial "collective leadership" testifies to the operations of this tendency and there is little question that each of the chief competitors in the succession struggle aspired to autocratic power. Certainly there can be little doubt that Khrushchev sought to aggrandize such power following his victory in the succession struggle. This seems clear, for example, from the way in which he treated his erstwhile rivals, for the evidence strongly suggests that Khrushchev wanted not only to expel the leaders of the so-called "anti-party group" of 1957 from the party (a desire that he ultimately satisfied) but also to bring them to trial on capital charges. These charges, moreover, were to pertain not only to crimes committed under Stalin but also to the crime of "conspiracy to seize power"—a new crime which was put on the books at Khrushchev's behest in 1958. What Khrushchev sought from such a persecution was clearly not only to retaliate against former opponents but also to deter future opposition and to create an atmosphere of terror within the current ruling elite. While he was anxious to observe legal forms, his goal was to rehabilitate the "ritual of liquidation" as procedure for settling leadership disputes. Moreover, at the same time that he sought to terrorize his closest colleagues and lieutenants, Khrushchev also began to propagate a new, Khrushchevian "cult of personality" and to pursue organizational and personnel policies that were clearly designed to maximize his own authority and power.

As during the succession struggle proper, Khrushchev now adopted tactics similar to those that Stalin had used in his quest for absolute power. In particular, he made a systematic attempt to reduce his dependence on the party *apparat* and enhance the authority of other power structures. For one thing, he repeatedly tried to bypass the party Presidium in his policy initiatives, going out of his way, for example, to "leak" plans and proposals that were still under discussion and had not yet been approved. In the

same vein, he sought to convert plenary sessions of the Central Committee into hortatory mass meetings in which the voice of the *apparatchiki*, who comprised the bulk of the Central Committee's membership, was drowned out by the voice of hundreds of technical specialists, state officials, and "rank and file" workers and peasants. Similarly, he developed an increasingly active personal secretariat, headed by his son-in-law Adzhubei, whom he eventually tried to co-opt into the party Secretariat proper. Again, he himself took over the premiership in addition to the first secretaryship of the party and even went so far as to have himself appointed to the new post of supreme commander-in-chief of the armed forces. Having thus enhanced his direct control over the state bureaucracy, he proceeded not only to sponsor a progressive recentralization of governmental and economic administration (which he had radically decentralized in 1957) but also, and even more importantly, to divide the previously "monolithic" party *apparat* into separate agricultural and industrial committees whose secretaries (now twice as numerous as before and perforce less powerful) were increasingly relegated to the status of low and middle level economic controllers.

All of these measures had a distinct dictatorial cast, and they were rendered the more ominous by the fact that they were accompanied by a marked acceleration of the "permanent purge." At all levels there was a systematic "renewal of cadres," and thousands of new men who owed their positions to Khrushchev were catapulted into high office. However, for all his exertions, Khrushchev's attempt to consolidate absolute power ended in defeat. Although he seemed to be on the verge of an autocratic breakthrough on a number of occasions, especially in late 1962 and again in late 1963, Khrushchev was consistently checked in the event. And when it finally became clear that he would neither moderate his personal ambition nor revamp a number of policies that seemed certain to eventuate in major fiascoes for the regime, he was decisively checkmated.

Khrushchev's ouster clearly suggests that the tendency toward one-man dictatorship that continues to operate within the Soviet system is not irresistible. Indeed, the "lesson" of October 1964 may be that one-man dictatorship cannot be attained so long as the would-be dictator is unable to resort to terror as a technique for controlling his colleagues within the ruling elite. Likewise, the relative stability that has characterized the Soviet leadership since Khrushchev's ouster suggests that "collective leadership"— for it is precisely such leadership that appears to obtain—may be a more viable system of rule within the Soviet context than most analysts would previously have supposed. At the same time, however, it remains true that Khrushchev almost succeeded in his drive for autocratic power. And it must be stressed that there is no guarantee against a breakdown in the present system of "collective leadership" and a consequent reactivation of the tendency toward one-man dictatorship.

Barring a very rapid growth in the procedural consensus which seems to be developing within the Soviet ruling elite, there seems no reason whatever to dismiss the possibility of a bitter and violent succession struggle in the near future. Signs of severe tension within the new leadership have been recurrent, and future developments may yet reveal that the solidarity that seems to exist within the Presidium is largely illusory. Should this in fact prove to be the case, there are as yet no institutional or societal restraints that would preclude the possibility of a younger and more ruthless Khrushchev type from successfully doing what Khrushchev tried but ultimately failed to do—i.e., from aggrandizing absolute power by liquidating his rivals, transforming the party Secretariat into a personal appendage, and using the techniques of "permanent purge" and perpetual reorganization in order to prevent the consolidation of insulated pockets of authority and power. The costs of such a process would, no doubt, be unprecedentedly high, but it would be premature to conclude that they could not be imposed or that their imposition would entail a breakdown in the system. Moreover, even if October 1964 did introduce a new stage in the evolution of the Soviet system, the ouster of Khrushchev and the emergence of a relatively stable "collective leadership" do not necessarily signify an extensive diffusion of power.

In the first place, it must be stressed that Khrushchev was ousted through a conspiratorial palace coup, participation in which was limited to a handful of top leaders. While the details of Khrushchev's deposition are still shrouded in mystery, it seems clear that the circle of conspirators was confined to members of the party Presidium and a few key officials in the state bureaucracy, military establishment, and security apparatus. To be sure, once the conspirators made their first overt move against Khrushchev, other participants were drawn in, and constitutional or quasi-constitutional forms were observed to the extent of immediately convening a session of the 200-odd man Central Committee to which

Khrushchev was allowed to appeal. However, the available evidence leaves little doubt that the real function of the Central Committee was to ratify an irreversible *fait accompli*. While the fact that procedural norms were observed is itself of some significance as an index of political change, it is doubtful that Khrushchev would have been allowed to appeal to the Central Committee if there had been any doubt as to the outcome of his appeal. Thus, at the same time that it testifies to the possibility of effective resistance to autocracy within the system, October 1964 also testifies to the highly elitist and exclusivist character of Soviet politics.

It is true that the Brezhnev-Kosygin government has given the various strategic elites in Soviet society a greater voice in the policy process. However, this is exactly what one would anticipate in the case of a new and as yet unconsolidated regime, and the present situation need not last. Moreover, even now effective access to the ultimate decision-making arena remains very strictly circumscribed. At best, it is only the top cadres of the various strategic elites who exercise decisional prerogatives on any other than a purely intermittent and particularistic basis, and the party *apparat* (which was quickly reunited after Khrushchev's ouster) continues to exercise an extensive power-political hegemony. Indeed, the party Presidium is now, even more than before, a veritable *inner sanctum* of leading *apparatchiki*. Thus, of the five men who have been promoted to the party Presidium since Khrushchev's ouster, four are men who have spent their entire careers in the party *apparat*. To be sure, the new premier Kosygin has made his career primarily in economic administration, but he is nonetheless a peculiarly "unmanagerial" manager who has always enjoyed the particular favor of *apparat*-dominated factions and groups. And, apart from his promotion, none of the personnel changes sponsored by the new regime suggest a break in the pattern of *apparat* primacy.

The Role of Administrators and Managers

Where there has been a marked change is in the amount of operational autonomy enjoyed by state officials and economic executives within the areas of their particular professional competence. However, this autonomy is designed to have a purely instrumental character, pertaining exclusively to the execution of centrally determined policies. Moreover, it is more likely now than ever before to retain precisely such a character. To an ever increasing extent, the men in whom administrative and managerial authority are vested are true professionals who are apolitical in their outlooks and are committed to implementing established policy in a more or less unquestioning fashion, and these men are unlikely to engage in extensive power-political maneuvers or seek to aggrandize personal power. While the growth of professionalism is often cited as a factor foreshadowing the erosion of totalitarianism, it can also facilitate central control, and past experience suggests that in the Soviet Union this is peculiarly likely to be the case. Furthermore, should practice confound this prognosis, it seems likely that the autonomy which has now been granted can and will be revoked without undue difficulty and that we will once again witness a rapid proliferation of *apparat* surveillances and control. Certainly, at a minimum, there seems no reason to anticipate anything approaching a "managerial revolution," let alone a managerial revolution that would eventuate in the acquisition by society of any substantial capacity for political self-determination. Although these two processes are often linked together, they have no logical connection, and a case can be made for the party *apparatchiki* being considerably more receptive to popular claims and demands than either the economic managers or any other major elite group. Be that as it may, however, there is no likelihood of society's soon attaining a significant voice in the policy process.

III. Prospect for the Future

The ouster of Khrushchev has not entailed any fundamental change in the political status of the non-elite groups and broad popular groupings of Soviet society. Now, as before, they are primarily objects of political manipulation rather than initiators of political action, and their claims and demands upon the political system remain unorganized and, from a liberal-democratic point of view, unrepresented. Moreover, it is by no means certain that the new regime—or its successors—will not once again revert to a policy of intensive social mobilization. Such a policy was, of course, part and parcel of the Stalinist system and it occupied a prominent place in the Khrushchev system as well, albeit it was pursued without recourse to mass terror. Thus, Khrushchev was the author of a multitude of measures assigned to undermine the authority of the family, to eradicate religious "survivals," to eliminate all forms of private property, and

to restrict sharply the sphere of personal privacy. These measures, which included the prosecution of a violent anti-religious campaign, the confiscation of a great deal of peasant-owned livestock and land, the institution of a far-flung network of boarding schools, and the creation of a variety of parapolice and parajudicial "public organizations" to administer a kind of organized vigilance justice, are too often overlooked in discussions of the political dynamics of the "Khrushchev era." Likewise, their significance is too often ignored in projecting future trends.

It is true that many of Khrushchev's mobilizational policies have been suspended or revoked by the new regime. However, a number have been retained and it is not unlikely that others will be resumed in the not too distant future. Most of the policies in question are firmly rooted in Marxist-Leninist ideology. They follow logically from the proposition that the Soviet Union is about to realize full-fledged communism. This proposition, in turn, continues to occupy a central place in the party program and is hence likely to have an important influence on future policy. This is true, moreover, irrespective of whether or not the Soviet leaders are ideological true believers. Whatever their beliefs, they all have immense vested interests in structures and procedures which incarnate ideological principles and can only be justified and rationalized in ideological terms. This point once noted, however, it is important to go on to note that one can query whether the erosion of genuine ideological commitment has in fact proceeded as far as many analysts believe. Certainly, for all his much vaunted "pragmatism," Khrushchev had a strong fundamentalist streak (viz., for example, his policy of confiscating peasants' private property in the midst of a massive agricultural crisis), and the fact that various of his successors have criticized him precisely for his excessive pragmatism may suggest that the new regime contains an even higher admixture of ideological militants. Moreover, such militants are unlikely soon to disappear.

While the younger members of the ruling elite are better educated than the present leaders, the educational system of which they are products is massively dedicated to the inculcation of ideological militancy, and the recruitment process through which they have been selected for elite positions continues even today to place very heavy stress on ideological and political criteria. To be sure, despite the regime's best efforts, cases of apoliticism and "technocratism" have become increasingly common among young party cadres, but there is good reason to believe that they are still the exception rather than the rule. Fairly extensive contact with Soviet youth has persuaded the present author that the regime's socialization and recruitment programs have operated successfully enough for most of the members of the emergent ruling elite to qualify for all practical purposes as "new Soviet men," attuned to the "imperatives" of modern technology but determined to maintain the traditional primacy of politics over economics and to base policy on ideological principle and the tenets of Marxist-Leninist doctrine. This determination could waver as the men in question acquire more responsibility, but it is unlikely to disappear. Its psychological roots are often extremely deep, and responsibility is as likely to reinforce ideological conviction as it is to generate ideological

agnosticism. Promotion is no certain source of critical acumen, and the tendency toward doctrinaire thinking that is characteristic of the men concerned may well be strengthened by the growing weight of institutional commitments and more intensive involvement in the party's on-going effort to legitimate its political sovereignty. That this quest is likely to encounter more and more obstacles does not necessarily mean that it will be pursued less vigorously, and it could mean precisely the reverse. History knows counterreformations as well as reformations, and in the Soviet Union the forces of ideological orthodoxy and organizational monolithism are well disciplined and occupy positions of vast strength.

In spite of the many factors that are operating to prevent Soviet society's acquiring a significant capacity for political self-determination, the dramatic changes that have ensued since Stalin's death should serve as a caution against excessive pessimism. There is, after all, no doubt that the past decade has witnessed many important victories for the anti-totalitarian forces within Soviet society, including, to name but a few, the elimination of mass terror, the cessation of "bacchanalian" planning, the allocation of many more resources to consumer welfare, and the spread of a multidimensional cultural "thaw." Moreover, there is no doubt that in some cases the term "victory" can be taken quite literally. That is to say, the changes in question have been wrested from a reluctant or recalcitrant regime by social groups (most notably, the liberal intelligentsia) that have backed their demands with sustained pressure and have shown great internal cohesiveness and solidarity in the face of official counterpressure. However, many of the changes that have ensued have been sponsored by the regime itself for the sake of its own interests. These changes, in turn, point more to the modernization of totalitarianism than to liberalization or democratization. Furthermore, many of the other changes have proved highly precarious when subjected to determined assault from above. Such militancy became more and more prevalent during the "Khrushchev era," and it may well prove common in the future.

There are those who argue that freedom is bound to grow at an ever quicker tempo. However, such arguments find little confirmation in past history and are often based on dubious premises. While freedom has grown, it has also declined, and it is well to remember that the freedom that has thus far emerged in the Soviet Union is essentially negative freedom—freedom *from* rather than freedom *to*. As such it is by no means illusory or nugatory, but it must be appraised for what it is and from a perspective that recognizes not only that benevolent dictatorship is nonetheless dictatorship but also that benevolence may actually serve to render dictatorship more effective and more stable. The "thaw" (using the

term in the wide sense) may be the prelude to a genuine spring, but Russian springs are notoriously late-coming and winter tends to be the longest, and, as it were, the characteristic season. As men, all we can do is hope that the political winter will at long last yield, as nature's winter always, finally, does. As analysts, we must, I think, be somewhat skeptical, if not precisely pessimistic.

To conclude, over the long run society may acquire a really significant capacity for political self-expression and self-determination and when it does it may be aided in realizing this capacity by the existence of the parliamentary forms and constitutional provisions that were described at the outset of this essay. Forms do have a way of taking on content, and there may come a time when it will be meaningful to discuss the legislative process in the Soviet Union in more or less conventional terms. This is a remote prospect, however, and it will require decades, not years, before the operation of the "legislative branch" of the Soviet government will acquire real political salience or representative government and parliamentary supremacy will be anything more than a hollow constitutional myth.

INTEREST GROUPS AND COMMUNIST POLITICS

H. Gordon Skilling

The idea that interest groups may play a significant role in Communist politics has, until recently, not been seriously entertained either by Western

political scientists or by Soviet legal specialists. The concept of "totalitarianism" that has dominated the analysis of communism in the West

World Politics, XVIII, No. 3 (April 1966), 435–51. Reprinted by permission. Footnotes omitted.

has seemed to preclude the possibility that interest groups could challenge or affect the single ruling party as the fount of all power. The uniqueness of a totalitarian system has been deemed to lie in the very totality of its political power, excluding, as it were by definition, any area of autonomous behavior by groups other than the state or party, and still more, preventing serious influence by them on the process of decision-making. Marxist theorists, starting from different presuppositions, have assumed that the single ruling party, the organization of the working class, best knew the "real" interests of the people as a whole, and have denied the possibility of fundamental conflicts of interest within the working class, or between it and associated friendly classes such as the peasantry. Within the ruling party itself, groups or factions opposing the leadership have not been admitted in theory or permitted in practice.

Although there has been by no means general agreement on the meaning of totalitarianism, and the term has been rejected out of hand by Communist scholars, it has been common in the West to treat it as a phenomenon unique in world history, sharply distinguished not only from Western democratic societies but also from traditional authoritarian regimes. It has usually been accepted that totalitarianism entails the widest possible extension of state power over society, thus tending to annihilate all boundaries between state and society, and destroying any associations or groups intermediate between the individual and the state. Zbigniew Brzezinski, having with Carl Friedrich (in their book published in 1956) established a syndrome of indispensable elements, argues also that the system involves an unavoidable compulsion on the part of the ruling movement to absorb or destroy all social groups obstructing its complete control of society. This line of thought assumes a totally organized or totally administered society, a mass community in which the individual is alone and helpless.

Yet even the most vigorous protagonists of the totalitarian model have admitted the existence of "islands of separateness," such as the family or religion, and others have written of the "limits" on totalitarian power set by the ability of the individual to resist the pressures put upon him. Perhaps even more destructive to totalitarian uniqueness is the suggestion, advanced by N. S. Timasheff, of a "democratic-totalitarian" continuum involving an infinite gradation of differing degree of totalitarianism and democracy. A specialist on Eastern Europe, Andrew Gyorgy, denies that the Communist states of that area were, at the time of writing, fully totalitarian, and suggests they were instead "partialitarian," thus implying the feasibility of a "relative," or nontotal, totalitarianism.

The totalitarian concept has also often implied a certain changelessness in the nature of Communist politics. Even after the death of Stalin, the likelihood of a decline of totalitarianism has been doubted by some. If anything, it has been argued by Friedrich and Brzezinski, Communist societies would probably become *more*, not *less*, totalitarian. Some scholars, however, have forecast the possibility that existing totalitarian societies might "mellow," or be "undermined" by their own features, thus opening up the perspective of nontotalitarian Communist systems as theoretically conceivable. Barrington Moore, in his *Terror and Progress USSR: Some*

Sources of Change and Stability in the Soviet Dictatorship, discusses several future alternatives, including nontotalitarian ones, and calculates the balance of social forces that might produce new political conditions. Writing some years later Alex Inkeles and Raymond Bauer argue that Soviet society is the product of the interplay of two elements: its distinctive totalitarian character and the pattern of an industrial society which it shares with others. The latter element had modified the former, producing changes similar to those in other industrial societies. Deliberate actions already taken to improve the system have made it "less totalitarian" and have reflected "the mellowing, even to some extent, the 'liberalization' of Soviet society."

Paradoxically, the wide-ranging re-evaluation of comparative politics which has been conducted during the past several decades has largely ignored the Soviet system. No doubt the use of the totalitarian concept, reinforced by the pressures of the cold war, has produced a propensity to think in black and white terms about Soviet and Western politics, and has tended to obscure the differences within the so-called totalitarian category as well as the common features of all political systems, the Soviet included. A gulf has opened up between two developing subdisciplines, comparative politics and Soviet political studies, each pursuing its own course largely unaware of, or at least unaffected by, the other's efforts. Needless to say, the comparative analysis conducted by David Easton, Gabriel Almond, and others is intended to be applicable to all types of states, including the Communist. Nonetheless the search for a new theory of politics has been based largely on materials and concepts derived from the study of American and other Western democratic institutions, enriched by postwar research and theoretical speculation concerning non-Western or developing societies. No serious effort has been made to test empirically concepts derived from these political experiences by applying them to Communist states; still less has any attempt been made to derive from Soviet political life concepts that might be useful in interpreting other systems. In the course of disquisitions on the comparative approach, there have been only random remarks referring to Soviet and Communist politics, and occasional warnings against a polarization of analysis of the totalitarian and democratic extremes.

On the other hand, a generally applicable concept such as that of the "elite" has sometimes been used as an instrument for the study of Soviet politics. Moreover several books, such as those of Sigmund Neumann and Maurice Duverger on political parties, and of Henry W. Ehrmann on interest groups, have embraced the Soviet system in a general comparative treatment. In both Neumann and Duverger, however, the bulk of the analysis is devoted to two-party and multi-party systems, and the one-party system is treated as a thing apart, sharply differentiated from the others and hardly comparable with them in function or organization. On the other hand, Professsor Djordjević, in his contribution to the 1958 conference proceedings edited by Ehrmann, recognizes the vàlue of the comparative approach for the study of interest groups in both Communist and non-Communist systems, and applies the group concept to Yugoslavia in an original manner (to be discussed more fully later in this article). His ideas are not, however, seriously incorporated in the general thinking of the conference. In all these cases, then, the traditional dichotomy between the Soviet and other political systems remains largely unbridged, and the general lack of systematic comparative analysis is pointed up still more sharply.

The model of Communist politics in most Western analysis has seemed, strangely enough, to be exclusively concerned with "outputs," i.e. the imposition of binding decisions, and to be entirely lacking in the "inputs" regarded by Easton as an essential element of every political system. Unlike all other systems, the Soviet has been often depicted as one in which struggles over ideas and interests, or conflicts of rival groups, are absent. Issues requiring decisions are raised not by society or social groups but presumably by the party, or better, by its topmost leaders, without regard for the values and interests of other entities. The monolithic party has been regarded as the only interest group, not itself differentiated in its thinking or behavior. Almond and Coleman, however, have offered the suggestive thought that the articulation and aggregation of interests characteristic of all systems take place within a totalitarian party, largely latently, through the interplay of interest groups and factions.

Western scholars were not fully prepared for the extraordinary changes that occurred in the Soviet political system after Stalin's death, and for the increasing diversity among the Communist countries. Many have continued to use the term "totalitarian" while the facts of Communist society are rendering it more and more obsolete and less and less helpful for satisfactory analysis. The evidence has steadily mounted that the Soviet system is far from being "conflictless" and that behind the facade of the monolithic party a genuine struggle has been taking place among rival groups or factions. Carl Linden speaks of a "continuing battle between powerful and entrenched elements in the party's higher echelons," and speaks of these as constraints built into the Soviet system of power," limiting the complete freedom of the top leaders. The conflict is sometimes interpreted as a mere personal struggle for power, largely divorced from issues of policy or ideology, or from the interests of social groups, and designed to secure control of the main institutions of power, namely the party apparatus, the state bureaucracy, the army, and the police. In other cases, however, the struggle is linked with major issues of public policy, and related to even more narrowly defined groups, such as the central or peripheral party organizations; the *apparatchiki* and state bureaucrats; central and local economic management; conservative, liberal and centrist factions; the intelligentsia and its various sectors; special interests such as heavy industry, agriculture, or arms production; the nationalities; and so on. Robert Conquest lists the "pressures"—including the peasantry, intellectuals, and national minorities—under which the struggle for power occurs, and the "institutional elements" involved, such as the various organs of party and government, and the army, police, and managers. Although he does not assign great influence to these groups, he views the power of Khrushchev as somewhat limited and not necessarily complete and final. T. H. Rigby, while insisting on the supreme power of the top leader, notes the foci of conflict, which he lists under twelve headings, including not only the conflicts obviously related to the struggle for power, but also those between different sections of the bureaucracy; between informal groupings of officials; between areas and occupational groups; between and within the groups purveying values in the arts and sciences, and even in ideology; and between the masses and the regime.

The study of political power in the United States and the USSR published in 1964 by Brzezinski and Huntington was a major break-through in comparative analysis. In this work the authors deal extensively with the role of interest groups, including "social forces" (aspirations of workers, peasants, and so on) impinging on Soviet politicians and creating the main issues of politics; "specific interest groups" (intellectuals, scientists, or minorities); and "policy groups" (the military, heavy and light industry managers, agricultural managers, and state bureaucrats) which participate in the formation of policy. Like most of the other specialists cited, however, they continue to regard conflict as taking place mainly at the peak of the Soviet political pyramid, with only the top party echelons making policy, and the other groups not enjoying much autonomy or influence.

It has thus become increasingly evident that a totalitarian concept which excludes group interest and conflict is no longer an appropriate means of analyzing Soviet politics, and that a more systematic study of the reality of group politics is overdue. In the Communist states of Eastern Europe there is even clearer indication of the growing importance of groups in the political process. This has even been acknowledged by Communist theorists themselves. Professor Djordjević has expressed the opinion that groups are inevitable features of every system, Communist as well as non-Communist, although they manifest themselves in different ways. The recognition of these groups has been hampered, he says, by absolutist and totalitarian ideologies, idealistic or legalistic theories of the state, and, in Communist countries, by "Stalinist dogmatism." "Modern society is a dynamic body, complicated and diversified in its structure, full of conflicting and even antagonistic interests. Consequently, the political affirmation, the role and influence of different interest groups, are the general tendency of human society.

More recently a Slovak theorist, Michael Lakatoš, writing in the legal journal *Právny obzor*, has argued that socialist society is characterized not merely by differences of class, but also by conflicts "evoked by the intraclass social differentiation of our society, i.e., by interest groups." These he terms "the real basis of the structure of the social and political system." The role of such groups in politics had been neglected in Europe until the late fifties, he says, both by bourgeois political science, with its emphasis on the individual and the state, and by Marxist scholars, with their exclusive concern with social classes. A scientific study of politics requires, he says, an investigation of "the interests of people in the entire complicated structure of socialist society, and especially group interests.

There can be no doubt that Communist society, in spite of its monolithic appearance and the claims of homogeneity made by its supporters, is in fact as complex and stratified as any other, and is divided into social classes and into other categories distinguished by factors such as nationality or religion. Each group has its own values and interests, and each its sharp internal differences, and all are inescapably involved in conflict with other groups. The novelty of the views expressed by both Djordjević and Lakatoš lies in their recognition, in the words of the former, that socialist society *is* "complex and heterogeneous." "In the sociological sense, society is a mosaic of larger and smaller, and highly different, interest groups." Djordjević refers also to amorphous groupings—ethnic, local, or regional in character—which might seek precedence over the national interest; the clashing of specialized interests, such as consumers and producers; and other influences such as those of "a backward environment," "bureaucratic and authoritarian groups," and "personal notions of individuals."

Lakatoš writes of the conflict between the interests of society as a whole and of individuals and groups, and recognizes that these are not mere vestiges of capitalism. In a list not meant to be exhaustive he suggests the following criteria of social differentiation: relationship to the means of production (state sector, cooperative sector, or small production); division of labor (industry, agriculture, intellectual or physical work); level of income; participation in the direction of society (Communists, nonparty persons, or organizers of production); ethnic affiliation; territorial divisions (different administrative entities); biological character (men and women); and so on. He refers to "inner conflicts which exist between society as the proprietor and interests of groups and individuals," and which call forth "a whole series

of conflicting relations in economics and in the social-political sphere," and cites the especially deep conflicts over the distribution of income.

More relevant for political analysis than such broad groupings of a sociological character are the organized political groups that claim to express the interests of the broad groupings and to exert pressure on government for their implementation. Djordjević defines three categories of organized political groups in Yugoslavia: (*a*) those participating directly in the process of governing (such as economic organizations and social institutions); (*b*) those holding "strategic positions" in the political system (such as the League of Communists); and (*c*) those representing the special interests of citizens (such as unions or churches). He recognizes that these might have their own selfish interests, and might also seek to impose their views on the social forces they are supposed to represent. There might also be conflicts of interests between the leaders of such groups and their members, or between their central and local organizations. Djordjević sees in the development of a public opinion favorable to "the general interest" the major safeguard of a correct relation between "rightful" and "selfish" group interests. The direct participation of many groups in the governing process (the "institutionalization") is regarded as a unique and valuable feature of the Yugoslav system. In similar vein Lakatoš expresses the opinion that groups might onesidedly pursue their own interests, at the expense of the general interest, or might, unless closely connected with the social forces they represent, fail to express real group interests and become mere arms of the state. An indispensable part of socialist democracy, in his view, are the "interest groups, the institutional expression of group interests"; to them, "as an integrating element, the guidance of society must be adapted."

In speaking of interest organizations Lakatoš has in mind mainly the societal or mass associations that exist in all Communist countries: the trade unions, youth leagues, women's committees, and a host of other bodies in specialized fields such as the unions of writers and journalists. Known in Stalin's times as "transmission belts," they were regarded as means of transmitting policy *to* the groups rather than as sources originating it, and had in fact no share in the shaping of public policy. Power was, in any case, concentrated in their higher echelons, so that each organization tended to stand not for the special interests of its members, or of a broader social group such as the workers or writers, but rather for a general "public" interest as conceived by the party and its spokesmen within the organization. In times of crisis, the mass associations have only occasionally emerged, as in Poland and Hungary in 1955 and 1956, as powerful pressure groups challenging the party itself. While it has rightly been assumed in the West that the mass organizations have not played an influential role in Soviet or Communist politics, we should be alert to the possibility of a shift in their role, and the strengthening of their position as articulators of the interests of specialized groups.

Much more powerful are those groups whose position has been institutionalized as part of the administrative machinery, but whose interests may be distinct and even in conflict with each other. These include the top party organs, the highest state officials (ministers and planners), the man-

agers of industrial enterprises, specialists in agriculture, the military and the police, all of whom by virtue of their official positions are able to influence the formulation of policy and its implementation. To some extent they defend the interests of extensive social groups, such as the "managers" or the "military"; to some extent, the standpoint of a particular department or sector. As noted above, the existence of these policy groups has been adequately recognized in recent writings, but much remains to be done in the way of a systematic analysis of their position.

Under Khrushchev a new element emerged in the form of a greatly expanded participation in decision-making in their respective fields by experts and specialists. In an increasingly vigorous debate on public policy, the specialized elites have been able to express their views and interests and to exert an influence on the ultimate decisions in such spheres as education, military strategy, industrial management, legal reform, science, and literature. In some cases initial proposals have been substantially altered as a result of the discussions. The cultural, professional, and scientific intelligentsia have thus emerged as one of the main pressure groups affecting public policy. Although their participation in policy-making is often linked with power-political considerations within the ruling echelons, the intelligentsia have also been drawn into a process of deliberation designed mainly to influence the shape of policy rather than to secure power. In this market-place of ideas, competition is highly imperfect, since the bounds of discussion are strictly drawn and the party authority has the last word. Nonetheless, sharp differences have been manifested between and within the groups (and no doubt within the party apparatus itself) on such basic questions as artistic freedom, historical truth, economic analysis, administrative management, the legal rights of the individual, and freedom of scientific research.

It is *not* true to say then, as Conquest does, that Soviet politics is quite unlike Western politics because there is "no mechanism in the USSR for social forces to express themselves." Nor are groups mere "formless clusters of vested interests," to use Aspaturian's term. The various sectors of the intelligentsia, for instance, exert their influence through their institutes and associations, and through newspapers, scholarly journals, and special conferences, and in varying ways express the needs and interests of broader segments of the population. Individual case studies already provide much data for further generalization concerning their role. Among the jurists, for instance, there has been substantial freedom of discussion and sharp cleavages of opinion, which have had considerable impact on legal reforms. On questions of planning and management there have been deep-seated differences among the economists and among managers, officials, and engineers between the extreme centralizers and others less centralist in attitude. Among writers and artists, a vigorous struggle between liberals and conservatives has occurred, with an embryonic public opinion emerging, and some success registered in resisting the party's policy of restricting freedom of expression. Discussion among educators exercised a definite influence on Khrushchev's educational reforms. National groups, such as Ukrainian leaders, have also not been without influence on party decisions. Scientists, although they are said not to have an influence on major policy, are important as "lobbyists," and the leadership is responsive to their argumentation. The military have been divided among themselves, and have differed with the political leadership on military strategy, and have sought to affect decisions on other matters of public policy affecting them. There is sometimes an interlocking of groups, as for instance between liberal writers and legal specialists on the necessity for a decrease of terror, or between managers and economists seeking a more decentralized system.

In the context of group conflict, the necessity arises of "sublimating" or "integrating" the competing interests and arriving at a decision that ostensibly represents the public or general interest. "The social interest in our society," writes Lakatoš, "can be democratically formed only by the integration of group interests; in the process of this integration, the interest groups protect their own economic and other social interests; this is in no way altered by the fact that everything appears on the surface as a unity of interests." The main burden of responsibility for this task falls to the groups holding "a strategic position," to use Djordjević's term (borrowed from David Truman), which he identifies in Yugoslavia with the League of Communists and the Socialist Alliance. Although it is not expressly stated, the function of these strategic groups is presumably to cultivate the public interest, and to subordinate to it special and partial interests. Lakatoš develops the same theme at greater length, referring at one point to the state as "an active organ capable of coordinating these interest conflicts, and under the pressure of these group interests, of forming a general social interest." The task, however, is shared, in his opinion, with the societal organizations, and with the Communist Party, all of which bear some of the responsibility for resolving the conflicts of class, group, and individual interests. "The party as the leading and directing political force fulfills its function by resolving intra-class and inter-class interests."

In the words of a Western commentator, the party is "an arena in which the various Soviet elites make known their demands on one another, articulate their special interests, and try to impose their desires as the unified will of society as a whole." It is no longer seen as completely monolithic, but as a "conglomeration of interests." Since it already possesses power, it need not be concerned with what is often the most important function of parties elsewhere, the acquisition of power. Nonetheless, within the party there is a hidden struggle for power, a subterranean rivalry over policy and the public interest, sometimes bursting into the open in purge and counter-purge. In the absence of an effective representative body, and also of independent and competing parties, the single party must fill many roles performed in other systems by various institutions and, above all, must serve as a broker of competing group interests. In the post-Stalin era, with the circle of decision-making widening and public discussion less restricted, the party chiefs must more and more give attention to forming a consensus among competing policy groups, specialist elites, differing viewpoints within the party, professional and other associations, and broader amorphous social groupings.

A new model of Communist politics is thus slowly emerging as a result of the changes that have occurred since Stalin's death and the shifting perspectives of both Western and Communist analysts. The model of a totalitarian system, in which a single party, itself free of internal conflicts, imposes its will on society, and on all social groups, is being replaced by a model that takes account of the conflicting groups that exert an influence on the making of policy by the party. This is not genuine pluralism, nor is it pure totalitarianism; it is rather a kind of imperfect monism in which, of the many elements involved, one—the party—is more powerful than all others but is not omnipotent. It might be called a "pluralism of elites," or to borrow Robert Dahl's expressive term, a "polyarchical" system, but oligarchical rather than democratic in character. As in all systems, the final product—policy—is highly political, reflecting the parallelogram of conflicting forces and interests within the structure of the single party, of the national Communist society, and, to an increasing extent, of the Communist world as a whole.

It was only in 1951 that David Truman directed attention to the role of interest groups in American politics. Since then there have been substantial efforts to adopt a similar approach in studying other political systems. Research is still, however, only at the beginning stage, and some doubts have been expressed as to the usefulness of this approach even for American politics. Nonetheless group theory is recognized as "a way one can talk about politics," and one that seems quite applicable to Communist politics.

On the basis of what has been said earlier in this article, it seems difficult to deny that there *are* in the USSR and other Communist states political interest groups in Truman's sense of the term: namely, groups which, "on the basis of one or more shared attitudes," make certain claims upon other groups in the society, and specifically "through or upon any of the institutions of government." These groups seek not so much to "become the government" as to "realize aspirations through governmental decision-making"—in other words, to influence policy rather than to seek power. As Truman notes, the interests "need not be 'selfish,' are not necessarily solidly unified, and may not be represented by organized groups." In Almond's terms, they may be "associational," i.e., "specialized structures of interest articulation," or "non-associational," i.e., groups that articulate interests informally and intermittently, through individuals, cliques, and such. As elsewhere, groups will differ in the scope and intensity of their activity, and in the success with which they influence governmental decisions. It is also quite likely that the nature of the groups and their mode of action will vary according to the issues involved, and the arena of action appropriate for their settlement.

The point has been well made by several analysts that the style of interest groups is always strongly influenced by the entire political culture within which they operate. In a system where decision-making is highly centralized, where several parties do not exist, and where the representative agencies and elections play a minor role, interest groups will take on forms appropriate to this setting. Soviet Russia is not a "pluralist" society with a long tradition of associational activity

and wide freedom of public discussion but is, on the contrary, one where Russian tradition as well as Communist theory and practice have been hostile to the idea of powerful interest groups, and where such groups have limited access to the public and restricted freedom of expression. In particular it is a system where there is not, as in the U.S., "a multitude of points of access" for pressure groups to the "points of decision." On the contrary, the main point of access is at the topmost level of the party, in its apparatus, secretariat, and presidium. Whether there are other such points (for instance, in the executive) or whether others may develop (for example, even in the legislature) should be the subject of further study.

Much remains to be done to apply the interest-group approach to Communist systems. Some lines of future inquiry have been suggested in this article. The questions for research that Truman set forth also seem relevant to Soviet and Communist politics today. "How do interest groups emerge? Under what circumstances do they make claims upon or through the institutions of government? ... What are the internal features of existing groups, the degree of cohesion they command under varying conditions, their resources? How are various groups interrelated ... ? In what fashion do groups operate upon the government and its subdivisions? With what frequency and degrees of intensity? What are the mutations of governmental institutions in response to group activity?" These and many other questions provide an imposing agenda for future research.

THE POLITICS OF SOVIET CULTURE, 1964–1967

TIMOTHY McCLURE

It is one of the ironies of the Soviet system that the Communist Party has built anti-intellectualism into its structure and outlook, yet finds itself ever more dependent on scientists, economists, writers and even artists. The party has tried to isolate the intellectuals by giving them a privileged position in society and at the same time controlling their output through an elaborate network of organizations and censors. But with the inevitable development of a more open and complex Soviet society, the party, its creature organizations, and the intellectuals have found themselves in a multisided tug-of-war—a struggle in which strange alliances develop and it often becomes impossible to tell the "good guys" from the "bad guys."

The tension resulting from this struggle has not as yet stimulated great cultural achievement; on the contrary, it has resulted in an enormous dissipation of intellectual energy and waste of talent. Yet out of the articulation of the conflict has come a meaningful dialogue, forcing the establishment along a course that has vacillated between grappling with the crucial question of greater freedom and reverting to the search for more effective ways to control and discipline the intellectuals. The trial of the two Soviet writers Siniavski and Daniel in February 1966 marked the latest stormy effort at discipline in the cycle of tempest and relative calm that has characterized the relationship between intellectuals and the regime since Stalin's death.

The "crisis of the intellectuals" in 1965–66 had much in common with the 1963 crackdown on the arts, which began with the bizarre visit of Khrushchev to the Manezh art exhibit on December 1, 1962, but dissipated only six months later with the June 1963 ideological plenum of the CPSU Central Committee. During both periods the heightened debate between "liberal" and "conservative" writers served as a surrogate battlefield for contending forces within the establishment and most likely within the Central Committee apparat and the Politburo itself. In both periods also, the authorities finally backed away from the threatened general repression of the liberals in the official family, while the liberals in turn felt vindicated and emboldened to risk even more daring excursions into artistic experimentation and social criticism. Furthermore, in 1963 as in 1966 the repressive actions that were sanctioned by the party resulted in an outpouring of shocked disapproval and indignation from foreign intellectuals, most particularly from Communists in Eastern and Western Europe.

At the same time, there are significant differences between the two periods of "crackdown," revealing a good deal about current Soviet politics and about the quality and extent of intellectual dissidence in Soviet society. One striking difference concerns the target of attack: in the 1962–63 crisis

Problems of Communism (March–April 1967), 26–43. Reprinted by permission. Footnotes omitted.

it was the young poets and the liberal wing of the official intelligentsia that bore the brunt of the leadership's wrath, whereas in 1966 the Soviet authorities directed their major effort against intellectuals who had sought to circumvent the party's controls by operating in the intellectual underground. Partly in consequence, official retaliation was more severe in 1966, resulting in stiff prison sentences for at least two Soviet writers (and reportedly several more) and in the expulsion from the country of a third writer critical of the regime. Yet meanwhile the targets of the 1962–1963 crackdown were left relatively unmolested and even flourishing; what fire these by-now not so-young writers and poets drew from the literary and bureaucratic conservatives served in large part merely to increase the demand for their publications and to make them even more inviolable institutions in Soviet society.

Another distinction between the two crises concerns the behavior of the top political leadership. The first crisis grew out of an impetuous political *volte-face* by Khrushchev at his most erratic and irascible, and his person continued to dominate the events that ensued. By contrast, during the 1966 crisis the leaders managed to stay out of direct involvement with the intellectuals and to leave the dirty work to lesser agents. Moreover, the decision to put Siniavski and Daniel on trial, risking the further alienation of the Soviet liberal intellectuals and universal disapproval from abroad, was surely not an easy or impetuous move on the part of the cautious coalition of Khrushchev's successors, who were otherwise demonstrating a desire to legitimize their right to rule and displaying a high degree of sensitivity to foreign

criticism. The decision that seemed to be so atypical for Khrushchev's heirs must have reflected, as Max Hayward observed, a leadership "torn between powerful conflicting trends and attempting to placate, or at least not to antagonize, violently opposed groups in Soviet society, if not in the party itself."

In the following pages a closer look will be taken at the events surrounding the recent crisis, though neither the trial itself nor the writings of Siniavski and Daniel will be dealt with in detail since these matters have already been covered extensively. For the purpose of analyzing the changing policies of Khrushchev's heirs it has been convenient to divide the time since Khrushchev's fall into roughly three phases: (1) the period of uncertainty from mid-October 1964 to mid-January 1965, during which the party leadership was too bothered with disestablishing Khrushchevism and establishing its own *bona fides* in the Communist world to concern itself with cultural matters; (2) the period of "liberal conservatism" from late January to mid-summer 1965, during which certain elements in the leadership were able to make important, if only moderate, overtures to encourage the intellectuals' participation in developing new programs and in expanding the arts; and (3) the period of reaction and disciplinary measures from September 1965 to the present. In the conclusion the political implications of the crackdown will be examined.

One note: Throughout this essay I refer to the various segments of the intelligentsia as "liberals," "moderates," "conservatives," "liberal-conservatives," *etc.*, to designate their political stance in the struggle between forces that seek and forces that oppose a more open society in the Soviet

Union. Such designations are necessary and valid within the context of the essay, but they perforce ignore the rich variety and multitude of crosscurrents that characterize the climate of cultural opinion within the intellectual community. It has seemed best to deal with some of the diverse cultural aspects of current intellectual ferment in a separate commentary so as not to blur the polarization of forces in the continuing political struggle.

After the Fall

By October 1964 the liberal writers and artists—most of whom had wisely chosen the "conspiracy of silence" during the conservative onslaught of 1963—had reemerged from the provinces and dachas and had actively resumed the game of who can publish what and where. A certain confidence was in the air in Moscow. The broadcasts of VOA and BBC had not been jammed for over a year. The year-old Nuclear Test Ban Treaty plus angry exchanges with the Chinese pointed to even closer relations with the West in the coming year—a development welcomed by the vast majority of the Soviet intelligentsia. The atmosphere in Moscow seemed so hopeful that the visiting Yugoslav Mihajlo Mihajlov, despite his pessimistic view of Soviet society in general, saw light ahead for Soviet artists: in his *Moscow Summer, 1964*, he predicted "a final liberation of literature and arts from all restrictions of dogmatism"—a surprising judgment from such a knowledgeable observer but certainly a reflection of the naive optimism that prevailed at the time among the younger intellectuals.

This air of general well-being was rudely jolted by the announcement of Khrushchev's fall on October 16. The immediate reaction of the intellectual community and probably of most citizens was understandably one of misgiving and uncertainty, but concern over what lay ahead no doubt outweighed concern over the change of regime *per se*. Among the intellectuals, the liberals' reactions were the most confused, for they had long felt ambivalent toward Khrushchev. They all knew that Khrushchev had been the first to open the floodgates of denunciation against Stalin; that he had personally authorized the publication of *One Day in the Life of Ivan Denisovich* and *The Heirs of Stalin*; that he had seemed impressed by certain independent artists like the sculptor Ernst Neizvestny and the poet Yevtushenko (both of whom had shown the bravado to talk back to the top man himself). On the other hand, Khrushchev's crude, peasant approach to culture had epitomized the party's philistinism and purely utilitarian view of art, and it was he who had placed the control of culture in the hands of the dogmatic and detested Ilichev. Furthermore, though Khrushchev had initiated destalinization, he had resisted yielding to its logical demands; indeed, as First Secretary, he had wielded his authority in the Stalinist style, making himself the final arbiter in all aspects of Soviet life.

Even more than the writers and artists, the scientific intelligentsia had reasons not to feel overly regretful about Khrushchev's downfall. Perhaps no segment of the Soviet establishment had been more contemptuous of his pretensions to expert knowledge and his various crash programs. The scientists were particularly antagonized by his often enthusiastic support for the charlatan geneticist Lysenko—an issue on which the liberals in the "creative intelligentsia" were solidly in agreement.

Thus a few reassuring developments under the new regime were enough to quiet the initial misgivings of the intelligentsia. Nothing could have offered quicker comfort than the post-Khrushchev attack launched in the press against Lysenko, his theories, and his supporters; an article by Vladimir Dudintsev published in *Komsomolskaia pravda* on October 23, only a week after Khrushchev's ouster, sparked an outpouring of abuse against Lysenko over the next few weeks that seemed clearly designed to win the support of the intelligentsia.

Also within a week of the ouster, word was passed that the authorities had dropped Khrushchev's pending project to combine the major literary and cultural newspapers into one organ. This was another easy way to win support from all sectors of the intellectual community, each of which had a stake in its own particular publication. The release of Pasternak's close friend Olga Ivinskaia from prison in early November (very possibly because she had already served out her sentence) was another means of picking up good will from the liberals. Word was also floated that the young Leningrad poet Yosif Brodski had been released from his place of exile near Archangel, where he had been sent six months earlier by a Leningrad court for "parasitism"—but this rumor later turned out to be false.

Among other signs encouraging to the liberals, *Pravda*, newly under the editorship of A. M. Rumiantsev, took to criticizing the conservative playwright A. Sofronov and the conservative stronghold *Oktiabr*. On Novem-

ber 30 Yevgeni Yevtushenko, Bella Akhmadulina and Rimma Kazakova—three of the leading young liberals—gave a poetry reading to some 1800 people in the Moscow Conservatory, the first such large reading by the liberal poets since the events of 1962–63. In late December, "Poetry Day" saw most of the liberal poets reading to small audiences.

All of these developments, however, were more or less wisps in the wind—or one might better say in the partial vacuum created by the turnover in the top leadership. Khrushchev's heirs had not as yet enunciated any official line in the sphere of culture—indeed in the first few months they showed little interest in the problems of the "culture lobby." They were concerned with the more pressing problems of tidying up the structural aberrations in the party, reassuring the nation's bureaucrats that they could rule better and more securely without that "subjectivist" Khrushchev, and mending fences with friends in the Communist movement. Cultural life seemed to proceed as usual in Moscow and Leningrad, reflecting—in many respects—trends that had been underway before Khrushchev's fall.

"Liberal Conservatism" The Rumiantsev Line

The first clear sign that some official sanction was being given to a moderate direction in cultural policies came with significant shake-ups in the literary and scientific bureaucracies. In late January 1965 the Moscow and Leningrad sections of the Writers' Union met in stormy sessions, with dramatic results. The Moscow meeting was highlighted by indirect but unmistakable criticism of Ilichev, the chief of the party's Ideological Commission, and of the hack-writer Nikolai Gribachev, who had thundered as one of the major conservative voices in 1963. The Moscow writers succeeded in removing from their directing board four of the most despised representatives of the old guard: besides Gribachev, they were *Oktiabr's* editor, Vsevolod Kochetov, the playwright Anatoli Sofronov, and the writer Georgi Markov. The four also failed to win election as delegates from Moscow to the upcoming RSFSR Writers' Congress, forcing them—as in 1962—to retire to the provinces where they could be assured of inclusion in other delegations. In Leningrad a similar triumph was scored: the Stalinist poet Aleksandr Prokofiev was not only removed as First Secretary of the Leningrad Writers' Union but was denied a seat on the new board and strongly criticized for his report to the meeting. Prokofiev was the symbol of old guard control over Leningrad's writers and had reportedly been the key advocate of harsh treatment for Brodski less than a year earlier.

The next straw in the wind was the report of M. A. Keldish, President of the USSR Academy of Sciences, to a February 1 meeting of the Academy, in which the officially condemned Lysenkoism and its negative effect on the development of biological and related sciences. The Keldish report (printed in *Pravda*, Feb. 4) was supported, as it turned out, by an earlier unpublished party-government decree on improving biology; the removal of Lysenko and his cronies from positions of power in genetics and in the biological and agricultural sciences became a foregone conclusion.

By mid-February there were other indicators suggesting that the moderately liberal line issued from the top party leadership—or at least an influential element of it: changes in the RSFSR Institute of Pedagogical Sciences and the formation of a new educational commission gave real hope that professionals would have a major voice in the restructuring of education, following the reversal of Khrushchev's ill-fated reforms. Similarly the economists, long isolated from policy-making, found themselves—to their great surprise—being approached for concrete proposals in anticipation of the overdue economic reforms that had been much discussed in Khrushchev's last years.

On February 21 *Pravda* published an editorial, over the signature of its new editor Rumiantsev, that seemed to herald a more enlightened period of cooperation between the party and the intellectuals. At long last the regime seemed to be recognizing that the economists, scientists, and writers could be of real value to the party if they were allowed experimentation, open disagreement, competition and considerable freedom. While the editorial clearly reasserted the primacy of the party, it appeared to represent an official view that might best be described as "liberal conservative"—a view implicitly acknowledging that the party's periodic confrontations with the increasingly influential cultural and scientific lobbies could only discredit the party itself and cause waste in the society. Among other key passages, Rumiantsev stated that it was necessary "to learn how . . . to open the road to everything talented and socially useful created by Soviet scientists and figures in culture and literature." And he declared: ". . . genuine creation is possible only in an environment of search, experiment, and the free expression and collision of opinions, the presence of various schools and trends, various styles and genres competing among themselves and at the same time joined by the unity of ... Socialist Realism." This was certainly a novel definition of Socialist Realism!

On the same weekend that the Rumiantsev editorial appeared, *Novyi mir*'s first issue of 1965 hit the news-stands, and it seemed to provide proof that the liberal lobby was to be given wide leeway. In the lead article poet-editor Tvardovski stated more emphatically and openly than perhaps ever before his magazine's liberal position on the arts and belief in the artist's right to express his "small truth."

Only a month later the March plenum of the CPSU Central Committee announced the demotion of L. F. Ilichev from his position as ideological boss of the Secretariat to a lesser role as a Deputy Minister of Foreign Affairs. Ilichev's place was taken by Piotr Demichev, who had been Party Secretary for the Chemical Industry under Khrushchev but who was promoted in November 1964 to the Politburo. From his earlier days in the Moscow city party organization, Demichev was known to be more moderate on cultural matters than Ilichev, and his first informal meetings with small groups of writers confirmed that he would be far less likely to meddle directly in their affairs than his predecessor.

As the long winter gradually gave way to spring, all these developments combined to nurture a growing sense of optimism among the liberals and moderates in the intelligentsia. At the same time, there were other developments that perhaps should have been recognized as harbingers of another sort of winter. The RSFSR Writers' Congress in March brought cold solace

to the liberals, as the conservative bureaucrats from the provinces vented their spleen on young writers in seeming sharp violation of the Rumiantsev line. The most ominous sounds came from Moscow party boss Yegorychev, who declared that the obsession of certain writers with the mistakes of the Stalin era "casts a shadow over the holy of holies—our socialist organization, Marxist-Leninist teaching, and the general line of the party." His call for less criticism of the Soviet past was a line that would be heard with increasing regularity and vigor over the coming months. Indeed, an effort to curb anti-Stalinist influences had already been evidenced by a significant decrease in the number of rehabilitations of the victims of Stalin's purges. The propaganda buildup for the May 9 celebrations of the 20th anniversary of VE Day was accompanied by the first public mention in years of Stalin in a positive vein. On May 8 Brezhnev himself uttered the terrible name, and the steely visage appeared on Moscow TV and in a documentary film on the war which was shown in Moscow.

This hint of a Stalinist revival, coexisting with the fresh sense of freedom among intellectuals—both following on the partial vacuum in cultural controls that was created by Khrushchev's ouster—resulted in a peculiarly restive and exciting atmosphere in the spring of 1965. In the arts, it had been the best season in years—there were two new experimental theaters in Moscow, and the plays of Berthold Brecht had burst on the stages of Moscow and Leningrad with full force. Voznesenski's "Oza" had dazzled both his admirers and his critics with its "formalist" tendencies. In April Yevtushenko's lengthy poem "Bratsk Dam," a restatement of many of his controversial themes, appeared in *Yunost*. *Novyi mir* outreached itself in its first six issues of the new year, particularly with the two tender and penetrating novels on rural life, *The Mayfly's Life is Short* by Vladimir Tendriakov (May issue), and *Seven in One House* by Vitali Siomin (June issue). *Yunost's* anniversary issue in June featured the young poets as well as a new story by prose writer Vasili Aksionov, whose play "Always on Sale," which had premiered in the spring at the Sovremennik Theater, marked the first important step by a modern Soviet playwright into the field of fantastic satire. And a new collection of Boris Pasternak's poetry was assigned to the press with an introduction by the devoted Pasternak scholar—Andrei Siniavski.

Even more striking than the quality of Soviet writing was the significant breakthrough in the foreign literature published in this period. For the first time, Kafka's short stories appeared in Russian, Faulkner's trilogy was finally put out in large editions, John Updike's "The Centaur" became the talk of literary Moscow after publication in *Inostrannaia literatura*, and a host of other major foreign writers began to appear in print. All of which suggested that the cultural "opening up" of Soviet society was a fact of life which neither the party bureaucrats nor the conservatives predominating in the publishing world could significantly retard.

The most unusual development was the degree to which young intellectuals and students were expressing themselves openly—aggressively showing, as one Soviet writer said, that they were the first Soviet generation "without the habit of fear." On April 14, 1965, a young organization of dissident poets, the *Smogisti*, marched from Maiakov-

ski Square to the Writers' Union club on Herzen Street, where they stood blocking traffic and reciting their unorthodox verse, to the utter amazement of Union officials who had neither seen nor heard of an unauthorized demonstration of Soviet citizens in Moscow for years. Another remarkable occurrence took place in the spring at a large organized student meeting at Moscow University; a young speaker who was ostensibly on the platform to condemn "Western bourgeois cynicism" for invoking the statute of limitations on Nazi war criminals in West Germany, shocked his audience by proclaiming that the real cynics were the leaders of the Soviet Union, who had revealed the horrible crimes of the Stalin era but had as yet failed to bring any of the perpetrators to trial.

It was also in the spring of 1965 that the eminent Ilia Ehrenburg, speaking to a group of writers at Moscow's Foreign Literature Library, declared that the time had passed when writers should describe how they suffered under Stalin—that they should now begin examining the question of "how Stalinism could have happened."

Looking back, the spring of 1965 seems to have been a period in which the leadership was perforce acting in a collective manner while groping for coherent programs—and for a more stable leadership alliance. In the process of developing such programs the new regime seemed more willing than its predecessor to turn for help to various segments of the intelligentsia. Thus, as it turned out, this period of "liberal conservatism" was not a policy line set down by the party leadership, but the result of several converging phenomena —a reaction to the excesses of Khrushchev's leadership style, the articulation by at least a segment of the party leadership (through Rumiantsev) of a moderate long-range approach to the intelligentsia, and the bolder action of liberal and young intellectuals encouraged by the apparent relaxation and increasingly confident of their cause. As viewed by the party, however, the "new conservatism" called for a strict limitation on writings or discussion that disparaged the Stalin era or the role of the party and the secret police in that era. In return, the liberals were to be allowed more opportunity to experiment with style and to be spared excessive attacks from their conservative critics.

The Reaction Sets In

The partial moratorium on heavy-handed conservative criticism was short-lived. By late July and August the conservative critics had opened up on their favorite targets—Aksionov, Voznesenski, Tendriakov, and Yevtushenko—and had found a new one in Vitali Siomin, whose aforementioned novel, *Seven in One House*, was the literary sensation of the season. *Pravda* printed a strong attack on Siomin, charging that he had dealt only with the "private truths" of a small group of isolated individuals and thereby distorted the big truth—the balanced picture—of Soviet reality. The issue of the "small" or "foxhole truth" versus the universal or big truth had been central in the liberal-conservative debate, particularly since the fall of Khrushchev. The liberals maintained that the private truth (*istina*) of the artist did not necessarily conflict with the big truth (*pravda*)—and that anyway it was the prerogative of a Communist artist to express his personal view of reality. This aspect of the debate also involved the issue of de-stalinization—*i.e.*, whether the revelation of individual crimes of the Stalin period distorted the entire reality of Soviet life. The cultural conservatives and many in the party obviously thought that it did.

The young prose writer Vasili Aksionov also drew major fire from the orthodox literary critics. The most serious attack came in *Izvestia* (August 13) which followed up a letter from irate taxi drivers in Yalta (the subject of a recent Aksionov story) with an editorial comment castigating all Soviet writers who painted a gloomy—and ergo distorted—picture of Soviet life. The *Izvestia* editors criticized the liberal journals *Novyi mir* and *Yunost* specifically, an unusual move even during the worst of times for Soviet writers.

Having been given the green light by *Izvestia* and seemingly by *Pravda*, the conservatives wasted no time in using their preponderant control over the literary journals and newspapers to focus on what they saw as the recent insidious trends in prose, poetry, drama, and films. Finally—as if to give the official seal of approval of the young party leaders to the conservative resurgence—Komsomol chief S. P. Pavlov, writing in *Pravda* (August 27), blamed certain journals and theaters for the malaise apparent among Soviet youth and exhorted the party's literary critics to be more harsh in judging such "trash." Most significant, Pavlov called for a revival of the atmosphere of the 1930's among the Komsomols and explained how the police organs, the Army, the border guards, and DOSAAF had all recently instituted new programs to restore respect among

Komsomols for past Soviet military glories.

At this juncture Rumiantsev published his second *Pravda* editorial (September 9), which in a highly polemical tone responded to the recent intemperance of conservative critics. In an almost unprecedented act, Rumiantsev reprimanded the government newspaper *Izvestia* (as well as the party agricultural newspaper *Selskaia zhizn*) for assaulting the liberal writers and journals. He strongly restated his case that the party needed to trust intellectuals and allow them more freedom for growth. In support of the liberal cause on the question of "private truths," Rumiantsev pointed out that it is "unrealistic to expect from an author absolute universality— with such a demand we wouldn't receive any artistic works," suggesting by implication that he also supported the continued examination of the errors of Stalin. Even more striking than his attack on the government newspapers was his charge that any effort "to place in opposition such concepts as intellectuality, party-mindedness, and popular-mindedness represents a dogmatic and stupid argument against a scientific world outlook," leading to the same type of arbitrary and crude direction of society for which the party had removed Khrushchev.

Just four days prior to Rumiantsev's article, *Pravda* (September 5) had carried an editorial on the nationality question which recalled, for the first time since the early postwar years, Lenin's demand for a constant "struggle against anti-semitism." In Soviet society the Jewish question inevitably comes to the forefront during periods of heightened anti-intellectualism, as it most certainly did during 1962–63.

What was clearly at issue in the early days of September 1965, then, was the growing atmosphere of anti-intellectualism, the mounting pressures to re-evaluate the Stalin era, and the conservative demands for more attention to the purification of ideology and the increase of discipline in society.

The Trial Célèbre

It was in this setting that Siniavski and Daniel were arrested in the second week of September. Some nine or ten days later Rumiantsev was removed as Editor-in-Chief of *Pravda*. That the two events were connected seemed patently clear.

Although Rumiantsev reportedly had been ailing, no such reason was given for his replacement less than a year after he had assumed the office. Furthermore, he appeared well enough to resume an active role in other fields within a month (more on which later). Whether or not he personally wrote the editorials in defense of greater intellectual freedom, their appearance over his name had publicly identified him with the most moderate semi-official approach to the intelligentsia since the pre-Stalin era. Thus his removal suggested strongly that either the cultural line was changing or that Rumiantsev was involved in a squabble of the highest order—or both.

There are very good reasons to assume that the pressures against the Rumiantsev moderate line were mounting anyway, but the Siniavski-Daniel case most certainly gave added weight to the conservative thrust and may conceivably have been used to precipitate the crisis. The arrest of the two writers—for publishing abroad "slanderous" literature about the Soviet state—was at the least timely from the conservatives' point of view. While it may seem astonishing that the KGB, with its network of informers and controls on foreign visitors, did not have some earlier clue to the writers' contacts, the evidence suggests that their activities went undetected until the spring or summer of 1965. In any event, this was the final "proof" the conservatives needed to support their case that the intellectuals couldn't be trusted. The party felt indignant and betrayed.

The developments directly related to the trial need little review, since so much has been written about the case. Suffice it to say that throughout the fall and into January of 1966, the crucial issue for Soviet intellectuals became the fate of the two arrested writers. Some members of the official intelligentsia felt that the offenders should not be put on trial but should instead be turned over to the writers' organization for appropriate punishment—as was done in the Pasternak case. On the other hand, 200 Moscow students who demonstrated in Pushkin Square on December 5 (Soviet "Constitution Day") demanded a trial—but one that was fair and open as required by Soviet law. Protests and appeals poured into the Soviet authorities from foreign intellectuals on behalf of the two writers.

On January 13, *Izvestia* published a viciously slanderous article against the writers, setting the stage for all ensuing propaganda and for the trial itself. The accusations in official Soviet newspapers seemed almost incredibly prejudicial to Western observers, and must have been totally disheartening to Soviet citizens who had been hoping for legal "guarantees" of their rights.

The macabre trial opened on a grey February morning in a small Moscow court building. It was not an open trial in that only a chosen few were issued tickets to attend. The text of the proceedings that was subsequently smuggled out and published abroad revealed a classic confrontation between two sensitive intellectuals and a frightened, philistine establishment. Daniel pointed out the irony of a powerful modern state trying two of its citizens for slander when he said at the trial, "I cannot think that a couple of books by us, or even a score, could inflict substantial damage upon a country like this." And Siniavski remarked in his final plea, "In the whole history of literature I know of no trial like this one." The fact that the writers refused to plead guilty forced the regime to present its flimsy case against them for the world to behold. The leadership, having apparently given them up as sacrificial lambs to the conservative camp and the KGB, looked on silently as Siniavski was sentenced to seven years and Daniel to five years in a labor camp.

It would be impossible to overstate the impact of the Siniavski-Daniel case on the Soviet intellectual community. The conservatives, not unsurprisingly, felt emboldened and vindicated, and their periodicals *Oktiabr, Molodaia gvardiia,* and *Neva* carried signed articles duly condemning Siniavski and Daniel. The conservative chief of the Moscow Writers' Unions, S. Mikhalkov, also lent his name to a pre-trial castigation of the two men in *Partinaia zhizn.* But the vast majority of Soviet writers and intellectuals, however they may have felt about the indiscretions and writings of the two imprisoned writers, were pained and disturbed by the trial and its implications for Soviet intellectual life. Some maintained an embarrassed silence. But in a show of strength almost unprecedented in the politics of Soviet culture, liberal intellectuals from widely differing professions—scientists, scholars, and cultural figures—addressed letters to the party leadership protesting the treatment of the writers and expressing concern over the possible rehabilitation of Stalin and Stalinist policies. The texts of many of these protest notes were later smuggled to the West for publication. The only really major Soviet writer to support the trial publicly was the recent Nobel Prize winner Mikhail Sholokhov, who earned the contempt of many of his colleagues by suggesting at the 23rd CPSU Congress (two months after the trial) that the sentences were not nearly harsh enough: for this act, one Soviet writer said, "literature has condemned Sholokhov to creative sterility."

Leadership Policy: Two-Fisted or Two-Faced?

The sensational stir created by the Siniavski-Daniel case partially obscured the importance of concurrent developments on the Soviet scene which, it has since become clear, marked the emergence of a new and distinct phase in Soviet cultural policy dating from mid-1965 to the present. In reviewing these developments, it seems simplest to trace two parallel yet, in part at least, contradictory trends that reveal significant ambivalence in the attitude of the leadership (the much clearer reaction of the intellectuals will be taken up later). On the one hand, a period of reaction set in that was marked by a

number of repressions as harsh, if not as well-publicized, as the trial of the two writers, and by a general effort of the regime to reassert discipline and respect for authority—most notably party and police authority—in the society at large. On the other hand, the top leaders persisted in striking an official stance that bespoke a middle-of-the-road outlook on culture, and took pains to demonstrate their support of the "trusted" intelligentsia (including liberals who stayed in line).

The conservative resurgence expressed itself with increasing insistence throughout the fall of 1965 and into the winter. Mounting criticism of the liberal writers was accompanied by loud demands for a more "objective" portrayal of the Stalin era. Military leaders entered actively into the intellectual tug-of-war, blaming the low state of discipline in the armed forces on the prevalence of ideologically impure literature and art. Marshal Krylov (in *Sovetskaia Rossiia* of October 8) laid out an elaborate program for the indoctrination of youth, much in the vein of Pavlov's August outline in *Pravda*. In December Pavlov again made headlines by unleashing a violent diatribe against *Yunost* and announcing further plans for Komsomol paramilitary activities. And at the turn of the year a curfew was imposed on young people in Moscow.

Meantime reports began to leak out of a number of repressive actions taken against intellectuals, mainly involving young dissidents. As the poet Yesenin-Volpin is reported to have said, Siniavski and Daniel were lucky in that "their case was taken up by the whole civilized world. There were so many others about whom the . . . world knew nothing—knew as little as people know of a rabbit eaten by the wolves in the forest." To cite some examples that have been reliably reported, the authorities tried to dissipate the *Smogisti* group of young poets after they helped to organize the aforementioned demonstration of December 5, and the KGB actually had one of their leaders, Vladimir Bukovski, interned in an insane asylum as an "invalid of the second category" (a euphemism for a political nonconformist) for six months or more in 1966. At least two other *Smogisti* were arrested but later released. A group of young Leningrad students who had published an illegal journal called *Kolokol* were arrested and their leaders sentenced to jail in the fall of 1965. In Moscow several other young students were arrested, and at least one reportedly sent to prison, when the police discovered their plan to hold an anti-Stalin demonstration in Red Square on March 5, 1966, the 13th anniversary of Stalin's death.

The worst repression took place in the Ukraine. Beginning in the late summer of 1965, as many as 70 Ukrainian intellectuals were reportedly arrested in Kiev, Lvov, Ivano-Franko and several other cities. Some of those seized were subsequently released, but many were put on trial in the first months of 1966. According to reports at least 20 were sentenced to two to five years in labor camps for disseminating and presumably writing anti-Soviet propaganda. Some verification of these actions has come from the Soviets. In December 1965 a spate of articles in the Soviet press reported on the problem of nationalist activities among Ukrainian intellectuals. And in the fall of 1966, a young Ukrainian poet, Ivan Drach, who was visiting the United States, publicly acknowledged the arrest and sentencing of several

Ukrainian writers, adding that the matter was painful for him since several of his friends were involved. While some of the defendants were no doubt carrying on anti-regime or nationalist activities, a number of the writers caught in the crackdown appear to have been guilty of nothing more than individualistic literary efforts that were unsavory to the authorities.

The repression against deviant artists and writers was supported by increased coercion in other areas of society. In March 1966 new laws were introduced imposing harsher restrictions on religious practices, and in subsequent months demonstration trials and campaigns made it clear that violators of the laws were being rooted out and disciplined. In July 1966 the central police ministry (the former MVD, now the MOOP) was reestablished and the militia force enlarged in a stepped-up campaign against "hooliganism" and crime. New legislation strengthened the hands of the militiamen and restricted the courts from being too lenient. Kosygin made it clear that the use of force would continue when he said in June: "It would be incorrect to think that since communism will finally lead to the disappearance of state organs of coercion, one need no longer bother about strengthening public order and can weaken the measures of coercion."

The campaign to build up the image of the police revealed the degree to which the "organs of coercion" had been undermined by Khrushchev's efforts to tame and even discredit them. In this respect the leadership's actions, particularly from September 1965 on, underscored its serious concern over the breakdown of order and discipline in Soviet society during the years of Khrushchev's rule and over the cumulative tendency of his policies to discredit the party.

To turn to the parallel course being pursued by the party leadership, throughout the entire period of disciplinary crackdown the top leaders struck a public posture of following a middle-of-the-road policy on culture. They refused to get overtly involved in the liberal-conservative tug-of-war, though it continued almost unabated. Moreover, they seemed to disassociate themselves from the Siniavski-Daniel case as much as possible. Cultural overseer Demichev is even reported to have passed the word that he felt the crude coverage of the case in *Izvestia* was overdone. At the 23rd Party Congress in the spring of 1966 First Secretary Brezhnev did refer to the case with a statement that "the Soviet people" would deal with such "renegades" in the manner they deserved. But other speakers seemed to avoid mention of the trial (though some of the conservatives used the Congress as a forum for attack on other liberal writers in the official family and on *Yunost* and *Novyi mir*). In general the Congress seemed to reflect an official effort to avoid opening any more wounds, while at the same time repudiating extremism of any sort. The removal of Tvardovski and Alexei Surkov from the Central Committee and of Kochetov and Prokofiev from the Central Auditing Commission had the effect of rescinding official recognition of the troublesome extremes; coincidentally it lowered the overall representation of the intelligentsia in the top party organs.

Even more interesting was the official treatment of the better-known liberal intellectuals, some of whom were the very men who had borne the heaviest fire in the crisis of 1963. In December 1965, just when the conservative campaign was mounting to full force, Voznesenki, Yevtushenko and Yefim Dorosh were proposed as candidates for the Lenin Prize in Literature for some of their most controversial works. During 1966 the regime permitted a number of the liberals to travel abroad; Yevtushenko, Voznesenki, and Aksionov each made several trips to various countries, and even Ernst Neizvestny and the ballad-singer Bulat Okudzhava were allowed their first foreign junkets. In the same period, the liberal intellectuals were making more frequent appearances before Soviet audiences. No doubt the regime was motivated in part by the desire to counter criticism of the Siniavski-Daniel trial with a demonstration of liberality. For their part, the young liberals—while not fully comfortable in their role as beneficiaries of the repression of the two writers—seemed to recognize the pragmatic need to keep their foot in the door with the party.

Throughout 1966 and into 1967, the pattern of events continued to reflect the two strands of the leadership's stance vis-à-vis the intellectual community. The party seemed to come to the tentative conclusion that by permitting cultural experimentation and foreign imports—within bounds—the intellectuals' energies could be sidetracked from potentially more dangerous anti-regime activity. At the same time, there was no let-up in the authorities' efforts to quell the intellectual underground; indeed, the recent strengthening of laws against anti-Soviet propaganda, as well as continuing reports of arrests among young intellectuals, seemed to reflect the regime's determination to impress upon the intellectual community the lesson that dissidence doesn't pay. Finally, while the top leadership continued to stand aloof from the conservative-liberal struggle, there were persistent indications that official pressure was being brought to bear in certain ideological "problem areas." For example, the editors of *Yunost*—the *bête noire* of the conservatives—were eventually induced to "confess" their ideological sins, and in the opinion of many observers the magazine's liberal stance thereafter showed signs of dilution; curiously, however, *Yunost* was allowed to raise its circulation to two million a month in 1966. There were also many signs that the authorities were pressing for changes in the editorial board and policies of *Novyi mir*.

The reaction of the liberal intellectuals to these various official policies and pressures was quite different from what it had been in the 1962–63 period of crackdown, when so many of them chose the "conspiracy of silence" as their best means of protest. We have already noted the remarkable strength and unity demonstrated by various segments of the moderate and liberal intelligentsia in protesting the trial of Siniavski and Daniel. Encouraged, perhaps, by this expression of an overwhelming consensus, the liberals did not retreat into silence, but rather sought other more subtle ways, in their writings and in their actions, to keep alive the crucial issues of the "little truth," the artist's freedom, the dangers of persisting Stalinism. The editors of *Novyi mir* continued to assert their independence— and courage—by publishing prose and criticism that expressed the liberal point-of-view, and *Yunost's* retreat was only marginal. The liberals also kept up their protest against censorship, holding that open criticism of Soviet society not only should be allowed but

was essential to its health—as one spokesman put it succinctly, "for Russia, the doctor is publicity [*yasnost*]."

Nor was the intellectual underground much intimidated. No greater act of defiance could have been devised than the smuggling abroad of the Siniavski-Daniel trial record and the protest notes on the case—the very crime for which the two writers had been incarcerated. The extent to which young dissidents and intellectuals remained recalcitrant was most recently revealed by two incidents in Moscow on the same day—January 22 of this year [1967, ed.]. In Pushkin Square some 25 to 50 young people put official tolerance to the test by a demonstration in protest against Article 70 of the Criminal Code—the article under which Siniavski and Daniel had been condemned and under which other writers have since been arrested. Elsewhere in the city, at a trade union club, 12 of Moscow's leading underground painters opened an exhibit of their paintings. The show was closed by the authorities within two hours, but only after over 500 people had managed to see it. Yevtushenko reportedly decried the closing, defended the artists, blamed the action on the bureaucrats in the Union of Artists, and suggested, according to one report, that the top party officials might have allowed the show to go on had they not been "too high up to be concerned with things like this."

Yevtushenko's remark reflected the degree to which liberals felt helplessly cut off from the top of the power structure, even as they continued to press for changes in cultural policy. Ironically—if what they wanted was some intervention from on high—they were about to get it. But the word that was issued, presumably with top-level sanction, was hardly what they yearned to hear. On January 27, 1967, an editorial in *Pravda* offered the first extensive policy statement on the arts since the removal of Rumiantsev in September 1965. The editorial had sharp criticisms for both extremes in the continuing "conservative-liberal" conflict, and was probably aimed at toning down the debate in preparation for the much-postponed Fourth USSR Writers' Congress, as well as for the general celebration of the 50th anniversary of the October Revolution. Yet there was no doubt where the most significant criticism fell. In the most explicit terms to date, the editorial spelled out the regime's objection to *Novyi mir's* editorial policies of publishing literature and critical essays that centered on the negative side of Soviet society, that defended "anti-heroes," and that failed to view the 50 years of Soviet history from the standpoint of "universality." The statement was a clear repudiation of the former Rumiantsev line defending the artist's privilege to write his "private truths," demonstrating the degree to which reaction had set in over the preceding 18 months. Though more than token criticism was directed at *Oktiabr*—for holding itself up as the only authority on "Socialist Realism," for producing "grey" literature, and for not accepting destalinization—this was little compensation to the elements in Soviet society who looked to *Novyi mir* as the conscience of the Soviet intellectual and the only real defender of the Russian literary tradition.

The editorial in *Pravda* marks the most definitive indication of the current trend of Soviet cultural policy as of this writing. It is time, then, to look backward over the past year and a half, to recognize that what has trans-pired on the cultural front is only part of the broad spectrum of what has been going on in the Soviet world, and to try to relate the cultural scene to the overall imperatives of leadership policy.

The Politics of Ferment

The developments in Soviet culture since the ouster of Khrushchev demonstrate what we already knew—that the intellectual currents in Soviet society are intertwined with the politics and policies of the party leadership in complex and confusing ways. The sequence of events described above does, however, suggest some observations on the manner in which the present leadership has evolved.

First, it seems clear that the changes on the cultural front in the summer and early fall of 1965 reflected the resolution within the party of broader political issues and most probably stemmed from a realignment within the top leadership. By September, party First Secretary Brezhnev seems to have reconciled to his advantage the disparate forces at work over the preceding ten months. A number of factors point to the conclusion that August-September of 1965 was a watershed in the leadership's programs and policies, and in the career of Brezhnev: (1) Rumiantsev's removal in September as editor of *Pravda* marked the end of that paper's short-lived practice of taking polemical and relatively "liberal" stances on key policy issues, suggesting strongly that he had been replaced in a policy controversy. (2) Within a few months after September, most of the major central newspapers and political journals were assigned new editors-in-chief, and important new assignments were made to the ideological and propaganda branches of the party and government, indicating that a new first team was being installed with new instructions. (3) Nikolai Podgorny, who had been one of Brezhnev's chief rivals under Khrushchev, was kicked upstairs in December 1965 to become titular chief of state; Podgorny had appeared on at least one occasion in the spring of 1965 as a chief spokesman for moderate policies in the economy, and his prior association with Rumiantsev allows speculation that he may have influenced Rumiantsev's appointment to *Pravda* immediately after Khrushchev's ouster. (4) Party Secretary Shelepin, who reportedly planned or made a move for more power some time in the latter half of 1965, was trimmed back in December 1965 when he was relieved of the party-state control apparatus. (5) After the fall of 1965 virtually every major appointment to the government or party was either a man long associated with Brezhnev or a figure representing Brezhnev's particular bias for older party leaders from the provinces. One seeming inconsistency in this picture is that many of the new appointments in the cultural and propaganda sector seemed to come from the younger party cadres, suggesting that in the September "reconciliation," the younger Politburo members, perhaps represented by Shelepin, Mazurov, and Demichev, were given an important voice in policies and personnel assignments in the field of ideology and culture.

The policy lines that emerged after September 1965 reflected on one hand the party's heightened awareness of the nation's economic ills and its preparedness to make some innovations to meet them, and on the other hand the party's proclivity in the social and political sectors to resort to old formulas. What has emerged over the last year and a half, then, has been a peculiar combination of programs for reform and retrenchment, relaxation and discipline: (1) The economic measures adopted at the crucial September 1965 Central Committee plenum were a moderate but important step toward reform of the economy—although the recentralization of the government and economic administration seemed to vitiate many of the reformist aspects. (2) Party officials were warned not to meddle too deeply in the economy—yet the changes made in the party structure and style were orthodox and fundamentalist. (3) In the face of evident opposition, particularly from the intelligentsia, the party was forced to slow down its campaign to rehabilitate the Stalin era —but increasing stress was put on refurbishing the image of the party, the heroic past, and the police. (4) New stress was placed on sociological and scientific work to determine public needs—yet in the much debated area of legal reforms and "guarantees," in the face of a continued high incidence of crime, there seemed to be regression to greater use of repressive organs. (5) The scientific establishment was restructured to encourage technological progress, and more latitude seemed to be granted cultural figures for experimentation—yet in the field of thought and expression in general, violators of official controls were severely punished in evident efforts to impose discipline by example, and censorship was tightened on writing critical of the party and police in the Stalin era.

The conclusion seems to be that Brezhnev patched together a conservative leadership bent on restoring the party's prestige but also seriously interested in improving the efficiency of the economy. In the deal, the moderate or "liberal conservative" line of Rumiantsev was moved out of the propaganda sector—but it has not been wholly abandoned. Rumiantsev himself has remained active in setting up the new work on sociology, and the policies he espoused still seem to be the unspoken rationale behind the official encouragement given to some segments of the intelligentsia. While the "hardliners" seem to have the upper hand in the Brezhnev coalition on matters of "legality" and discipline, it is unlikely that the leadership is prepared to introduce extreme enough methods of control and repression to retard significantly the breakdown in the authority and ideology of the party. Therefore, the "liberal conservatives" in the party are relied upon to seek out more subtle methods to tame the youth, channel their intellectual vigor, and—insofar as possible—reinforce their patriotism.

There seems to be little hope that the Brezhnev leadership as it is now constituted will ever allow a major relaxation of controls over the intellectuals. The provincial party and the military and police lobbies have too strong a voice in the Brezhnev collective leadership and in any foreseeable coalitions to allow hope that "liberal conservative" elements will gain dominance in the cultural field. At the same time—barring the unlikely return to extreme repression—the gains in the expansion of culture over recent years will not be undone, and the various intellectual forces in the Soviet Union can be expected to continue pressing forward with marginal moves to open up the society.

Brezhnev, however, is still faced with the same dilemma Khrushchev had—how to adapt the party to its leadership role and keep its ideology relevant to Soviet society and the Communist movement. For a short period in 1965, when the leaders were most unsure of their directions, they seemed cautiously to seek the assistance of the intellectuals in taking some moderate steps toward adapting the Soviet establishment to modern needs. However "scientific" their orientation has been since that time, the leaders have demonstrated that the party's bias remains anti-intellectual, resistant to change, and distrustful of the artist. One Soviet intellectual who lived through both the 1953–54 and 1964–65 "thaws," and who understood clearly this persistent inflexibility of the party leadership, has suggested that what the Soviet Union obviously needs is frequent leadership changes, so that during the confusing interregna, the management of the country can be left to those who know what must be done and the intellectuals can benefit from the relative freedom that flows from disorientation at the top.

IV

THE PARTY AND
THE IMPLEMENTATION OF DECISIONS

It is one thing for a small elite, the Communist Party of the Soviet Union, to arrogate to itself the function of political leadership. It is another for the decisions reached by this elite to be implemented efficiently and effectively. The manner of implementation, especially the broader and more general the decision, often becomes in itself an act of decision making. The way in which details are filled in, or broad policy statements or goals are interpreted, can affect the spirit if not the letter of the decision. In a country as large and as populous as the Soviet Union, with a complex and sophisticated economy, it is impossible for the decision makers themselves to serve also as the implementors and administrators. For this reason, the party leaders have always been concerned with how and by whom its decisions are put into practice.

Given the prevailing political norms and the scope of decision making, whether in imperial Russia or the Soviet Union, a large and extensive state administrative bureaucracy became inevitable. After the revolution, especially after the introduction of the Five-Year plans in 1928, managers and directors for the productive enterprises—the factories, mines, power generating stations, and transportation and construction facilities—were required. A vast array of planners, statisticians, auditors, investigators, not to mention ministers, bureau chiefs, and other line administrators, spread throughout the Soviet economy. After the collectivization of agriculture, collective and state farm managers and the vast bureaucracy in the countryside concerned with planning, procurement, and distribution of agricultural products emerged.

A key issue for the Soviet leaders has been how to define the relationship between this huge administrative apparatus and the party. Should they be fused, in that the lower echelons of the party would provide the administrative services required to implement decisions? Or was the party to remain institutionally aloof from the administration of state affairs? It was decided at an early date to separate the state organs from those of the party. The ill-defined relationship between the party and the soviets that existed immediately after the revolution was soon clarified. The local party organs were provided with their own budgetary sources of support, independent of the local soviets, upon which the party organs had theretofore been dependent for funds. This step was taken in the context of a general concentration of power in the hands of the party at the expense of the soviets.

This structural separation of party and state has been maintained to the present. The separation remains only structural, however, because the party, particularly the lower echelons, continuously has had the responsibility of supervising and controlling the state apparatus. It is the party that is to be "the organizer of the economy" for the entire country. With the party "as the highest form of the social and political organization of all the Soviet people," the apparatus of the state becomes subordinate, but by no means inconsequential, in the eyes of the party. Every party member has as his most important task to "exercise political control over the implementation [by the state administrative apparatus] of the party's programs, directives, and decisions, of its general line, and the mobilization of the working people for their implementation."[1]

Recognizing that implementing broad policies itself becomes a process of decision making, the top party leaders have sought to assure party control by seeing to it that the lower party organs, themselves under the discipline of the party leaders, play a paramount role in the making of these lower-order decisions. The persistent difficulty has been how to avoid both too much and too little party intervention in administrative affairs. If the party organs become too involved in administration, they cease to be an independent instrument of supervision and control. If they remain too aloof, they cease to exercise the political control demanded of them—they cease to be supervisors and stimulators, and effective antennae through which the top leaders become informed quickly of difficulties and problems.

This latter point emphasizes the fact that in addition to its political function, the party's control responsibilities may serve other equally important purposes. Jerry F. Hough, writing in the context of the specific organizational forms (*sovnarkhozy*) that existed from 1957 until shortly after Khrushchev's removal at the end of 1964, explores the vaguely defined relationship between the lower party organs and the state administrative apparatus (especially industrial), the roles of the lower party organs in decision making, and the ambiguities in the notion of "political control" over implementation of party decisions. He argues that beyond the political reasons there are administrative and organizational rationales for the extensive role of the party in administrative affairs. Given the decision "to create a unified bureaucratic society," certain functions have to be performed—

---

[1] See *Current Digest of the Soviet Press*, XIX, No. 52, 22–24.

provision of information to top decision makers, the need to assure a broader outlook at the lower and middle administrative levels, the need for regional coordination. These functions are now performed by the lower party organs because they aid in "the smooth operation of the administrative system and the fulfillment of rational-technical goals."[2]

An example of how the leadership expects the lower party organs to supervise and control can be seen in connection with the recent economic reforms, which granted more scope for independent judgment to the managers of productive enterprises in the Soviet Union.[3] At the same time that the party was taking this broad policy decision, it was setting out the duties and obligations of the basic party organs, the primary party organizations (PPO), with respect to checking up on management's work. A "paramount role" is assigned to the PPOs, and the right is granted to them "to delve deeply into the state of affairs, familiarize themselves with the appropriate documents, hear reports from economic executives, raise their responsibility for assigned sections of the work and help them expose and eliminate defects." The party organizations are to "keep all the central questions of production under constant control," in the sense of scrutiny or auditing. The control commissions set up by the primary party organizations are to be the focal point of this work. The major purpose of this recent emphasis on the supervisory functions of the primary party organs appears to be the rapid exposing and elimination of defects, and the putting of "unutilized potential into operation."

Through what institutions are the broad, fundamental decisions of the top party organs implemented? What structural form does the state administrative apparatus take? Constitutionally, binding decisions with the force of law (laws, decisions, orders, decrees) are made by the hierarchy of soviets and their inner bodies, from the villages and hamlets to the USSR Supreme Soviet. That the decision-making role of the higher soviets (apart from the most important inner body, the Council of Ministers) essentially is one of ratification of decisions made elsewhere can be seen in the report of any session of the USSR Supreme Soviet. In one recent session[4] the two chambers of the Supreme Soviet, meeting separately twice, and jointly three times, transacted several rather important items of business in two and a half days with a minimum of discussion and apparently no debate. A considerable portion of the time was taken up in the hearing of reports. Unanimity appears to have prevailed on all occasions when the delegates were called upon to take formal action. This may be important to the party

---

[2] See also Professor Hough's new book, *The Soviet Prefects: The Local Party Organs in Industrial Decision-Making* (Cambridge, Mass.: Harvard University Press, 1969).

[3] See *Current Digest of the Soviet Press*, XIX, No. 37, 8–10.

[4] See *Current Digest of the Soviet Press*, XX, No. 26, 14–15.

in perpetuating the myth of unity of will and purpose under party leadership, but as Jeremy Azrael has noted, it leaves many doubts as to its being an expression of significant decision making.[5] The purposes of the Supreme Soviet procedures are to impart an aura of constitutional legitimacy to party decisions, to symbolize national unity, and to mobilize "leading" elements of society for the task of implementation.

There is a wider scope for decision making and administration permitted and encouraged at the lower levels in the structure of soviets, but this is carefully contained through party control of delegate recruitment and by other means. The soviets at each level formally elect an executive committee (or council of ministers), and charge it with the task of implementing decisions. This network of administrative bodies, with all of their subordinate and auxiliary committees and commissions, constitutes the state administrative apparatus. These executive bodies are the source of administrative leadership. The higher up one goes in the structure the more likely one is to find the executive organs staffed with party members.

A very important division exists within this administrative structure. Those administrative functions that are performed directly by the hierarchy of local soviet executive committees are limited, for the most part, to what can be called the "public services"—education, local public works, health care and other forms of social welfare, retail trade, and maintenance of public order. The vast array of productive enterprises (with some exceptions for local industry) are administered separately from the local soviets and directly by the USSR Council of Ministers or the councils of ministers in the individual union-republics. One productive area in which the administrative arm of the local soviets does play a major role is that of agriculture. Under central administrative direction from Moscow and the capitals of each republic, the executive committees at the *oblast* and *raion* level are responsible for "operational direction" of the individual farms. An agriculture committee is found as part of the executive committee substructure in each *oblast* and *raion*.

L. G. Churchward provides a discussion and evaluation of recent trends in Soviet local government. Local government in the Soviet Union consists of three levels: (1) *oblast* (region or province) and large city (such as Moscow, Leningrad, Kiev); (2) *raion* (district or county), towns and cities subject to *oblast* supervision; and (3) village, city *raion* (district or borough), and towns subject to *raion* supervision. Mr. Churchward dis-

---

[5] Even in the Supreme Soviet there may be pressures for changes. Some observers view the increased number of legislative committees now found in the Supreme Soviet, and evidence of what might be more activity on their part, as concessions to demands for more meaningful participation. Of particular interest is the recent formation of a Committee on Youth Affairs in each chamber of the USSR Supreme Soviet (See *Izvestia*, December 11, 1968, p. 5).

cusses the changing character of Soviet local government, emphasizing the effort of the Community Party to increase the degree of popular participation in the work of the local soviets. Many administrative functions appear to have been turned over to the growing body of "social organizations," with a corresponding decline in the size of the professional or bureaucratic administrative apparatus. As Mr. Churchward notes, however, this effort to "democratize" local administration remains under the pervasive influence of the appropriate party organs.

The really significant administrative structure is that which is concerned with the economic life in the country. With some few exceptions, the whole of the industrial means of production, including all of the means of transportation and construction, are owned and centrally administered by the state. As noted by professor Richman, both micro- and macro-management of the economy are concerns of the state—and behind the state, the party. Although the current movement toward economic reform has modified the norms of economic organization and management somewhat, the broad outline remains the same: central guidance and direction through the imposition of essential indices, with an increasing decentralization in operation.

One can gather some idea of the degree of central direction of the economy from the recently published General Statute on USSR ministries.[6] After the removal of Khrushchev in October, 1964, his successors took immediate steps to dismantle his administrative innovations. One of the most important of these had been a change in emphasis away from the industrial principle of administration (according to industry) to the territorial principle (according to region). The system of regional economic councils (*sovnarkhozy*), which had been set up first in 1957, was abolished. The country had been divided into a number of economic regions, and administrative responsibility devolved to a committee representative of the breadth of all economic activities within the region. Khrushchev's successors re-established the system according to which a central ministry administers each branch of industry.

Right at the very outset, the General Statute provides that each economic ministry is responsible not only to "the state and the people," but first to the party. The tasks of the ministry, as opposed to the productive enterprises under the ministry's direction, are broad and concerned with macro-management—planning, assuring the maximum application of technological developments, the efficient use of capital investments, and the assuring of adequate numbers of trained personnel for the productive enterprises.

Administrative coordination is provided through a council of ministers, both at the national level, and in each individual union-republic. A great

---

[6] See *Current Digest of the Soviet Press*, XIX, No. 37, 3–8.

deal of the attention of the councils of ministers is devoted to "trouble shooting," or coping with "new problems arising in the course of development of the economy."[7] The broad outlines are laid down for the economy by the economic plans (twenty-year, five-year, annual), but adjustments and revisions are constantly being made as unforeseen contingencies arise or as the inadequacies of the planning process lead to problems in operation.

How capable is the Soviet administrative system and its personnel of coping with the problems it faces—"with the growing diversification and complexity of a modern industrial society"? Alf Edeen suggests that the problem of administrative efficiency is becoming more and more difficult, and that it "has a bearing on the Soviet capacity for further overall expansion." Mr. Edeen emphasizes the problems that have been created for the administrative structure by the decisive influence exercised at all levels by the party. The very important question that Mr. Edeen raises is: can the Soviet administrative machinery, at a time when the industrial and social structure is becoming more complex, provide "the really sophisticated planning, coordination, integration, and timing of various economic and social activities" that the party's commitment to central direction requires?

Considerable pressures on the administrative system and on the party leaders come from the economic and social environment. There are continuing efforts on the part of the party leaders to find a way to economic rationality in both industry and agriculture that would not undermine their political position.[8] As many observers have pointed out, the problems raised for the economic administrative structure in the Soviet Union are a product of forty years of economic growth and development. The central planning organs and the ministries, formed on the basis of industry, became overloaded with communications and decisions as the economy became more sophisticated and complex, and as efficient utilization of resources rather than gross volume of output became the objective. Khrushchev sought to cope with these difficulties by decentralizing decision making on a regional basis, with other undesirable consequences. His successors, still committed to firm central direction of all economic activities, have sought to ease the burden on central authorities by freeing them from the myriad of petty, microeconomic problems arising from day-to-day operations.

The persistent difficulties that the party has faced since 1928 in the agricultural sector appear no closer to remedy today than before. As Stalin and Khrushchev before them, the current party leaders have been looking for ways in which to improve agricultural productivity, without changing significantly the pattern of agricultural administration. The latter remains

---

[7] See *Current Digest of the Soviet Press*, XIX, No. 43, 34–35.

[8] See, for example, Keith Bush, "The Reforms: A Balance Sheet," *Problems of Communism* (July–August 1967), and Roy D. Laird, "New Trends and Old Remedies," *Problems of Communism* (March–April 1968).

essential to the party, both for ideological reasons, and for more immediate political reasons. The return of the Brezhnev and Kosygin leadership from Khrushchev's innovations to a strongly centralized form of organization makes a basic change in the existing system very unlikely.

This leaves the pertinent questions with respect to the Soviet economy unanswered. Is the economic and social environment, in great measure the product of earlier party decisions, inevitably forcing changes in economic administration that will have undesired political consequences for the party, or can the party leaders cope with the pressures by adjustment and adaptation? Can agricultural productivity be improved so as to meet the demands of a growing population with more sophisticated tastes; can the style and material content of rural life be improved, within the existing administrative structure? Can these aims be achieved, as in industry, without changes bearing with them far-reaching political consequences?

THE SOVIET CONCEPT OF THE RELATIONSHIP BETWEEN THE LOWER PARTY ORGANS AND THE STATE ADMINISTRATION

JERRY F. HOUGH

To Westerners one of the most confusing aspects of the Soviet administrative system has been the role played by lower officials of the Communist Party. It has long been clear that the top policy decisions are made within the central Party organs, but the relationship between the lower Party officials and the governmental administrators has been obscured by a number of seeming ambiguities and inconsistencies in Soviet administrative theory. The Party apparatus has been assigned the duty of supervising and controlling the state administration, but the mandates and powers of the two hierarchies appear ill-defined and overlapping.

On the one hand, Soviet legal and textbook discussions of the administrative system seem to indicate the necessity for a strict line of command (particularly in such realms as industry) with single and undivided responsibility in the hands of the governmental administrator at each level. Organs such as the *sovnarkhozy* (regional economic councils) are said to "bear full responsibility for the fulfillment of the production plan [and to have been] granted all the powers necessary for carrying out their economic and financial activity." Lower managers perform their duties in accordance with the principle of *edinonachalie* (one-man management and control), a principle which "demands the complete subordination of all the employees in the production process to the will of one person—the leader—

Slavic Review, XXIV, No.. 2 (June 1965), reprinted by permission. Revised by the author for this volume. Footnotes omitted.

and his personal responsibility for the assigned work." These managers, according to one authority, enjoy "the right of decision" for all questions within the jurisdiction of their organization.

Yet Soviet administrative theory contains equally emphatic statements that "the leading and directing role of the Communist Party is the foundation of Soviet state administration." Indeed, the standard Soviet textbook on administrative law declares that "not one important question is decided without supervisory instruction of the Party organs." There are many indications that these quotations are not merely formal generalities. For example, we may find in the Soviet press a matter-of-fact report that a Party *obkom* "obligated the *sovnarkhoz* to prepare 300 bulldozer attachments for the DT-54 tractor" or that the bureau of another *obkom* "removed M. R. Kulik from his duties as regional prosecutor (*prokuror*) because of his unsatisfactory supervision of the procuracy."

The first purpose of this article is to explore these apparently conflicting concepts of the Party-state relationship and to attempt to clarify the ambiguities involved. In doing this we hope to illuminate the operational principles implicit in the formal administrative theory and to explain them in terms familiar in Western administrative theory.

The second purpose is to suggest the reasons why the Party organs have been assigned control responsibilities and to speculate on the effect of lower Party participation in decision-making upon the nature of the decisions being made. To use the categories suggested by Barrington Moore, we shall ask the questions: To what extent have the responsibilities of the Party apparatus reflected the desire of the leadership to solidify its political power? To what extent have these responsibilities resulted in decisions which deviate from a "rational-technical" norm?

The Limited Meaning of "Edinonachalie"

For a Westerner the most unfortunate aspect of Soviet administrative theory is its failure to use familiar concepts in discussing familiar administrative problems and situations. To a large extent the problem is one of language. For instance, the word "policy" and the phrase "policy implication" are covered by the Russian word "*politicheskii*," a word usually translated into English as "political"; or, the phrase "delegation of authority" has no easy Russian equivalent. Consequently, in grappling with the problems of "delegation of authority" and "the policy implications of administrative decisions," Soviet administrative theorists have often used language that has often been understood by Westerners to mean a chain of command far clearer and an allocation of power far broader than the Soviet leaders ever intended. In particular, the concept of *edinonachalie* has a much more limited meaning than the usual English translation would indicate.

Although all lower officials work within the framework of higher policy, Soviet administrative theory implicitly recognizes that the decisions delegated to each level often may entail policy considerations, and it attempts to distinguish between these decisions and those that are truly routine. The sweeping statements in the legal documents and textbooks about the authority of the state official pertain almost exclusively to the location of the power to take "non-policy" decisions and the power to issue the formal decrees by which all decisions must be implemented; these statements do not imply that the "policy" decisions at a given level are within the sole jurisdiction of the one-man manager.

If our understanding of *edinonachalie* is correct, then it is—and always has been—a very limited concept that denotes only three things: (1) Hour-to-hour, day-to-day decisions of a fairly routine nature are to be made by a single man, the duly constituted administrator. He need not clear each of these routine decisions with the Party or trade-union organization. (2) Although important decisions can and must be influenced by groups other than the state officials (notably the Party organs), every decision must be formally implemented by a governmental organ, specifically by the man or institution which has the legal, formal authority to do so. This aspect of Soviet administrative theory is epitomized in the well-known regulation that Party organizations desiring some action must work "through" the state organs, not "apart from them." Even when Party organizations have been granted the power to take a particular kind of decision, they cannot issue the necessary formal decree themselves but must compel the appropriate governmental official or agency to do it. (3) An employee is obligated to obey any order or instruction emanating from his formal administrative superior. He has no right to appeal to any Party or trade-union organization to have any specific order countermanded, or at least he has no such right of appeal if the order requires immediate execution.

The meaning of *edinonachalie* is illustrated in a practice that is sometimes mentioned in the Soviet press. This is the willingness of many managers to use even design engineers for such tasks as unloading vital supplies from a truck if the rush for plan fulfillment at the end of the month demands it. Even though this practice has been severely criticized by the Party leadership, an engineer receiving such an order from his superior is bound to carry it out. This is the essence of *edinonachalie*. The engineer does, however, have the right and even the duty, to protest later through the Party organization and to demand that the manager be punished and prohibited from repeating the practice. Of course, the effectiveness of such a protest will depend upon the attitude of the higher authorities, particularly the Party organs.

Any reader familiar with the long Western discussion about "policy" and "administration" knows how difficult it is to distinguish between a routine administrative question and one that has policy implications, and Soviet theorists frankly admit they have not solved the problem. Lower Party officials themselves have inquired as to what kind of questions should be decided by soviet organs and what kind by Party organs, and have been answered by the foremost of Soviet theorists that it is impossible to give a recipe or some sort of catalogue. This official, the head of the "Party Life" department of *Pravda*, cautioned that in certain cases there might be questions which seemed minor at first glance "but which in reality should be raised to the level of important political significance."

The inability of Soviet administrative theory to distinguish precisely between a policy and a non-policy question inevitably means a certain ambiguity in the Soviet administrative system, but it is an ambiguity that in one form or another is inherent in large-scale organization everywhere. Once it is conceded that lower-level decisions may have policy implications —and all Western administrative theorists would concede that point—then the Soviet distinction makes at least some sense. For the sake of convenience here, a lower-level policy question may be defined as one on which two technically qualified persons, both working within the framework of central directives and rules, might still arrive at different decisions. Thus, a policy question arises when a Party secretary differs with the decision made by the state administrator or feels it necessary to advance a suggestion himself. The "political maturity" of the Party secretary becomes defined in terms of "his ability to pick out the most significant matters from the mass of current business."

Admittedly, our hypothesis about the reconcilability of *edinonachalie* and official statements about the Party's role is not the usual one. It is difficult to prove its correctness conclusively because a question of interpretation and translation is involved. The hypothesis does, however, "work" in the sense that it explains a considerable body of data which must otherwise be dismissed as inexplicable or deliberately confusing.

First, the interpretation fits the history of the concept of *edinonachalie*. *Edinonachalie* was not invented by Stalin as he moved to reduce the independence of the Party apparatus that had placed him in power; rather it was vigorously advocated by Lenin in

the first months after the Revolution— a period when he surely had no desire to limit the authority of lower Party officials.

When quoted in the abstract or in a contemporary Soviet source, there seems to be a categorical quality to an assertion by Lenin that *"incontrovertible subordination* to a single will is unconditionally indispensable for the success of work . . . [in] large-scale industry." Yet, in the context of early 1918, such statements surely were not an appeal for a plant manager who would be an independent decisionmaker subject only to higher administrative authorities. They are much better understood as an attempt to combat the utopian interpretations of workers' control and trade union control prevailing in this period (and encouraged by Lenin's own prerevolutionary slogans).

From this perspective the advocacy of *edinonachalie* and "incontrovertible subordination to a single will" represented little more than Lenin's conviction that the complicated processes of industry would require planning, coordination, and labor discipline under socialism as well as under capitalism. Although the worker would have to accept orders from a directing figure, Lenin had no intention of suggesting that the orders of the "single will" would be based on the manager's independent decisions. It is for this reason that the early debate about *edinonachalie* hardly touched on the question of the role of the Party.

In the second place, the hypothesis is in accord with the examples which Soviet spokesmen use to illustrate the importance of *edinonachalie*. When Party organs are criticized for interfering in the business of management, the examples almost always involve very minute details rather than questions of any significance. Thus, one Party handbook argued against excessive Party involvement in the following terms: "What would happen if the district (*raion*) Party committee told a collective farm chairman where to send a particular tractor or instructed the shop heads of an enterprise as to which worker should be placed on a particular operation?" Similarly, after Khrushchev's removal the *Pravda* criticisms of local Party organs which usurped the functions of the administrative organs featured such examples as Party determination of traffic rules, the location of a street sign, the method of street cleaning, or the schedule for digging the foundation of a building. It is particularly instructive that "such a style of work" is criticized on the grounds that "it does not permit the political leader to concern himself with his real job—the resolution of the important problems which are within his competence."

Finally, the interpretation offered here makes sense of one of the most puzzling paradoxes in Soviet administrative theory, namely, the repeated instruction to Party organs to strive "to strengthen *edinonachalie*" and the assertion that "the Party committee of the plant, in using its right of verification (*pravo kontrolia*), is strengthening *edinonachalie*." If *edinonachalie* implies autonomy for the manager in decision-making, this type of statement obviously contradicts other statements about the role of the Party, and in some formulations it becomes ridiculous; but, if *edinonachalie* has the more limited meaning suggested here, then the strengthening of *edinonachalie* can mean little more than the strengthening of labor discipline—a much more understandable demand.

The Relationship of Party Organs and Governmental Administration

To state that *edinonachalie* is compatible with an active Party role in decision-making is not to indicate the nature of that role. This will be the subject of the remainder of the article.

It is actually misleading to speak of "a" role for the lower Party organs in Soviet decision-making, for, in reality, there is more than one Party-state relationship. The role of the primary Party organization (summarized in the term *pravo kontrolia*, that is, the right of verification) is different from that of the local (*mestnye*) Party committees (summarized in the terms *rukovodstvo* and *napravlenie*, that is, executive leadership and direction, respectively). An understanding of the distinctions made in Soviet administrative theory between these two roles is vital for a comprehension of the complex role of the lower Party apparatus in Soviet decision-making.

The relationship of the primary Party organization and of its secretary to the chief administrator of an enterprise or institution can be quite varied. If the organization is located within a governmental administrative office (for example, a ministry, *sovnarkhoz*, or department of a soviet), it has no right to interfere in policy decisions but should simply ensure that decisions are made smoothly and that a "bureaucratic" atmosphere with red tape, toadyism, and excessive self-satisfaction does not appear. If it is located within a factory, collective or state farm, construction site, design bureau, or store, however, it has been specifically assigned the so-called *pravo kontrolia*, the right to check on the substance of managerial decisions.

In this article only those primary Party organizations with the *pravo kontrolia* will be discussed specifically. Yet, while the discussion will be totally irrelevant to the situation within governmental administrative offices (there the role of the Party secretary is quite weak, and Party supervision is exercised instead by the territorial Party organs), the general points to be made apply also to several institutions in which there is no formal *pravo kontrolia*; these include schools, colleges, army units, and perhaps hospitals.

It is quite clear that the *pravo kontrolia* can involve the Party organization deeply in decision-making and in conflicts with the plant director, but the precise meaning of this phrase is not clear at first glance. Part of the difficulty in understanding the *pravo kontrolia* stems from the fact that the word "*kontrol*" does not really reflect the real nature of the work of the primary Party organization. *Kontrol* has entered the Russian language from the French and has a much more limited meaning than the English word by which it is usually translated. The English verb "control" can often imply the providing of policy direction, but *kontrol* has more the connotations of the word "controller." Consequently, the phrase "*pravo kontrolia*" conveys the impresssion of a primary Party organization checking, verifying, inspecting the work of the manager and enforcing his adherence to laws and plans established elsewhere.

However, the role of the primary Party organization and its secretary is stretched far beyond the literal meaning of *pravo kontrolia* by the nature of the instructions and directives that the plant receives from higher Party and state organs. As American authorities have long noted, the Soviet leadership does not provide an enterprise or institution with a precise plan or program to fulfill. Instead, the plant, the farm, the store, is ordered to overfulfill its plan by as much as possible, to do so with optimal efficiency, and to continue to improve the production processes as rapidly as possible. Further complicating the situation is the extreme tautness of the plan in relation to resources. Because of the resulting low levels of inventories, any mistakes in the planning process or any failure of a supplier to meet his schedule can lead to serious difficulties. Consequently, a manager finds it virtually impossible to fulfill his overall plan without sacrificing some of the plan indicators or violating some of the regulations that are supposed to govern the work of the enterprise. Schools, colleges, and institutes do not face precisely the same problem, but even they are obligated to achieve an ideal in education or research that can never be reached in the real world.

The effect of this situation on the role of the manager has long been recognized. Because he has no precise set of rules and regulations to follow, he has much more room in which to maneuver than might be expected for an official low in a very centralized hierarchy. Indeed, an American author, David Granick, concluded in 1954 that the plant manager has so much freedom of action that he cannot rightfully be called a bureaucrat in the Weberian sense.

If the nature of the Soviet planning system leaves the manager with some freedom of action in relation to his superiors, it has had a corresponding effect on the nature of the *kontrol'* exercised by the primary Party organization. Since there is no precise plan or set of regulations, the *kontrol'* cannot be a routine "verification of performance" in the usual sense. The party organization cannot merely check off regulations which have been violated, for, as one higher official expressed it, regulations are constantly being broken "for the sake of production." To be sure, the organization is interested in gross machinations and law violations, but its basic role is much broader. In checking on the overall performance of the enterprise, it inevitably becomes involved in decision-making, if only for the reason that the mere choice of the indicator or regulation to emphasize constitutes a decision of significance.

Moreover, since the Party organization has the duty of preventing mistakes as well as of reporting and correcting them, it has in effect an opportunity to discuss with the manager any question which it deems important. The official Party handbook is filled with demands that the organization as a whole "raise questions about production," "recommend various measures," "bring up various problems to the administration," and so on. In the realm of personnel action, the Party bureaus do not have the right either to appoint personnel or to confirm appointments, but they do have "not only the right but also the duty to consult with the economic leader and to recommend that this or that official be promoted."

In short, the right of *kontrol* entails both the right to check *after* a decision has been made, and also, more importantly, the right to participate intimately in policy-making *before* the decision is made. It means that the Party committee or bureau of the primary Party organization is the real board of directors of the plant—the place where the top administrative officials together with the Party secretary, the trade union chairman, and a few workers, discuss the major questions facing the enterprise and make the decisions concerning them.

Although the Party bureau is primarily an "inside" board of directors (that is, composed of men from inside the plant who are subordinate to the manager in their daily work), it does contain at least one man who is always supposed to maintain a position independent of the manager—the secretary of the Party organization. Of course, the crucial question is: what happens when this official and the director do, in fact, "argue about questions of principle"? In cases of disagreement, do the Party organization and its secretary have the authority to compel the manager to accept their position?

There are, unfortunately, few other matters on which there are so many contradictory authoritative statements as on the proper relationship between the manager and the plant Party secretary. If at times Soviet officials (for example, Zhdanov in 1939) have criticized "Party organizations [which] take on themselves the improper functions of *executive leadership* (*rukovodstvo*) in economic matters," others have spoken of the "leading (*rukovodiashchaia*) role" of the primary Party organization in the enterprises or of its "providing of political leadership." In one place it is declared that "the decision of the meeting [of the primary Party organization] expresses the opinion and will of the Party collective, [and] it is binding on every Communist" (including, presumably, the director). In another place the statement is made that "the Party organization and its leaders cannot directly give any operational instructions, [nor] can they even require that the director clear his orders and commands with them." It is asserted that a situation should never develop in which "it is not the director who supervises the enterprise but the Party organization which commands the director."

Perhaps the strangest formulation of all appeared in an authoritative attempt to clarify the situation for a confused employee. The director at his plant admitted that the *obkom* and the *sovnarkhoz* could obligate him to take action, but he objected to attempts by the primary Party organization to do so, in addition. The employee wrote for support to the journal of the Central Committee, *Partiinaia zhizn'*. It answered as follows: "Comrade Razumovskii is mistaken if he thinks that only higher-standing Party and economic organs can obligate him. . . . But it would be incorrect [for the primary Party organization] to abuse its authority by addressing the director in such categorical phraseology as 'obligate,' 'propose,' 'demand.'" Despite the blatant contradictions which seem to exist in these statements about the role of the primary Party organization, Soviet administrative theory is actually not nearly so ambiguous on this point as it appears on the surface.

Part of the explanation for the contradictions has already been suggested in the discussion of the phraseology used to describe *edinonachalie*. For example, the assertion that the primary Party organization "cannot *directly* [my italics] give any operational instructions" is surely a reflection of the Soviet insistence that Party officials

work through the duly constituted governmental officials in carrying out their decisions. Prohibitions against commanding the director and against forcing him to clear his orders with the Party organizations are likewise expressions of the Soviet belief that managers should be permitted to make minor day-to-day decisions on their own. (The word *komandovat'* tends to connote an excessive ordering around of people.)

A second partial explanation for the ambiguities in statements about the primary Party organization lies in the diversity of the types of decisions that the primary Party organization may take. Zhdanov's reference to "the improper functions of leadership *in economic matters*" (my italics) reminds us that other decisions of the Party organization deal with various intra-Party matters. Here the authority of the organization and its secretary may be unchallenged.

Even within the economic sphere itself there are many kinds of decisions that may be taken. If the local Party organs issue a *formal* decision about an enterprise, the decision is often directed at the primary Party organization rather than solely at the management. The decision is then echoed by the primary Party organization, its decision obligating all Communists to carry out the different points decreed by higher officials. In such cases there is no questioning the obligatory nature of the "decision of the primary Party organization" for the manager.

There are other decisions of the primary Party organization so general that it would seem strange if the word "to suggest" were to be used instead of "to obligate." In 1952, for example, "the Party committee [of the giant plant Elektrosila] obligated comrade

Shevchenko [the director] to be attentive to the workers, to have more contact with them, to take into account criticism which comes from below." A similar obligation was stated in 1965 by the Party conference of the Tbilisi Electric Locomotive Works: "A decision was taken which obligates the Party committee and the Communists: To raise the level of the technical leadership of production. To devote serious attention to the scientific organization of work. More boldly to introduce new techniques and progressive technology into production. . . . To strengthen labor and production discipline, to obtain a rise in labor productivity, to guarantee rhythmic work, to lower costs, and to raise the quality of production."

If it were categorically denied that the Party organization has the right to obligate the manager, then the general decisions quoted above, as well as those on intra-Party matters and those embodying higher Party decisions, could not have been phrased as they are. When the editorial board of *Partiinaia zhizn* states that the director can be obligated by the primary Party organization but that the organization should not abuse its authority by using the word "to obligate," it is possible (or even probable) that it is tacitly differentiating between the type of decision we have been examining and those that deal with specific production questions.

A third step in understanding the role of the primary Party organization and its secretary lies in making a distinction between the organization and the secretary which Soviet theorists are frequently eager to blur. If we closely examine two contradictory statements about the primary Party organization, we often find that one statement refers to the powers and functions of the Party organization as a whole, while the other actually describes the powers and functions of the secretary alone.

Although the primary Party organization has been assigned the right to verify the work of management, we must never forget that the organization also, in fact, contains nearly all of the top members of management itself. From the point of view of Party theory, the organization as a whole (including the managerial team) occupies a special position in relation to the enterprise employees who are not Party members. The organization is part of the vanguard of the proletariat, and its relationship to the proletariat is depicted in the same terms as those used to describe the general role of the Party.

The really sweeping statements about the "leading role" of the primary Party organization almost always refer implicitly to this relationship of the Party organization to the enterprise and to the men in it who are not members of the Communist Party. They do not refer to the relationship of the Party secretary or of a majority of the members to those Communists who occupy the top administrative posts in the enterprise. This is vital to understand if a very frequent type of Soviet press report is not to be misinterpreted. Take, for example, the assertion that "the Party committee [of the Orekhovo-Zuevo Cotton Combine] . . . skillfully directs the efforts of the Communists, of the 26,000-man collective in finding and using the internal reserves, in perfecting production, in raising productivity of labor and profitability." This statement does not necessarily imply any limitation on the role of the top managerial officials, for they are among the most important members of that Party committee. It means simply that the major plant decisions are made—or formalized—at a meeting of the plant's "board of directors"; it does not necessarily mean that the Party secretary has had any real impact on the decision.

On the other hand, much Soviet discussion of the primary Party organization is implicitly based on a much narrower conception of the organization—that is, as consisting of the Party secretary at the head of the rank-and-file members. The whole concept of *pravo kontrolia* does, of course, imply a Party organization apart from the top administrators of the unit, and in practice it tends to refer to the role of the Party secretary. Because of the democratic mythology surrounding the primary Party organization, Soviet administrative theorists sometimes find it awkward to discuss the legitimate authority which the leadership really intends to be vested in the Party secretary. However, many of the narrow definitions of the powers of the organization were written with the secretary in mind. When Zhdanov denied that the primary Party organization was to have the role of executive leadership, when *Partiinaia zhizn'* stated that it would be improper for the primary Party organization to use the words "obligate" or "demand" in its decisions, they were thinking of the Party secretary and the rank-and-file members he leads.

All Soviet officials interviewed in 1958 and 1962 agreed that both in theory and in practice the powers of the secretary are limited to those of persuasion and of appeal to higher officials, and that the secretary cannot (without the support of higher officials) force the managers to accept

his opinion on policy questions. Those interviewed stated that the decision of a meeting of the primary Party organization or its bureau usually does not bind the manager unless he has concurred in the decision. Even a non-Party director of a textile factory insisted that the primary Party organization would take no decision concerning the economic side of the enterprise's life without clearing it with him first.

The interviews indicate that if there is disagreement between the director and Party secretary the secretary's only recourse is appeal to the local Party organs for support. However, one authoritative post-Khrushchev statement about the primary Party organizations suggests that in the realm of personnel selection, at least, it is the director who must take the initiative if he is not to be bound by the opinion of the Party organization. After asserting that the Party committees' "decisions, proposals, and recommendations are obligatory for the [director]," this statement continued, "If the economic leader ... considers the decision of the Party organization mistaken, he should turn to a higher-standing Party organ and ask it to correct the mistake of the Party organization and to annul its decision."

It is not certain whether the burden of making the appeal has been placed on the director only in the post-Khrushchev period or whether it actually represents a long-standing operating procedure. In fact, the statement does not make clear whether this procedure applies to all decisions of the primary Party organization or just to those involving personnel changes. Another 1965 *Partiinaia zhizn* statement about the primary Party organization defines its role in such a way as to suggest that it still may be compelled to initiate most of the appeals in cases of disagreements with the manager: the Party organizations should, the statement demanded, "work out effective recommendations for the administration and *place important problems* before higher-standing Party organs." The three underlined words were in heavy dark print in the original.

Whoever must make the appeal to the local Party organs, neither the director nor the plant Party secretary can force the other to accept his opinion without the support of higher Party officials. As a result, the essential image of the relationship of the director and the Party secretary emerging from Soviet administrative theory is that of a policy-making team within the enterprise. These two officials, together with the trade union chairman, are to form a three-man directorate— the triangle (*treugolnik*), a term from the 1920's still used today.

Within the policy-making team the director is primarily responsible for day-to-day decisions, but when broader questions arise he must discuss them fully with the secretary, and the two must find a common language, an *obshchii iazyk*. On certain questions dealing with dismissals, housing distribution, and so forth, the agreement of the trade union chairman is also required, but he is closely supervised by the Party secretary and is scarcely an independent power center within the enterprise.

This relationship between administrator and Party secretary in the situation when the Party organization has the *pravo kontrolia* seems also to apply to many other enterprises and institutions in which there is no formal *pravo kontrolia*. To be sure, it has no relevance for the relationship within the central and regional administrative organs, but it is implied even in discussions of such an institution as the army. Marshal M. V. Zakharov, then head of the General Staff of the Soviet Armed Forces, wrote of "the persistent need for businesslike, Party-like cooperation of the commanders and the political workers in the struggle to strengthen the fighting capcaity and military discipline of the troops." He criticized "individual political workers who think that they have no obligation to investigate military matters thoroughly," and he condemned any attempt to limit the cooperation of the commanders and the political workers "only to Party-political matters."

Within the policy-making team the two leaders are in a roughly equal position, at least in the sense that neither can compel the other to take a particular action. It is safe to say that the relative influence of the administrator and the secretary varies from enterprise to enterprise, depending upon the personalities and abilities of the two men. No doubt it is also safe to say that most frequently the director is first among equals, both because he has been granted higher prestige and pay and because he is in charge of day-to-day administration. In the army, for example, the head of the political administration (at least at the military district level) seems always to have a lower rank than the commander. In any event, the author has never seen a case in which the political officer had a higher rank. All in all, the relative position of the secretary of a primary Party organization is best expressed in the fact that he may become the chief administrator in his enterprise or unit, but the chief administrator never becomes the Party secretary. Nevertheless, the mere existence of the right of appeal is surely a powerful weapon for the secretary, ensuring a role for him even when that right is not exercised.

The Soviet leaders have realized that a policy-making team within an enterprise can create difficulties, and they have taken a number of steps to avoid them. To prevent one member of the team from becoming dominant, they periodically vary the balance of emphasis between the two roles, and they also follow a policy of replacing Party secretaries after a very short tenure.

The Soviet leaders have also used a number of devices to thwart the development of irresponsibility and indecisiveness in this system. They have held the administrator and the Party secretary strictly responsible for results (basically the same results in each case) and then have given them an extremely difficult plan to fulfill. In this way the two men are given to understand that any poor results ensuing from a failure to work together effectively will bring their prompt removal. Another device has been the insistence upon *edinonachalie*—the insistence that orders be carried out along the administrative line and that the administrator have the authority to carry through action which he thinks is needed immediately. Finally, the local Party committee has been given the right and the power to settle any conflict that arises between the administrator and the secretary of the primary Party organization and that cannot be resolved by them.

Above the primary Party organizations in the Party hierarchy we find a series of Party committees, one located within each territorial unit in the Soviet Union—the rural district, the borough, the city, the region

(oblast), and the republic. Like the primary Party organizations, these middle-level committees (termed "the local Party organs") are held strictly responsible for plan fulfillment by the state institutions within their jurisdiction. They too are instructed to intervene to help achieve that plan fulfillment. Yet the relationship of the local Party organs to the state administrators is strikingly different from the relationship of the primary Party organizations to those administrators.

In Soviet administrative theory the key determinant in the relationship of any local Party organ to any state administrator is the territorial level at which the two are located. If the state administrator works at a higher territorial level than the Party organ, the Party organ's position with respect to him is quite weak. In theory the interaction of a Party committee with a higher state official is not that of team decision-making but rather a supplicant-superior relationship. A Party committee can request that a higher administrative official take some action, it can appeal one of his decisions to higher Party officials, but it is not in any real sense an equal. The percentage of success for its requests and appeals is not particularly high; indeed, the well-known difficulties of the local Party organs with the industrial ministries prior to 1957 are a typical reflection of the weakness of the Party organ in this type of relationship and of the unlikelihood of its obtaining consistent support from higher Party organs in its disputes with higher administrators.

If, on the other hand, the state administrator is located at the same territorial level as the local Party organ or a lower territorial level, the Party organ has a very different relationship to him. In fact, in this case the position of the local Party organ is far stronger than that of the primary Party organization within the enterprise. The local Party organ is not called upon simply to exercise *kontrol'* over the administrators within its area; instead, it is instructed (in the words of one of the last *Pravda* editorials of the Stalin era) "to realize leadership of the soviet, economic, and public organizations ...'" to unite, to direct (*napravliat'*), and to control (*kontrolirovat'*) [their] activity."

This difference in the role of the local Party organs and of the primary Party organizations was expressed very well in a 1940 editorial in *Pravda:* "Checking (*kontrol'*) by the *plant* Party organization in a given case is combined with correct and capable *leadership* (*rukovodstvo*) of the plant from the side of the Leningrad City Party Committee—daily leadership which is concrete and deep." In the editorial only the two words *plant* and *rukovodstvo* were printed in bold-face type.

The words *napravlenie* (direction) and *rukovodstvo* imply far broader powers than *kontrol'*. While *kontrol'* implies the absence of the authority to obligate an administrator, *rukovodstvo* denotes its presence. This authority derives formally from the relationship of the local Party organ to the primary Party organization as defined in the Party Rules, specifically from the clause declaring that "the decision of higher [Party] bodies are unconditionally binding upon lower ones." Since the important administrative personnel are for the most part Party members and are enrolled in the primary Party organization at the place where they work, they, too, are subject to the de-

cisions of the local Party organs which supervise their primary Party organization.

That these powers are more than formal and are not limited simply to intra-Party matters is graphically shown in the many references in the Soviet press to local Party organs which "obligate" managerial personnel and which also "promote" or "remove" them. A striking illustration appeared several years ago in a *Pravda* article about the compilation of the plan at the Elgav Agricultural Machine-building Plant in Latvia. The plant had been ordered by the *sovnarkhoz* to produce air conditioners, and with difficulty its managers succeeded in setting up the necessary rigging. At this stage, however, "officials of the Latvian Party Central Committee suggested that the production of air conditioners be discontinued." The article did not specify which officials were involved, but their "suggestion" was decisive. The plant management vigorously objected to the decision, and they were supported both by the Elgav City Party Committee and by the *sovnarkhoz*. Indeed, the *sovnarkhoz* twice appealed the decision to the bureau of the Latvian Central Committee, but the production of air conditioners continued to be deleted from the enterprise's plan.

After Khrushchev's removal the Soviet press carried a number of articles indicating that the local Party organs had been calling special operational sessions (*operativki*) and planning sessions (*planerki*) at which they directed the work schedules of state administrators (particularly those associated with construction) in a most immediate way. "At the operational sessions the *gorkom* and *raikom* secretaries distribute labor force, urge on the suppliers of materials, establish [daily or weekly] work schedules."

While this article and others like it criticized the Party organs, they accused the Party organs not of exceeding their authority but of using it unwisely. It will be recalled that the plant director who questioned the right of the primary Party organization to obligate him to take action conceded readily that the *obkom* had this authority, and none of the post-Khrushchev articles suggest that there has been any change in this respect. It was still reported in a matter-of-fact way, for example, that the Kamchatka *obkom* had established a schedule for mail delivery in the oblast and that the Grozny Party officials had required the city's enterprises to send 200 metalworkers to a key construction project temporarily. In short, it was not at all misleading to describe a *gorkom* first secretary in a novel as "the highest authority in the city," or to refer to a *raikom* secretary as "the head (*glava*) of the raion."

As these examples indicate the local Party organs use their powers to do far more than simply provide general ideological and inspirational leadership for the state administrators. The "leadership" which Soviet administrative theory demands from the local Party organs is that associated with the job of a chief executive. A description of the actual work of the local Party organs is not within the scope of this article, but their duties are as broad—and as difficult to define —as those of any chief executive. They include such functions as selecting important administrative personnel, providing policy direction to the state administrators on "questions of principle," maintaining standards of per-

formance, and, most important of all, coordinating the work of the different administrators and resolving disputes which arise among them.

In carrying out these functions, the local Party organs are to conduct themselves in accordance with the principles implied in *edinonachalie*. The Party Rules obligate the Party organs "not to supplant (*podmeniat'*) the soviet, trade-union, cooperative, and other public organizations of the toilers, not to permit a mixing of the functions of the Party and other organs or unnecessary parallelism in their work." "The Party organs cannot take on themselves the function of direct administration"; there should be no "detailed interference of the Party committees in the work of the economic organs and their leaders."

These statements are nothing more than the Soviet method of demanding delegation of authority on detailed questions from the Party to the state organs. This is most graphically demonstrated in the fact that Soviet administrative theorists use identical language when they discuss delegation of authority from a superior to a subordinate in the state apparatus: "The higher standing administrative bodies in exercising general supervision of the organs subordinate to them do not supplant (*podmeniat'*) them."

The essence of the relationship of a local Party organ to a state administrator within its area was best summarized in a 1957 statement by the second secretary of the Sverdlovsk *obkom* about the relationship of the *obkom* and the newly-created *sovnarkhoz*. After stating that "the oblast Party committee should not and must not supplant [the *sovnarkhoz*]," the second secretary continued: "The impression might be created that our Party organ takes on the role of a passive inspector.... In actuality, this is not so." He then made the crucial distinction: "There is a line where concrete, operational leadership of the enterprise ends and where economic policy begins." Even though the Sverdlovsk *sovnarkhoz* was then headed by a former USSR minister—a man who was a candidate member of the Party Central Committee—the secretary made it clear that questions involving "economic policy" should not be left to the *sovnarkhoz* to decide. While, of course, the relationship between an *obkom* and a *sovnarkhoz* changed with the raising of the *sovnarkhoz* above the oblast level in 1962, the secretary's distinction has general applicability to the relationship between any local Party organ and a state administrative agency at its territorial level or below.

Since the local Party organs are located at middle levels in a highly centralized hierarchy, naturally there are many questions of "economic policy" which are not left to them to decide either. In general terms the local Party organs are required to operate within the directives and plans established by higher Party and state agencies. (As the state officials at a higher territorial level receive their policy direction from the Party officials at their level, it would be illogical to permit a lower Party committee to thwart a governmental policy which embodies higher Party policy.) In practice, however, the orders which come down the different governmental lines of command are often all-embracing and conflicting, and this increases the scope for action of the local Party organs just as it does that of the

lower administrator and the secretary of the primary Party organization.

In our opinion the most important functional responsibility of the local Party organs has actually always been the adjustment of disparities and contradictions in the various plans, directives, and regulations which flow into the area from the various ministries and departments. While all of these plans and directives ultimately derive from the policy of the same Party leadership, they inevitably diverge somewhat as they descend the lines of command and become a bit distorted in meaning and emphasis by different departmental self-interests and perspectives. Moreover, the many regulations which have been issued by the leadership to control undesirable behavior may have untoward results in certain instances and create the need to make exceptions.

A whole series of conflicts and problems result from the contradictions and rigidities in the detailed plans and directives which reach the operational level. A local educational plan for in-factory training may require so much manpower and material from local factories as to threaten the fulfillment of parts of the industrial plan. The completion of the construction of a school by the beginning of the school year may depend upon an extraordinary (outside-the-plan) priority in the delivery of some key item. The harvesting of the local crop may be unsuccessful unless the farmers receive the help of "volunteer" labor from city enterprises and institutions. Some local construction emergency may demand the waiving of certain operating regulations if loss is not to be sustained.

In all these cases the administrators involved may take their problem to a local Party organ, and it has the authority to decide the relative priority of two plans or directives, to demand that one institution help another in important marginal cases, or to authorize a state administrator to disregard a particular regulation. And, of course, it also has the power to enforce its decision.

In short, the general authority relationship which Merle Fainsod found existing between the Smolensk *obkom* and the oblast soviet in the 1930s is that which the Soviet leaders intend to prevail generally between a local Party organ and a state administrator within its territory. In this respect there has been very little if any change in three decades.

Indeed, as early as 1923 we find Stalin noting with the greatest approval and encouragement that "the *guberniia* [Party] committees have got into their stride, they have taken up construction work in earnest, they have put the local budgets in order, they have taken control of local economic development, they have really managed to take the lead in the entire economic and political life of their *guberniias*." As the 1940 and 1953 *Pravda* editorials which we have quoted indicate, the mandate of the local Party organs to lead and direct the work of their area's administrators was not abandoned in the last years of the Stalin period.

But to say that the conception of the Party-state relationship at this level has been relatively stable is not to say that the influence of the local Party organs on Soviet decision-making has remained unchanged. When middle-level industrial administrators were moved into the region with the creation of the *sovnarkhozy*, the local Party organs (especially the *obkomy*) were obviously in a position to influence their decisions far more than when they worked in the ministries in Moscow. On the other hand, when the amalgamation of the economic regions raised the *sovnarkhozy* above the oblast level, the principles defining the Party-state relationship dictated a significant reduction in the influence of the *obkom* on *sovnarkhoz* decisions.

Many other factors vary the influence of the local Party organs. When, as in the case of the Smolensk committee in the 1930s, the Party officials in an area were judged primarily on the basis of the performance of one sector of the economy of the region (in the Smolensk case, flax production), the influence of the Party officials might be quite selective as they concentrated their attention upon the particular administrators in charge of that key sector. When, as in the Saratov oblast in 1959, the Party leadership removes from the first secretaryship an old-line Party official with long experience in agricultural regions and replaces him with a former factory director who has been in industrial management until the age of forty, the supervision over both agriculture and industry takes on a different character (in fact, in the Saratov case that was precisely the result looked for). And, finally, when the secret police became a less feared instrument after the death of Stalin, the local Party organs were clearly able to establish a real superior-subordinate relationship, which had been psychologically difficult to achieve earlier.

Yet, for this discussion, the important point is that (except in the role assigned to the Party committee of the kolkhoz-sovkhoz administration) the Party leadership has changed the influence of the local Party organs not by redefining the basic Party-state relationships but by changing the technical qualifications of Party officials, the relative priority of plan fulfillment in different sectors of the economy, the territorial level at which administrators are located; by dividing the Party into industrial and agricultural components to allow Party officials more time for each branch; or, most recently, by reuniting it.

The Rationale of the Party-State Relationship

We have seen that officials of the lower Party apparatus have been assigned rather substantial responsibilities in decision-making. Now we turn to an examination of the rationale for this policy of the Soviet leadership.

Unquestionably one of the major reasons has been a desire to strengthen the political control of the leadership. During the early Soviet period the state administration was, in Trotsky's words, "a cell of world counterrevolutionaries, a durable, solid economic nucleus which fights us with weapons in its hands." Even when the administration became increasingly staffed by Party members, the leadership recognized the political dangers of a simple chain of command with only one line of communication open to the center. Under such a " 'simplified' apparatus," Stalin feared, "the ruler, in governing the country, receives the kind of information that can be received from governors and comforts himself with the hope that he is governing honestly and well. Presently, friction arises, friction grows into conflict, and conflicts into revolts."

The desire for political control seems, however, an insufficient expla-

nation for the degree and type of Party participation in decision-making—particularly for the continuation of this scale of participation in recent decades. Given the progresive sovietization of the administrative elite, the development of other lines of communication upward, and the concentration of attention on industrialization, education, science, and public health, the Soviet leadership would certainly long ago have restricted or redefined the supervisory and control functions of the Party apparatus if they had seriously hindered the achievement of the programmatic goals. We submit that the Party organs have continued to be assigned these functions (indeed, in practice, to have their involvement deepened and intensified by the increasing appointment of technically qualified personnel to Party posts) because the Party leadership has found that their presence in the decision-making process helps to resolve several important problems inherent in very large organizations.

One such problem is the persistent inability of administrators to obtain all the information they need in order to make intelligent decisions. Few questions are so widely discussed in American administrative theory as that of difficulty faced by administrators in receiving a proper "feedback" of information from lower levels and of the continual necessity for them to make decisions with insufficient information. The Party organs facilitate the flow upward not only of information useful for political control but also of information which will contribute to optimal decisions from a rational-technical point of view.

The primary Party organization is particularly useful in ensuring that more information does flow to those who need it. The higher Party officials receive from the institutions and enterprises independent reports filled with criticism and self-criticism and are also able to participate in the resolution of disputed issues that are likely to provoke major disagreement between the director and the Party secretary. Moreover, the existence of the primary Party organization guarantees that the director (and the secretary) will be provided with a steady stream of information about conditions and trouble spots at lower echelons of the enterprise and will receive alternative suggestions for action.

The local Party organs serve both as a continuation of the line of communication upward and as an important independent source of information. As the local Party organs are the only institutions in the territorial subdivisions responsible for all aspects of life within them, they alone have the proper perspective to point out regional disparities and strains and to speak out for integrated regional development. The very localism that interferes with the performance of the local Party organs as a nationally attuned control instrument is quite functional from the point of view of information flow.

A second problem of large-scale organization which helps to explain the functions assigned to the lower Party apparatus is the amount of discretion which in practice tends to accrue to administrative officials at lower and middle levels of the organization. While the Weberian model implies that decisions within a bureaucracy can always be made correctly and predictably by any technically competent official who applies rules determined by higher policy-makers, Western social scientists have long since realized that this is not necessarily the case, particularly in administrative situations (such as are found in industry) in which many decisions are not routine.

In theory the development of a perfect incentive system might provide a set of "rules" which would ensure that the "independent" decisions of the administrators conformed either to the specific preferences of the leaders or to their generalized desire for efficiency and growth. However, such an incentive system is difficult to achieve within a hierarchical order. The establishment of a measure for success may distort decisions, as the administrators come to focus on the indicator rather than the goal behind it, while the existence of many diverse units in a hierarchy (particularly in the Soviet Union, where all organizations are really part of the same hierarchy) make it quite difficult to ensure that the incentives in the different units do not lead to conflicting actions. Even if these obstacles can conceivably be overcome, it is clear in any case that they have not been in the Soviet Union.

The problem of the discretion to be left to lower officials is complicated by the possibility that the training of these officials may not prepare them well for the exercise of discretion. A number of Western authorities have expressed concern about the type of habits and technique a future executive develops in his first, more detailed jobs and about the isolated environment in which he works (Peter Drucker speaks of the environment in the corporation as being that of a monastery). They fear that this environment tends to produce a parochialism and a mechanical attitude toward men that may seriously limit the executive's effectiveness as he rises to posts in which more and more policy-making is involved.

Soviet authorities on the Party-state relationship show a keen awareness of the problems relating to the discretion exercised below the top policy-making levels. All of the discussions about "democratic centralism," "Leninist principles of administration," and the advantages of "collective" decisions continually express concern about the danger of one-sided, arbitrary decisions by administrators. On the surface, at least, the Soviet leadership worries less about these arbitrary decisions involving too much political independence than about the fact that they will not be well thought out and well rounded. The existence of the secretary of the primary Party organization and of specialized officials within the local Party organs increases the probability that at least two men will be considering questions relating to policy, and this, in the opinion of the Soviet leadership, contributes to decisions which are generally sounder from a rational-technical point of view.

Moreover, the involvement of Party officials also ensures that men with wider responsibilities and often with a less specialized background participate in the solution of many of the most important questions. Even in cases in which the Party officials do not have the general, nonspecialized background to start with, their responsibility for political stability and (in the case of the local Party organs) for many sectors of life gives them a perspective which a man who has always been responsible only for plan fulfillment in one specialized hierarchy might not develop.

Indeed, paradoxically, the existence of the Party organs makes it easier for the administrators themselves to develop the breadth of perspective which is needed. For a number of reasons important administrative personnel are selected for membership in the bureaus of the primary Party organizations and in the committees and bureaus of the local Party organs. While they may be chosen largely because of their technical expertise or because of the desire to give them symbolic recognition, the administrators so selected are compelled to become acquainted with many problems outside their narrow professional field. Those who head the most important enterprises and who are named to the bureaus of the local Party organs have an unparalleled opportunity to observe the interplay of all administrative and social forces within the local area.

It cannot be said with any certainty that the involvement of the Party organs in policy-making does contribute to sounder decisions from a rational-technical point of view. It is interesting to note, however, that Arthur M. Schlesinger, Jr., has suggested that the decisions of the Roosevelt administration were more creative because of the conflicts between men who had been given responsibility for much the same policy realm. It is interesting to read the proposal by Harold W. Dodds that the president of a large college or university should have "a different kind of personal staff officer, one who is fitted by temperament and experience to share his thinking at the highest levels at which he operates ... one person who will not be troubled, dominated, or compromised by operating responsibilities ... [who] may discover trouble brewing of which the president otherwise might not be aware until it explodes ... [who] can render an invaluable service by telling the president when he is wrong ... [and] can serve as a watchdog to see that his chief is not neglecting major matters because of other pressures." It is interesting to note that in American industry the existence of an active chairman of the board in addition to the corporation president is often justified in language very similar to that used by Dodds.

A third major problem of large-scale organization alleviated by the Party organs is the need for regional coordination, particularly the need for the resolution of conflicts among different administrators in the region. While this problem may not be great in a very specialized organization, it becomes much more serious in any organization with a number of divisions, each of which has subordinates interacting in a particular region (the WPA would be a prime American example). The disparities in plans, directives, and regulations which we discussed in the last section demand adjustment, and the only apparent means is through the creation of a regional coordinator, whatever the effect may be on the neatness of the organization chart. This, in fact, has been the solution chosen in such organizations as the WPA.

In the Soviet Union the executive committees of the local soviets are able to serve as a regional coordinator to some extent, but many key officials —including most of those in industry, construction, and transportation as well as all those in the "public organizations," for example, the trade-union and the Komsomol—are not in any way subordinated to the oblast, city, or raion soviets. Consequently, two officials or organizations which come into conflict will often have no common governmental superior below the republic or even the all-Union level to which they can take their problem (in fact, if an official of a "public organization" is involved, there is no common governmental superior at all). Even when there is a common superior at the next hierarchial level, it may be inconvenient to take a problem to him because (as in the case of two factories subordinated to the *sovnarkhoz*) the superior may be miles away and too preoccupied to be conconcerned with some relatively minor question.

It would be possible to create governmental super-coordinators to fill this gap in the administrative structure (perhaps by widening the responsibilities of the local soviets). In fact, the present practice of subordinating construction to an administrative hierarchy separate from both the soviets and the *sovnarkhoz* requires such detailed and intensive Party coordination of construction activities that some type of reorganization in this realm may be considered.

However, while general regional coordination could be assigned to a governmental body, the local Party organs are in many ways especially well adapted to perform this function. It is interesting to note that the "broker" function is often the responsibility of a political party, and there are a number of reasons why this occurs in the Soviet Union as well. Part of the answer, no doubt, is found in the type of persons who are likely to be attracted to political work. Moreover, while any regional super-coordinator held responsible for the plans of all phases of life in the area would be compelled to develop great sensitivity to the scale of priorities set up by the leadership, the political organ is far better able to take the demands of political stability into consideration in evaluating the relative priority of the factors involved in a particular case.

Another advantage of the local Party organs is their ability to operate with a degree of flexibility that a governmental super-coordinator would find hard to match. It is difficult to imagine precisely how the powers of a governmental super-coordinator would be defined in legal terms. Would the factories, stores, schools, and so on, be subordinated to all of the coordinators at the various territorial levels? If so, would not the legal statutes be extremely complicated? If not, could one coordinator solve the problems which arise at the different territorial levels? The rules of subordination found in the Party principle of democratic centralism are sufficiently generalized so that the duties and powers of the local Party organs can be defined flexibly by instructions and by custom.

The powers of a governmental coordinator in relation to the "public organizations" would be especially difficult to define. Whatever their democratic mythology, these organizations are an integral part of the administrative system and serve a number of useful functions. They interact with the officially recognized governmental administrators, and there must be some effective way of ensuring that this interaction is relatively smooth and that conflicts are resolved along lines corresponding to the leadership's priorities. Yet, if they are to remain "nongovernmental" agencies, it would seem crucial to subordinate them informally to another nongovernmental organization such as the Party rather than directly and explicitly to the government.

A final advantage derived from using the local Party organs as the regional super-coordinator—and probably the most important advantage—is the special mystique which they possess as being part of the ruling party. Just as the position of the President of the United States is en-

hanced by the fact that the possesses the aura of the chief of state, so the regional coordinator in the Soviet Union has stronger position and may be able to resolve conflicts with greater ease because he can speak as "the Party." This is particularly important because, as James Fesler has pointed out, the area coordinator is inherently likely to be in the weaker position than the functional hierarchies in the type of dual subordination found in the Soviet Union.

In this concluding section we have explained the role of the local Party organs and the primary Party organizations largely as a response to real problems of very large organizations. While this response may not have been a completely conscious one, we have suggested that the role of the Party organs in decision-making would have been modified had it not been at least partially conducive to the smooth operation of the administrative system and the fulfillment of rational-technical goals.

We have not meant to suggest that there are no costs for the use of the Party organs in decision-making. There is an increase in staff involved and a resulting drain of trained personnel from other work. Moreover, as Stalin admitted, the deviation from a simple line of command "will complicate the work of administration." There are additional conferences, additional conflicts, additional need for clearance.

Yet the costs can be overemphasized. While the lines of authority and influence become rather complex, there is little evidence that the complexity "destroys all sense of responsibility and competence." From the outside the organization chart may appear almost hopelessly confused with its interlocking Party and state hierarchies, but from below (that is, from the point of view of the lower administrator) it is much clearer. When one explores this matter with plant managers, for example, it is obvious that they know the relative standing of the different officials and they have a good idea as to how important a question must be and what type it must be before it is taken to a particular governmental or Party official. Moreover, they insist that basically there is order within the enterprise itself—that the Party secretary is usually consulted regularly and that he and the manager are normally able to find a common language without referring questions upward.

This evidence is scarcely conclusive, but it remains true that, whatever the possibilities of chaos, the administrative system in the Soviet Union does function and has functioned for many years. If we are to judge by such indicators as industrial growth, development of education and science, and progress in public health, the administrative system has functioned reason-ably well, and at the least it has produced results in the areas of priority.

It may be that the attempt to supervise all phases of life directly within the framework of a single hierarchical system will ultimately prove impractical as society becomes more complex. Perhaps the system will have to be abandoned in favor of one in which the bureaucracies are more autonomous and are controlled by more indirect ways (such as through the manipulation of the price system). Yet, *once* the leadership has decided to create a unified bureaucratic society, it is difficult to avoid the conclusion that the advantages of Party participation outweigh the costs, for some of the functions the Party organs fulfill seem absolutely required in such a unified system. If for some reason the Soviet leadership decides to restrict the lower Party organs to ideological work, it would seem certain that they will have to create other institutions to carry out at least some of their responsibilities.

SOVIET LOCAL GOVERNMENT TODAY

L. G. CHURCHWARD

From September 1964 until May 1965 I enjoyed a sabbatical leave in Europe. I spent several months in Britain studying various problems of Soviet politics, in particular local government. I spent a week in Moscow in September 1964 and a further three months in the USSR from 9 February to 8 May. Apart from a week spent in Leningrad late in April, I was in Moscow for the whole of this period. I was a guest of the USSR Academy of Sciences and was attached to the Institute of State and Law, Moscow. During my stay in the Soviet Union I made a survey of the elections to the local Soviets (14 and 21 March) and also investigated other aspects of local government. I

Soviet Studies, XVII, No. 4 (April 1966), 431–52. Reprinted by permission. Footnotes omitted.

had discussions with many academics and local Soviet officials, attended various election meetings, investigated the work of various electoral agencies and observed the voting in two Moscow electorates. I was also able to extend my reading of Soviet newspapers, periodicals, pamphlets and books. The report which follows represents a summary of my findings on the present situation in Soviet local government. It does not provide a general picture of Soviet local government such as I attempted in an earlier article in *Soviet Studies* (January 1958). At the most, it provides some material on a limited number of problems of Soviet local government and certain personal evaluations of recent changes.

1. Factors of Change in Soviet Local Government

Local government is never static. It changes in response to a variety of factors. The first factor producing changes in the structure of Soviet local government is that of long-term economic and social development. Gradual but fundamental social changes, such as urbanization, industrialization, the settlement of new areas, and even the enlargement of the size of agricultural units, produce adjustments in the local administrative structure. Such changes, as far as local government structure is concerned, are 'objective developments', although in a larger context they might be regarded as a consequence of the remoulding of the economic environment on the basis of conscious political decisions. Thus continued urbanization results in a steady increase in the number of urban-type settlement Soviets and town Soviets. Thus 170 new town Soviets were established over the years 1955–60. The

settlement of new areas produces new local government units, especially village Soviets. Thus, 1,220 new village Soviets were established over the years 1955–60, mainly in the virgin lands areas of southern Siberia and northern Kazakhstan. The consolidation of collective farms prompted the reduction in the number of village Soviets. Thus 10,396 village Soviets were abolished over the years 1955–60.

Secondly, administrative theory on such things as the optimum size of various units of local government, rationalization, administrative costs, etc., clearly prompts a tailoring of the administrative structure. The effect of administrative theories on administrative structure is most noticeable in recent years at the raion level, but it has also influenced reorganization at the level of village Soviets and oblast Soviets. In consequence, the number of rural district Soviets fell from 4,418 to 3,433 between 1 January 1955 and 1 July 1961. The number of raion Soviets in cities fell from 511 to 337 over the same period, while the number of oblasts fell from 144 to 108.

A third factor producing alterations in the Soviet administrative structure is that of political ideology. Thus an important booster to certain trends in local Soviets since 1961 was the new evaluation of the role of local Soviets made at the XXII party congress. While earlier congresses and Central Committee meetings had stressed the connection between the increase in the powers and activities of local Soviets and the development of communist self-government (*samoupravlenie*), the XXII congress brought this to a new theoretical level by coining the concept of 'the state of the whole people' (*obshchenarodnoe gosudarstvo*). The XXII congress also stressed the expanding role of public organizations (*obshchestvennye organizatsii*) in local Soviets and declared that they held the key to the eventual withering away of the state under communism.

A fourth factor producing changes in the structure of local government is the alteration of the structure of the Communist party. Because of the underlying principle of the parallelism of party and state structures, any adjustment of one structure means a readjustment of the other. This applies irrespective of whether the modification is first introduced into the state or into the party structure. Thus in 1953–54 the relations between the two state agencies, the raiispolkom (Executive Committee of the district Soviet) and the Machine Tractor Station were changed. The agricultural departments of raion Soviets were liquidated and their functions transferred to the MTS. This led (February 1954) to the regrouping of the raikom instructors on the basis of the Machine Tractor Stations instead of on a zonal basis. The establishment of kolkhoz-sovkhoz administrative boards in March-April 1962 covering a wider area than the existing rural raions produced strains on both Soviet and party administrative structures. The November 1962 Central Committee meeting decided not merely to enlarge the area of party committees in rural areas but to establish a separate agricultural party organization. Soviet organization had to fall in line. More recently, the restoration of a single party structure (November 1964) was matched by the restoration of a single Soviet structure.

Fifthly, purely subjective factors, in the shape of the personal preferences of the party leader or leaders, clearly affect the shape of the state structure. Unlike Stalin, Khrushchev was an innovator, an experimentalist as far as administrative arrangements were concerned. Thus he sponsored five reorganizations in the rural administrative structure between September 1953 and the end of 1962. Only the last of these represented a really fundamental change. It was a fundamental change for the following reasons. Unlike the changes of September 1953, July 1958, 1961 and March 1962, it involved a major disturbance to more than one administrative level. It was not confined to the raion level but affected the oblast and krai level. Unlike earlier reorganizations it involved a virtual abandonment of the basic principle of territorial Soviets, hierarchically organized. Before this, while there had been some overlapping of Soviets (as in cases where a district town was simultaneously the centre for a raion Soviet and a town Soviet), there was only one oblast Soviet, to which all Soviets on its territory were subordinated. From the end of 1962 until the end of 1964 there were separate industrial and rural Soviets in two-thirds of the oblasts and territories and separate Soviets right down to the first level of Soviets. This resulted in a good deal of administrative confusion as subordinate Soviets were hastily detached from their customary supervisor and reallocated to a new one. The difficulty of keeping the new party and state structures strictly parallel added to the confusion. Finally, the November 1962 reorganization resulted in a reduction of the powers of the oblast (regional) leaders, both party and state. While some benefited by the promotions involved in the enlarged provincial party and state structures, the more entrenched leaders suffered a reduction of their powers. Whereas Khrushchev's industrial reorganization of

May 1957 had secured strong support from the provincial leaders, his November 1962 reorganization tended to lose him that support. This, amongst other factors, turned the pro-Khrushchev majority of June 1957 into an anti-Khrushchev majority in October 1964.

2. The Structure of Local Soviets, November 1962–March 1965

The decision of November 1962 did not refer explicitly to the reorganization of the local Soviet structure, although Khrushchev had recommended this in his report to the Central Committee. As applied to local Soviets the decision meant the establishment of separate provincial and territorial Soviets wherever separate party committees were established. By early 1963, separate Soviets had been established in 70 out of 104 provinces and in 5 out of 9 territories. Consolidated Soviets survived in 4 territories and 34 provinces and in all 8 autonomous provinces.

The 1962 reorganization was quickly abandoned. A month after Khrushchev's removal the Central Committee decided on the restoration of the traditional united party and state administrative structures. An *Izvestiya* editorial of 19 November 1964 summarized the experiment of 1962 in these words:

The division of party, Soviet, trade union and komsomol organs greatly complicated their work, gave rise to countless difficulties, resulted in a confusion of functions in the localities, limited the possibilities of rendering efficient help to the village from the side of the industrial cities, and created distinct inconveniences for the population. The administrative apparatus during the last two years did not become

either simpler or more economical, but, on the contrary, inflated. Because of this, the raion link was noticeably weakened. In short, the reorganization not only did not bring the desired results, but in relation to the most important parts of economic construction it led to the weakening of the influence of party organs in production activities.

Even before the removal of Khrushchev some criticisms of the consequences of the 1962 reorganization had appeared. In the two months that followed the November 1964 Central Committee meeting a considerable volume of specific criticism appeared in various newspapers and journals. The reorganization was hastily conceived and recklessly implemented. Apparently the suggestion was first put to Khrushchev in September 1962 and it met with his enthusiastic acceptance before the full implications of the scheme had been examined. The decision of the November 1962 plenum was implemented within six weeks, the new divided provinces and territories being proclaimed on 26 December in Russia, 29 December in Uzbekistan, and 30 December in the Ukraine, Belorussia and Kazakhstan. Whether because of the speed of the reorganization or because of other reasons, some anomalies resulted, especially in the relationship between party and state structures at the lower levels. In most cases, however, the provincial party authorities followed the guiding principle of the reorganization quite faithfully and agricultural oblast Soviets were left in control of only local industry concerned with the processing of agricultural products.

Some anomalies have already been reported. Other consequences of the reorganization were more widespread.

Thus the reorganization of the party structure, which was directed towards making party organs more effective agencies for leading and controlling economic agencies, increased the tendency of party organs to usurp the administrative functions of economic agencies. Many examples of such interference were quoted in *Partiinaya zhizn'*, 1964, no. 19. The journal accused many party committtees, especially those based on the kolkhoz-sovkhoz production administrations, of 'petty guardianship' which resulted in the 'freezing of the initiative' of Soviet and economic cadres and weakened their work. As the editorial in *Kommunist*, 1964, no. 16 recognized:

The production principle of constructing party organizations, as experience proved, led objectively also to confusion of functions, powers and responsibilities of party, Soviet and economic organs, forced party committees to substitute for economic organizations, gave rise to parallelism and duplication of leadership.

Apart from unnecessarily complicating party-state relations, the new organization produced many new problems for the local Soviets themselves. The weakening of the district apparatus was frequently commented on during November-December 1964. There can be little doubt that this took place on a wide scale. The new districts were on the average more than twice as large as those they replaced. Not only did many district centres suddenly cease to exist, but people now had to undertake much longer journeys (sometimes 100 kilometres or more) to reach the district officials, and district officials found it difficult to supervise agencies in the remote parts of their district. The problem was complicated by the sudden reduction of staff in the party and state apparatus. This was only partly offset by the quick expansion of nonstaff departments and inspectorates.

The division of the Soviet structure at the province level complicated relations between the Soviets and the sovnarkhozes. The reduction in the number of economic regions at the end of 1962 ended the situation in which the boundaries of most provinces and territories coincided exactly with the boundaries of an economic region. Henceforth each region covered two or more provinces and each sovnarkhoz had to work through three to five Soviets. Thus the Lower Volga Sovnarkhoz had to coordinate the economic plans of the Volgograd Agricultural Oblast Soviet, the Volgograd Industrial Oblast Soviet, the Kalmyk ASSR Supreme Soviet, and the Astrakhan Oblast Soviet. This region established various coordinating agencies, including a Coordinating Council of the Sovnarkhoz on which the chairmen of all four Soviets sat. Despite this, cooperation was often faulty and there were frequent complaints from deputies that sovnarkhoz enterprises were not meeting their obligations to supply local trading establishments with consumer goods.

The division of Soviets produced another administrative problem. With the division taking place along economic lines there was the problem of what to do with non-economic fields such as police, health, and education. Various arrangements were made here, some very ingenious but none really satisfactory. These included the establishment of duplicate departments for some of the existing oblast departments but not for others. Thus in the Perm oblast each oblispolkom was to have a planning commission and departments of finance, education, municipal economy, services, social security, culture, building and architecture, and a general department. In addition, the industrial oblispolkom was to control boards of trade, supplies and sales, communications, defence of public order and departments of health, archives, the oblast court and procuracy, the oblast committee on radio and television, the oblast statistical board, etc. which were to operate over the entire oblast, rural and urban. On the other hand, special departments of the agricultural oblispolkom such as the board of production and requisitioning of agricultural products were to be confined to the rural population. In some cases joint departments responsible to both executive committees were established. Joint sessions of agricultural and industrial province Soviets were sometimes convened to discuss common oblast matters such as public health. Joint sessions of Soviets were also held in December 1964 to discuss the economic plan and the re-amalgamation of Soviets.

It is probable that the experiment with divided Soviets produced some good results, at least in certain areas. Certainly many local leaders reported during 1963 and early 1964 that the work of local Soviets in the fields of social and municipal services, trade, and control of some economic enterprises, had improved, and such improvements were often linked to the new administrative structure. It is also probable that the sudden reduction in the size of the district apparatus accelerated the use of non-staff persons and public organizations in the work of local government.

The decision to abandon the 'so-called production principle' and the return to the 'territorial-production principle' of organizing party and state structures was taken on 16 November 1964, a month after the dismissal of Khrushchev. The decision promised a restoration of a single party and Soviet organization for each province and territory, the restoration of the traditional rural district (and with it the traditional district authorities of raikom and raiispolkom) and the abolition of the industrial districts. Regional party conferences were announced for December 1964 for the election of new regional committees, and the Presidium of the CC was directed to prepare plans for the reuniting of party and Soviet organs in the provinces and territories.

Party leadership was evidenced at all levels in the reorganization. Thus the Central Committee of the CP of the Ukraine met on 8 January 1965 and decided on the breaking-up (*razukrupnenie*) of the large rural districts established in 1962. Details for the administrative structure in each province and territory were worked out in party conferences and in joint sessions of Soviets in each province or territory where the administrations were divided. Usually the report to the joint session was given by the first secretary of the newly restored consolidated obkom. These sessions took place in December 1964. In January 1965 the Presidiums of the Supreme Soviets of the Union Republics approved the new administrative arrangements. The speed of the reconstruction was undoubtedly influenced by the fact that local Soviet elections were due in March 1965 and the new boundaries had to be completed by mid-January. Because of this haste it is certain that some decisions will be reconsidered and further adjustments made in the future.

What exactly was restored by the decisions of December 1964 and January 1965? The first achievement was the restoration of united Soviets at all levels. Secondly, industrial district Soviets disappeared. Thirdly, the rural district was re-established with an average size intermediate between that of the rural district of pre-November 1962 and post-November 1962. Thus the number of rural districts increased from 1,711 (April 1963) to 2,544 (March 1965), but this was still well below the November 1962 figure of 3,421. Fourthly, while many of the smaller towns and settlements were restored to district Soviet supervision, this did not happen in all cases. Larger towns tended to keep the 'status position' they had secured in December 1962. Thus in the Russian Republic only 40 towns out of about 140 which came under province and autonomous republic supervision at the end of 1962 were restored to district supervision in January 1965. In some provinces the number of towns of province subordination actually increased with the reorganization of January 1965. Thus in Chelyabinsk oblast the number of towns of this category increased from 17 to 18. No special changes were required to the pattern of village and settlement Soviets. There were 39,623 village Soviets and 3,252 settlement Soviets in March 1965, as against 39,898 and 3,255 respectively in April 1963. The number of territories was reduced to seven by the liquidation of two territories in Kazakhstan. The number of districts within cities rose from 384 in April 1963 to 398 in March 1965. In all, there were 47,736 local Soviets in March 1965 compared with 47,339 in April 1963.

3. Local Soviets and Social Organizations

Social or public organizations (*obshchestvennye organizatsii*) have always played a large part in the work of local Soviets. The XXII congress merely added emphasis to this established role and gave it a new theoretical basis by a more careful formulation of the theory of the transformation of the state in the transition from socialism to communism.

As socialist statehood develops, it will gradually become communist self-government of the people which will embrace the Soviets, trade unions, cooperatives, and other mass organizations of the people. This process will represent a still greater development of democracy, ensuring the active participation of all members of society in the management of public affairs. Public functions similar to those performed by the state today in the sphere of economic and cultural management will be preserved under communism and will be modified and perfected as society develops. But the character of the functions and ways in which they are carried out will be different from those under socialism. The bodies in charge of planning, accounting, economic management, now governmental bodies, will lose their political character and will become organs of public self-government. Communist society will be a highly organized community of working men. Universally recognized rules of the communist way of life will be established whose observance will become an organic need and habit with everyone.

While few western writers have attempted to assess the role of social organizations in Soviet local government, there is a vast and growing literature on this subject in the Soviet Union. It is not my intention here to duplicate what has already been covered by others. I want only to consider a few aspects of this development. Firstly, how extensive are social organizations and how many are involved in their work? The general figure of 23 millions involved directly or indirectly in local government work has been given several times in recent years. More detailed statistics have sometimes been given for the USSR as a whole, for individual republics or for particular provinces or cities. Thus a recent handbook, *Sotsializm i narodovlastie* (Moscow, 1965), p. 88, gives the following statistics for the Russian Republic (see Table below).

Many recent local lists suggest that up to one in five of the adult population is engaged in local Soviet work. Thus Orlov oblast claimed that it had 9,800 social organizations functioning in 1962 with 86,000 persons engaged. Belgorod oblast claimed 13,360 organizations in 1964 with 116,000 persons participating, while Novgorod oblast claimed 7,323 social organizations with 56,000 persons participating. Many of these organizations have only a paper existence and others operate spasmodically. However, my general impression of social organizations, especially in the larger cities, is that they are a pretty effective means of spreading the burden of local government.

A second question that arises is that of the rate and direction of their expansion. That an important expansion has occurred since 1959 is clear enough. Volunteer Militia squads and Comradely Courts, which today occupy more than 40% of volunteers in all social organizations, have mainly developed since that date. It is probable that the rate of expansion of social organizations, especially in the rural

Data on social organizations in the RSFSR (1964)

Type of Organization	Number of Organizations	Number of Members
Street and house committees	170,346	919,722
Parents' Committees in schools, kindergartens, creches and flats	172,388	1,138,507
Councils in Medical Institutions	10,600	127,451
Councils of Clubs and Libraries	64,549	454,524
Councils for assisting the improvement of living conditions	7,174	99,537
Women's Councils	32,607	297,904
Pensioners' Councils	9,531	194,479
Volunteer Fire Brigades	38,072	707,269
Volunteer Militia	85,182	3,351,078
Comradely Courts	112,372	693,434
Commissions on Control of socialist property	3,391	25,688
Technical-Production Councils in enterprises, state and collective farms	12,201	164,030
Councils of kolkhoz brigades	16,554	95,947
Shop and Restaurant Commissions	107,402	386,282
Councils of Elders	1,151	13,487
Sanitary posts and brigades	90,811	485,423
Pensioners' Commissions in establishments and enterprises	2,498	16,535
Other organizations	29,583	571,075
Total	966,412	9,774,372*

* [The figures add up to 9,742,372. The discrepancy is in the original. ED.]

regions, was accelerated during the years of divided Soviets. If this was so, it resulted not so much from the division of Soviets as from the emphasis in the November 1962 decision on Soviets doing more in the fields of welfare and social services and that they do this on a reduced staff. Consequently there was an impressive extension of non-staff departments and inspectorates in these years. Thus there were 9,166 non-staff departments in local Soviets functioning throughout the USSR at the beginning of 1964 on which 98,518 persons served. In the Russian Republic there were 5,901 non-staff departments of local Soviets in which 64,497 persons worked. In addition here were 23,662 non-staff Vice-Chairmen of Executive Committees of local Soviets, 10,745 non-staff inspectors of Executive Committees, 84,734 non-staff inspectors of departments of local Soviets, and 930,012 social inspectors and agents working under the control of Executive Committees of local Soviets.

Has this development resulted in a reduction in the size of the administrative appartus of local government? The answer is clearly in the affirmative although no overall figures seem to be available. What figures are available, however, do suggest a further reduction of the apparatus of local government during 1959–64. Thus the number of persons employed in the apparatus of local government in the Buryat ASSR fell from 2,009 in 1960 to 1,680 in 1962. The replacement of paid staff by non-staff personnel has proceeded most rapidly in local departments of trade, housing services, education, health, culture, and organization-instruction. Thus in the Kirov district of Rostov-on-Don there is only one paid instructor concerned with

mass-organizational work, but there are ten public instructors. In the organizational-instructional department of Rostov City Soviet there are only four paid workers as against thirty unpaid social inspectors. As early as 1961 there were over forty non-staff departments and inspectorates operating under the Executive Committee of the Leningrad City Soviet. The Frunze raion (Moscow city) has only fifty staff personnel. Six out of twelve Executive Committee members are non-staff persons. Three departments of the Executive Committee (Culture, Social Security and Housing Services) have non-staff heads. There are about 300 non-staff persons working either in departments of the Executive Committee or in inspectorates controlled by it.

Non-staff departments have all the powers of staff departments. As one writer rather laconically put it:

The work of non-staff departments differs from that of staff departments only in that it is done in spare time and without pay.

They are staffed predominantly by pensioners, including retired civil servants. In view of this it is difficult to accept at face value the claim that:

Non-staff organs are schools of training workers in the art of administering state affairs, of educating them to the feel of lofty public duty.

A third problem of the recent extension of social organizations in local government is that of their location within the structure of local government. While the Party Programme clearly envisages the Standing Commissions of the local Soviets as the key organs in this extension of mass participation and control over administration, the most impressive developments have been in the direction of transferring administrative functions to non-staff departments and commissions. Such agencies are of course directly controlled by the executive committee, although they might be linked to one or another Standing Commission of the local Soviet. An alternative line of development has been to liquidate local departments and to transfer their functions to Standing Commissions. This has happened most often in the fields of culture, trade, health, and education. Soviet authorities are clearly divided in their attitude to this development. While some acclaim it as democratic and in line with the party programme, others abhor it and argue that in involves a confusion of the legally distinct functions of executive committees exercising the executive and administrative functions and the Standing Commissions and the Soviets as being merely advisory and control agencies. If there is any confusion here it is also to be found in the party programme.

It is probable that the transfer of administrative functions to Standing Commissions has progressed more in the case of village, settlement and rural district Soviets than of the large city Soviets. Certainly in Moscow the Executive Committee of Mossovet has firmly directed the expansion of the social organizations. In fact only a minority of deputies in Mossovet actually serve on Standing Commissions. This is because the number of deputies on each of the present seventeen Standing Commissions averages fifteen, but there are 1,104 deputies. The majority of deputies maintain their contact with various social organizations via the deputies' groups in the microraions (sub-division within districts) and not through the Standing

Commissions. Local Soviets have not been consistent in the manner in which they have extended the powers of their Standing Commissions. Thus one Soviet might transfer the functions of a department to a Standing Commission and abolish the department (Leningrad oblast), another might transfer only some functions to the Standing Commission and retain the department (Gorky oblast), another might simply make decisions of Standing Commissions obligatory (Moscow City). As is usually the case with local Soviets, the regulations (*polozhenie*) on standing commissions have not kept up with changes in their functions.

The role of the 'deputies' groups' in local Soviets has already been discussed by Wesson. In the larger cities deputies' groups are organized on the basis of the microraion, a segment of a city district which coincides with a Housing Exploitation Office (Zhek —*Zhilishchnoekspluatatsionnaya kontora*) and also with an educational zone, the children of the microraion all attending the one school. Such a deputies' group would normally consist of 7–11 deputies of district and city Soviets. In other cases deputies' groups are based partly on economic units and partly on electoral sub-divisions. Deputies' groups exercise control over the activities of the Housing Exploitation Office, over trading enterprises, restaurants and cafeterias, over cultural and health agencies in the area. They direct or coordinate the work of social organizations functioning in their area and they make recommendations to the Executive Committee of their Soviets on the allocation of housing space in their area. They are obliged to help the Standing Commissions in their organizational work and to carry out Soviet and party decisions, and to implement the demands of the electors. They do not act as micro-Soviets and they have neither legislative nor administrative powers. The only cases in which they have threatened to usurp the powers of established Soviets are in villages which no longer have a Soviet. In these cases deputies' groups sometimes tend to act as semi-autonomous agencies. This is even more the case in villages where social councils (*obshchestvennye sovety*) or village committees have been established, the members of which are elected by a general meeting of the villagers.

A fourth problem of the expansion of mass organizations in local Soviets is the role of the party. The expansion of social organizations has been largely initiated and directed by the party, a fact which seems to negate the claim that these are voluntary organizations. Party direction is admitted, although the admission are usually couched in very general terms. Still, a careful analysis of recent Soviet press, pamphlet and periodical material does reveal some interesting detail on the means and avenues of party control. Party control of local Soviets continued to be exercised along traditional channels of directives, fractions operating in local Soviets and executive committees, and cadre control. New developments in the field of local government produced some modifications and extensions to the established control network. Party control over volunteer militia squads is acknowledged in the regulations governing the *druzhiny*. The district headquarters of the *druzhiny* are invariably headed by a member of the district party committee, usually the second secretary. The district party committee confirms the membership of the headquarters staff.

Volunteer militia squads are formed in factories and localities under the direct leadership of the party primary, the secretary of which is usually the chief of the militia squad. The staff of the volunteer militia report on their work both to party primaries and to raikoms and gorkoms. Party training and allocation of cadres was stepped up during the reorganization of the Soviet structure at the end of 1962. Most provinces and territories had two-year state-party schools for training cadres for the provincial and local party and state apparatus. While the party controls the main appointments to local Soviets (including the Chairman, Vice-Chairmen and Secretary), the key agency is the organizational-instructional department of the local Soviet. The instructors, amongst other duties, assess the performance of local cadres and recommend promotions or transfers to the Executive Committees of local Soviets.

Party primaries and party groups seem to have increased rapidly during the period of the divided party structure. This expansion was accompanied by an increase in their direction of local Soviets. In many places party fractions operated not merely within the Executive Committees and local Soviets but within Standing Commissions and local government departments. With the emphasis on party supervision of the expanding activities of local Soviets it is not surprising that both during 1962–64 and since there have been rather more than the usual number of complaints that party organs are exceeding their role when they tend to substitute themselves for local Soviets. But it is difficult to see how the situation could be otherwise when the party insists on such detailed supervision of the work of local Soviets.

One final question relating to the role of social organizations in local government is the assessment of their success and importance. With over a million organizations and over ten million persons engaged in them there is obviously a wide range in their achivments. Many organizations function spasmodically and ineffectively. Most operate at a pedestrian level, so that it requires some deeper conviction to accept the claims of Soviet writers that they herald the growth of communist self-government of the future. On the other hand there can be little doubt that public participation in local administration has been steadily expanded over the past decade and that fundamental local matters such as housing allocation and maintenance, expansion of kindergartens and nurseries, allocation of places in boarding schools, health, and social services, are being increasingly controlled by these grass-roots organizations.

4. The Elections to Local Soviets, March 1965

For a number of reasons the elections to local Soviets in March 1965 promised to be unusually interesting. The elections followed close on the abandonment of the experiment of divided industrial and agricultural Soviets. Hence it seemed likely that additional information on this experiment might come out during the election campaign. The elections came shortly after the fall of Khrushchev. Hence national policies might be expected to play a greater role in this year's local government elections than they usually do. Furthermore, the renewed emphasis on collective leadership and strength-ening democratic forms in government that accompanied the removal of Khrushchev might be expected to find some echo in the elections. These at any rate were my expectations when I arrived in Moscow on 9 February to begin my survey of the election campaign. However, I was doomed to disappointment. Although I found plenty to interest me in the elections, they proved unexceptional. Scant reference was made to Khrushchev or to any of his administrative aberrations. National and international politics rarely obtruded into the campaign. There is no evidence that there was any more competition in this campaign than in earlier campaigns. Certainly nothing so rash as a two-candidate ballot was attempted.

The election campaign divided itself fairly naturally into two phases. The first phase (from early January to mid-February) saw the definition of the electorates, the election of the network of electoral commissions, the reporting back to Soviets of Executive Committees and reporting back of deputies to electorates, and the forwarding of candidates by the various collectives entitled to nominate candidates under the electoral law. It also saw the mobilization of agitators, the establishment of agitation points and the early canvassing of the electorates. The second phase of the campaign saw the finalizing of the electoral lists, the formal nomination of candidates by electoral meetings ('meetings of candidates with electors'), the registration of candidates (completed fifteen days before the day of the election), the final canvassing of the electorates and the organization of the poll itself. Press, radio and television publicity continued throughout both phases of the campaign, but became more frequent and more specific as the campaign progressed.

Soviet election campaigns are not, as is often held in the west, merely formal displays designed to produce a facade of democracy and to obscure the Communist party's monopoly of political power. They serve a variety of purposes. In the first place they allow the party and government agencies to bring their past achievements and future plans before the public for criticism, alteration, and endorsement. The reportage and editorial comment on the 1965 elections frequently emphasized this role of elections. The press reported many instances of this advice being followed in practice. Newspaper comment on the nomination of candidates emphasized thorough discussion and the forwarding of really active and conscientious candidates.

Official campaigns in the various localities took their cue from the economic plan for 1965 (adopted by the USSR Supreme Soviet in December 1964) and emphasized additional housing, kindergartens, transport, trading establishments, cultural buildings and social services. Thus the Moscow press frequently noted that over the past two years 6.8 million sq. metres of new housing had been built in Moscow (new housing for 800,000 persons), 554 new department stores and 800 other service agencies opened. Moscow planned 3,540,000 sq. metres of housing for 1965, 25 new polyclinics, 42 schools, 119 kindergartens and nurseries, 210 new department stores, 150 public eating places and 10 new cinemas.

Elections serve to test out the popularity of new plans and to correct deficiencies. Electors' views are canvassed individually by an army of hundreds of thousands of agitators (canvassers) and also through the means of meetings of collectives called for the purpose of nominating candidates, at report-back meetings of retiring deputies, and at the later meetings called to hear the candidates speak and pledge their determination to carry out the mandates (*nakazy*) of the electors. Indeed, not to carry out the mandates of the electors is regarded as a breach of the deputy's duty and is in itself sufficient ground for his recall and replacement, as official comment and electors' letters frequently pointed out during the campaign. Election meetings vary tremendously in size and performance. Some produce no questions and little discussion but others produce lively interjections, suggestions from the floor, and sharp criticism of retiring deputies or of suggested candidates.

Secondly, elections to local Soviets certainly produce massive participation on the part of the electorate. While the number attending election meetings would run into millions, even more people are actively engaged as agitators, members of electoral commissions, and as retiring deputies or candidates for deputy. The total number would perhaps be in excess of twenty million. The agitators are recruited mainly from the party, komsomol and trade union organizations. They operate over several weeks, and their work includes not only going around to work places and home canvassing but also assisting in meetings arranged at various 'agitation points,' red-corners, schools, institutes, etc. They assist the Electoral Commissions by providing a roster to man the electoral office and to help answer the queries of voters. In the Frunze district each agitator had a list of fifty voters whom he visited several times during the campaign and also on election day if it was necessary to remind voters of their civic duty. From discussions I had with various agitators in this district, I formed the impression that they rarely had lengthy discussions with electors on domestic or foreign policy issues, although this sometimes happened. It seems probable that, as was claimed during the election, the agitator's job is more demanding and less a routine matter than it was a decade ago. The number of agitators in the Moscow city area ran into several hundred thousand. Kiev district had 164 agitation points and 20,000 agitators, October district had 7,000 agitators, and Kuibyshev district over 3,000.

The electoral commissions are an elaborate machinery for involving millions of citizens. No doubt the essential duties of the commissions could be handled by some tens of thousands of paid professionals, but the Soviet system every two years provides a two-month course in electoral procedure to millions, an achievement of some public importance. This year 8,751,540 persons served on the electoral commissions required to handle the elections to local Soviets. In Moscow alone there were 2,734 electoral commissions functioning at the ward (*uchastok*) level with 29,173 members, including 13,838 women. Direct representation of the communist party on the electoral commissions is kept low—the rule in Moscow during the last election would seem to be one representative of a party organization for each commission, i.e., 1 out of 7–13 members. Since electoral commissions exist not only at the level of the individual electorates (whether for city Soviet or for district Soviets within the city) but also for voting wards (*uchastki*) within the

electorates, there is an elaborate network of these commissions. They are not neutral in the sense in which electoral offices are expected to be in most parliamentary states, but they are required to assist and further the electoral campaign at all stages. There is no evidence that they ever exclude candidates. In fact the mechanics of the Soviet electoral system is such that there is rarely more than one candidate nominated in any electorate and the role of the electoral commission is merely to record this nomination. Nor is there any evidence that members of the electoral commissions influence the balloting or threaten independent voters. The members of the commissions are far too busy during the polling in checking the credentials of the voters and distributing the necessary papers. Secrecy of ballot is meticulously observed by the commissions, but only about one in fifty voters bothers to enter the screened-off sections of the polling booth. Nobody pays any attention to those that do.

The third important function of Soviet local elections is to elect a new body of citizens to take their turn at work in local Soviets as deputies, as members of executive committees and as members of various standing commissions. Rotational retirement operates in a rudimentary fashion by the requirement (adopted at the XXII congress, 1961) that at least one-third of deputies elected should not have been deputies in the previous Soviet. The elections last March returned 2,010,303 deputies of whom 56.6% had not been deputies in the previous Soviets. Even in the Moscow City Soviet, where experience might be considered to have a premium, 556 deputies (50.36%) out of 1,104 had not been members of the previous Soviet.

Fourthly, Soviet elections do allow the electors to play an important, if carefully circumscribed, part in the choice of their representatives. The mechanics of this system is not fully evident either from press comments during the elections or from descriptions by Soviet experts. Thus one Soviet expert, after claiming that several persons may be put forward within one electorate, states that:

In order that collectives possessing the right to nominate candidates may come to an agreement on a general candidate, practice has developed such a form of consulting opinion as a meeting of representative persons of collectives. At this meeting, not only do they decide on which candidate to put up for balloting in a given electorate, but how to develop the campaign for that candidate.

In fact, the normal procedure is for only one candidate to be nominated for a particular electorate. Some collectives even seem to secure a temporary claim to a particular electorate and provide the candidate in two or more consecutive elections. Such a system has advantages, since it tends to establish regular links between collectives and particular local Soviets, and also reduces the burden on party and state instructors, who do not find new collectives for each electorate in each election. Since there are over two million places to be filled, most, if not all, sizeable collectives will secure the right to nominate to one or more of them. But competition between collectives of the sort suggested by Soviet writers is so rare as to be almost nonexistent. I found no cases to investigate during the recent elections, although I was several times assured that it did happen occasionally. The nearest approach to 'competition' at this level

was in a report of a preselection meeting at the Orlov Stocking Factory (Moscow). The workers' collective recommended one candidate but another candidate was recommended by the chairmen of the social organizations operating within the factory. The latter held that the first candidate could not be spared from the factory for work in Soviets as she had just started a new production process. The meeting eventually decided to support the alternative candidate put forward by the chairmen of the social organizations.

Whatever the degree of competition within the Soviet electoral system in the preselection stage of the campaign, only one candidate is registered and only one candidate's name appears on the ballot paper in each electorate. Official biographies are prepared by the electoral commission and circulated throughout the electorate. Press and radio provide publicity for only a small percentage of the candidates and, of course, there is no such publicity for candidates prior to the preselection meeting at which the candidate is nominated.

As far as the voter is concerned, he has no choice on polling day other than to vote for or against the official candidate by leaving his name on the ballot paper or by deleting it. He is not permitted under the electoral law to write in the name of another candidate. Hence most voters merely check the names on their ballot paper and drop them into the ballot box. As mentioned above, only about one in fifty enters the screened-off booth to delete or otherwise to mark his ballot paper. In the 1965 elections 1,891,400 votes were cast against official candidates, less than 1% of all votes cast. In all Soviets, 208 candidates (187 of them in village Soviets) were defeated. Irregularities occurred in eighteen electorates and elections did not take place in eleven further electorates. Fresh elections were therefore necessary in 237 electorates a fortnight after polling day.

All Soviet elections are carefully regulated and controlled by the Communist party. Not only do all Communist party organizations have the right to nominate candidates, but communists represent a strong core (and sometimes a clear majority) in all nominating agencies. The evidence suggests, however, that many candidates are not sponsored by the Communist party, although few if any are nominated without the approval of the party. Central party organizations decide the social and political (percentage of non-party) composition of the Soviets. Thus the Central Committee clearly decided prior to the 1957 local Soviet elections to increase the percentage of workers in town Soviets, and the carrying out of this decision was reflected in the percentage of workers in town Soviets rising from 27.7% of deputies in 1955 to 45.2% in 1961. In like manner, the percentage of women deputies, non-party deputies and collective farmer deputies has varied according to party policy on what the social composition of Soviets should be. On the other hand, variations as between one republic and another do reflect in a general way variations in economic structure and cultural patterns within the USSR. Thus only 11.1% of Kazakhstan deputies returned in 1965 were collective farmers as against 57.8% of deputies returned in Moldavia. Only 38.3% of Kazakhstan deputies returned in 1965

were women as against 47.0% of Moldavian deputies. The crucial social factor behind each difference is probably the relative strength of state and collective farms in the two republics. At lower levels, district and town party committees, and even party groups, take more specific decisions involving whom to nominate for specific electorates.

5. Conclusions

Soviet local government is changing steadily. It is becoming less official and more 'voluntary', more broadly based and less bureaucratic. If mass participation in the process of government is the key to democratic government then local Soviets have progressed some way towards democratic government. Public participation is greater than it is in most other countries and it is increasingly effective at this local level. But the amount and success of public participation lessens in the higher levels of government. It is generally less at the provincial level than at the district or town Soviet level, and it is less again at the level of the republican Supreme Soviets and the USSR Supreme Soviet. For this and other reasons it is clearly too soon to accept the official Soviet claim that the seeds of communist self-government are to be found in the recent expansion of social organizations. The achievement of communist self-government in the Soviet Union clearly demands other changes besides changes in local government. Not least it requires wider choice in elections and a retreat by the party from its present all-pervasive position in government.

MICROMANAGEMENT, MACROMANAGEMENT,
AND ECONOMIC ACTIVITY

Barry M. Richman

*Management and the Critical
Economic Functions*

In any economy human beings make
the necessary economic decisions and
human beings must carry them out.
Since human beings do not react
by biological instincts, they must somehow be induced to do the right things
at the right time if the critical economic functions are to be carried out in a
manner consistent with economic progress. The effective and efficient performance of the critical economic functions is the task of management in all
its forms.

Management entails the coordination of human effort and material resources toward the achievement of
organizational objectives, as well as the
organization of the productive functions
essential for achieving stated or accepted economic goals. Certain common functions of management must be
performed whether productive enterprises are state or privately owned and
whether resources are allocated through
state planning or through a competitive market price system. Whether and
to what degree self-interest is to be
used in motivating managers is a most
important practical question.

*Micromanagement and
Macromanagement*

In discussing management in any
country it is best to distinguish between
macromanagement and micromanagement. The latter is the management of
individual productive organizations on
the lower operating levels of the economy. In any modern society there are
thousands of productive units which
contribute to and determine over-all
national economic performance. Managers at this level coordinate human
effort and material resources toward
goal achievement in their respective
organizations by the common managerial functions of planning (which
includes decision-making), controlling,
organizing, staffing, and directing. In
any complex productive organization
plans must be established; activities
must be controlled; duties must be assigned; departments must be set up;
authority must be delegated and responsibility exacted; and personnel
must be obtained, trained, appraised,
motivated, supervised, and led. The
administrators of a given organization
must also devote some time to managing external relations with other organizations and persons with whom
they must deal. Moreover, managers
are generally expected to improve
operations and results through innovation where feasible.

On the microlevel are found the
production managers in factories, vice-
presidents of finance, and all other
persons concerned with the management of individual productive organizations, large and small. Such managers may be working in public or
private organizations. A plant super-

Barry Richman, *Soviet Management*, pp. 7–9, 14–20, © 1965. Reprinted by permission
of Prentice-Hall, Inc., Englewood Cliffs, N.J. Footnotes omitted.

intendent and a company sales manager are clearly micromanagers, as is a steel company president—until the one steel company, as is common in some smaller countries, is the only firm in the industry. In Communist countries micro- and macromanagement clearly represents a continuum of control. It is difficult to determine at times where one leaves off and the other begins.

The industrial enterprise is the key focal point of all the critical economic functions in the Soviet Union. Although production is the primary function of the enterprise, it is also involved in research and development and in distribution and financial activities. The enterprise also has a comprehensive statistical and accounting system which provides both its management and the government with pertinent information for decision-making.

Macromanagement denotes the management of an entire economy. In this study macromanagement is defined as that portion of the economic, political, legal, cultural, and social structure of a given country which bears on or influences the activities of micromanagers. Here the problem of interpretation can be quite vexing. In some countries, particularly Communist states, macromanagement is pervasive and detailed. All significant phases of economic activity are regulated through comprehensive national economic plans. In other countries, most typically those considered capitalistic, such management is often by law, tradition, or custom rather than by design. But in either case, the macromanagerial structure imposes various restraints on micromanagers. How well the critical economic functions are performed in a given society depends largely on the macromanagerial rules within which micromanagers must operate.

The U.S. Federal Reserve Board is practicing macromanagement when it alters interest rates; so is the U.S. government when it approves changes in corporate tax rates and antitrust laws. So, for that matter, is a Soviet central planner who makes investment or resource allocations for the steel industry.

Macromanagement is not normally considered management in the sense the word is used in business administration; but in fact it is since it involves decision-making and policy formulation. In the Soviet case it also involves the performance of the other basic managerial functions. The Soviet macromanagerial structure encompasses the entire governmental economic and planning apparatus apart from productive enterprises. Various governmental macroagencies play a significant role in planning, controlling, staffing, directing, and even organizing the activities of the tens of thousands of Soviet industrial enterprises. This is far from the case in privately owned American enterprises.

In general, societies have endless ways of organizing and performing their productive functions. In political terms, the possible range is from laissez-faire capitalism through monolithic totalitarian communism. In every case the over-all macromanagerial structure determines the rules for micromanagers at the operating level. The Soviet macromanagerial structure differs significantly from the typical capitalistic macrostructure. . . .

Economic Organization and the Interaction of Macro- and Micromanagement: U.S.S.R.

Soviet communism came to power on the doctrines of Marx, following his notion of inevitable class conflict—notably the exploitation of labor—in the capitalist system. Marx said little about the future Communist economic system, and what he did say was vague. He did point to state ownership of productive resources and some sort of planned economy as being distinctive features of the future Communist society, but he left no blueprint or operational theory describing how the Communist economic system was to function.

As the Soviet state evolved after 1917, it became clear to the Soviets that state ownership was the basic means by which the pure Communist state could be developed. By the end of the 1920's, the state takeover of all productive assets was well under way, and within a few years all major and most minor material means of production were in state hands. Today the Soviet government either owns outright or decisively controls all non-human factors of production, in agriculture as well as in industry.

The virtually complete state ownership of productive enterprises had the effect of destroying the market price system, since without competition among rival firms there could be no meaningful price competition. This in turn rendered the profit motive impotent as an automatic economic regulator. With the collapse of the competitive market price system, another means for solving the basic economic problems and performing the critical economic functions common to all societies had to be developed. The automatic regulators of economic activity inherent in a capitalist system, however imprecise they may be, were now gone. To date there has been only one known, logically consistent economic system, that of general equilibrium developed by Walras and am-plified by Leontief in his input-output analysis. This system forms the basis for all capitalist and mixed economies.

The method of deciding key economic questions in the Soviet Union—that is, what should be produced, how much, how, for whom, when, where, and the allocation of resources necessary to achieve the production desired—was to be comprehensive national economic planning. Hence, what is done primarily by market forces in the U.S. must be consciously done by bureaucratic action in the U.S.S.R. In such a system there is a fusion of political and economic leadership, and all economic activity tends to be subordinate to the politically motivated decisions of the state. By the state is meant the highest party and governmental bodies in the land, namely, the Central Committee of the Communist Party and the Council of Ministers of the U.S.S.R., which are interlocked at the apex of the economy. At the top of the economy the central planners decide all major economic questions in the light of goals and values set forth by the leaders.

In a capitalist, price system economy, it is implicitly assumed that individual consumers will themselves determine whatever goals they desire, and their expressions, indicated by effective demand, will determine the course of economic activity. On the other hand, a society with specific ideas about the goals of the economy, be they rapid industrialization, growth in military power, or higher living standards, must plan in detail how economic resource allocations are to be made. The leaders must determine their important objectives and plan the economy to meet them.

In such a system long-range economic planning is essentially investment planning, and annual planning is basically production planning. The annual national plan is the operational document for the individual Soviet productive organizations. The planners must decide how to divide production between consumer and producer goods, and the rate of accumulation (savings) necessary for desired future economic expansion must also be determined. Each production target must be limited so that the total of all targets does not exceed the productive power of the nation. The plan must also provide for allocations of economic factors into the necessary sectors in light of national objectives. In other words, the plan must be all-inclusive.

Although Marx never clearly indicated whether he was for or against consumer sovereignty, in this kind of economy it is not possible to have consumers determine the course of production. Such interference would tend to deflect scarce productive resources from other planned uses, thus upsetting the entire plan. Prices in such a system also have little guiding function; rather they are subservient to the plan. Commodity prices are used chiefly for aggregation, control, and evaluation, although retail prices for consumer goods are used as a rather crude device of equating demand with supply (rather than vice versa). At the same time, wage differentials are needed to channel manpower resources into productive sectors in accordance with the requirements of the plan because some occupational choice, as well as a limited amount of labor mobility, is tolerated. Unequal income distribution also serves as an incentive for improving human capabilities and performance.

This type of planned system necessarily requires that central planners make a vast number of ethical decisions which in a free market economy are left to individuals. The stipulated national goals are in themselves value judgments. The volume of consumer goods production has traditionally been dependent on available resources after the resources required to achieve the other aims of the plan are accounted for. National production has been influenced by consumer demand only to a limited degree, and free consumer choice is limited to the goods the government decides to produce for the consuming public. Although the planners are not entirely insensitive to the desires and needs of the population, the planners' preferences do essentially take the place of the consumers' preferences—which implies that the planners know better than the public what is good for them. It was noted above that in a market economy, similar decisions about the propriety of certain commodities are made; but these decisions are regarded as aberrations from the ideal rather than a necessary and critical part of the economic system.

In the planned state, it may be decided at the top that consumers should have more bread and less shoes than they would desire if they had free choice. Or certain highly desired commodities, such as chewing gum, rock-and-roll records, and automobiles, may be produced in negligible quantities or not at all. The setting of basic wage rates for different occupations also involves value judgments. Hence, if the national economic plan is really comprehensive and complete, as it must be to function properly, a very high degree of centralized ethical decision-making is built into the system.

Instead of the apparent chaos of the capitalist economic system, all is in order in the Soviet system—at least on paper. The macrorules for micromanagers, rather than being of the "thou shalt not" variety, are of the "thou shalt" type. In reality, the complexities and problems involved in planning the economic activities of an entire country, such as the Soviet Union, are beyond human imagination. The literally billions of planning decisions that must be made to achieve consistency result in a complex and complete interlocking of macro- and micromanagement. Predetermined tasks and resource allocations, rather than competitive buying and selling, regulate the activities of the myriad interdependent productive organizations on the basis of one comprehensive national plan. The number of planned interconnections called for increases more rapidly than the size of the economy, and since 1953 the Soviet economy has doubled in terms of national production. The job of planning, coordinating, and controlling national economic activity may be mathematically compared to the square of the number of the different commodities produced plus the number of productive units.

A modern industrial society will produce perhaps 20,000 identifiable classes of output (that is, steel, bolts, shoes, radios, and so forth). Each class of output may have dozens of subcategories of products (that is, bolts of various sizes, made of various steels: brass, copper, and so forth). Even with the most sophisticated mathematical techniques and electronic computers, the task of interrelating demands and factor inputs for every possible item by every possible subcategory becomes impossible for the central planners alone. A gargantuan intermediate bureaucratic apparatus is

needed, and the micromanagers themselves are called on to participate in the planning process and to make operating decisions.

The various types of productive organizations in the system are assigned to one or more of the critical economic functions, and their duties are spelled out in considerable detail. The state carefully guides the emergence and development of all productive units and consciously fashions their forms of organization. The result is a degree of homogeneity which is of doubtful pleasure to those who live in the society, but which nevertheless serves to greatly facilitate central planning and control. The American businessman who sets about establishing a new enterprise is limited only by his imagination and by his assessment of the advantages of the different types of opportunities open to him. By contrast, the Soviet administrator authorized to set up a new productive organization, or to manage an existing one, has the basic structure laid out for him in advance.

In the Soviet Union certain types of organizations are charged with the production function, others with distribution or finance, and still others with research and development. In addition certain agencies are charged with collecting detailed accounting and statistical data from all the productive organizations. Such data are crucial for macrodecision-making and control. The macromanagerial apparatus must have at its disposal information on all economic activity if the economy is to function properly.

Productive organizations in the Soviet Union do not deal with each other through mutual consent or free choice, but rather, by higher decree.

Since all economic activities are assigned somewhere in the system, no competition is allowed; the organization which bears the responsibility need not worry about aggressive competition from outsiders. The system is orderly, neat, and horribly complex for the micromanagers charged with carrying out directives from above.

There are about two million separate organizations in the Soviet Union, each one of which has its own plan and objectives subordinate to the national plan. A great many of these organizations are not directly involved in performing critical economic functions, for example, schools, hospitals, libraries, and so on.

Of major concern in this study are the more than 200,000 Soviet industrial enterprises engaged in the production of goods. It was stated previously that the industrial enterprise is the key focal point for all the critical economic functions in the U.S.S.R. It is here that the key economic questions—what to produce, how much of each item, how and when to produce each item, and for whom—are translated into detailed enterprise operating plans in a manner which should be consistent with the national economic plan. The national plan must allocate to each enterprise adequate resources and funds if the desired production is to be forthcoming. It is from the industrial enterprise that goods are distributed to their intended destinations; and it is at the enterprise that new technical processes are introduced and new products are developed and produced. Moreover it is from the enterprise that the government obtains a major portion of the accounting and statistical information necessary for planning, coordinating, and controlling over-all economic activity.

The Soviet manager is not concerned with the survival of his enterprise since, as long as the state wants the enterprise in question to continue functioning, its future is provided for in the national plan. The earning of profits is not a requisite to survival, and 20 per cent of all Soviet industrial enterprises operate at a planned loss.

The state prescribes the ultimate objectives to be pursued by all industrial establishments. Each enterprise is supposed to achieve as great a quantity of production as possible with given resources; or, given certain production targets, they should be achieved with minimum practical resources and costs. The production program is supposed to be carried out in accordance with a predetermined time schedule. Within the over-all output targets and resource limits prescribed by the plan, the detailed product mix, including the quality of output, is supposed to conform to the requirements of customers. A balance between short-run and long-run considerations is also called for so that current decisions and activities should not endanger future operations, but rather, should enhance them and further the future needs of society.

In addition to these ultimate objectives or basic desiderata of enterprise performance, the state prescribes certain policies to be followed for their achievement, for example, the use of the most progressive utilization norms in planning and the constant improvement of technical processes, products, and quality.

Since the ultimate objectives to be pursued by the Soviet enterprise represent a high level of abstraction (in the same way that a profit maximization goal does in an American company), they must be translated into concrete operating terms. A system of interconnected plan indices which constitutes the annual enterprise operating plan, and which is directly linked to the national economic plan, is the device utilized for this purpose. Each Soviet industrial enterprise receives an annual plan having quarterly subdivisions. If the plan is sound, and if the managers do their jobs properly, the result should be the production of the right amount of goods and services, of the right assortment and quality, delivered to the right place at the right time. In theory, the proper design and execution of the plan means that resources are efficiently utilized and that nothing is wasted, since no unneeded excesses or shortages of goods would appear at any point. It is also hoped that enterprise managers would tend to innovate in both products and processes.

Although the micromanagers are narrowly confined by the targets and resource limits prescribed in the plan, their expert knowledge and participation are indispensable to its formulation and execution. It is physically impossible for superior authorities to plan in detail without close consultation with plant executives, or to exert instantaneous effective control over the execution of plans at the vast number of industrial establishments. The men on the spot are in the best position to determine the capabilities and resource needs of their enterprises and to adjust the plan to unforeseeable changing conditions. In addition, enterprise innovation depends greatly on what the micromanagers choose to do or not to do. Those who imagine the Soviet economy to be a pure "totalitarian command economy" in which enterprise managers merely carry out orders have no conception of reality.

Hence, in the absence of a competitive market price system, detailed directives and rules of behavior from above must guide managerial decision-making at Soviet industrial enterprises. Monetary incentives are also used in an attempt to achieve an identity between managerial self-interests and the interests of the state.

Management within the Soviet enterprise is quite similar to management within an American company, particularly an American factory. The same managerial functions are performed in many similar ways. However, the external relations that Soviet micromanagers engage in differ rather dramatically from those of their American counterparts. The capitalist enterprise is related to other organizations only through the market; it buys and sells according to price-cost relations and not to fulfill predetermined quotas; it expands and contracts as profit expectations dictate. In all these actions there is no red tape of the kind with which a Soviet executive must cope. The bureaucratic impediment lies primarily in the external relations of the Soviet industrial enterprise rather than in its internal structure.

The Soviet enterprise administrator is not charged with the major task of achieving desired contributions from other organizations by generating enough inducements to insure their participation. This delicate balancing job is, in the main, done for him. With very few exceptions, the plan prescribes the relationships among productive organizations, the contributions forthcoming from each, and the payments to be made for the contributions rendered. For example, a Kharkov enterprise engaged in the production of ventilation machinery had the following external relationships prescribed from above for 1961: It was to receive

supplies from about 40 other producers; it was to produce goods for
approximately 60 different assigned
customers; it was to deal with 4 research and design institutes on a continual basis, as well as with various
other institutes from time to time; it
was to maintain accounts at 2 state
bank branches; it was to deal with a
number of transportation organizations; and its management was to have
continuous contact with various higher
authorities.

. . . a system of prescribed relationships among productive organizations,
rather than a system based on free
choice and mutual consent, does not
necessarily provide for mutual self-
interest, cooperation, and interdependence.

THE ADMINISTRATIVE INTELLIGENTSIA

ALF EDEEN

Many aspects of Soviet society have
been seriously and thoroughly investigated and analysed in the West. One
important sector seems, however, to
have been somewhat neglected in the
overall assessment of Soviet achievements and strength, namely, the performance of the Soviet administrative
system and personnel, and particularly
its capacity to cope with the growing
diversification and complexity of a
modern industrialised society. This is
rather strange, because there is no lack
of interesting material. On the contrary, in the Soviet press we read daily
about appalling instances of mismanagement and deficiencies—often making the Soviet administration a laugh-
ing stock in both the West and the
East. We usually leave it at that—
adding perhaps that they will muddle
through somehow or that similar instances could be found in any country.

The administrative problem is the
more serious and vital in the Soviet
Union as almost every social activity
is centrally directed and controlled by
an elaborate system of administrative
organs and agencies. Among western
observers the level of efficiency is generally rated very low—with the exception perhaps of military matters and
defence-related activities. Even a cur-.
sory reading of the Soviet professional
reviews indicates that Soviet political
scientists are of the same opinion,
though the 'system' in itself, of course,
is 'best'. A most illuminating example
is to be found in an article published
in 1965 in *Sovetskoe Gosudarstvo i
Pravo*: 'The practical organisation of
the execution of decisions is still the
weakest link in the work of the government administration'. This is certainly
a surprising statement, since to get
things executed seems to be the very
point of having an administrative body
at all.

The problem of administrative efficiency is not a new one—it can be
traced far back in Russian history. But
all the evidence suggests that it is becoming more and more difficult and
complex in the country's new industrial
setting, and certainly has a bearing on
the Soviet capacity for further overall

Survey, No. 65 (October 1967), 61–74. Reprinted by permission.

expansion. To understand the nature of the problem today it is useful to recall some background factors which are particularly relevant to a discussion of the notorious Russian administrative mess.

Development under communist rule provides many important lessons, particularly concerning the effects of forced and rapid social change. The new rulers were probably serious when at the start they thought it would be easy to do away with the old Tsarist establishment and social system. They also appear to have believed that administration was a simple job, to be carried out in the not too distant future by a comparatively small staff of administrative personnel, most of them unpaid volunteers. But despite their ambitious goals and the repressive means adopted in the attempt to attain them, they had to yield to the deeply rooted social and psychological forces of an old agrarian society, governed for centuries by a centralised and swollen bureaucracy.

Many solid reasons can be put forward to show why the communists had to accept both a centralised governmental system and a large staff of administrators in order to build up the new society. The mere size, the diversified geographical and ethnic structure of the country, not to mention external dangers, made some sort of centralised power essential, as the practical experience of centuries had shown. The main instruments to enforce policies were traditionally the military and the police—bodies which by their very nature require centralised command. Moreover, the lack of strategic mobility forced the central government to keep strong standing forces in remote areas. It was vital for the existence of the whole system that

the central government should be able to rely upon and enforce its power through these channels. The civilian local authorities played at best a subsidiary role, and the inadequacy of their personnel, both in number and training, was notorious. These are familiar features of the scene even today —the government system, the status of the local administration, the logistics problem, and the need for large standing forces more particularly on the periphery, and an omnipresent police force for internal security. But there are differences too. One completely new feature, and the most prominent, is the party machine—the supreme channel of command running parallel from top to bottom with the already existing administrations as an extra control of the controls. This important innovation has created a specific *modus operandi* in the Soviet administrative machinery and has given rise to a multitude of new institutional problems and ambiguities.

The heritage from the Tsars is but one factor explaining the propensity to centralisation and bureaucratisation in Soviet society. The communists have themselves made an ample contribution, above all at the ideological level. It is true that the idea of government ownership and active state interference in domestic affairs has a long tradition in Russia. But the socialist or communist basic idea was that the state should control *all* sectors of the society. This was and is looked upon as a *sine qua non* for the successful construction of a new society and a new administrative system. Thus, the communists enthusiastically supported the centralist forces inherent in the old Russian society.

Even more important in this development was the industrialisation drive to achieve in the shortest possible time political, military, and economic independence. The Industrialisation in any country means a radical reallocation of manpower and brings with it especially a sharp increase in the number of administrators, directors, managers, engineers, statisticians, planners, bookkeepers, clerks, and other office personnel. Even before the industrialisation started there was a weighty administrative apparatus, composed of the inherited impressive Tsarist government machinery and of the many new administrative organs required by socialisation. Owing to the traditional lack of reliable statistics it is difficult to make an exact estimate of what industrialisation really meant in employment of new civilian personnel in industry, agriculture, building, trade, banking, and social services. What figures there are suggest a fivefold or sixfold increase within a decade or two.

This rapid expansion of administrative personnel created many problems for the leadership—the problem of their social origin, their education, training, social attitudes, the question of wages versus salaries, differentiation between various categories of salaried personnel, etc. One serious dilemma was the choice between employees with the 'right' background and the 'wrong' background. The surprising fact is that many old *chinovniks* managed to stay in office. Professionally they were certainly the best that could be found in Russia at that time, but their value to the regime from a political and psychological point of view was doubtful indeed. Their attitudes and values were bound to have a strong impact on the new inexperienced civil servants of worker and peasant origin. It is admittedly difficult to pinpoint this asser-

tion, but the fact remains: no matter whether you read a prerevolutionary or post-revolutionary paper—including the most recent—the complaints are invariably the same: inefficiency, red tape, bullying, indifference, not to mention embezzlement and fraud. The artificial and ideological character of the regulations governing wholesale trade makes it almost impossible for honest administrators to act efficiently, and the necessary job is left to so-called *tolkachi*, often very useful agents but of rather dubious character. This is another case in which old Tsarist habits are reinforced by the communist heritage.

These tendencies are bad enough. But the rapid and sharp increase in the number of functionaries in the military and civilian sectors automatically created a fundamental change in the entire social system and its prevailing values. At first almost imperceptibly a process of social stratification opened a widening gap in economic, social, and cultural status both *between* different social groups and *within* each particular social group. But it is worth mentioning that the tendency to social stratification was apparent much earlier. The hard fact was that the regime from the very beginning of its existence was involved in warfare. It had to build up a military organisation. And it is unavoidable—no matter what the ideology— to have commanders of larger or smaller units, which in its turn means a differentiation in rank and for practical reasons in titles and uniforms for different services, reflected in an elaborate system of marks and insignia. Clearly, what happened in the armed forces had a pronounced psychological impact on the entire social and administrative framework of the Soviet

Union, as, indeed, elsewhere in the world. A corresponding development was soon found natural in the foreign service—yet another sign of greater Soviet stability and 'respectability'. This process of greater visible social stratification was given a further stimulus during the second world war, particularly, of course, in the armed forces and the police, and reached its peak in the later forties, when civil servants even in many economic departments not only were classified in a very detailed and precise ranking order, which was the general rule, but also got special uniforms for each branch.

In his mania for secrecy and in his constant resort to administrative reshuffles and reforms, Stalin followed the Russian tradition. It is too easy and superficial to regard these reorganising attempts as no more than manoeuvres on the part of a dictator to stay on top, though of course the element of 'power struggle' was often involved. But at bottom these frequent changes reflected serious maladjustments, imbalances in the whole society and especially in the structure of the administrative system. There was always an obvious and rational objective in these different moves, an effort to deal with equally obvious and acute troubles.

Turning to more recent times—the Khrushchev era—a most remarkable increase in the number of sudden, far-reaching reforms is to be noted. This was certainly not accidental. The abruptness, the dashing to and fro, and the general clamour can be attributed to Khrushchev's personality. But in this period the Soviet Union reached a very critical stage of development; it was making the transition from an agrarian society into a complex, modern industrial society. The planning of the economy—one of the central tasks of the administration—had formerly been comparatively easy. It had centred on the problem of constructing heavy industrial plants—almost anything was an improvement on the earlier state of affairs. With industrial progress and the end of post-war reconstruction, conditions changed. The problem now was to make the right choice between a variety of possible courses: alternative economic policies—high growth rate, rearmament, better living conditions, foreign aid—optimal product mix, investment in new industries such as chemicals, and, finally, concessions to the maltreated ordinary consumer, whose non-planned preferences introduced some confusion into 'scientific planning'. The remedy was seen in decentralisation; in 1957 Khrushchev introduced his own new system for industry and agriculture.

The idea behind the reform was indeed reasonable. The rigid central command and control of the Stalin era, with its comparatively simple economy, was naturally seen as the main obstacle to economic progress in a society where the officially proclaimed goal was to catch up with and surpass the United States in the shortest possible time, while at the same time every increase in overall output not only put a heavy strain on the entire economy but, above all, required extremely careful resource allocation and a smooth operational system between and within all administrative levels down to the individual enterprise.

From the broad political point of view the decentralisation scheme implied an opening for regional and local initiative and ambitions, not unreasonable, having regard to the increased number of educated and trained personnel. This was, of course, particularly important in the national minority areas, where the local national intelligentsia could at last see a chance to conduct a local policy not exclusively dictated from the central power in remote Moscow. Decentralisation also had the beneficial effect of easing overcrowding in Moscow by a forced exodus of ministers, directors, and managers to the newly established provincial *sovnarkhozes*. There was in this an element of political tactics, namely, to remove from the political centre the conservative hard core in the administration, who could be exploited by opponents of Khrushchev's radical plan.

Strategic considerations also played an important role, working strongly in favour of decentralisation. A highly centralised government machine located in one single area is extremely vulnerable to nuclear attack, and the entire command system could be knocked out by the first strike, with disastrous effects for the country's overall defence capacity. Though some decentralisation measures must have been embodied in defence planning, it is interesting to note that no visible administrative changes followed in the military sector. It would have been logical to appoint defence ministers in the Union republics, in accordance with the provision in their constitutions. This would also have been in line with the administration of the police system, or the foreign service, where some republics are allowed their own foreign ministers. The management of military affairs seems to be too delicate a matter, and the central power was not prepared to sanction any institutional new order that might eventually encourage military 'localism'.

The decentralisation plan was, however, not at all a success when put into effect. The basic weakness became apparent at the very start—the difficulty of reconciling the political-administrative with economic-administrative rationality. This is clearly shown by the size of the new regional areas. The country was divided into rather more than a hundred small *raions* without an adequate economic basis. The point was that these *raions* coincided with the *oblast* organisation, that is, the apparatus of the provincial first party secretary. An economic-administrative rational size would have meant a merger of several *oblasts*, leading to most intricate competence conflicts and, above all, to a substantial reduction of power for many provincial party bosses. In the spring of 1957 Khrushchev's position was very exposed, as we know. He could not risk adding to his troubles by challenging this influential party body, which constituted the largest single 'professional' group in the Central Committee and whose support was essential to Khrushchev's bid for supreme power. Thus from the beginning the rational basic concepts of the plan were distorted.

It has been argued that the plan did not lead to any decentralisation at all. But it all depends on which level of the administrative system is in question. In this complex system of relations a certain measure may be looked upon as a decentralisation of power at one particular level, but may represent increased supervision from above at another level. It seems clear that decentralisation was neither felt nor intended at factory level. On the contrary, pressure and interference from the *sovnarkhoz* were probably stronger and more direct than under the old system of ministerial control from distant Moscow. The point of the new system was rather to delegate some power to the regional bodies; that is, it was an attempt to alter the relations between these organs and the central authorities. And within a short time the predictions of some western observers and the warnings from the author of the scheme himself came true. The new regional leadership rapidly acquired a strong local bias— *mestnichestvo*—the technical term for promoting regional and local needs and ambitions at the expense of national interests. This localism became no doubt a serious problem, particularly in areas where political, national, and economic borders coincided. In Latvia, for instance, the chief economic planner even talked about 'exports' and 'imports' in business deals with other republics within the Union.

The central authorities reacted as might be expected: in the early sixties recentralisation measures were gradually introduced and after the removal of Khrushchev in 1964 the new leaders resolutely returned to the old ministerial system. This time they tried yet another variant to tackle the old trouble: to combine strong centralised planning and control with decentralisation at the factory level, particularly in the consumer industries, where some element of market economy is supposed to operate. Recentralisation was very likely also connected with other important internal and international developments, especially the vigorous rearmament in 1961–63. This national effort, which laid heavy new burdens on an already strained economy, was not to be delayed or hampered by regional or local obstruction. The ministerial system with its proved chains of command would guarantee the smooth running of the economy in accordance with supreme national interests. On the other hand, this development again poses the uneasy problem of a highly centralised administrative machine and the effects of modern weaponry.

Another most interesting example of Khrushchev's passion for reform was the change made in 1962, when he split the party cadres into 'industrialists' and 'agrarians'. This sudden and unexpected move seems also to have reflected the growing complexity of the Soviet structure, and particularly the need for specialists with professional knowledge even within the party, in place of the verbose, pushing, and bullying party official of the old type. And this too presents the dilemma of specialised professional knowledge versus the status of the party member in Soviet society.

The fact is that the earlier fairly clear distinction between party and government officials has become increasingly blurred. The modern party man of the younger generation has acquired higher education, mostly in engineering, in no way inferior to that of his opposite number in government service, and this educational fusion is further underlined by the fact that party officials serve alternately in party and government jobs, and in many cases are civil servants in central or local administration for considerable periods. This exchangeability has been on the increase lately.

A similar development is noticeable in the relations between the professionals and the politicians in the armed forces. Today the professional officer is expected to be able to perform the duties of the political officer and vice versa. This may seem strange and perhaps recall the amateurish experiments of earlier periods. But the statistics given in Soviet military journals show an increasing number of political officers with higher or middle military education, while professional officers are reported as holding the post of party secretary in the political organisations of the armed forces. How far this dilution of functions has proceeded and how successful the substitution is, it is hard to say.

In the civilian sector there was a problem of similar complexity which Khrushchev no doubt had in mind when he proposed the change—the endless troubles caused by direct party interference in daily administrative work. On paper the tasks and duties of the two parallel hierarchies are clearly defined. The administration's job is to administer; the party's job is to guide and supervise the activities of the administration and its personnel. At every administrative level the ultimate power *and* responsibility lies in the hands of the corresponding party organ. If something goes wrong, which it does very often, the party organ is in its own interest forced to intervene. The borderline between 'intervention' and *administrarovanie* is, of course, hazy, and more a matter of the inclinations and ambitions of the responsible party man.

Khrushchev's idea of the division of the party into 'industrial' and 'agrarian' could be interpreted as an attempt to resolve conflicts of competence and to accelerate a party-government integration in order to promote a more rational, efficient, and less personnel-absorbing administrative system. The controversial point was the potential danger to the party's position in society. The obvious risk was that an integration or fusion might lead to a 'withering away' of the party as the supreme and autonomous organisation, responsible for the development of the entire society. There was also the danger of clashes between industrial and agricultural 'fractions' within the party, representing strong vested interests.

The party reform, like so many of Khrushchev's projects, was short-lived. It is hard to say whether his opponents regarded the bold and novel ideas it embodied as completely wrong and dangerous or just premature. But no one can deny that Khrushchev vigorously tackled both old and new ills in Soviet society. He may not have been very successful as reformer. But it is now up to his successors to present better ideas to meet the challenge of the new Russia. After the downfall of Khrushchev the party reform was immediately cancelled. This is a sort of reform, too. But by merely restoring the old order it leaves the old administrative problems untouched.

Central to the performance and efficiency of the administrative machine is the leadership's attitude towards the administrative intelligentsia. This covers the general atmosphere created by the leaders, and the social, economic, and cultural status of the officials. Stalin's traditional pragmatic approach has been mentioned. He organised a strict command system, which even in civilian departments had a definite touch of the military about it. He also oiled the machinery with a large dose of terror—to such an extent that at one time the entire system almost broke down. In certain circumstances a reign of terror may be effective, but certainly nor for very long, and not in a mature society. Almost immediately after Stalin's death his heirs started to introduce new methods. The more lenient attitude affected the whole of society, but the intelligentsia was most concerned. The keen awareness of the specific problems of the administrative class was shown by the measures which brought some elementary order into office hours, which earlier had been determined by the nocturnal working habits of the dictator.

Fear was certainly a constant element in Stalin's technique of rule. On the other hand, it was under him that the administrative intelligentsia acquired social and economic status. Under Khrushchev the threat of jail and prison camps was reduced. But his radical and egalitarian inclinations were combined with a deep, rather vulgar resentment towards officialdom and expertise. He himself posed as the common-sense representative of the ordinary people. Stalin was on the right track when he once contemptuously called Khrushchev a *narodnik*. Khrushchev's arrogant self-sufficiency often brought him into conflict with the economic experts, as in 1957, when he said that the Soviet Union could out-produce the USA in meat production 'in a couple of years'. His garrulity and dilettante approach to intricate problems at home and abroad, and his occasional crudity of manner, no doubt caused a lot of irritation among upper civil servants and educated people in general. These characteristics became quite dangerous when he presented himself as military strategist and intervened in matters of military organisation and defence.

Khrushchev's reforming activities were particularly annoying and disturbing for the administrative intelligentsia, civilian and military. A bureaucracy is by nature inclined towards routine, strict rules of procedure, stable organisation, and this is especially true of the Soviet type of administration. Khrushchev inclined in the opposite direction, and was constantly searching for new organisational arrangements and improved methods of management. Planning in a Soviet-type economy is a very complicated matter indeed, requiring at least a minimum of consistency and stability. His impulsive and frequent reshuffling of economic priorities must have driven Gosplan officials to despair. It is true that a huge and sluggish administration must have a leader with a strong will and initiative. But Khrushchev's excessive élan and arbitrary interference created a very unfavourable atmosphere for rational long-term planning and the smooth running of day-to-day administration.

The present leaders seem to have a quite different approach to the administrative intelligentsia. Both Brezhnev and Kosygin have higher professional education and long administrative experience. So far they have acted very cautiously in administrative matters and—after cancelling out Khrushchev's whims—seem anxious not to introduce disturbing innovations. Consequently the administrative machinery has regained stability and the administrators have recovered their authority and status. It was significant that Kosygin in his maiden speech to the managerial class made a special point of management's right to office cars. The same tendency is obvious in the new plans for increased production of consumer durables, including private cars. Figures on output and on wages and salaries indicate that the well-paid officials in government service are among the first to benefit from the expanded production of luxury items. Though conditions and resources differ, there is undoubtedly a Stalinist touch in the positive attitude of the present leaders towards the administrative intelligentsia.

In their turn, professional attitudes and technical expertise have made a strong imprint upon the political climate in the Soviet Union. There is now a notable absence of inspiring and visionary appeals; the conduct of the leadership seems efficient and rational, but at the same time colourless and unimaginative. This is perhaps a natural development and may well be suited to a more advanced stage of industrial evolution. But in view of the traditional inertia and indolence in the Russian state service, this carries with it the risk of stagnation, leading to negligence and the sending to and fro of papers, instructions, and reports. The delicate problem the present leaders have to tackle is to strike a nice balance between the bureaucracy's need for stability and consistency and society's growing need for innovation and new administrative techniques.

The degree of appreciation of the administrative intelligentsia may vary from one to the other, but, fundamentally, the Soviet leaders have always had an ambivalent attitude. This is not surprising. The increasing stratification, partly inevitable and partly deliberate, has in fact created a gap between hard social realities and the still vivid memory of earlier utopian or romantic views on the evolution of society. This contradiction explains both the psychological obstacles to a rational, scientific approach to managerial problems and the officially sponsored confusion on these matters. There is pride in the increased output of engineers and other specialists, but when these categories enter on their

professional career in the state service, they feel uneasy about the social (and for that matter economic) effects of this process, and an attempt is made to conceal these continuous additions by way of artificial definition and classification devices. The political scientists indulge in endless and quite irrelevant discussions about categories in the 'productive' sphere, or 'directly connected with production', and categories which are said to be 'unproductive'.

Two other questions of interest arise: first, the composition and training of the administrative intelligentsia; the second, strictly technical, is the provision of modern office machines. Again, the statistical material is sadly inadequate, but it does warrant a few general conclusions. Organisationally, the present set-up of the administrative intelligentsia is top-heavy; there are too many in the higher ranks of management, and too few in the lower. The table gives the composition of the administrative personnel in the Ukraine in 1964.

These figures must be read with some caution. But top management is a comparatively distinct group and represents no less than about 30 per cent of the administrative personnel. The figure of 6–7 per cent for clerks and other office workers, including typists and stenographers, may be slightly underrated, because this group causes some 'ideological' uneasiness in general and is a headache for Soviet sociologists, who

Occupation	As percentage of total
Directors and deputies	25.6
Chief specialists and deputies	2.4
Engineers, etc., in administrative jobs	9.4
Engineer-economists, economists, planners	4.8
Bookkeepers and statisticians	30.5
Office personnel	6.6

are at a loss where to place this diffuse and transitional category—in what 'class' or 'stratum' (*prosloika*). Still, this distribution is almost incredible and certainly creates one of the most serious bottlenecks in the Soviet administrative system. It leads automatically to extremely irrational ways of handling administrative duties and explains the continuous complaints about the misuse of qualified officials. These are up to their ears in all sorts of minor jobs and details, and are at the same time supposed to perform responsible duties.

Connected with these tendencies are the troubles created by crash programmes to mass produce certain types of 'status' specialists. The outstanding example is the impressive production of civil engineers (university level), which has caused a rather awkward imbalance between this category and the technicians (middle-school level). Since there is a considerable relative shortage of this latter group, the same story is repeated: many university engineers are placed in functions below their educational level and qualifications.

There is, secondly, the intricate problem of what type of professional training is required for different stages of the industrialisation process. The first generation of industrial leaders and managers consisted largely of self-made men—represented in Russia by the party official whose lack of education and expert knowledge was to some extent compensated by his capacity for leadership. At the second stage of a still comparatively unsophisticated economy, the need for expert technological knowledge is strongly felt. This explains the great emphasis on enginering and technical education in

the Soviet administration as well as in the party machine. The rule is the engineer-boss in the factories and next to him the chief engineer. But as soon as this second generation of industrialists is in due course installed in office, industrialisation has reached a far more complex stage of evolution, and another generation and type of industrial manager is needed. Symptomatic of the present trend and the new requirements is the appointment of a chief economist in the factories on a par with the old chief engineer. This innovation has been stressed by Premier Kosygin, who has publicly complained of the shortage of personnel with economic training, and more particularly of the very low output rate of economists from universities and other higher professional schools. The problem of engineer versus economist in the administration is reflected in the table above, where the figure of the relative share of the economist group is improved by the inclusion of the hybrid 'engineer-economists'.

Office equipment is a particularly weak point in the Soviet administrative system. Much has been written lately in Russia about computer techniques as the grand solution for the administrative mess. Some enthusiasts seem to believe that it is only a short and easy step from the still widely used abacus to the refined electronic computer. This school of thought also predicts that within a couple of decades the whole adult population will have to be engaged in administrative jobs and planning, if the present outmoded system continues. Now the fact is that the production of computers in the Soviet Union is still very low, and all the evidence suggests that the relatively few data machines in use are largely 'consumed' by the military sector or in defence-related activities. There are, of course, exceptions: the surprisingly rapid and comprehensive publication of the results of the 1959 census must be credited to the extensive use of computers.

But quite apart from these obstacles, the real trouble here is that there are no computers with the capacity to swallow the mass of data from such a giant monster as the Soviet planning system. Thus, the computer offers no overall means of mastering Soviet administrative and planning complexities in the foreseeable future. The more serious problem today is rather the appalling lack of simple and ordinary office machines and means of communication—typewriters (even carbon paper), calculating machines, dictaphones, and telephones. These deficiencies tend to reinforce each other, and to set in motion a downward spiral of efficiency. The shortage of clerks and secretaries means that oral communication predominates over written, but since there are not enough telephones or other communication equipment, managers have either to devote a good deal of time to walking around the factory or office to get in touch with subordinate personnel, or to summon their staff to lengthy and numerous meetings. Whether the managers choose the first or the second method or both, they are not easily available for other people, who may be in urgent need of information or orders and who, consequently, in their turn have to spend hours passively in waiting-rooms. The Soviet leaders are, of course, aware of all this, but perhaps do not realise the real scope and importance of these very efficient obstacles to administrative efficiency, and how far Russia is lagging behind the West in this respect.

And if they do, it may be that they find it impossible at the moment to allocate more hardware for administrative rationalisation.

This brief survey gives a rather gloomy picture of the present situation; nor do the prospects for the coming decades seem very bright either. The problems involved cannot be resolved overnight by some ingenious technical device. We have here to deal with deep-rooted, institutionalised factors and irrationalities, which the Soviet leaders will have to live with for a considerable time. An established bureaucratic machine seems to live its own life, and if it changes, it will do so grudgingly and according to its own inherent 'laws': it would rather change the people it deals with than be changed by them. Efforts to provide the administration with modern business equipment can certainly make things better and easier, but, basically, the question is one of changing people's attitudes. It is hardly possible to do this with people who have grown old in the old ways, and hopes must be set upon the coming generations, largely unaffected by the terror of the thirties and the horrors of the war.

There still remains the extremely complex and delicate problem of power relations in the administrative system —the party machine versus the state and local administration, the command system from central organs via regional and local organs down to individual enterprises in industry, agriculture, trade, etc. In spite of frequent and sometimes vigorous attempts to bring about a change in these relations, nothing like a modern, efficient, and smooth-running organisation is in sight. The leaders obviously understand the need for substantial reforms and particularly for a delegation of power to the lower administrative levels. But caution sets a limit; the greater autonomy now granted to enterprises could lead to polycentric tendencies at the base of the economy, with possible repercussions on central planning and might—in combination with other liberalising measures—even endanger the entire political command and control system.

The central difficulty is that these problems seem to be eternal in the sense that a decentralisation scheme can solve *some* problems and bottlenecks at *some* administrative levels, but tend at the same time to pose a threat to what is seen as a national interest. And, conversely, a centralised system can certainly safeguard the latter, but requires an extremely cumbersome management at the top, wastes local resources, and suppresses local initiative. So the whole system oscillates back and forth in slow motion; adjustments and readjustments are introduced, when one particular reform has caused too many and too serious troubles at one administrative level or another.

In a less advanced society these frequent shifts and reforms would perhaps do no harm. But the Soviet industrial and social structure is steadily growing more complex, and this makes the job of the planning authorities more and more difficult. An interesting and significant symptom is the new emphasis on economists rather than engineers: with perhaps the exception of completely new industries, the question now is not so much one of production as of the really sophisticated planning, coordination, integration, and timing of various economic and social activities.

The steady increase in the number of officials and of the personnel in service industries is a positive trend, because it will probably promote a higher rate of social mobility, counteracting the tendency of the intelligentsia to recruit exclusively from its own ranks. On the other hand, the relative share of workers and peasants will rapidly decrease; the Soviet Union is fast moving from its 'proletarian' social origin to a middle-class society, an evolution strongly reinforced by the official endorsement of typical middle-class social values and attitudes. These changes, both economic and social, and the accompanying administrative complexities, are a challenge to Soviet political scientists and most particularly sociologists. Are they well enough trained, and are they allowed to investigate freely delicate social questions and administrative practices, thus helping to resolve both present and future problems? The fact is that Soviet sociologists, like Soviet social scientists in general, work in an adverse intellectual climate, and seem to have very limited opportunity to influence the bureaucrats. It is true that sociological research has improved considerably during the last five to ten years, and has touched many sore points. So far, they have succeeded in producing embarrassing statistics and analyses which reveal the wide gap between the official propaganda and Soviet social realities. In fact, they are making a nuisance of themselves to the ruling circles and leading bureaucrats, who may set limits to further inquisitive investigations. Perhaps the increasing complexities of social engineering are outpacing the speed of intellectual liberation, and both the bureaucrats and the social scientists will lag behind the requirements of social and economic development.

V

THE PARTY
AND SUPERVISION OF SOCIETY

Compliance with, and the Enforcement of, Decisions

In the Soviet political system the right to exercise power, to lead, to make decisions, is arrogated by a self-appointed elite, and is not based on a broad mandate from the people as a whole. Rather, it is derived from *a priori* assumptions about history, social classes, and the role of the Communist Party. In these conditions, supervision of society takes on considerable importance. Under a direct mandate, those who rule can expect something more than minimum support for decisions and commitment to the system. The system is "legitimate" in that it is accorded respect and the decisions made through it are generally obeyed by those who created it, and the individual can identify the satisfaction of his interests with the system. One of the continuing problems facing those who rule in the Soviet Union has been how to establish and to maximize their legitimacy—how to develop sufficient acceptance of the system and its rationale by the population as a whole so that discontent and disaffection will be kept to a tolerable minimum. Even more important, as the Soviet Union has grown to a modern industrial society, with efficiency and increased productivity becoming essential to further development, those who reserve to themselves the right to make decisions have had to be concerned with evoking an active commitment, as contrasted with a passive acceptance, of the system from the broader masses of the population.

As the party strives to widen its base of support and to legitimize its role in society, it must seek continuously to exercise sufficient supervision of society so as to assure compliance with party decisions. In this context, supervision means: (1) the prohibition of any overt opposition to the party's role or the decisions made by the party; (2) the overcoming of apathy and indifference; and (3) the inculcating of a positive commitment to the system, to develop sufficient legitimacy for the system so that the individual will not engage in anti-system behavior, and at best, will eagerly get on with his assigned tasks.

By what methods does the party leadership seek to assure compliance with its decisions? How does it supervise society? How successful are they? Have the instruments used by the party been changed? If so, for what reasons, under what pressures, and what might the consequences be for the future? The readings in this part all address themselves to one or more of these questions.

One of the most important changes in the Soviet political system since Stalin's death has been the abolition of the overt use of terror, of the forced labor camps, and of the existence of the secret police almost as a "state within the state." The police and security apparatus have been placed, at least so far, under firm party control, and their functions severely limited in practice. This undoubtedly has had the beneficial effect of increasing the sense of physical and psychological security on the part of both the party member and the individual citizen. It also has broadened considerably the limits within which public and private discussion may be carried on free from arbitrary interference by the police and other organs of social control.

A considerable element of coercion remains, however, in contemporary Soviet society.[1] Coercion here is defined as the use of state power to punish, or threaten to punish, behavior considered to be antistate or antiparty, or political behavior unacceptable to those who currently occupy the positions of authority and power. One of the intriguing issues that appears to occupy the attention of the leadership in the Soviet Union is just what behavior is to be permitted, and what is not. Divisions in the leadership on this have appeared from time to time, and will more than likely continue to exist.

This coercive aspect remains quite arbitrary, for apart from criminal behavior regulated and punished by most states, there is no clear definition of what specific behavior is to be considered deserving of punishment. The proscribed behavior is set forth in broad, vague terms subject to great differences in interpretation. What is and what is not "anti-state" or "anti-party" behavior? What constitutes "anti-Soviet agitation and propaganda"? At best, if a "coercive atmosphere," as one observer characterizes it, does not exist, then at least some sense of psychological insecurity remains for the individual Soviet citizen.

With the removal of terror and the creation of a less coercive atmosphere than had existed before his death, Stalin's heirs have come to rely on other means for supervising society, maximizing the legitimacy of the system, and attaining compliance with their decisions. Although the party organization, the legal system, the electoral system, bureaucratic and administrative controls, social compulsions, rewards and incentives, and the socialization process had been used under Stalin for these purposes, one of the major developments since his death has been the greater dependence upon these instruments by the elite.

---

[1] See Jeremy Azrael, "Is Coercion Withering Away?" *Problems of Communism* (November–December 1962).

The party organization itself provides the basic instrument of social control. Its supervisory and control functions in the economic life of society were discussed in Part IV. Primary party organizations, however, exist in all places of work, whether specifically related to what would be termed economic activities or not. Schools, military units, communications media, the arts—all places of work have their PPO and come under party supervision. As one goes up the hierarchy of party organs through the various secretariats, one finds the same function being performed. The various secretaries receive information, investigate, prod and push, and make recommendations to higher authorities in cases beyond their immediate power to solve. The higher up one goes, the broader the view and range of concerns with which the secretariat has to cope. Supervision over party members themselves, apart from the top leaders, is maintained by the Party Control Committee.

Eugene Kamenka outlines the development of the highly instrumental Soviet view of law. Most all societies, certainly all modern nation-states, have a legal system more or less well developed in terms of scope, precision, and acceptance by the population. The human instinct for order and security appears to demand at least an elementary system of rules and regulations governing conduct, personal relations, and property relations. Further, the democrat's concern for justice has led to demands for the "rule of law": for due process and the avoidance of arbitrariness in the application of the law.

It is only in passing that the Soviet view of law takes note of man's concern for personal security. Law is to serve, in the words of Vishinsky which have not as yet been repudiated, "the interests of socialist construction, the interests of the state of the proletarian dictatorship." In contemporary terms, this means that "in the conditions of the complete victory of socialism and the gradual transition to communism, the Soviet state and the law act as exponents of the will of all the people and become still more effective levers of communist construction."[2] It is argued that law and morality are united organically to "serve a single historical idea, the construction of communism."

Thus, law in the Soviet Union serves the function of regulating traditional antisocial behavior—criminal and civil—as in all modern societies, and it also exists as an instrument to limit or inhibit political behavior that in other societies would be considered outside the scope of the law. It also is supposed to serve a more positive function. "Soviet socialist law not only acts as the direct regulator of highly important social relations, but also serves as an effective tool of communist upbringing of the working people." The legal system in the Soviet Union is a means by which compliance with

---

[2] See *Current Digest of the Soviet Press,* XIX, No. 35, 24–25.

economic, social, and other decisions of the party leaders can be facilitated.

This role of the law, and the effort of some party leaders to perpetuate and extend it, does not go unchallenged. A running debate within and among the legal profession and party circles in the Soviet Union finds some seeking to control and regularize the more informal and arbitrary elements in the law—to create a "rule of law."[3] The effect of doing this, of course, would be to limit or eliminate the instrumental character of the law, and could well make it more difficult for the party to rationalize its position in Soviet society and assure compliance with its decisions. This has become another of the problems facing the party leadership: how to adapt and make concessions in the name of efficiency and rationality, and in order to broaden its legitimacy, without endangering its position of power and authority.

A vast network of bureaucratic and administrative controls has been created within the state administration in the Soviet Union.[4] These range from the extensive planning apparatus, through personnel and financial/budgetary controls, to the legal restrictions or inhibitions already mentioned. The multiplicity of bureaucratic control mechanisms, often overlapping and inherent in the centralized economic administrative structure, not only enables the bureaucracy to function by serving as a channel of communication and exhortation but provides an important means by which autonomous tendencies, inefficiency, and malpractices within the bureaucracy are uncovered and uprooted.

One way by which the party leaders can hope to control "bureaucratism" and the inefficiencies and arbitrariness of the bureaucracy is through popular pressure. In addition to illuminating the problems the individual citizen can encounter in a highly bureaucratized society, Robert Osborn has shown how the party attempts to use complaints from the citizenry, and turning "a spotlight of publicity on offending bureaucrats and impermissible bureaucratic practices," as a means of controlling the administrative bureaucracy.[5] He has noted also the desire of some Soviet critics of the bureaucracy for better administrative organization, and the emergence of pressures for the development of a body of administrative law, "a regular system of administrative procedure."

In recent years social compulsion, an instrument for social control which has existed for some time in the Soviet Union, has been given much greater emphasis. This involves the use of contemporary social values for the benefit of the system—values some of which the party itself has sought, not without

---

[3] See A. J. C. Campbell, "The Legal Scene," *Survey*, No. 57 (October 1965).

[4] See Merle Fainsod, *How Russia is Ruled*, rev. ed. (Cambridge, Mass.: Harvard University, Press, 1963), Chap. 12, especially 403–17.

[5] Robert J. Osborn, "Citizen Versus Administration in the USSR," *Soviet Studies*, XVII, No. 2 (October 1965).

success, to instill in the population. It seeks to use systematically the social pressures toward conformism that the community exerts on the individual, pressures that in most cases are apparently desired by the individual. By holding the deviant or wrong-doer or economic "slacker" up to opprobrium from his neighbors and fellow workers and citizens, the party hopes to reduce, if not eliminate, such behavior.

The forms in which these social compulsions appear are varied: the anti-parasite laws, the volunteer police brigades, the comrade's courts, the appurtenances of the local soviets (apartment or street committees, commissions on juvenile affairs and the administrative commissions, and the standing commissions, local soviet "activists," social inspectors, instructors, and "trouble-shooters"). Leon Lipson traces the development of the anti-parasite laws and the rationale for the use of social pressure as a means of control and assurance of compliance with party policies and values. He also notes the opposition that existed, and presumably continues, if only passively, when the anti-parasite measures were revived in 1957, and while the laws were being worked out.[6]

One, ideological, objective of increasing the number of "social controllers" is to take what party ideologues hope might be the first steps toward "communist self-government" by widening participation in the administration of justice. Aside from this are some other, perhaps more immediately practical, objectives. As one observer has noted, the new emphasis on social control through drawing in more individual citizens: (1) provides more checks at the lowest level of society on the execution of policy and the observance of the imposed values, a level where compliance is hardest to assure, (2) perhaps makes it harder for a bureaucracy to establish itself and to resist that which it disapproves of, and (3) gives the force of moral and social authority (the "voice of the people") to more of the decisions from the top, and makes it more difficult for the individual to stand up against these decisions.

The most pervasive and important means, in terms of individual desires and aspirations, by which the party seeks to acquire legitimacy for its decisions and its role in society and to assure compliance with its decisions is its conscious use of the process of socialization. In the Soviet Union, the socialization of the individual to political affairs has been a matter of highest interest to the party. The party has sought to monopolize this process and to provide its content. It has striven to condition the individual to accept, unquestioningly, the goals and values of the party, as determined by those who occupy the highest positions of power. Perhaps many of the problems that the party faces today, much of the discontent and unrest,

---

[6] Professor Lipson provides in his comments a further example of how the decision-making process can be influenced by professional considerations and pressures coming from outside the party elite, and from both inside and outside the party.

especially among youth and the intellectuals, can best be explained as opposition to and resistance of the party's effort to guide and form the values of society.

The ultimate goal of the party is to resocialize the individual so that he becomes a "new man." "At the center of the communist dream is its unique vision of society and its view of man in that society. The new social order will be cooperative rather than competitive; altruistic rather than selfish."[7] In order to create such a society, human nature will have to be remodeled so that the individual will behave totally in a cooperative and altruistic manner.

Short of such utopian hopes, however, the party can be satisfied if it has socialized the individual such that each has internalized the party's more immediate goals and the party's rationale for the existing political system. Compliance will be assured because the individual accepts the party's claim to legitimacy. Each individual will want to implement party policy properly because the party, through the socialization process, has succeeded in evoking from him an *active* commitment to the system. The program adopted by the Twenty-Second Congress of the CPSU in October, 1961 articulates the party commitment to socializing the Soviet citizen to party-determined values and goals in the following fashion:

The party considers that the paramount task in the ideological field in the present period is to educate all working people in a spirit of ideological integrity and devotion to communism, and cultivate in them a communist attitude to labor and the social economy; to eliminate completely the survivals of bourgeois views and morals; to ensure the all-round, harmonious development of the individual; to create a truly rich spiritual culture. Special importance is attached by the party to the molding of the rising generation.[8]

The effort of the party to socialize the population takes several forms: control over the structure and content of the educational system; the creation of youth organizations encompassing the complete age span from the earliest years to young adulthood, and control over all formal youth activities; an enormous apparatus whose sole purpose is the indoctrination of the individual, both the citizen at large and the party member; and the electoral system.

A recent *Pravda* editorial exemplifies the commitment of the party leaders to "theoretical activity," and its importance for "communist construction."[9] The "ideological and political upbringing of the working people" is the phrase used to describe the pervasive system of agitation and propaganda

---

[7] Herschel and Edith Alt, *The New Soviet Man* (New York: Bookman Associates, 1964), p. 19.

[8] Herbert Ritro, *The New Soviet Society* (New York: The New Leader, 1962), p. 202.

[9] See *Current Digest of the Soviet Press*, XIX, No. 36, 23–25.

and party education to which so much time, effort, and manpower is devoted by the party. Among other things, the press in the Soviet Union is called upon to help "actively mold the communist way of life."

Also evident in this editorial are the problems facing the party in formulating theory and values, in finding capable cadres to "spread the word," and in finding a receptive audience. Exhortations are made to cadres to become better informed and politically educated, and to succeed in their tasks by persuading their audience and overpowering opposition or reluctance to accept or commit by the force of the argument. Failure to do so never is attributed to the weakness or sterility of the argument, but rather always to inadequacies of the propagandist.

Allen Kassof has provided us with an illuminating study of what the party would like to achieve with respect to character and value formation through its control over organized youth activities.[10] An equally important and concomitant aspect of the process of political socialization in the Soviet Union is the educational system. Jeremy Azrael discusses the degree to which the Soviet educational system has been successful in instilling new values in the younger generations of Soviet citizens. Despite its many achievements, the educational system has failed "to create the sort of all-inclusive, monolithic, and homogeneous political culture that the rulers desired." The problems facing the party in accomplishing this task are several and serious. The educational reforms initiated in 1958 by Khrushchev were intended to cope with these problems, but created as many, if not more, than they helped to alleviate. The Brezhnev and Kosygin leadership has returned to many of the pre-1958 forms and procedures without a complete return to the *status quo ante*, having initiated some major changes of their own.[11]

One notes in Professor Azrael's study of the educational system yet another example of the tension created in Soviet society by the party's continued efforts to impose its values, and the counterpressures from not only the environment, but equally, if not more importantly, from human nature. How to adapt and make concessions under pressures for change without conceding away the basis for party rule? This remains perhaps the cardinal problem for the party in the Soviet Union today.

A final example of the party's effort to assure compliance with decisions through maximizing their legitimacy can be seen in Jerome Gilison's discussion of the theory and practice of Soviet elections, emphasizing their essentially educational, symbolic, and legitimizing role, and analyzing the

---

[10] Allen Kassof, *The Soviet Youth Program* (Cambridge, Mass.: Harvard University Press, 1965). See also Ralph T. Fisher, Jr., *Pattern for Soviet Youth* (New York: Columbia University Press, 1960).

[11] See Jeremy Azrael, "Fifty Years of Soviet Education," *Survey*, No. 64 (July 1967).

evidence of dissent that has appeared. He concludes that "increased liberalization of Soviet society, and the general improvement in living conditions, results in a decreased use of elections as a vehicle for the expression of dissent." Although one can continue to analyze the source and nature of dissent in the Soviet Union through studying electoral results, argues Professor Gilison, it would appear that the electoral system will continue as an instrument by which the party leaders hope to legitimize their authority and their decisions.

THE SOVIET VIEW OF LAW

Eugene Kamenka

"Law," said Lenin, "is a political measure. Law is politics." No one can examine the foundations of legal doctrine in Russia without the sense of the completeness with which this conception has permeated the whole fabric of the law. Behind all of it is the relentless purpose of consolidating the dictatorship of the proletariat. In every phase of the law, property, contract, tort, crime, this note is the threefold one of crushing counterrevolutionary resistance, of freeing the workers from the impact of what are regarded as capitalist habits, and of building up a social outlook able to work the principles of the Communist society.—Harold J. Laski, *Law and Justice in Soviet Russia.*

Karl Marx had a profoundly negative attitude towards law. He dismissed sharply all talk of "legality," abstract "justice," and abstract "right" as having any theoretical value: for him, such terms were, at most, sops to be resorted to occasionally in dealing with the woolly-minded liberals who made up much of the First International. Law to Marx was an instrument of oppression and class rule, a system of sanctions designed to safeguard the fundamental principles of class rule and the particular interests of the ruling class. At a deeper level, he regarded law as resting on the abstraction of the individual from his social background and his social life: just as the capitalist market converted men's products, men's work, and thus men themselves into commodities, so law enslaved man to something outside himself, made him the object instead of the subject of social life. Law, in his view, arises and maintains itself in a society rent by antagonistic classes, where men live at one another's expense. When private property has been abolished and the social organization of production has taken its place, when the true social interest has established itself and man has become the subject and not the object of history, the need for coercion disappears, and law and the state wither away and die. "Rights and duties," Marx wrote in the *German Ideology*, "are the two complementary sides of a contradiction which belongs only to civil society." Seven years later, in an article for the *New York Tribune*,

---

Problems of Communism (March–April 1965), pp. 8–16. Reprinted by permission. Footnotes omitted.

he wrote: "Punishment, at bottom, is nothing but society's defense of itself against all violation of its conditions of existence. How unhappy is a society that has no other means of defending itself than the executioner!"

The history and social condition of prerevolutionary Russia did much to lend plausibility to Marx's onslaught on law. The "emergency conditions" under which the eastern Slavs spent so much of their history—the battering they received at the hands of Mongols, Swedes, and Livonian Knights; the emergence of the centralized Muscovite state; the crushing of the Boyars; the institutions of state lands and state peasants, of a service nobility and of serfdom—all helped to create and consolidate a situation in which government was held to be necessarily autocratic and law readily became a series of decrees. Before the judicial reforms introduced by Alexander II in 1864, writes Michael Florinsky, the judicial system was characterized by "inhuman severity of punishment, multiplicity of judicial agencies, complexity of procedure . . . secrecy and arbitrariness and heartless formalisms." To most of the Russian intelligentsia, as much as to the peasant, law meant the knout. It was a means of suppression—of intellectuals by the state, of peasants by their masters, of wives by their husbands. Even where the law guaranteed formal rights, these had no value in the material context of an autocratic society. As the Russian revolutionary, N. G. Chernyshevski observed at the time that Marx was writing *Das Kapital:*

Man is not an abstract legal person, but a living creature . . . a man who is dependent for his material means of existence cannot be an independent human being in fact, even though his independence is proclaimed by the letter of the law.

True, in the period from the 18th century up to the Russian Revolution, there were men like S. F. Desnitski (c. 1740–89, translator of Blackstone's *Commentaries* into Russian), A. D. Gradovski (1841–89), and M. M. Kovalevski (1851–1916), who played a prominent part in liberal constitutional discussion. But such men tended to belong to the liberal wing of the academics (public servants), and not to the true, largely revolutionary intelligentsia; their influence on events and on the revolutionary movement proved negligible. By 1909, writing in the collective *Vekhi (Landmarks)*, V. Kistiakovski felt that he had to defend the rule of law and the concept of legality against Russian intellectuals of all political shades, from Leontiev and the Slavophiles to Herzen and both Marxist and non-Marxist radicals.

The Soviet state, Communist jurists have stressed, "emerged not on the basis of some written statutes, but as a result of the direct initiative of the masses, which in the course of the Revolution destroyed the old order, the old legality, the old system of authorities, and created in their stead their own system of power, their own governmental agencies." The profession of advocate (private attorney), the old courts of justice, and the old Procuracy (Department of Public Prosecutions) were abolished by the Decree on Courts No. 1, December 7, 1917; and the new People's Courts were instructed to apply "the laws of the overthrown governments only insofar as they were not abrogated by the Revolution and did not contradict revolutionary conscience and the revolutionary concept of law."

The first decrees of the new Soviet government were not regarded by their promulgators as laws in the traditional sense. "Not the *corpus juris Romani* but our revolutionary consciousness of justice ought to be applied to 'civil law relations,'" Lenin wrote to People's Commissar of Justice Kurski in 1922. Five years earlier, in 1917, he had written:

It does not matter that many points in our decrees will never be carried out; their task is to teach the masses how to take practical steps... We shall not look at them as absolute rules to be carried out under all circumstances.

In other words—the words Trotsky was to use later in his autobiography—the decrees were "the program of the party uttered in the language of power... a means of propaganda rather than of administration."

The courts were to be guided by "conscience" rather than by law. Thus, the rules of the Provisional Revolutionary Court of the Government of Novgorod—which were typical of many such rules—provided:

[*Sec. 15*] The court decides on the issues by conscience, on the basis of its own conviction. [*Sec. 18*] In imposing punishment upon the guilty person, the court is not bound by any existing laws, but is authorized to use the existing criminal laws for non-obligatory reference.

Or, as Kurski was to put it later:

The bourgeois judge could only supplement the statute by interpretation. The scope of the proletarian People's Court is much wider. In its basic function—criminal prosecution—the people's court is absolutely free and is guided above all by its *consciousness* of law. [Stress added]

Writing in 1927, P. J. Stuchka, then Chairman of the Soviet Supreme Court, affirmed that "communism means not the victory of socialist laws, but the victory of socialism over any law, since with the abolition of classes with their economic interests, law will disappear altogether." This certainly seems to have been the attitude with which the Bolsheviks entered upon their reign. The various decrees promulgated between 1917 and 1921, it is true, showed a certain amount of vacillation on the relationship of the revolutionary tribunals and people's courts to prerevolutionary legal relationships and legal concepts that had not been specifically abrogated by the new regime, but the main tendency was to elevate consciousness, loyalty to the Revolution, and Bolshevik discipline above any concept of law as such. Revolutionary law was seen as a system of decrees designed to suppress class enemies and to facilitate the construction and initial functioning of socialist institutions. It would wither away once the whole country had become truly Bolshevik.

With the New Economic Policy (NEP) of 1921–28, however, there was in certain respects a basic reversal of the trend towards governing by revolutionary justice. The Soviet authorities now permitted—indeed facilitated—the reappearance of money, private trade, kulaks, and private business managers operating under state license. A detailed system of law and legal procedures designed to fit these conditions quickly emerged. In 1922 and 1923, the Soviet authorities promulgated a Judiciary Act, a Civil Code, a Code of Civil Procedure, a Criminal Code, a Code of Criminal Procedure, a Land Code, and a new Labor Code.

The NEP, however, was only a temporary, partial, and strictly controlled restoration of the capitalist market. The laws required were therefore seen not as lasting socialist laws but as temporary legal arrangements on the capitalist model which would disappear when the concessions to capitalism were once more eliminated. The drafters of the new codes frankly based them on the codes of the non-socialist world—of Germany, Switzerland, Imperial Russia and France. Legal capacity, persons, corporations, legal transactions, statute of limitations, property, mortgages, landlord-and-tenant relations, contracts and torts, unjust enrichment and inheritance, were all dealt with in traditional terms, although subordinated in the last resort to the supposed economic interests of the proletariat. Article 1 of the Civil Code stated: "Civil rights shall be protected by law except in instances where they are exercised in contradiction with their social-economic purpose."

At the same time, legal representation and legal education were again formalized. Following the abolition of the old professional bar in 1917, the Decree on Courts No. 2 of March 1918 had provided for the formation of special colleges of persons—not necessarily legally trained—devoting themselves to legal representation, while also maintaining the right of any citizen present in court to act as an accuser or defender. These colleges had likewise been abolished in 1920, after which the courts had been empowered to draw up special lists of "defenders" consisting mainly of officials in public enterprises and unions who were not normally lawyers. Now, in 1922, a bar of professional attorneys-at-law (*advokatura*) was set up; university law training or two years of actual legal work was made mandatory for admission to practice; and attorneys'

fees were fixed on the basis of a percentage of the client's income.

Meanwhile, genuine—though politically circumscribed—juristic discussion and legal research accompanied the drafting of the new codes. If many of these documents nevertheless showed signs of having been drawn with haste, Soviet lawyers still could point with pride to the modernity of some of their theoretical views on crime and criminology. Thus, Soviet courts applied such humane methods of correction as the suspended sentence, public censure in place of fines, and constructive labor in place of confinement. The purpose of penal measures, it was proclaimed, was the defense of society and the reformation and reeducation of offenders, not retribution.

Nevertheless, all this juristic work was seen as purely transitional—*i.e.*, as consisting of measures directed against a necessarily dwindling group of class enemies and socially irresponsible elements or of regulations made necessary by the continuing but only temporary existence of property. In the view of such Soviet legal theorists as Reisner and Pashukanis, Stuchka and Krylenko, there still was no such thing as socialist law. Law, they argued (following Marx at his subtlest level), was a reflection of the laws and assumptions involved in the exchange of commodities and the organization of production on the basis of private property. The essence of law, wrote Pashukanis, is the contract of commercial exchange: man as a juridical person is a right-and-duty-bearing unit involved in "exchanges" with other right-and-duty-bearing units. This is so not only in civil law, but also in domestic law, where marriage and adoption are seen as contractual relationships; in public law, where the state is seen as standing in a "social contract" with its citizens; and in criminal law, where the idea of retribution has given way to the notion of the contract *ex post facto*—of the punishment as "payment" for the crime. Law thus develops fully only in bourgeois society, Pashukanis argued, because only there do the laws and assumptions of commerce fully develop; with the birth of communism, with production for use and the supersession of private property and commercial exchange, law necessarily dies.

After the abandonment of the NEP and the launching of the first of the Five-Year Plans in 1928, those espousing this view saw the withering away of bourgeois law and its replacement by the socialist plan as close at hand. The teaching of civil law was abandoned at Moscow University, where Pashukanis was dean. Speaking in 1930 on "The Soviet State and the Revolution in Law," Pashukanis said:

In bourgeois-capitalist society, the legal superstructure should have maximum immobility—maximum stability—because it represents a firm framework of the movement of the economic forces whose bearers are capitalist entrepreneurs.... Among us it is different. We require that our legislation possess maximum elasticity.... law occupies among us ... a subordinate position with reference to politics. We have a system of proletarian politics, but we have no need for any sort of juridical system of proletarian law.

Pashukanis' work is, without question, the most interesting produced by Soviet jurisprudence precisely because it is the most closely linked with the more subtle aspects of Marx's critique of commercial civilization—that is to say, because it pursues, in essence, the since popular theme of alienation and puts very little weight on the cruder

Marxist line about class interest and class domination. But theoretically capable as Pashukanis undoubtedly was, the practical effect of his work was to strengthen the Bolshevik line that the party was above the law, that the party, indeed, *was* Law. It helped to produce the atmosphere in which new Soviet administrators were trained to calculate the effects of their actions on the party and their political position, and not the relationship of these actions to law. It made possible the ideological justification of arbitrary arrest, administrative punishment, secret trials, etc. By placing "socialist construction" above and against the law, it made it possible for Andrei Vyshinski, then Deputy Procurator-General, to say in his report to the General Assembly of the College of Defenders on December 2, 1933:

The defense in the Soviet court must be based on profound principle. The principles of the Soviet defense must be those of socialist construction ... [the advocate must present] all his proofs in defense of the accused without descending from the terrain of principle held in common with the court, with the prosecution, with the whole country—from the terrain, that is, of the interests of socialist construction, the interests of the state of the proletarian dictatorship.

Further, Pashukanis' ideas created an atmosphere in which professional lawyers were looked upon with suspicion except where they were acting as investigators or prosecutors for the state. The drive for collectivization in 1929 was extended, by pressure instead of legislation, to the professional bar, which was transformed from an organization or union of private practitioners into a collective. The high proportion of attorneys with prerevolutionary legal training made them especially vulnerable to political purges: in Moscow alone, according to a Soviet émigré who was present at the time, 200 members of the bar were arrested in 1931, another 400 in 1935, and 165 in a single night in 1938. Almost all of these were sentenced administratively, without trial, and never heard of again.

Meanwhile, however, certain tensions were building up between the Soviet desire for complete and untrammeled powers of political direction and the newborn desire for a certain stability and regularity in the day-to-day affairs of Soviet life. According to the recollections of Professor Boris A. Konstantinovski, there was a steady stream of cases passing through the Soviet courts—commercial disputes between enterprises or between enterprises and their employees, thefts and misappropriations, abuses of official authority, and cases of official negligence. These were often handled by the judges much as they might have been by a Western magistrate— and on occasion the accused might, with luck, even score a minor triumph over a low-ranking party official.

That Soviet judges were under pressure to show their zeal in convicting, especially in cases of misconduct regarded as setting a socially dangerous example, there can be little doubt. But there was a growing emphasis, at least in minor matters, on formal legality. Then, in 1936, this suddenly became a major political slogan. The period of social reconstruction, Stalin announced, had ended: the Soviet Union was entering the era of socialism with a new (Stalin) constitution and a new concept—socialist legality. Law was not to begin withering away; on the contrary, as Soviet jurists were told at their general convention in

Moscow in 1938, "under socialism . . . law is raised to the highest level of development." Pashukanis and Stuchka were now denounced as counter-revolutionaries, traitors and wreckers, and accused (by their former colleague, Vyshinski) of sliding into the bog of economic materialism, of liquidating law as a specific social category, drowning it in economics, and depriving it of its active, creative role. Must those laws which govern marriage and family relationships also be regulated from the viewpoint of "socialist planning"? Vyshinski asked rhetorically. He went on to quote Article 112 of the Stalin Constitution, stipulating that "judges are independent and subject only to law," as proof that law had its own specific role under socialism and was not merely subservient to politics and economic planning.

For the philosopher of law, the theory of "true socialist law"—"perhaps bourgeois in form, but socialist in content"—developed during the post-1936 period of Stalin's dictatorship is totally uninteresting. Vyshinski's chief theoretical work, published in 1948, shows a conspicuous decline from the intellectual standards established by Reisner, Stuchka and Pashukanis in their theoretical writings. In that work and other subsequent writings, Vyshinski adheres inflexibly to the class view of law, formulated in crude, conspiratorial terms. Law, he asserts, represents the interests of the dominant class and those common rules of community life which are advantageous to the ruling class. Socialist law, however, differs from bourgeois law in that in socialist society the ruling class itself represents "the true interest" of the people, of all Soviet citizens. The onslaught on "capitalist law" throughout this period—and even subsequently —degenerated into the coarsest kind of falsification, exemplified by Vyshinski's treatment of the Dreyfus case, the prerevolutionary trial of Beilis on a trumped-up charge of ritual murder, and the Sacco-Vanzetti scandal as "typical" examples of bourgeois justice.

"Socialist legality," then, did not mean to Vyshinski and Stalin—any more than it does to their present successors—the creation of a *Rechtsstaat* in which political power is subject, both in principle and in practice, to legal restraints, legal rules, and legal challenge. Throughout the period of "socialist legality" under Stalin, the security police had the power to investigate crimes and to execute or deport persons under special rules, without the intervention of the courts or even of the Procurator-General of the USSR. Military courts and special secret-police tribunals had wide jurisdiction over civilians; and laws enacted in 1934 and 1937 permitted the trial of accused persons *in absentia* and/or without representation by counsel. In connection with the purge trials, Vyshinski elaborated the doctrine that confessions had special value as evidence in cases of serious political crime (on the specious ground that no one would confess to such crimes unless guilty), and that in such cases the burden of proof rested on the accused. Not only did the statute books carry such vague offenses as "committing a socially dangerous act," but they even revived the old Tsarist doctrine of "analogy" (abolished in 1903), under which a man might be convicted and sentenced for an act not specifically covered by existing criminal laws but "analogous" in some respects to an act that was. Above all, behind these formally questionable provisions lay the stark reality of one of the most brutal and pervasive police terrors ever known.

The irony of Stalinist legal doctrine lay in the fact that it was an attempt to do precisely what the cruder sort of Marxist writing accused capitalist law of doing. Having once been dismissed as a bourgeois institution, law was converted by Stalin into an instrument of party dictatorship. Its function was to create a certain amount of regularity and predictability in routine social affairs and, *above all*, to invest the decrees of the Soviet state with that magic aura of impartiality and impersonality which the law provides simply by being "the law." When Stalin spoke, as he did increasingly, of the creative role of Soviet law, he had in mind precisely the capacity of legal forms to instill awe and respect in the Soviet population and to gloss over the arbitrariness and sectional nature of political power in the USSR.

The death of Stalin, the rise of "collective leadership," Khrushchev's secret speech and the destalinization campaign, the various "thaws," and the fall of Khrushchev himself have not resulted in any fundamental revolution in the Soviet "philosophy of law" comparable to that initiated by Yudin and Vyshinski (presumably under Stalin's orders) in 1936. "Socialist legality," after all, was originally a Stalinist slogan. Like Stalin, his successors have continued to claim that law and the state will "wither away" under true communism, while the family—originally expected to wither away as well—will remain and blossom forth in its true glory. Stalin, in line with his coercive interests and inclinations, argued by Hegelian dialectic that before the state and law could wither away, they must reach their greatest peak of development—that is, they could die only by first becoming stronger. Since his death, the CPSU has proclaimed—if not very convincingly—that the era of communism is now being approached, and that the withering-away of the state and law may thus be expected to begin.

In the process of explaining this, however, the party leaders have subtly changed the content of the original expectations. What is now to wither away is not coercive power itself, but merely the formal state and judicial organs of coercive power, which will first be supplemented and then gradually supplanted by citizens' assemblies acting as tribunals and volunteer brigades and committees acting as popular vigilantes. Even while these new instruments of arbitrary power are coming into being, the Soviet regime proclaims that it is continuing to strengthen "socialist legality." Such are the contradictions allowed by the dialectic!

The contradictions, however, are no longer primarily of the regime's making. The outstanding feature of the post-Stalin period is neither a radical break with the formal principles of Stalin's brand of Marxism nor a wholesale institutional change; it is rather a relaxation of terror and the consequent opening to view of some of the pluralistic tensions and contradictions that have been building up in Soviet society over the past few decades. As the writer has argued elsewhere, these are primarily connected with the inevitable tensions between growing professionalization and the demands of an advanced industrial society on the one hand, and the party's anxiety to maintain both decisive political control and its claim to ultimately absolute author-

ity in all fields on the other. The party, in seeking to alter the mixture of persuasion and coercion (on which all dictatorships rest), has been balancing on a tightrope, gauging the winds of change it helped to liberate, leaning sometimes with them, often against them.

In these circumstances, the attempts of Soviet jurists to systematize a post-Stalinist Marxist philosophy of law have completely lost their theoretical unity and thrust and have become little more than barometric indications of the relative strengths of competing pressures within Soviet society. Marxism as an ideology with pretensions toward theoretical coherence is patently falling apart, and the tensions within Soviet juristic theory and practice no longer have a characteristically Marxist flavor. Fundamentally, these tensions reflect the impact of basically non-Marxist—one might even say "Western"—demands for legal protection, certainty and independence vis-à-vis possible administrative abuses, even by the Communist Party itself, and the attempt of the party to meet and at the same time counterbalance some of these demands.

"Socialist legality" and the gradual normalization of Soviet society, even under Stalin, produced and strengthened a new class of Soviet lawyers with a growing claim to special expertise in their field. In 1946, the CPSU Central Committee noted that there were insufficient cadres of jurists and that the teaching of law had become sadly neglected. The number of institutions of higher legal education was increased, and courses for lawyers were lengthened. The steady and very significant rise in the number of law students and trained lawyers brought with it a growing, albeit stifled, demand for greater recognition of the value of the lawyer's work.

It was only after Stalin's death, however, that these demands were openly voiced, and to some extent met. The lawyers' journal *Sovetskaia yustitsia* began stressing the need for raising the standards of the bar, pleading at the same time that it be afforded proper respect and cooperation. Khrushchev's secret speech of February 1956, with its admission of malpractices under Stalin, and the review of political sentences that went on between 1953 and 1957, resulting in many "rehabilitations," created a climate in which it became permissible to stress the need for formal respect of human and legal rights and the desirability of safeguards that would make administrative disregard of such rights difficult or impossible. Against this background, Soviet jurists began stressing the advantages of certain Western formalist conceptions—in particular, the concept of a trial as a contest between an equally-favored prosecution and defense in the context of a presumption that anyone accused of a criminal offense was innocent unless proven guilty. There were even suggestions that still stronger safeguards might be obtained by introducing a sort of jury system, although the authors attempted, unsuccessfully, to hide the radical nature of their proposal by framing it in terms of increasing the number of people's assessors from two to six.

The party met some of these demands in the wholesale revision of codes begun after the constitutional amendments of 1957. The Special Board of the Ministry of Internal Affairs, which had the power to send people to labor camps without a hearing, was abolished. The security police were placed under the supervision of the Procuracy. The special procedures for cases involving the most serious counterrevolutionary or anti-state crimes were taken out of the law, and Vyshinski's doctrines shifting the burden of proof to the accused and lending special importance to confessions in cases of counterrevolutionary crime have been repudiated. Military courts have been deprived of their jurisdiction over civilians except in cases of espionage. The law permitting the punishment of relatives of members of the armed forces who desert abroad has been abolished. The Fundamental Principles of Criminal Law, promulgated in 1958, stipulated that no criminal law could be retroactively applied unless the law itself specifically so provided. The status of the defense lawyer is in the process of being redefined more carefully and more favorably, while the active participation of attorneys' organizations as well as of law faculties and institutes has been sought in formulating the preliminary drafts of new legal codes. Great significance is now being attached to the Procurator-General's powers to review the records of court trials and institute proceedings for revision of sentence as a further safeguard against repetition of the criminal violations of socialist legality that occurred in the past.

On the other hand, the drive to strengthen "socialist legality" has been carefully contained. The suggestion for a jury system was rejected as a return to a Tsarist institution, and the presumption of innocence has not been incorporated in the Fundamental Principles of Criminal Law. While federal jurisdiction in the making of codes has been heavily curtailed, the Procuracy has been strongly centralized. A number of procedural guarantees suggested by the legal profession for inclusion in the codes have been stricken out in the draft stage. Capital punishment has been restored for certain economic crimes, and in one case this penalty seems to have been imposed retroactively in spite of the specific prohibition contained in the Fundamental Principles of 1958. The "anti-parasite" laws adopted by several union republics at the end of 1957 and by the RSFSR in 1961 have restored to the statute books a crime as vague as the old "socially dangerous acts." The *druzhiny* (people's militia), established in 1958, were already said to have grown to 2.5 million by 1960; they actively and officiously call Soviet citizens to order for minor infringements, while the *bytovyie otryady* (volunteer patrols) of the Komsomol visit Soviet citizens in their own homes to settle disputes and inculcate collective principles. In 1962, violent resistance to arrest by either police or members of the *druzhiny* was made a capital offense. Meanwhile, the growth of "comrades' courts," empowered to try minor matters informally, has been actively encouraged as part of the movement towards true communism.

All this points to the conclusion that the Soviet view of law has not simply and completely broken with its recent past. As Professor Harold J. Berman, of Harvard University, has written:

If one looks behind the structure to the purposes of Soviet law, it remains a totalitarian law, in the sense that it seeks to regulate all aspects of economic and social life, including the circulation of thought, while leaving the critical questions of political power to be decided by informal, secret procedures beyond the scrutiny or control either of legislative or of judicial bodies. It remains the law of a one-party state. It remains the law of a planned economy. It remains a law whose primary function is to discipline, guide, train and educate Soviet citizens to be dedicated members of a collectivized and mobilized social order.

At best, the "philosophy of law" approved by the Soviet party leadership is akin to that which might guide a Western juvenile court: the duty of the Soviet citizen is to be a good child, to work hard, to obey his elders, and to learn to live and play with others. Against this "philosophy" stand the pressures exerted by Soviet citizens who no longer feel themselves to be entirely dependent children, who want guarantees, rights, and some recognition of their human and professional dignity. Mostly they express their demands in Marxist jargon, but this only robs their point of its effectiveness.

The complexity of the Soviet situation lies in the fact that the tension between "socialist legality" (reflecting the impact of Western concepts) and Bolshevik coercive paternalism has to some extent penetrated to all levels of Soviet society and certainly into the party itself. At the present moment, the Soviet leaders are trying hard to have it both ways, and so are their critics at home who cannot hope to speak unless they at least pay lip service to Bolshevik paternalism. The practical results are indeed considerably better than in Stalin's day, but the accompanying eclectic apologies for a legal philosophy or a Marxist view of the world can hardly be taken seriously as theoretical contributions to the understanding of law and its role in society.

HOSTS AND PESTS:
THE FIGHT AGAINST PARASITES

Leon Lipson

Like many other countries, the Soviet Union has people of varied habits, tastes, morals, and ways of life. Unlike many other rulers, Soviet leaders find this diversity repugnant. To their mind, the team must pull together, and no one must be allowed to pull the wrong way. When some players act as if they did not even know they were on a team and pulling, they are suspect: Could they, in stealth, be playing on another?

The metaphor of the team is but a metaphor. It exaggerates the definiteness of the rules to which the team adheres, and it understates the size of the stakes in a contest that the managers take in dead earnest. Yet it will profit us to follow the metaphor a little further still.

The managers of Soviet society believe that society, like a team, is no mere aggregation or even congregation but an organism aimed at a goal. It is the managers who define the goal and aim the organism. As in a game, the goal can be reached only by defeating the opponents who (though doomed to defeat) are assumed to be well organized, perservering, and equipped with tools and strategy.

The players count for less than the managers, but they need to be looked after. From time to time they need rest, reward, and refreshment. From time to time they need exhortation and morale-boosting; at all times they need strong and confident leadership. The health of the team demands vigilant attention; certain players must be relied on to observe and report on the rest. When a player falters or is faint of heart, he must be sent to the sidelines lest he corrupt his teammates. Weakness, illness, and betrayal differ more in origin than in effect, and the response must be uniformly decisive. Occasional exemplary punishment acts as a stimulus to the others.

Not all of the objectives pursued by the Soviet leaders can be fitted readily into the team-metaphor. Coercion to virtue is esteemed not only for virtue's sake but also as a means of reducing the incidence of lawbreaking. The number of violations of public order is swollen by the difficulties of the society and by the broadly inclusive notion of what *amounts* to a violation. The more precarious the equilibrium of the state, the greater the perceived danger of subversion; the narrower the line, the harder it is not to deviate from it. Even short of disorder, subversion, and deviation, the failure to do one's part in raising the wealth of the state is an offence against the presuppositions of the leaders and thus against the laws of the realm. If *homo oeconomicus* is not yet respectable enough to be allowed on the stage, let his lines be given to *homo juridicus:* Soviet morality permits the government to threaten pain in order to push the citizen to many acts to which it cannot yet pull him by hope of reward.

Problems of Communism (March–April 1965), pp. 72–82. Reprinted by permission. Footnotes omitted.

Under Khrushchev's rule the Soviet state apparatus lightened its grasp a little. Much has already been written about the reduction of penalties for some crimes, the abolition of certain forms of criminal liability side by side with the hardening of repression in other fields. Observers of the Soviet scene have described the decline in (not the elimination of) the power and conspicuousness of the internal security police, as well as the partial reform of the procedure of investigating and prosecuting crimes.

What has thus far received insufficient attention in the West has been another mode of control that has spread widely over the Soviet Union, covering a wide variety of criminal acts, anti-social behavior, unorthodox views and "un-Soviet" attitudes. The institutions through which the control is exercised, though tied closely to the State, lack a full-time paid professional staff, formal procedural rules, and bureaucratic traditions; indeed, that is counted to their credit. These institutions may be described as the non-courts (in the first place, the comrades' courts and the anti-parasite tribunals) and the im-police (the DND, or volunteer people's guard). The importance of these "civic" organizations for the Soviet administration of justice is equalled by the place they have come to occupy in Soviet constitutional theory: the non-courts are the foremost installments by which Khrushchev made partial delivery on his promise, or threat, to transfer more and more functions of government from the State to the people. Soviet jurists seldom choose to illustrate this process with the anti-parasite tribunals, which sometimes seem as awkwardly marginal in Soviet theory, and almost as awkwardly prominent in Soviet practice, as the death penalty.

The Party Leads the Way

The anti-parasite laws began their modern career before the revival and reformation of the comrades' courts and the volunteer people's guard. Draft statutes appeared in party newspapers through the Union in early 1957. Under those drafts, "able-bodied citizens leading an anti-social, parasitic way of life, deliberately avoiding socially useful labor, and likewise those living on unearned income" could be tried at a public meeting of fellow-residents. In cities, the meeting would be convoked by a street committee or apartment house management's committee for cooperation in maintaining public order; in rural areas, by a village soviet. Sentence could be passed by a majority of those attending, who in turn had only to be a majority of the adult citizens of the given local unit. Although the meeting could confine its action to a warning for a period of probation, the primary sanction was exile at forced labor for two to five years. The sentence would be subject to no judicial review, but would go into effect on being confirmed by the executive committee of the local soviet.

The drafts met opposition, some of which was made public in articles and letters to the newspapers. A number of people asserted that the definition of living on unearned income was vague; that sham-workers should be included beside non-workers; that the requirements for a quorum at the public meeting should be tightened. Someone urged that the government prosecutor (*prokuror*) should be present at the trials to watch over legality; it was suggested that the power of the general meeting should be limited to the uncovering of facts to be brought to the attention of the *prokuror* for further action in the course of regular criminal prosecution; others urged that the public meeting be vested with a wider range of possible sanctions than the choice between a warning and two-to-five-year exile.

The anti-parasite measures were nonetheless enacted, mostly in a form close to the drafts, in nine "outlying" republics between 1957 and 1960. In the Russian Republic and the Ukraine, no anti-parasite law was enacted until 1961; opposition there may have been even stronger though less visible.

There is reason to think that between 1957 and 1961 the opponents of an anti-parasite law sought to play off one non-court against another. The draft statute for the comrades' courts in the Russian Republic, published in 1959, included a provision that would have let a comrades' court hear parasite cases. As the sanctions available to the comrades' courts did not include anything so drastic as exile to forced labor for two to five years, the suggestion to bestow parasite jurisdiction on comrades' courts may have come from those who thereby desired to forestall the adoption of an anti-parasite law.

In late 1959 and 1960 the drive for more drastic punishment of parasites in the Russian Republic was renewed. A lead seems to have been taken by officials of the Young Communist League (*Komsomol*), whose institutional connection with the internal security apparatus has long been apparent. First, the Komsomol has administrative responsibility for many of the "welfare" activities aimed at combating the rise of juvenile delinquency. Second, it has special duties in organizing and controlling public demonstrations and the more carefully planned "spontaneous" demonstrations. Third, the Komsomol has played an active role in the establishment and staffing of local volunteer people's guards (*druzhiny*) and the units that the guards superseded. Fourth, the Komsomol, in its public pronouncements, has tended to uphold a stern, xenophobic, and maximalist standard on questions of ideological purity and public morality. Fifth, the leaders of the organization appear to form a pool from which the senior Soviet security apparatus draws its staff.

In early 1960 the Komsomol Central Committee urged its local organs to work with and reform young ex-convicts and idlers, to help comrades' courts, to fight drunkenness, to help parents in the upbringing of children. In April a Komsomol newspaper objected to a prosecutor's leniency in remitting to the custody of her father a pampered girl who with her husband had taken to theft. Later the tone grew harsher. In August, in a pair of articles on a young drifter whose main offenses seemed to be that he could not hold down a job and that he aped foreign ways, the newspaper's correspondents complained that others like him could sin undeterred because they knew that he was not threatened "with even 15 days, much less 15 years, for his parasitism." They asserted that comrades' courts had no jurisdiction because "these people have no comrades," and they recommended that "the people's volunteers, who know these idlers well, should be granted the right to try them and hand down stern sentences in the name of Society, the right to turn them out of the Peking Restaurant [in Moscow] and send them to construction sites and logging camps, to make them work." Letters from readers upheld these suggestions, recommending with vigor that "loafers like these should be expelled from big cities and settled in special colonies"; that "hooligans, drunkards, and all other loafers must be categorically barred from living in the big cities," especially Moscow; that "these 'heroes' must be sent to special correction colonies to be taught respect for labor."

Other Soviet papers paid their respects to parasitism in the same period but tended to fit their accounts more closely to a particular offense which was, or in the writers' view ought to have been, made a regular crime.

Important, though still general, guidance came in September 1960, through a leading article in the official party theoretical organ *Kommunist*. The writers of this article acknowledged that "the struggle against parasites is being intensified at the present time"; attributed the persistence of parasitism to private-property psychology, which was nourished by contemporary influences from the bourgeois world; recommended stricter enforcement of existing laws and less emphasis in the press on speculators' ill-gotten gains; and ominously concluded with a word of praise for the anti-parasite law passed shortly before in Georgia and a call for new legislation making it possible to bring "administrative or criminal proceedings" against all parasites.

Comments and Response

Jurists moved into the discussion in the latter part of 1960. Two of them agreed that new penalties on parasites had to be set, but they advocated the use of sanctions adjusted to the offense. Thus, said one, it might be possible to deprive parasites of a right to state housing, to rescind permits on land used for rental speculation, to take licenses away from drivers who used their cars for illegal transport at a profit, to deny parasites admission to health resorts, to exclude them from medical facilities except in dire need, to keep them out of educational institutions and libraries. The other expressed himself against the withholding of medical care and access to libraries, but he favored settlement in special corrective-labor colonies; condemnation as a parasite, he held, ought to be pronounced either by a comrades' court or by a public meeting.

Shortly thereafter a people's judge voiced two recommendations which found their way into an RSFSR decree six months later: one, that property acquired by means other than labor be forfeit; the other, that parasites should be not simply banished from the city where they happened to be offending but settled in definite areas and compelled to work there, on pain of criminal punishment.

It was just this element of forced labor that troubled other jurists. A leading article in the journal of the RSFSR Ministry of Justice and Supreme Court, preferring the denial of various social benefits, objected:

...it is hardly possible to accept as correct the assertions of some readers who propose that parasites should be forced to work by administrative bodies, inasmuch as forced labor, widely resorted to under capitalism, is alien to socialism.

The article did, however, agree with the adoption whenever necessary of the hearing procedure familiar from the existing anti-parasite laws: sentence by public meeting, and confirmation by the local soviet executive committee.

The year 1961 was marked by the campaign against economic crimes and the expansion of the death penalty; it is not surprising that during that year public opposition to the stiffer form of anti-parasite law came to a halt. On May 4, 1961 the RSFSR at last enacted its decree, to which in the following months the legislation of almost all other union republics was substantially conformed. The opponents of anti-parasite legislation had lost. Comrades' courts, with their lighter sanctions, were not given authority over parasite cases as such; the new legislation retained the sentence of two to five years of exile to specially set-off regions, with compulsory labor at the place of settlement.

Opposition, however, had not proved altogether vain. The 1961 decree did contain one important change from the 1957 drafts, and thus also represented a departure from the legislation of the 1957–1960 period. This was a change in the procedure for hearing cases. In the 1961 decree no role was left for the residential public meeting, and the lowest state court of general jurisdiction, the people's court, was assigned important duties. A procedural distinction was drawn between cases of parasites who did not work at all and cases of parasites who had been registered in a job but did not report for work. The parasite who held no job was placed under the exclusive jurisdiction of a people's court, which, however, was supposed to try the case non-criminally and thus without such safeguards as were contained in the Code of Criminal Procedure. The parasite who was enrolled in a sham job could be tried by a people's court or by a public meeting of workers; discretion to select the forum was not expressly lodged anywhere, but subsequent commentary has made it clear that it is the government prosecutor's office that makes the decisions.

According to the decree, cases heard by a people's court are not subject to review in ordinary appeal but may be protested by the prosecutor to higher courts. Cases heard by a public meeting are subject to no review in court, but the sentence does not take effect until it has been confirmed by the executive committee of the local soviet, which therefore is in a position to conduct an administrative review of the file; as the convocation of the public meeting may have come at the initiative, or at least with the approval, of the executive committee of the local soviet in the first place, the administrative review probably persuades the reviewers in most cases that the sentence was right and should be confirmed.

Another change was that under the 1961 decree the warning became not one of the consequences but one of the prerequisites of the trial. An anti-parasite proceeding now is not to be instituted until after the offender has been warned by the authorities to mend his ways and has disregarded the warning. Some convictions have since been set aside, on protest, by appellate courts on the ground that the necessary warning had not been given; more have been set aside on the ground that too little time had been allowed for the warned offender to reform. The warning may be given by "civic organizations or state organs," including the police, the public prosecutor, a trade union, a comrades' court, and perhaps others. In most cases the way for a man to comply with a warning is to get a job, or, if he is already on the rolls, to work regularly at his job; however, sometimes it is hard to tell what the offender could have done after the warning to avert the subsequent proceedings. If the parasite has gone to work by the time his case comes to trial or even by the time it comes to the attention of a higher court (where that is possible), the exile is wrongful and must be set aside even though the offender took the job only after the expiration of a realistic term of warning; but he has to be supervised closely in his work lest the employment prove to have been a maneuver to circumvent the decree.

Casting the Net

The Soviet statistics on crimes and quasi-crimes are, "as is well known," not well known. Even if we had numerical data on the operation of the anti-parasite laws, we should be unable to infer the number of proceedings against "parasites." Those laws do not reach all who in Soviet terms are parasites, and other laws reach some of the offenders who could otherwise be held liable under the anti-parasite laws: the overlap touches on one side the regular criminal code and the comrades' courts and, on another side, the administrative proceedings taken to deprive certain speculators of the property used in the speculation, such as rental housing.

Still, some semi-statistics can be put together. From a study of parasites sentenced in the first six months after the enactment of the decree of May 4, 1961, we can infer that at least 600 cases led to a conviction. Furthermore, it appears that 96 per cent of the parasites given a warning in the early months were not prosecuted, because they heeded the warning and found proper work. Arithmetic calculations suggest that during the time in question at least 15,000 warnings were administered. As to convictions, a Soviet researcher suggested informally in mid-

1963 that the index of convictions, by calendar quarters, might look something like this:

	1Q	2Q	3Q	4Q
1961	—	100	150	200
1962	150	120	110	100
1963	75	50		

The role of the public meeting, reduced by the jurisdictional provisions of the 1961 decree, was reduced still further in operation. Most of the prosecutions under the law had to be brought before people's courts because the defendants were unemployed and thus not attached to any occupational collective. It has been said that the sham workers were too often protected by their fellows. Even the few sham workers who were tried were usually brought not to the workers' public meeting but to the people's court. The government prosecutors may prefer this route because they regard the public meetings as too lenient, too different from ordinary criminal prosecutions, or too unfamiliar.

The laws against parasites seem to look two ways at once. One edge of the sword is turned against the violent drunkard, the wife-beater, the man who has never made it. Thus an American observer describes the trial in Moscow of one Zbarski—drunk, loathsome, scandalous, without work—who was exiled under the decree for three years. Sometimes the decree is used to get rid of prostitutes, as appeared to be the case with one Maiseva, sentenced to five years after trial in the city of Chita. The woman who instead of working spends her time slandering her neighbors and complaining to the authorities about imaginary threats is also a fit subject for exile. Many of the offenders are young ne'er-do-wells who are depicted as living off their poor but industrious parents and spending their nights in drinking bouts.

The other edge of the sword is turned against the man who disrupts the economic order by turning an illegal profit, the over-privileged scion who seeks shelter behind the broad backs of his rich and powerful relatives, the *stiliaga* in narrow trousers and duck-tail hair-cut lounging on the sidewalks of Gorky Street, the snob who likes to sport Western clothes and a Western nick-name.

Yet it is also possible to speculate that the thrust of the sword is really all one, and that the weapon is being wielded in the interest of the values of a lower middle class rising to power. After all, many of the virtues celebrated in anti-parasite proceedings and in the literature about parasites are just those so often ascribed to the lower middle class: the glory of work in one's appointed calling; modesty in dress, toilet, deportment; adjusting to one's surroundings, making one's peace with the organization. In defense of these values the anti-parasite laws, like the comrades' courts and the volunteer people's guard, are used to repress "excesses" characteristic of either the lower or the upper class. On this view the self-appointed gravediggers of the bourgeoisie are now busy making the land safe for the *petit bourgeois*.

Ironical though it may be, this explanation of the anti-parasite laws has much in its favor. As a part of the truth it must not be neglected; yet there are other facts in the picture which it fails to fit. First, the men and women in the party establishment do not seem effectively subject to the anti-parasite laws or other non-courts in the public sector, though party discipline may be exerted from time to time for similar reasons on some "upper-class" cases. Second, the Soviet ideologists would deny that a social class structure in this sense exists in Soviet society; anyone in any station can be part of the *narod* (the people) just as anyone in any station can be an *obyvatel* (Philistine, selfish vulgarian). Third, the procedures used to further these lower-middle-class values are derived from rather unlikely models, such as the village assembly and the pattern of peasant collective censure. Fourth, certain values usually associated with the lower middle class in European and American society are not only absent from Soviet ideology but attacked as unworthy: one thinks in particular of the value of personal thrift (or personal accumulation) and of the value of privacy or discretion in personal relations. The individual pioneer, the self-reliant Titan raising his edifice of thought or invention or production, is not an approved model in collectivist society.

We do not know whether the anti-parasite law is used to punish, or to discourage, political opposition. There seems to be no evidence that the trial proceedings are concerned with directly political matters. No doubt a man who tried to devote any substantial time to building an independent political group or theory would qualify as a parasite in the Soviet sense, but he would thereby have offended other and sterner prescriptions also, and other bodies would handle his case.

The emphasis on the prosecution of young men who affect foreign ways probably has political significance for at least some of the participants. Other political bias is shown in the prosecutions of evangelists and unorthodox artists. The recent conviction of a young Leningrad writer and translator of poetry, Yosif Brodsky, has become well known outside the Soviet Union because detailed notes of his two trials have been published in Europe and the United States. Brodsky left school at 15 and worked briefly at many jobs. Senior writers and critics submitted testimonials vouching for his diligence and competence. The accusers at his parasite trial charged him with having written pornographic poems and corrupting the young. They attacked lines in his poems: "I love another homeland," "I have long thought about going beyond the Red line," and, in a letter, "I felt like spitting on Moscow." Brodsky was sentenced to five years and, according to report, was sent to a state farm near Archangel; since then, conflicting rumors have been circulated about his release, transfer, and continued detention. The trial notes indicate that the judge and some others exhibited a harsh and flippant anti-intellectualism, with undertones of anti-semitism.

Dubious Successes and Embarrassing Failures

Soviet commentators sometimes treat the parasite laws like a nuclear arsenal, maintained more in order to make threats credible than to be regularly invoked. Mere enactment and dissemination of the anti-parasite decrees, some have claimed, have driven the great majority of parasites into regular work. Of the rest, all but a few are said to have been reformed by the obligatory warning.

The Soviet study of six hundred parasite convictions in 1961 indicated that the maximum sentence of five years was passed on 43 percent of the cases; 25.5 percent got three years, 20 percent two, 11.5 percent four. The Supreme Court complained in the same period that sentences below the minimum were being passed by people's courts; perhaps some lower courts had taken too seriously the assertion that anti-parasite penalties were not criminal.

Very few of the sentences have included confiscation of the property earned by means other than labor. The reason has not been made clear. It is not very probable that the authorities would be stopped by the difficulty of tracing the property if they determined to search for it, but they may not think it worth the effort, or most of the defendants may not in fact have acquired much property by the means indicated, though it can be argued that possession of such property is a principal index of probable guilt and even that it is a necessary element in the offense; or some of the offenders who have such property may be guilty of some regular crime, like speculation, and thus in theory not liable to trial as parasites. A more speculative possibility was raised by an official opponent of a dissertation on the interrelationship of norms of law and morality, submitted in the Institute of Philosophy: he referred to the practice in the administration of the anti-parasite laws that require the defendant to show how he obtained the property, and hinted that it might violate the presumption of innocence.

The place of ex-settlement is not specified in the decrees. In the Russian Republic most of the offenders appear to be settled in the Krasnoiarski Krai. Many of them come as unskilled (non-) laborers. They are put to work on collective farms, in factories, at construction sites, in lumber camps.

Though there are criminal sanctions for refusing to work at places of ex-settlement, some—again we do not know how many—refuse and are subject to "corrrective labor" at docked pay and, if they persist, to "deprivation of freedom."

The failures of re-education have been attributed to the solidarity of the parasites, or their mutual contagion; being settled together, they continue—again, in an unknown percentage of cases—to encourage one another to shirk, to drink, to loaf, to steal. One writer has recommended that they be dispersed singly or in small groups among healthy collectives. The managers of the enterprises to which the exiled parasites are assigned do not seem to be overjoyed by the abundant supply of labor; there have been reports of managers falsely attesting to a parasite's reform, so as to be allowed to ship him back home.

In Siberia, the authorities have gone so far as to protest the transportation of parasites. Many of them, it seems, not only continue to lead a parasitic way of life but disturb public order, commit more serious offenses, and even corrupt others. Still other parasites, the authorities contend, begin to behave well only after serving half of their term so as to take advantage of provisions for parole. To put an end to these trends, a solution opposite to that of dispersal has been suggested—namely, that the parasites be concentrated in special work colonies, presumably far enough from normal civil life to lessen the danger of contamination.

It is safe to assume that the stories of rehabilitation, written from Moscow (as most of them appear to be), are not very representative. The home team may be glad to hear that the transported parasite is making good Out There if only he stays Out There; the men who are responsible for public order in the places of settlement have a different outlook.

The People and the State

One of the claims made for the non-courts in the Soviet Union is that they bring the processes of justice closer to the people and at the same time induce the people to take part in the processes of justice. In part, the claim is justified. When a civic accuser or defender speaks in a criminal trial, he does represent an organization or collective even though the collective decision authorizing his effort may have been inspired and guided from above. When a court holds sessions in the Little Red Corner of an apartment house or the club-room of a trade union local, many attend who otherwise probably would not, and the responses of the audience frequently interact (not always in the interest of justice) with the proceedings "on stage." The speeches made by members of the audience toward the end of a trial in a comrades' court, while some of them appear to reflect the instructions of the local *aktiv*, do convey a sense of popular morality—channeled into a state-established, though nominally unofficial, sanction. The authorities go to considerable trouble before and during the trials of accused parasites, both in people's courts and at public meetings of workers, to mobilize the expression if not the reality of public sentiment.

Nonetheless, it is clear that the "popularization" of justice tends to bring an ever larger portion of life under the eye of a watchful regime.

The non-courts do not—as is sometimes asserted—merely relieve the official courts from that portion of their case-load that can be handled with less formal procedures and less drastic sanctions. A comparison between all the cases handled by the regular courts in, say, 1956 and those handled by the courts and non-courts together in 1964 would reveal that the range of supervised conduct has markedly increased. So have the number of sanctionable offenses, the total number of cases, the amount and probably even the median severity of the penalties handed down. The comparison would very likely hold good even if the 1956 figures were augmented by the caseload handled by the predecessors of today's comrades' courts and of today's volunteer people's guard. The Soviet regime has become less repressive; but it does not show many signs of becoming less comprehensive.

Procedures in cases against parasites fit into a pattern that has been described more thoroughly in its application to small and limited organizations than in relation to an entire polity. In many countries, certain types of institutions share an approach to the individual, an official ethic, and a mode of operation that have led a sociologist to call them "total institutions." Examples may be found in the work of many mental hospitals, insane asylums, prisons, reformatories, army camps, concentration camps, some preparatory schools, and the training programs of certain religious orders. Some of the features of these institutions closely resemble ordinary life in the Soviet Union as a whole, and one of the most striking resemblances is the practice that the sociologist has called "looping."

Looping takes place between institution and individual and appears most clearly when the institution is most nearly "total." In those cases, officials of the institution, doing their duty as they see it, have acted upon or against the individual (patient, inmate, prisoner, recruit, novice—or, in the Soviet Union, citizen). The subject responds by defensive reaction. Then—and here is the place where the loop is made—the officials of the institution treat the subject's defensive response as evidence confirming the rightness of their initial judgment or diagnosis or punitive measure, and inflict more of the same. Sometimes the loop is traveled through several circuits.

How does looping occur in the operation of the anti-parasite laws in the Soviet Union? One instance is the counter-response to the Grin. In anti-parasite cases, as well as in comrades' courts, the defendant often reacts to his odd and unpleasant situation (no matter whether he deserves, by his or the regime's criteria, to be put in it) by a tight, fixed grin. This grin thereupon becomes an added offense; prosecutors, civic accusers and judges comment on the grin, "which shows that this defendant has no respect for our Soviet laws, has a frivolous attitude toward his social obligations, and mocks the authority of this tribunal." The judgment itself, though it may not mention the grin specifically, will refer to the defendant's contemptuous attitude in court as one of the signs that he is in need of correction. The grin has its counterpart in the smaller "total institutions" when the subject is not permitted the luxury of an autonomous facial reaction (sneer, pout, disgust, frown) and must keep a blank face lest the severity of the sanction be increased.

Another example lies in the blurring

of the lines between various parts of a subject's existence. In the mental hospital what the patient does or says on the ward where he sleeps or in the shop where he works is observed, perhaps by different officials, but it is part of the job of the institution to collate the observations, to relate them to a picture of the whole man. The freedom of ordinary civil life, where work, play, family, public service, social life can be kept in separate though not completely sealed compartments, is infringed in the total institution for the subject's own good—as the institution views it. Correspondingly, in the Soviet Union it is not only permissible but obligatory for the authorities to collapse the separate structures of a subject's daily life by piecing together the observations recorded by his family, his colleagues, the housing committee, the union officials, the party representatives.

A third example lies in the use made by the official of information elicited from the subject himself in the interests of the program of the institution (again ostensibly for the good of the individual as well as society). A mild form of this can be seen in the use made of interviews and questionnaires in market research and political polling. A more intensive form is practiced in certain kinds of psychotherapy. In the Soviet Union, the authorities profess to encourage candor but in practice reserve the privilege of using the elicited material to justify further sanctions.

To a lawyer, the closest parallel in a looser society is the process by which a convicted defendant is sentenced. At the point of sentencing, the privacy and autonomy that have been preserved at least in the public forum are discarded; testimony, under safeguards of no great rigor, is taken from the district attorney, police officers, welfare workers, and others; the convict himself is heard, but what he says is likely to be used against him. Not only the Soviet anti-parasite proceeding but also Soviet life as a whole is governed to some degree by similar rules. It is almost as if a Soviet citizen came into his society already convicted and ripe for the sentencing.

THE SOVIET EDUCATIONAL SYSTEM AND THE PROCESS OF POLITICAL SOCIALIZATION

JEREMY R. AZRAEL

I

With a few notable exceptions, students of Soviet politics have largely neglected, or at best treated only indirectly, the process whereby Soviet citizens, and more particularly Soviet youth, acquire their political values, atti-

Jeremy R. Azrael, "Soviet Union," in James S. Coleman, ed., *Education and Political Development* (Princeton, N.J.: Princeton University Press, 1965), pp. 233–57, 265–67. Reprinted by permission of Princeton University Press. Footnotes omitted.

tudes, perceptions, and sentiments. The task of this chapter is to help fill this gap by discussing one major agency involved in the process of political socialization in the USSR—the educational system.

There are good reasons for making a study of the educational system the first toward a broader study of the process of political socialization in the Soviet Union. In the first place, a good deal of relevant data, though by no means enough, is available. In the second place, the Soviet rulers aspire to transform the educational system into *the* primary agency of political socialization for Soviet youth. However, the present effort is limited in scope. There is, for example, no discussion of pre-school institutions or "schools of special purpose" such as military and party schools. Similarly, the focus is almost exclusively on the past two or three decades of Soviet educational history. No attempt is made to discuss the first period of Soviet education during which a combination of revolutionary zeal for "progressive" pedagogical experimentation and concern to undercut the authority of the temporarily irreplaceable "bourgeois" teachers led to a thorough-going transformation of the traditional educational system.

In addition, another, more fundamental, word of caution is in order. Those suggestions which follow and attempt to correlate the influence of the educational system as an agency of political socialization with the political behavior of those who have passed through it (or for that matter are still in it) are at best very general and tentative; they are offered with extreme trepidation. In the first place, the educational system is but one agency of political socialization, and

its influence cannot be appraised with confidence unless the roles of other critical agencies such as the family, the peer-group, the communication media, non-school institutions and organizations, etc., are analyzed in some detail. In the second place, political behavior cannot be viewed simply as a product of political socialization unless political socialization is treated in a purely reductionist fashion—i.e., unless all other variables are reduced to the single variable "political socialization." Political socialization often determines the tenor of political behavior, sets limits to it, etc., but behavior is determined by situational and other variables as well. What is true of the political behavior of individuals is even more true of the processes of political change in society at large. Thus, if the suggestions which are offered on the interrelationship between the functioning of the educational system and political behavior are very general and tentative, those which are offered on the interrelationship between the functioning of the educational system and basic processes of political change are doubly so.

Given this orientation and these limits, the central question which is posed in this essay might be put as follows: what degree of success has the Soviet educational system achieved in meeting its assigned task of creating a "new man"? To put the question in this way suggests the existence of a number of potentially instructive comparisons, since in other countries as well, and notably in some of the newly independent nations, the political rulers have assigned the educational system a key role in the transformation of traditional values, beliefs, attitudes, and sentiments. However, if the Soviet educational system is considered in its own terms, comparisons of this sort can be valid only up to a point. The "new *Soviet* man" whom the Soviet educational system is supposed to produce is not merely "civic man" and "industrial man" but also "totalitarian man." There is persuasive evidence that *ultimately* political cohesiveness and rapid economic development are merely instrumental values for the Soviet rulers, and that the latter's end goal is the construction and consolidation of a political system in which total power is concentrated in their own hands. As leaders of the Communist Party, the Soviet rulers have claimed that status of exclusive custodians of an all-embracing, action-oriented ideology—Marxism-Leninism. Since at least 1928, they have interpreted this ideology as postulating and legitimizing the creation of a polity in which the entire populace is kept in a state of perpetual mobilization, all primary groups and secondary associations are transformed into malleable "transmission belts" controlled from the center, and all traditional loyalties are subverted or uprooted. They have attempted to establish a totalitarian political culture—an all-inclusive, monolithic, and homogeneous political culture characterized by values, beliefs, attitudes, and sentiments which foster absolute devotion to the Communist Party, undeviating adherence to the principles set forth in the party line, and enthusiastic obedience to the directives of the party leadership. Few, if any, of the rulers of the "new nations," even where they have borrowed Soviet organizational techniques, aspire to such total power. Nor is a nationalistic ideology conducive to the creation of such a polity or the establishment of such a political culture, since, no matter how revolutionary its spirit, na-

tionalism usually implies and entails some legitimation of and respect for traditional social arrangements and cultural principles. In the Soviet system, as will be shown, the attempt to achieve political cohesiveness and rapid economic development has forced modification in, and in some important respects placed obstacles in the course of, the quest for total power. However, that quest has been persistent, and its pursuit has had a decisive influence on the nature and functioning of the Soviet educational system. In the next section of this chapter the nature of this influence will be described; in the third section the obstacles which the educational system has encountered in its effort to induct Soviet youth into the totalitarian political culture will be analyzed, and in the fourth and fifth sections an attempt will be made to discuss and appraise recent changes in the educational system.

II

In this and the following section the discussion will be focused on the educational system during the decade or so immediately prior to the "Khrushchev educational reform" of 1958.

Structure and scope

In the period prior to 1958 (and still today) the educational system was part of the monopolistic, centrally controlled communications network of Soviet society. The Department of Schools of the Party Central Committee supervised the functioning of the entire system and each link of the latter was subject to tight control by local party organs. Policy-making authority in the sphere of higher education was officially centralized and in the remaining spheres, which were formally under the jurisdiction of the several republics, the Russian Republic Ministry of Education set the basic policy line on all important educational issues. What operative decentralization there was derived from the need to take special local conditions into account in order better to realize centrally determined objectives and tended to be almost exclusively administrative in character. A single basic pattern of school organization prevailed throughout the entire country. The law provided for universal, compulsory, seven-year, or *incomplete* secondary education beginning at age seven, although, in fact, in the years immediately preceding the 1958 reform, only 80 per cent of Soviet children who entered the first grade finished the seventh. Upon completing their compulsory education, the overwhelming majority of students followed one of three paths. One group went more or less directly into the work force. A second group enrolled in *technicums,* where they received *complete specialized* secondary education which qualified them, after three or four years' study, as low- or middle-level technicians. A third group, consisting of those whose parents could meet the moderate, but by no means inconsequential, tuition payments which applied from 1941 on and who received the highest scores on the rigorous qualifying exams which were instituted in 1944, was allowed to enter the so-called "complete secondary" or ten-year school, where, for three years, they received a *complete general* secondary education. During most of the period under discussion, the first group constituted approximately 60–65 per cent of the total; the second, 15 per

cent; and the third, some 20–25 per cent; although, as we shall see, in the years immediately preceding the 1958 reform the relative size of the first group decreased and that of the third grew rapidly. Of those students who entered the work force, the preponderant majority pursued their education no further, although there did exist a skeletal network of so-called "schools of working and rural youth" in which they could continue their studies in their free time. Similarly, graduation from the *technicum* was ordinarily the final step in the education of students in the second group, although the top 5 per cent of *technicum* graduates were permitted to apply for immediate admission to higher education, and the remainder could do so after having worked at state-assigned jobs for at least three years. The normal route to higher education was graduation from the ten-year school, and, in fact, prior to 1954, a complete general secondary education was not only a virtual prerequisite for but also a virtual guarantee of admission to higher education. Higher education, which normally lasted five years, was provided in universities or technical institutes and was culminated by enrollment in the lower ranks of the Soviet elite.

Curriculum

Just as a single pattern of school organization prevailed throughout the entire USSR, so a uniform core curriculum was found in all schools of the same basic type. The only significant variations had to do with the language of instruction and, at the upper levels of the educational system, with the particular technical specialty that was stressed. Ideological consideration militated against the development of special programs for "gifted" or "backward" pupils, since the desire for political homogeneity led to an insistence that, within fairly narrow limits, all students were equal or could become equal if they so chose. The same factors led to the politicization of the entire curriculum, although the major indoctrinational burden was carried, as one would anticipate, by the social sciences and humanities. In these fields politicization was particularly intensive and proceeded according to a carefully organized plan designed to synchronize substance and method with the maturation process as understood by Soviet educational psychologists. Broadly speaking, the indoctrinational techniques used corresponded to those which were characteristic of the rest of the Soviet communications network. At the lower levels of the system primary reliance was placed upon *agitation*, with the main effort devoted to inculcating the "spirit" of Bolshevism, conditioning responses to a few relatively simple symbols, acquainting the students with the party's slogans and principal platform planks, and "explaining" in gross outline the policies of the regime. At the upper levels, and above all in the universities and institutes, increasing reliance was placed upon *propaganda*, with the main effort devoted to "the intensive elucidation of the teachings of Marx, Engels, Lenin, and [prior to 1956] Stalin, and of the history of the Bolshevik Party and its tasks." At all levels, however, the general outlines of the "message" were the same.

In the primary and middle grades an intensive effort was made to establish in the minds of students a full identity among political community (nation), regime (party), and government (state system and ruling authorities) and to channel commitment from one to another "level" of the political system without discrimination or differentiation. Early initiation into the cult of Lenin and—prior to 1956—into the cult of Stalin was considered an especially useful means of cementing this identification. According to Soviet educators, experience had shown that "children progress most easily to the feeling of love for their motherland, their fatherland, and their state through a feeling of love for the leaders of the Soviet people— Lenin and Stalin," that "they [the children] associate with the concrete images of Lenin and Stalin, the Party of Communists, the Party of Bolsheviks created by [the] great leaders," and that "they quickly begin to perceive that under the leadership of the Party of Lenin and Stalin we both build and defend our Soviet state, our fatherland." The desired orientation toward the monolithic political system was summed up in the concept "Soviet patriotism," and the supreme task of the curriculum was to inculcate "Soviet patriotism."

At the lower levels of the education system, "Soviet patriotism" was interpreted primarily in terms of the political community. Thus, history texts —and the primary school song book and readers as well—were designed to convince students that "everywhere, in all spheres of science and art, industry and agriculture, in the works of peace and on the battlefields, the Soviet people march in the forefront of other nations and have created values which are unequaled anywhere in the world." As this suggests, a dichotomous image of the world was an integral part of the inculcation of "Soviet patriotism." While elaborating the glories of the Soviet Union, teachers were instructed to regale their students with vivid "human interest" stories of life in the West—stories of a sort which would insure that students knew "not only with their minds, but with their hearts that capitalism is hunger, unemployment, and eternal fear of tomorrow." It was expected that an emotionally charged juxtaposition of the glories of Soviet life and the horrors of life in the West would "foster a hatred for the exploiters," "teach the students to struggle," and reinforce the students' love of the Soviet system. Out of this syndrome of emotions, in turn, the students would develop a feeling that they stood in debt before their own society and were obliged to repay its beneficence with endless and unstinting service.

The type of service which was expected was made clear to school children by appropriate models. Primary school readers were replete with tales of the careers of political leaders (above all Lenin and Stalin), valiant soldiers, famous scientists, and production heroes. The style of these "biographies" was at once hagiographic and intimate, and they were designed not merely to exemplify right conduct and inspire reverence, but also to facilitate the internalization of desirable "ego-ideals." Full identification was encouraged by including many "heroic" children, ranging from the notorious Pavlik Morozov to young partisans killed in the "Great Fatherland War" (World War II). In addition, almost all the "biographies" of adults began with glimpses of the childhood years of their heroes. The fact that the Great Lenin was once *Volodya* Ulyanov and the Great Stalin was once *So-So* Djugashvili was stressed, and the idea was constantly

driven home that the character traits of the heroic adult were consciously cultivated by the child. As for the character traits themselves, those which were most exalted were love of labor, and, in general, the "protestant" economic virtues so central to industrial development; "personal self-sacrifice with the aim of bringing victory to the fatherland"; and "devotion to revolutionary and scientific ideas." And, once again, as in the case of the picture of the world at large, graphic examples of "negative heroes" were juxtaposed to the portraits of "positive heroes" in order to reinforce commitment to the character traits of the latter. The dichotomous image of the world was complemented by a dichotomous image of human nature, and every effort was made to inculcate a radical intolerance of ambiguity.

At the upper levels of the educational system, the indoctrinational themes were essentially the same. However, the approach became increasingly sophisticated. One change of note was the devotion of progressively more time and energy to the development of proper orientations toward the regime and governmental "levels" of the political system. All complete secondary school students were required (usually in the tenth grade) to take a course on "The Constitution of the U.S.S.R." Here the status of the Soviet state as "the most democratic in the world" was elaborated, the institutional setting of Soviet politics was clarified, and students were instructed in the nature and norms of "socialist legality." History was increasingly party history, and more and more time was devoted to the contemporary period. While the inculcation of absolute devotion to the nation as such was by no means abandoned, and history texts continued to cultivate not merely chauvinism but xenophobia, the concept of "Soviet patriotism" was more and more infused with manifest political content. Increasing attention was devoted to cultivating a "class point of view" and to training students to "unmask" and "expose" the "class essence" of ideas. Prior to 1953, all students from the senior grades on were required to be intimately familiar with the *History of the Communist Party of the Soviet Union: Short Course*, with its exaltation of Stalin, its cries for vigilance against any political deviation, and its vigorous assertion of the vanguard role of the party. After Stalin's death, texts and guides of generally similar character, though minus the somewhat hysterical tone and the "cult of personality," were gradually substituted.

In the middle and senior grades there was no separate study of Marxism-Leninism or, as the sequence ran prior to 1953, Marxism-Leninism-Stalinism. The role of the party as exclusive custodian of the ideology was stressed constantly, but no effort was made to cultivate real ideological sophistication. The fact that the party had a "scientific" theory at its disposal was emphasized in order to generate "convictional certainty." This "convictional certainty" was to rise out of but transcend the emotional predispositions built up in the earlier grades. To the students' emotional revulsion against the West was added a "conviction in the inevitable victory of socialism." However, emphasis was *not* placed upon the niceties of historical and dialectical materialism. What was sought was total loyalty to the party, and there was an implicit recognition that until such loyalty was secured, familiarity with the ideology *per se* could lead to "confusion" and provide

a standard by which to judge the party and resist changes in the party line. It was only in the institution of higher education—after the students had been exposed to an all-out attempt to socialize them into party loyalty—that the formal study of Marxism-Leninism was introduced. At this level, however, it was a required subject and occupied an important place in the curriculum. Instruction in ideological theory was designed to consolidate the world view of that segment of Soviet youth which was destined to enter the ranks of the Soviet elite. It was designed to insure that they would not approach their future assignments from a "narrowly professional" point of view and would make the proper choice—i.e., the choice in conformity with the regime's current schedule of priorities—among the conflicting goals which would confront them as they moved up the ladder of success and were accorded more and more operational autonomy. It was designed to insure that they would become worthy members of an *aktiv* on one or another of the "fronts" of Soviet life. And, finally, it was designed to guarantee that they would be sensitized to the special semantics of Soviet political life and hence able properly to "interpret" the measures of the regime to the masses. It was designed, in other words, to prepare them to serve as agitators in their own right, thus perpetuating the cycle of indoctrination through which they themselves had passed.

Atmosphere and spirit

Within the educational system, manipulation of the atmosphere and spirit of school life was considered at least as important as manipulation of the formal curriculum in guaranteeing the proper "political upbringing" of youth. Throughout the system, the atmosphere was pervaded by a spirit of discipline and hierarchy. At the lower levels, lessons were marked by the formal recitation of material drawn from the assigned textbooks and by catechetical drill, while at the higher levels standardized lectures propagating the official version of the Truth predominated. Among the very first requirements imposed on entering pupils was that of memorizing and obeying the highly authoritarian "Rules for Schoolchildren" which constituted "a program for the cultivation ... of habits of disciplined and cultured behavior" both inside and outside the school. It was hoped that behavior, become reflexive, would produce corresponding thought-patterns and that habituation would be the first step in the development of self-discipline. Self-discipline was desired, in turn, because with it *"conformity and obedience [would] become more perfect."* The ultimate goal, in other words, was the internalization of the attitudes toward authority that the "Rules" reflected. Teachers were reminded that they were the principal authority figures with whom school children had contact and that they had to conduct themselves accordingly, never forgetting, as the late Soviet president Kalinin put it, that "a pedagogue is an engineer of human souls." An authoritative text, after pointing out that "submission to the will of a leader is a necessary and essential mark of discipline," directed teachers to "assume from the outset a firm and impressive tone" and warned them not to coax students but rather to demand obedience, for only in this way would students develop the desired moral qualities.

"Conformity and obedience" were

secured not only by casting the teacher in an authoritarian role and imposing rigid rules upon the individual pupils, but also by carefully structuring relationships among the pupils. Here the role of the *kollektiv* was crucial. Indeed, *Pravda* proclaimed a strong *kollektiv* to be "the foundation of foundations of the Soviet educational system" and stressed that it was essential that "the organization of a *kollektiv* and the cultivation in each child of a feeling of collectiveness ... [begin] from the first grade." Teachers were instructed in the ways and means of shaming recalcitrant students into obedience by mobilizing the *kollektivs* against them, thereby at once buttressing their own authority and training students from a very early age to use and respond to such fundamental institutions of Soviet political life as criticism, self-criticism, denunciation, confession, and recantation. However, the *kollektiv's* area of "legitimate" concern was considered to extend well beyond the walls of the classroom, and it was manipulated to break down all attempts on the part of students to develop or maintain a "private" sphere of existence. An attempt was made through the *kollektiv* to exploit the natural vulnerability of youth to peer-group pressure. This was a particularly strategic control technique because, as Kassof has pointed out, the *kollektivs* operated on such a highly personal level and, where they were successful, turned "the abstract question of obeying official norms into issues of friendship and personal emotional security." The first step was to create "citizens ... able to put social above personal interests," but the long-run goal was "to educate a person ... who [had] no interests opposed to the collective interests." The hope was that the student would ultimately come to make his standing in the *kollektiv* the basis for self-appraisal and would develop such a "passion for unanimity" that coercion would be superflous.

The *kollektiv* functioned as an agency of mobilization as well as an agency of control. Here the involvement of the *kollektiv* in "socially useful labor" was considered to be of particular importance. At the lower levels of the educational system, class and school *kollektivs* competed with each other in the collection of scrap metal, the planting of trees, the tending of public parks, etc., while at the upper levels Komsomol organizations mustered their members for "Saturdays" and "Sundays" of labor on nearby construction projects and for summer stints on collective or state farms. The objectives which were sought through student participation in "socially useful labor" were chiefly political and ideological, and in only a few instances was student labor of major economic significance. In the first place, participation was designed to inspire respect for physical labor, thereby, at one and the same time, strengthening the appeal of the regime's image as a bulwark of the proletariat and inhibiting the growth of "class-consciousness" within Soviet society. In the second place, it was designed to bring home the reality of socialism. There appeared to be faith in an inverted Lockean logic, whereby, by dint of mixing their labor with the construction projects of the regime, students would develop a sense of the reality of *their* ownership—socialist ownership through membership in the *kollektiv*—of all of the resources of Soviet society.

Finally, the *kollektiv* functioned as an important channel of political recruitment. This function was most marked, of course, at the upper levels of the educational system, but even in the primary grades the operations of the *kollektiv* were considered particularly useful in permitting teachers to identify "children of initiative." Once the latter were identified, the task was to discipline them without reducing them to apathy. On the one hand every effort was made to insure that "initiative not be exhibited impulsively." On the other hand something more than "just blind obedience" was desired. The objective was to restrict the exercise of intiative to a purely instrumental level where it would find expression as "an independent search for the best way to fulfill a command." To accomplish this delicate task, initiative had to be "directed into organized channels." Here again the *kollektiv* occupied a key position, serving as a forum and a framework for the development of initiative of the desired sort and guaranteeing that "out of children of initiative good organizers ... [would] come." In the earliest years the position of "class monitors," which entailed assisting the teacher with such things as distributing supplies and maintaining classroom discipline and "cultured" standards of student behavior, served as a training ground for "children of initiative." In addition, from the primary grades on, such children were encouraged to assume special "social obligations" above and beyond their participation in "socially useful labor." "Social obligations" in the lower grades ranged from aiding more backward classmates with their school work to writing articles for local children's newspapers. Later "social obligations" entailed such things as the assumption of leadership (under the guidance of the teacher concerned) of a lower-level class *kollektiv* or Pioneer detachment, participation in the regime's various agitational campaigns, etc. Those students who undertook major "social obligations" and fulfilled them with enthusiasm and skill were singled out, in turn, for further and more intensive initiation into the rites of responsibility. They were apt to be moved into the Komsomol apparatus itself, to be accorded early party membership, to be enrolled in the special "cadres reserve" maintained by leading party committees, and thus to be placed on a course which could lead not merely to elite status, but to membership in the "power elite" itself.

III

The educational system prior to 1958 accomplished many of the tasks set it by the Soviet rulers and, in the process, won admiration and prestige for the regime abroad and support for the regime at home. It transformed an overwhelmingly illiterate population into an almost universally literate one. It fought a largely successful battle against the influence on youth of such traditional institutions as the church. It helped socialize a predominantly tradition-oriented population into the cultural patterns of an industrial society. It trained the technical and managerial cadres without whom rapid industrialization and the maintenance of a high tempo of industrial growth would have been impossible. It educated scientists whose researches enabled the regime to pioneer new developments in a wide variety of fields. It played an important role in persuading the bulk of Soviet youth of the merits of socialist principles of production and distribution. It helped generate enough con-

sensus to enable the political system to survive severe shock from within and without. And, finally, it was instrumental in producing enough highly motivated, ideologically committed, and politically active young people that the regime was able to institutionalize tremendously rapid social and economic change and to establish a "permanent purge" of key officials without losing its essential political continuity.

These were no small accomplishments, and the foregoing catalogue is by no means exhaustive. However, despite its many "successes," the educational system had not managed to create the sort of all-inclusive, monolithic, and homogeneous political culture that the rulers desired. Its efforts to create such a political culture had been beset by a number of problems which it had been unable to resolve. To be sure, in many cases, the fault lay not with the educational system proper but rather with forces in the broader economic, social, and political environment within which it functioned, but the problems at issue were often rendered more acute by the consequences of its functioning. The most critical of the problems which beset the educational system were those which derived from (1) the multinational character of Soviet society, (2) the tendency of the rigid status hierarchy which the regime had established to turn into a general system of social stratification and take on "class content," and (3) the capacity of the human mind to resist, remain immune to, "misinterpret," or become apathetic in the face of intensive indoctrination.

The problem of nationalities

The educational system was still far from having eradicated all of the sources of tension and discord inherent in a multi-national polity. It had accomplished a great deal in this direction and had in large measure succeeded in creating a sense of shared destiny among the polyglot nationalities of the USSR. Even in this respect, however, there were significant exceptions, and, although reliable data are scarce, there is persuasive evidence that educational successes in the area of political socialization were consistently greater among Russian than among non-Russian youth. In part this was a consequence of the fact that the launching of the five-year plans had produced a more far-reaching social and cultural upheaval in many of the non-Russian regions than in Russia proper and, quite apart from any strictly political considerations, had engendered widespread hostility against the Bolsheviks as agents of "modernization." Moreover, there was a not altogether unjustifiable tendency to identify the Bolsheviks as Great Russians. This introduction of a nationalistic dimension into an already complex situation made the task of the educational system more difficult. The difficulty was further compounded because the regime had assimilated many —though by no means all or the most important—of the traditional values and attitudes of the Russian people in an effort to win support among the dominant nationality during the "transitional period" to full-fledged totalitarianism. For example, throughout most of the period under discussion, the concept of "Soviet patriotism" was heavily infused with the spirit of Russian nationalism. This unquestionably heightened its appeal to Russian youth, but this was scarcely the case where Ukrainians, Uzbeks, or Tadzhiks were concerned.

One step which the regime had taken to make its indoctrinational "message" more palatable (as well as to insure its wider diffusion) was to propagate "socialist content" in "national form," and most non-Russians were given an opportunity to receive their education, including their higher education, in their native languages. This unquestionably tended to appease nationalist sentiment in some respects, but it also had dysfunctional consequences. For one thing, the perpetuation (or in some cases creation, at least in written form) of native languages served almost automatically to preserve and in many cases to strengthen consciousness of a separate identity. In addition, it reduced the incentive to learn or teach Russian well and contributed the rise of a situation in which, although the intensive study of Russian was required in all native-language schools, even graduates of native-language secondary schools and institutions of higher education were not really fluent in Russian. This was dangerous for the Soviet system because Russian was the primary language of science, technology, and administration, and was hence a prerequisite for "progress" as the regime conceived it. The existing situation made it difficult for the regime to utilize native cadres and, at the same time, meant that non-Russians educated in native-language schools faced more limited career prospects than Russians with equivalent education. They could normally make their way at the local level, but the odds were disproportionately against them at the national level. The aspirations of the most ambitious were thus apt to be frustrated, while many other educated non-Russians had their tendencies toward "local nationalism" reinforced precisely because their occupational and professional frames of reference were "sensibly" local in character. Opportunities for advancement and access to positions of responsibility were extensive enough that there did not appear on the scene a wholly alienated native intelligentsia similar to that produced by the functioning of so many other "imperial" educational systems. Concessions to national pride were extensive enough that little real separatist spirit developed. However, "localist" tendencies were prevalent, and forthright nationalist sentiment was by no means eradicated among highly educated non-Russian youth. That this should have been so graphically demonstrated by the violent reaction of Georgian university students to the destruction of the "personality cult" of their co-national Stalin was ironic but, at the same time, both symptomatic and symbolic.

The problems of status, mobility, and stratification

The Soviet rulers accompanied their turn to a policy of rapid industrialization and total planning with the establishment of a rigid status hierarchy in all walks of life. Extreme wage differentials, clearcut symbols of rank and office, etc., were introduced in an effort to buttress managerial authority and to create a system of incentives which would draw maximum effort from the labor force and attract the ambitious, but ideologically hostile or indifferent, to the service of the regime. At the same time, however, the rulers were committed to the maintenance of a rapid rate of vertical social mobility. The establishment of a rigid status hierarchy constituted a clear betrayal of those key tenets of Marxist-Leninist ideology which posited social egalitarianism, and the rulers

hoped to mask this betrayal by pointing to universal *equality of opportunity* and the complete dependence of status on achievement. More important, the rulers counted upon a rapid rate of vertical social mobility to play a significant part in preventing the transformation of the status hierarchy into a general system of social stratification. Fearing a system in which status would cease to be wholly impersonal, a mere reflection of the regime's evaluation of the benefits which accrued to it through the exercise of various social and economic functions, the rulers hoped that rapid mobility would inhibit tendencies toward the consolidation of privilege and automatic transmission of privilege independently of the direct sanction of the regime. Rapid mobility was viewed as a desire to help insure against the status gulf's growing into a class gulf and unleashing pressures for social "routinization" and a reduction in the "tempo" of Soviet life. In sum, the commitment of the rulers to the maintenance of a rapid rate of vertical mobility within the established status hierarchy was part and parcel of their commitment to the consolidation of total power in their own hands and to the creation of a totalitarian political culture.

The rulers always expected the educational system to serve as a major channel of rapid social mobility. In fact, as industrial maturation made problems of management and administration both increasingly critical and increasingly complex, the educational system almost perforce became the primary channel of social mobility. However, although it trained hundreds of thousands of "proletarian specialists," the educational system never managed to create a situation of equal opportunity for all, and in the period after World War II it began to show signs of functioning more and more as an instrument of social stratification. Note has already been taken of the fact that in recent years, despite the seven-year compulsory education law, only 80 per cent of Soviet children who entered the first grade actually completed the seventh. The great bulk of the "delinquents" were concentrated in rural areas. The "delinquency" of rural children was attributable in large measure to the low quality of rural education, the necessity most of them faced of having to transfer to schools in towns and cities in order to continue their education beyond the fourth grade, the inadequacy of transportation and near absence of boarding facilities for transferees, etc. The "under-representation" of the peasantry increased as one ascended the educational ladder. This was due to the operative effects of low social status which were not confined to the peasantry although it hit them with particular force.

Among the urban population also differential rates of access to the upper levels of the educational system had become characteristic. Universal seven-year education was a reality in the cities, but the children of the workers were increasingly underrepresented as one moved into the upper reaches of the educational system, access to which had become a virtual prerequisite for entrance into the elite. The necessity of paying tuition fees in the ten-year schools and institutions of higher education, which applied between 1941 and 1956, militated against the children of workers continuing their education. An additional factor was the inability of working-class parents to bring pressure or influence to bear in order to secure places in institutions of higher education for their children. This factor acquired great importance in the years following Stalin's death, for in these years, due partly to widespread knowledge that the abolition of tuition fees was imminent and partly to a rise in income which made the payment of fees less burdensome, more and more working-class children did enter and finish the ten-year schools. Since the institutions of higher education did not increase their enrollments, an intensive competition for openings began, and parental status determined the outcome in many instances. The combined effect of the fee system and parental influence is suggested by the fact that in 1958 60 to 70 per cent of the students in institutions of higher education were children of "officials" and "members of the intelligentsia." This represents a marked change from the situation which prevailed in the early 1930's, when the drive to "proletarianize" education was at its height and a significant change from the situation which prevailed in 1938 (after the "proletarianization" drive had been relaxed) when only 42 per cent of university students were children of professional, administrative, or white-collar parents. This change could not but be highly disturbing to rulers whose ideology posited a movement toward "classlessness," whose political system numbered a widespread opportunity for education among those of its attributes which attracted major support from the population at large, and who were desirous of preventing the transformation of a "service elite" into a "social elite." It was the more disturbing because it was accompanied by a growth of "class consciousness" which the schools seemed powerless to prevent and often subtly encouraged, e.g., by stressing that the fate of academic failures was to become common workers. The growth of "class consciousness," in turn, threatened to generate patterns of solidarity and antagonism in society which the regime could not wholly control, and which could undercut its drive to eliminate all dimensions of autonomous social interaction. It also was largely responsible, in the eyes of the regime, for a disturbing tendency on the part of many students to take their privileged status for granted and respond with indifference or hostility to the educational system's attempts to mobilize them.

The problems of disaffection and apathy

Had the Soviet educational system fulfilled the entirety of the political socialization plan that was assigned it during the period under discussion, the official "de-Stalinization" campaign that began in 1956 would, in one way or another, have resulted in the disintegration of the entire fabric of Soviet life. At a minimum it would have resulted in moral anarchy among the younger generation of Soviet citizens. According to Soviet sources, "de-Stalinization" did cause "a trauma in [some] impressionable young souls" and led a certain number of students to become "skeptics" and "nihilists," believing in nothing and no one. However, despite its disorienting consequences, it would appear that "de-Stalinization" did not profoundly disturb the bulk of Soviet youth, and it is the author's distinct impression that it left the majority of students remarkably untouched. In launching the "de-Stalinization" campaign, Stalin's successors gambled that the educational system had failed in its ultimate task

of inculcating an undifferentiated image of community, regime, and government, with faith in Stalin as the unifying cement. They won their gamble, but their very victory could not but disturb them, for it was clear that in part it was due to pervasive political indifference among a sizeable segment of Soviet youth, and they were no more willing to tolerate indifference than Stalin had been before them. Moreover, the relaxation of control which accompanied "de-Stalinization" quickly revealed that there was a group of students at the upper levels of the educational system who were politically disaffected and whose disaffection could not be eradicated by the kind of political changes which they, Stalin's heirs, proposed to institute.

Disaffection, derived from a wide variety of sources, took diverse forms and appeared with varying degrees of intensity. Here only a few major variants can be noted. Among some students disaffection took the form of "pandering to Western tastes." Often this amounted to little more than *stilyagism* or "style chasing," indulged in more or less for its own sake as a protest against the drab, puritanical atmosphere of Soviet life and the depressing uniformity of official Soviet style. Sometimes, however, "pandering to Western tastes" involved genuine cultural "cosmopolitanism" and represented an effort on the part of some of the most cultured members of the younger generation to break free of the stultifying esthetic canons of the regime and to reestablish contact with the main streams of Western art, literature, and music. In a few cases, there was concern with Western political concepts and institutions as well, but most of those who cultivated an interest in the West were not interested in political liberty so much as in liberty from politics. They tended to be apolitical, although in the Soviet context to be apolitical was to be politically defiant.

The major substantive sources of articulate and directly political disaffection were not to be found in the contemporary West, but rather in Marxist-Leninist theory and in the Russian cultural heritage. The students concerned tended to elaborate an "immanent critique" of the political system, contrasting Soviet reality with the theories which were used to legitimize it. The imagery they developed was that of "Russia betrayed" or "the Revolution betrayed," and their goal was to recover the pure nucleus which they believed had been present at the inception of the political system, but had been stifled and contaminated by the bureaucratic rigidities and institutionalized brutalities of Stalinism. They were, in a word, idealists—but idealists whose zeal the educational system had failed to harness to party loyalty and whose enthusiasm it had failed to discipline and direct into "constructive" channels. Although the source of their disaffection was Stalinism, their conception of Stalinism embraced almost the whole of the contemporary Soviet system, and the selective "de-Stalinization" and wary return to Marxism-Leninism that Khrushchev was attempting seemed merely hypocritical.

The disaffected students, while disturbing, were nonetheless a small minority among the student body. A much larger group was politically indifferent and apathetic. As was the case with disaffection, the sources, forms, and degrees of political apathy were highly varied. A sizeable group of students, including many of the best students in the pure and applied natural sciences, had developed a deep sense of professionalism and a somewhat technocratic orientation which made them shun political involvement and become restive at political interference in their own sphere of primary interest, be it interference in the form of demands that they perform political functions or that they pursue their professional callings from a "Marxist-Leninist perspective." Another group was apathetic from sheer overwhelming boredom aroused by the dogmatism and repetitiveness of all political communication sponsored by the regime, whether in the classroom, the Komsomol, or the mass media. And yet a third group—perhaps the largest of all—developed an attitude toward politics that was purely instrumental. Political involvement was for them but a part of the process of acquiring prestige and status. The students in the group were adept at expressing zeal and enthusiasm at appropriate moments and were politically active when occasion demanded, but they were basically self-satisfied and complacent. The artificial quality of the activism of this group was demonstrated with particular force in the years after 1954 when the number of ten-year school graduates began greatly to exceed the number of openings in institutions of higher education. A great many of those ten-year school graduates who were denied admission to the university or institute of their choice refused to enter the labor force and engaged in endless attempts extending over a period of years to gain admittance to *any* department of *any* institution of higher education. They were unwilling to serve the regime in any but a "suitable" station despite the fact that the regime was facing a manpower shortage and could offer such challenging perspectives as labor in the Virgin Lands. As Khrushchev put it, they disdained and had a contemptuous attitude toward labor, and this was not only ideologically disturbing but also boded ill for the quality of their work when and if they achieved "suitable" positions. Soviet executives no less than Soviet laborers were supposed to be "shock workers," and "disdain for labor" was unlikely to be translated into the desired entrepreneurial behavior. . . .

V

The "Khrushchev school reform" [of 1958] should be viewed as an effort to overcome many of the "failures" of the old educational system in its endeavor to socialize all Soviet youth into the official, totalitarian political culture. As has already been noted, these "failures" are far from telling the entire story of how the Soviet educational system functioned prior to 1958. Its "successes" were manifold and impressive, and, in a number of important instances, the "failures" were at least partially direct or indirect consequences of these "successes," although this made them no less intolerable from the point of view of the regime. The "failures" of the educational system became particularly intolerable after the death of Stalin in view of the succession leadership's decision greatly to curtail the application of terror. To a degree this decision itself was no doubt a consequence of the "successes" achieved by the system. In the first place, Stalin-style terror had become increasingly costly with the economic development of Soviet society, and the educational system played a significant role in the process of economic devel-

opment. In the second place, the educational system had created enough consensus and support that Stalin-style terror was no longer absolutely essential to the retention of governmental power in the hands of the Party leadership.

The decision to curtail the application of terror also was prompted by a desire on the part of the leadership to rally further support, and there was no doubt that the decision would make it easier for the educational system to contribute to this process. Terror had made the tasks of the educational system more difficult by discouraging initiative, by heightening the tension between family and school, by enlarging the gap between professed theory and reality, etc. At the same time, however, terror had tended to compensate for (as well as to conceal) the "failures" of the educational system. It had functioned to uproot traditional loyalties, to inhibit the growth of group solidarity (among co-nationals, co-professionals, etc.), to frustrate attempts to consolidate and transmit status, to prevent the growth of class-consciousness (partly by making the possession of privilege less enviable since it meant a vastly increased likelihood of arrrest), to maintain rapid social mobility, to enforce conformity, and to produce activist and entrepreneurial behavior. These were crucial functions in the totalitarian scheme, and a mere increase in generalized support and consensus did not render their exercise superfluous.

Generalized support and consensus, while desirable in many respects, did not guarantee the sort of behavior that the leadership considered essential to the maintenance and consolidation of its total power, and they were positively dangerous if they were rooted in a spirit of demobilization and were oriented toward the *status quo*. Terror and education had been harnessed to the same goal in Stalinist Russia; their joint task had been to facilitate the accumulation of total power in the hands of the party elite. The succession leadership's decision to relegate terror to the background meant that the educational system was called upon to assume a double burden. The ultimate goal of the educational system had been to render terror superfluous by establishing a *totalitarian* consensus in society and creating a "new man" characterized by the sort of self-control and self-mobilization that would permit the establishment of a wholly "consensual" or "popular" totalitarianism. Now, with terror held in abeyance and with the possibilities of its extensive use perhaps increasingly atrophying, this ultimate goal has taken on much more immediate and pressing operational significance. . . .

ELECTIONS, DISSENT, AND POLITICAL LEGITIMACY

JEROME M. GILISON

A few questions are still hotly debated among students of the Soviet political system, but certainly the nature of Soviet elections is not one of them. Everyone agrees that they are more interesting as a psychological curiosity than as a political reality. They are seen by various writers as ritualized affirmations of regime legitimacy, as methods of involving the masses in supportive activity, as a means of publicly honoring model citizens, and as a crushing display of unanimity designed to isolate the potential nonconformist. Both Western and Soviet writers see Soviet elections from the positive side, from the side of the dutiful 99 percent who invariably vote for the single candidate on the ballot.

In fact, Soviet and Western writers are in very close agreement on the major functions of elections in the Soviet Union, although their value judgments tend to differ along the lines one would expect. Taking one typical example from the general Western literature on the Soviet political system, we find the purposes of a Soviet election defined as "a public demonstration of the legitimacy of the regime . . . an invaluable education and propaganda exercise . . . and perhaps most important of all, . . . proof that the system of control is unimpaired." In the more detailed Western works on Soviet elections we find the same approach. Thus, Howard Swearer, in a very insightful and valuable article on Soviet local elections, states that "in the Soviet Union, the formal act of voting is comparable in purpose to such civic rituals as singing the national anthem or saluting a country's flag. It is a public display of personal reaffirmation of

From "Soviet Elections as a Measure of Dissent: The Missing One Percent," *American Political Science Review*, LXII, No. 3 (September 1968), 814–26. Reprinted by permission. Footnotes omitted.

the Soviet way of life and the party leadership." Swearer further suggests that the function of Soviet elections "is not only to legitimize the leadership in the mass mind and to help identify the people with its policies, but also to reassure the leadership itself of its popularity and infallibility." In a similar vein, Richard M. Scammon, after personally observing a Soviet election, reported that Soviet elections reflect "the need felt by every regime (even a one-party regime) for popular endorsement and consent to its program, no matter how unreal the conditions under which that endorsement be produced." Max E. Mote, after studying an election in Leningrad at close hand, suggests that the very idea of an election as a choice between alternatives is not comprehended by the average Soviet citizen, who thinks of voting as "both a patriotic and a social activity, invested with the diverse pleasures which most people derive from performing a commendable action."

Soviet writers agree with the Western analysis of Soviet elections as essentially positive, participatory, legitimizing, demonstrative, educational and patriotic. One of them writes: "Our elections are not simply acts of selecting people's representatives for the organs of state power. They are a most important form of participation of the masses in the implementation of state power, and of their education and organization in the struggle for socialism and communism." Generally, Soviet commentators see elections as expressions of the pervading unity of Soviet society, a condition brought about by the absence of class conflict. The fact that only one candidate is nominated for each elected position is explained in

terms of this assumed underlying unanimity of the Soviet "working masses." Michael Kalinin, titular head of state during Stalin's reign, remarked that the single candidate is "a feature of socialism, a sign that amongst the working masses there is not and cannot be any internal disagreements such as is found within bourgeois society."

Thus on both sides of the political fence that used to be an iron curtain, observers have fixed their glance firmly on the positive role of Soviet elections as massive demonstrations of ritualized affirmation. Ninety-nine percent support is indeed a dazzling achievement in an age when many governments achieve power without even receiving the votes of a majority of the registered electorate—and some achieve power without even receiving a majority of the votes cast. It would be difficult to quarrel with the prevailing view of Soviet elections in regard to the functions they perform *for the ninety-nine percent*. But what of the others? Every year in which elections are held (actually three out of every four years), approximately two million votes are cast against the official candidates, under an electoral procedure which, as we shall see, makes this act difficult, at least potentially disadvantageous, and largely ineffectual. All the positive functions described by Soviet and Western observers have no meaning when discussing these nonconformists. These people have apparently taken the word "election" literally, and have made the only choice Soviet procedure allows.

It is therefore useful to consider whether Soviet elections may be studied as elections are studied in other countries where two or more candidates are usually nominated for each elected position. Such a study could be made if the following conditions do in fact exist:

1) If the Soviet electoral procedure, while heavily biased toward achieving affirmative unanimity, does permit the possibility of registering dissent, and the possibility of avoiding consequent sanctions against the dissenter.

2) If reasonably detailed and comprehensive data are available.

3) If the data are accurately and honestly compiled, or if the falsification and inaccuracy are randomly or evenly distributed.

It is obvious that under present conditions, Soviet electoral results cannot be considered an accurate reflection of the true state of Soviet public opinion. A heavy bias in favor of the regime is introduced by the well-established system of pressures, controls and propaganda, and until this system is dismantled the relationship between Soviet voting and Soviet public opinion will remain an enigma. This does not mean, however, that there is nothing to be gained by studying Soviet electoral statistics. If the study is restricted to a systematic comparison of groups, areas and periods in the Soviet system, the environment of pressures—which produces the ninety-nine percent—can be considered either a constant or a random variable, and the variations in results can be analyzed for clues to the *location* and *relative incidence* of dissent to be found in the Soviet Union. For comparisons, we require only the three conditions mentioned.

There can be no doubt that the first precondition does exist in the Soviet Union. Curiously enough, Soviet electoral law is written as though the drafters expected contested elections. The present statute governing election of deputies to the USSR Supreme Soviet states that "the voter, in the place set aside for filling out the ballot, leaves on each ballot the name of the candidate for whom he wishes to vote, and crosses out the names of the others." In actual practice, of course, only one name appears on each ballot, the name of the candidate representing the "people's bloc of Communists and non-party members." The voter can cast his ballot for the "bloc" candidate by simply folding and depositing his ballot in the appropriate receptacle. In order to vote against the candidate, he must repair to a booth or room, provided by law to ensure "secret" balloting, and cross out the name of the candidate. Since this act invites attention, the Soviet voter's reluctance to take the legal guarantee of secret ballot seriously is quite understandable. Nevertheless, the possibility remains that he will take the risk or will mark the ballot surreptitiously. Many Soviet voters, wishing to demonstrate their superpatriotism, take pen in hand and write patriotic slogans on the ballot, and this practice could distract attention from the occasional dissenter who crosses out the approved name while proceeding to the ballot box. Regardless of the technique used, the fact that it is possible both to cast a negative vote and to escape serious sanctions is amply evidenced by Soviet statistics. Since approximately two million negative votes are cast year after year, and since many of these votes must be cast by the same people who have become habitual dissenters, it follows that the act of voting "no" does not bring about sufficient sanctions to cow a rather large number of brave Soviet souls. Indeed, the futility of the act, rather than the danger, might very well be the major deterrent for many potential dissenters who follow the crowd without enthusiasm, and are counted in the ninety-nine percent.

The second precondition, the availability of detailed and comprehensive data, places some limitations on any examination of Soviet elections, but does not eliminate the possibility of making such a study. In the Soviet Union, publication of data is a "sometime thing," sometimes remarkably consistent, sometimes exasperatingly incomplete. The best data, including not only percentages but also absolute numbers of voters, are published for the elections to the local soviets, which occur every even-numbered year. These data are the most detailed, and therefore the most useful for the purpose of comparison.

The existence of the third precondition, honesty and accuracy in compiling electoral results by Soviet officials, is not so easily determined. We know that the electoral laws have been amended to provide heavy criminal penalties for "a responsible person or member of the electoral commission who commits a forgery of the electoral documents or deliberately miscounts votes or violates the secrecy of balloting," but we cannot be sure that such strictures are always observed. A further check on possible corruption is provided by the electoral laws in the provisions that "certified representatives of public organizations and workers' associations, and representatives of the press have the right to be present during the counting of ballots." Leonard Schapiro's evaluation of these safeguards is that "it is less likely now than in the past that blatant electoral fraud could be practiced in the presence of so many witnesses," and one would have to agree that the presence

of witnesses from outside organizations makes obvious fraud rather unlikely. But if one is disinclined to accept the reality of these formal safeguards from a system notoriously contemptuous of formal rules, there is another argument which seems more convincing: the environment of pressures is so effective that the desired result—a rousing affirmative vote of over 99 percent—could be achieved without recourse to such dirty business as falsifying election returns. Furthermore, in those relatively few cases where the local candidate is very unpopular, it is probably more advantageous for the regime to permit his defeat than to falsify his victory, since it is quite simple to find a more suitable candidate for the required second election in that district. In a system so heavily biased in its favor, the regime can well afford to "let the chips fall where they may," especially since this attitude may provide the leadership with a useful source of information on the location of dissent and the efficiency of local party and government organizations.

It should be emphasized, however, that we don't require a perfect record of honesty and accuracy of the Soviet Electoral Commissions. Our requirements in this regard are reduced by the fact that in dealing with Soviet electoral data we do not have merely a small *sample* of the voting population, we have in effect the *entire population*. This means that we can afford to be tolerant of isolated incidents of fudgery and forgery. In addition, since we will deal only with *comparisons* of data within the system, we can permit uniformly distributed falsification of even major proportions, such as would be produced if every affirmative vote across the country were raised by five percent. Thus our modest requirements, in combination with the Soviet leadership's need for accurate feedback information and the legal safeguards provided by the electoral statutes, permit a certain degree of confidence in asserting that our requirements have been met.

I. The Theory and Practice of Soviet Elections

Soviet voters cast ballots for delegates ("deputies") to the soviets (councils) established on all levels of governmental administration. From the spontaneous and often riotous gatherings that the soviets were during the revolutionary year of 1917, they have become docile tools of the party-state leadership, although with increasing administrative responsibilities involving limited discretionary powers. Nominations of candidates for the soviets are endorsed by open meetings of various public and work organizations, but it is no secret that these nominations are actually decided by the party nucleus in prior, closed meetings. Nomination for candidature is considered a reward for model behavior and outstanding achievement in work, and these are the criteria apparently used in making the selection. Indeed, in the few cases reported in which the pre-selected nominee was rejected by the open meeting of the collective, the major difficulty seems to have been that the party nucleus had chosen someone who did not possess sufficient Soviet virtue. Because the nucleus takes some considerable care in selecting fitting objects for public approbation, the nomination procedure at open meetings tends to be *pro forma*. It would seem that most Soviet citizens have accepted the idea of nomination as reward for virtue rather than as the first step in a competitive selection process. Max E. Mote reports that a typical Soviet response to the question of why only one candidate is advanced would be: "You see, it would indicate a lack of confidence in the candidate if you were to nominate two men for the same post. It would mean you think one of them is not good enough for the office. We don't want to insult our candidates."

After nominations are completed, a "campaign" of about six weeks ensues, with daily press coverage in the form of biographical sketches of the candidates, reports on the progress of organizing electoral commissions and of establishing agitation centers (*agitpunkty*). Press coverage is generally more complete and intensive during elections for soviets at the all-union level (USSR Supreme Soviet) and republic level (Supreme Soviets of the republics) than it is for local elections, in which there are thousands upon thousands of candidates. Nevertheless, even during local elections, many a homely, honest and happy face appears under the heading, "Candidates of the People."

The scope of Soviet organization for elections is truly impressive. This is certainly one area where the system demonstrates its great ability to mobilize large numbers of people to accomplish a short-term, and clearly defined task. Before the "campaign" reaches its closing hours, a significant proportion of the electorate becomes involved in one or another of the many electoral organizations. (In 1967, one out of every 16 qualified voters in the U.S.S.R. was involved in the work of the electoral commissions alone.) The Soviet electorate is divided into precincts (*izbiratel'nye uchastki*) and constituencies (*izbiratel'nye okruga*), the former being temporary units for the counting of ballots, and the latter being actual units of representation in the various types of soviets. There is virtually no escape from the all-embracing organization of the precincts. They are established on board ships with 20 or more voters, in hospitals, rest homes and sanatoria, in railroad stations, airports and on board long-distance trains—in fact, wherever human life is to be found within the borders of the U.S.S.R. The invalid is visited in his home by a representative of the local electoral commission, accompanied by a portable ballot box; the isolated weather-observation team sends its votes from the northern frozen wastelands by radio. The network is so all-inclusive and so carefully articulated that it is virtually impossible to avoid voting—in fact, it is probably easier to vote against the nominated candidate than it is to escape the grasp of the local precinct organization and abstain. In this regard, as in so many others, the system demands active involvement, participation that gives visible evidence of one's loyalty. From this point of view, inaction, purposeful non-involvement, is just as despicable as negative action.

The regime attempts to make each election a plebiscite, in which the sole issue, as George Barr Carson puts it, is "support or non-support on a question which no one publicly dares reject —do you favor the soviet system?" The front page of all newspapers on election day is decorated with a standardized drawing of stalwart voters ready to deposit ballots marked "For Communism." Press reports of interviews with voters invariably yield such remarks as: "I voted for the candidates so that our splendid Motherland would develop even further, and the cause of peace would win," or "I voted for peace and the flowering of our great Soviet Motherland." Thus the vast array of propaganda media attempts to bend the attention of the voter away from local issues—and real potential grievances—and toward the ultimate question of loyalty to the regime and "Soviet patriotism." In other words, the regime attempts to remove issues from the elections entirely. This is done not only by a propaganda campaign and by choosing model, "non-controversial" candidates, but also by a positive attempt to satisfy local grievances in advance of election day. Thousands of "agitators" are sent out to explain the causes of past deficiencies, laud past accomplishments and promise all sorts of future improvements in local living conditions.

The reason for this emphasis is not hard to discover. The Soviet voter has been molded in a political environment which permits the voicing of dissent *exclusively* on local issues, on issues that essentially involve the implementation by local officials of policies decided at higher levels. Thus if these issues of local implementation were thrust into the forefront of the election campaign, there is every reason to suspect that the negative vote, and the number of defeated local candidates, would rise sharply. This is particularly true of certain regions where the local party and state organizations have been thoroughly roasted in the official press for shortcomings in past performance. In a country still far short of Utopia, still displaying its full share of corruption and mismanagement, it is still necessary to make each vote against every last officially-sponsored candidate a vote of "no confidence" in the entire regime, and thus a potentially traitorous act.

By this means, the regime attempts to remove elections entirely from the area of limited grievances and to make it a simple test of allegiance to the system. The Soviet voter, in effect, is told to seek redress of his grievances through other administrative channels, and at election time to stand and be counted on the ultimate issue of loyalty. Soviet propagandists make the point that on certain local issues "all the instructions of the voters are collected after the election, and measures are taken to carry them out." It is quite clear, however, that such "instructions" are communicated to the candidates informally, and are in no way, either in theory or in practice, connected with the act of voting.

But what of the negative voter? Is he, by reverse logic, dissenting against the entire Soviet system when he crosses out the name of the "bloc" candidate on the ballot? Some Western observers, such as Mote, make this simple reversal: "If casting a vote on election day is a sign of support of the regime, then not casting a vote is a sign of opposition." Unfortunately, the matter is not quite so simple. It cannot be assumed that all negative votes and abstentions are expressions of total rejection of the system. These negative votes may also express disapproval of the particular candidates, or local grievances, or personal grievances (resulting from bureaucratic bungling, being passed over for job promotion, etc.), or crankiness, or eccentricity, or even frivolity. Finally, such a negative vote may actually express genuine antagonism to the values of the regime or its basic structure, but this is only one possibility which must be weighed with the others. Some Soviet voters simply may not heed the warnings of

the regime that voting is a test of loyalty, and not a means of expressing particularized dissent. They may derive psychological satisfactions from negative voting; they may be deluded into thinking that positive results will issue from this act, or they may simply take Soviet propaganda at face value when statements are made that "the electoral system in the U.S.S.R. shows that constitutional principles combined with practical guarantees ensure genuine democracy and respect for the rights of citizens."

As this quotation from a typical Soviet source indicates, the dissenting voter does have some support from official Soviet doctrine. The question of elections illustrates the basic ambivalence of current Soviet ideology, which stands athwart two contrary notions of human society and personality. On the one hand, there is the commitment to the model of the conflictless social monolith, and its assumption that there is a single "correct" answer to every problem to which all will agree, once their basic interests are harmonized by the removal of classes. On the other, there is the idea of "the free development of the individual human personality," with its assumptions of great creativity and variety of expression. The two principles are not miscible, despite the vigorous efforts of Soviet ideologists to shake up a single solution. As we have already seen, Soviet elections contain elements of both principles, the idea of the monolithic plebiscite on the one hand, and the legal provisions for secret ballots, several competing candidates, and run-off elections on the other. Even though the heavy emphasis in the propaganda—especially in the press—is on the plebiscite theme, the knowledgeable Soviet dissenter can take refuge in the contrary, thoroughly respectable concept of Soviet ideology if he wishes. This is especially important since he would most likely justify his negative vote in terms of the inadequate qualifications of the particular candidate. This interpretation of his negative vote would be unanimously seconded by the learned Soviet experts on ideology. In explaining why some candidates are defeated in local elections, two such experts write:

This act [i.e., defeat of a candidate] is only evidence of the high activism of the voters and of the fact that the public organizations and meetings obvious made a mistake when they nominated the candidate. The mistake has been corrected. As a result of new elections in all such areas, other deputies will be elected.

Thus the dissenter could conceivably relate his negative vote to his high sense of public responsibility and "activism" when confronted with a "mistake" of the nominating organizations.

In any case, one need not accept the interpretation that all negative votes are anti-regime votes in order to conclude that the phenomenon bears closer investigation than has been accorded it in the past. In the absence of opinion polls, we cannot determine the distribution of dissenting views, but the existence of electoral data does permit some analysis of the location of dissent and the frequency of its expression through the ballot.

II. Measuring Dissent

The present study of electoral returns is restricted to the biennial elections for the local soviets. There are two reasons for this approach: the reported data are more complete and detailed for these elections, and the

TABLE 1. Mean size of electoral units, U.S.S.R., 1967*

Unit	Registered Voters Per Unit
krai	1,603,717
oblast'	887,946
city raion	89,566
okrug	53,861
city	41,895
raion	26,477
poselok	3,767
selo	1,525

* Data calculated from Pravda, March 26, 1967.

relative closeness of these soviets to local issues, and of the candidates to the electors, makes the dissenting vote in these elections more interesting and significant. As already mentioned, the Soviet regime is more permissive toward localized dissent than toward dissent on national issues, and the Soviet voter has consequently become depoliticized on the larger issues. Furthermore, even though negative votes are registered in elections for the all-union Supreme Soviet and the Supreme Soviets of the republics, the candidates for these soviets are relatively remote from the voter and their qualifications are generally of a higher, more irreproachable level than the local candidates. In fact, as we shall see from the data, the frequency of dissent is inversely related to the size of the electoral units when other factors are held constant.

As indicated in Table 1, the size of the electoral units is extremely variable in local elections. The average krai, with more than 1.6 million voters can hardly be considered a unit of "local" representation at all, especially since these units are generally vast and sparsely populated. On the other hand, the selo (village) unit is more than 100 times smaller than the krai, and can be considered truly local in character. The *poselok* (settlement), with almost four thousand electors, can also be counted as a local unit. It is a peculiarity of Soviet electoral organization that such small units are found only in rural areas, for the smallest unit of urban voters (the city soviet) numbers approximately forty thousand.

Two kinds of information reported in the Soviet press are useful for analysis of dissent: the number of negative voters and absentees, and the number of defeated candidates. Since it is virtually impossible to miss voting by accident, only design or sheer physical incapacitation can account for absenteeism. In fact, the vote-getting machine is so marvelously efficient that in the Tadzhikistan *raion* elections of 1957, 1961, 1963 and 1965, with over 400,000 registered voters, not a single lonely Tadzhik absented himself from the polls. Because of this rather awe-inspiring organization, one can assume that in the vast majority of cases, absenteeism is the result of purposeful abstention—one must be an artful dodger, and not merely absent-minded!

Thus it seems reasonable to add the number of absentees to the number of negative voters as an indication of total dissent expressed through the ballot. Since this information is given for the various administrative units shown in Table 1, and since it is given separately for each union republic in the union-republic newspapers, a useful basis of comparison can be established. This figure, expressed as a percentage of the total registered voters for the various units will be termed the Individual Dissent Index (IDI), since it is essentially a measure of *individual* negative choices, made presumably without communication or discussion with others. It represents the acts of a

small minority, engulfed in an atmosphere of conformity.

The other piece of published information, the number of defeated candidates, leads to a rather different analysis. The data reveal that candidates are *never* defeated in any but local elections, and that even in local elections candidates are defeated only in the smaller electoral units. In fact, 98.2 percent of all defeated candidates in the elections studied systematically (1957, 1961, 1963 and 1965) were from the smallest electoral units, the *selo* and *poselok*. There was not a single recorded instance in the elections studied of a defeated candidate in any unit larger than the city soviet. This is certainly not the result of increased pressure on the voter in balloting for larger units. In order for a candidate to be defeated, he must receive less than a majority of the votes cast, and under Soviet conditions this can occur only in small, relatively cohesive and relatively isolated communities. Only in a small, cohesive community could there be sufficient communication of the dissenting view prior to the election to assure each voter that he would actually be a member of the *majority* by voting "no." Only as a majoritarian could he be absolutely assured of being counted as an "activist" who corrected a "mistake" of the nominating organizations. Only in an isolated community, far from the party-state control levers, could discussion be open enough to achieve a dissenting consensus. Thus the published information on defeated candidates serves as a measure of *group* dissent rather than individual dissent in the Soviet Union. Since the different units and republics elect vastly different numbers of deputies, a convenient unit of comparison would be the number of successful candidates for each defeated candidate, which we shall call the Group Dissent Index (GDI). As one might expect, this number in all cases is quite large, for the defeated candidate is a rather rare animal in the Soviet Union, generally representing less than .001 percent of all candidates in any given election.

These two indices are readily obtainable from published Soviet data and provide excellent measures of comparison for two different types of dissent: the dissent of the individual nonconformist surrounded by conformity, and the dissent of the small, cohesive group against the local authorities. The two indices are almost completely independent, for the votes cast against the defeated candidates form a very small proportion (less than one percent) of the total negative vote. In adjudging the reasons for individual dissent, the full range of possibilities already discussed must be considered. The IDI is important as an over-all measure of dissent on all levels in the Soviet Union. Group dissent, because of its rarity and its heavy concentration in small, rural communities of the RSFSR, is not as useful as a comparative measure of dissent in different areas of the Soviet Union—for example, in three elections studied, the Turkmenian and Tadzhik Republics did not report a single defeated candidate—but it does provide us with a clearer picture of a particular type of dissent, based on a consensus opposed to local conditions or candidates.

The two indices can be compared both statically (eliminating the time dimension by averaging results from different areas or electoral units over a period of years) and through time (by following trends shown in successive elections). Because of limitations of data, nine of the fifteen union re-

publics of the U.S.S.R., representing 89.2 percent of its population, have been included. Complete data for calculation of the IDI were reported by the Soviet press only for the local elections of 1957, 1961 and 1965, although data on defeated candidates have been reported for all local elections.

Static Analysis. A quite revealing comparison can be made of variations of IDI among the nine union republics studied. Table 2 shows the average IDI of the nine republics for three elections, and reveals a striking difference in the amount of dissent registered by the voters in differing areas. Although

TABLE 2. Mean IDI by union republic, elections of 1957, 1961 and 1965*

Republic	Mean IDI (%)
Estonia	1.18
RSFSR	0.86
Kazakhstan	0.55
Latvia	0.44
Turkmenistan	0.32
Belorussia	0.29
Ukraine	0.27
Lithuania	0.25
Tadzhikistan	0.21

* Sources:
Sovetskaia Rossiia, March 19, 1965; March 12, 1961; March 8, 1957
Pravda Ukrainy, March 20, 1965; March 10, 1961; March 7, 1957
Sovetskaia Belorussiia, March 19, 1965; March 24, 1961; March 7, 1957
Kazakhstanskaia pravda, March 20, 1965; March 11, 1961
Alma-Atinskaia pravda, March 14, 1957
Turkmenskaia iskra, March 19, 1965; March 9, 1961; March 7, 1957
Kommunist Tadzhikistana, March 20, 1965; March 17, 1961; March 7, 1957
Sovetskaia Litva, March 26, 1965; March 9, 1961; March 7, 1957
Sovetskaia Latviia, March 20, 1965; March 22, 1961; March 14, 1957
Sovetskaia Estoniia, March 26, 1965; March 22, 1961; March 15, 1957

the republics in general are distinguished by differing national cultures, large-scale population movements of past decades have complicated the picture. Particularly in some of the smaller republics, the in-flow of ethnic Russians and Ukrainians has tended to dilute the distinctive national culture of the area. Nevertheless, national differences do remain, and the borders of the union republics can still be taken as approximate lines of division between different peoples.

As shown in Table 2, Estonians are significantly more likely to be dissenters—at least at election time—than any of the other national groups. One can easily relate this opposition sentiment to Estonia's troubled times in the recent past, its brief period of independence, forced entry into the Soviet Union during the Second World War, and Stalin's post-war repressions and the settlement of many ethnic Russians in Estonia. One would be satisfied with this explanation were it not for the fact that the Lithuanians, who for the most part shared the Estonians' fate, indicate very little dissent at election time. This difference in frequency of dissent can only be explained by a careful study of contemporary conditions in the two neighboring republics, a subject beyond the scope of this essay.

Another result which bears some discussion is the high IDI for the Russian Republic. It must be kept in mind that the Russian Republic, which stretches from the Baltic to the Pacific, and contains more than half the population of the Soviet Union, also contains many non-Russian nationality groups living quite remote from the power centers in Moscow and Leningrad. All indications are that these groups, and the Russians who have

TABLE 3. Mean GDI by union republic, elections of 1957, 1961, 1963, and 1965*

Republic	Mean GDI
RSFSR	6630
Estonia	7353
Latvia	8022
Lithuania	11220
Belorussia	12117
Ukraine	28120
Kazakhstan	28629
Turkmenistan	—**
Tadzhikistan	—**
Mean (above nine republics)	8344

  * For sources see Table 2
  ** No defeated candidates reported in three elections
  Note: High numerical values of GDI indicate low incidence of dissent.

settled in the austere new towns of the Siberian plains, contribute more than their share to the amount of dissent shown in Russian Republic elections.

The average GDI for the union republics during these years is shown in Table 3. Three republics, the RSFSR, Estonia, and Latvia show markedly less reticence in defeating candidates than the others, and these three republics also score high in individual dissent as shown in Table 2. Over-all, the rank-order correlation of GDI and IDI for the nine republics is +0.62. Kazakhstan's pattern of relatively high IDI and low GDI fits very well the picture of a district which has seen a large influx of young people (during Khrushchev's Virgin Lands program) who have subsequently become disillusioned but who have not yet established solidary groups. This hypothesis is supported by the figures, which indicate a rather high level of dissent manifested almost exclusively through individual action.

Another method of comparison has been used to determine if any significant differences exist between urban

TABLE 4. Mean IDI for different electoral units, nine republics, elections of 1957,
1961, 1965, and 1967*

Electoral Unit	IDI (%)
Large urban	0.75
Small rural	0.64
Large rural	0.48

* Data in *Pravda*, March 26, 1967 permit
this calculation, but not comparison by republic. For other sources, see Table 2.

and rural areas, and between large and
small electoral units, in the expression
of electoral dissent. In this study three
types of electoral units were compared:
large urban (city soviet), large rural
(*raion* soviet), and small rural (*selo*
and *poselok* soviets). The IDI's for
each of these units were aggregated
for all nine republics, with the results
shown in Table 4.

The results indicate that individual
dissent is highest in urban areas, which
might indicate a weak Soviet reflection
of the urban malaise that has afflicted
other industrial or industrializing nations. Another interesting result is that
small rural units show considerably
more dissent than large rural units,
*even though for the most part the same
voters are involved in both cases.* This
means that there are thousands of rural
voters who cast their ballots for their
raion candidate, and at the same time
vote against their local candidate. Thus
the evidence supports the hypothesis
that rural voters are more likely to
voice their discontent over local conditions than over larger, "political"
issues.

Table 5 gives a further indication
of differences between urban and rural
voting patterns. The results clearly
show that the urban voter is more
likely to show his opposition by staying
away from the polls than the rural
voter. It is plausible to conclude that

TABLE 5. Absenteeism as a percentage of
total negative choices

Electoral Unit	Absenteeism (%)
Large urban	11.3
Large rural	7.9
Small rural	5.9

the difference lies not so much in the
psychology of the voters, but in the
increased opportunities for evasion that
are provided by the mass concentration of voters in the cities. The rural
voter might be just as apathetic, but
he is organized in smaller, more self-
contained groups making escape more
difficult. This conclusion is given added
support by the fact that in rural areas,
absenteeism is higher for the large
units than for the small units, even
though the large units have a lower
IDI.

Comparison of urban and rural
units for indications of group dissent
shows, as already mentioned, that this
phenomenon is almost exclusively found
in rural areas. Of 910 candidates defeated in five local elections (1957,
1961, 1963, 1965, 1967) throughout the
U.S.S.R., only ten were candidates for
city soviets. The fact that defeated
urban candidates represent only 1.1
percent of all defeated candidates is

TABLE 6. Mean number of electors for
each candidate, U.S.S.R., 1967*

Candidate for:	Mean Number of Electors
krai soviet	5432
oblast' soviet	4355
okrug soviet	571
raion soviet	339
city soviet	328
city *raion* soviet	430
poselok soviet	68
selo soviet	48

* Calculated from data in *Pravda*, March
26, 1967

directly related to the size of urban and rural electoral units, as shown in Table 6. It is quite apparent that on the average it would take only a bare majority of 48 voters to defeat a candidate for the smallest rural unit (*selo*), while it would take a majority of 328 voters to defeat a candidate for the smallest urban unit. If the hypothesis is correct that pre-election communication of dissent among the voters is required to defeat a candidate, it would follow that the process would be much more difficult in a group of over three hundred than in a group of less than fifty. In addition, the urban group is far less likely to have developed the necessary group solidarity because of the greater fluidty of movement in the urban environment.

Based upon the record of past local elections, then, one can draw the following general conclusions about voting patterns and dissent in the Soviet Union:

1. *The amount of individual dissent indicated in elections is inversely related to the size of the electoral unit.* The Soviet voter is more likely to dissent against local conditions than against policies of wider importance. In this attitude, he reflects the values of the regime, which permits criticism of local implementation, but not of national policies.

2. *There is more individual dissent in the cities than in the countryside.* This may be the result of the greater education, "sophistication," and diversity of the urban population in comparison with the peasantry of the villages.

3. *There is far more group dissent in the countryside than in the cities.* This clearly demonstrated phenomenon can be related to the greater solidarity, cohesiveness and isolation of rural groups, as well as the much smaller size of the minimal rural electoral units (*selo* and *poselok* soviets). It is probably true, however, that this rural group dissent is not directed toward politically significant issues.

4. *Opportunities for abstention from voting are greater in the cities than in the countryside.* This conclusion, which emerges from the data on urban and rural absenteeism, is based on the assumption that absentees are for the most part willfully abstaining.

5. *There is significantly more individual and group dissent in the Russian Republic (RSFSR) and Estonia (followed closely by Latvia and Kazakhstan) than in the other republics studied.*

Trend Analysis. Some very interesting and quite unexpected results were obtained from analysis of trends in Soviet voting during the past ten years. As shown in Figure 1, there has been a general and steady decline in electoral dissent over the past decade in both urban and rural areas. This would seem to contradict the expectation that with increased liberalization of Soviet society, with the growth of diversity and stratification of the population and with loosening of controls over political expression, there would be an increase in nonconformity and diversity of opinions. This cherished idea—or perhaps hope—need not be discarded on the "garbage heap of history," as Trotsky was wont to say, if we recall the previous conclusion that most negative voting throughout the Soviet Union is probably based on economic and local issues rather than on "purely political" issues of national policy. In this case, the decrease in negative voting can be related to the general improvement in living conditions which has occurred in the Soviet

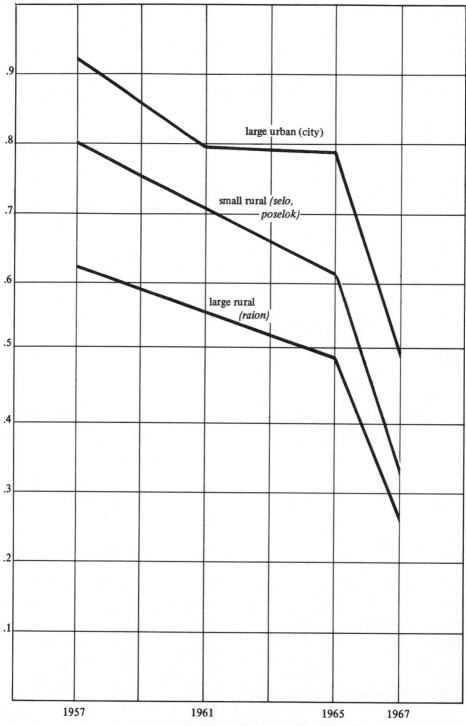

large urban (city)

small rural *(selo,
poselok)*

large rural
(raion)

Fig. 1. Decline in IDI by Electorial Unit 1957-1967

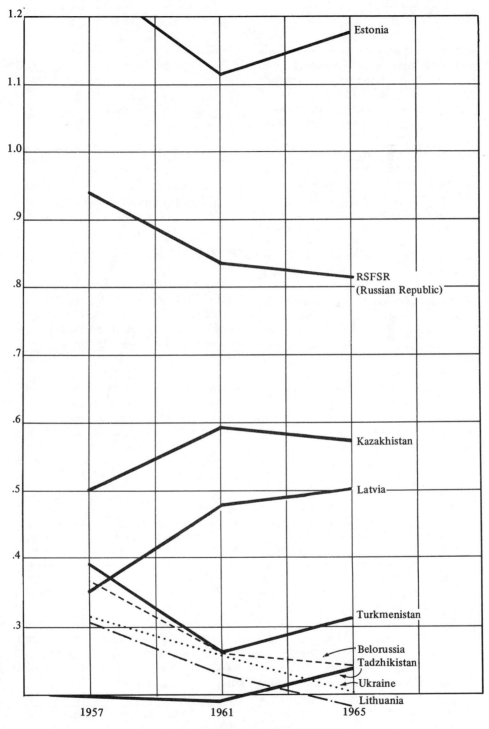

Fig. 2. IDI by Union Republic 1957-1965

Union in the past ten years. As already suggested, the typical dissenting voter has probably resisted the regime's heavy-handed invitation to vote on the ultimate issue of loyalty to communism, and has instead cast his *"Nyet"* as a little reminder that he hadn't been pleased with the last pay raise, or the increase in food prices, or the lack of adequate recreation facilities in his village. Students of American voting habits will realize that this is far from a frivolous or fanciful explanation of voting behavior. It is far less fanciful under Soviet conditions, where the government, if not each candidate, is clearly and wholly responsible for the economic problems that trouble the souls of Soviet voters. A corollary explanation would be that the increased liberalization of Soviet society has opened up more effective channels for the communication of moderately dissenting views and grievances than existed in the past, and that some negative voters have abandoned an act they always knew was more symbolic than effective, and taken advantage of those new channels that can achieve demonstrable results.

The general pattern of decline in individual dissent is repeated in all the union republics studied (see Figure 2), except Tadzhikistan, Kazakhstan and Latvia, which show a slight to moderate increase. A roughly comparable decline in group dissent is indicated in Table 7, although the poor agricultural conditions of trade in 1961 resulted in a sharp increase in group dissent (i.e., lower GDI) during the election of that year. The general decrease of rural group dissent can be ascribed to well-known improvements in the conditions on the collective farms. The effects of the Brezhnev-Kosygin "new deal" for agriculture,

TABLE 7. U.S.S.R average GDI for four local elections

Year	Average GDI
1957	9278
1961	7316
1965	9664
1967	15855

announced in March 1965, may possibly be related to the marked decline in rural group dissent shown (in Table 7) for 1967.

III. Conclusions

If our hypothesis is correct that increased liberalization of Soviet society, and the general improvement in living conditions results in a decreased use of elections as a vehicle for the expression of dissent, the study of Soviet elections might prove to be a less rewarding enterprise in future years. On the other hand, there is the possibility that in the long run the idea of an election as a choice between alternatives could make some headway. It is not altogether unreasonable to suggest the possibility that:

Russians are being educated in the procedures of modern elections, and some day in the future may be allowed a choice of candidates on election day.... Certainly there can be no argument that the legal machinery for elections on western European or American lines is all present. Not a word of the present laws would need to be changed.

Even this prospect, however, should be treated with caution. It is not enough to offer "a choice of candidates on election day," if these candidates are all hand-picked selections of a single ruling party. This sort of system has been used in Poland without producing any notable increase in the democratic content of Polish politics.

The Soviet regime has not permitted even this limited choice, and has chosen to emphasize the ceremonial aspects and the theme of social unity. As a result it has had to face the inevitable consequence of social apathy. The long-term problem is that Soviet elections in their present form present a basic contradiction between structure and function. The structure of Soviet elections in its formal aspect conforms to the functional requirements of a contested election between candidates representing differentiable alternatives. The function of Soviet elections at present, however, is to symbolize mass patriotism and allegiance through a day-long public ceremony. The contradiction is not subtle, and one can assume that it is recognized by many Soviet citizens. By ritualizing the elections, the regime has removed the element of uncertainty and drama which make elections intrinsically interesting, even when the choices offered to the electorate are not. But when choices are not even offered, excitement disappears, and the regime must struggle mightily with pen and loudspeaker to generate enthusiasm.

Under such circumstances, one could imagine two possible alternatives to the present system: the Soviet authorities could eliminate elections entirely, or they could permit a limited choice between pre-selected candidates, as in Poland. The first choice could be easily justified in ideological terms, under the assumption that the stage of pure communism is being approached; it would save money and time, and it would remove the patent ambiguity of the present electoral practices. Still, the regime would lose the positive symbolic benefits, and the citizen's commitment-through-action that the elections provide. The second choice might therefore seem more advantageous since it would retain the symbolic and active supportive elements and at the same time permit a competitive—and possibly even interesting—campaign based on the qualifications of the candidates.

One suspects, however, that the most likely future for Soviet elections will be a continuation of the present. They have become entrenched through time as a symbol of regime legitimacy, and as the Soviet regime passes its fiftieth anniversary, it seems more reluctant than ever to tamper with such symbolic institutions. Although Soviet elections do not create much excitement, they still provide a splendid opportunity for the regime to test its mobilization powers, and to prove to the world—and to itself—that it can make just about every able-bodied adult in the Soviet Union perform a useless task at a prescribed time and place—and do it with a smile! But as long as it does this, the few scowling faces in the crowd will provide us with some useful information on dissent in the Soviet Union.

VI

THE COURSE OF CHANGE

If indeed the Soviet political system today is characterized by tensions created by the interaction between environmental influences and the con-sciously-directed actions of a small elite group, and if those tensions are producing changes in the political system and perhaps even in the position of the elite group itself, what might be said about the future? Is the small elite group succeeding in coping fast enough with the pressures generated in society? If not, what might be required for it to do so? Can it manage to cope at all with the problems facing it, short of a drastic "transforma-tion" of the political system?

Most of the authors included or refered to in this volume offer sugges-tions or predictions as to future developments, some more explicitly than others. During the years 1966–1968, however, *Problems of Communism* featured a continuing symposium directed specifically to questions of the future. Professor Brzezinski's article and Michel Tatu's commentary on the book by Michel Garder provided the point of departure.[1] Professor Barghoorn's article provides a point of disagreement with Professor Brzezinski's conclusions.

Professor Brzezinski isolates as key areas where developments (or lack of them) will be critical for the future of the Soviet political system: the character of the top leadership, the way in which leaders acquire power, and the relationship of the party to society. Unless certain institutional reforms are implemented, he argues, which "would eventually lead to a profound transformation of the Soviet system" apparently closer to a liberal-democratic model, the system will be likely to "degenerate". He sets forth the conditions in which a political system can be said to be degenerating, and implies that degeneration means the incapacity to govern effectively and the inability to provide continued economic and social "progress" and the increased satisfaction of societal demands. Professor Brzezinski has been

---

[1] For Professor Brzezinski's reply to his critics see *Problems of Communism* (May–June 1968).

criticized, perhaps unfairly, for leaving no option or possibility for the elite to adapt to the pressures for change short of transformation in the image of Western democracy.

A salient point raised by Professor Brzezinski refers to the party's rationale of its position in society. Heretofore the party has argued in theory for, and in great measure carried out in practice, a radical transformation of society, and insisted that this could be accomplished only through party leadership. As has been seen in the preceding readings, the political system has been structured so as to facilitate this objective. Brzezinski argues that the achievements already attained toward this objective have created a fundamental problem for the party, and the political system which it maintains. "What is to be the function of an ideocratic party in a relatively complex and industrialized society.... ?" Why must a political system, including the position of the party, formed for social revolution be maintained in its essential form when that goal is no longer being pursued? Might not managing a modern industrial state, and the maximization of economic productivity and development, be better assured by less restrictive political processes and institutions? Can the party leaders succeed in maintaining their position of power in Soviet society, while they make the transition in roles from leader of an economic and social revolution to manager of an increasingly stable society?

The significance of current developments, and their consequence for the future, cannot be determined to everyone's (or perhaps *anyone's*) satisfaction. Substantial answers to these and other such questions remain elusive. Perhaps the best that can be expected is an elaboration and refinement of the various alternatives—a task only just begun—leaving each to be measured by developments as they unfold. The selections in this part will provide the reader with an exposure to some differences in view,[2] and lead him to greater appreciation for the complexities of predicting the future of the Soviet political system.

---

[2] For other perspectives on how the Soviet political system may develop see: Raymond Aron, "Soviet Society in Transition," *Problems of Communism* (November–December 1957); Bertram D. Wolfe, "Reflections on the Soviet System: The Durable Core of Totalitarianism," in Samuel Hendel and Randolph L. Braham, eds., *The U.S.S.R. After 50 Years, Promise and Reality* (New York: Alfred A. Knopf, Inc., 1967); Isaac Deutscher, *The Ironies of History: Essays on Contemporary Communism* (New York: Oxford University Press, 1966); Milovan Djilas, *The Unperfect Society* (New York: Harcourt, Brace and World, Inc., 1969); and T. H. Rigby, "Security and Modernization," *Survey*, No. 64 (July 1967) and "Traditional, Market, and Organizational Societies and the U.S.S.R.," *World Politics*, XVI, No. 4 (July 1964), Paul Hollander, ed., *American and Soviet Society: A Reader in Comparative Sociology and Perception* (Englewood Cliffs, N.J.: Prentice-Hall, Inc., 1969), Part VII; Allen Kassof, ed., *Prospects for Soviet Society* (New York: Frederick A. Praeger, 1968); Cyril E. Black, ed., *The Transformation of Russian Society* (Cambridge, Mass.: Harvard University Press, 1960), Conclusion; and Jan Tinbergen, "Do Communism and Free Economies Show a Converging Pattern?", *Soviet Studies*, Vol. 12, No. 4 (April 1961).

THE SOVIET POLITICAL SYSTEM: TRANSFORMATION OR DEGENERATION

ZBIGNIEW BRZEZINSKI

The Soviet Union will soon celebrate its 50th anniversary. In this turbulent and rapidly changing world, for any political system to survive half a century is an accomplishment in its own right and obvious testimony to its durability. There are not many major political structures in the world today that can boast of such longevity. The approaching anniversary, however, provides an appropriate moment for a critical review of the changes that have taken place in the Soviet system, particularly in regard to such critical matters as the character of its top leadership, the methods by which its leaders acquire power, and the relationship of the Communist Party to society. Furthermore, the time is also ripe to inquire into the implications of these changes, especially in regard to the stability and vitality of the system.

The Leaders

Today Soviet spokesmen would have us believe that the quality of the top Communist leadership in the USSR has been abysmal. Of the 45 years since Lenin, according to official Soviet history, power was exercised for approximately five years by leaders subsequently unmasked as traitors (although later the charge of treason was retroactively reduced to that of deviation); for almost 20 years it was wielded by a paranoiac mass-murderer

who irrationally slew his best comrades and ignorantly guided Soviet war strategy by pointing his finger at a globe; and, most recently, for almost ten years, by a "harebrained" schemer given to tantrums and with a propensity for wild organizational experimentation. On the basis of that record, the present leadership lays claim to representing a remarkable departure from a historical pattern of singular depravity.

While Soviet criticism of former party leaders is now abundant, little intellectual effort is expended on analyzing the implications of the changes in leadership. Yet that, clearly, is the important question insofar as the political system is concerned.

Lenin was a rare type of political leader, fusing in his person several functions of key importance to the working of a political system: he acted as the chief ideologist of the system, the principal organizer of the party (indeed, the founder of the movement), and the top administrator of the state. It may be added that such personal fusion is typical of early revolutionary leaderships, and today it is exemplified by Mao Tse-tung. To his followers, Lenin was clearly a charismatic leader, and his power (like Hitler's or Mao Tse-tung's) depended less on institutions than on the force of his personality and intellect. Even after the Revolution, it was his personal authority that gave him enor-

Problems of Communism (January–February 1966), pp. 1–15. Reprinted by permission. Footnotes omitted.

mous power, while the progressive institutionalization of Lenin's rule (the Cheka, the appearance of the *apparat*, etc.) reflected more the transformation of a revolutionary party into a ruling one than any significant change in the character of his leadership.

Lenin's biographers agree that here was a man characterized by total political commitment, by self-righteous conviction, by tenacious determination and by an outstanding ability to formulate intellectually appealing principles of political action as well as popular slogans suitable for mass consumption. He was a typically revolutionary figure, a man whose genius can be consummated only at that critical juncture in history when the new breaks off—and not just evolves—from the old. Had he lived a generation earlier, he probably would have died in a Siberian *taiga*; a generation later, he probably would have been shot by Stalin.

Under Stalin, the fusion of leadership functions was continued, but this was due less to his personal qualities as such than to the fact that, with the passage of time and the growing toll of victims, his power became nearly total and was gradually translated also into personal authority. Only a mediocre ideologist—and certainly inferior in that respect to his chief rivals for power—Stalin became institutionally the ideologue of the system. A dull speaker, he eventually acquired the "routinized charisma" which, after Lenin's death, became invested in the Communist Party as a whole (much as the Pope at one time acquired the infallibility that for a long time had rested in the collective church). But his power was increasingly institutionalized bureaucratically, with decision-making centralized at the apex within his own secretariat, and its exercise involved a subtle balancing of the principal institutions of the political system: the secret police, the party, the state, and the army (roughly in that order of importance). Even the ostensibly principal organ of power, the Politburo, was split into minor groups, "the sextets," the "quartets," etc., with Stalin personally deciding who should participate in which subgroup and personally providing (and monopolizing) the function of integration.

If historical parallels for Lenin are to be found among the revolutionary tribunes, for Stalin they are to be sought among the Oriental despots. Thriving on intrigue, shielded in mystery, and isolated from society, his immense power reflected the immense tasks he succeeded in imposing on his followers and subjects. Capitalizing on the revolutionary momentum and the ideological impetus inherited from Leninism, and wedding it to a systematic institutionalization of bureaucratic rule, he could set in motion a social and political revolution which weakened all existing institutions save Stalin's own secretariat and his chief executive arm, the secret police. His power grew in proportion to the degree to which the major established institutions declined in vitality and homogeneity.

The war, however, as well as the postwar reconstruction, produced a paradox. While Stalin's personal prestige and authority were further enhanced, his institutional supremacy relatively declined. The military establishment naturally grew in importance; the enormous effort to transfer, reinstall, and later reconstruct the industrial economy invigorated the state machinery; the party apparat began to perform again the key functions of social mobilization and political integration. But the aging tyrant was neither unaware of this development nor apparently resigned to it. The Byzantine intrigues resulting in the liquidation of the Leningrad leadership and Voznesenski, the "doctors' plot" with its ominous implications for some top party, military and police chiefs, clearly augured an effort to weaken any institutional limits on Stalin's personal supremacy.

Khrushchev came to power ostensibly to save Stalinism, which he defined as safeguarding the traditional priority of heavy industry and restoring the primacy of the party. In fact, he presided over the dismantling of Stalinism. He rode to power by restoring the predominant position of the party apparat. But the complexities of governing (as contrasted to the priorities of the power struggle) caused him to dilute the party's position. While initially he succeeded in diminishing the political role of the secret police and in weakening the state machinery, the military establishment grew in importance with the continuing tensions of the cold war. By the time Khrushchev was removed, the economic priorities had become blurred because of pressures in agriculture and the consumer sector, while his own reorganization of the party into two separate industrial and rural hierarchies in November 1962 went far toward undermining the party's homogeneity of outlook, apart from splitting it institutionally. Consequently, the state bureaucracy recouped, almost by default, some of its integrative and administrative functions. Khrushchev thus, perhaps inadvertently, restored much of the institutional balance that had existed under Stalin, but without ever acquir-

ing the full powers of the balancer.

Khrushchev lacked the authority of Lenin to generate personal power, or the power of Stalin to create personal authority—and the Soviet leadership under him became increasingly differentiated. The top leader was no longer the top ideologist, in spite of occasional efforts to present Khrushchev's elaborations as "a creative contribution to Marxism-Leninism." The ruling body now contained at least one professional specialist in ideological matters, and it was no secret that the presence of the professional ideologue was required because someone had to give professional ideological advice to the party's top leader. Similarly, technical-administrative specialization differentiated some top leaders from others. Increasingly Khrushchev's function—and presumably the primary source of his still considerable power—was that of providing political integration and impetus for new domestic or foreign initiatives in a political system otherwise too complex to be directed and administered by one man.

The differentiation of functions also made it more difficult for the top leader to inherit even the "routinized charisma" that Stalin had eventually transferred to himself from the party as a whole. Acquiring charisma was more difficult for a leader who (even apart from a personal style and vulgar appearance that did not lend themselves to "image building") had neither the great "theoretical" flare valued by a movement that still prided itself on being the embodiment of a messianic ideology, nor the technical expertise highly regarded in a state which equated technological advance with human progress. Moreover, occupying the posts of First Secretary and Chairman of the Council of Ministers was not enough to develop a charismatic appeal since neither post had been sufficiently institutionalized to endow its occupant with the special prestige and aura that, for example, the President of the United States automatically gains on assuming office.

Trying to cope with this lack of charismatic appeal, Khrushchev replaced Stalin's former colleagues. In the process, he gradually came to rely on a younger generation of bureaucratic leaders to whom orderliness of procedure was instinctively preferable to crash campaigns. Administratively, however, Khrushchev was a true product of the Stalinist school, with its marked proclivity for just such campaigns at the cost of all other considerations. In striving to develop his own style of leadership, Khrushchev tried to emulate Lenin in stimulating new fervor, and Stalin in mobilizing energies, but without the personal and institutional assets that each had commanded. By the time he was removed, Khrushchev had become an anachronism in the new political context he himself had helped to create.

Brezhnev and Kosygin mark the coming to power of a new generation of leaders, irrespective of whether they will for long retain their present positions. Lenin's, Stalin's, and Khrushchev's formative experience was the unsettled period of conspiratorial activity, revolution, and—in Khrushchev's case—civil war and the early phase of communism. The new leaders, beneficiaries of the revolution but no longer revolutionaries themselves, have matured in an established political setting in which the truly large issues of policy and leadership have been decided. Aspiring young bureaucrats, initially promoted during the purges, they could observe—but not suffer

from—the debilitating consequences of political extremism and unpredictable personal rule. To this new generation of clerks, bureaucratic stability—indeed, bureaucratic dictatorship—must seem to be the only solid foundation for effective government.

Differentiation of functions to these bureaucrats is a norm, while personal charisma is ground for suspicion. The new Soviet leadership, therefore, is both bureaucratic in style and essentially impersonal in form. The curious emphasis on *kollektivnost rukovodstva* (collectivity of leadership) instead of the traditional *kollektivnoe rukovodstvo* (collective leadership)—a change in formulation used immediately after Khrushchev's fall—suggests a deliberate effort at achieving not only a personal but also an institutional collective leadership, designed to prevent any one leader from using a particular institution as a vehicle for obtaining political supremacy.

The question arises, however, whether this kind of leadership can prove effective in guiding the destiny of a major state. The Soviet system is now led by a bureaucratic leadership from the very top to the bottom. In that respect, it is unique. Even political systems with highly developed and skillful professional political bureaucracies, such as the British, the French, or that of the Catholic Church, have reserved some top policy-making and hence power-wielding positions for non-bureaucratic professional politicians, presumably on the assumption that a free-wheeling, generalizing and competitive political experience is of decisive importance in shaping effective national leadership.

To be sure, some top Soviet leaders do acquire such experience, even in the course of rising up the bureaucratic party ladder, especially when assigned to provincial or republican executive responsibilities. There they acquire the skills of initiative, direction, integration, as well as accommodation, compromise, and delegation of authority, which are the basic prerequisites for executive management of any complex organization.

Nonetheless, even when occupying territorial positions of responsibility, the *apparatchiki* are still part of an extremely centralized and rigidly hierarchical bureaucratic organization, increasingly set in its ways, politically corrupted by years of unchallenged power, and made even more confined in its outlook than is normally the case with a ruling body by its lingering and increasingly ritualized doctrinaire tradition. It is relevant to note here (from observations made in Soviet universities) that the young men who become active in the Komsomol organization and are presumably embarking on a professional political career are generally the dull conformists. Clearly, in a highly bureaucratized political setting, conformity, caution and currying favor with superiors count for more in advancing a political career than personal courage and individual initiative.

Such a condition poses a long-range danger to the vitality of any political system. Social evolution, it has been noted, depends not only on the availability of creative individuals, but on the existence of clusters of creators who collectively promote social innovation. "The ability of any gifted individual to exert leverage within a society . . . is partly a function of the exact composition of the group of those on whom he depends for day-to-day interaction and for the execution of his plans." The revolutionary milieu of

the 1920's and even the fanatical Stalinist commitment of the 1930's fostered such clusters of intellectual and political talent. It is doubtful that the CPSU party schools and the Central Committee personnel department encourage, in Margaret Mead's terms, the growth of clusters of creativity, and that is why the transition from Lenin to Stalin to Khrushchev to Brezhnev probably cannot be charted by an ascending line.

This has serious implications for the Soviet system as a whole. It is doubtful that any organization can long remain vital if it is so structured that in its personnel policy it becomes, almost unknowingly, inimical to talent and hostile to political innovation. Decay is bound to set in, while the stability of the political system may be endangered, if other social institutions succeed in attracting the society's talent and begin to chafe under the restraints imposed by the ruling but increasingly mediocre *apparatchiki*.

The Struggle for Power

The struggle for power in the Soviet political system has certainly become less violent. The question is, however: Has it become less debilitating for the political system? Has it become a more regularized process, capable of infusing the leadership with fresh blood? A closer look at the changes in the character of the competition for power may guide us to the answer.

Both Stalin and Khrushchev rode to power by skillfully manipulating issues as well as by taking full advantage of the organizational opportunities arising from their tenure of the post of party First Secretary. It must be stressed that the manipulation of issues was at least as important to their success as the organizational factor, which generally tends to receive priority in Western historical treatments. In Stalin's time, the issues facing the party were, indeed, on a grand scale: world revolution *vs.* socialism in one country; domestic evolution *vs.* social revolution; a factionalized *vs.* a monolithic party. Stalin succeeded because he instinctively perceived that the new *apparatchiki* were not prepared to sacrifice themselves in futile efforts to promote foreign revolutions but—being for the most part genuinely committed to revolutionary ideals—were becoming eager to get on with the job of creating a socialist society. (Moreover, had the NEP endured another ten years, would the Soviet Union be a Communist dictatorship today?)

Stalin's choice of socialism in one country was a brilliant solution. It captivated, at least in part, the revolutionaries; and it satisfied, at least partially, the accommodators. It split the opposition, polarized it, and prepared the ground for the eventual liquidation of each segment with the other's support. The violence, the terror, and finally the Great Purges of 1936–1938 followed logically. Imbued with the Leninist tradition of intolerance for dissent, engaged in a vast undertaking of social revolution that taxed both the resources and the nerves of party members, guided by an unscrupulous and paranoiac but also reassuringly calm leader, governing a backward country surrounded by neighbors that were generally hostile to the Soviet experiment, and increasingly deriving its own membership strength from first-generation proletarians with all their susceptibility to simple explanations and dogmatic truths, the ruling party easily

plunged down the path of increasing brutality. The leader both rode the crest of that violence and controlled it. The terror never degenerated into simple anarchy, and Stalin's power grew immeasurably because he effectively practiced the art of leadership according to his own definition:

The art of leadership is a serious matter. One must not lag behind the movement, because to do so is to become isolated from the masses. But neither must one rush ahead, for to rush ahead is to lose contact with the masses. He who wants to lead a movement and at the same time keep in touch with the vast masses must wage a fight on two fronts—against those who lag behind and those who run ahead.

Khrushchev, too, succeeded in becoming the top leader because he perceived the elite's predominant interests. Restoration of the primary position of the party, decapitation of the secret police, reduction of the privileges of the state bureaucrats while maintaining the traditional emphasis on heavy industrial development (which pleased both the industrial elite and the military establishment)—these were the issues which Khrushchev successfully utilized in the mid-1950's to mobilize the support of officials and accomplish the gradual isolation and eventual defeat of Malenkov.

But the analogy ends right there. The social and even the political system in which Khrushchev came to rule was relatively settled. Indeed, in some respects, it was stagnating, and Khrushchev's key problem, once he reached the political apex (but before he had had time to consolidate his position there) was how to get the country moving again. The effort to infuse new social and political dynamism into Soviet society, even while consolidating his power, led him to a public repudiation of Stalinism which certainly shocked some officials; to sweeping economic reforms which disgruntled many administrators; to a dramatic reorganization of the party which appalled the *apparatchiki*; and even to an attempt to circumvent the policy-making authority of the party Presidium by means of direct appeals to interested groups, which must have both outraged and frightened his colleagues. The elimination of violence as the decisive instrumentality of political competition—a move that was perhaps prompted by the greater institutional maturity of Soviet society, and which was in any case made inevitable by the downgrading of the secret police and the public disavowals of Stalinism —meant that Khrushchev, unlike Stalin, could not achieve both social dynamism and the stability of his power. Stalin magnified his power as he strove to change society; to change society Khrushchev had to risk his power.

The range of domestic disagreement involved in the post-Stalin struggles has also narrowed with the maturing of social commitments made earlier. For the moment, the era of grand alternatives is over in Soviet society. Even though any struggle tends to exaggerate differences, the issues that divided Khrushchev from his opponents, though of great import, appear pedestrian in comparison to those over which Stalin and his enemies crossed swords. In Khrushchev's case, they pertained primarily to policy alternatives; in the case of Stalin, they involved basic conceptions of historical development. Compare the post-Stalin debates about the allocation of resources among different branches of the economy, for example, with the

debates of the 1920's about the character and pace of Soviet industrialization; or Khrushchev's homilies on the merits of corn—and even his undeniably bold and controversial virgin lands campaign—with the dilemma of whether to collectivize a hundred million reticent peasants, at what pace, and with what intensity in terms of resort to violence.

It is only in the realm of foreign affairs that one can perhaps argue that grand dilemmas still impose themselves on the Soviet political scene. The nuclear-war-or-peace debate of the 1950's and early 1960's is comparable in many respects to the earlier conflict over "permanent revolution" or "socialism in one country." Molotov's removal and Kozlov's political demise were to a large extent related to disagreements concerning foreign affairs; nonetheless, in spite of such occasional rumblings, it would appear that on the peace-or-war issue there is today more of a consensus among the Soviet elite than there was on the issue of permanent revolution in the 1920's. Although a wide spectrum of opinion does indeed exist in the international Communist movement on the crucial questions of war and peace, this situation, as far as one can judge, obtains to a considerably lesser degree in the USSR itself. Bukharin *vs.* Trotsky can be compared to Togliatti *vs.* Mao Tsetung, but hardly to Khrushchev *vs.* Kozlov.

The narrowing of the range of disagreement is reflected in the changed character of the cast. In the earlier part of this discussion, some comparative comments were made about Stalin, Khrushchev, and Brezhnev. It is even more revealing, however, to examine their principal rivals. Take the men who opposed Stalin: Trotsky, Zinoviev, and Bukharin. What a range of political, historical, economic, and intellectual creativity, what talent, what a diversity of personal characteristics and backgrounds! Compare this diversity with the strikingly uniform personal training, narrowness of perspective, and poverty of intellect of Malenkov, Kozlov and Suslov. A regime of the clerks cannot help but clash over clerical issues.

The narrowing of the range of disagreement and the cooling of ideological passions mean also the wane of political violence. The struggle tends to become less a matter of life or death, and more one in which the price of defeat is simply retirement and some personal disgrace. In turn, with the routinization of conflict, the political system develops even a body of precedents for handling fallen leaders. By now there must be a regular procedure, probably even some office, for handling pensions and apartments for former Presidium members, as well as a developing social etiquette for dealing with them publicly and privately.

More important is the apparent development in the Soviet system of something which might be described as a regularly available "counter-elite." After Khrushchev's fall, his successors moved quickly to restore to important positions a number of individuals whom Khrushchev had purged, while some of Khrushchev's supporters were demoted and transferred. Already for a number of years now, it has been fairly common practice to appoint party officials demoted from high office either to diplomatic posts abroad or to some obscure, out-of-the-way assignments at home. The total effect of this has been to create a growing body of official "outs" who are biding their time on the sidelines and presumably hoping someday to become the "ins" again. Moreover, they may not only hope; if sufficiently numerous, young, and vigorous, they may gradually begin to resemble something of a political alternative to those in power, and eventually to think and even act as such. This could be the starting point of informal factional activity, of intrigues and conspiracies when things go badly for those in power, and of organized efforts to seduce some part of the ruling elite in order to stage an internal change of guard. In addition, the availability of an increasingly secure "counter-elite" is likely to make it more difficult for a leader to consolidate his power. This in turn might tend to promote more frequent changes in the top leadership, with policy failures affecting the power of incumbents instead of affecting—only retroactively—the reputation of former leaders, as has hitherto been the case.

The cumulative effect of these developments has been wide-ranging. First of all, the reduced importance of both ideological issues and personalities and the increasing weight of institutional interests in the periodic struggles for power—a phenomenon which reflects the more structured quality of present-day Soviet life as compared with the situation under Stalin—tends to depersonalize political conflict and to make it a protracted bureaucratic struggle. Secondly, the curbing of violence makes it more likely that conflicts will be resolved by patched-up compromises rather than by drastic institutional redistributions of power and the reappearance of personal tyranny. Finally, the increasingly bureaucratic character of the struggle for power tends to transform it into a contest among high-level clerks and is therefore not conducive to attracting creative and innovating talent into the top leadership.

Khrushchev's fall provides a good illustration of the points made above, as well as an important precedent for the future. For the first time in Soviet history, the First Secretary has been toppled from power by his associates. This was done not in order to replace him with an alternative personal leader or to pursue genuinely alternative goals, but in order to depersonalize the leadership and to pursue more effectively many of the previous policies. In a word, the objectives were impersonal leadership and higher bureaucratic efficiency. Khrushchev's removal, however, also means that personal intrigues and cabals can work, that subordinate members of the leadership—or possibly, someday, a group of ex-leaders—can effectively conspire against a principal leader, with the result that any future First Secretary is bound to feel far less secure than Khrushchev must have felt at the beginning of October 1964.

The absence of an institutionalized top executive officer in the Soviet political system, in conjunction with the increased difficulties in the way of achieving personal dictatorship and the decreased personal cost of defeat in a political conflict, create a ready-made situation for group pressures and institutional clashes. In fact, although the range of disagreement may have narrowed, the scope of elite participation in power conflicts has already widened. Much of Khrushchev's exercise of power was preoccupied with mediating the demands of key institutions such as the army, or with overcoming the opposition of others, such

as the objections of the administrators to economic decentralization or of the heavy industrial managers to non-industrial priorities. These interests were heavily involved in the Khrushchev-Malenkov conflict and in the "anti-party" episode of 1957.

At the present time, these pressures and clashes take place in an almost entirely amorphous context, without constitutional definition and established procedures. The somewhat greater role played by the Central Committee in recent years still does not suffice to give this process of bureaucratic conflict a stable institutional expression. As far as we know from existing evidence, the Central Committee still acted during the 1957 and 1964 crises primarily as a ratifying body, giving formal sanction to decisions already fought out in the Kremlin's corridors of power. It did not act as either the arbiter or the supreme legislative body.

The competition for power, then, is changing from a death struggle among the few into a contest played by many more. But the decline of violence does not, as is often assumed, automatically benefit the Soviet political system; something more effective and stable has to take the place of violence. The "game" of politics that has replaced the former mafia-style struggles for power is no longer murderous, but it is still not a stable game played within an established arena, according to accepted rules, and involving more or less formal teams. It resembles more the anarchistic free-for-all of the playground and therefore could become, in some respects, even more debilitating to the system. Stalin encouraged institutional conflict below him so that he could wield his power with less restraint. Institutional conflict combined with mediocre and unstable personal leadership makes for ineffective and precarious power.

Party and Group Interests

In a stimulating study of political development and decay, Samuel Huntington has argued that stable political growth requires a balance between political "institutionalization" and political "participation": that merely increasing popular mobilization and participation in politics without achieving a corresponding degree of "institutionalization of political organization and procedures" results not in political development but in political decay. Commenting in passing on the Soviet system, he therefore noted that "a strong party is in the Soviet public interest" because it provides a stable institutional framework.

The Soviet political system has certainly achieved a high index of institutionalization. For almost five decades the ruling party has maintained unquestioned supremacy over the society, imposing its ideology at will. Traditionally, the Communist system has combined its high institutionalization with high pseudo-participation of individuals. But a difficulty could arise if division within the top leadership of the political system weakened political "institutionalization" while simultaneously stimulating genuine public participation by groups and institutions. Could this new condition be given an effective and stable institutional framework and, if so, with what implications for the "strong" party?

Today the Soviet political system is again oligarchic, but its socio-economic setting is now quite different. Soviet society is far more developed and stable, far less *malleable* and atomized.

In the past, the key groups that had to be considered as potential political participants were relatively few. Today, in addition to the vastly more entrenched institutional interests, such as the police, the military, and the state bureaucracy, the youth could become a source of ferment, the consumers could become more restless, the collective farmers more recalcitrant, the scientists more outspoken, the non-Russian nationalities more demanding. Prolonged competition among the oligarchs would certainly accelerate the assertiveness of such groups.

By now some of these groups have a degree of institutional cohesion, and occasionally they act in concert on some issues. They certainly can lobby and, in turn, be courted by ambitious and opportunistic oligarchs. Some groups, because of institutional cohesion, advantageous location, easy access to the top leadership, and ability to articulate their goals and interest, can be quite influential. Taken together they represent a wide spectrum of opinion, and in the setting of oligarchical rule there is bound to be some correspondence between their respective stances and those of the top leaders. This spectrum is represented in simplified fashion by the chart on the next page, which takes cumulative account of the principal divisions, both on external and on domestic issues, that have perplexed Soviet political life during the last decade or so. Obviously, the table is somewhat arbitrary and also highly speculative. Individuals and groups cannot be categorized so simply, and some, clearly, could be shifted left or right with equal cause, as indeed they often shift themselves. Nonetheless, the chart illustrates the range of opinion that exists in the Soviet system and suggests the kind of alliances, group competition, and political courtship that probably prevail, cutting vertically through the party organization.

Not just Western but also Communist (although not as yet Soviet) political thinkers are coming to recognize more and more openly the existence of group conflict even in a Communist-dominated society. A Slovak jurist recently observed:

> The social interest in our society can be democratically formed only by the integration of group interests; in the process of this integration, the interest groups protect their own economic and other social interests; this is in no way altered by the fact that everything appears on the surface as a unity of interests.

The author went on to stress that the key political problem facing the Communist system is that of achieving integration of group interests.

Traditionally, this function of integration has been monopolized by the party, resorting—since the discard of terror—to the means of *bureaucratic arbitration*. In the words of the author just cited, "the party as the leading and directing political force fulfills its functions by resolving intra-class and inter-class interests." In doing so, the party generally has preferred to deal with each group bilaterally, thereby preventing the formation of coalitions and informal group consensus. In this way the unity of political direction as well as the political supremacy of the ruling party have been maintained. The party has always been very jealous of its "integrative" prerogative, and the intrusion on the political scene of any other group has been strongly resented. The party's institutional primacy has thus depended on limiting the real participation of other groups.

If, for one reason or another, the party were to weaken in the performance of this function, the only alternative to anarchy would be some *institutionalized process of mediation,*

Policy Spectrum USSR

Systemic Left	Marginalist — Left	Centrist	Right	Systemic Right
Malenkov	Khrushchev Podgorny	Kosygin Mikoyan ¦ Brezhnev	Shelepin Kozlov Suzlov Voronov	Molotov Kaganovich
Consumer Goods Industry	Light Industry Regional Apparat		Central Apparat Agitprop	
		Military Innovators	Conventional Army	Heavy Industry
Scientists	Agronomists		Ministerial Bureaucrats	
Moscow-Leningrad Intellectuals	Economic Reformers (Liberman)		Economic Computators (Nemchinov)	Secret Police

replacing the party's bureaucratic arbitration. Since, as noted, group participation has become more widespread, while the party's effectiveness in achieving integration has been lessened by the decline in the vigor of Soviet leadership and by the persistent divisions in the top echelon, the creation and eventual formal institutionalization of some such process of mediation is gaining in urgency. Otherwise participation could outrun institutionalization and result in a challenge to the party's integrative function.

Khrushchev's practice of holding enlarged Central Committee plenums, with representatives of other groups present, seems to have been a step towards formalizing a more regular consultative procedure. (It also had the politically expedient effect of bypassing Khrushchev's opponents in the central leadership.) Such enlarged plenums provided a consultative forum, where policies could be debated, views articulated, and even some contradictory interests resolved. Although the device still remained essentially non-institutionalized and only *ad hoc*, consultative and not legislative, still subject to domination by the party *apparat*, it was nonetheless a response to the new quest for real participation that Soviet society has manifested and which the Soviet system badly needs. It was also a compromise solution, attempting to wed the party's primacy to a procedure allowing group articulation.

However, the problem has become much more complex and fundamental because of the organizational and ideological crisis in the party over its relevance to the evolving Soviet system. For many years the party's monopoly of power and hence its active intervention in all spheres of Soviet life could indeed be said to be "in the Soviet public interest." The party provided

social mobilization, leadership, and a dominant outlook for a rapidly changing and developing society. But, in the main, that society has now taken shape. It is no longer malleable, subject to simple mobilization, or susceptible to doctrinaire ideological manipulation.

As a result, Soviet history in the last few years has been dominated by the spectacle of a party in search of a role. What is to be the function of an ideocratic party in a relatively complex and industrialized society, in which the structure of social relationships generally reflects the party's ideological preferences? To be sure, like any large sociopolitical system, the Soviet system needs an integrative organ. But the question is, What is the most socially desirable way of achieving such integration? Is a "strong" party one that dominates and interferes in everything, and is this interference conducive to continued Soviet economic, political and intellectual growth?

In 1962 Khrushchev tried to provide a solution. The division of the party into two vertically parallel, functional organs was an attempt to make the party directly relevant to the economy and to wed the party's operations to production processes. It was a bold, dramatic and radical innovation, reflecting a recognition of the need to adapt the party's role to a new state of Soviet social development. But it was also a dangerous initiative; it carried within itself the potential of political disunity as well as the possibility that the party would become so absorbed in economic affairs that it would lose its political and ideological identity. That it was rapidly repudiated by Khrushchev's successors is testimony to the repugnance that the reorganization must have stimulated among the professional party bureaucrats.

His successors, having rejected Khrushchev's reorganization of the party, have been attempting a compromise solution—in effect, a policy of "muddling through." On the one hand, they recognize that the party can no longer direct the entire Soviet economy from the Kremlin and that major institutional reforms in the economic sphere, pointing towards more local autonomy and decision-making, are indispensable. (Similar tendencies are apparent elsewhere—*e.g.*, the stress on professional self-management in the military establishment.) This constitutes a partial and implicit acknowledgment that in some respects a party of total control is today incompatible with the Soviet public interest.

On the other hand, since obviously inherent in the trend towards decentralization is the danger that the party will be gradually transformed from a directing, ideologically-oriented organization to a merely instrumental and pragmatic body specializing in adjustment and compromise of social group aspirations, the party functionaries, out of a sense of vested interest, have been attempting simultaneously to revive the ideological vitality of the CPSU. Hence the renewed stress on ideology and ideological training; hence the new importance attached to the work of the ideological commissions; and hence the categorical reminders that "Marxist education, Marxist-Leninist training, and the ideological tempering of CPSU members and candidate members is the primary concern of every party organization and committee."

However, it is far from certain that economic decentralization and ideological "retempering" can be pushed forward hand in hand. The present leadership appears oblivious to the fact that established ideology remains vital only when ideologically motivated power is applied to achieve ideological

goals. A gradual reduction in the directing role of the party cannot be compensated for by an increased emphasis on ideological semantics. Economic decentralization inescapably reduces the scope of the political-ideological and increases the realm of the pragmatic-instrumental. It strengthens the trend, publicly bemoaned by Soviet ideologists, toward depolitization of the Soviet elite. A massive indoctrination campaign directed at the elite cannot operate in a "de-ideologized" socioeconomic context, and major efforts to promote such a campaign could, indeed, prompt the social isolation of the party, making its dogmas even more irrelevant to the daily concerns of a Soviet scientist, factory director, or army general. That in turn would further reduce the ability of the party to provide effective integration in Soviet society, while underscoring the party *apparatchik's* functional irrelevance to the workings of Soviet administration and technology.

If the party rejects a return to ideological dogmas and renewed dogmatic indoctrination, it unavoidably faces the prospect of further internal change. It will gradually become a loose body, combining a vast variety of specialists, engineers, scientists, administrators, professional bureaucrats, agronomists, etc. Without a common dogma and without an active program, what will hold these people together? The party at this stage will face the same dilemma that the fascist and falange parties faced, and that currently confronts the Yugoslav and Polish Communists: in the absence of a large-scale domestic program of change, in the execution of which other groups and institutions become subordinated to the party, the party's domestic primacy declines and its ability to provide social-political integration is negated.

Moreover, the Soviet party leaders would be wrong to assume complacently that the narrowed range of disagreement over domestic policy alternatives could not again widen. Persistent difficulties in agriculture could some day prompt a political aspirant to question the value of collectivization; or the dissatisfaction of some nationalities could impose a major strain on the Soviet constitutional structure; or foreign affairs could again become the source of bitter internal conflicts. The ability of the system to withstand the combined impact of such divisive issues and of greater group intrusion into politics would much depend on the adaptations that it makes in its organization of leadership and in its processes of decision-making. Unless alternative mechanisms of integration are created, a situation could arise in which some group other than the top *apparat*—a group that had continued to attract talent into its top ranks and had not been beset by bureaucratically debilitating conflict at the top—could step forth to seek power; invoking the Soviet public interest in the name of established Communist ideals, and offering itself (probably in coalition with some section of the party leadership) as the only alternative to chaos, it would attempt to provide a new balance between institutionalization and participation.

The Threat of Degeneration

The Soviet leaders have recognized the need of institutional reforms in the economic sector in order to revitalize the national economy. The fact is that institutional reforms are just as badly needed—and even more overdue—in the political sector. Indeed, the effort to maintain a doctrinaire dictatorship over an increasingly modern and industrial society has already contributed to a reopening of the gap that existed in prerevolutionary Russia between the political system and the society, thereby posing the threat of the degeneration of the Soviet system.

A political system can be said to degenerate when there is a perceptible decline in the quality of the social talent that the political leadership attracts to itself in competition with other groups; when there is persistent division within the ruling elite, accompanied by a decline in its commitment to shared beliefs; when there is protracted instability in the top leadership; when there is a decline in the capacity of the ruling elite to define the purposes of the political system in relationship to society and to express them in effective institutional terms; when there is a fuzzing of institutional and hierarchical lines of command, resulting in the uncontrolled and unchanneled intrusion into politics of hitherto politically uninvolved groupings. All of these indicators were discernible in the political systems of Tsarist Russia, the French Third Republic, Chiang Kai-Shek's China and Rakosi's Hungary. Today, as already noted, at least several are apparent in the Soviet political system.

This is not to say, however, that the evolution of the Soviet system has inevitably turned into degeneration. Much still depends on how the ruling Soviet elite reacts. Policies of retrenchment, increasing dogmatism, and even violence, which—if now applied—would follow almost a decade of loosening up, could bring about a grave situation of tension, and the possibility of revolutionary outbreaks could not be discounted entirely. "Terror is indispensable to any dictatorship, but it cannot compensate for incompetent leaders and a defective organization of authority," observed a historian of the French revolution, writing of the Second Directory. It is equally true of the Soviet political scene.

The threat of degeneration could be lessened through several adaptations designed to adjust the Soviet political system to the changes that have taken place in the now more mature society. First of all, the top policy-making organ of the Soviet system has been traditionally the exclusive preserve of the professional politician, and in many respects this has assured the Soviet political system of able and experienced leadership. However, since a professional bureaucracy is not prone to produce broad "generalizing" talents, and since the inherent differentiation of functions within it increases the likelihood of leaders with relatively much narrower specialization than hitherto was the case, the need for somewhat broader representation of social talent within the top political leadership, and not merely on secondary levels as hitherto, is becoming urgent. If several outstanding scientists, professional economists, industrial managers, and others were to be co-opted by lateral entry into the ruling Presidium, the progressive transformation of the leadership into a regime of clerks could thereby be averted, and the alienation of other groups from the political system perhaps halted.

Secondly, the Soviet leaders would have to institutionalize a chief executive office and strive to endow it with legitimacy and stability. This would eventually require the creation of a formal and open process of leadership selection, as well—probably—as a time limit on the tenure of the chief executive position. The time limit, if honored, would depersonalize power,

while an institutionalized process of selection geared to a specific date— and therefore also limited in time— would reduce the debilitating effects of unchecked and protracted conflict in the top echelons of power.

The CPSU continues to be an ideocratic party with a strong tradition of dogmatic intolerance and organizational discipline. Today less militant and more bureaucratic in outlook, it still requires a top catalyst, though no longer a personal tyrant, for effective operations. The example of the papacy, or perhaps of Mexico, where a ruling party has created a reasonably effective system of presidential succession, offers a demonstration of how one-man rule can be combined with a formal office of the chief executive, endowed with legitimacy, tenure and a formally established pattern of selection.

Any real institutionalization of power would have significant implications for the party. If its Central Committee were to become in effect an electoral college, selecting a ruler whom no one could threaten during his tenure, the process of selection would have to be endowed with considerable respectability. It would have to be much more than a mere ratification of an *a priori* decision reached by some bureaucratic cabal. The process would require tolerance for the expression of diverse opinions in a spirit free of dogmatism, a certain amount of open competition among rivals for power, and perhaps even the formation of informal coalitions—at least temporary ones. In a word, it would mean a break with the Leninist past, with consequences that would unavoidably spill over from the party into the entire system and society.

Thirdly, increased social participation in politics unavoidably creates the need for an institutionalized arena for the mediation of group interests, if tensions and conflicts, and eventually perhaps even anarchy, are to be avoided. The enlarged plenums of the Central Committee were a right beginning, but if the Committee is to mediate effectively among the variety of institutional and group interests that now exist in Soviet society, its membership will have to be made much more representative and the predominance of party bureaucrats watered down. Alternatively, the Soviet leaders might consider following the Yugoslav course of creating a new institution for the explicit purpose of providing group representation and reconciling different interests. In either case, an effective organ of mediation could not be merely a front for the party's continued bureaucratic arbitration of social interests, as that would simply perpetuate the present dilemmas.

Obviously, the implementation of such institutional reforms would eventually lead to a profound transformation of the Soviet system. But it is the absence of basic institutional development in the Soviet political system that has posed the danger of the system's degeneration. It is noteworthy that the Yugoslavs have been experimenting with political reforms, including new institutions, designed to meet precisely the problems and dangers discussed here. Indeed, in the long run, perhaps the ultimate contribution to Soviet political and social development that the CPSU can make is to adjust gracefully to the desirability, and perhaps even inevitability, of its own gradual withering away. In the meantime, the progressive transformation of the bureaucratic Communist dictatorship into a more pluralistic and institutionalized political system—even though still a system of one-party rule—seems essential if its degeneration is to be averted.

THE BEGINNING OF THE END?

MICHEL TATU

Michel Garder's *L'Agonie du régime en Russie soviétique* is a change from the scholarly treatises to which the Sovietologists have accustomed us; it is a study, to be sure, but also much more —a manifesto. The author, a French officer who has long specialized in Eastern affairs, decided this time not to worry about nuances and details. His conclusions—not unlike those of Valery Tarsis—are radical: the Soviet regime is doomed to collapse. He even foresees the date of this collapse: about 1970—or, to be more precise, *before* 1970. And he sets out to prove it in a little more than 200 pages.

The apocalyptic character of the author's conclusions naturally dictates the style of the book, which is written in anything but academic language; certain excesses will seem shocking, others quaint. Thus, for example, M. Garder insistently pictures the party as a clergy, discussing the role

Problems of Communism (March–April 1966), pp. 44–47. Reprinted by permission. Footnotes omitted.

of the "Pope-Emperor" (Stalin) and referring to Khrushchev as the "self-styled vicar." Or, on post-Stalin Russia, he writes: "Rid of the terror, the huge country rapidly adopted a spirit of free-for-all"—obviously, somewhat of an exaggeration of the relaxation that has taken place. Or, a striking thumbnail sketch of Khrushchev in late 1963 and early 1964: "The Pope-Emperor, who had beamed with self-assurance in the preceding years, gave way to a worried old man seeking to square the circle." On a few occasions, the book shows how dangerous narrow convictions can become. Completing his book early in 1965, M. Garder deemed it necessary to add a footnote reporting as a fact the completely unverified rumor that First Deputy-Premier D. F. Ustinov had been arrested. Clearly the rumor fitted in too well with the notion of the regime's "death throes" for the author to resist the temptation of using it. He would have done better had he waited until 1970, since that is precisely what he advises us to do.

Yet all this being said, it is not a bad idea occasionally to leave the beaten path and, even at the risk of oversimplification, to unfold a fearless vision of the future. By the very radicalism of its conclusions, a work of this kind may force useful reactions. It may stimulate some to reexamine a few pat ideas; to others it may offer a "working hypothesis." In any case, no one can remain indifferent to the prospects the author holds out. In fact, any study of Soviet society written without a general idea about the Soviet future, whether short or long-term, is likely to be sterile. Hypotheses such as those put forward by M. Garder—or equally well-defined hypotheses expressing an opposite view—have the ad-vantage of introducing a dynamic element into an analysis.

Now a few remarks on M. Garder's thesis. It is, of course, perfectly true that conservatism is the main ill from which the Soviet system suffers at the present time. As the author puts it in his customary "shock" terms, "the most conservative Western bourgeois is a revolutionary next to the *apparat-chik*." Before M. Garder, the Yugoslav writer Mihajlo Mihajlov had already come to a similar conclusion, and so have many others, including Soviet writers, though the latter prefer to speak of "dogmatism" or "clinging to the old ways." But it is really necessary to go one step further and conclude with Garder that the "Leninist-Marxist clergy" and its ideology cannot change; at best, it can only perpetuate itself.

It is also true that the best formula for preserving the system would have been to maintain absolute power in the Stalinist manner. "Only the formula 'God is dead, long live God!,' could have saved the theocracy," remarks Garder with respect to the year 1953. It is indeed difficult to conceive of a religion without a pope; Khrushchev had hoped to be a "Pope-Emperor," but he failed because he did not have at his disposal his predecessor's Draconian means. And if a conclusion can be drawn from Khrushchev's ill-fated reign, it is that one man cannot rule alone without resorting to police power. Not only must the leader in power gain obedience from his subjects, but he must, above all, eliminate recalcitrant "cardinals."

M. Garder attributes Khrushchev's fall, a little hastily perhaps, to a mere accumulation of problems and failures for which a "scapegoat" had to be found. It would seem that a more convincing explanation of the event lies in the institutional changes introduced by the first post-Stalin reforms: the termination of the political terror and its corollary—the right, claimed more and more openly by the "cardinals," to share in the exercise of supreme power. In any event, this development seems to rule out absolute one-man rule for the foreseeable future, and it consequently further weakens the cohesion and effectiveness of the "clergy."

In contrast to the immediate advantages seen in the present course by the incumbent leaders—the return to "reason" and "scientific leadership," confirmed by certain efforts at a rationalization of economic management—a major drawback stands out in the longer-range perspective: the loss of political impetus. For what more can be expected from a collective leadership than the lukewarm breath of a bureaucracy propping up its power? Tendencies toward rationalization may be in evidence, to be sure, but they are weakened by the need for negotiation, compromise, and respect for vested interests. Despite certain appearances, conservatism is thus very likely to become more pronounced rather than weaker as a result of Khrushchev's fall. In the beginning, at least, the former First Secretary deserved credit for having given new impetus to the regime through destalinization and a dynamic foreign policy.

This brings us to the most crucial of M. Garder's premises. "The mounting conflict," he writes, "between a decaying regime that no longer has any other justification than the personal interests of those who profit by it and the population of a young, healthy country awakening after a long period of torpor cannot end in a compromise." In brief, M. Garder dismisses the possibility of a peaceful transformation of the regime. But here a distinction must be made.

If it comes to a direct confrontation between the regime and its *apparatchiki* on the one hand, and the "young and healthy" population on the other, the author is quite likely right. The known aspirations for individual freedom in the USSR, particularly among the young people, the "radicalization" found among their conservative opponents, the general lassitude, to say the least, toward worn-out slogans, and the dissatisfaction with the prevailing standard of living—all this is abundant evidence to lead one to conclude that the day everybody is left to himself in the Soviet Union the situation will soon be out of control. The fact that accounts have not yet been settled for the "excesses" committed during the Stalinist era only adds to the uncertainty. And the party leaders now know that the grant of partial freedom only whets the appetite of those to whom it is given, and that it cannot therefore solve their problem. (Those in the West who continue to foresee a progressive "convergence" of the Soviet and Western systems disregard this fact. Aside from the economic questions involved, which deserve to be discussed separately, the major flaw in this theory is that it ignores the Russian people, their reactions and frustrations.)

On the other hand, insofar as the confrontation between the party apparatus and the other organized forces of the regime is concerned, there is no reason why a compromise should be impossible; or, to be more precise, a series of compromises solving all the more or less serious but not necessarily violent crises that may arise in this contest. Unquestionably, the party machine —the "clergy"—is today the most conservative element in the system and the principal curb on progress. Opposing it is the slightly more "progressive" state economic bureaucracy, which, impelled by the need to resolve serious technical problems seeks to free itself from party tutelage. M. Garder foresees this conflict between the *apparatchiki* and the technicians, especially at the lower echelon, and it is imaginable that the former may be bribed into making certain concessions. The party, of course, loudly proclaims its determination to resist even the slightest transfer of power, but the day may come when it will find a compromise preferable to more serious upheavals. Some more "enlightened" *apparatchiki* may help in this direction.

Above all, however, there remains the possibility of a transfer of power to the military and the police, the principal organized forces outside the party apparatus. M. Garder rules out this possibility, alleging that the military are too divided and infiltrated by the party. He believes that the role of the KGB will be much more important, while at the same time admitting that this is the great unknown of the equation, which indeed it is.

While it is true that traditionally the army has been strictly subservient to the party, this does not mean that this relationship can never change, especially in the face of a divided and uncertain political leadership. There have been many indications in the past year that Khrushchev's fall has widened the autonomy and authority of the marshals, and this seems true also of the police. Assuming, as M. Garder

does, that the gravity of the problems facing the USSR, coupled with the impossibility of defining collectively a valid policy, dooms the members of the party Presidium to a struggle for power—a power which is becoming increasingly elusive—is it really so absurd to think that one or more marshals might decide, in a day of crisis, to "take charge" of the government to save the country? A regime of this kind, rid of the ideological chaff (of which it would retain only the patriotic content), would have a fair chance of staying in power. Since it would be inclined to leave the economy in the care of the technicians, even of the producers themselves, it would probably prove much more effective in economic administration than its predecessors. Politically, it would maintain a strong government, and it would find in the *apparatchiki* the perfect scapegoats for all the mistakes of the past. But with or without such army intervention, freedom would not be likely to arrive by 1970.

There are still other possible hypotheses. For instance, a member of the collective leadership might strengthen his authority step by step as Khrushchev did between 1953 and 1957; but, unlike the latter, he might want to use the police apparatus for his own ends. Unquestionably, the obstacles to such a course would be enormous in view of the determination of the party cadres to protect themselves against a repetition of Stalinist terror. Resistance at all levels would thus be considerable; but then, what is the aim of terror if not precisely to break down all resistance? M. Garder rules out this theory on the ground that going back to police pressures would be detrimental to the interests of the economy. This is undeniable, but it is equally true that there are times when economic considerations carry little weight compared to political interests, particularly when the preservation of the system is at stake. It must be granted —and above all ardently hoped—that the probability of a return to police terror is slight. Besides, many gradations in this respect are possible, as the history of the 1930's attests. But the "law of irreversibility" of political changes in the Soviet Union remains to be proven.

In brief, then, there are three main approaches for projecting the present Soviet situation into the future. The first rests on the conclusion that the USSR finds itself in a typically prerevolutionary situation; that its ruling regime is in conflict with the dynamic social forces of the country and must inevitably be swept away. This is M. Garder's view—and also, incidentally, the belief of many authentic Marxists, including members of reputedly orthodox Communist parties. Another, less "linear" approach takes into account various accidents of history and leads to the conclusion that the conservatism of the regime and its leadership has not yet come to full fruition, that it can still mature and harden. Lastly, one can envisage a gradual transfer of authority from the party to other centers of power—the army, the economic cadres, the police —a transfer half-negotiated and half-conquered, which under conditions of "controlled violence" would transform the regime into a more effective, if still dictatorial, system of government. Let us leave to M. Garder the responsibility for his "wager," and let us wait for his 1970 rendezvous.

CHANGES IN RUSSIA: THE NEED FOR PERSPECTIVES

FREDERICK C. BARGHOORN

This symposium confronts the difficult but rewarding task of evaluating several thoughtful studies pertaining in one degree or another to the Soviet future.

Before commenting in detail on the fundamental issues posed by the studies in question, especially Professor Brzezinski's ingenious and original analysis, I should identify my point of view. Since political systems are the product of men's experience, they can change when there are changes in the environment by which they have been shaped. When political structures and the belief systems which legitimate them cease to be "functional," tensions develop between them and their internal and external environments. Institutions and practices which become obsolete must be either modified or replaced by new ones more appropriate to the tasks which confront them. Of course, political behavior is influenced not only by the experience of the living but also to some degree

Problems of Communism (May–June 1966), pp. 39–42. Reprinted by permission. Footnotes omitted.

by living memories of the experiences of earlier generations. Hence, practices which have outlived much of their earlier relevance may, because of historical inertia, persist for a very long time indeed. The concept of the political system as a set of interdependent processes and structures, adapting to but also influencing its domestic and foreign environments, is of course no magic key to political analysis. Its usefulness in the study of any system depends upon scrupulous regard to the unique history and characteristics of the particular system examined.

I shall comment briefly on the essays in the "Progress and Ideology" issue of *Problems of Communism*. These competent surveys of post-Stalin developments in several fields of social and natural sciences suggest, in my opinion, that the Soviet "creative intelligentsia" is an increasingly autonomous and politically influential subcommunity of the overall political community. However, Soviet intellectuals are still constrained to seek limited objectives, pursued largely by such indirect means as behind-the-scenes pleading with party overseers, who are sometimes inclined for various reasons to support particular aspirations of the intelligentsia. The limited but real progress toward intellectual freedom made by the groups whose problems and prospects are examined in these essays tends to confirm Robert C. Tucker's view that the contemporary Soviet political system, having at least partly shaken off the heritage of the unique pressure of Stalin's personal rule, "should be pronounced, at least provisionally, post-totalitarian." Still, the continued, if diminishing, frustration by the party and state of unfettered intellectual inquiry and artistic expression—especially Moscow's ob-

structiveness toward the practical application of innovative thinking—indicates how vigilantly the party still shepherds "its" intellectuals. The satisfaction of Soviet liberal intellectuals—and their well-wishers abroad—with post-Stalin gains must be tempered by realization that these gains are still not protected by firm legal guarantees or even by explicit revisions of obsolete and stifling ideological dogmas. Some of the partial reforms granted by the Soviet Establishment were after all, reluctant, possibly temporary concessions, impelled by domestic economic difficulties and by such expediential foreign policy calculations as the desire to achieve respectability in the eyes of leftist French and Italian intellectuals.

I share so fully Michel Tatu's skepticism, expressed in his review of M. Garder's *L'Agonie du régime en Russie soviétique*, about Garder's prediction of the collapse of Soviet communism by 1970 that I can deal very briefly with his article also. Garder's book is the latest of a long line of apocalyptic predictions of the collapse of communism. Such prophecies ignore the fact that great revolutions are most infrequent, and that successful political systems are tenacious and adaptive. Vigorous elites, such as the Soviet party and police cadres, also are ruthless in acting to suppress threats to their power. Perhaps the most sensible aspect of Garder's analysis is his insistence that the disappearance of the Soviet regime would still leave Russia a very great power. Even this assumption is perhaps somewhat debatable, for the collapse of Soviet authority might be accompanied by the breaking away from Russia of some of the non-Russian nationalities. Tatu's observations—especially his succinct discussion of a possible military takeover in Russia, and his opinions on the political implications of economic reform—are very perceptive, but since they closely resemble those of Professor Brzezinski, I shall confine myself to registering general approval without elaborating. Tatu is, however, less convinced than Brzezinski that the Kremlin stands at a crossroad of historical destiny.

Brzezinski's brilliant article may well signal a new stage in Western analysis of Soviet politics. It deserves most careful scrutiny. Brzezinski combines systematic analysis of the development and present state of the Soviet policy, with provocative forecasts of its various possible futures. Forecasting the political future is hazardous, and many scholars regard it as an idle exercise. However, the hypothetical futures forecasted by Brzezinski have considerable value in helping to orient us toward various contingencies. Moreover, they may spur us to a sharp look at the warp of the past in search of intimations of the woof of the future. Brzezinski avoids overcommitment to a particular hypothesis by making his predictions contingent upon a variety of possible conditions. However, I think that his use of the "ideal type" mode of analysis, which for clarity and effectiveness selects aspects of a problem considered particularly significant, leads to some oversimplification. I share what I regard as his underlying assumption that a political system designed for the conduct and consolidation of a revolution is not necessarily suited to the needs of a relatively modernized society. The latter may be most simply characterized as a society whose members would like fewer jails and jailers, more comforts and conveniences, less propaganda and more uncensored information.

Brzezinski frames his analysis largely in terms of the concepts of political "degeneration," or decay, and "institutionalization," a proper level and quality of which he regards as essential to the constructive guidance and control of the emerging demands of productive social groups for access to the making of national policy. I agree with Brzezinski that important adjustments, and perhaps fundamental reforms, are necessary if the Soviet Union is to preserve stability and achieve continued dynamic growth in popular welfare. I believe also that without such reforms the USSR will eventually lose ground in international competition.

However, it seems to me that Brzezinski exaggerates the clear and present danger of "degeneration" in the Soviet political system. Incidentally, or perhaps not so incidentally, it is very difficult to gather from Brzezinski's article any very precise indication of just when political decay began to set in and how far it has proceeded or will, within any specific period of time, develop. Possibly Brzezinski will wish in the future to further refine his predictive techniques.

Secondly, Brzezinski's somewhat schematic use of the concept of institutionalization leads him to exaggerate the imminence of decay, and to underestimate the difficulties of institutionalizing the fundamental reforms which he regards as anti-decay prophylactics. The reforms which he suggests are so fundamental as to amount, in effect, to the adoption by Soviet Communists of some sort of limited parliamentary or constitutional regime. Certainly this would be highly desirable, but how likely is it to occur in the foreseeable future?

The Russian political tradition is woefully defective in the prerequisites for gradualism. Russia's tragic history

390 The Soviet Political System

hindered the acquisition of a mature, balanced political character. Both the Tsarist and the Soviet political cultures have exalted the virtues of a stern social discipline and of unquestioned acceptance of the ruler's commands by his subjects. Most citizens, in my opinion, are still so awed by authority and so unsophisticated politically as to be easily manipulated or at best cowed by a display of determination from on high. In the Soviet era especially, citizens have been heavily indoctrinated in an anti-liberal spirit not calculated to foster sympathy for a wide sharing of authority and responsibility among even highly placed elite groups, and still less receptive to notions of governmental responsiveness to the wishes of the "masses." The elite elements are probably united both against internal subversion of their privileges, and against "imperialist" threats from abroad. If the present Soviet political system disintegrates within the next few years, it will probably be replaced at least for some time by a nationalistic oligarchy, representing a coalition of forces, dominated by moderate, production-oriented party leaders, scientists, industrialists and military figures. However, I think that the more desirable outcome envisaged by Brzezinski as one of his hypothetical variants, namely, gradual constitutional development, might eventuate after a long period of international tranquility and increasingly rewarding Soviet contact with the West.

In my opinion, fundamental change —or collapse—can only occur when at least the following conditions exist. First, the leadership must be badly split, or paralyzed by indecision. Second, there must be widespread loss of respect and support for the political authorities. Finally, it must become possible for some sort of organized political opposition with a clear conception of an alternative to the present system to organize, covertly or overtly, for effective political action. It seems reasonable to assume that some years will pass before these conditions are fulfilled.

Moreover, it will probably be possible to make partial reforms, short of those suggested by Professor Brzezinski, which will enable the present Soviet political system to continue to function fairly effectively for at least another ten or fifteen years. I am not persuaded that it would be impossible to retain the present centralized system of policy formation for some time, while granting increasing autonomy to the economic bureaucracy, to the scientific community, etc. Also, it seems to me that within the party itself, improved training and a more efficient method of recruitment of party executives, especially those assigned to coordinating the efforts of and maintaining liaison with the leaders of the various professional communities, could go far toward gaining increased support by the latter for the political authorities. To the extent that the party can recruit top executives capable of perceiving early enough the need for adjustments and taking initiatives to make them before pressures become explosive, it may be able to survive, and even to flourish. The burden of proof is upon anyone who takes the view that the Soviet political elite has lost or will soon lose the touch that has enabled it to perform its functions thus far with a relatively high degree of effectiveness. It is not irrelevant to note that the post-Khrushchev leadership, despite its perhaps excessive caution, has taken important steps toward improving the relationship between the political system and the Soviet national economy. If the reforms instituted at the September 1965 plenum prove successful, the economy, and indirectly the political system, will be considerably strengthened—even though the uneasy compromise effected at the plenum between centralized organization and managerial autonomy is likely to fail.

In foreign affairs, at least, the Brezhnev-Kosygin leadership has displayed considerable skill in steering a course between the other two giants of the international arena, Communist China and the United States. Kosygin, in particular, seems a more skillful diplomat than any of us would have predicted before his mediation between India and Pakistan.

Despite my reservations, I agree with Brzezinski that existing Soviet political structures and the ideology which serves as a major source of their legitimacy are increasingly irrelevant to a more and more diversified society. Whether or not the specific institutional changes he regards as necessary for the effective processing of social demands by the polity are necessary or feasible remains largely unpredictable. There are so many unknowns and unknowables! For example, how sure can we be that a dynamic leader may not arise in the coming years—or months—to replace the colorless Brezhnev-Kosygin team and once again get Soviet society moving?

We must beware of confusing the desirable with the real. Fundamental social and political changes usually occur slowly, unevenly, and in a zig-zag fashion. Some parts of the system may change more rapidly, or more slowly, than others, although it is doubtless true that profound changes, for example, in the recruitment of leaders,

eventually affect the functioning of all the structures of a system.

Institutional changes are usually preceded by broad changes in attitudes and ways of thinking. The erosion of ideological dogma among intellectuals is undoubtedly helping to undermine the psychological foundations of rule by a party which still makes a demigod of a man who died almost fifty years ago. There has recently been an encouraging revival of rational and empirical thinking in many fields. Its exponents, however, still constitute a small if growing minority, and they function in a considerable degree of isolation from one another. Still, empiricism, in science and social science, in economic administration and even in such fields as law is increasingly challenging traditional Communist orthodoxy. Related to these positive developments is the tendency for liberal, nonconformist Soviet writers to ally themselves with, and in a sense to act as spokesmen for Soviet natural scientists—a trend symbolized by the fact that physicists are among the best patrons of avant-garde writing and "abstract" art.

However, the dominant political culture in which the rational, liberal factions of the Soviet intellectual community must cautiously maneuver is still characterized by a great deal of arbitrary administrative behavior, cloaked in secrecy and justified with sacrosanct dogma and official lies. I was vividly reminded of the seamy side of the political culture when on October 31, 1963, I was abducted on a Moscow street and detained in total isolation for nearly three weeks on a fabricated charge of military espionage.

The growing demand of various segments of the Soviet intellectual community for greater autonomy has forced the Kremlin to recognize grudgingly the need to relax controls over the trained and talented professionals upon whose willing and efficient performance national power depends. Concessions have even been made to that most troublesome group, the creative writers, at least to those not openly in opposition to official doctrine and policy. Party spokesmen still warn that "groupism" (*gruppovshchina*) is incompatible with the proper behavior of Communist intellectuals, thus acknowledging the existence of group consciousness among professionals. However, Soviet social scientists, and even *Pravda* editorial writers, instruct researchers and youth leaders to take account in their work of the diversity of interests of Soviety society.

There has been a great deal of behind-the-scenes bargaining between the Kremlin and the Soviet intelligentsia since the death of Stalin. One of its products has been the creation for the first time in the history of the USSR of the rudiments of a free, critical public opinion. Although still shackled, the Soviet intellectual community today is at least free to defend its views and interests against the cruder forms of arbitrary political interference, provided its members do not openly flout doctrines and symbols still regarded by the party leadership as above

criticism. A poor sort of freedom? Yes, but almost unimaginable when measured by the Stalinist yardstick.

The possibility that the progress which has been achieved since the death of Stalin—toward personal security, the rule of law, limited intellectual freedom, and partial access to the exciting "bourgeois" world—might still be swept away by a relapse into Stalin-like terror seems remote even if it cannot be completely excluded. In terms of a rational Kremlin approach to the Soviet national interest, the price of such a relapse would be prohibitively high. Its consequences could be dire for the lives and fortunes of many party and government leaders. It would cripple an increasingly sophisticated economy, and it could undermine support for Kremlin policies among important segments of Soviet society and among Western intellectuals, including many Communists.

The foregoing considerations seem to me to support the view that the Soviet political system will continue to adapt more or less successfully and positively to pressures arising in the intrasocietal and extra-societal environments. It seems likely that the CPSU will be with us for a while before it accepts Professor Brzezinski's blithe recommendation that it wither away.